TAPE OP

The Book about Creative Music Recording, Vol. II

Edited by Larry Crane
Introduction by Steve Albini

TAPE OP

The Book about Creative Music Recording, Vol. II

Edited by Larry Crane
Introduction by Steve Albini

ISBN 0-9779903-0-3
978-0-9779903-0-6

The beginning of anything is always exciting. Excitement is for kids. Makes sense, since everything's new for kids, and they see a lot of things for the first time. They're easily excited. Peeing in the grown-up toilet, Pogs, Power Rangers, Harry Potter, chronic masturbation, 'shrooms, guitars, a flanger... You get the idea. When you're young and everything is new, you're coasting downhill on it. You couldn't go slow if you tried. Everything comes and goes and it's all whoosh-whoosh happening fast. You can go a long way downhill like that.

Newness will only get you so far, but you build up speed and coast for a way, and when that peters out, well... Then you have to get out and push. That's where we are now with this thing, in the middle. Newness all wore off, we're out here in the middle, pushing ourselves along. Someone asked, so I counted, and I've been making records on-and-off for 25 years now. Fuck me running, I never thought I'd say that. That means I've probably been in the middle for a while and just didn't notice it. I tricked myself with periodic novelties, like a new microphone or control room or telephone system or building or intern or accountant or TiVo or Internet porn or poker table or 100 shares of Krispy Kreme. I guess those are artifacts of the middle too, all these no-longer-new things, acquired to maintain the illusion that everything was happening fast and I wasn't out here in the middle, pushing myself along.

But I have respect for the middle. It's where the experiments bear fruit and are not just nonsense done to feel clever. No longer baffled by every request, we can say, "I've been here before, and this - this right here - is what solved the problem." The alien becomes familiar and the path worn in the linoleum denotes the fastest route to the basement, where the flashlight is hanging where it should be, but you don't need it, because that breaker is like an old friend and you can find it in the dark. Once a month or so, when the dehumidifier and the fridge and the SVT all spike at once, and, well I've been meaning to get that fixed. And no, I don't think we should try it just one more time. After thirty takes we pretty much know what take thirty-one's going to sound like, give or take a who-gives-a-damn. Sure, double it. Whatever. Uncle. It's your record. Like The Beatles, I get you. With or without the harmony, sure.

Did I mention the backing vocals? Last minute like always, "Let's put some harmonies on there..." Baby Jesus, I beg you, kill me now. This instant. It's like looking in the rearview mirror and seeing the trooper's gumball lights fire up. You just know you're going to be in for hours of bullshit and recrimination, it's going to cost a fortune and all you'll get out of the experience is that you're four hours late getting to bed. In the end, some of it will be on the record, out of respect for the effort expended, but criminy, why bother? Has it ever made a difference? Sure, has anybody ever run barefoot up Mount Hood? Any non-zero probability is bound to occur, given enough trials. There's a gambler somewhere in Vegas down to his last $40 who knows that line. It has to come an eight eventually, right? It's all in the odds. Maybe if we put down a piano as a guide and then do it one at a time. Which part are you doing again? No, wait.

The cat, or the cats, or the current cat (we have been through several cats, but many more NS10 woofers) are no longer startled by any of it. I'm no longer startled by any of it. The demo is, of course, better than the record. Of course it is. You already love the demo, and now you're trying to make something identical to it, but somehow better than the thing you love. Can you carve yourself a new mom out of butter? Embrace the mom you already love and release the goddamn demo already. Speaking of which, you will eventually lose your parents. Whatever you're doing right now, it will mean nothing to you once they are gone. Drop it and call your mom. She'd love to hear from you. Tell her you tried to carve a new one out of butter, and have decided it's not worth it and you're sticking with her and releasing the demo after all.

ward

by Steve Albini

And getting the job done is what it's all about, right? In the beginning, you want everything to be amazing, and it is. It is amazing because you're dumb as a stump and water falling out of the sky amazes you. You push the lever and the machine shaped like a throne makes a noise and swirls your poo away. Amazing. It's all new, remember? Lets double it. Oh... My... God... Did you hear that? That's amazing. I'm going to do that to everything. That's amazing. I'm dumb as a length of pipe, and I think what I just did here is amazing. Thank you. Did you get my name? It's got an unusual spelling... here, I'll just write it down for you. Amazing, wasn't it? Did I play you the amazing part? The thing I did was, well, I had her sing it twice, and then I played them both back. I call it "doubling".

But not now. Now it's all about getting it done. We have three days and five hundred dollars. Chop-chop! Let's get this turkey in the shop! Keep them all and decide later? Dude, there is no later. Later is now. Can you pick one? No, I'm not going to pick one, they all sound the same... I mean, they all sound great to me. Okay, we can do another one.

And getting it done is not to be sniffed at. You can only buy a record if it has made it through the grinder and actually been manufactured. The best record ever is one of those in the store over there. The record being slaved-over by genius-boy over there, the one that will never be finished because it isn't yet perfect - that record is nothing at all. An unfinished record is nothing. Pure bullshit. Spend years wooing some unattainable goddess, rending garments and crying pools of teardrop? So you can die a victim, ignored? A martyr to your stubbornness? Fuck that, just troll your dick through a tavern and land the first thing that nibbles. If it gets weird, make your excuses and make another cast. You can throw a lot back before you land a keeper, but you never land the keeper without that first, "Fuck it, I'm going to the bar." You will recognize the keeper, don't worry. Do you know how many beautiful relationships have been forged from that simple get-it-done dick-trolling? Uncountable millions! Grandparents celebrating their golden and more! Deeply in love for a lifetime! It started when young grandpa couldn't take it any more and decided to get it done. Finish your goddamn record. Get out and push.

So it is with *Tape Op*. Many, many issues. So much paper, so many words. In the beginning it was a fanzine, now it has its own convention. Millionaires and huge companies vie for its attention. Can you believe this shit? From that to this? Incredible. Just incredible. They made it out of nothing. Well, not nothing. They made it out of what they were doing anyway. Taping everything, playing it back. All new. Oh... My... God... Did you hear that? All new. Write that shit down so we don't lose it. I'll bet there are a bunch of us out there...

And there were. We are all here now, out here in the middle, banded together by that what we do. We are all getting it done. We all know that another take is seldom the answer, but sure, it might be, so what the heck. We're all working late and forget what day it is. We're all wondering how long we can keep it up. We keep it up first with the downhill glide of New, when everything is amazing, then we coast on momentum gathered then. Now we're out of all that. We know what to do now, and we just do it. We get out and push and sure as shit, we get there.

The middle is grand, ain't it?

Welcome to the middle, and congratulations.

Hello and Welcome to...
Tape Op Magazine's
second book-

TAPE OP: THE BOOK
ABOUT CREATIVE MUSIC
RECORDING, VOLUME II!

The book you hold
in your hands

is a collection of most (but not all) of the articles from issues
11 to 20 (covering the years 1999 through 2000) of
Tape Op Magazine. Tape Op is dedicated to being
"The Creative Music Recording Magazine", and whether that means
the music or the recording is "creative", we look for music and
recordings that we find interesting for many different reasons.

I assume that many of you readers have read our previous book, *Tape Op: The Book About Creative Music Recording* - **a collection of articles from issues one through ten of** *Tape Op Magazine* **(spanning the years 1997 to 1998, and published by Feral House). I also might assume many of you are subscribers to** *Tape Op Magazine*. **While it was tempting to update, or editorialze, some of the pieces in this book we ultimately decided not to, and to just let them stand as they were originally published, a glimpse into that point in time. Please also note that while the book is broken up into four basic sections, the logistics of laying out some pages in color while most were black and white, dictated that there are some pieces within a section that don't strictly fit that section. Think of these pieces as a neat little surprise, like a french horn solo on a death metal track.**

Look forward to more books in this series, collecting articles from *Tape Op* **by the year. In any event, the world of** *Tape Op* **has a lot to offer to anyone that is interested or involved in the recording of music.**

Please enjoy this book. Inside are a wide variety of opinions on how to record music, make albums and pick gear. The art of recording is a wide-open world, where there is no "right" or "wrong" - learn to embrace that and celebrate making music.

-Larry Crane, Editor

www.tapeop.com

TAPE OP: II

THE BOOK ABOUT CREATIVE MUSIC RECORDING

VOLUME

RECORDING STUDIOS:

13	Abbey Road Studios: Elliott Smith
18	Chicago's AACM
22	Toe Rag Music Studios
26	Suma Studios
30	Wharton Tiers
36	The Blasting Room
42	Butch Vig and Smart Studios

RECORDING TIPS:

48	Studio Supplies
50	Recording Recipes 4
52	Recording Recipes 5
54	Recording Recipes 6
56	Recording Recipes 7
58	Recording Recipes 8
59	Recording Recipes 9
60	Analog Tape Deck Calibration
62	How to Build a Microphone
64	Resistors
66	Headphone Splitter Box
67	Recording Recipes 11
68	Tape Splicing, Editing & Loops
70	Calibration for 2-Head Machines

ENGINEERS & PRODUCERS:

72	Andy Hong
74	Phil Brown
78	John Agnello
82	Jim O'Rourke
89	Oz Fritz- Visual Images
90	Jon Brion
96	Joe Chiccarelli
102	Bob Weston
108	Jack Endino
114	Adam Lasus
117	Oz Fritz - High Velocity Sound Engineering
118	David Barbe
122	Roger Moutenot
126	Tchad Blake
134	Dave Trumfio
140	Grant Showbiz
144	Dave Fridmann
150	Ken Nordine
152	Moby
153	Digital vs. Analog
154	Stuart Hallermann
156	Jim Dickinson
162	Scott Colburn
164	Some 4-track Cassette Tricks
165	Make Your Own Piezo Drum Triggers
166	John Hardy
169	Introduction to Digital Audio
170	Dave Botrill

ARTISTS:

178	Sparklehorse
181	Howe Gelb
184	Mayo Thompson
190	Fugazi
194	J. Robbins
198	DJ SHadow
200	Neutral Milk Hotel
202	Mercury Rev
206	Calexico
210	Death Cab For Cutie
214	DJ Spooky
216	Robyn Hitchcock
218	Elliot Peter Earls
222	Ani DiFranco
230	Ex
234	Ween
237	NS-10 Mod
238	Andy Partridge of XTC
244	Spot
249	Top 10 Recording Tips
250	Macha
253	Recording Drums
254	Jeremy Enigk
257	Used Gear
258	the Go-Betweens
262	Eric 'Roscoe' Ambel
266	Scott Fritz of KCRW
269	Notes From Under the Ground

Editor
Larry Crane

Publisher & Design Director
John Baccigaluppi

Book Designers
Brian Shelvin and Brandy Faucette

Assistant Book Designer and Pre Press
Scott McChane

Contributing Writers & Photographers
Steve Albini, Chris Carnel, Liam Watson, Tony Michels, Jim Newberry, Chris Brunkhart, Joseph Cultice, Jane Cowan, John Heaton Jones, Albert Sanchez, E.J. Gold, Gilson, VI Foot Sloth, Archer Prewitt, Jeff Kriege, Adam Selzer, Barbara Moutenot, Barry Rudolph, Ben London, Ben Werth, Bill Carter, Brad Gobdel, Bryan Bingold, Chris Eckman, Chris Wills, Craig Smith, Curtis Settino, Danny Clinch, Darron Burke, David Patterson, Dewey Mahood, Donald Bell, Eric D. Morrison, Eric Stenman, Ferriou Sanjar, Geoff Farina, Graeme McIntyre, Greg Roberts, Heather Mount, Henry Owings, Hillary Johnson, J. Robbins, Jef Brown, Jeff Gros, Jenny Toomey, Joanna Bolme, Joe Chiccarelli, Joel Cameron, John Askew, John Holkeboer, John Vanderslice, Joseph Cultice, Kelly Huckaby, Kevin Coral, Kevin Robinson, Larry Hirshowitz, Leigh Marble, Mary Fridmann, Nicole Radja, Oz Fritz, Paul C. Fitzgerald, Pete Weiss, Phil Clark, Phillip Stevenson, Roman Sokal, Scott Craggs, Sonny Mayugba, Stephen Murray, Steve Gullick, Steve Silverstein, Syd Kato, Tommy Ryan & Val Canez

Cover Art
Brian Shevlin

Transcription
Anne Elchikawa, Bryan Bingold, Jane Cowan, Mark Ellsworth, Matt Mair Lowery, Ted Brack

Special Thanks
Hillary Johnson, Tim Starback, AJ Wilhelm, Laura Thurmond, Craig Schumacher, Andy Hong, Liz Brown, Jenna Sather, Kendra Lynn, Holly Abney, Catlin Gutenberger, Sam Toll, Alexander Lawson, and Nadia Osta. Rob Christensen and Under The Radar Sonny Mayugba & Patty West

Tape Op Editorial
Jackpot! Recording Studio, Inc.
P.O. Box 14517, Portland, OR   97293
(503) 232-6047
john@tapeop.com

Tape Op Publishing
SingleFin, Inc.
P.O. Box 160995, Sacramento, CA 95816
(916) 444-5241
john@tapeop.com

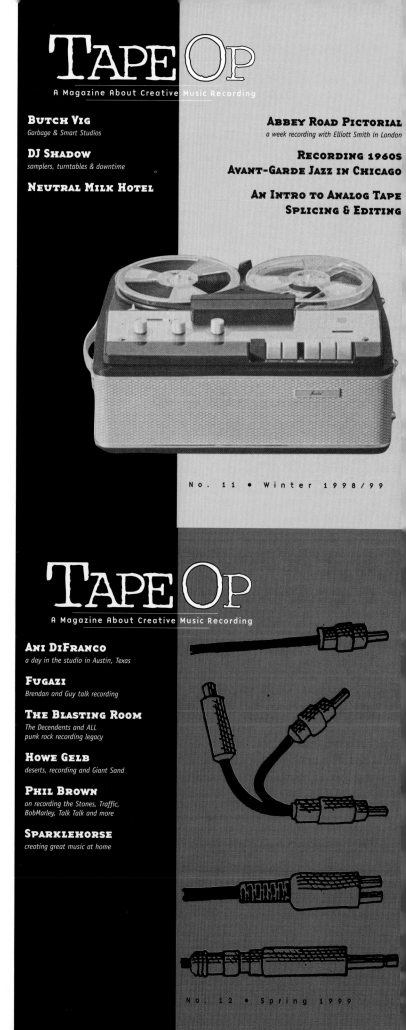

TAPE OP
A Magazine About Creative Music Recording

BUTCH VIG
Garbage & Smart Studios

DJ SHADOW
samplers, turntables & downtime

NEUTRAL MILK HOTEL

ABBEY ROAD PICTORIAL
a week recording with Elliott Smith in London

**RECORDING 1960S
AVANT-GARDE JAZZ IN CHICAGO**

**AN INTRO TO ANALOG TAPE
SPLICING & EDITING**

No. 11 ● Winter 1998/99

TAPE OP
A Magazine About Creative Music Recording

ANI DIFRANCO
a day in the studio in Austin, Texas

FUGAZI
Brendan and Guy talk recording

THE BLASTING ROOM
The Decendents and ALL
punk rock recording legacy

HOWE GELB
deserts, recording and Giant Sand

PHIL BROWN
on recording the Stones, Traffic,
BobMarley, Talk Talk and more

SPARKLEHORSE
creating great music at home

No. 12 ● Spring 1999

TAPE OP

A Magazine About Creative Music Recording

JACK ENDINO
Seattle's King of Rock Production

SPOT
Hüsker Dü, the Meat Puppets & more

ERIC 'ROSCOE' AMBEL
one of 'alt-country's' best producers tells all

WGNS
this DC studio's wacky history

SUMA RECORDING
Ken & Paul Hamann make recording history

RESISTORS

No. 13 • Summer 1999

TAPE OP

A Magazine About Creative Music Recording

DJ SPOOKY
Defying expectations

TOE RAG
London's fab studio

MACHA
Ethno-indie rock & field recordings

KEN NORDINE
Father of 'Word Jazz'

JOHN HARDY
Builder of mic preamps

BASEMENT RECORDING

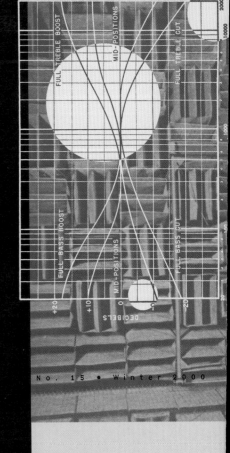

No. 15 • Winter 2000

TAPE OP

A Magazine About Creative Music Recording

JOE CHICCARELLI
Top LA producer secrets!

JOHN AGNELLO
Producer of Jawbox & Varnaline among others

DAVID BARBE
Sugar, Son Volt, Macha & home in Athens, GA

JEREMY ENIGK
of Sunny Day Real Estate

THE GO-BETWEENS
A Recording History

ELLIOTT EARLS
Multi-media that doesn't suck

No. 14 • Fall 1999

TAPE OP

A Magazine About Creative Music Recording

TCHAD BLAKE
Recording Guru's Tales & Tricks

JIM O'ROURKE
Superchunk, Aluminum Group & more

DAVE TRUMFIO
Interviewed by Joe Chiccarelli

GRANT SHOWBIZ
The Fall, The Smiths, Billy Bragg...

MAYO THOMPSO
Red Krayola recording his

BUILD YOUR OWN MI

RECORDING RECIP

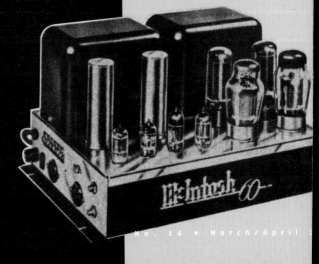

No. 16 • March/April

TAPE OP
The Creative Music Recording Magazine

DAVE FRIDMANN
...oducing the Flaming Lips and more

MERCURY REV
...lk about Dave Fridmann

WHARTON TIERS
...cording Sonic Youth and more

ROBYN HITCHCOCK
...ngs, not sounds

...EEN
...cording vocals in car trunks

RECORDING RECIPES

RECORDING DRUMS

No. 17 • May/June 2000

TAPE OP
The Creative Music Recording Magazine

JIM DICKINSON
Legendary Memphis Producer

ANDY PARTRIDGE
XTC's Home Studio

DAVE BOTTRILL
Working with Peter Gabriel, Tool, Eno...

VISUAL IDEAS
for the studio by Oz Fritz

THE EX
European Punks & Steve Albini's Mics

DEATH CAB FOR CUTIE
Home Production Tricks

RECORDING RECIPES
MIXING TIPS
RECORDING TIPS
4-TRACK TIPS

No. 19 • Sept/Oct 2000

TAPE OP
The Creative Music Recording Magazine

...GITAL V.S. ANALOG
...Tools lovers and haters

...N BRION
...ucer, musician and film scorer

...B WESTON
...rding Sebadoh, Polvo and more

...UART HALLERMAN
...neer and studio owner

...KE YOUR OWN
...UM TRIGGERS

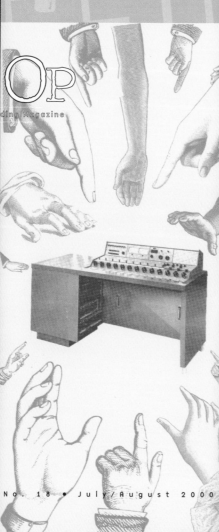

No. 18 • July/August 2000

TAPE OP
The Creative Music Recording Magazine

ROGER MOUTENOT
Producer for Yo La Tengo, Sleater-Kinney...

ANDY HONG
One of Boston's finest

BROOKLYN STUDIOS
With Rare Book Room & Fireproof Studios

PHILL NIBLOCK
Minimalist speaker placement

UNCLE PUNCHY
Embracing digital

TOBIN SPROUT
Post Guided by Voices

SCOTT FRITZ & KCRW
Live radio recording

DIGITAL AUDIO INTRO

ANALOG BIAS
& CALIBRATION

No. 20 • Nov/Dec 2000

Part 1 RECORDING STUDIOS

RECORDING STUDIOS:

13	Abbey Road Studios: Elliott Smith
16	Chicago's AACM
22	Toe Rag Music Studios
26	Suma Studios
30	Wharton Tiers
36	the Blasting Room
42	Butch Vig and Smart Studios

page

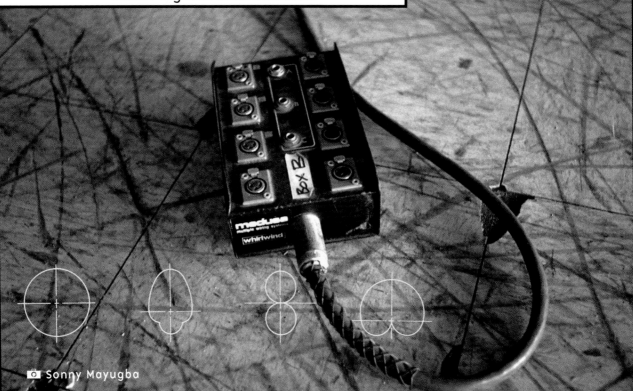

Sonny Mayugba

Elliott Smith, Sam Coomes, Rob Schnapf, and Tom Rothrock
live out their Abbey Road Studios fantasy.

This is a story about how I got to live my fantasy of walking through the door of the building at 3 Abbey Road and saying, *"We're working in studio two."* It's second only to the one where I walk through the door and the receptionist says *"Good morning Mr. Martin."* This was made possible by my generous friend Elliott Smith, whom I believe had a similar fantasy. We were joined by our buddies Rob Schnapf and Tom Rothrock, who took care of the recording duties, and Sam Coomes from Quasi, the best rock band in the world.

Excuse me Tom, who's the Nuge? -Paul

Elliott, Sam and I arrive at studio two around noon. We walk into the control room and meet friendly house engineers Paul Hicks and Chris Bolster. Rob and Tom have taken a wrong turn and are now heading farther and farther away from the studio. Let's have a look around, shall we? The mixing board is a Neve VRP Legend with flying faders, not a little EMI board with a grinning St. George and Geoff Emerick permanently attached to it like my fantasies have led me to believe. Oh no! One of those screens with the EQ display. I'll get sucked in I know, just like those dryers at the laundromat. A Studer A820 24-track analogue tape machine. There's a machine bay, so you can wheel in whatever you want, digital or analogue. They have a lot to choose from. Assorted outboard gear that Rob and Tom decide not to use. A comfy couch and chairs. Coffee! Okay, now for the studio downstairs. It's huge. The ceilings are 24 feet high and the floor is 38 feet x 60 feet On the studio statistics sheet they list the reverberation time at 1.2 seconds. Mounted on hinges and wheels against the main walls are four acoustic screens that are nearly as tall as the room, and about 1/3 the width, so you can break it up. There are lots of smaller screens you can use for isolation. We've got a Steinway grand piano, a Steinway tack piano *(actually there are no tacks, just very stiff, ridged hammers)*, a Hammond C3 organ with two Leslies to choose from, and an electric harmonium. Let's see, microphones. Hmm, Neumann, Neumann, Neumann... you name it, they got it. I go over to check out the rented Ludwig vintage drum kit. Cute. Those cymbals look like trouble though. There are a pair of very weathered looking Coles 4038's perched nearby. "Hey Paul, how old are these?" "Pretty old." "Like Beatles old?" "Yeah." I press my cheek against one of them. *(Insert Beatles fantasy here.)* I open my eyes. Rob and Tom have arrived and are inspecting the drum set. All the cymbals but the hi-hat have been nixed. The heads have to go too. They want Remo Ambassador coated top and clear bottom. "Excuse me Tom, there's a Joey Waronker on the

phone for you." Everyone, "Tell him to come over!" Joey played drums on a couple songs from Elliott's album, *XO*, and happened to be in town with R.E.M. He has just arrived at the studio and is now on the phone with another music store. It seems to be a bit more complicated to rent gear in London than LA. He is being very patient and speaking very calmly. He sounds like my chiropractor right before the big adjustment. "Now what I would like to do, is have you bring me some of these cymbals, and some of these, and two of these, and I'll try them out and send back the ones I don't want to use. Do you think we can do that?" After 15 minutes of hypnosis, they agree. Elliott is downstairs working on a new song, the rest of us discuss very important things while we wait for the gear to arrive. "Excuse me Tom, who's the Nuge?" asks Paul. Okay we're recording now. Sam is attempting play without using headphones. This turns out to be impossible as the delay from one side of the room to the other is too long for him to keep time with the drums. After a good take we listen back. We all marvel at the sound of the room. It really has a sound. "Now if we just had an old board instead of this damn thing." says Rob.

We should smash them to smithereens. -Rob

Abbey Road has an extensive list of floating equipment you can bring in, Rob and Tom have requested some EQs that were originally part of an old EMI board. Not only does the old stuff sound better, it looks better. Why is modern recording equipment so ugly? They have also brought in Summit mic pres, a Fairchild limiter, a Tube-Tech CL 1B compressor, an SSL compressor and some other preamps. Studio two has exclusive use of the legendary echo chamber. Located in the back of the room , it was just recently reinstated for work on the Beatles *Anthology*. All studios have access to the EMT reverb plates. Hey, have I mentioned there's a pub in the basement? It's part of the cafeteria, which offers up the usual casserole style cuisine, but the beers on tap are great. You can order a pint of Guinness, light a cigarette and take a little stroll through the halls if you want to. We decide to order out for Indian food tonight. After dinner, the band heads downstairs to work on another song, I have a stomachache, and fall asleep on the couch imagining what the *Odessey and Oracle* sessions were like. (Insert Zombies dream here). The band returns to the control room just as Rod Argent delivers a kick to my stomach because I won't let him sit down. *"How did that sound?"* asks Elliott. *"Well ..."*

Are you taking the Mickey out of me? -Paul

It seems after spending enough time with us Paul and Chris have figured out that half of what we say is bullshit, and have started dishing it back at us with gusto. Now we're one big happy family. Elliott and Sam lay down some vocals (U47) on the track started last night. They sound great, but Mr. Smith, is unhappy with the words and the song is shelved for now. He begins work on another song. He lays down acoustic first (KM56), then electric guitar through a Leslie (U47 on bottom 2 SM 57s placed at an angle of about 130 degrees [for more spin, according to Rob] on top), and drums (just make something up). Mr. Waronker isn't here today so Elliott plays. Once again he lays down one of the weirdest and coolest drum tracks you ever heard. "Okay Sam, think you can play bass over that?" Excellent! Sam opts to stay up in the control room to record it. We enjoy delicious frothy pints while he works away. Rob has something to show me downstairs. Tucked away at the end of the hall is an old EMI board. There's compressors built right in to every channel. In fact, the VU meters on top show compression not signal. Chris comes over and tells us that the board no longer belongs to the studio but to one Michael Hedges who produces a lot of bands I don't listen to. He just keeps it at Abbey Road to use when he works there. I stash a pen behind it to use next time I'm working there.

On that note, I'm disappointed to discover that out of a staff of 80 people, only eight are engineers, and all are boys. Paul assures me it's not sexist hiring policies, just lack of applications from the girls. I think of the Spice Girls and decide he's not taking the Mickey out of me. Come on ladies of London, out of 7,000,000 people, *One* of you must be interested in recording! Back at the ranch Elliott is laying down an organ part. The organ sound is great. *"Hey, how long has that been here?..." "Really? That long? So that's the one they used on 'Blue Jay Way'?"* The tack piano's been here for a long time too. *Penny Lane!* I run down and touch them both again. We forget to eat, the cafeteria stops serving food at 8:30 and London turns into a pumpkin at 10. We all go to bed hungry.

I'm gonna put some gooey schmutz on the oohs. -Rob

We went to bed hungry, not necessarily sober. The bar in our hotel stays open later than the pubs so we wrapped up the night there. I wake up at 3 pm. Everyone else left at noon. When I get to the studio they have already recorded basics for another song. Joey has played drums and left by now. Sam is doing his bass part again. Let's take a little time to get to know *"The Abbey Road Kids."* Paul is only 24 years old and has been working here since age 19. He spent six months splicing tape by hand with Geoff Emerick for the Beatles *Anthology*. *"So, were you freaking out?" "Actually no, not really."* He's so cute. Chris is a New Zealander who moved to London in March. He landed his job at Abbey Road within three months. Not too shabby! He is a wee 23. He also informed me that the term for ice cream bar in England is "icy lolly." Elliott is adding piano and organ. Now I forgot to tell you about studio one. It's even bigger than two. 92 x 55 feet., and 39 feet. high. This is where they record most of the orchestras and film scores. It's the only other studio I check out because number three gives me a weird vibe every time I walk by. Later I find out this is where *Dark Side of the Moon* was recorded. No wonder. I do read a little info on it though. It's smaller than the other two, and includes a separate 19 x 12 ft live room which has no parallel surfaces and tile floors. The board is a 72 channel SSL G. It has a kitchen and shower. The Spice Girls, Morrissey, and (shudder) Phil Collins have all used this room. There is also the smaller penthouse studio, used mostly for vocals, overdubs and mixing. It has a Neve Capricorn board and is the only studio with full digital capabilities. You know, if you're one of *those* people. Abbey Road also has a cassette duping suite, CD pre-mastering room, a disc cutting facility, a classical editing room, and separate digital re-mastering suites for pop or classical music. Whew, now that that's out of the way, we have moved on to slide guitar.

There is a story about George Harrison's iron fist while recording Badfinger's 'Day After Day.' He insisted on doing the double slide parts at the same time, one played by him and the other by Pete Ham. Of course this was no easy task and took a bunch of takes. Now when I hear the song I don't know if I'm crying because its so beautiful, or because the idea of recording something that many times is too stressful. *(Insert Badfinger nightmare here).* Vocals added, the finished product is a rocker called *Brand New Game*. Some of you may recognize this as the song Mr. Lawrence Crane and I recorded a demo of in the short film *Strange Parallel*. Isn't Larry photogenic? Now adding vocals to the one from yesterday. Elliott does a lead vocal and doubles it. Moving on, he wants to try some harmonies but clarifies more than once that he's not sure what he's going to do. He's just "sending out a probe" if you will. He declares after the first couple of passes that "the probe has discovered nothing" but by the next one he's off and rolling. I lost track of how many harmonies he added but I think Brian Wilson would be jealous. While making a rough mix, Rob talks me through what he's doing including putting some gooey shmutz on the oohs. Damn his techie talk.

I'm just futzing around in here. -Rob

Today the orchestra arrives. Another Studer has been brought in as a slave deck. We've got eight violins, four violas, four cellos, three basses and four French horns. They are mic'd as follows, four U67s on the violins, two on the violas, two U47s on the basses, two on the cellos, and the 4038s on the French horns. There are two M50s out front by the conductor, and very high above, a pair of KM56s. Did I mention the special love that developed for the KM56s? Aside from the acoustic guitar, they were also used as drum overheads, on a piano track or two and probably some other things I'm forgetting. A+ for versatility. The arranger/conductor arrives and goes over the sheet music with Elliott. Both satisfied, he goes downstairs, gives some brief instructions to the players and we're ready to go. They put down a few different arrangements of the song and are done within an hour. Some of them thank Elliott for an easy day of work and head downstairs to the pub. Tom now bounces these tracks onto the original so Elliott can sing to it. The rest of the day is spent mostly on vocals and assorted bits here and there, interrupted only once so Blondie can check out the studio. I resist taking their picture and settle for waving to Clem Burke from the control room. Control tower is more like it. At about 15 ft. above the studio, you kind of feel superhuman. Just by adding some reverb to the talkback and speaking in a deep voice you can almost live the dream. Another day finished, we head back to the hotel bar for overpriced drinks.

Take your time, as an error would be disastrous at this juncture. -Tom

Last day and I'm feeling a little teary-eyed. Elliott wants to try one more song that he's been messing around with, temporarily called 'Honky Bach' because of the piano style. Rob sets up the mics on the tack piano, and recording begins. Listening back, we realize the tape had started rolling before Rob made it up the stairs and shut the door. Sounds great, we move onto the harmonium. He adds some low stuff that sounds like a tuba, and some high stuff that sounds like an accordion. Sam adds a bass part and the song is now called 'The Lost and Found.' Lyrics not quite finished, we move on to mixes. Rob asks Paul if they ever use any API stuff there. He's heard of it but we're in Neveland and nobody he knows seems to have actually used it. Maybe next time...

We wanted to take "the Kids" out at the end of the day, but once again it's very late. No one seems too anxious to leave our new little home, but Paul has to work early tomorrow. We're reluctantly getting ready to leave when Chris rushes out and returns with a bottle of champagne and some gifts. The boys get the standard Abbey Road T-shirts, and I get the supercute baby tee. Which would look great if I didn't have shoulders like Greg Louganis. We make a toast and hang out for just a little while longer. ☮

TAPE OP: BOOK II | PAGE 15

Elliott, Rob & Tom going over the arrangement.

Elliott & Sam reaching for a high note.

A pint and playback.

The Orchestra.

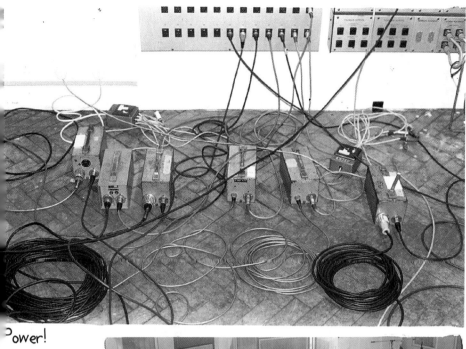

Power!

Chris (L) & Paul (R).

Waiting.....

Rob and the old board.

Elliott, Joey and Sam.

RECORDING HISTORY: The AACM and the Chicago Avant-Garde Jazz Scene of the Mid-Sixties by Steve Silverstein

While some of my favorite albums were made in huge studios with big budgets, I'm also very excited about records made under less ideal circumstances. I find it really inspiring when timeless records can be made by people with limited experience and resources. For this reason, I find the early records from Chicago's Association for the Advancement of Creative Music (AACM) exciting. At a time when avant-garde jazz was developing in new directions, without an obvious market for these records, no one invested huge resources in recording them. In the mid-1960s, recording technology was far less available than it is today. The music was also drastically different from so much of what had been recorded before that I expected it may have presented particular challenges in recording.

L to R: Malcolm Chisolm, (engineer), Joseph Jarman & musicians listening to playback

Malcolm Chisolm, moving mic, Charles Clark on cello. Both photos from the *As If It Were The Seasons* album sessions by Joseph Jarman. Summer 1968 at Per-Mar Studios at Chess Records in Chicago. Both photos by Greg Roberts.

The AACM was a nonprofit co-op, led initially by Muhal Richard Abrams, which helped to produce concerts of experimental jazz. The organization evolved in part out of the work of the Experimental Band, which began in 1961, also under Abrams's leadership. The first recording of these musicians was the Roscoe Mitchell Sextet's *Sound*, which was released on Bob Koester's Delmark label in 1966. Up until that album, the Chicago-based label had released blues, traditional jazz, and bebop. While Delmark had not previously been involved in releasing such aggressively avant-garde music, Koester did have experience with recording studios. He was very happy with his experience recording at Hall Studios with engineer Stu Black. When Black went to work at Sound Studios, a converted radio station at 230 N. Michigan Avenue, Delmark's business followed. Sound Studios had a Neve board, a 3-track recorder, and a good variety of microphones. While the main room at Sound was neither as large nor as live as that at Hall Studios, it was big enough to comfortably position all of the musicians and their many instruments.

Stu Black engineered Mitchell's album at Sound Studios, and Chuck Nessa, who managed Koester's Jazz Record Mart at the time, supervised the two sessions. Despite Black's experience as "a journeyman engineer," Nessa says that "by far this was the strangest stuff he'd ever encountered."

Nessa describes his job as producer "as a liaison between the techies and musicians, between the money, which was Koester, and the musicians." He was not concerned about recording the variety of instruments used on the album ("you can fake it in the mix later"), and his advice to Black for recording the harsh overtones used by the reed players was "that the music was going to get very loud, so leave plenty of headroom."

All of the musicians were in one large room, with some small baffles around the drums that would not obstruct anyone's view. Nessa's sole strategy to deal with bleed was to try to guess while setting up. He feels that making adjustments later "screws up people's concentration," and prefers to "go with the decision you made at the beginning and live with it." This approach illustrates his broader philosophy that "if there's a choice between musical problems and technical, always err on the side of the music and deal with the other shit later." No overdubs were used on *Sound* or any of these records.

Nessa was concerned about the music's ability to communicate with new listeners, and felt that achieving this goal was one of his tasks as producer. He explains: "When we recorded *Sound*, the first day, we had run through the pieces. I realized that this was the first AACM music to appear and it was the first Roscoe Mitchell record. We'd recorded *Sound* and we'd record-

ed *Ornette*, and there was no place that you heard Roscoe Mitchell playing with drums behind him. Afterwards, I said to Roscoe, 'We're going to be giving this to a lot of people who don't know anything cold about this; they're going to be coming to it blankly. To have the leader of the group, who is the saxophone player, never playing when there are any drums playing is kind of bizarre.' I said, 'Maybe on *Ornette* you could do it with drums behind you.' On the first take that we did the first day, it's a cello behind him, playing pizzicato like crazy, and it's wonderful. But I said, 'Maybe we could do that with drums behind you.' So the next date when we came back, he did it again with drums behind him. And that's what came out."

In addition to containing the original take of *Ornette* described above, the CD reissue contains two separate takes of the piece *Sound*, which were edited into one piece for the original vinyl. Nessa explains that one take was too long, and that the parts of the two takes which they used worked together. This fits Nessa's idea that a record does not need to reflect a live performance. He says, "You can't always do what you hear in your head on stage either, or at a rehearsal."

The next two albums were recorded under similar circumstances. Sound had upgraded to a 3M 1/2" 4-track deck before the recording of Joseph Jarman's *Song For*. Delmark's third AACM release,

Muhal Richard Abrams's *Levels and Degrees of Light*, was recorded in 1967. While the album's first session was recorded at Sound, the second session was recorded at Chess/Ter-Mar Studio, where Stu Black now worked. Chess had a bigger live room and an Ampex 1/2-inch 4-track.

Chuck Nessa had left Delmark, so Koester began to supervise the sessions. Koester's approach to production was even more hands-off than Nessa's. He says, *"Most of those records were really produced by the artists anyway. That's essentially true of any jazz record. I'm not a guy who's going to say, 'You play this.' I can't do that; I'm not a musician. I'm a fan, and I'm not a terribly erudite fan. When it came to the AACM, I was scared to death. I realized quickly that between the engineer and Muhal and the sidemen, that I had nothing to worry about."*

The big change with *Levels and Degrees of Light* was the active use of electronic processing in the mix. The application of reverb makes it sound very different than the Mitchell and Jarman albums, though the recording process was otherwise similar. Electronics were already common by 1966, Abrams says, just not frequently used in jazz records. He points out that such effects have become even more common today. While Koester gives "100% freedom" to musicians on Delmark, he found the reverb *"a little bit corny."* He prefers recordings which more closely resemble live performances. When Stu Black once suggested to him moving drums subtly left or right, Koester replied that *"they don't put the drums on a cart in a club and carry them across the bandstand. When they do, I'll maybe record them that way."*

After leaving Delmark, Chuck Nessa started his own label, Nessa, to release Lester Bowie's *Numbers One and Two* and Roscoe Mitchell's *Congliptious*. These two albums, both recorded by Stu Black, mark the beginning of the core that would evolve into the Art Ensemble of Chicago. *Numbers One and Two* introduced the use of a single overhead microphone, which Nessa felt would "get a blend of what the group sounded like."

Delmark's next three recording sessions continued in the by-now established pattern. Anthony Braxton's first album as leader, *Three Compositions of New Jazz*, was recorded at Sound Studios, with its new staff engineer Ron Pickup. Koester says that *"they'd brought an engineer into Sound from England, who'd once done a Beatles demo. That was his claim to fame. He made them re-equip to some extent."* Koester describes Malcolm Chisholm, who recorded Joseph Jarman's, *As If It Were The Seasons*, as *"one of the deans of the Chicago recording field."* At the session for his second Delmark album, *Young at Heart/Wise in Time*, Muhal Richard Abrams was concerned about the recording of Leo Smith's trumpet. Koester explains that *"there was a metal horn, and a metal microphone, and he got upset because there was a plastic windscreen on the mic. He thought that was a bad idea, because the metal wouldn't reach the other metal because of the plastic screen."*

In addition to its own productions, Delmark also licensed an album of Anthony Braxton's own recordings. He had bought a tape deck in Korea, and used it to record his solo performances in the basement of the Parkway Community Center. The double-album, *For Alto*, which collects these recordings, came out in 1969.

In 1969, with the Art Ensemble of Chicago and Braxton's Creative Construction Company leaving for Europe, many of the AACM musicians had left Chicago. The last three Delmark productions were two records by Kalaparusha Maurice McIntyre, *Humility in the Light of the Creator* and *Forces and Feelings*, and Muhal Richard Abrams's, *Things to Come for Those Now Gone*. When the Jazz Record Mart bought a building, funds were no longer available to produce records which took so long to recoup their expenses. Delmark did license two final AACM releases, after which Koester says, "We went to sleep for a long time."

In 1975, Nessa released *Old/Quartet*, which included basement recordings of early configurations of the Art Ensemble. More of these home recordings appeared on Nessa's 1993 CD box set *The Art Ensemble 1967/68*. Journalist Terry Martin recorded many of these practices solely for his own listening. He had a Wollensak 2-track reel-to-reel which he'd bought for playback. The deck came with 2 microphones, which went direct to stereo. Martin recorded with these mics, and ran the deck at its fastest speed, 7 1/2 ips.

Martin claims no credit in the good sound of the recordings. *"It had nothing to do with my abilities. I just used common sense in setting up the two mics."* Nessa describes the site of the earlier recordings as *"a big square Victorian house, with a large basement, brick walls, wood stud ceiling."* Martin says that the room was *"acoustically very suitable."* With only two microphones, he *"had one mic overhead, which was picking up the horns, mainly, and the drums."* He put the mic slightly closer to the reeds than the slightly louder brass instruments. The other mic *"was directed towards Malachi Favors's bass, that could also pick up some of the drum sounds."* He also credits the *"musicians' ability to interact and form their own group dynamics"* as contributing to the recording quality.

Nessa describes the site of the later recordings as *"a more modern townhouse with a finished basement and a finished ceiling."* Martin found that room inferior sonically. *"The session would not necessarily have been so promising,"* he says, *"except there was a large group of musicians coming into a fairly small space."* The musicians' bodies reduced the echo which would otherwise have been prominent.

Bob Koester now runs Riverside Studio. Here's some choice observations on the recording sessions that take place there and the state of musicianship these days.

> **Only our clients ever put drums in the drum booth, and some of them take the hint and don't.**

> **It seems they keep finding more reasons to use more mics and more channels on drums every year.**

> **'20s jazz mixes itself because we didn't have the disadvantage of sophisticated public address systems. They had to mix it to play it. I just wish jazz would go back to that way, we could save hours of time.**

> **Musicians come out of college knowing more about how to record than they do about how to play sometimes. We have guys who look at our studios and kind of snicker.**

> **Layering, I hate layering. I hate isolation booths. Jazz is not the kind of music you can manufacture that way.**

> **You spend half your time deciding who you can believe in as an engineer and then you spend the other time trying to keep him from bob-bugging the musicians.**

While I didn't find as much naivete as I'd expected, I was excited by so much of what I did discover about these records. I had known nothing about Ter-Mar or Sound Studios, and learned that they were well-equipped studios staffed by experienced engineers, rather than the more naive settings I'd visualized. Without today's abundance of cheap and small equipment, it's not surprising, in retrospect, that such facilities really were the only available option. Given the cost of these full-equipped studios and the labels' tight budget, it's impressive that so many records did get finished. Joseph Jarman's gratitude in describing Stu Black as an "excellent engineer" was especially nice to hear. Most exciting of all, for me, is learning that people involved with making these records still do recording 30 years later. Delmark now has Riverside Studio in its own building, and Bob Koester supervises sessions there. Chuck Nessa does recording and mastering work. Terry Martin is *"still interested in amateur recording."*

If not in the ways that I expected, I find the early AACM recordings even more inspiring now that I know so much about them. Ⓐ

(ENDPAGE RANT) JUST LISTEN!

Photo by Chris Carnel

Tape Op gets a lot of CD's in the mail. Some are great, and we play them to death, but many just plain stink. Why?

Maybe nobody is listening. The recording process is great. You can create amazing sonic landscapes that draw the listener in. You can bolster the mood of a song with great overdubs and studio tricks that would be impossible in a live setting. There's just one problem. You must have a great song to begin with.

The songwriting process is beyond the scope of this short column, but it's obviously the most important element. Recording only exists to capture the song and music and is not the most important part! It seems that many songwriters, especially in the "indie/alternative" rock world, have incredibly small record collections or a really narrow perspective on what they plan to achieve with their music. This is a big problem. I'm not saying that schizophrenic genre hopping is cool (`cause it usually sucks) but one thing I've noticed about all great artists is that they draw inspiration from many diverse sources and often times the music they create is vastly different from what they listen to. Songwriting should be familiar without being obvious. If you can guess, on first listen, what lyrics are coming up or what chord progression the chorus will use, then a song is predictable and weak. If the lyric line follows the chords so close that they're nearly one-in-the-same, then the whole tune feels one-dimensional. Arrangements are very, very important too. Cutting out 'dead' spots in the songs is very crucial, as can be repeating an earlier part in order to reinforce thematic elements or to give a sense of resolve. All of the above can be learned by listening. When you put on your favorite record, listen to how the songs are structured. How do the vocal melodies fit the chords? What's the song structure? You'll be surprised at how simple some songs are and how complex some that appear easy really are. Listening is also incredibly valuable to the engineer/producer/recording geek. Maybe even more valuable to the recordist than the artist. When I hear poorly done home recordings, what usually strikes me first is how the piece doesn't sound 'right'. This 'right' isn't a rule laid down by some god of music, it's what we've grown accustomed to hearing from the last 90 years of recorded music. Not that I'm saying rules shouldn't be broken, but if you're trying to get someone to listen to a recording of a band, it should sound similar to records by bands that pursue a common aesthetic. What I hear is people trying too hard. Every piece of the drum kit has been close mic'd and EQ'd drastically and the bass has been tampered with until only the lowest lows ("Make it sound deep, man!") and highest highs remain. What bugs me is, that with a proper amount of listening and perspective, all this could be avoided. Just as a songwriter should listen to the music of others to know what works and what doesn't, recordists should listen to records, a lot, to know what makes them tick.

Personally, I'd be wary of working with anyone, engineer or artist, who hasn't done a lot of listening. If you're gonna bend the "rules" of songwriting or recording, you have to be familiar with the "rules". If you haven't put in the time at home listening to records, how fine tuned will your ears be when it's time to mix an album? It's music, and it all starts with keeping your ears open.

-Larry Crane

Let's get one thing out of the way first: I love old technology. If I had the space, I'd have a workshop full of old radios, open reel tape and wire recorders, valve amps, old keyboards and vintage guitars. (Thinking about it, there are those who would say my house is getting that way already). I also dig obsolete and forgotten recording formats – the more obscure the better - send 'em my way (say, has anyone else come across those weird 8-inch magnetic disc recording machines from the pre-tape 1940s?). I've always loved this kind of stuff. When I was small, in the mid-1960s, I can remember my dad reading the radio hobbyist magazines and building radios and tape recorders with great-sounding names... Leak, Quad, Truvox and Ferrograph... those names alone conjure up a bygone era and a pioneering, experimental spirit. To paraphrase Phil Spector, back to mono, kids! The digital domain just doesn't do it for me in the same way.

Toe Rag Music
London's Swinging Studio
by Phil Clark

Up until just a few years ago, vintage musical equipment was fairly easy to find here in London. Nobody seemed to want the old stuff, and music shops couldn't give it away! Things are changing now though. Vintage instruments and recording gear are becoming scarce and sought-after, so when these items come onto the market, they are often snapped up straight away. Folks seem to be re-evaluating gear previously thought to be obsolete or mundane... it's as if they're discovering a forgotten world; "Hey, maybe there is something worth using here!" Well this newly acquired "retro-vision" is no news to me, and it won't come as any surprise to the folks at Toe Rag, either, because they've been there all along.

Toe Rag is an East London recording studio operating very much in the classic style. Here's an antidote to the sometimes-too-sterile world of modern digital recording: an entirely analogue studio, fitted out with an impressive collection of vintage recording equipment and instruments, salvaged over the years from auctions and studio graveyards, and carefully restored by the studio's resident engineer and manager, Liam Watson. Liam has run Toe Rag since 1992 and has just relocated the studio to a specially designed new space, so I was delighted to visit and check it out.

The studio room (see picture) is 17ft by 14ft with an 11ft high ceiling and nifty retro-style black-and-white-squared lino floor. Straight away

I was reminded me of how I imagine an EMI studio might have felt in the mid-1960s. I was half-expecting to hear one of those stereotypical white-coated studio boffin on the talkback any second: "That's a take, boys!" That feel is captured so well that two film crews have recently been in to shoot sequences amongst the authentic period studio fittings. A large retro "Recording" light above the window into the control room is a nice touch and a collection of vintage condenser mics is arranged along one wall. Outside in the hallway there is a wonderful selection of valve guitar amps, an old tone wheel Hammond L102 and a Vox Continental organ, the latter as used by legendary garagepunkers, ? & The Mysterians on their recent London visits.

The control room (see second picture) is 14ft by 9ft and is dominated by four huge tape recorders including a striking BTR (British Tape Recorder) Model 2 one-track 1/4-inch mono deck from the mid-1950s which, true to form, is painted battleship green. Liam is still restoring this machine and hopes to have it working soon. In the meantime all recording takes place on either of two Studer multitracks: a 1-inch A80 8-track and a 1/2-inch J37 4-track. This latter machine previously belonged to Fab 208 Radio Luxembourg, and was apparently used for a lot of their radio sessions. Mixdown is to a third Studer A80 1/4-inch machine. Mixing desks are a Calrec M Series dating from the

1970s, bought from the BBC, and an EMI Redd 17 desk from 1956 which previously belonged to Abbey Road until EMI had their famous equipment auction in the early 1980s.

Outboard effects include some classic names with compressors from Cinema, Altec, Pye and Gates and an AKG reverb chamber. Most striking of all, in the corridor between the studio and the control room there is a large rectangular wooden box stacked up along one wall, measuring at least six feet long. Liam explains that this is an original EMT 140 reverb plate, and gleefully demonstrates the single large dial looking rather like a water stopcock on the top of the case. The EMT is of course a complete classic, and didn't Abbey Road at one time have a roomful of these monster machines? It's great to see one still in captivity.

So what sort of bands record at Toe Rag? As might be expected, the studio has always been very popular with the bands on London's retro music scene, which revolves around such groovy go-go clubs as Frat Shack and the Dirty Water Club. Toe Rag has been central to capturing the sound of the bands on that scene, and over a hundred records have so far been cut there. Liam: "People like the fact that we're analogue, and that we do things in the classic, or perhaps the 'old-fashioned', way. Also we're ideally set up to do live recording. Quite often, in fact, bands want to record completely live, including the vocals!

So when we start a new session, I'll talk to the band about how they want to work. I'll get them to run through their songs so I can see how they work together. I'll look out for the obvious stuff like drummers playing one side of the kit harder than the other – there, for example, I'd know to compensate when we start recording. Then we'll either start doing live takes, with everyone in the studio at the same time, each musician in a different corner, or we'll be doing the bass and drums first, getting the rhythm track down. Then I'll mix that to two, maybe three tracks and build it up. We're eight-track, which might sound at first like a limitation, but I like working with eight-track tape. There are more than enough tracks there for whatever you want to do, and it demands discipline and skill to get good results out of the equipment. Anyway I wonder sometimes how many favorite 1960's records were recorded on four-track."

Having expanded into their new premises, the Toe Rag team is seeing a wider range of musicians coming in for sessions. Liam: "I don't think we're a purely RETRO studio, that's too narrow a description and it alienates people. The equipment here is all classic designs and good quality gear, and we're set up for a wide range of music. Just lately I've been doing rock and roll and rockabilly with a band called Number Nine. Also, possibly surprisingly, we do quite a lot of country type stuff with accoustic guitar and stand-up bass, with a traditional sound. Just before that, we had a punk band in, and then a couple of weeks ago I was with this ska or reggae band. That was quite different. It was very instrumental, with a big brass section who played completely live, apart from the conga player, who couldn't make it on the day and came in later. So I've been doing all sorts of things."

I ask Liam what was the most bizarre or unexpected thing he's found himself doing on a session. "Well, there was a band called Vibrasonic; I did two albums with them. Take their first album in particular... they were a psychedelic group, there were two of them and they played guitar and would get other people in to play drums and then maybe they'd put down bass – fine. Then they'd spend hundreds of hours overdubbing millions of the weirdest things you've ever heard! Nothing was recorded at the right speed; we tried everything backwards and everything was phased - of course this was all done in the

old way, we don't have any digital effects here - we do it all with tape recorders. By the time this all came to the mix, there was one song in particular which was about ten minutes long and we'd done so much that the guitar bass and drums were all bounced on to one track, with the other seven tracks filled up with these different sounds. In the end, I found myself having to try and convince the band that it sounded good, and that they had put enough down on tape. It was already quite a challenge to keep track of what was going where. It was good fun though, I enjoyed doing that and I learnt a lot with it."

How would Liam react if a mainstream act called him up and wanted to come down for a session? First of all, I suggest UK indie outfit Blur. "Sure ... as long as they were aware that we do things in a traditional way here, I'd be up for that." Then I suggest a Top 40 pop act. "Dance music.... That's not really my scene, and anyway we're not set up to do dance stuff here - for a start, we don't have any computers!"

Finally, I ask Liam to name two big influences and he cites two of the great British producers from the 1960s. Shel Talmy (producer of classic mid-'60s British freakbeat including the Kinks, Creation and early Who [and expatriate American]) and Joe Meek (legendary maverick producer of early to mid-'60s British pop, a true genius and years ahead of his time; famous for his wholly unconventional, self-taught approach to recording and also for being the first of the independent tape-lease record producers). "I remember when I was about eleven or twelve, this was around the time that punk was going strong. I heard those old Kinks records they made with Shel Talmy, especially "All Day And All Of The Night" and I thought to myself, this is nothing new – punk was going years ago! And of course there was Joe Meek. He was a real big influence on me too, in fact he was probably the reason I got interested in recording technology itself in the first place. I remember reading about his home-made studio where he made all these strange, pioneering records, some of which were just way over the top – The Tornadoes' "Jungle Fever" for example, and The Syndicats' "Crawdaddy Simone" I loved as well."

So, kids, if you've ever wanted to capture that classic 1960s sound, or just make a record using classic techniques, Toe Rag is the place to do it! ☙

Liam Watson's Eleven Favourit
Toe Rag Production
(Not in any particular orde

The Kaisers: "There's lots of great stuff by this group, b
I especially like the *Wishing Street* CD (on Imperi
Wireless/No Hit) and the two 45s on Spinouts: "She
Gonna Two Time" and "Liquorice Twitch". (Kaisers releas
are available in the US via Get Hip

Big Joe Louis And His Blues Kings *Big Sixteen* CD on A
Records and the two 45s on Spinout, "Rock & Roll Bab
and "Wine-Head

Sonny George *Truckin' Country* CD on Spinou

The Bristols *Introducing* CD/LP and "Questions I Car
Answer" 45, both on Damaged Good

Fire Dept *Elpee For Another Time* on Ye

Splash Four 2 LPs on Estru

Television Personalities *I Was A Mod Before You Was A M*
LP on Overground and the "Seasons in the Sun" 45 on Twi

Neanderthals *Menace to the Human Race* LP on No Hit a
the "Aru-la-mata-Gali" 45 on Spinc

Eddie Angel Various stuff especially the "Casbah" 45 a
the *Guitar Party* LP, both on No Hit/Spinc

Quant "Play With Mary" 45 on Detc

Country Teasers Their 10" LP on Cry

Toe Rag Studio Kit Lis

Mi

AKG C12; C12A; D12; D19; D
Neumann U
STC 4021; 4033; 4035; 4037; 4038; 4
ElectroVoice
Altec
Shure

Mixing Des

EMI Redd 17, ex Abbey Road, 1
Calrec M Series, ex BBC, 19

Tape Recorde

Studer A80 1" eight track, 19
Studer J37 1/2" four track, ex- Radio Luxembourg, 1
Studer A80 1/4" two track mastering machine, 19
EMI BTR2 1/4" one-track mono machine, mid 1950s (undergo
overha

Effec

Langevin EQ units, early 19
Cinema EQ units, mid-19
Altec, Pye and Gates compressors (compressors are also b
into the Calrec de
Ashtronic Response Control Grap
EMT 140 Reverb Pl
AKG Reverb cham

Monito

2 x Tannoy 15" dual concentric speakers with original Lockw
cabinets, mid-19
2 x Quad power amps,

Various vintage instruments and amplifiers are also availab

GEAR

by Larry Crane

For the last three years, TAPE OP was created on a Packard Bell PC computer, a 486 with a small hard drive. It's rather slow with a small memory. With the switch to having a new company publishing the magazine, the text files needed to be in Microsoft Word 4 in a Macintosh format. The crew were kind enough to send up an "extra" Macintosh Classic which was sitting around the offices. I went and got an old dot-matrix printer, new keyboard and new mouse for $90. I asked about used laptops and the woman told me I could get a faster laptop than the Mac I had for $169. This means that for $259 I can have enough computer power to edit this magazine and even bring some of the work home on the portable computer when I need to; not a bad investment.

In 1991 this computer was brand new, and probably cost a bit and was "state of the art" to some. Now you can pick them up for $100. People were laughing when I set it up at the office. But shit, it does the job I need to do and it was cheap.

My friend Craig and I were driving around the other day, checking out the monster Quad-Eight console that my studio has in storage (because it's too big to install!) and picking up some drum parts. Craig "manages" a studio in town here, although he also engineers there and owns a lot of the gear too. We were talking about how he and the studio's owner are looking to upgrade the console, maybe even to purchase an API (legendary mixing boards, if you didn't know). Anyway, one of the reasons that they want to have an API is that no one else in the area does, it would lend a "world-class" image to the studio, and that it would attract business. I can see their point, it makes sense to me, but on the other hand I disagree. I don't see that at the level their studio is at (less than $500 per day) that people expect or can demand that kind of gear and with the cost involved, it seems like they'll spend years paying that kind of gear off. That scares the shit out of me.

Gear is something that comes up all the time. Anybody who records is concerned about what they use to capture and create sound on. Is my deck working properly? Do I need a new one? Will "better" gear make me sound better? There's probably more options for purchasing new recording equipment these days than there has been at any time in history, and that's great. Plus, the fact that there's more stuff out there means there's more *affordable* gear than ever before. That rocks. But gear isn't really all that important. I mean, once you get past a microcassette*, recording mediums all have a certain quality that can work for making music on. **This is true of the simplest Fostex 4-track cassette up to 48 tracks of 24 bit Pro Tools. They work and you can get sounds on them that are pleasing.**

My point is that I think it's much more important what you are doing with this gear than what it is. I know that I reiterate this in every issue of TAPE OP but it's damn important. If you are doing home recording learn to maximize the potential of your 4-track. If you are running a commercial studio make the best possible recordings you can. When people hear it on record, that's when you'll get some calls.

So gear, you gotta have it to do anything, but don't look at as the be-all, end-all of recording. Just because you're recording on the best equipment in the world doesn't mean it's better than someone making an album on a 4-track at home. And the best thing? We can all learn from what other people are doing with the gear they've got... ☻

Actually, if anyone knows of an album recorded on a microcassette please let me know! I'm fascinated by the idea.

Looking at my Pere Ubu liner notes, I noted the frequent appearance of the last name "Hamann". After some confusion, I realized that there were two different first names which accompanied it. I learned that Ken Hamann was the father of Paul Hamann, and poked around to find that they'd recorded a Styrenes single and a Girls single. A friend added that Ken Hamann had recorded a Grand Funk album. It wasn't until I talked to the Hamanns that I discovered the extent of their history in recording and the rest of the story behind their studio, Suma, in Painesville, Ohio.

HAVE YOU HEARD ABOUT THIS HOUSE?

Ken and Paul Hamann and the old house that is Suma Studios

by Steve Silverstein

Ken Hamann began recording as a staff engineer at Cleveland Recording Company. His earliest recordings were *"some polka things back in the 1950s. Frankie Yankovic, Georgie Cook, Eddie Habat, and a few of the other famous Cleveland-style polkas."* The first rock recording of his that *"broke out was the Outsiders with 'Time Won't Let Me'."* It was recorded on a 3-track. *"The first run-through was strictly drums, guitar, bass. There were solos with the baritone sax, the organ, and so forth on another track. All of the vocals and other effects were on a third track. It took a lot of anticipation because we had to do a lot of sub-mixing. At the time, I remember I thought the organ was too hot, but that turned out to be one of the features of the record."*

The equipment at Cleveland Recording was evolving over this time. *"At the very beginning we used RCA broadcast equipment. I found that to be alright but not suitable for some of the things [I was recording]. Having gone to Germany to tour some studios then, in the late 1950s, we decided to move over into German-type of technology, with the use of the flat desk and the faders as we do today. So, I built one. I was able to buy some of those faders out of Germany and I built my own console. The first one was a 3 channel output, and I think it had 10 channels of input. It was modest. That was sufficient to work with 3-track recording, which was then just beginning, on tape, and then mix down to 2 track, of course."* Both the 3-track and 2-track decks were Ampex 351s, and he used 3M Scotch tape.

The next widely-remembered Hamann recording from that era was *"Nobody But Me"* by Youngstown's Human Beinz, from 1967. *"We had two studios available. They had people hitting shovels and Coke bottles while doing certain other tracks in the front studio. This is still 3-track."* Not too much later, Cleveland Recording upgraded to a 4-track deck. *"I found, in New York, a Studer J-37, the same kind that*

the Beatles used recording 'Strawberry Fields'. Th[ey] used 1 inch wide tape for 4-tracks of recording, and w[e] started using that. [It was] fantastic. We still hav[e] the machine; we still use it. But I determined that [it] wasn't enough, so I was able to buy some 8-trac[k] heads and adapt them to that machine. We made th[e] Studer into an 8-track 1 inch. We did many recording[s] with that."* Other well-known Hamann recording[s] from this era include later Outsiders albums, th[e] Lemon Pipers' "Green Tambourine", and some of Er[ic] Carmen's earliest recordings.

"We went through a period when we were tryin[g] to imitate Motown sounds in the late '60s. They ha[d] unique sounds then. I became very good friends wi[th] their chief engineer, Mike McLaine, who is more [a] technical person than a music person. All of th[e] ideas we picked up were not from Mike, but rath[er] from their records. Mostly their snare drum soun[d] and the bass. We discovered that a lot of the sou[nd] was due to how the drums were tuned and mic'd. W[e] did a lot of experimenting. The bass drum was a [bit] stiffer usually, and there's padding put on the surfa[ce] of the head."

The next few years brought two bands to Hamann and the studio which influenced the techniques which he used at the time. *"Jimmy Fox came in with a group called the James Gang, featuring Joe Walsh. Then Terry Knight came in with a new group called Grand Funk Railroad. I did their first several albums, including* Closer to Home, *which is still one of my favorites."* The first Grand Funk album marked the first use of the studio's new Ampex MM-1000 16-track two inch, which still resides at Suma. *"We're pack rats around here; we keep everything."* He also developed techniques for recording bass with Grand Funk, *"using a microphone and distorting the speaker, without distorting the microphone or distorting the amplifier. The actual JBL speakers would distort, and this gave us a very unique bass sound. The amplifiers were West amplifiers, which are hard to come by anymore. They were tube; everything was tube then, thank goodness. The first half of* Closer to Home *was done in that mode, and then we switched when all of the sound effects come in with the ocean, etc. We switched to a different bass sound. You can actually hear a change, a more modest bass without distorting."*

While Wild Cherry (*"Play That Funky Music"*) were the most commercially successful of Ken Hamann's projects at that time, his work with Pere Ubu has led to a successful long-term relationship. *"It could be said that they found me. They had recorded '30 Seconds Over Tokyo' and ['Heart of Darkness']. It was a single, a 45,*

The Hamanns had relocated to Suma by the time he recorded Pere Ubu's first album, 1977's *The Modern Dance.* By this point he had developed a *"standard setup in the studio. The drums were in the same room, a wood-surfaced room in an old house that was built 70, 80 years ago. We had the drums sitting in one corner, on a small platform, 20 inches high. It had gobos around it. We were able to isolate it somewhat, to focus the sound. The other instruments were generally in the room at the same time. We did have isolation booths nearby, adjacent to the studio, so we could put a vocalist or whatever in there. Most of the recordings were done with the basic tracks first, embellishments second, that is guitar things and so forth, and then the vocals last."*

Drums were *"mostly close mic'd, with a pair of overheads. Snare usually was either from the top or the bottom; the bottom was good. The bass drum, the front was usually open and the mic was in the drum. And the toms frequently we mic'd from underneath. That's the floor tom. The other toms we might have done micing from the top. Generally speaking, the bottoms of the drums were all removed. It removed unwanted resonances, gave them a tighter sound."* He most often used Neumann KM-56s on the toms and snare and as overheads, with a Beyer dynamic microphone on the kick drum. Neumann U-47s were common on bass and guitar amps. Allen Ravenstine's EML synthesizer went direct. *"I was quite taken by how he was able to provide exactly the right sound that was needed."*

quite a bit. And, of course, then we started getting into DAT tapes. Today we're using DA-88s and 98s for primary recording and DAT tapes for mix down. I did build quite a few interfaces so that all of these different formats, the AES format, the Pro Tools format, and so forth, were able to talk to each other through the interfaces I've put together. We can handle most anything that a client brings in. Our process today is generally to record a multi-track 32, 48 tracks, whatever, and transfer that in groups of eight tracks, to Pro Tools in a Mac environment. There we can do quite a bit. We're also using a Finalizer for EQing and other processing. Plus some of the software that I developed many years ago."* Suma still has its 2 inch 16- and 24-track decks, and many bands still record in analog there.

Paul Hamann got involved with Cleveland Recording in 1973. He was involved in building that facility too. *"That's how I basically started was helping to build the console that we use. It just sort of rolled over that way."* The first recordings of his that I've encountered are Pere Ubu live recordings from 1978 on the *390 Degrees of Simulated Stereo* albums. Ken and Paul Hamann recorded the Girls single on Hearpen together, with David Thomas producing. The first Pere Ubu studio album which Paul Hamann recorded was *The Art of Walking.* He attributes the diversity of material to the simple fact that *"the songs were very different from each other."*

The David Thomas solo albums of the next several years were among Hamann's most visible work in the '80s. The first of these albums, *The Sound of the Sand* was recorded in England, but Hamann did all of the mixing. The next David Thomas studio album was *Variations on a Theme.* Hamann played bass on all of this album, but what stands out to him is Richard Thompson's guitar playing. *"It was great working with Richard. It was absolutely wonderful."* Much like his father, he has a fairly consistent process for recording. He also tends to have everyone play in one room as much as possible. *"Drums were always done in the live room. Always close mic'ing and always far mic'ing."* He tended to use Neumann U-47s as room mics, Sennheiser 441s on toms and Sennheiser 421s on a snare. He prefers mic'ing snares from the top. *"I'm not into the gritty stuff from the bottom."* The mic on the kick drum varies, often based on the song that's being recorded. He sometimes uses a Sennheiser 441 on the kick drum. For the acoustic instruments that were prominent on these albums, he always uses U-47s. *"I do have one of the largest collections in the state of tube mics that were all purchased new back in the '50s and '40s. So I do have that luxury, and I really don't know any other way."*

Hamann tends to use the solid-state mic preamps that are built in the studio. *"A properly working solid-state mic pre and a properly working tube mic pre are very very similar. When you get into the improper use of it is where you start noticing the difference."* He tries to use compression infrequently. *"If I get into compression, depending on the effect, old Urei 1176s. If I was using it, that was a phase when I was using it as an effect, not as a crutch. Which so often those things*

"I was able to buy some of those faders out of Germany and I built my own console."

and they had recorded it and wanted a master. We had the facility to cut 45 masters, and still do as a matter of fact. I did not [record it], but I did make their master disc. They were impressed with the studio. 'Final [S]olution' I think we did."*

In 1970, Cleveland Recording owner Greg Wolf had [s]old his studio to its two staff engineers. *"In 1976, we [s]plit the studio. I formed Suma Recording Studio and [m]oved out into the country. The reason was that at that [t]ime, in the early '70s, it was the rage to create studios [o]ut in the country. George Martin did it, the group Chicago [d]id it, some others. I emulated them in a small way."* The [n]ew studio brought a new tape deck, a 2 inch 24-track [A]mpex MM-1200. *"We still have that, actually; we still [u]se it."* Hamann built a board for Cleveland Recording in [1]973, and it moved to Suma in 1976. *"It's a 48 channel, [a]ctually 24 mics and 24 lines. It's a dual board, so that [o]ne can mix at the same time as recording. It has the [a]ppropriate number of outputs and mix combining buses. [I]t's all solid-state. At the time I was building consoles for [o]ther people, as well, other studios. I decided to get out [o]f that business when it became a little cut-throat. About [t]he same time that Rupert Neve was starting in England. [I] decided to focus more on the actual recording. I did [b]uild equipment for my own use in the studio. Originally [i]t was all discrete, but we have updated it continually to [k]eep it up to date with modern standards."* Some of the [n]ewer parts of the board include ICs.

He says that David Thomas's vocals were recorded *"carefully, sometimes phrase by phrase, which is still the case."* He often used a U-47 with a windscreen. While Thomas typically sang in a live room, his vocals were *"close mic'd so the room didn't really figure into it, so we would have to add reverb. We were using an EMT-140 at that time, we had two of them—that was the big plate. We first acquired that in the early '60s."*

One song from *The Modern Dance* which stands out to Hamann is "Sentimental Journey", which features the sound of breaking glass. *"We have a huge, stone fireplace at one end of the studio—it's about 15 feet wide. They asked if we could do it. We said, 'Sure, why not, as long as you don't hurt yourself.' That was done as an overdub. At that time, we had 24 tracks, so we had the tracks to spare."*

While his son Paul has taken over much of the recording at Suma, Ken Hamann is still involved with the studio. He does a lot of work with equipment, and has been especially involved with the installation of digital recording equipment in the studio. *"First we bought a Sony M-1, a 2-track. That was very good. We modified it so that we could interface with certain other digital equipment for the purpose of getting it into the computer, and I wrote some programs for equalizing and that kind of processing, in addition to using Digidesign software. We borrowed on occasion the Sony 3/4" format video, the 1610/1620 format, and we used that* are used for, as crutches. They're much more interesting to use as an effect." He previously used 3M 996 tape, but now uses BASF 900. While Suma has always used Hafler amps, they try many different monitors. "I'm never happy with monitors. What I usually use is some JBL product. My main monitors are either 4350s or 4430s. I've got 4430s in there now. The majority of the mixes I do are done, and have been all along, on a pair of Minimus 7s. Little Radio Shacks."

Hamann adds that some of these records employed tape loops. "Some of it was 1/4 inch tape, and some of it was 16-track 2", where we'd have the stuff stretched across the room. The 16 track machine was the only one we could abuse that way. The 24-track wouldn't operate in loop situations—the holdback on it wouldn't permit that kind of thing."

The David Thomas album which stands out to Hamann is 1986's *Monster Walks the Winter's Lake*, which was recorded live to a Sony F-1 digital 2-track. It "was all basically acoustic instruments. There were no drums. There was just people out there beating on chair mats with drum sticks, and that was basically the drum set." While all of the instruments are clearly recorded, it can sometimes be hard to distinguish which unusual sound comes from what instrument.

"At the same time that was all going on, if I remember, we were pretty heavy in the local metal scene. That was kind of the contrast that's been going on out here. And then interspersed with all of that was the jazz, local jazz guys, too." While he finds isolation challenging with a piano and drum set in the same room, he considers jazz and rock recording similar. "I treat them all pretty much the same, it's up to the players." Most of the bands that he recorded at the time were not known outside of Cleveland. Eddie Kramer, who produced Jimmy Hendrix, Blue Cheer, and Traffic, produced a Michael Stanley Band album which Hamann engineered. He found Kramer great to work with.

The use of two drummers, Scott Krauss and Chris Cutler, stood out to Hamann as the most interesting challenge with Pere Ubu's *The Tenement Year* album. It was recorded "primarily live, with both players at once. Then we just basically pick and choose parts during the mixes. Sometimes it was both sets; sometimes it was Scotty's bass drum and Chris's snare, and we'd mix parts back and forth. We'd try to arrange the parts as we went. Usually Scotty was holding the beat down and then Chris was doing the cool stuff on top. Again, that was always done live, the two kits together. Isolation was not an issue, not at all. The only place that there would have been any leakage would have been in the overheads and of course the room mics, but the rest of it, no, it was all close mic'd." To reduce bleed, he used "creative placement, creative EQ," and "a lot of times it just didn't matter."

Pere Ubu's *Cloudland* was "mixed up with a whole slew of different people." Hamann enjoyed mixing parts of the record at Paisley Park, although he never got to meet Prince. "He'd call at 11 o'clock at night wondering when I was going to be done so he could get in there." Paisley Park had an SSL board and Studer 800 multi-tracks. "The only thing he didn't have was Dolby, which

was hilarious, because they had to rent Dolby's all over the place. So I had everything from the little cat cards to old ones all piled up on top of the 800. Everything we do [at Suma] is Dolby A, if I'm using the 2 inch. With the higher operating levels of Dolby A, I can get away with it. I have to be careful with tapes that are going to be mixed elsewhere, because of the availability of it [now], but I like it. It's at least financially kept us from having to get into SR."

The next Pere Ubu album, *Worlds in Collision*, started at Suma. In the effort to achieve more commercial success than Ubu had in the past, it was finished elsewhere. "A lot of that we had recorded once, and then that's when Stephen Hague came on. He went and re-recorded a lot of it. How much of it, I don't know, from the original stuff that was re-done. Before he got it, it was all pretty much laid out, the form was there, the tunes were there. And then he went back and re-recorded everything."

While none of Ubu's *Story of My Life* was recorded at Suma, the band returned for 1995's *Raygun Suitcase*. The first sessions for the album were with a line-up that included founding Pere Ubu drummer Scott Krauss and cellist Garo Yellin. Hamann describes the rest of the album as "done inside out. That one primarily was recorded with the guitar and the bass and whatever synth there was, and then afterwards the drums were added. Everything was done to a click track and then the drums were added after the fact. That's why I say it was sort of done inside out." The album also began a more experimental approach to recording. Distance mic'ing was used more often. "A lot of the stuff would wind up going out through studio monitors out in the studio, and re-record it from that point. There may have been some guitar parts where I put literally a wall of Marshalls outside and recorded that way. Since I'm out in the country, in the woods, I've got a valley behind us. I do have a considerable collection of old Marshall and Hiwatt stuff. I'd put that stuff outside, you can hear it all over the city, but it sounds cool."

For Thomas's vocals, while he'd "start with a U-47", he also experimented with a wider range of microphones. He'd sometimes use a Neumann M-49 or M-50, a Neumann stereo SM2 in MS mode, or three U-47s in left/center/right. "I'd have the mics splayed out in front of him so he could move around. Some of the vocals we did send back through the speakers. Some of them were done through a window fan. We used the window fan and a Variac, to slow the thing way down. The window fan thing I think came from one of David's tours, one of the Ubu tours, which turned out to be pretty amazing."

With the popularity of heavy metal declining, more jazz and folk was recorded at Suma. Steven Stills and Lenny Kravitz both did recording with Hamann, and some of the Kravitz tracks were released on the Kiss tribute album. David Thomas and Two Pale Boys' 1996 CD *Erewhon* was built in the studio around samples, "and bad ones at that. We had to do something to create the illusion that something was going on. A lot of that was peculiar mic'ing. At that point we were screwing around using speakers, horn drivers [as mics]. One of the

cuts is strictly done with a telephone handset. Another one was vocal tracks that [Thomas] had sung in his little portable tape recorder, with the DAT machine playing in the background. I had to fly them back in onto the master tape." The album was recorded to DA-88s.

Erewhon was recorded with "excessive improper use of phase" which would have made a vinyl release in stereo impossible. Hamann takes pride in the record's ability to make him queasy, but explains that such a situation is atypical of his recordings. "Before and afterwards I'm usually pretty conscious of [stereo phase issues] because we also do have a [vinyl] lathe. So, I'm quite well aware of what the problems are about working with that. And what makes an easy job for the engineer and what doesn't." Other stereo effects were achieved by using military surplus engines as auto-pans.

Some of the mixes on *Erewhon* are also unusual. "One of the mixes I blew through a Leslie, and I recorded it through a door from the next room. That comprises a good portion of one of the mixes. It was all done live while the mix was going on. You got the microphone in the next room and the Leslie screaming in another room."

Pere Ubu's most recent album, *Pennsylvania*, was a return to live band recording, but it follows *Erewhon*'s use of unconventional microphones. "Since I had track space, we were using other things again, such as speakers, horn drivers, that kind of thing. Quite literally, I was using various and sundry 15 inch and 12 inch speakers, down to little computer ones. Some of the guitar sounds were primarily computer speakers sat next to the amplifier. Some of the bass drum sounds are JBL 15 inch speakers sitting on the floor next to the drum set. I'd pick and choose there. Some of the ones that I have have melted voice coils, so they scrape. Other ones are in good shape. So we pick and choose whether we want the scraping sound or something cleaner."

Aside from Pere Ubu and David Thomas, Hamann has recently recorded Robert Lockwood, Jr. and Buddy Miles. He also received an Emmy award for a video soundtrack.

Ken and Paul Hamann reminded me of the simple need for balance in approaching recording. Each has developed a set of techniques that work reliably without letting it constrict them or prevent experimentation. They trust well-known equipment which works, like their Urei compressors and Neumann microphones, but also build their own boards and use West bass amps. They're comfortable working with old and proven technologies but also willing to incorporate newer equipment. And while they understand the value of musicians performing live in a room together, they also construct tracks in small pieces when it's appropriate. This basic mindset which has led to so many memorable recordings continues in a still active but often overlooked studio. ☉

The first time

by Larry Crane

I ever went in to a studio to record was in the summer of 1985. Our band, Vomit Launch, had been around for almost six months, and we decided it was time to hit the studio and make a "demo". Our drummer at the time, John, suggested a place that we always saw advertised in the local weekly, so we gave them a call. John, having done this a few times before, suggested we go to the place and check it out before committing to recording time. We found ourselves 30 miles from town in the middle of some olive orchards looking for the place. Eventually we came upon a small house sitting on a barren hill with a shack next to it. The shack was the studio. Inside was a Fostex 16-track 1/2", a small mixer, a few other pieces of gear and a live room the size of a small kitchen. The control room was like a closet and the studio owner looked like a troll. We played him some board tapes from recent gigs and he seemed to be into it, comparing one song to the Doors, which seemed weird to us. When we showed up to start our two days of recording there were goats and kids running around and it was pushing 100 degrees outside. We brought our motley collection of amps but he wouldn't let us use them, instead running

everything direct with the option to overdub later. I was sitting in the control room when I noticed a little mirror and razor blades on a shelf under the mixer. Tracking went fairly fast; we weren't perfectionists. In between takes we'd turn the air conditioner on to cool off. When we set up Lindsey's two amp guitar setup the guy was skeptical. We won out, and got a pretty decent stereo sound with it. I remember him wincing as I demanded to use my overdriven bass sound. Trish nailed her vocals pretty fast. The troll had been drinking a few wine coolers by the time I was trying to lay down backing vocals. He kept recording them and then couldn't find them on the tape. I thought this was a little weird. When we finished all the tracking the troll suggested we could stay overnight with him at his house. We declined. The next day we showed up to mix. After a while it became apparent that he was gonna mix our songs with a wildly different idea in mind than what we had. John and I eventually commandeered the mixer from him and balanced the mix out to our taste while he drank wine coolers. We paid our bill ($360, I think) and on the way home were pretty excited about the sounds we got. Eventually we used the songs, with some horrible sounding live tracks, on a cassette that we called *Fishbutt*. We sold a lot in town and at gigs for a few years. It really wasn't that good. A year later I got a call from my pal Mike, asking if I wanted to go out to the same studio to help mix some local band that had asked Mike for assistance. Feeling like I didn't know shit but interested in recording and getting some more studio experience I agreed.

When we got there nobody was awake. Eventually a few people stumbled out of the troll's house. Apparently they had partied all night, getting drunk and having a "jam" session in the studio. The singer was supposed to do all of his vocals today but had fried his voice out during the "jams". To top it off, he was drinking a big glass of milk for breakfast. The musicians started moping around with nobody taking initiative to get anything done. We left. Over the years I'd run into the troll at local shows. He told me that he didn't let people take over the control room the way we had anymore. I wasn't so sure that was a good thing. He had moved into an old quonset hut north of town where he shared the space with some weird yuppie band that played covers in bars around town. The studio disappeared and we heard a story about the yuppie band beating him up while they videotaped the proceedings. Small town cocaine dealings were blamed. Vomit Launch ended up obtaining the building they had been in. It made a pretty nice practice pad. ☻

WHARTON TIERS

WHARTON OUTSIDE HIS STUD

BY LARRY CRANE AND HILLARY JOHNSON

Wharton Tiers has run Fun City studios out of his Manhattan basement since 1981. He's record
some of the finest records by Sonic Youth, Dinosaur Jr., Helmet, Unrest and many more. It's
unimposing place, and not very large, but the records he makes sound amazing. For the last f
years he's also been helping Sonic Youth set up and run their Echo Cañon studio, where they
recorded recent releases
the band and their si
projects. He also leads
Wharton Tiers Ensemble
riveting instrumental com
that he composes for o
plays drums in (check
Twilight of the Computer A
on Atavistic). Hillary an
dropped in at Fun City o
had a great ch
The following day we visi
Echo Cañon and chatted w
Lee Ranaldo (of So
Youth - see sideb
about working w
Wharton and sett
up a private stu
for their ba

INSIDE WHARTON'S STUDIO

In 1981 you started in this spot?

Yes.

What were you doing before '81, recording wise?

Playing in about 20 bands. No, actually at my peak I was playing in five bands, no money in any of them.

Playing guitar?

Playing guitar in a couple, but mostly drums. I was always a busy guy.

Had you been going into studios with any of the bands as a musician?

Yes, in a bunch of New York studios, basically we were rehearsing stuff down here. We used to put a cassette down with a couple of mics and people were saying, "This sounds better than the studio." I had a 4-track, which I ran into the ground by recording on it. I ended up getting an 8-track and then I had Sonic Youth here a month later.

That would have been *Confusion Is Sex*?

Yes. They never made another one that sounded exactly like that again. [laughter]

I kind of wish... it's so raw.

It was an 8-track with no outboards, I think we had one compressor.

Had you been using this place as a practice space then?

Yes

How does that work with people living up there?

My apartment is directly over the studio and this is all brick and stone. For a New York space it's pretty isolated.

I think Lee [Ranaldo] had said you had some problems awhile back with someone.

I had a problem with a person in the building next store.

Did you off them or anything? [laughter]

No, we worked it out.

Did you set up some times or something?

It was just one those people that you find in New York, nothing happens in their own life and they're like, "Everything bothers me." She's complaining about the studio at the same time she's complaining about her neighbor closing his door or having his girlfriend over.

I think when people see studios, they see bands pulling up and coming in and out, they probably think a drug deal is going on half the time.

People knew what I was doing. In New York it's better to have people around than to not have people around. If you have people around... half these buildings are empty during the day, everyone leaves for work and that's when all the robberies happen. So you're much better off having people around.

So you had a 4-track initially and then went to eight and did the Sonic Youth stuff right after you got the 8-track going?

Pretty much, it was a Tascam 38, it had just come on the market, it was a couple thousand dollars. I thought that was a lot of money to spend for my personal use so maybe I'll get some people in to record.

What kind of jobs did you get after *Confusion Is Sex*?

Just a lot of local bands. I, of course, from playing in bands had a lot of contacts from different bands.

What kind of board were you using then?

Kelsey, it was a Pro Club 12 channel. I got two of them at one point and spliced them together for 24 channels. Basically, when Kelsey was over Crest Audio blew out all of the stuff they had and I bought a whole lot of it.

I've never seen one of these.

I don't know how many of them they made. It's an amazing board, it was designed by some guy in England, I think he worked for Neve. The circuitry is very similar to the Neve VR except it's basically half as much. It's the most economical straight-line design as opposed to outbands at every stop. It always had a really cool sound so I stuck with it.

How many channels do you have now?

I've got the 24 and the 12 and the Mackie [1604] for effects returns. I've got the Pro-Mix here which I use to automate stuff.

What are you tracking to these days?

A 1" MSR24 [Tascam].

You don't see too many of those around anymore.

No, it's really a shame because I think it was the last analog tape machine that was ever designed. It's a spectacular machine but of course the ADAT revolution was already underway by the time it hit the market. The ADATs came out about three or six months before that machine was released and everyone was like, "Yeah, digital, digital!"

What do you think of ADATs?

I've worked with them. 16-bit audio is a little thin for my taste as a rule, some of the 20-bit ones that are out now sound pretty good. I think that as the high bit stuff starts happening, the sound will catch up.

After the 8-track, what did you move to?

A 16-track 1" Tascam. I was always into Tascam because they use to have a great service center in New Jersey.

What projects were you doing when the sixteen came around? I think you had Dinosaur Jr. and Unrest.

I think the first Unrest I did was 16-track and the second album was 24-track.

How did you get to do Dinosaur Jr.?

That was a Sonic Youth referral.

It seems like that was a good band to get working with originally.

Absolutely. *Confusion is Sex* did really well; it got a lot of press and everything. I think it took me another four years to get something that had that level of visibility. Eventually, people were happy with what they were getting so they came back and told friends about it. I never really had to advertize, it's all been through word of mouth.

Now you're at the point where you're doing lots of work.

Yeah, now you walk around and it's like, "Blah, blah, blah was a classic record to me!"[laughter] It's fun when all that kind of stuff survives.

Think of all the recording sessions that you've done that don't go anywhere. You never know when you're working on something which ones are the ones people are going to hear.

It's not always the best stuff either. Sometimes it's just people who have the right connections and their stuff comes out, other bands do this incredible material and sit home and smoke pot and never get any further with it.

As far as recording, how do you use the space in here?

It's set up now for my band, there's something about the way this room is; you get incredible isolation. There's nothing parallel about this room, the floor slopes down, the ceilings are all curved, if you look at these walls they're not straight, they're kind of angled a little.

You didn't even have to build it this way.

This was totally one of those lucky, fortuitous things. I just kept moving stuff around until it got to this point where things worked really good.

Do you ever try to do vocals live with the band going?

Yes. Usually if I do vocals live I'll just use a mic that hardly picks up anything except for what's right on it.

A dynamic mic?

Yeah, like an Audix or an [Beyer] M500, something like that. If you get a good vocal take it's great because you've got plenty of isolation, you can compress it or put effects on it without getting instruments in it. A lot of times if you get a cool sound and later on you try a better mic on the vocals they end up liking the rough tracks better. Not everyone needs to sing through a super expensive clean mic. It doesn't really help a lot of people at all. Especially with rock'n'roll singers, high end condenser mics pop, sputter and hiss from their singing styles and it's just not the right mic. One of the best parts about recording is trying a few different mics out on a vocalist and seeing what really gives it character. Every mic has it's own character, you find the right match with the person. Helmet, for example, Page sounded great through this 635 Electrovoice which is an $80 mic. The guy from the label practically had a shit when he came over and saw... "This is your vocal mic?" Of course he called up a rental company and got four tube mics. We put them up together and tracked with them but in most cases the 635 was the one, it just sounded perfect on his voice.

I heard about that session, they were even fighting with you about the tape speed.

Yeah well, some A&R people know a little more than you do. [laughter] If they worried about selling the records the music business would improve immensely.

LEE RANALDO

You had worked with Wharton on *Confusion Is Sex* ages ago. As far as bringing someone in - how did you pick Wharton for the job?

We had been good friends for a long time and in the years after *Confusion*... we worked with Wharton periodically on all kinds of things. Never really big album projects, but lots of EPs or singles, or one-offs. It was always easy and comfortable to work in his studio and he seemed to have the most savvy grasp on the whole thing. When we decided to set or own place up and get our own gear, he was a big part in being a consultant – as far as what stuff we were going to buy and what was going to be good for us. He knew what our preferences were at this point... the analog stuff, the Neve, the 15 ips 2" 16-track. He was consulted a lot as we were purchasing this stuff. It was always assumed that he would be the "Tech King" and wire all of it up. It just worked out that it was the perfect time, because things weren't happening in his building – he wasn't working a lot there and he had a chance to come here and work with us. We wanted to do an album with him, so it all kind of came together. With the Neve coming from the BBC, it had its idiosyncrasies and quirks – it took him a long time to figure it out.

He told me about trying to figure it out and firing it up.

Yeah, we basically drew a lot on his information and John Siket's information. John turned us on to the dealer in Detroit that sold us the Studer and the Neve. John, himself, sold us the Ampex 1/2". They were both instrumental in sort of guiding us to the equipment that we wanted.

You had an 8-track right?

Yeah, before this we had a Tascam 8-track 1/2" and a Soundcraft Spirit board. That was a cool step... Me being someone that's fascinated with recording and recording gear, I was always pushing for that stuff. We use to have a 4-track that we did some stuff on, but when we got the 8-track, we really got serious about incorporating the recordings into the working method of the band. We had always recorded stuff on cassette and listen back to it, trying to figure out what the good parts of the songs were. Once we got the 8-track, we would come back from doing something really good and one of us would be like, "Well I don't remember what I played on that part." We would just solo the track. We got a lot of use out of that studio, it was fairly inexpensive to set up – a few thousand dollars for the gear. Again, Wharton helped us with the mics and the purchase of all that gear as well. Around the time that we were doing Lollapalooza, we realized that they were going to pay us enough to make the jump to something serious, if we wanted to. For the last three or four albums we had

been recording on Neves, mixing to 1/2", working at 15 ips on both machines. We just finally realized that we should buy this gear and have it for ourselves. Eventually it'll be a cost-effective measure. We've only done one album... well we've done the album, but we've also done the fourth [SYR] EP on it. So, it's definitely proven very cost-effective, in spite of Manhattan rent.

Wharton was talking about when you had to have a place to store your gear, you had a place to practice... you had to rent all of these different places, now it's kind of like your little complex.

It's great, it's the total clubhouse... It's really good. It's allowed us to work in a way that we were never able to work in. That's the coolest thing about having our own place, it's not a commercial venture. We let our friends come in when we're not in here and a couple of us have done other projects in here. The best thing is that we come in and play in our natural, relaxed environment and we tape everything. It's not like you go to a studio after you've rehearsed the songs 50-million times and you're under that pressure – both financially and time wise... "We've got to do the best version of this song we ever did in our lives right now." Our whole thing is that we really like the idea of versions where the song is just starting to coalesce. All the elements are there, they're not all dusted and perfectly shined and polished and in place, but it's all there at that point. We feel like we can hear the newness of it - the sort of still inventive quality of the music, that's what we're going for. Whenever we're here Wharton is in there rolling tape, whether we're just doing a freak out jam for a week on end or... It's really the perfect way for us to work. What we realized, as far as capturing the sound of the band, it was not an overdub situation as much as the band playing live. When you heard old records from the '50s, Buddy Holly or whatever, they stuck a couple mics in the room and the band was really there playing. It wasn't like the drummer came in and did his part and the bass player layered over it. That was more interesting to us, even if it meant sacrificing – we play in here with not that much baffling, there's bleed all over the place. It's not really up our alley to worry too much about that stuff because it's all going to come back together at some point anyway. We are just looking for a natural situation to play in and having are own gear and our own place to do it...

Has it changed the way that you write and operate as a band?

In a way. I think it's just allowed us to be looser and free. It sort of coincided with a push in all of us to want to just blow everything wide open and forget about song form. It sort of started with *Washing Machine* - getting more into extended songs like "Diamond Sea", that just went a million places in 15 minutes. Since then, we just stopped worrying about record company bullshit and tried to just

please ourselves. It was kind of a coincidence, the fact that we were able to have our own space at the same time meant that we could stretch out here and as long as the tape would roll... "Diamond Sea" is actually an early example of this. The song wouldn't fit on one reel of tape, so we had a DAT machine covering the interim while we swapped reels. We still put songs together that way, where there's a piece in the middle that is a DAT edit that we spliced in.

You guys seem to always be rejuvenating yourselves.

Yeah, having a studio has helped with that in a way. Since '90, when we signed to Geffen there's always been this record company umbrella over everything and we finally got to the point where we were like, "Somebody will put out our records." We got very loose and I think the solo stuff that all four of us were doing really helped – to sort of challenge the band and bringing back new stuff back into the band. We're having as much fun making music the last few years than as we've ever had, so that's a good sign.

WHARTON CONTINUED

In the position you're in now, how busy are you? Do you have to field everything that comes in and decide which things you have time to work on?

I've been basically trying to get more time for myself. I'm trying to get a little less busy. I've been working with Sonic Youth a lot in the last couple of years, which has taken a lot of time between all of their individual projects. A lot of the local bands which I used to record, don't even call at this point. They just figure that I'm too busy or I'm too expensive or I'm unreachable. I generally have enough to keep me busy.

You're not having to scramble and record blues bands?

I don't really do anything like that. I've been spending a lot of time on my band and my stuff and that's totally rewarding. I've been doing a lot of mastering which is a lot of fun because you can get something to sound good with no commitment to spend 80 hours doing the thing.

When you're doing the mastering what kind of gear are you using?

I basically just use the Sound Designer.

It's all in the computer?

I use the analog tape machine a lot because I get a lot of stuff that's totally digital and the best thing to do is to put it on tape.

So you take it from DAT and dump it down to 1/4"?

Yes, usually I'll EQ the DAT or compress the DAT a little when going to tape and then the tape to the computer is pretty clean. Once it gets into the computer I try to do as little with it as possible. I don't really like the way that the manipulation makes things sound. It's pretty much just a straight line in with a maximum level.

Cool. What kind of projects are you getting for that?

All kinds of strange things. My cousin's actually got a recording studio in his basement now in Brooklyn. He's been recording a lot of stuff that I probably would have done ten years ago. A lot of them will come here to master stuff. Labels will send me stuff.... It's basically people that can't afford to go to Masterdisc and get the super high-end deal.

How much are those kinds of places?

Hundreds.... hundreds an hour, depending on whom you're doing it with. You can literally spend a few thousand dollars mastering something these days. They don't cut deals. It's hard to find off-hours, those places are really expensive. Obviously they have all the latest gear continually rolling in so I'm sure there's some little measure of benefit from all of that, but in reality, when your starting with tapes that are basically raw anyway, you don't want to clean them up. You're really just looking to get a good maximum level and a nice sound spectrum.

When did you start doing the mastering?

Obviously the software became available and it really started about a year and a half ago when I was having some problems with the cassette machine and I thought "Well, I'll just go buy a new cassette machine." The quality control on the cassette world has gone to where the machines don't play at the right speed. They don't track correctly... this is brand new out of a box! I started out spending a few hundred dollars and kept ratcheting my way up figuring sooner or later there's got to be a good cassette machine out there and there wasn't. I ended up taking the money and getting these two tape machines, a Nakamichi and a Teac and I got them completely rebuilt because I was happy with the sound of them. I figured it doesn't really pay to give people demos on cassette anymore so I just got a CD burner. Then I experienced the usual dilemma of how do you really make a CD sound good, because so much of the software is geared towards not peaking out so you end up with these things that are really flat sounding and don't have the correct level. So I went through this whole intensive period of studying and talking with people who worked with the big mastering houses and figuring out my chain to do stuff. When it got to the point where I was able to make my stuff sound as good as it would've sounded if it went somewhere else I figure I was ready to master.

Initially you were doing it so you could give people a good sounding CD at their sessions.

Yeah, if they wanted something to give to someone that really sounded right. I would always experience bands taking off with cassettes and coming back and saying that the mix doesn't

sound good. I'd say, "You're listening to a cassette." I can't even guarantee that when it leaves here it's going to sound right because your cassette player may be playing it at different speed or blah, blah, blah. If you give them a CD you stand a better chance of them getting an idea of what it really is going to sound like. Amazingly enough, cassette tapes survive better than reel to reels, which I haven't quite figured it out. I think in an effort to create a better tape, I think they just fucked up and didn't realize that climate would affect the tapes the way it did. New York City is horrendous on reel to reel tapes. They have ways of aging things to try and emulate what's going to happen. I guess they think that everyone stores their reels in underground humidity controlled vaults. I think it's the lubricant, when the lubricant breaks down that's when you start losing your takes.

It replaces it with humidity.

Hillary: that's where tape baking comes in.

I got the full thing on how to build it.

Hillary: I got a whole set of instructions from Ampex on how to do it; I'll put it up on the web site.

It's like a three day process if you're doing it right. Have you ever done that?

Yes. I had to do that on a couple of old Heartbreakers tapes that Richard Hell found. They were mush but we baked them and we got it off, I think after the baking you lose a little of the sound quality but if that's all there is then you're happy that you can get it at all.

Was it studio stuff?

It was some stuff that they had done in the studio when he was in the band.

How did you get involved with Echo Cañon [Sonic Youth's studio]?

I guess for the last record, *A Thousand Leaves*... I guess, basically, most bands without studios would spend large sums of money to make their records. For a band like Sonic Youth, it really made sense to have their own studio because every one of them, individually, has their own projects going on. They called me up and asked me to help them put something together. I put an 8-track studio together for them some years before so they would have something to at least do demos and things like that. They had accumulated a bunch of stuff for that, then they went and bought an old 16-track 2" and an old Neve BBC broadcast board. We found a space downtown and the stuff showed up... the boxes, no manuals, no documentation. I got to sit down there and figure it all out.

Hillary: Was it fun?

Yeah, it's kind of like discovering a wreck, and trying to figure out... I always feel like the spaceship that lands and someone goes in and says, "How does it work?" I had worked with Neve consoles before and you learn that every one of them is different. So many of them are custom built, this one was on a BBC remote truck so it was definitely a custom built console.

The faders go the wrong way right?

The faders go backwards.

So if you want to hear more, you're pulling it towards yourself.

Yeah.

Hillary: There's a story as to why that is.

Just to screw everyone else up? [laughter]

Hillary: The BBC engineers wore suits, so the cuffs from the suits...

No way.

Yeah. When you're on the air and you send out the wrong signal it'll just blow everything to a million pieces. The BBC is entirely anal about that anyway so that was exactly the reason that they did that. It's also got another feature where you push the control up a little you could actually solo. The fader actually solos, like a cue.

When you buy a new Soundcraft or Mackie you just patch cords into the back. When you get a board like the Neve there are tie-points and you have to figure out where the wiring is all going.

Fortunately, there was a built-in patch bay and the jacks on the back we basically don't even use. Most of it was on the patch bay and what was on the back was labeled so it wasn't like totally being in the dark. One interesting thing I found was that they flipped the inputs and outputs on the outputs of the board so they were reversed on the labeling. You could be there for hours trying to figure out that the inputs and outputs were flipped. It took me awhile to figure it out. It looks right but it sounds all weird. I think they just flipped it around as a real easy way to screw people up that weren't BBC engineers, it was a union thing.

With Abbey Road too, it was a very regimented thing.

Yeah, and that's totally what the BBC's about too. It's quite easy to imagine them doing that. I would like to find that out, that would be a good story. I suppose it could've been an accident, someone just wired it wrong.

They got a Studer 16-track?

Yeah.

That's kind of rare as far as I know, I've never seen one. It's not set up to do 24 at all, right?

Well it's pre-wired for another 8-channels. I've tried to get them to get those 8 channels while they can. Of course everyone is into the macho 2" 16-track kind of aspect of it.

I can't say that I'm not but....

I don't really think it's a valid consideration unless your talking of long-term storage on tape, maybe there's some advantage to it. Maybe there's some advantage from going from studio to studio because the heads will line up better. I could tell that the Tascam 1" is a quieter machine with a greater dynamic range.

But you're saying that there's not that much of a difference in what you hear?

Well I could tell you that this machine [Tascam 1"] is quieter with the noise reduction, there's no doubt about it.

They have no noise reduction?

Right, no noise reduction.

And they're running it at 15ips or 30ips?

Usually, if it's quiet we'll run it at 30ips and of course that cuts the hiss out.

The low-end changes a little.

The low-end changes a little, which I never liked. I like the low-end at 15ips.

Steve [Shelley] was telling me that they kind of just do a lot of rehearsing onto tape.

That's basically how they've always recorded. I keep trying to convince them to write the song and the vocals and then record, but I don't think I'm going to win that over. The only thing that's on my side is that the record company... "Sunday" is the last track to release as a single off of A Thousand Leaves and that was the only song that they had actually done like that because they had recorded it once before for a movie. The song was already together so when they recorded it they were recording the vocals and the music and everything else. The record company picked up on it right away and said, "This is the single." And they asked, "Why do you think they picked that?" I said, "Well, it may be because it was something that was already completed when you were recording it." They just like working the other way so it's a hard sell.

It seems like you have a lot of give-and-take with them though.

Yeah, I've been working with them for a long time. I know what they're going to agree to and what they're not going to agree to. I'm comfortable enough with them to say whatever I feel or think and they tell me whatever they feel or think. It's a perfect working relationship really.

As far as them doing lots and lots of recording, do you get called in every time they rehearse?

Things are set up to run in a way that I try and be there as much as possible. Especially, with the machine and the dynamic range of that machine, you have to be really careful about setting the levels than you would if you had higher headroom. One track on the last record I didn't actually... I wasn't there when it was recorded. It's the crappiest sounding thing on the record because of it; there's a lot more hiss and noise on that track. It took a lot more work, mixing it, to get it to sound as good as the other things. In a way it's good to be there. I basically worked out an arrangement with them... to be there when they're ready to do stuff like that. They never usually get together for more than three or four hours so it's always an easy day. It's really like hanging out with your friends for a few hours and pushing a few buttons. It doesn't get much more perfect than that.

When they do that, is there any specific goal in mind or does someone have some new ideas that they're going to run through?

They approach everything a little bit differently. They get together and it's like, "Well blah, blah, blah wants a track for this" and " We should really think about some stuff for the next record."

The three EPs that came out before A Thousand Leaves, were those all things that were coming together before they tried to make a new album?

The whole idea behind that was that they could record these instrumental versions that will evolve into the next record and they could release the instrumental versions as a thing. When the record comes out with the vocals, it'll be a different thing. In some cases that's what happened, in other cases it was just a jam or something that seemed like it would be cool on that record.

I really like the EPs; they seem kind of informal.

I was trying to get them to put out the third EP as the Geffen record. [laughter] Which would have been a very radical step; it's the weirdest one. It would have been pretty amazing. Months later after the record came out they reviewed both the record and the E.P. and they actually gave the E.P. more stars than the record. I felt like it was some vindication, even though vindicated by Rolling Stone seemed so horrible. Maybe I was wrong! [laughter]

With the Sonic Youth studio, what things did they buy? Did you get to advise gear after the main two purchases?

After they started off with a couple of things I basically helped them fill out the stuff. There's nothing really super complex, they bought a U-47 [Neumann] which is the good microphone down there. I got them a bunch of other mics... Sennheisers and EVs. Outboard is pretty minimal, a few reverbs and a Harmonizer and a few compressors. The board sounds pretty decent so we don't need a lot of outboard EQ.

Did you mix the album on that..?

Yeah, it was done quickly down there.

What are you mixing through down there?

They bought an Ampex 1/2". The classic repair special. You never know when you throw the switch if it's going to go on or not. It's really not my favorite kind of tape equipment to work on. That's one of the problems with a lot of the vintage stuff, I try and make them understand that. That stuff is expensive to fix, it's hard to find parts. I'm sure that once that machine is done they'll have spent as much on repairs as they did buying it.

Hillary: What do you think about recapping Neves?

Well, they run extremely hot because of all the circuitry packed in on it. I think when they're actually shot, if there's a problem that's usually the answer. As far as taking the entire board apart and recapping it, uh... Caps should be caps but there's a broad range of... Anything you change is going to change the sound. People buy these vintage amps and they

take it to someone and the guy changes everything in it. You could of just went out and bought an "off the shelf" amp at that point. It really is trying to figure out what's not happening; maybe it's just some output caps that need to be changed.

Has anyone done sessions at Echo Cañon?

Lee [Renaldo] and I did a record for a Spanish singer and that came out on Warner Spain. Steve did the Two-Dollar Guitar record there; Thurston has done a bunch of stuff there, Kim's working on her record there.

Is she doing a solo record or...

She's doing a trio with DJ Olive and Ikue Mori. It's a really cool record.

Who engineers on stuff like that?

I actually engineered that record.

What kind of gear, both here and at Echo Cañon, have been cool finds that you've had lately?

These Orban compressors are cool. You can find them around for not a lot of money. They really make things sound incredibly strong. They're not for everything, I use them for vocals, especially with hardcore bands because no matter what goes through it, it'll cut through anything in the mix. You get those screaming vocals that are sheeted by guitars; it really works well to bring it forward.

They're old radio compressors right? For radio stations mostly?

I think radio stations probably bought them but... they're from the early '80s, before the tube thing really happened. They're all solid state, but they're cool. I have a Dynaco PAT-4 preamp that's great for putting shine on anything. The treble control on it is just amazing. I've seen them all over eBay for under a hundred dollars. You get a couple channels of cool, two band EQ. [laughter]

I noticed you got a couple of [Radio Shack] Realistic graphic EQs here.

I'm totally into the Realistic things for really grunging down something.

Just insert it into a channel?

Yeah, it definitely gives you a different sound. What else have I got there...?

These little APIs.

Well, APIs, they're not cheap on any level, but they are really nice.

Oh, the Alesis MicroEnhancer. What have you been able to find that you can do with it?

I honestly don't use it that much anymore. It's good for brightening things up a little.

You've got some higher end stuff, lots of it...

There was a point where I was definitely an equipment junkie. I had probably twice as much stuff here at one point. My cousin's studio has a bunch of it, Sonic Youth's studio has some. I just kind of work it down to the stuff that I really use. If something just sits there for six months and doesn't get turned on, you might as well sell it to someone that's going to use it. The Orban spring sounds amazing. These things are beautiful sounding reverbs... amazing on guitars.

Hillary: You don't have any problem with bass vibrations?

It's actually really solid down there. I don't really have problems with bass vibrations, because it's all stone. It's not like a floating room, you don't have too much bounce.

Those Klipsch speakers, those are home speakers right?

Yeah, that line came out in the early '50s and was made up until the '80s. Of course now you can't find that kind of stuff anymore. They're the Klipsch Heresy, it's basically a 12" woofer and two mid-range horns and a high-end horn. They were under a thousand dollars when I bought them, I don't know what they would go for now. They are very dynamic, they can rip your ears off. It's really useful playing back basic tracks for bands. I really don't mix on them, I'll put stuff up there to hear how they sound but...

What do you mainly mix on, the Yamahas?

I switch between the three here, a lot.

What are the bottom ones?

Those are Cambridge Acoustics... The Optimus are kind of...

Radio Shack... You're a big supporter of Radio Shack here.

Radio Shack is not so bad, for the money. They always come up with some cool stuff.

What do you use for mic pres in here?

I throw them into the Kelsey.

Did you get heavy into the electronics yourself then?

Yeah, I do a lot of that kind of stuff. It's a good thing to know if people are going to get into a studio, unless they're made of money.

You've been making your own mic pre or...

I basically changed the ones that were in the Kelsey... Jensen transformers and better op amps and better connectivity. For awhile I was totally into it, to the point where... tracking things with both of them and listening to it for hours afterwards trying to figure out which one sounded better. I'm sure we've all been through it...

You gotta' give it up at some point.

Like I said, I went through my whole period of buying stuff and everything, now I'm into just using what's around. The level of stuff has gone up to the point where you can get good sounds out of tons of stuff. Why be ffixiated... "I can't do my record unless I have this..." As long as I have some speakers that I know what's happening I can walk into a studio and deal with it.

Have you done a lot of work out of different places besides these two?

I've been to various places... in town, in England, in Spain and the west coast...

Just for different album projects?

Yeah, for different stuff.

What do you take with you?

I took a few microphones, I always take a couple of Sennheiser 421s if they don't have those. I always take some 57s if they don't have those. I generally don't carry high-end mics around.

I can't believe a studio that wouldn't have 57s but...

They might have them, but they're stomped on or... It's good to have one for the snare that you know sounds right. I like the 421s on guitars, either alone or in combination. If I don't have them I get a little freaked out.

Do you take any gear or rack stuff?

Generally not. This record I did in Spain was basically 1" 16-track Tascam. This guy was running a lot of stuff at 30 (ips) because the machine had gotten so out of spec and it worked just a little better like that. The first day I re-aligned his machine without a test tape because it would take him a week and a half to get test tape.

He had a studio and didn't have a test tape for his machine?

It's not so surprising. You get into a place and you realize how great it is to be in New York, where you can go to 48th street and find stuff.

Hillary: Spa didn't have one for a really long time.

We bought that when we got our machine because the tech said he wasn't coming over if I didn't have a test tape.

If you're going to take stuff from one place to another, you need the test tape. There's no other way around it. I knew I was going to finish the whole project in the studio so I knew if I aligned the machine and it was a little off it would play back right. Just make sure everything goes in at zero and comes back at zero, that would be a good start [laughter]. They had a Topaz console, which I think is a good alternative to the Mackie. I think it's a little better sounding EQ than a Mackie and it's in the same price range. I basically did the record on that. They had a few compressors and they were all the strange brand things I've never heard. Most of them didn't really do the right stuff. I brought the stuff back here to master figuring I could... it came on DAT so it sounded very thin and strange and I just EQ'ed a little and put it on tape and it came back to life.

How did you get a job like that?

I'm not sure how I got hooked up with that band, I think they either found me on my website or... they were big Sonic Youth fans. Doing Sonic Youth doesn't hurt, lots of people listen to them. Usually people that call me, that listen to them, are into good music which is really nice. Its always nice to do something that's good... in a way it's easy for me because I know what they expect.

Do you have any kind of manager?

I've got a manager in Europe, in Germany, so far she hasn't helped me get my record out there, but she exists. I made an attempt to find a manager to do the production stuff here, figuring I could get more into the record company stuff, but the music business is in such turmoil at the high-end.

When you get bands, how do you work out a production fee or engineering fee? Do you ask for points on records?

Yeah, I ask for points on records. I do that across the board now, for anyone who's there, it's part of the agreement of recording with me. It makes sense. There's tons of records that I didn't do that on and I think it's only fair; you're a big part of it and you should be compensated.

Has that paid off on some of the work?

On a bunch of stuff, it's always fun to get checks. But, I had an agent here for awhile and she would call me up in tears, "I can't get you anything."

Hillary: What's a typical amount of points?

I'd say three would be typical, I'm usually quite happy to do a two point deal with a band and split production credits or however they want to work it. The basic justification for a production is that your bringing something to the final product that wouldn't be there otherwise. It breaks down across a couple lines: The engineering line and the mixing line and the pre-production line... In most cases, bands I work with I don't get all that heavily involved in pre-production, unless it's a big record company project and they want me to. I'm not really in to rearranging songs for bands. I'll always make suggestions and things but my idea is to take the band and take what they're doing and make it sound as good as it can. I think that should be enough. If I'm going to make someone sound like someone else I'll turn them into the Backstreet Boys - why not, they sell a bunch of records - if you really want to go that route. I guess that's my hallmark and because of that, a lot of people will say, "Well, he didn't really do anything." I get that from people in the industry sometimes. It's like, "You send them to somebody that does something with them and then see what happens." What happens is the band is unhappy with the record, the record doesn't sell anyway and they've spent a lot of money on this guy to sit there and change them.

It's a fine line between... "Are you just an engineer or are you producing?"

You say, "Just an engineer." In a way engineering is just as important too. People find that out when they build a home studio and say, "Why doesn't it sound like the record I did with... this is what blah, blah, blah used to make their record, but mine doesn't sound that good." One of the nicest things of having done all of this stuff and having a gold record on your wall is that people start to take what you say seriously. I'm sure everyone's been through the fighting with people over things. I went through that for years, with bands. If you don't really have all these records that you've done, they're not as willing. Now people are more willing to accept what I say, which is wonderful. ⏣

The Descendents, and subsequently **ALL**, are the manifestation of what I like about punk rock and music in general: energy, humour, and musicianship above everything else. This group of guys have changed the way that punk is played, infusing the idiom with interesting arrangements, strange time signatures, and a keen sense of melody. Stephen Egerton has prospered alongside the freneticism of bassist **Karl Alvarez** and drummer **Bill Stevenson**. As a guitar player, he has developed a singular angular approach and an eccentric harmonic imagination in a genre of music which can be intolerant to either of these attributes. Egerton and his ALL/Descendents cohorts have toured incessantly since the middle of the 1980s. They have remained steadfast in their commitment to their music, weathering yet another rise and fall in the popularity of punk rock and a major label debate. ALL have emerged stronger as a result, releasing two of their finest records (Descendents - *Everything Sucks* and ALL - *Mass Nerder*) with their new label, **Epitaph**. For Mr. Egerton, the last few years have seen a move to **Fort Collins, Colorado**, co-ownership in a 24-track analog studio (**The Blasting Room**) with members of ALL/Descendents and ex-members of **Black Flag**, the launching of a new label (**Owned & Operated Records**), and the continuation of a prolific engineering/producing relationship with ALL/Descendents drummer Bill Stevenson. Normally reticent about doing standard band interviews, I found Mr. Egerton extremely affable and very willing to share his thoughts on the subject of studios and the recording process. In retrospect, I think our conversation was analogous to the never-ending argument between analog and digital. That is, analog is continuous, digital is discrete. We spoke on a cold **Toronto** evening about the importance of getting good performances rather than a series of disjointed musical chunks, and the general lack of this kind of recording occurring within the industry today.

Here's what made it on to tape.

wanted to ask you first about your early studio experiences at Radio Tokyo. What was the setup like in there?

Radio Tokyo was the first studio that I worked at that wasn't just a small 8-track studio in somebody's house. The Descendents, before I joined, did the *Enjoy* record there, and then I joined and we did the Descendents *ALL* record there. They mostly did demo work there and managed to build up over the course of a few years. The guy who owned the place was a keyboard player in Blue Cheer at one point. Interesting history the guy had... I believe it was Blue Cheer. He put this place together. It was just a very small house, totally dead, carpet-covered walls, and no windows just a few blocks from the beach near Venice Beach, California. It was a very strange setup. By the time I got there, it had graduated recently from a 2 inch/16-track 3M format to a 2 inch/24-track 3M format. That machine was a nightmare. They were always kicking the cards to try and get it to work right. That's very much the kind of studio it was - very seat-of-your-pants kind of studio. I wouldn't even be able to tell you the name of the board, but the board was really funny. It was a 20 channel board designed to work with a 16-track machine and have four extra

worked with on many records after that, they both had very good ears and had really learned to maximize what they had equipment wise. I think they did a really good job as engineers. Richard and our drummer, Bill Stevenson, really taught me how to engineer. Richard knew more technical stuff than Bill did, but Bill had been involved in tons of records dating all the way back to the Black Flag records that he'd been with and the early Descendents records. He'd always had his hands pretty deep in the recording process. They did that Minutemen *Double Nickels on the Dime* record which is, to me, just a really very plain, nice, natural sounding record - very cool. It's not bombast or kick-ass sounding, but it's just a good straight-ahead plain recording. I really like some of the stuff that was done in Radio Tokyo.

Do you know what the *Ride the Wild* 7" [first Descendents release in 1978] was done on?

Ride the Wild, I believe, was done on 16-track/2 inch in...

...the worst of conditions?

Yeah, in like four hours. I mean, it was literally just throw the mics up and that was it. I know they spent a little more time on *Milo goes to College*. I don't know too

Yeah, 'cause at Radio Tokyo the SM-81's were THE cymbal mics [laughs]. Everything else was [Shure SM] 57's and an [EV] RE-20 for the kick. It was very straight ahead in that way. Third Wave had a little bit more variety that way. They had a couple of Neumann microphones and several AKG microphones. It was a very dead room. We were still recording things very dry because that was our ethos anyway.

I was going to ask you about that [very dry, tight sounding records are a trademark of the band].

During the 80's there was a lot of reverby, overblown production stuff that didn't make any sense when you were playing as fast as we were going. It didn't really add up.

Allroy Sez [first ALL recording] was pretty reverb.

Everything was experimental for us at that point, so we tried it on that. We've been back and forth through that whole thing a lot of times. [laughs] Our records were very much a testing ground for us. We recorded some live records for the Descendents. We did one in Berkeley, California *Hallraker* and one in Minneapolis *Liveage*. We

---

"During the 80's there was a lot of reverb, overblown production stuff that didn't make any sense when you were playing as fast as we were going"

---

rails left over. They had this funny little really shitty line mixer thing that they would use for the other tracks for bringing up effects. The patchbay you had to punch every once in a while to keep it working. They had a PCM-70 [Lexicon outboard unit].

That's a pretty nice piece of gear to have in that kind of studio at that time.

Yeah, they had some nice outboard gear - that was the thing. They had a couple of UREI EQ's that were decent, they had some [UREI] 1176 compressors, some pretty decent stuff.

Sounds like they blew all their dough on outboard gear.

Well, the stuff just built up little by little over time and their place was the kind of place where microphone selection was, you know, more or less like this is the vocal mic... [laughs]. U87s, and then a couple of SM-81s probably, that kind of stuff. So it was very, very basic. Everything was played in the same room with a bunch of baffles. The control room was only slightly larger than this truck we're sitting in. Personally, I was only involved with one record that we did there, but later on I did record some other bands. I did a little bit of recording for Gwar there once.

For Gwar?

Yeah, it was something that never ended up coming out. It was supposed to be for a SubPop singles compilation. They ended up signing their major deal and the thing never actually came out. I'd always wished I could hear it 'cause the drummer that played on it (they were in between drummers) was really excellent. The guy that ran Radio Tokyo, Ethan James, and another guy, Richard Andrews, who we

much about the specifics of that recording. Spot, who worked on a lot of the early SST recordings, engineered the Milo Goes to College record.

When you moved from Radio Tokyo, how did you decide on using Richard Andrews to start doing the ALL records for Cruz?

Well, this guy Ethan primarily ran Radio Tokyo and did most of the recording. Richard was more like a junior engineer kind of a guy who had learned largely from Ethan. During the *Enjoy* sessions, I think Ethan got sick and Richard came in and started doing some work. Billy [Stevenson] felt comfortable with him and they got to be friends. We'd developed a good relationship with Richard, so we did the Descendents *ALL* record with him. We decided to try to move up into maybe a little nicer studio. The next place we went to work was called Third Wave in Torrance, California. It's now gone as is Radio Tokyo. The Third Wave studio had been there a long time.

Was it a nice 'normal' studio?

Yeah, it was definitely built to be a studio. It was an old style studio, very dead rooms, but big. It had a lounge. It was more like a regular kind of a studio.

Did it have a vocal booth?

Not really. They did have a couple of isolation booths, but pretty much everything was done in the main big room. It was maybe a 20 foot by 15 foot room or something. Maybe even a little smaller. They had a better selection of microphones than we had been using. We'd seen our first [AKG] 414.

Did you start experimenting with mics?

decided to go into a little better studio to mix them, which is how we got to Third Wave. Third Wave had a Harrison console, which wasn't too bad for time, and a JH-24 MCI 24-track tape machine mixed to 1/2 inch Fostex. They had a PCM-70. They had a nicer console than Radio Tokyo, but maybe not as nice as selection of outboard gear as Radio Tokyo.

Did you start using gates and some of the more advanced outboard stuff at that time?

They had been experimenting with gates going back pretty far. We were using noise gates on Descendents ALL and they used them on *Enjoy* and on a few songs on *Milo goes to College*. I didn't know anything about that stuff until we got to Third Wave. That's when I started asking, "What does this do?" They had a couple of Drawmer gates and a bunch of Gatex gates, which we started using pretty heavily. Gates were always a part of the process for us.

If you did stuff live off the floor, how did you get everything so separated?

Yeah, we were nuts about that stuff. Plus, we were recording in really dead rooms and ambient room mics just didn't matter. We sought that really isolated thing in a lot of ways. We learned about mix compression and just started using a lot of compression all the way around. We knew about Steely Dan. We didn't aspire to having really awesome production, but we would try to compare things from time to time to use as a reference point. For us, when we were kids, Steely Dan was like the highest order of recording.

Where they would spend a week moving their chair around at $200 an hour.

[laughs] Yeah, exactly. They still sound pretty good. Those records still have quite a bit of chutzpa to them for the time. We knew they were compressing every channel. You know what I mean? We were definitely guilty of really overusing compression on a number of things we did. We'd really go overboard. All of ...Sez, ...Prez, ...Saves, ...Revenge, and Trailblazer were done at Third Wave as well as the Doughboys Home Again record. We also mixed a Big Drill Car record there that we had recorded at Radio Tokyo with Richard [Andrews]. After all of that stuff, we moved away from Los Angeles to rural Missouri. Our next record, Percolater, was recorded at a studio similar to Third Wave, it was a

brought an engineer with us. He had worked on an automated console and was the only person we knew who had ever worked on one. We ended up being in the 'A' room with the Neve automation. It was a Neve VR, I guess, a 56 input console. I'd never seen anything like that before. Ardent has been around since the '60s... they've got a bunch of amazing vintage gear and all kinds of shit. Anyway, our record was really panning out the way we'd liked. The engineer wasn't familiar with that style of automation. So they said, hey we'll give you an extra day with this house guy, Hampton. He did a fucking awesome job. Hampton's great. He's done lots of big records, lots of big country records. He produced the Gin Blossoms [and the Replacements Pleased to meet Me] and has been working at Ardent for years.

I really like the way the guitars sound on that record.

Oh yeah. I am a wholly reactionary creature. I just g[et] "I hate that, I hate that." ...and I go the oth[er] way. I've never been able to keep my shit togeth[er] that way, so my sound is changing all the time. W[e] did some very unorthodox recording durin[g] ...Saves, like gating and compressing everythin[g] to tape, which, you know, nobody does that, yo[u] just don't do that. But we had to learn. That['s] where Billy and I cut our teeth engineering stu[ff] by ourselves. We brought some of those tapes u[p] recently and we were like "Oh, brother..."

It's hard to have to learn and the[n] put out the record.

Yeah, and ultimately we did the right thing. I thin[k] that's how a lot of engineers learn. You just tr[y] it, and you fuck a bunch of shit up. Fortunatel[y] we fucked up our own records and not someboc[y] else's. Or not too bad on other people's. We di[d] a lot of records for the Chemical People. We wer[e] utilizing whatever we knew at the time, whic[h] might have meant that their record came ou[t] sounding like Allroy Saves. They didn't mind a[t] the time and neither did we.

What was the first record you and Bill di[d] for another band? Do you remember[?]

I know one of the first things we did was a spl[it] recording with two bands from Washingtor[,] one of which we're still basically recording, M[y] Name. The other band was called Hest[er] Prynne. They've been broken up for a number c[f] years now. They came down together and w[e] did a split recording with them at Third Wav[e.] That was one of the first things that we di[d] totally alone. We did another Big Drill Ca[r] record, Batch, which I think came out real[ly] good for the time. I can't remember what th[e] actual first one would've been. We got quite [a] bit of work right around that time. There's [a] Chemical People record we did in there b[y] ourselves. We started doing some stuff once i[n] a while at West Beach Recorders. We did th[e] Chemical People record up there and the di[d] the Tony-All [with original Descendents bassis[t] Tony Lombardo] record. The drums for tha[t] were actually the same drums we used o[n] Saves. They were done at the same sessior[.] We did all the other tracking at West Beach.

How did you split up the duties?

Originally, it was just like we'd get up, one guy woul[d] start, the other guy would sleep, and then the othe[r] guy would take over. That was really how it worke[d.] Whoever was around did whatever needed to get don[e.] We would just swap until the record was done. That['s] how it worked for a long time. Now we have anothe[r] guy, Jason Livermore, who we work with regularly a[t] the Blasting Room. Livermore was from Seattle and h[e] had some basic 8-track home recording setup and wa[s] experimenting with and wanted to come out an[d] learn. So, when we built the Blasting Room, he cam[e] out and helped while we were finishing wiring th[e] studio. He's been there since day one.

"We were into Black Flag. We didn't give a fuck about, you know, Janet Jackson"

---

legit studio built to be a studio. The guy that ran the place was an older guy. He could cut his own vinyl and had a ton of ancient equipment in there that I had never seen before. Most of the work that they did there was advertising work. This place was called Chapman, a very small studio. We tracked all the Percolater stuff there. We rented some Focusrite mic preamplifiers and EQ's and tracked through that stuff. They had a Neotek console and a old Studer 2-track machine there and quite a bit of good outboard gear. We didn't get to use a lot of it because we were just tracking. We decided that we would try mixing some of our stuff, like singles, in a really good studio as an experiment for Bill and I.

There were songs that you mixed separately from other ones?

No, it didn't work out that way. That was the theory at the time.

Do you remember which songs you were thinking of doing that with?

Not really, maybe "Hotplate" would have been one of them at the time; we thought that was kind of funny. "Dot" I think was maybe going to be one. What ended up happening is I started calling around and going through MIX magazine to find out where the nearest studios were. The closest good ones were in Nashville, Memphis. We were getting packets and client lists from all of these studios. These guys all had Neve consoles and SSL consoles, stuff I'd just started reading about. It just seemed like whoa... this heavy thing. I had been recording for years before I even laid eyes on one of these consoles. Ardent were willing to work with us within our budget to try and make it possible for us to come down there to do some stuff. We didn't know anybody there, so we

On Percolater? Really? We mixed it real quickly. We ended up mixing that record in three days. We ended up just doing the whole thing with him [John Hampton]. That started a really cool relationship with him. We did a Big Drill Car record with him and did our whole next record Breaking Things with Hampton in the 'A' room in 19 days. We worked with him for a long time. A band called the Lemons we took down there with us to do. Another band, My Name, we tracked all the stuff at Chapman like we had with Percolater and mixed it with Hampton at Ardent on the Neve. That's where Billy and I got a taste of the real equipment.

Was Allroy Saves the first record where you and Bill were alone to do everything?

That was the first record where Billy and I did the whole thing by ourselves. It wasn't because of a falling out with Richard [Andrews]. Richard was an excellent engineer. I can't complain a bit about Richard. But, Richard was the kind of engineer that was familiar with good sounding records. Billy and I didn't care about good sounding records. We were into Black Flag. We didn't give a fuck about, you know, Janet Jackson... that didn't mean anything to us. We might have some of these things around as comparative analysis, but we weren't production hounds in that way. To us, that Black Flag Slip It In record, we consider that, in its own way, to be an excellent production. We just thought we could do it more efficiently and cheaper ourselves. So, we did ...Saves that way and we fucked it all up. [laughs] We did a terrible job.

What was going on with your sound on that record? Your sound more than anybody I know has just been all over the map.

and a little bit of outboard gear and it was set up originally so you could track really effectively and then take it to Ardent, or wherever.

What did you do with *Pummel*? [Interscope release]

Pummel was tracked at the Blasting Room and mixed at Ardent with Michael Barbiero.

Did the record company want some big name guy there to watch over you guys?

No, we were experimenting. We'd been interested in trying some of these other guys that were out there, in particular Andy Wallace [Rage Against the Machine, Nirvana, Jeff Buckley, etc.]. Bill and I were both really into the way he mixed stuff. He was busy right then doing Blind Melon, so he couldn't do us. Then somebody just suggested Mike Barbiero and we just kind of went "Shit, why not? Let's try it". He's done some pretty big records.

And you got the big dough from Interscope to do the record.

Yeah, when we signed with Interscope we used the recording budget basically to build the studio. We more or less told them going in that that's what we wanted to do. We told them we know what we're doing, we've done lots of stuff and they were like "Yeah, these guys are total idiots." And its worked out really well [pauses] for us anyway. [laughs] So, we recorded the stuff ourselves. We had John Hampton come up to the Blasting Room to help us do the first alignment to the machine and helped us get the place going and get some sounds. We tracked *Pummel* using some sounds he'd kind of worked on with us. That was really cool. We went and mixed with Mike Barbiero and it was, in some ways, successful. *Pummel* took a lot of work. It's one of those records that only now, years later, am I able to sit down and listen to it without remembering all the heartache that went into making it. I listen to it now, and there's some things I don't like the sound of, but it's pretty good. A lot of people actually really like the sound of it and point out that one as a really good sounding record. I think I just don't give it a fair shake all the time. Billy thinks it sounds pretty good, he's pretty happy with it. Mike Barbiero was an excellent engineer and really neat to watch. His orientation doesn't include the bass guitar in the way that we need it. In that way, it took some work to get there with that. But that's just one thing.

I guess that's probably from working with all the hard rock guys where the bass is really an afterthought.

Yeah, where it's just like a low end glue for everything else. We don't work that way. That was new for him. He got very good, solid sounds and I learned a lot watching him. At that point, I still hadn't touched an automated board. Bill and I would be over these guys shoulders telling them what to do. The next thing that ended up happening at the Blasting Room was the Hagfish *Rocks Your Lame Ass* album for London. Hagfish just said, "No, we want to do it all at your place. Fuck it.". I said, "You realize I have a $4000

mixing board". They said, "Fuck it. We don't care." So, whatever. You don't care, I don't care. We had a few really good pieces of outboard gear we bought. We had an Eventide H-3500 which had some excellent reverbs in it, we had an SPX-900, an SPX-1000, you know, just enough stuff to get it done. Very base level, plain, straight ahead stuff. Good compressors, good gates, that kind of shit. So we mixed this Hagfish record for London on our Mackie. [laughs] That was definitely cool. The album came out really great. The album is really a testament to how much import good playing has over what equipment you're recording on. If most major labels had really thought about the fact that we were mixing their record on a Mackie, they would've had a fucking heart attack. Haqfish kicks ass, so it doesn't matter. They're just good and solid, you couldn't fuck them up. You know what I mean? You'd have to really blow it to screw their record up. We ended up doing another band, the Lemons, who are big favourites of ours. We did their record for Mercury.

I love the Shades Apart *Seeing Things* record that you guys did. The guitars on that record sound so big. Great big sounding guitars are a real rarity right now with all the indie rock stuff.

Sometimes we use direct guitars.

Did you do that on *Everything Sucks*? [latest Descendents release] There's a little extra high end in the guitar sound.

Yeah, we did. And Andy [Wallace, who mixed *Everything Sucks*] mixed them pretty bright. But, that's the way we like 'em.

He's a bass player too, so I guess you didn't have any problems with getting the bass really present in the mix.

The beauty of Andy is you can hear everything all the time no matter what. There's never a time that you can't hear every single thing exactly right on an Andy Wallace mix. It's just amazing. If you go back and listen to his records, that's always true. And the bass always has a great voice in an Andy Wallace mix. He's just fucking incredible. It was great working with him. I always like to say that he's forgotten more than I know. He built his first studio when I was eight. He mixed that Cult *Electric* record manual. Unbelievable... The *Seeing Things* record was pretty basic, but again, when you've got a band like that, playing is production. If you record the greatest band in the world, you can record them on a fucking blade of grass and it'll sound pretty good. Shades Apart, if you ever get a chance to see them, they're a fabulous band, fucking incredible.

I missed them on the last Descendents tour they did with you guys in Vancouver. The show started so early.

Shades, you just can't screw 'em up. You can't. They just kick butt. His guitars just sound like that. They just finished a new record I just heard. They did it with Mike Fraser for a major label, Universal or something.

Had he done your live sound before that?

No, he hadn't. But he has since for other people. He actually did tour with us doing monitors at one point when the studio was still just us and the few recording projects we would have every year. Now, at this point, that's Jason's main thing. He records more than Billy and I do. He does a lot of the smaller gigs, but he does a fair amount on really every record we do. He taught me how to use the automation on the SSL, because I was on tour when they brought the SSL in. I've imparted him with every piece of knowledge I ever got and he's taught me a lot, too.

Did you move to Ft. Collins with the idea of building a studio there? Was the building already there?

We built the place completely ourselves. Billy and I had been talking for a long time about putting a studio together. So, we decided on going with a 24-track 2-inch machine and we bought six good mic pre's and EQ's, a bunch of Focusrite mic pre's and some API EQ's. So we had these six good microphone preamps and a Mackie console. The plan was, really more than anything, to track the stuff as high quality as we could get away with. We bought some decent microphones

They got signed to a major?

Yeah, they've been recording this record for a long time. I heard it. It sounds good. It's a good solid record. The guitars sound basically that same way.

I wonder if it was your production job that got them signed.

You know what it was? It was actually a demo that Livermore did with some of their newer songs. That was one of the first things that was recorded after we got our SSL. Jason had been doing a lot of engineering over that period and he really did a great job on these demos. I think they got signed on the strength of those demos. There's a couple of songs on there, that when I heard them I was on tour when they did that and when I came back it was like, "Holy Shit!" You could see where that was headed. These boys are going to get famous now and that's how it's going to work.

Were you at all swayed by the ADAT craze when they first came on to the scene?

We considered it, and it's funny, Billy mixed the first Lemons record on ADAT. I personally have never used one, so I don't know too much about them.

Was it a sound thing?

We just asked around a lot, talked to a lot of people. We heard many horror stories about lock-up problems, the whole rewinding business, and how long it takes to shuttle and lock up. It sounded like a fair amount of work, whereas the 24-track 2 inch machine was a known quantity. That's what I learned on and every record I've done, other than when I was a kid, was done on a 24-track 2-inch machine. So it was very natural. We went with it because we knew it would be good.

What do you think the cost difference for you guys would be between doing an album on ADAT instead of 2-inch tape?

Well, you can do them cheaper on the ADAT. Definitely. I think the ADAT thing is pretty effective and I think the way that recording is going, and is going to need to go now in this kind of music, since that's what I'm most familiar with, ADAT will be a player. It will have to be. The days of punk being the biggest thing in the world. It's not that way any more. It's not going to be that way. It's shrinking back down. That's totally fine with me. We'll get back to how it was just like we said when it all started to take off. 'We'll just keep on cruising.' That's what all the bands from that

time and this size, we're back where we started. It's no different for us. We sometimes did stuff at 15 ips to lower our tape costs, but ultimately, I like 30 ips better. There is a definite low end advantage. Jack Endino was really set on 15 ips at one point in time.

Do you use the natural compression you can get with analog tape a lot?

It goes by instrument. Not at all on cymbals. But I'll beat the crap out of the kick drum. It seems different every record. It depends on how the guy plays and what you can pull off that way. I would say that there are people out there who hit the tape quite a bit harder than me. We definitely get into it on certain sounds. Kick, snare, toms, we tend to hit it pretty hard. Not with guitars. Sometimes the vocals depending on the guy.

What did you do with your sound on the new record, _Mass Nerder_? There's a lot less gain.

Yeah. The guitar sounds that I had been listening to were a lot of the early punk rock records I grew up with, Generation X, Sex Pistols, The Ramones. What I'll call a rock n' roll guitar approach as opposed to a metal sound. I've listened to some metal. I grew

DRUM ROOM

up in punk rock, that was the first music that I really had a strong attachment to.

It's a hard thing when you're playing in a trio setting like you are. You have to worry about filling that space with either sound or lots of activity.

A lot of the music we've done over the last couple of years, our interests aren't so much in a complicated arrangement or a complicated chord part. I used to be more into jazzed up wild shit. I've been trying to come to terms with my own songwriting. I had never really been much of a songwriter until just a couple of years ago. I'd never really written any kind of songs. It was more like I would just write pieces of music. The rest of my band were always songwriters first. At the point that I started writing songs, I pretty much dispensed with most complicated guitar stuff [laughs] and really started to want to play the kind of music that I first learned... you know 60's music, like Chuck Berry. That was the first stuff that I ever learned, "Johnny B. Goode." Stuff my mother taught me.

Is that where the double stops thing comes from?

Yeah, totally. I mean, that's what I grew up on. It was the simplest music going and it was something that my mother could teach me. A, D, and E, you could play half the songs on _the American Graffitti_ soundtrack. This stuff was very much an influence on the early punk bands that would influence me. Richard Hell and the Voidoids were based more in a rock sound, a cleaner sound, not quite as high in the gain department. I've used a lot of gain on a lot of records. _Pummel_ was like that.

Was it all amp gain or were you using pedals?

No, all amp gain. I can't really hang much at all with pedals. I've just never gotten along with them.

Have you tried the standard stuff like the [Ibanez] Tube Screamer?

Tube Screamers I like okay, and I think some of that stuff can be pretty useful, but for the most part I just want to get it out of my guitar and my amp. Over the years I've tried to rid myself of all of the elements in the guitar path, to the point where the guitars I play now don't even have volume knobs. I'm digging these guitar sounds on Mass Nerder. I finally found a few things that

> **"If you record the greatest band in the world, you can record them on a fucking blade of grass and it'll sound pretty good"**

I had been trying to get in my head.

I guess it helps when you have your own studio. You can just sit there and move stuff around.

Yeah. I spent a week on guitar sounds and I have to admit I worked hard. The sound on the record came largely from the 'A' channel on a Marshall JCM-900 50 watt and I used that a lot with a DOD compressor/sustainer pedal with the compression off just to bump up the output of my guitar just slightly without going active specifically, just to drive the front end of the Marshall a little bit harder. Then I used an old Sound City 50 watt head that I bought when I was 18. It was laying around in my basement and I had a guy refurbish it to stock. Then I've got another JCM 900 100 watt that I used on the dirty channel for some of the slower songs where I needed some more sustain. I wanted you to be able to get a sense of how fast and hard I was picking. Sometimes when you've got a pretty distorted guitar, it levels all of that shit off. _Mass Nerder_ is more like a Malcolm Young kind of a guitar sound. I wanted the sound to represent the physicality of the playing the way that it does with the drums. ☮

What is a Producer?
by Larry Crane

What is a producer? This is opening up a potential can of worms/Pandora's box, but what I will give is an example, only one, of what a producer can be.

I often wonder what the word "producer" means. When people ask me if I produce records I answer with a hesitant "yes." I don't know. I feel like a lot of times I co-produce with a band. I don't feel like I'm running sessions with an iron fist, rewriting songs, dictating tempos and forcing my own vision on the band. Instead I play it pretty mellow, trying to capture what's best about the group, offering sonic ideas and such. I've worked in a few sessions where there was a producer on hand but it wasn't until recently where it became apparent what a producer could be.

The band was well rehearsed and had even demoed many of the songs at home. The producer showed up the day before the session with a bunch of notes culled from the demos and sat in on a practice suggesting ideas. They came in the next day and I concentrated on being an engineer - getting good sounds, watching levels, keeping records, making rough mixes and all. The producer worked on getting guitar tones, watching the tempos, keeping an ear out for tuning problems and, most importantly, looking for the best take of each song. His ideas on how the instruments would fit together and what made a great take made my job easier - I could just focus on getting what was happening onto tape.

In four days we tracked over an albums-worth of songs. All the takes were sounding great, and despite some long hours everyone seemed to be in pretty good spirits. On day five the producer had to leave for another job and I was to start on guitar overdubs for three days. We had a listening session and took notes on what each song could use. No problem, right?

Day five just didn't work. We kept trying to guess if what we were doing was what the producer had in mind. Band members were edgier without the producer there taking charge. It felt like someone was missing.

Photo by Steve Silverstein

The band had put a lot of their trust and faith into the producer. Insecurities and worries about the work were assuaged by gentle positive comments when he was there. Instead of trying to "produce" the record by committee within the band, a large amount of decisions and fears had been placed in the producer's hands, most of which were never even discussed. It made the job that the band had to do much easier, allowing them to concentrate on playing to their utmost and getting the mood of the songs right. Without him these things rose to the surface and stopped the session dead in it's tracks. The band decided to wait and do the rest of the album with the producer present.

Did I feel slighted? Not in the least. The presence of a producer whom they put their faith in would take a load off of the band. I wasn't the person for this job or this band, though I think I have been for others. The album is going to be amazing and when we resume sessions I'll bet it goes very smooth. And I think I'm one step closer to knowing what a "producer" is.

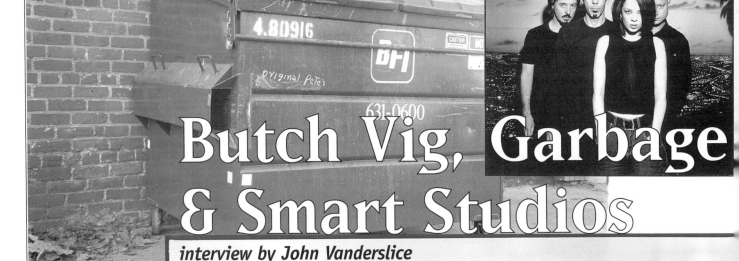

Butch Vig, Garbage & Smart Studios

interview by John Vanderslice

Butch Vig has created a big name for himself in the recording world. In 1984 he and **Steve Marker** founded **Smart Studios** in Madison, Wisconsin, and started working with tons of indie bands (like **Killdozer**, **L7**, **Urge Overkill**), including quite a few albums for records labels like Touch and Go, Slash and Sub Pop. As time went by his reputation got bigger, leading to work with **Smashing Pumpkins**, **Nine Inch Nails**, **Nirvana** (*Nevermind*) and **Sonic Youth** (*Dirty*). Then, as if this wasn't enough, he and Steve put a band together with **Shirley Manson** and **Duke Erickson** and called it **Garbage**. When we got the opportunity to interview Butch, it was originally going to be in San Francisco. After some contemplation, **John Vanderslice** of **Tiny Telephone** studio (himself a former *Tape Op* interview victim) came to mind. John runs a very analog-orientated studio, so I figured with him chatting up Butch, who works extensively in Pro Tools, we'd get some sparks flying. And what happens? They got along like peas in a pod...

You started Smart Studios (in Madison, WI) a while ago, and you used to record a lot. Do you miss engineering as much as you used to when you first started Smart?

Yeah, I guess I do. Even though we made Garbage's *Version 2.0*, our guitar tech, Billy Bush, by default became the engineer and he handled a lot of the technical aspects, particularly because this is the first time we jumped into using the full-on Pro Tools system. But, I still get behind the board all the time and even now as I'm talking to you, I've got my laptop and a Kurzweil, a little keyboard, and this Yamaha speaker set-up 'cause we're working on some B-sides and we spent most of yesterday programming some loops and things. I like to tinker with stuff. I was never really classically trained as an engineer; never went to any of those schools. I always just did it by the seat of my pants. I still like to get a new piece of gear and just plug it in and fool around with it; see what you can do with it. I'm also not a good manual reader.

Did you start Smart to record your own band? What was the reason behind starting it?

Steve and I met in film school and he had a 4-track in his basement at the time. I was recording electronic ambient things for a fellow film student's soundtracks.

Yeah, your already un-watchable films.

Exactly, they were very un-watchable. But, some of the soundtracks were pretty interesting. They were very inspired by John Cage and even more accessible stuff like Brian Eno's solo things, or Stockausen. I can't even remember what I was listening to back then. I was really into it, and at the time also playing in bands and we couldn't afford to go into proper studios. So, we started doing little demo things in Steve's basement and when I finished college, Steve and I had the idea that we could make a go of this, so we rented a space in a warehouse and bought an 8-track. We had very little gear. I think we had a spring reverb unit, we had a handful of mics, all 57s or even cheaper stuff than that; that was the most expensive mic we had. We had one DBX-160 compressor that we bought used for fifty bucks.

You probably used that on everything.

On every single thing. And we had a Roland Space Echo. The first board we had was an Allen and Heath. It was all kinda' to record our own stuff. We knew a lot of other musicians from the local scene, so we were like, "If you guys can go out and buy the tape, we'll charge five bucks an hour just so we can get fifty bucks for the night so we can get some money to pay our rent here. We got a lot of work off of that. Everything that we started making we put back

into the studio. It was like, "We need to get a better monitor system, we need to get more reverbs, we need to get more compressors, we need to get better mics," and the list, of course, if you own a studio never stops. Everything we made we pretty much plowed back in. Over a period of time, we went to a more sophisticated 8-track to a 16-track to a 24 to a 48, to now a full-on Pro Tools system. It was a slow evolution. There were a lot of bands and albums between all those steps.

I checked out your website and I couldn't believe all the bands you had recorded. It was absolutely phenomenal! You have a Studer deck, an A827, were you syncing up two of those and doing Pro Tools on the new record?

Yeah, we recorded most of the tracks into Pro Tools, then we would edit or process or whatever we ended up doing, which we do actually a lot, and then when it came time to mix the rhythm tracks, stuff was all transferred to the Studers; the drums, bass, some of the guitar and vocals. Any of the weird little sound effect things, if we were to use them, we would leave them in Pro Tools so we use Microlynx to lock them up, so we had the two 48-track Pro Tools and the 48-track Studers.

In general, do you use a lot of compression when you track?

It depends on what it is. I usually don't compress drums until they've been recorded. I do more compressing post. A lot of times if I'm looking for compression, I want something that really screws with them or over-pumps them or shreds them out. I always compress the bass and usually compress some acoustic things, like acoustic guitar, even piano sometimes we'll compress a little bit. Shirley's vocals, I always use a solid TLA-170. That's the stun. Whenever she starts singing it kicks down, even if it's quiet, it kicks down a -10 dB.

Do you mix a song differently if you know it's going to radio, or do you just let radio compression do its job?

Years ago I always used to use bus compression. I've got a Daking compressor that I've been using lately. I like it a lot. I'll put it across the bus sometimes just while we're tracking to make sure if something gets really loud, it's not going to blow the monitors up. I will occasionally do mixes with it, but I have a tendency to wait till mastering to do that. I always go to Masterdisk and I work with Scott Hull and Howie Weinberg. They're both really good and I always go to the sessions there so I can listen to the EQ and make suggestions, but let them do their thing. I'm well aware of how radio can affect it but I try and also compress it, so like *Version 2.0* sounds as loud as anything else, but there's still really strong dynamics. A lot of times you're

four photos of Smart Studios

"*We need to get a better monitor system, we need to get more reverbs, we need to get more compressors, we need to get better mikes' and the list, of course, if you own a studio never stops.*"

doing things to trick the compression. Little frequency things or things that sound like they come in loud and then ease-off right before it comes back in 'till the next section of the song.

Do you like the sound of radio compression?

Yeah, sometimes I do. I don't like it when it's so severe; like when a song starts out with a vocal and an acoustic guitar and the band kicks in and the band sounds like they drop down 20 dB or lower.

It's amazing how radio stations vary in how much compression they use. Alternative stations seem to use a lot of compression. Sometimes it sounds good and sometimes it just sounds really extreme. When you track, do you track with a mix in mind, like say Tchad Blake, or do you try to get good tones down onto tape?

We just try to get interesting sound on tape. Fortunately, we have no idea what the mix is going to sound like when we start and we have a tendency to record a lot of ideas. We constantly cut the song up and chop it up in Pro Tools. "This chorus sucks. Let's just erase it. Let's take this sound thing from this other song and transpose it to this key." We do a lot of really weird things and it isn't until the actual mixing process begins that we define how the songs are going to sound. The record took us a year and the mixing took about six weeks at the end of that. Four or five of the songs had over a hundred tracks by the time we mixed, so we had a huge puzzle. At that point, a lot of the things are kinda defined around your lyrics after we've gone through and we're happy with our vocal performance. No matter what we do sonically, it needs to work around Shirley because she's definitely the center. She's the mouthpiece for the band, so whether we make it noisier, more poppier, more organic, or weird layers going on, it somehow has to work with the songs and with Shirley's vocals.

When you're not in your own studio and you're recording another band, are you flexible about what gear is available or do you always bring your own racks with you?

I'm flexible, although there are a few things that I do like to have. I've got an API Lunchbox that I've used for a while that I really like a couple pieces of Summit gear, but the TLA-170, I cannot live without. It's by far my favorite compressor. I like that Daking, that compressor that Geoff Daking came out with a couple years ago. It's very simple to use but it sounds really good. I will occasionally use that on some tracking, but I like to leave it on the bus. The other thing I probably always use lately, is I have an old ELA-M, I think from 1957-that's an old tube mic. It sounds amazing,. It's one of these mic's that has this incredible high-end, "haaah" all the steam and crunch, that goes on the vocals.

What's the difference between a 250 and a 251?

I do not know.

My friend has a 251 and those are Telefunken mic's right? I don't think I've even seen one. Our highest end mic is a Neuman 67. What dynamic mics, maybe more esoteric dynamic mics, do you rely on for guitars or drums or other instruments?

I love a fet U-47, the big chunky mic. It's kinda dark sounding.

It's a solid state version of the U-47?

Right, but it takes a lot of level on bass and guitars and kick drums—it's thumpy. It's not as clear as other mic's. I've used that on a lot of things. We use Audio Technica 4050s, 57s and 421s and m88s on guitars sometimes. We have a couple of Coles mics, but I'm not always a huge fan of those. They have a tendency to be back a ways. And if you want something recorded really closely, to me they don't sound quite as good and they can't handle a lot of pressure.

If a band was going to start a studio with a minimum amount of money, what would you advise that they spend most of their money on? EQ's, microphones? What do you think is a really essential link in the chain?

I guess if they're going to be recording bands with live instruments, you'd almost have to say it's the mics and the preamps. If you've got a good mic and a good preamp, and you move the mic around, you're probably not going to have to EQ very much. Sometimes you can even go directly to tape on whatever you're recording on. I remember when we first started, we had really shitty mics and I had to EQ a lot. I just couldn't get things to sound good. You'd have to bottom-on, or high-in, or screw around with the mid-range, whether you're cutting it or boosting it. Going back to Nirvana's *Nevermind* , I don't think I've EQed a guitar going onto tape for eight years now.

Do you usually brighten it up on the way back or do you usually tweak it all in the mix?

In the mix, but usually at that point, it has less to do with EQing, and what we call our processing point, where we take things and re-sample then and change the bits or, it might be some strange EQ or it just might be some effect that gets put on them that gives them a totally different timbre. I don't really EQ the bass when it gets recorded and I don't really EQ the guitars and the same with Shirley's vocals. I don't EQ those, just go flat to whatever we're recording on.

Does the TLA-170 tend to brighten up vocals at all?

It seems to be fairly neutral. I think obviously any compression will bring out more sibalence, but that's just the nature of compression. But, this mic, as I said, has a really soft, nice smooth crunch to it when the tubes kind of overload on the high-end. We'll sample stuff on the Kurzweil 2500s and those get thrown in too. Then we'll process them into Pro Tools. We have a ton of programs to do processing, DSP and things, plug-ins basically and filters and compressors and stuff. We'll use a lot of those on just about anything.

For all those people out there who have 8 and 16-tracks, which are probably the majority of the Tape Op readers, if you had four tracks to record drums, how would you mix and assign them?

Four tracks, depending on what the band plays like, if it was a jazz band or something that was very quiet, I would probably put the kick on a separate track and then stereo mix the toms and snares and overhead into two tracks. If it was a rock thing where there's a lot of kick, snare and back-beat, where they were playing a lot of grooves, I'd put the snare on a separate track. Possibly take a top and bottom mic and run them together and then put the overheads on track three and four. I used to do that a lot when I had our 8-track. I used to commit drums stereo. I wouldn't even put the kick on a separate track back then.

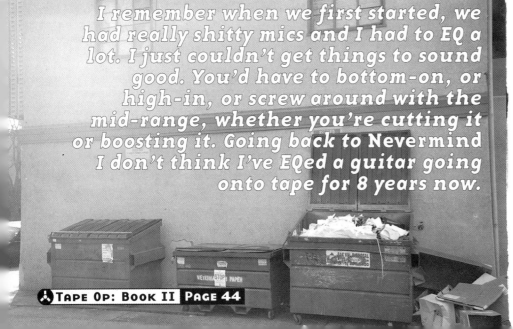

I remember when we first started, we had really shitty mics and I had to EQ a lot. I just couldn't get things to sound good. You'd have to bottom-on, or high-in, or screw around with the mid-range, whether you're cutting it or boosting it. Going back to Nevermind I don't think I've EQed a guitar going onto tape for 8 years now.

That sharpens your skills too.

Well, sometimes in the mix early on you realize you should've had the kick a little louder or the kick is awful loud compared to the rest of the drums. But usually you can get it pretty close, once you've got the mix down and the band is playing together. You can listen to it with the bass and the guitar and the vocals. You're almost kinda listening to a slight rough mix at that point.

Our engineer Greg Williamson, showed us this trick when we were mixing down where he would just send the snare out through a speaker into a room and prop the speaker on top of the snare and get the snare to rattle and then he would just mic it and mix it during the mix and get this really nice separate bottom snare sound. So, that was like the coolest thing I've learned in the past year as far as mixing on drums. It's nice because you save yourself a mic and it's totally clear.

"Getting back to your question, depends on what we're recording."

A couple times on *Version 2.0*, we would take a drum loop or some sort of groove thing, and run it through an old Auratone, that we've had since 1983, that's pretty blown up. So any low-end, it just distorts right away. We put a mic on top of that and run stuff onto it and re-mic it and send it back into Pro Tools and get these amazing crunchy mid-range drumloops.

Have you ever used a Shure Bros. Level Lock?

No.

It's like an old PA compressor that's really junky. Must've been like 20 dollars when it came out. The threshold is 6 inches, 12 inches and 18 inches, for the distance from the speaker to the mic. If you slam stuff through that, you get just absolutely bizarre distorted compression sounds. When you record do you always separate instruments from drums, or do you like bleed?

No. I mean the bleed is what makes stuff sound cool. When we started tracking on this record, we spent a month. We took a Pro Tools, a Mackie and all of our live gear and for a month we basically jammed and improvised and came up with some song ideas. It was set-up very loosely, not pristine at all. It was like a big parlor room. It had a pool table in the middle, amps were set-off to the side and the drum-kit was kinda off in the corner. Shirley could sit in the middle and then basically, we could run tape, record, and bounce around between the samplers and the keyboards and guitar and bass and drum-kit stuff. A lot of things came from that, that made it into the final mix. Might have been a drum loop or a guitar thing or a vocal that made it into the final mix. We're not particularly concerned with something matching or being pristine. Even vocal takes, if they sound different from day one to day two, we don't care that much. A lot of drum stuff, tons of drum things are mixed down to mono on this. It's like I didn't even want to bother with doing things, where I knew there might end up being 15 drum tracks on a song. I didn't want to have 15 tracks with separate bass drums and snares. So I just mixed drums down to mono in a lot of instances. They got filtered, EQed, in one or two or four or eight bar loops. It's basically just the grooves that work in the context of what we're recording and this is easier to deal with than a mix. A lot of times when we would mic them, you'd start putting on all these little things and I find that I use very little effects. I'll usually use something on Shirley's vocal if it was recorded dry. Use an Eventide harmonizer for a double effect. We'll use the 4000 sometimes for a reverb patch. We use the Roland Space Echoes for a lot of tape-slap type things. The mix is pretty dry. I remember when Billy and Mike had to do the recall on the first mix, I think we had three stereo effects on them. But, as I said, so many things are processed by the time you start throwing up all the faders, all these weird things are happening like ambient tracks. A lot of times if there's a main drum groove that would be down the center, which maybe has more of a live feel, I may take another two or three loops and just pan them all left and the other two or three loops pan them hard right. They all have different frequencies and play at different times in the songs, so you're constantly getting this pretty wide set of things coming from the spectrum. I guess getting back to your question, it depends on what we're recording. A lot of things I record flat, a lot of things we will process once we get them in there.

When you record, say piano, do you like things in stereo pairs or do you like having stuff in mono because it's so much easier to deal with and it also gives a solidity to the instrument.

Both, I think. For instance, rather than hearing a stereo guitar, I'd rather double track the guitar, left and right because they're two discrete things, and sound even wider when you pan them. I do have a Calrec Sound Field that sounds amazing. It's got an incredible stereo mic that works really good on drums. I ran piano on it, acoustic guitar. We've used it on a couple of vocal things, where Shirley's singing more ambiently. But, I have a tendency to record things on mono and not worry about them.

What records have you heard recently that you really, really like engineering wise, or sound wise?

I really love Massive Attack's new album, *Mezzanine*. The way they approached their arrangements, it's all moody and dark and very atmospheric. It's great, great late-night-turn-off-the-lights and play-it-really-loud music. I like this band Flick, I like the way their record sounds; like indie recorded, lo-fi fuzzy, power-pop. I like the songs and their singing. There's some elements of Big Star and even the Pumpkins' mellower songs. It's a really cool record. It's walking that line of trying to do it yourself in the indie world and also just approaching greatness, to mix a timeless sounding record.

Who are your favorite engineers right now? And not necessarily ones that are active right now.

I like Tchad Blake a lot, I think his mixes always sound really interesting. I'm very partial to Flood's work. He's been acting more as a producer these days, but he's been an engineer. His records sonically always have a great darkness to them. He always lets a lot of the room bleed into the tracks and that gives them a lot of character. I like the new PJ Harvey record that he did.

Of all the records that you've done, which one is closest to your true sonic vision?

God, I don't know.

Or the one that you put on and say, "Damn, that's the sound that I was going for?"

It would probably have to be *Siamese Dream*. I worked really hard on that record, as did Billy, as did the band. I knew what he kinda wanted to do going into that record, and I knew he wanted to do a lot of layering. I knew because I worked with *Gish* on him. It was a really intense album to make because they were also under a lot of pressure internally and from outside sources. I particularly remember, when I finished it, I knew we made a good record. ☻

-band photo by Stephane Sednaoui
-portrait by Joseph Cultice
-Studio photos by Tony Michels
-Garbage can photos by John Baccigaluppi

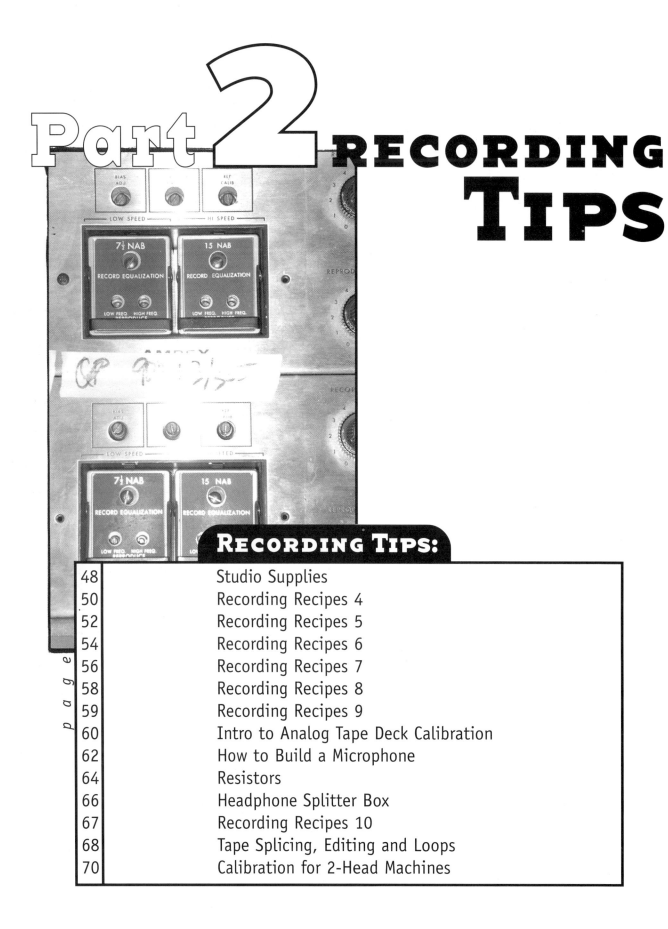

Part 2 RECORDING TIPS

RECORDING TIPS:

page		
48		Studio Supplies
50		Recording Recipes 4
52		Recording Recipes 5
54		Recording Recipes 6
56		Recording Recipes 7
58		Recording Recipes 8
59		Recording Recipes 9
60		Intro to Analog Tape Deck Calibration
62		How to Build a Microphone
64		Resistors
66		Headphone Splitter Box
67		Recording Recipes 10
68		Tape Splicing, Editing and Loops
70		Calibration for 2-Head Machines

Mixing Tips & Tricks

by Pete Weiss

When I first sat down to write this piece I was a bit apprehensive. Over the years there have been countless magazine articles on mixing techniques and tips. I kept thinking, "Man, every *Tape Op* reader probably already knows this stuff. I'm going to get hammered with 'duh' email." But then I remembered that whenever I had read any of those 'tips' pieces, I almost always picked up a new trick or two. So, as a green comedian in the Catskills was once heard to say, "Bear with me if you've heard these before..."

Some of these techniques have been around for decades, others were developed out of necessity. Equipment limitations can force a creative engineer to approach a mix from a fresh angle. Often a great mix trick is discovered by accident; it can be a beautiful thing when you forget to unplug a random patch cord from a random piece of gear.

An important reminder: nothing is absolute. Please take my suggestions with a shaker of salt. There are no rules in creative recording. Music and sound mean a lot of different things to a lot of different people and lemme tell ya, there are a LOT of people in this world who listen to recorded music. If the art of recorded music is going to progress, the participants in the art had better learn to free their minds, be open to wacky new ideas, and above all, trust their own taste. If, in this article, I say "always", what I really mean is "usually". If I say "never", I mean "rarely". Dig?

Let's dig into a mix.

WATER + DIRT = MUD

Remember the "mud factor." You know what I'm talking about. That dreaded frequency area roughly between 180 and 350 Hz. Seems like such a small range... why are there so many problems associated with it? A lot of instruments used in popular music have fundamental tones falling in the "mud range": the low strings on an acoustic guitar; the low notes of most electric guitars (the nifty "thump" of a Les Paul thru a Rat pedal thru a Marshall stack comes to mind); the majority of male vocals; certain bass guitars; the tone (not the impact) of many snare drums; tom-toms; etc. etc. Anyway, while they may sound great on their own, in a lot of cases, these elements tend to pile up and muddify your mix - if you're not careful.

MUD AVOIDANCE: Don't touch that "solo" button!

Well, you can touch it, but try not to rely on it for EQ-ing. The point of mixing is to get all the instruments and vocals to sit together, not necessarily to sound amazing by themselves. Mixing acoustic guitars in the context of a rock song is just one good example: if you solo the acoustic track and EQ it by itself, you're liable to make it sound very full-bodied - which would seem desirable. However, with drums, bass, electric guitars etc. competing for space, you'll probably want to thin out the acoustic a bit so that the instrument's upper harmonics are emphasized. This way, the acoustic can sit lower in the mix, still be heard and it won't contribute to the "mud factor." Anyway, try to do your overall EQ-ing with all the faders up. Once you get used to EQ-ing this way, you'll find your mixes go a lot faster.

...AND FOR MORE REFINEMENT...

EQ the mix initially in mono. It sounds easy, but it can be very tricky. During tracking it's sometimes tempting to layer, layer, layer (hey, we all know it's fun...) But too many elements in the mix can add up to audio claustrophobia. All too often we take the easy way out and pan similar-sounding instruments away from each other in order to give them their own sonic space. But it takes discipline, good judgement, and perky ears to be able to make sonic elements fit together in mono. You may need to emphasize or cut frequencies in a way that seems counter-intuitive. You may want to consider axing a part or two. It's a studio hyper-cliche, but less sometimes is more. I'm not saying mix totally in mono (go for it, if you want...) I'm just saying if you can get the mix to sound halfway decent in mono as a starting point, it'll be a breeze to make it sound great in stereo.

DE-ESSING BEFORE REVERB

A fave of mine. It's a subtle thing, but it can open up a bit of extra sonic space. If you want to avoid the exaggerated essi-ness encountered when adding digital reverb to a vocal, of course you can try de-essing the vocal. Often, though, this can make the vocal sound lispy and artificial. A technique I've used for a while is to split the vocal track into two channels, using one in the mix and heavily de-essing the other. Then the heavily de-essed vocal (which isn't in the stereo mix) can be sent to a reverb unit. The resulting reverb is warm and clear, yet contains much less of that awful "reverb essi-ness" since it originates from the de-essed vocal. Meanwhile the "mix" vocal, still with a bit of essiness to it, sounds bright and natural. This technique has worked really well for me when I want to stylize a bright female vocal by drenching it in a long hall or plate reverb.

"GHOST" GATING THE SNARE

Similar in principle to the above in that you're able to retain a snare track's natural attack and decay while stylizing with non-sloppy effects. Try splitting the snare track into two channels, gate one severely and send that signal to a reverb, but keep the channel itself out of the L-R mix. Use the ungated snare channel for your main snare and the reverb from the gated channel for your main reverb. By doing this you can avoid cymbal and hi-hat leaking into the reverb while being able to use a nice natural-sounding snare in the mix. Like the above vocal de-essing trick, this technique is especially nice if you're looking to add a big hall or plate reverb that would normally become sloppy and distracting-sounding if it had cymbals, etc. leaking into it.

A related snare trick that's subtle but effective is recording the top and bottom of the snare onto separate tracks (a common practice if you have the tracks) so that you can only send the top to your reverb. This allows you to judiciously add the rattly bottom of the snare (a little goes a long way) into the mix without it becoming too magnified because of reverb. ✪

OH, AND TRY TO HAVE SOME FUN

Studio Supplies

Recording Recipes #3
by Curtis Settino

If you're setting up a recording space (commercial or personal) there are numerous items you have to obtain in order to get up and running. Obviously, a recording device, mixer, monitors, and microphones are the essence of any studio. Less obviously though are all the little non-musical things that you'll need. Below is a checklist of these session saving items. You may not need all of them, but you'll definitely need some.

❑ **Studio Name**
This is the most important thing!

❑ **Guitar, Microphone, and Speaker Cables**
These can be forgotten or fry out without any warning.

❑ **Music Stand** *(preferably a tall one)*
You don't want anyone holding their lyrics. rattle, rattle, rattle.

❑ **Pop Screen**
Quell the popping "P"s and "B"s.

❑ **Guitar Stands**
When guitars fall over they tend to go out of tune.

❑ **Instrument Strings, Drum Sticks, Reeds, Etc.**
Stock whatever you go through the most of.

❑ **Tuner**
Everyone loves A-440!

❑ **Click Track Source**
Nail that 120 bpm disco beat on the head!

❑ **Computer**
It looks really cool to have one sitting around regardless of whether you use it or not.

❑ **Microphone Stand Clips**
They're always breaking.

❑ **CD-Rs**
People like to leave with a copy of what they've done.

❑ **Track Sheets**
If you don't use these you'll erase something by accident eventually. Also, make room on it to list the artist, date, and any other important session info.

❑ **Clipboard**
Holding track sheets and looking official

❑ **Ball Point Pens, Pencils and Paper**
Taking notes, writing lyrics, doodling

❑ **Memo Pads**
Handy reminders

❑ **Sharpie Pens**
Labeling cables and boxes

❑ **China Marker**
Marking tape (editing) and reels

❑ **Razor Blades**
Splicing tape, chopping cocaine (only if you're working in the '70s)

❑ **Q-tips and Isopropyl Alcohol**
Cleaning tape heads, contact points on electronics and ears

❑ **Masking Tape**
Many uses (great for marking notes on a keyboard for non-keyboardists to play!)

❏ **Duct Tape**
Many uses (to the 10th power)

❏ **Allen Wrenches**
For setting up guitars

❏ **Screwdrivers**
Have a variety of sizes available, especially teeny tiny ones.

❏ **Soldering Iron, Table Top Vise, Wire Cutters and Strippers**
Instrument and cable repairs

❏ **Pliers**
Tightening and loosening mic stands, drum hardware

❏ **Lug Wrench**
Tuning drums

❏ **Drum Heads**
Having a few extra around, especially for snare drums, is a good idea

❏ **WD40 or Sewing Machine Oil**
Silence those squeaky drum thrones and pedals.

❏ **Flashlight**
It's dark inside your rig.

❏ **Power Strips and Extension Cords**
Get the best you can.

❏ **Ground Lift Plugs**
It's good to keep electricity straight.

❏ **9-volt batteries**
Effects pedals eat these, as well as guitars and basses with active electronics.

❏ **AC adapters** *(wall warts)*
Get ones with adjustable DC output and connectors.

❏ **Milk Crates**
Get those amps off the floor!

❏ **Bricks**
Anchoring kick drums, steadying mic stands, settling arguments

❏ **Rope and Twine**
Hanging microphones in impossible to reach locations, binding things/people

❏ **C-Clamps**
They'll mount almost anything in a jiffy.

❏ **Refrigerator, Coffee, Tea, Water, Etc.**
Properly nourished musicians play better.

❏ **Chairs, Stools, and a Couch**
Asses need friends too.

❏ **Inspiration and Entertainment**
Books, magazines, music, games, and TV are good for jogging stagnant musicians and baby-sitting those who are done with their tracks.

❏ **Personally Meaningful Knick Knack**
Set it out somewhere and never explain its significance to anybody.

❏ **Ambiance**
Sometimes black lights, lava lamps, strobe lights, candles, and/or incense make musicians feel more at home.

❏ **Blankets and Pillows**
kick drum damping, making it cozy for sensitive singers *(a la Stevie Nicks and Edie Brickell)*

❏ **Camera**
Document the session.
It's nostalgic *and* scientific to do so.

❏ **Calculator**
"You owe me..."

❏ **Change**
"Can you break a hundred?"

❏ **Receipt Book**
"Taxman! yeah!"

This list is in no way complete (How could it be?).

Thanks to Larry for his fine contributions.

Recording Recipes, No. 4

Flying Musicians
by **Curtis Settino**, art by **Jeff Kriege**

In *Recording Recipes No. 2* (TAPE OP No. 10), I wrote about flying microphones. This time I'll set forth a few recording techniques involving flying *(roaming, really)* musicians. As with the microphone techniques, the goal when using flying musician techniques is to create and capture unique volume, position and/or timbre changes in the performance you're recording. It's a roundabout approach to orchestration and dynamics. The following methods can work in a variety of recording situations *(4-track and beyond)* and are designed for vocals and hand-held acoustic instruments.

Volume Changing

Did you know that an automated volume control technique was used with Elvis Presley when he first started recording? An assistant engineer would stand behind him, clutch his shoulders, and physically pull him away from or push him closer to the microphone depending on Elvis' volume. In those days, this technique was crucial since everything was usually going down live. No one had the ability to fix it in the mix. But even if you've got the space to isolate a vocalist, or other volatile sound sources, onto a single track, this approach could save you some mixing hassle. Also, too often people record the various parts of a piece of music without a clear picture of the desired end result. So when it comes time to mix, they're left with the chore of juggling those parts within the mix and taming volume fluctuations within the parts.

When you prepare to record a song, try writing down the song's structure in a linear form before you start. This is generally referred to as a "chart". You don't have to know how to read or write music to do this. I find using different shapes to represent the different sections of the piece helpful. You can even use magic markers and crayons if you want. Then, once you have the entire piece laid out, choose which sections will serve what purposes *(i.e., this will be the loud part, this will be the catchy part, etc.)*. Once you have a clear picture of how you'd like the song to unfold before the listeners' ears, you can address all your performances to suit this plan.

Back to flying musicians. Like the voice of the young Elvis Presley, some sounds are difficult to control volume wise. Or they take on a considerably different timbre when played quietly. A lot of percussion and wind instruments fall into this category. Luckily though, many of them are hand-held. For this recipe, you'll need one microphone, a vocalist or carryable instrument, and a song in need of track-embedded dynamic performances that require no adjustments during mixing.

1) Set up the microphone so there's room to roam away from it either directly in reverse or off to the side *(each has a different effect)*. Don't forget to lose the clomping shoes if you're on wood or cement floors.
2) Get a level on the vocal or instrument up close at a moderate to loud level. Mark the spot on the floor with tape*.
3) Have the performer move away from the microphone *(still singing or playing at the same volume)* until he or she has reached a spot that reduces the volume to a level that'll work well as the quiet level in the song. Mark this spot with tape, too. I often set this level at about one-third of the loudest level on my meter.
4) Record. If you're doubling any vocals or instruments, replicate the maneuvers for each one. And as always, if you can get a few people to perform the same part at once, you'll get something you can't fake with overdubs–charming chaos. Here are a few possible applications: Start the song at the furthest distance and naturally "fade-in" the intro by walking toward the microphone. Do the same, but in reverse, for the song's fade-out. During a solo, have everybody but the soloist step back from the microphone. As the song progresses, with each section change, move the performer a step closer to the microphone.

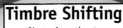

Timbre Shifting

Changing the tone of a vocal or instrument during a song is another way of aiding the dynamics in your composition. Here's a simple technique. You'll need a microphone, of course, and a rug.

1) Set up the microphone near a highly reflective wall. Position it and thevocalist or instrument so the reflected sound is easily heard. This may require the performer to be a little off axis from the microphone.
2) While recording, have someone hold the rug up against the highly reflective wall, thus damping the sound. You may need to drape the rug over a pole and use that as a handle. Otherwise, it's hard to get the rug in between the wall and the microphone without the person holding the rug getting in the way.

Possible applications: During the verses put the rug up, then during the choruses, take the rug down. Start with the rug up, then gradually lower it to the floor over the course of the song. Switch between the rug, a wood surface *(the wall),* and a metal sheet throughout the course of a song.

Hands-Off Auto-Panning

This approach is easiest with lots of tracks available, but can definitely be done with a 4-track. You'll need two microphones *(the same brand and model is preferable)* and two free tracks.

1) Set up the microphones a couple feet apart facing the performer. The three of them should form a triangle.
2) Set the levels on the individual tracks so that they are just below optimum.
3) Have the performer take a step or two to each side from this central location and check the individual levels. They should be optimum for one side and much quieter on the other.

Possible applications: Have the background vocals travel from the left to the right, then right to left in unison. Have contrasting sounds criss-cross each other while they are being performed. When a supporting instrument takes a solo, have the performer step into the center for the solo from one of the sides, then go to the other side for the remainder of the song.

Flying Musicians and Flying Microphones

This is an idea I've had for a long time and haven't tried yet, but it's one of my favorites. Record using all the techniques in this article, and the flying microphones from *Recording Recipes No. 2 (depending on the instruments)*, at the same time and on every performance. This will require lots of planning and patience. My hope is to do an entire album this way one day. To mix, I want to be able to bring all the faders up to unity and just let it play.

As a last thought, I'd like to add that these techniques aren't intended to save your songs. They are intended to help elucidate the musical nuances and to add color and interest. A great song can shine through even the most inept or unconsidered recording and stick in your memory. A bad song can sneak by with the help of studio trickery, but usually only for the duration of the song. Once it's over, it's forgotten – unless it's really bad.   ⊛

*With vocalists it may be better to hang something from the ceiling at head height as a marker for the close up position *(just like when people hang tennis balls in the garage so that they hit the windshield when the vehicle is pulling in and has reached the perfect depth without crunching the trash cans)*. If the singer is looking down at the floor for their mark, it could significantly change the close-up volume and timbre, thus ruining the whole effect.

Recording Recipes, No. 5

by **Eric Morrison,** art by **Jeff Kriege**

Microphones, I hardly knew thee.

Here's a few "input devices" that I've discovered through the ineptitude and squalor of my youth. Although I've since bought some real microphones, I'm still foolish enough to use the following on occasion, and I encourage you to expand your microphone paradigm as well.

1. "Mister Microphone", although it's been a while since I've seen the original brand-name on sale, there are always knock-offs in the toy stores. In addition to the ultra-compressed quality of these lo-fi FM transmitters and the ease of taking a line out of a stereo receiver, there's a lot of room for exploration. For instance:

a. Find different zones of transmission quality in the room and use them to color the different parts of the song (i.e. Start the track crackly and broken up and get clearer as the song goes on).

b. Keep the receiver's speakers loud enough to produce feedback; your Mr. Microphone suddenly becomes a Buck Rogers-era theramin type instrument, squealing new tones and timbres as you swish it around the room like a light-sabre (sorry to mix my sci-fi metaphors).

2. The guitar-pickup as microphone. Just take your average electric guitar and gain it up as far as you possibly can (I usually use two distortion pedals). Due to the noise factor, you'll need a loud source (like screaming your fool head off), and a gate helps. You can either:

a. Damp the strings and use the pickup as a straight up microphone, or...

b. Try tuning all of the strings to the key of the song (or part). The vibration of your voice and the breath of your consonants will start to activate the strings and cause a lovely "vocoding" drone.

3. Headphones as microphone. Most of the guerrilla engineers I know have resorted to this at some point in their escapades, but why not kick the concept up a notch? My favorite arrangement goes like this:

a. Use coconut-shell type headphones; the more cavernous the better.

b. Use a Y-splitter to separate the left from the right (you'll obviously need two tracks).

c. Hold the headphones laterally in front of your mouth and move your head around as you sing.

The end result can be quite dynamic and jarring (like a madman flailing about in a wooden box). As with the pick-up method, lots of gain, careful EQing, and gating can be used to keep the noise under control. So remember... Just because an object is not clearly marked "MICROPHONE" doesn't mean it isn't one!

A bed of loops with no sampler?

Don't leave the joys of sonic loops to the techno/dance hippies, it belonged to us avant-types first (e.g. Reich, Cage), so let's recomandeer! Gardens of loops can be used in so many wonderful ways: undulating ambiance, exploration of spatial mechanics, and of course providing rhythm tracks when your drummer is on a week-long bender.

Ingredients:
A multi-track recorder
A delay pedal

1. Set your delay pedal at 100% feedback
2. Find a nice loop to start with (get crazy, even the most non-musical sounds make sense when repeated over and over).
3. Lay it down to a track. (on some delay pedals 100% actually means 99%, so you might need to ride the gain up as the loop starts to wither).
4. DON'T TOUCH THE DELAY LENGTH!
5. Find another loop you like (depending on how cohesive you want the end product to be, it can be helpful to listen to the first track - but as for me, I like to do the whole thing blind).
6. Lay the second loop down (minding how tracks 1 and 2 are coexisting).
7. Repeat 4-6 until you've exhausted your tracks or your patience.
8. Now go back and play your recording-deck like a damn bagpipe; isolate, overlap, structure and love them.

Advanced tip

Try doing the whole thing at double speed, dropping it down to normal speed for mixing. This will double your delay length, and produce a less "sampley" sound. ⊕

The Organic Phase

Most "tape ops" know the ear-tickling fun that can be had with the phase-shifters, but don't you ever tire of the predictable algorithms that pre-fab outboards offer? Take charge! Play the phase yourself!

Ingredients:
A multi-track recorder with the pitch-wheel
An additional tape deck

1. Select a track you want to phase (my favorites are soloing instruments and room tone)
2. Isolate the track and record it onto an outside tape.
3. Record this back onto a new track on your multi-track deck (it takes a little persistence and luck to sync it up with your original track).
4. As you are recording, slide your pitch to and fro (keeping in mind that small moves produce the classic phasing sound, big moves will just send the whole thing out of sync).
5. Experiment extensively. If you have the luxury of lots of tracks, save all your passes and composite them in your final mix.
6. When you mix down, try various panning strategies. I usually use hard left and right positions, as the two tracks move from identical to "slightly different" and back, they will spatially widen and shrink by themselves.

There are a million happy accidents that you can stumble upon using these basic parameters, and you'll have the pleasure of knowing the effect sprung forth from your hand, mind, and soul... not some damn sine wave!

Recording Recipes, No. 6

by Curtis Settino

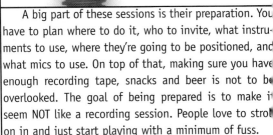

Capturing Improvised Music

In 1995, I had my first opportunity to try a musical experiment I'd been concocting in my head for a good 10 years. In short, the idea was merely to record some improvised music. In long, it's been an attempt to create a situation in which a group of musicians spontaneously write and perform pieces of music that sound like they were preconceived and/or prewritten. It is the antithesis of "jamming." It's composition. Needless to say, it's been an elusive prize to create and capture. Each session (I've done 14 so far) has been recorded onto an ADAT or two. One nice thing about this medium for this situation is that I can let tape run almost the whole session without worrying about tape costs adding up. Afterwards, I can mix the whole thing down and try to push and pull a little more coherence out of it. Eventually, I'll probably end up dissecting some of these things in a digital editing program. But my hope is to not have to – for it to happen the way I want it to while we are performing live.

A big part of these sessions is their preparation. You have to plan where to do it, who to invite, what instruments to use, where they're going to be positioned, and what mics to use. On top of that, making sure you have enough recording tape, snacks and beer is not to be overlooked. The goal of being prepared is to make it seem NOT like a recording session. People love to stroll on in and just start playing with a minimum of fuss.

Each time I do one of these improv sessions, I learn something new. And that knowledge is then applied to the next one. I make notes, draw diagrams, and take pictures to help me remember the details. In this Recording Recipes, I'm going to go through the first seven of these sessions and list out what ingredients went into them and what the results tasted like. Regardless of whether or not you're into this kind of music, there's definitely tips and tricks that can be gleaned and applied to where *you* need them.

Improv #1 - 11/28/95

Participants: 8

Space: The Shed – a 9' x 12' x 8' room with carpeting on the floor and walls, and foam on the ceiling.

Recording set up: I hung two PZMs in the center of the room in a stereo configuration and four dynamic microphones each pointing at a different corner of the room. Each corner had two musicians and two similar instruments (two hand drums, two acoustic guitars, marimba and glockenspiel, cello and banjo). This was an attempt to produce a doubled-quartet sound by having each duo try to play as one person.

Lesson(s) learned: Each participant had to be able to think ahead *and* play on time at the same time to achieve our goal. If they weren't able to do this, they would drag the whole performance down. I also learned that the mic setup made for a great quadraphonic playback, especially when we walked in a circle around the room while playing. Lastly, I learned to never invite anyone who's going to ask to play something less "out there"–poison.

Improv #2 - 4/14/96

Participants: 3

Space: The Living Room – a 12' x 25' x 10' room with wood floors, plaster walls and lots of broken planes.

Recording set up: There were two percussion stations and an acoustic guitar. The percussion was captured with a dynamic mic on each station and a PZM in between to capture the room sound. The guitar had a condenser mic on it. We barricaded the guitar with a couch to isolate it a bit from the percussion. Also, a click track and headphones were used.

Lesson(s) learned: Using less instruments and a click track made it easier to keep the tempo solid and more satisfying to go back and overdub on these recordings. I filled in the arrangement with bass and more percussion later. This, however, took the recording away from the original intention and it came off a little less spontaneous feeling. I cut the treble and boosted the bass on the PZM track. and it helped bring out the lower tones of the percussion.

Improv #3 - 5/25/96

Participants: 3

Space: The Living Room

Recording set up: Electric guitar, piano and bass were the instruments used. The bass went direct. The guitar amp was mic'd and placed on the opposite side of the room from the piano. PZMs were used in a stereo setup between the guitar and piano. Again, a click track and headphones were used to help with tempo.

Lesson(s) learned: For this kind of recording, relying on a click track for rhythm support and wearing headphones ended up feeling more restraining than helpful.

Improv #4 - 8/30/96

Participants: 4

Space: The Living Room

Recording set up: A piano, banjo, marimba and cello were each closely mic'd. Two PZMs, again in stereo, divided the group spatially. The piano and marimba were on one side, and the cello and banjo were on the other.

Lesson(s) learned: Having at least four people helps keep things more solid, eliminating the need to resort to a click track. Keeping the instrumentation diverse helped everyone find their place in the mix. The PZM setup helped reinforce this.

Improv #5 - 11/8/96

Participants: 5

Space: The Living Room

Recording set up: This session was essentially the same as with the previous improv. The additional person played percussion and helped anchor everything.

Lesson(s) learned: Discussing dedicated roles prior to recording (you're the leader, you're the follower, you're the glue, etc.), made it easier for everyone to understand how their instrument fit into the big picture. With the additional person, though, separation of the instruments became harder to achieve because of space limitations. So we spread out into the room's corners. But then everyone had a hard time hearing the other instruments. Thus, the performance turned out a bit more sloppy and tentative.

Improv #6 - 12/6/96

Participants: 4

Space: The Shed

Recording set up: Once again, a stereo setup of instruments was used with the PZMs in the middle as room mics. Electric guitar, cello, and percussion were closely mic'd. A keyboard was sent direct. Also, we set up two vocal mics.

Lesson(s) learned: Trying to capture vocals turned out to be a mess. The two vocal mics ended up picking up so much room sound (even when they were being sung into) that they negated the PZMs. Moving back into the smaller space helped everyone hear each other better, though.

Improv #7 - 1/11/97

Participants: 6

Space: The Shed

Recording set up: Two stereo keyboards (direct), bass (direct and mic'd), electric guitar (mic'd), drum set (in stereo), percussion, three vocal mics, and the PZMs made this the most complex session yet.

Lesson(s) learned: Too much is too much. But it was fun to overdo it. In general, the problem here was too many mics in a small space. In a nice big room with headphones and baffles between the instruments, this would have been a perfect set up. Also, with six people and lots of electronics going, it got really hot and claustrophobic in there. Creativity and technical proficiency tend to freeze up under those circumstances. ☮

It's been really hard to get just the right combination of players, instruments, and environment. On top of that, trying to get professional sounding recordings of these performances has been a technical challenge at times. In general though, the approach is solidifying, and the percentage of successful pieces of music increases with each session. By looking at all these sessions in consecutive order you can see the growth process. The one thing that seems to be the biggest asset is a shared vision. With *any* recording session a pre-performance discussion can help focus everyone onto a single agreed-upon goal. This is the most important thing.

Recording Recipes, No. 7

Sing, Surprise and Share.

by Curtis Settino, illustration by Jeff Kriege

SINGING

Only a few bands can use the exact same instrumentation setup in every song and still sound fresh. This is personal taste, of course. But listen to your favorite band's recordings and see if they NEVER stray from their *sound*. By "sound", I don't mean just the musical instruments, but the vocals, too. Below are two somewhat silly but very effective ways to alter your vocals.

Vocal technique #1: Straining to be heard

My friend Vince, who agreed to try this technique, also made me promise not to tell anyone that he did it. It's really not that embarrassing, so here I go. We were working on a piece of music that required a strained vocal–something that said to the listener, "Call 911." I had Vince lay on the floor on his stomach. I placed a mic stand and microphone directly in front of his head. But instead of putting the microphone down near his mouth, I kept it about a foot above his head. Next, I instructed him NOT to use his arms to raise his mouth nearer to the microphone. Instead, I asked him to arch his back to raise his head upward. So he would arch upward, say his line, then collapse onto the floor to catch his breath. This worked really well and was very amusing to watch. When trying this technique, you'll need to adjust the microphone height depending on your performers' physical fitness and/or yogic ability.

Vocal technique #2: Swallowing your words

Tired of sounding clear and highly enunciated? Well, then this is for you! Get a bag of cotton balls, stick as many as you can handle into your mouth, press record and sing! Done right, this can make you sound down right *muffled*. I've found that the exact amount of cotton balls isn't as important as their dryness. Performing a whole vocal passage in one take is the way to go with this technique. If you have to punch in a line or pick up after restuffing your mouth, the sound will be inconsistent with what's already on tape. What happens is that while you sing, saliva issues forth and condenses the cotton balls making them less effective. When this occurs during a complete vocal take, it's not that noticeable. It becomes a subtly changing vocal texture-- something I love. But if the muffledness of each line is drastically different it can be too distracting (or maybe not). It helps to have a garbage can and a towel on hand when doing this.

SURPRISING

Composer Erik Satie was notorious for being an odd duck. And I mean that with the utmost respect *(for him and the duck)*. One of things he did to stir things up musically, was to include written notes in between the staves. These little bits of text weren't intended to be read or sung aloud–in fact he expressly forbade it! They were meant to jostle, steer, and amuse the performer only. It is thought that this would then affect the performance. So, if you've occasion to supply notated music or charts for a group of musicians, feel free to slip in a little blurb like, "Laugh without anyone knowing".** in with the music. If you're not using written material try some of these visual techniques to affect a performance. The key element here is surprise.

Surprise techniques 1-5

1) Shut off the lights when the laid back part of the song comes in and see if everyone doesn't slow down a bit and get quieter.

2) Turn on a strobe light at some crucial moment. Can you say, "Space Jam"?

3) If it's possible, open an outside door, again, at the perfect moment, so that either freezing cold or sweltering heat infiltrates the performers' space.

4) Throw anything Nerf at someone right as they're getting a little too pompous with their performance.

5) Have hangers-on burst into the room and shake booty like mad, then walk like zombies, then fall on the floor and writhe - nudity optional.

SHARING

The following paragraphs are not really techniques, but observations. I'm into my eighteenth year of music recording *(does that really matter?)*, and reflecting upon that, I noticed these two overriding characteristics of my musical art.

Shared characteristic #1: Musical sketchpad

Reading about techniques is fine, but trying things out is the only way to really learn anything. What I suggest is to start a tape that is strictly for musical experiments. On this tape record pieces of music that explore ideas, not songs. These ideas can be things like, "Is it possible to use percussion to convey melody?" or "Is it possible to groove with no instruments hitting the downbeat?" or "What happens when I..." These self-designed exercises can be very short. If they are kept short, the results will be learned more quickly *(and you can get back to "serious" recording)*. When you play back your experiments, don't just look for the success or failure of your main query. You should also take a step back *(literally?)* and see if this piece of music begs further or different exploration. The next step is to keep at it and apply what you learn where and when it is needed.

Shared characteristic #2: Eclecticism as education

Being a somewhat diehard "Jerk of all Trades"** I'm forever trying musical instruments that I have no business playing. But my motto is, "If you can repeat yourself on it, then you can play it." This, of course, is not for everyone. Some people spend their whole lives mastering one instrument. I think that's great–for them. But to me, it's a bit boring. I started off, as many of us do, playing guitar. But as soon as I could, I started trying other instruments the second their owner stepped away from them. Next, I started obtaining these other instruments, rather than upgrading my guitar. So, instead of focussing entirely on one thing, I've spread myself around. This has landed me with a collection of mediocre to good instruments that I can play good to well, rather than an exquisite guitar that I am a master at. But, playing these other instruments has given me a better perspective on the guitar as an instrument among instruments, which is what it is to me. At the same time, I've never listened to, played, or recorded just one style of music. I feel this eclecticism has given me a better understanding of music in general. So go out there and play, record, and/or listen to some music that you're sure you'll hate. Your Rock will rock harder if you've experienced New Age music, and vice versa.

---

* Taken from Erik Satie's piece of music, "The Monkey's Dance (no.4)," which is part of "Medusa's Snare: A Lyrical Comedy in One Act," also by Satie.

** For more on the tyranny of specialization see R. Buckminster. Fuller's "Operating Manual for Spaceship Earth," chapter two. New York: Pocket Books, 1973.

Recording Recipes, No. 8

by Curtis Settino

"Let It Bleed"

Mic #1 - Room
Position this mic (preferably an omni-directional) centered above the amps. This mic will pick up the majority of your "bleed."

Mic #2 - Amp
Guitar #1

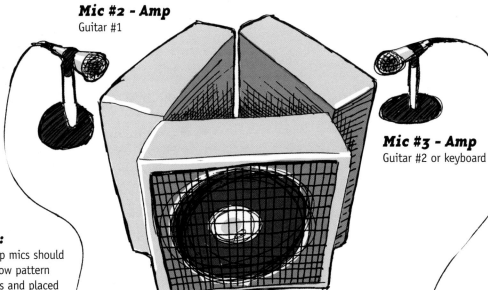

Mic #3 - Amp
Guitar #2 or keyboard

Note:
The amp mics should be narrow pattern cardiods and placed fairly close to their individual speakers. Also, each amp should be about the same volume.

Mic #4 - Amp
Bass guitar

Note:
If you don't have enough mic stands, try a stack of books with a towel on top (to keep the mics from rolling around).

Mic #4 → Mic #3 → Mic #1

Mic #2 →

Recording Device:
You can either record each mic onto its own track or mix them in stereo. If you do stereo, you can play with the pan positions as they go to tape.

An Aside:
When you're trying to learn a song off of a CD, you can use a graphic equalizer to boost the frequency of the particular instrument (or vocal) that you're focusing on so that it is louder in the mix, and its nuances will be more easily discerned.

Recording Recipes, No. 9

Random Thoughts on Music and Recording
by Curtis Settino, art by Jeff Kriege

«When overdubbing, perform your parts while blindfolded, or with minimal light. This will help you focus on the "sound". Our brains tend to give most attention to visual stimuli.

«Only perform two to four takes in a row, then move on. Your spontaneity and energy begins to fade after too many takes of the same thing. The end result shouldn't feel labored - unless you prefer perfection over personality.

«Recognize that your recording tools have a signature sound. For example, a lot of music today is being "created" (composed and arranged) in the computer. This is not the same as fixing music (adjusting timing and removing errors) in the computer. Unfortunately, much of what comes out of the computer studio is too perfect and lacks flow. Fixing every note sounds as tedious as it is to do it. And a song rearranged in the computer usually sounds that way, too. Natural transitional elements that tie one section of music to another (inherent in a live performance) will often go missing. This is why so much current music sounds disjointed and oddly sectional. This "cut, paste and tweak" music will be the late '90s/early '00s version of the '80s' "overly gated everything with a crappy sampler." Of course, everything comes back in style again (but usually with a wink of self-knowing, pretentious, ham-fisted kitsch). But you know, only the good songs survive - in general.

«Listen to some music. Don't eat, clean, drive, talk, read, think, work, walk or run while listening. Just listen. When was the last time you did just that?

«People mostly listen to music in their cars and at work. Do you want to have your music heard by people in these situations? If so, then consider what kind of music "works" in those circumstances, then cater your recordings to match.

«Study the song structures of your favorite artists. Actually sit down and chart out the parts to every song on a record. Look for patterns and techniques that repeat. Sometimes a song that you thought was simple is really quite convoluted. Not every song is intro/verse/chorus/verse/chorus/solo/chorus. Sometimes a song IS just that simple and ordinary, but it doesn't sound that way. Why?

«Study the song order and quantity of all your favorite records. Again, make a chart. Use any descriptions that you like (fast, catchy, dark, etc.). Where does the hit single fall? Is the record front loaded (all the best tunes first). Is there a lull at any point? Is there a song that doesn't fit stylistically and/or sonically? Does one song stand out as an odd duck? ("We're only at 35 minutes total. What else do we have?"). Do several songs sound like filler? ("But a CD can hold 70 minutes. I must fill every nook and cranny!")

«When settling in to make a record, reference other records that sound like the one you think you're making.

«When settling in to make a record, don't listen to any music at all. Only listen to the stuff that springs forth from inside you.

«Totally rip somebody else's song off (but change the words, key and tempo) and see how many people can pick up on it. Then realize that this is a commonplace activity.

«Reinvent the wheel every time you sit down to write a song.

«Rework really old material of yours and see if it works this decade.

«Keep your work space clean and organized, but not too much so.

«When recording vocalists, try hiding them behind a screen or in a booth. This can help them feel less self-conscious about the fact that everyone in the control room is scrutinizing each little squeak they make.

«When you're singing in the studio, try not to give a flying fuck what anyone thinks.

«When listening to a playback or critique of your performance, try not to take anything personally. It's all supposed to be about the song, remember? If it seems that someone is picking on you, it's because either you're defensive about something or the person has a hidden agenda. It's so hard to tell the difference, isn't it?

«Don't have an argument with someone while you're standing near a microphone. Some engineers are prepared to record your full-blown freak-out straight to DAT without anyone realizing it. Later, they'll share the hilarious recording with everyone. You don't want this kind of acclaim.

«Remember that nearly everyone in the world can make CDs now. It's very affordable. This is good and bad. Some really great independent records have surfaced because of this. But there is also a glut of home-wrung schlock. I guess, like everything else these days, there's too much music for any single person to check out. But there are those who try.

«Don't worry if you're not up to date on all the latest gear, either. As with the multitude of records, lots and lots of new gear hits the market every month. If anyone ever tries to make you feel bad about your ignorance, try one of these three responses: 1) "I'm so out of it! Hey, have you heard about the [insert fake product name here]? It's really cool." 2) Smile and realize that without vapid modern culture and all of its accouterments, this person would probably evaporate. 3) Walk away and never talk to them again.

«Remember why you're making music. Who's it for? Why's it for? Do you even know why you spend all your money on gear, all your time staring at meters, and all your brain power pondering Ab versus G#?

«It may be helpful to think about your recordings as though they were beach art - that is, temporary. Completely erase a song that you spent a week on. Do it! Sometimes the memory of the song is more helpful than the actual recording.

«If you're stuck not knowing what to do next on a recording, move on to the next song or clean the heads on your deck.

«Have at least one functioning microphone that you wouldn't mind a three-year-old (or the rock band equivalent) handling.

«Enjoy what you're doing.

AN INTRO TO ANALOG TAPE DECK CALIBRATION FUN

by David Patterson & Larry Crane

Bias and equalization; you've probably heard and used the terms for years, possibly without really understanding their effect on the quality of your recordings. If you're an engineer working with analog tape decks, you should know how to set decks up for different operating levels, bias for varying brands and formulations of tape, and how to calibrate your deck for a flat EQ response. Your recordings will sound better (than if you left it uncalibrated for years!) and you won't be afraid to try new tape formulations or work on tapes from other studios. Keep in mind that this is just the tip of the iceberg - there's enough info and tips on this to fill a book - but don't be afraid to learn how to do this yourself - you need this knowledge! Here's how it works:

The bias oscillator in your analog tape machine serves two purposes: it erases the tape as it passes the erase head, and it provides recording bias, as a smaller amount is sent to the record head. Well, if the tape's already been erased, you might wonder, why do we need more of the same signal fed to the record head? Turns out that magnetization is not a linear function. The tape needs a bit of a shove to get it into the linear part of its transfer function. That shove is provided by high-frequency bias. Since the bias frequency is way beyond our hearing range (100-200 kHz. in pro decks), it doesn't affect the audio being recorded too much. There is some low-level intermodulation distortion, however.

We all understand the purposes of equalization. In analog recording, a built-in EQ is applied at both ends of the process. Recording equalization (set to AES/NAB or IEC/CCIR standards in most cases) is applied before our audio gets to the tape. Its purpose is to compensate for the characteristics of the recorder and the tape. Playback equalization must be applied to compensate for the nature of the medium. On playback, magnetic tape exhibits a 6 dB per octave rise in output. Thus the tape deck uses a -6 dB per octave low-pass equalization to obtain flat frequency response.

Armed with this knowledge, we are now ready to match the tape machine's electrical characteristics to the tape we wish to use for recording.

You will need the following:

1. A magnetic reference tape. This is a tape, which has been recorded at a known level of magnetism for at least three frequencies, 100 Hz, 1 kHz, and 10 kHz. You will use this to set playback levels and EQ. These tapes, frequently from Magnetic Reference Laboratories and known as MRLs, are fairly expensive. You can get around buying one if you happen to have a tape from a pro studio, or from school, which has test tones recorded on it at a known level, although these can sometimes be misleading ("what operating level?"). Make sure the tape is the appropriate speed you plan to run your deck at and that (duh!) it is the right width (1/2", 2" etc.). Generally test tapes featuring AES/NAB EQ are desired, although there can be advantages to using IEC/CCIR EQ for recording – look for this in a future *Tape Op* article. AES is the only EQ setting for 30 ips whereas 15 or 7.5 ips can be run at AES or IEC EQ. Check your machine for what it's capable of using – many have internal switches for different EQs.

2. You also need a sine-wave oscillator capable of output at those same frequencies. For this, you can substitute a test CD with those frequencies, but a pure oscillator is best. Some consoles and decks have built-in oscillators.

3. A tiny screwdriver will be needed to tweak the adjustments.

4. It also helps to have an AC voltmeter to double-check your levels.

STEP I: Clean the heads and anything which the tape touches (guides, lifters, capstans). Do not use head cleaner on the rubber pinch roller or tach roller unless it is formulated to be safe on these parts (like that S-721 stuff). If you have a demagnetizer, follow the instructions that came with it to demagnetize the heads. Be sure to turn off the deck, remove all tape from the room, and leave your wallet and your watch in the next room (no

sense erasing your credit cards while you're at it). If your demagnetizer has an on/off switch be careful not to turn it on or off near the deck! Consult the service manual for your tape machine to be sure that you know where to find all the correct potentiometers for alignment. Also, switch off any noise reduction (dbx, Dolby) during the calibration and biasing process.

STEP II: Load your magnetic reference tape and set all channels to REPRO/SAFE. Play the 1 kHz tone and observe the VU meters. If you plan to record at the reference tape's level, all the meters should read 0 VU. Adjust the REPRO LEVEL pot on each channel to obtain this level. If you desire a higher or lower level, adjust the REPRO LEVEL until the meters read under 0 by the amount you wish to record over 0. For example, say you have a 250 nWb/m reference tape but you wish to record at +6 dB (370 nWb/m), you would adjust the REPRO LEVEL so that each meter reads –3 dB (See the chart here for quick conversions). There is one warning, though. Some recorders cannot supply enough bias current to record at elevated levels. If proper results cannot be obtained in the next step, you might be stuck with a lower level. Repeat this procedure with the 10 kHz tone, adjusting the HF (high frequency) REPRO pot (HF EQ, HF, EQ - whatever it may be called). Repeat this procedure at 100 Hz. Adjust LF (low frequency) REPRO for your reference level if that adjustment is available on your recorder (although this may change later...). Recheck the levels at 1 kHz, and adjust if necessary. Now do the same thing for SYNC/CUE playback - this time adjusting the SYNC LEVEL pots to obtain the same levels. Rewind and store your reference tape. You have now set all the reproduction levels and EQ for flat response. Do not skip this part, as everything else depends on having the playback circuitry properly adjusted.

STEP III: Load a new reel of the tape you wish to use. All channels should be set to RECORD/READY and the monitor switch set to TAPE/REPRO. Input 10 kHz at 0 VU from your oscillator. You can check for the correct input level with a voltmeter set to read AC volts. If your deck operates at +4 dBu (most pro gear), your meter should read 1.23 volts AC across the hot and cold outputs (tip and ring on 1/4" and pins 2 and 3 on XLR). If your recorder operates at -10 dBu ("home" recording gear), it should read 0.316 volts AC. While recording this tone, observe the meters. Turn the BIAS pot counterclockwise and notice the peak output on the VU meters. Now, turn the BIAS pot clockwise until the level peaks again then starts to fall. If the needle pegs the meter and stays there, reduce the level from the oscillator during the biasing, but remember to reset it to +4 or -10 after this

What VU to calibrate your repro level to:

Operating Levels	desired operating level	But your reference tape is (n/Wb/m)					
		185	200	250	320	370	520
+9 = 520 nWb/m	0 db	0	+1	+3	+5	+6	+9
+6 = 370 nWb/m	+1 db	-1	0	+2	+3	+5	+8
+5 = 320 nWb/m	+3 db	-3	-2	0	+2	+3	+6
+4 = 290 nWb/m	+5 db	-5	-4	-2	0	+1	+4
+3 = 250 nWb/m	+6 db	-6	-5	-3	-1	0	+3
+1 = 200 nWb/m	+9 db	-9	-8	-6	-4	-3	0
0 = 185 nWb/m							

...ep. This peak is your reference bias level. Turn the
...t further clockwise until the level drops from the
...ak level by the amount specified in the literature
... your tape or listed in the manual for your tape
...chine with the brand of tape and the tape speed
...u use. This level is known as the "recommended
...er-bias" (see the other chart for this info).
...peat this procedure for each channel.

...Now, we have repro level and recording bias
...justed.

STEP IV: Switch your oscillator to 1 kHz @
...VU and send the tone to the inputs of each track,
...her through a buss, or multed, or one at a time,
...through a test tone input like on Otari decks.
...ile recording this tone and watching the meters
...repro/tape, adjust the RECORD LEVEL/GAIN pots
...obtain 0 VU at the meters for each channel. (You
... switch between INPUT and TAPE monitoring,
...h level should read the same.) On some tape
...ks, like MCI gear, there's a REC CAL pot on the
...ord card. You'll need to fine-tune this to 0 while
...nput mode while switching to repro to set the
...ord gain (and go back and forth till both read

...Switch your oscillator to 10 kHz and record, this
...e adjusting the HF RECORD EQ for 0 VU output
...le monitoring in tape mode. Sometimes this is
...led simply as EQ on the record card.

...With the oscillator set to 100 Hz record yet
...ther pass and monitor in repro while adjusting
...LF/LO FREQ on the repro card (that we set
...ore) and set it to zero. You can even skip the
...ustments of this during the reference tape ses-
...earlier if you feel comfortable doing so.

...Re-check the levels at 1 kHz and readjust them
...ny have changed.

...Now you have set the bias to optimize the
...e and your deck and you should be reading
...levels on all your test tones when you record
...n and monitor in repro. You can print tones
...to 60 seconds per tone) at the top of a new
...(or reel number one of a session) for your
...future reference or for the poor engineers at
...e other studio that may have to work on your
...ks. This will enable them to set up their
...hine to sound as much like yours was set up
...ng tracking. If you have a feeling a project
...be travelling to a number of studios you can
...rve a space on the first reel as a "bias pad".
... is a stretch of tape (3 minutes is nice)
...e the next studio can set the bias on their
...hine without worrying about running over a
... or test tones. Always separate test tones
... bias pads by tape leader if you can.
...ember to label the reels as to where the
...s are (head or tail?), what the frequencies
...1 kHz, 10 kHz and 100 Hz being pretty stan-
...but you never know), what tape speed it is
...ing at, and operating level (+6/185 nWb/m
...g an example). This will make somebody's
...lot easier in the future.

Recommended Overbias Settings

Tape Speed (ips)	Record Gap			Tape/Type
	.25	.30-.40	.50	
30	1.75	1.5	1.25	Quantegy GP9/499
15	4.0	3.5	3.0	Quantegy GP9/499
7.5	7.0	5.5	4.0	Quantegy GP9/499
30	1.5	1.25	1.0	Quantegy 456/478/480/406
15	3.0	2.5	2.0	Quantegy 456/478/480/406
7.5	5.0	4.5	4.0	Quantegy 456/478/480/406
30	1.5	1.25	1.0	BASF/Emtec/RMGI SM 900
15	4.0	3.5	3.0	BASF/Emtec/RMGI SM 900
7.5	6.5	5.0	4.0	BASF/Emtec/RMGI SM 900
30	1.5	1.25	1.0	BASF/Emtec/RMGI SM 911
15	3.0	2.5	2.0	BASF/Emtec/RMGI SM 911
7.5	6.0	5.0	4.0	BASF/Emtec/RMGI SM 911
30	1.5	1.25	1.0	BASF/Emtec/RMGI SM 468
15	4.0	3.5	3.0	BASF/Emtec/RMGI SM 468
7.5	5.0	4.5	4.0	BASF/Emtec/RMGI SM 468
30	2.0	1.75	1.5	3M/Scotch 996
15	4.0	3.5	3.0	3M/Scotch 996
7.5	6.5	5.25	4.0	3M/Scotch 996
30	2.0	1.7	1.4	ATR Magnetics
15	4.5	3.75	3.0	ATR Magnetics
7.5	8.5	7.15	6.0	ATR Magnetics
15	1.0	.75	0.5	3M/Scotch 808/809
7.5	3.0	2.5	2.0	3M/Scotch 808/809

Record Gap Lengths

.25 mils: Otari (most), Studer (all), Tascam (all)

.30-40 mils: Ampex ATR-124 (2")/MM 1100/MM 1200, Lyrec (all), MCI (all), Otari MTR-10 (1/4"), MTR-12 (1/4"), MTR-15 (1/4"), Scully (all), Soundcraft (all), 3M M79

.50 mils: Ampex ATR 100 series, Ampex MM 1000, Otari MX-5050 (full track)/MX-7800/MkII-I, Stevens (all), Ampex AG 440

Now record some great music.

Perhaps you see yet another reason why digital recording is so dang popular. You don't need to go through all this crap to get a decent recording on digital, but I swear there's nothing like the feeling of security you get after setting up your deck for optimal levels before a big session. ☸

NOTES: 1. Frequently people lump "alignment" in with biasing and calibration. Alignment specifically refers to setting up the actual tape heads for optimal performance by adjusting the axis so that tracks 1 and 24 (or whatever is highest) read the tape at the same time, by making sure the head is perpendicular to the tape, and that the tape is equidistant from the top and bottom of the head.

This is a more involved process, and requires an oscilloscope, though you can be reckless and eyeball these settings in an emergency!

2. Many decks have different names for all the adjustments on the repro, record, bias and control cards. Read a manual if one is available to make sure. Be wary of turning controls labeled BIAS TRAP or BIAS CAL or ERASE PEAK as they do other things.

3. If you have a two head machine, check the article on page 70 for information on how to align your machine.

(Many thanks to Jeff Saltzman and Craig Smith who forced me to learn this dying art and to Greg Norman at Electrical Audio who threw in some tips. -LC)

How to build a microphone

for decades condenser microphones have been the staple for high-quality recording and live sound assignments. Unfortunately, not everyone can afford to own a good one. Well that's about to change. i've written this article so that anyone who wants a great condenser mic (or those who just want more of them) can have their wish. for around $20 (US) anyone can build an eXtremely accurate, life-like condenser microphone. DO NOT let the cost fool you, this mic's frighteningly good performance will blow your mind—and it's easy to build! -Joel Cameron

This microphone is largely based on a posting I found on the internet showing how to modify Realistic (Radio Shack) PZMs for better performance. I have simply finished the design so people can build a complete mic from scratch. After making a pair of these, I was shocked to find out how amazing they sound. In fact, these little buggers have become my first choice for capturing unhyped, totally natural stereo images, beating-out pairs of choice small and large-diaphragm condensers, and some nice ribbons too!

There are several good points worth a quick mention regarding this microphone:

Firstly, it uses an extremely simple circuit with very few components. As such there's not much stuff in it to screw up the sound. In audio design simple is generally better, and this is the epitome of simplicity.

Secondly, because it is such a simple circuit, it is very easy to build, even if you have no previous electronics building experience. With moderate care and attention anyone can easily build a pair of these mics in an afternoon.

Thirdly, this mic uses a proprietary, portable power supply instead of phantom power. This makes it a great choice for location recording, binaural nature recordings, or anyone forced to rely on dynamic mics because their gear lacks phantom power capability.

Lastly, because this mic uses a tiny 6-mm diaphragm, it has incredibly fast impulse response, which essentially means that its sound reproduction is extremely accurate and life-like. This factor has contributed to the recent popularity of ultra-small-diaphragm condensers. Larger diaphragms (even those used in traditional, high-quality small-diaphragm pencil mics) simply cannot reproduce this kind of accuracy. Recording with a pair these mics sounds just like being there!

Enough rambling—let's get started.

Circuit components

(1) http://www.jlielectronics.com/transsound/electrets/ts-60a.htm

IMPORTANT NOTE: When this article was originally run, a Panasonic element was specified which is no longer available. The above part number is a substitution that was kindly supplied to us by Brad Avenson of Avenson Electronics. But, it has NOT been tested. We have had many requests for this article to be reprinted so we are doing so, but please consider this a bit of a science project and please don't call us or Brad with questions!

(1) 1000 pF ceramic disc capacitor
(1) 10uF mylar or metalized polypropylene capacitor (DO NOT substitute an electrolytic!)
(1) 2.2Kohm 1% metal-film resistor
(1) 9-volt battery terminal w/leads
(1) 9-volt alkaline battery
Insulated copper wire

Hardware:

(1) *Metal* enclosure for the power supply (important for proper grounding)
(1) 9-volt battery mount (clip types can be purchased at Radio Shack or you can use industrial velcro, etc...)
(1) Panel-mount male XLR connector
(1) Panel-mount female XLR connector

(1) Male XLR cable connector (for the mic output to PSU)
(4) Rubber feet (not necessary, but I like them for the bottom of the PSU!)

This project consists of two main parts: Fig. 1 - the microphone, and Fig. 2 - the power supply. Fig. 2a is power supply used when driving a balanced input. This is the one most people will want to build. When using it to drive an 1/8" unbalanced mic input (such as those on many cassette and mini-disc multitracks), simply use an XLR female to 1/8" male adapter cable connecting pin 2 to tip and pins 1 and 3 to sleeve. If you are certain that you will *never* want to drive a balanced input, you can opt for the supply shown in Fig. 2b designed for use with unbalanced inputs only.

You may notice that there is no "power" switch on the power supply diagrams. This is because the battery will only drain when the mic is plugged in. Each time you finish using the mic, simply unplug it from the supply. There is no need to remove the battery.

FIG. 1 - MICROPHONE

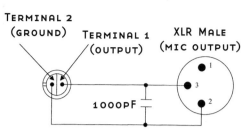

TERMINAL 2 (GROUND)
TERMINAL 1 (OUTPUT)
XLR MALE (MIC OUTPUT)
1000pF

Note: The bottom of each cartridge is marked with a white positioning dot used to determine Terminal 1 from Terminal 2. With this dot in the 12 o'clock position Terminal 2 is left while Terminal 1 is right.

FIG. 2A - POWER SUPPLY FOR BALANCED XLR INPUT

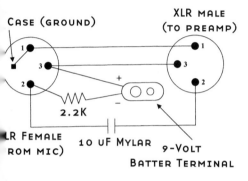

CASE (GROUND)
XLR MALE (TO PREAMP)
2.2K
XLR FEMALE (FROM MIC)
10 uF MYLAR
9-VOLT BATTER TERMINAL

2B - POWER SUPPLY FOR BALANCED 1/4" INPUT

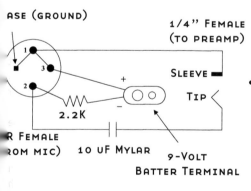

CASE (GROUND)
1/4" FEMALE (TO PREAMP)
SLEEVE
TIP
2.2K
XLR FEMALE (FROM MIC)
10 uF MYLAR
9-VOLT BATTER TERMINAL

Construction tips:

- When building the circuit make sure to shrinkwrap all bare leads to prevent the possibility of shorting against the chassis or other leads. If shorting occurs, your mic won't work. Shrinkwrap is available from any electronic supply store.

- After you connect the wire leads to the mic cartridge seal the entire back of the cartridge with non-conductive epoxy making sure to overlap a touch where the back meets the sides. This seal provide additional dampening of the phenolic backplate of the capsule which further extends its low frequency response.

- You can mount the cartridge just about any way you want. I chose to mount mine in the end of the rubber boot of a Neutrik XLR connector (see photos). This allows for a compact package, reasonable sonic neutrality, and perhaps even a touch of shock-mounting because of the rubber's ability to damp vibration. If you choose to mount your cartridge the same way, sink it by pressing gently on the *edges* of the cartridge. *Do not* mash down dead center or you risk damage to the diaphragm. Note that mounting the cartridge this way will also require that you handle the finished mic with care so as not to damage the exposed capsule.

- Buy or borrow a simple multi-meter for use during construction. Mine is an inexpensive Radio Shack model 22-802 which costs about $25. Use this to check all solder points *as you go* just to make sure that they are good (sometimes a connection may look good, but, for some reason, won't be making solid electrical contact). By checking as you go you can identify a problem when it occurs rather than having to go through the entire, completed circuit to find a single cold joint (which can easily become a hair-pulling experience!).

- For my power supply chassis I used a single-wide electrical junction box which cost me 79-cents at Home Depot. The solid cover for it (to complete the enclosure) cost another 35-cents complete with screws! This is an excellent choice because it's cheap, it's metal, it's sturdy, and the punch-outs are already the right size for most XLR panel mount connectors. I used Neutrik XLRs which required that I file four grooves around the edge of the hole for the right fit, but the hole was already there!

- Work slowly! This is not a complicated project, so it won't take long. Check and recheck your progress. I know it's easy to get impatient and want to have it done, but work methodically. When you are finished the mic will give you years of excellent performance!

Using your new mic(s):

Despite the fact that these mics are omnidirectional they do possess directional characteristics at higher frequencies. Therefore using a pair in an X-Y configuration can yield an incredibly natural stereo image. This also allows you to back-off the top-end a touch (acoustically!) by simply pointing the tip of mic 90-degrees from the source. The impulse response and realism remain unaffected!

These mics are awesome for stereo recording. Try them as drum overheads and room mics. Jecklin-disc and spaced-omni stereo techniques also work fabulously. They are great for acoustic guitar, piano, percussion, choral groups, or just about anything that you want to sound like "being there".

If you have never used omnidirectional mics before, be aware that they hear much more of the room in which the source is recorded than cardioid mics do. Therefore, if you want a "dead" sound, you will need to either record in a "dead" room or use baffles and/or strategic placement to reduce ambience. I was able to effectively control the ambience in a vocal track by placing the mic below the singer's head in a carpeted room, pointing up at him while he sang down at the mic. Since his voice projected primarily into the carpet, much of it was absorbed leaving very little to reverberate in the room.

Also, omnidirectional mics do not exhibit the proximity effect (low-end boost when used up close) that directional mics do, so you can place these mics extremely close to a source without the unnatural boominess that can result from using a cardioid. This also means that when you *want* that low-end effect (for say, a lead vocal) then you will need to dial in a touch of low-frequency equalization.

Because these mics sound so natural, they are great for capturing just about any good-souding source. Use them on guitar cabinets, acoustic instruments, brass sections, ensembles, inside kick drums, you name it. Experiment and have fun!

A word of caution: NEVER connect these mics to a phantom powered input without first turning off the phantom and allowing 5-10 minutes for discharge. Though it is designed to drive a balanced input, the mic's output is not a true balanced design, so the DC-voltage provided by phantom power on pins 2 and 3 will not cancel as it would with a balanced mic. This could easily damage the cartridge, which is rated for a maximum of only 10-volts DC!

Many thanks to Phil Rastoczny for writing the article on the Realistic PZM modification that is the basis for this microphone and to Brad Avenson for the updated part number. ☉

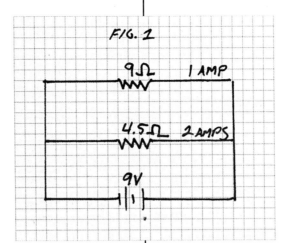

FIG. 1

9Ω   1 AMP

4.5Ω   2 AMPS

9V

I'M NO EXPERT #3: RESISTORS

by Geoff Farina

You might remember the last time we met I explained how capacitors worked in your gear, and how you could change the filter capacitors in your guitar amplifier to beef things up a bit. This time I'd like to give the same treatment to resistors. In this column I'll illustrate what resistors are, what they do, how to identify them, and then offer some real-world tricks that will allow you to use resistors to soup up your amp a bit.

DISCLAIMERS

#1: TAPE OP and I are not responsible if you kill your amplifier or yourself! Tube guitar amps carry enough voltage to kill you **EVEN WHEN THEY ARE TURNED OFF AND UNPLUGGED!** Do not open up your amplifier unless you know how to discharge filter caps and have a good idea of what you are doing! NEVER open up your amplifier when it is plugged in!

#2: **I'm no expert.** I learned everything I know from reading and blowing shit up. I do not guarantee the accuracy of the information in this column and I welcome all additions and corrections.

RESISTORS ARE EVERYWHERE

Even the casual geek knows that resistors are everywhere. They're the little color-coded tubular components that are a fundamental part of everything from your high-end mic preamps to your rack gear to your Roland Juno-106 and right down to your Tube Screamer. Even your silly looking G3 uses resistors, and in some cases, the tone controls on your guitar or bass as well. To gain an understanding of what they are and what they do, we need to take

a minute (surprise) to revisit your high-school physics class, so bust out your Trapper Keepers.

CIRCUIT THEORY 101

You'll remember from high school (and from my previous two articles) the analogy of electricity as water that flows down the path of least resistance. To keep things simple, imagine that electricity flows across wires just like water flows through a pipe. We can imagine that there are three elements that control the flow of water through a pipe: the water pressure, the amount of water, and the size of the pipe. Likewise, the flow of electrons down a wire is dictated by the pressure **(voltage)** pulling the electrons, the amount of electrons **(current)**, and the size and material of what the electrons are flowing through **(resistance)**. A thick copper wire has very little resistance, but if we cut the wire and put a piece of carbon in the gap, we add resistance to the flow of electrons. This, just as if we put dirt and gravel in the middle of the water pipe, we impede the flow of the water. With me so far? No? Well, it's sort of like when the screen in your bong gets all clogged with resin and...

In any case, if everything else escaped you from Physics 101, you surely remember that **Ohm's Law** is best way to explain the relationship between these three elements—current, voltage, and resistance.

Now, before you nod off or start carving Van logos onto your desktop, take a minute to vis this relationship. Ohm's Law can be thought of amount of current (in amps, usually expresse for some stupid reason) in a circuit is equal voltage (volts, or V) divided by the amou resistance (or R, expressed in Ohms). In geek this looks like **I=V/R**. As you also know from A 1, you can express this equation in two other V=IR and R=V/I. This simple equation allows figure out any one of the three factors in a cir you know the other two. So how much curr flowing through a wire with a 400 volt power through 100 ohm resistor? If you said four am to the head of the class.

WHAT RESISTORS DO

Although basic Ohm's Law has little value you're poking around your gear wondering what, we can use it to understand how am (and other gear) actually use resistors. For th part, resistors do two main jobs: limit curre divide voltage. For example, lets say you stompbox with a power supply of a 9-Volt b The design of the stomp box requires that you one point in the circuit with 1 Amp, and a point with 2 Amps. You can create this situatio resistors in parallel. As you can see in Figure put two resistors in parallel with the 9-volt battery, we can split the current between them. We can use Ohm's law to figure out just what size resistors we need: if we know we need 1 Amp, we can use Ohm's Law to figure out that 9 volts divided by 1 Amp leaves us with a 9 Ohm resistor. Likewise, 9 Volts divided by 2 Amps leaves us with a 4.5 ohm resistance. Here we see that **RESISTORS IN PARALLEL ACT AS CURRENT DIVIDERS, AND THAT THE VOLTAGE REMAINS CONSTANT THROUGHOUT THE CIRCUIT.**

You can use similar logic to see that **RESISTORS IN SERIES ACT AS VOLTAGE DIVIDERS.** Consider figure 2. We have three resistors in series with 120 volts. The voltage between the the resistors is different from the voltage at the positive or negative lead of the battery because some of the voltage is dissipated by the resistance, just as water pressure is dissipated as it tries to push water through the clog in a pipe. The important thing to remember is that the current remains constant in this situation, just as the same amount of water still travels through the pipe, it just arrives at a slower rate and with less pressure then it began with. So, given the resistance values of 10 ohms, 20 ohms, and 30 ohms, figure 2 illustrates how we can figure out the voltages between the resistors, and the constant amount of current flowing through all of them.

Also, notice from these two examples that **THE TOTAL RESISTANCE IN A CIRCUIT WITH RESISTORS IN SERIES IS THE TWO RESISTORS ADDED TOGETHER, AND THE TOTAL RESISTANCE OF A CIRCUIT WITH RESISTANCES IN PARALLEL IS THE RESISTANCES ADDED AND THEN DIVIDED BY THE AMOUNT OF RESISTORS.** In other words, in a series circuit, R=R1+R2+R3 where there are three resistors in series and R is the total resistance.

In a parallel circuit, 1/R = 1/R1+1/R2+1/R3, where the circuit has three resistors in parallel and R is the total resistance. So, in figure one, the total resistance is a little less than 7 ohms (13.5/2), and in figure two the total resistance is 60 ohms.

This column just glosses the surface of circuit theory. You can use Ohm's Law to calculate the resistances, voltages, and currents in more complex circuits that have resistors in both parallel and series. If you're interested in learning more, any high school physics text will do. The purpose of this introduction is simply to illustrate how resistors do the job of dividing voltages and limit current in your amps and other audio gear. Next I'll show you how to recognize them and then a few ways you can manipulate them to beef up your Fender amp.

RECOGNIZING RESISTORS

Unlike the obscure and proprietary markings on capacitors, most resistors are clearly color coded with an international standard that makes them easily identifiable. There are usually four color bands around the resistor that indicate its value and

tolerance. The last band will usually either be silver or gold. This indicates the tolerance of the resistor. If the band is silver, the resistor is within 10% of it's indicated value. If it's gold, it's within 5% of its indicated value. Don't worry too much about the tolerance of the resistor. Usually 5% or 10% tolerances will work fine for most applications. (Sometimes resistors have a red tolerance band, indicating they have a 2% tolerance. Others have no tolerance band at all, indicating a 20% tolerance. But for the most part, you'll find gold and silver bands on the resistors in your audio gear.)

The remaining three color bands indicate the actual value of the resistor. The following chart will help you decode the values:

Opposite from the tolerance band, the first and second bands indicate the first two numbers in the value, and the final band indicates the number of zeros that follow. So, for example, if you see a resistor that has blue, gray, brown and silver stripes, it has the value of 680 ohms and it has a tolerance of 10%. One thing you should know to make this easier is that for most gear you'll usually be using only a few values over and over again. In Fender amps there are usually no more than 10 or 15 different values for the most part, so you don't have to spend all your time decoding values. Also, when you buy resistors at Radio Shack they usually come packaged with a little chart that you can tack up to your work bench for easy access. (Not that I advocate buying anything from the Shack!)

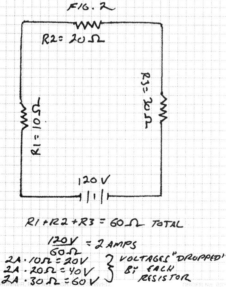

FIG. 2

R2 = 20 Ω
R3 = 20 Ω
R1 = 10 Ω
120 V

R1 + R2 + R3 = 60 Ω TOTAL

$\frac{120V}{60\Omega}$ = 2 AMPS

2A · 10Ω = 20V
2A · 20Ω = 40V
2A · 30Ω = 60V
} VOLTAGES "DROPPED" BY EACH RESISTOR

The other thing you should know about resistors is that you'll usually find three different sizes: 1/4 watt, 1/2 watt, and 1 watt, from smallest to biggest. All that this means is that the bigger resistors have a better capability for dissapating heat produced by the higher voltages in older gear. Most vintage amps use 1/2 watt and sometimes 1 watt resistors. Today, 1/4 watt are the most common by far because of the lower voltages used in solid-state gear.

Finally, there are too many different kinds of resistors to address in this column. Most vintage amps use carbon-composition resistors, but you can

usually replace them with metal film resistors. If you're a purist and want to dig up the real deal, you'll have to check the Mouser or Digi-Key catalogs and see if they have any in stock. I bought a bunch in bulk years ago and I'm glad I did because they're hard to find these days.

| BLACK = 0 |
| BROWN = 1 |
| RED = 2 |
| ORANGE = 3 |
| YELLOW = 4 |
| GREEN = 5 |
| BLUE = 6 |
| VIOLET = 7 |
| GRAY = 8 |
| WHITE = 9 |

AMPLIFIER SPEAKERS

Okay, you've done your homework for the day. Now it's time for some real-world applications of what you have learned. There's no better way to apply what you've learned than to address the ubiquitous confusion over the wiring of your favorite resistors of all, the speakers in your amplifier. Technically, speakers are not simple resistors. Speakers are transducers, or components that turn current into physical motion (and sometimes vice versa, for example, on the "out" RCA jack of your spring reverb tank or a dymanic microphone). Also, although speakers are rated with Ohms, these are not static resistances. They are impedance ratings, or resistances that change with frequency. (Ever wonder why your 8 Ohm speakers never show up as 8 Ohms on your multi-meter?) However, for our purposes and for the purposes of illustrating the proper wiring of speakers, we will treat them as simple resistors. Take my favorite amplifier for example, the lovely Fender Twin Reverb. This amplifier requires a 4-Ohm load and has space for two speakers. What impedance speakers do we put into this amplifier, and how do we wire them? Two 8 Ohm speakers wired in parallel will work just fine. From here it's easy to apply this knowledge to using different speaker configurations and external cabinets with your amps.

A CAVEAT ABOUT SPEAKERS

Keep in mind that there are two other factors that change the way your speakers work together:

1) Phase: Speakers must all be in phase with each other. This means that the cones must all be moving in the same direction at the same time. To check, place the leads of a 9 volt battery on the respective positive and negative speaker leads. If the speaker travels forward, away from the spider, it's fine. If it travels backward or toward the spider and the magnet, the positive indication on the speaker is wrong and the leads should be reversed. Many older speakers, like vintage Jensons, are reverse-marked.

2) Impedance mismatching: Remember earlier that I said that the Ohm ratings on your speakers are actually impedances, which are resistances that vary with the frequency. Although the most accurate signal transfer comes when the impedance of the output transformer is an exact match to the impedance of the speaker load, you will never get an exact match because the impedance is always changing with the frequency of your guitar notes. Also, most tube amps can easily tolerate an impedance mismatch of 100%. This means that if you have an amp that wants to see an 8 Ohm load, two 8 Ohm speakers wired in parallel (four Ohms) won't hurt the amp. However, a 2 Ohm load (for example, two 4 Ohm speakers wired in parallel) will almost look like a direct short to that amp and make it run too hot, probably damaging it.

MODS USING RESISTORS

Here's a few mods that involve resistors that you can try on your silverfaced/blackfaced Fender amplifier. I won't go into the theory of why they work, but using what you know, you should be able to gain an understanding yourself.

1) Instant Overdrive: Here's a great mod that I used on my Fender Twin on many of the Karate recordings. It gives you a nice overdrive if you're willing to sacrifice your reverb. Get a 470K Ohm, 1/2 watt resistor and an RCA cable. Cut the RCA cable in half and hook up the hot wires to the leads of the resistor, taking care not to short out the ground wires. Then unplug your reverb tank from the Reverb In and Reverb Out connections on the back, and plug in your resistor so that the reverb signal is now running through the resistor. Now hook up a foot pedal to the Reverb On/Off foot pedal jack and you're good to go. The Reverb knob on your amp controls the amount of overdrive, and the foot pedal turns it on and off. I've found that this mod works better with nice, high-wattage speakers that don't break up as much.

2) Cleaner Sound: Most older Fender amps have a 1500 Ohm resistor going from the cathode of the preamp tubes (pin 3 on a 12AX7) to ground, in parallel with an electrolytic capacitor. Changing this resistor from 1.5K Ohms to 2.7K Ohms will clean up the tone of your amp and give it less preamp distortion.

3) Higher Fidelity: You can improve your sound by eliminating series resistance on your Fender. Most Fenders have two 68K ohm resistors that go from the input jacks to the preamp stages of the amp. You don't need these unless you're using both jacks simultaneously. Simply remove them and connect the hot lead (the one that touches the tip of your guitar cable) of the jack you want to use directly to the wire that was soldered to both resistors. This puts less garbage in your signal path and improves the clarity of your sound.

4) More Mids: If you have a Fender amp that only has a Treble and Bass control, you can still adjust the mids. Adjust the size of the 6.8K resistor soldered to the back of the bass potentiometer. You can go from grounding it out completely all the way up to 25K, but use your ear. You can even try replacing the resistor with a 25K (audio-taper) potentiometer to give you total control. After all, all a pot is is a resistor that allows you to vary it's value by turning the knob.

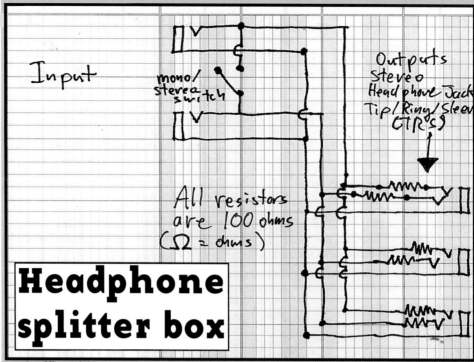

Headphone splitter box

Geoff's article on resistors inspired me to share a few cool 'resistor-only' projects that can come in super handy in just about any studio large or small. - *John 'I'm No Expert Either' Botch*

1. The first hand-drawn schematic is for a headphone splitter box. This box ensures that the impedance the amplifer sees is more or less the same regardless of how many headphones are plugged in. This will work with any old junky power amp you might have lying around and headphones of all impedances. Get the largest wattage resistors (1/2 watt or even 1 watt if you can find 'em) you can find however, because I did have one of these catch on fire once when some death metal guitar player needed the 'phones really loud for a feedback solo. I only show three headphone jacks on my badly drawn diagram, but you can put in as many as you want. The switch for mono/stereo is optional and you can hardwire it one way or the other if you like. This box will get lots of abuse, so make sure to use a sturdy case and good switchcraft jacks.

2. The second schematic is for a 20 dB pad. You can build these inline into those Switchcraft XLR barrel plugs if you need to pad down signals. You can also use these barrel things without any resistors to make phase reversal barrels if your board doesn't have a phase switch. I took the resistance values from the *Audio Encyclopedia* by Howard Tremaine (Howard Sams). The formulas are a little too lengthy to re-run here, but you can make pads for any amount of attenuation and impedance matching you might need from the formulas in this book. This circuit is un-balanced; the balanced circuit is more involved but that's in the book too. The Audio Encyclopedia is over 1500 pages and has lots of other technical info like this from very basic to very arcane.

Thanks to everyone who's written and emailed me with great questions, info, or just to shoot the shit about mutual interests. ☺

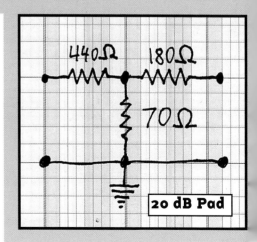

Recording Recipes, No.10
by Curtis Settino

"Mega In, Mega Out"

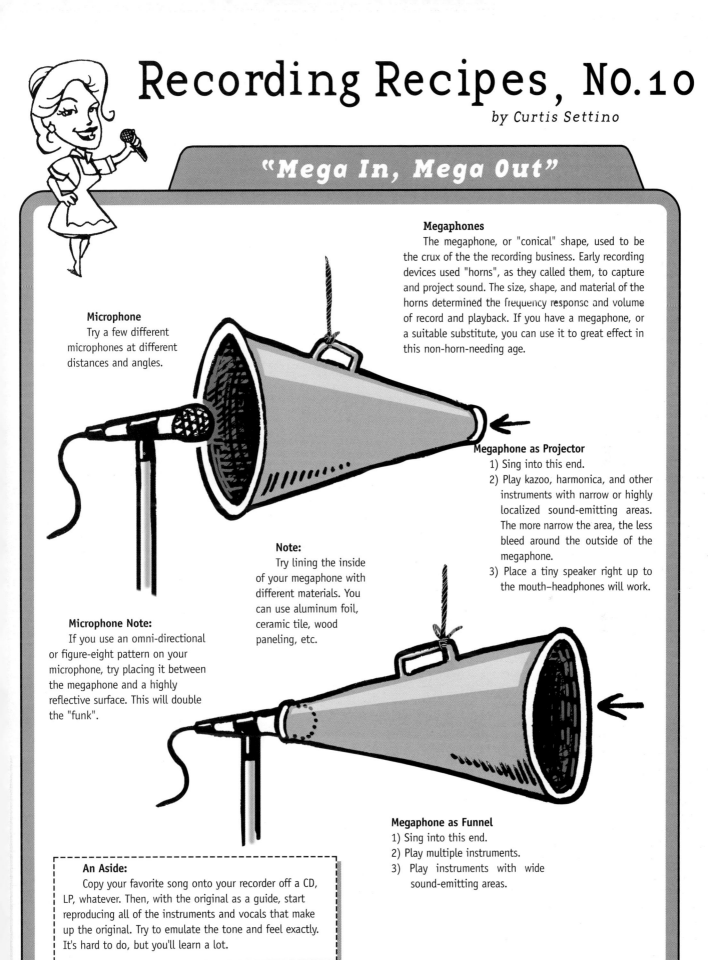

Megaphones
The megaphone, or "conical" shape, used to be the crux of the the recording business. Early recording devices used "horns", as they called them, to capture and project sound. The size, shape, and material of the horns determined the frequency response and volume of record and playback. If you have a megaphone, or a suitable substitute, you can use it to great effect in this non-horn-needing age.

Microphone
Try a few different microphones at different distances and angles.

Microphone Note:
If you use an omni-directional or figure-eight pattern on your microphone, try placing it between the megaphone and a highly reflective surface. This will double the "funk".

Note:
Try lining the inside of your megaphone with different materials. You can use aluminum foil, ceramic tile, wood paneling, etc.

Megaphone as Projector
1) Sing into this end.
2) Play kazoo, harmonica, and other instruments with narrow or highly localized sound-emitting areas. The more narrow the area, the less bleed around the outside of the megaphone.
3) Place a tiny speaker right up to the mouth—headphones will work.

Megaphone as Funnel
1) Sing into this end.
2) Play multiple instruments.
3) Play instruments with wide sound-emitting areas.

An Aside:
Copy your favorite song onto your recorder off a CD, LP, whatever. Then, with the original as a guide, start reproducing all of the instruments and vocals that make up the original. Try to emulate the tone and feel exactly. It's hard to do, but you'll learn a lot.

An Intro to Analog Tape Splicing and Editing and Tape Loops.

By John Holkeboer (with Larry Crane)

Who among us hasn't wanted to take a razor blade to our tapes for no other purpose than malicious destruction? Through the ancient art of manual tape editing and splicing, you now have a practical reason for doing just that!

Basic materials for tape splicing and editing.

✓ recording tape *(basic magnetic tape, e.g. Ampex, Maxell)*
✓ razor blades
✓ leader tape *(white, clear)*
✓ timing tape *(yellow, red)*
✓ adhesive splicing tape *(blue, best on a weighted desk dispenser, 1" for 2" tape, otherwise use 1/2")*
✓ editing block *(usually mounted on your console reel to reel recorder with grooves for hard cuts [vertical] or soft [diagonal])*
✓ grease pencil or china marker *(white, yellow, any color that stands out against brown tape)*
✓ ruler

Tape splicing and editing is essentially cutting and pasting tape by hand. It's organic and crafty. Instead of working with digital, virtual sound, you are manipulating the tape with your bare hands. In any other sense, however, there is no comparison. A comparison would be analogous to the difference between using a typewriter and a word processor. Manual splicing and editing is time consuming, and the results are irreversible. It is simply the old way: no better or worse than modern methods, only very different.

Whether you use digital or analog editing, the basic techniques of splicing and editing *(leader tape, tape loops, and cut and paste editing)* are essential skills for anyone who uses analog tape. Most console-style reel to reel recorders come with a factory installed editing block. It's a rectangular piece of milled aluminum or steel with one flat groove across the middle for holding the tape in place. This shallow, wide tape groove is intersected by one deeper, thin, vertical groove for cutting the tape with a razor blade *(hard cuts)*. Next to this is a similar, but 45 degree diagonal groove *(soft cuts)*. Most editing blocks have only these two razor grooves, but some have one more 30 degree diagonal razor groove for a super soft cut *(see diagram 1)*.

If you have an upright reel to reel recorder or your reel to reel is not equipped with an editing block you can buy one or in desperate situations only, go without. I have gone without an editing block in a pinch and it just takes lots more manual precision. And then, only for the most basic operations like adding leader tape to the front of a master reel. If you buy an editing block you just have to mount it firmly to your workspace *(as close as possible to the tape recorder and horizontally or at a low angle)*.

Leader tape application

Leader tape is made from polyester and is theoretically soundless. It's sold by the reel like recording tape and is usually white or clear with black stripes which denote time, i.e. 30 per minute at high speed, 15 per minute at low speed. It's mainly used at the beginning and end of a reel to protect the first and last few feet of tape, just like on a cassette.

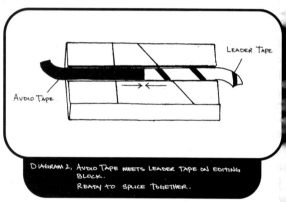

LEADER TAPE

AUDIO TAPE

DIAGRAM 2, AUDIO TAPE MEETS LEADER TAPE ON EDITING BLOCK.
READY TO SPLICE TOGETHER.

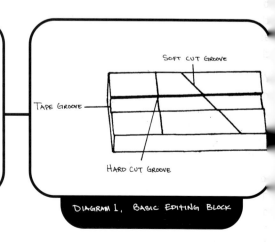

SOFT CUT GROOVE

TAPE GROOVE

HARD CUT GROOVE

DIAGRAM 1, BASIC EDITING BLOCK

To apply leader tape, follow these procedures:

1) Locate the beginning *(or the end)* of the recorded sound on the tape, rewind *(or fast forward)* a little bit to insure that you won't cut into the recorded sound you want, then mark *(on tape)* the intended cut with grease pencil *(always make the mark on the tape facing away from the side of the record/playback heads. i.e. the dull, darker brown non-magnetic tape).*

2) Place the marked segment of tape in the editing block *(you can pull the tape away from the tape heads with the tape still on the reels).*

3) Align the grease pencil mark with the desired razor groove *(vertical for a hard, instantaneous sound cut, or diagonal for a soft, more oblique cut).* Then with a clean, swift stroke cut through the tape.

4) Keeping the tape held in the shallow groove, match end to end *(no gaps, no overlaps)* then cut master tape with length of leader tape, cut the same way *(see diagram 2).*

5) Using the razor blade, cut off enough blue adhesive tape to cover the splice vertically. Affix the blue adhesive tape across the cut and joined magnetic and leader tape *(use the handle side of the razor blade or a fingernail to rub the adhesive tape on and to smooth out the air bubbles).* Trim the blue tape from the top and bottom of the audio tape by holding the razor at an angle and sliding it along the groove that holds the tape in the splicing block.

You can cut the leader tape to any length depending on how much dead silence you want. You can experiment with timing in this way. Incidentally, timing tape is essentially the same thing as leader tape, except it's yellow or red and sometimes it's useful to differentiate between timing and leader functions. The above procedure is useful for inserting breaks in your master tape, between songs or programs. Again, leader or timing tape is essentially endless, so you can also use it whenever you don't want tape hiss or want to permanently remove stick clicks.

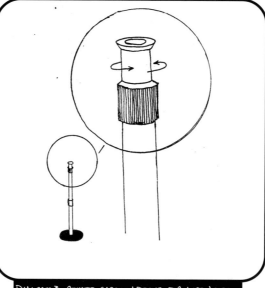

DIAGRAM 3, REMOTE CAPSTAN DEVICE FOR TAPE LOOPS. NOTE: THIS CAN BE DONE A NUMBER OF WAYS. HERE, A CAPSTAN (OR OTHER SPOOL-LIKE TOOL) IS MOUNTED ON A MICROPHONE STAND.

DIAGRAM 4, FINISHED (SPLICED) TAPE LOOP.

ADHESIVE TAPE

SPLICE LOCATION

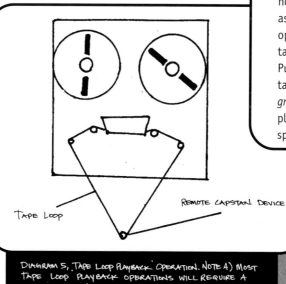

DIAGRAM 5, TAPE LOOP PLAYBACK OPERATION. NOTE A) MOST TAPE LOOP PLAYBACK OPERATIONS WILL REQUIRE A CONSOLE, OR HORIZONTAL REEL TO REEL MACHINE, SEE DIAGRAM 5A. B) ACTUAL REELS AREN'T INVOLVED IN TAPE LOOP PLAYBACK AT ALL.

TAPE LOOP

REMOTE CAPSTAN DEVICE

Tape Loops

Before sequencers and drum machines, enterprising people made tape loops to achieve endless repetition of a given sound sequence. If you've never seen or made one, the tape loop is a disarmingly easy and logical device.

To make and playback a tape loop, follow these procedures:

(The only item you need for tape loop playback in addition to the aforementioned materials is a floating capstan or spool, mounted on a portable stand, such as a mic stand. See diagram 3.)

1) Find the exact beginning and end of the tape segment you wish to loop and mark the cutoff points with a grease pencil.

2) Cut out the desired segment *(see step 3 of above procedure for cutting instructions. In the case of loops, either hard or soft cuts are fine. Again, hard for a sudden attack, soft for a more gradual attack.)*

3) Make into a continuous loop *(see step 4 of above procedure).* Be sure loop has no twists.

4) Splice together *(see diagram 4).*

5) To play back loop: Run the loop around capstans, through place holders, and in front of tape heads as you would for normal playback operation, but run the remaining tape around the remote capstan. Pull taut-not tight, making sure the tape can move normally *(see diagram 5).* Press play. Tape loop will play back repetitiously at regular speed until you press stop.

Cut and Paste Editing

Say you have two takes of a song. One take has an unfixable flaw in the last section of the song. Another take however, had better results over the same section. Isolate the flawed part in the first take, cut it out and replace it with the better part from the other take and splice it on. This type of editing is obviously risky and has potential to cause serious continuity problems. But sometimes it is the only solution. This same type of edit was used famously on 'Strawberry Fields Forever.' Other uses for this technique are to edit out overly long portions of a song, mix edits, and even slicing out small pieces of tape to remove stick clicks during a sloppy drum fill!

Other more advanced techniques refined by earlier electronic music

composers made use of such things as simultaneous tape deck playback: music comprised of separate parts played on separate tape decks timed to sync up by carefully measured *(by ruler)* lengths of leader tape. This type of music, also known as musique concrete, was originated by **Pierre Schafer** and **Pierre Henri**. Their piece, 'Symphonie Pour un Homme Seule,' is widely regarded as the first musique concrete composition. Other notable pieces done in this method include **Karlheinz Stockhausen**'s 'Kontakte' and 'Gesang' or **Iannis Xenakis**' 'Orient/Occident' or 'Bohor.' **Mario Davidovsky**, **Otto Luning** and **Gyorgy Ligeti** have also made significant contributions to this repertoire. This music also utilized backwards tape wherein you cut out a tape segment, flip end over end, and splice in for desired backward envelope. Also artificial tremolo, achieved by cutting many equal-size segments of tape and equal-size segments of leader tape *(by the use of a ruler)* and splicing them together *(see diagram 6)*.

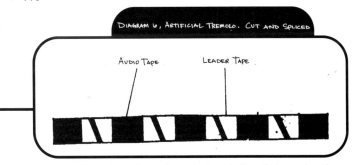

DIAGRAM 6, ARTIFICIAL TREMOLO. CUT AND SPLICED

AUDIO TAPE LEADER TAPE

These are very labor intensive and seemingly archaic techniques, but there are few very good reasons to use them. If you do it a lot, your technique improves and you even discover options unavailable with a computer. In sum: If you're looking new ways to be creative in your editing, it pays to have these options at your disposal. There is also the element of control. This kind of editing gives you a kind 'no-turning-back' decision-making power over your recordings. Perhaps more importantly, experimentation with manual tape splicing and editing is enlightening and informs one's own understanding of how sound engineering has evolved. ✆

What's a Repro???: Calibration for Two-Head Machines *by Jeff Saltzman*

I'm sure that more than a few *Tape Op* readers are like me and own a narrow format(1/4" 8, 1/2" 8 or 16, some 1" 16, and 1" 24-track.) analog deck by either Tascam or Fostex. To keep construction costs, and the physical size of these units tidy, the manufacturers designed their recorders with an erase head and a combination record/playback head only (sort of like most cassette decks). The lack of a dedicated playback (repro) head after the record (sync) stage in the tape path makes it impossible to see the adjustments being made in real time while calibrating - but with time and A LOT of patience on your part, your multi-track can be aligned (almost) like it's three-head brothers.

First off - if your machine sounds fine to you and it is NOT showing the signs of a tape recorder out of alignment - i.e. tracks coming back off tape much hotter or weaker than your initial input level and/or tracks coming back sounding inordinately brighter or duller than what you originally heard - this process is probably not something you want to get into. It's especially unnecessary if all your projects are recorded and mixed on the same machine and you use the same type of tape every time you work. Second - obviously this procedure can be done by a tech with a volt meter pretty easily, so I guess the following information is for those who want to learn more about their tape machine and experience the satisfaction of setting up their own deck.

Okay, start with an MRL tape and reference your units service manual for the manufacturer's recommended operating level (my Tascam MSR-16 manual suggests +3 or 250 nWb/m.) If the MRL is rated at a different level than what you need use the chart on page 60. Access the calibration adjustment pots on your deck (again - the service manual) and thread up the MRL. With your machine's noise reduction

off, play the 1 kHz segment of the test tape and find the pot designated "reproduce gain" or "reproduce level". Adjust each track to the desired level and now find the "reproduce EQ" control (making sure you are tweaking the right speed - there is usually a "hi" and a "lo"). Play 10 kHz off the MRL and trim these pots to the same level as your previous "gain" setting.

That was the easy part - now remove the MRL and thread up a blank reel of the type of tape you usually/or want to use. Put a track in record and feed the machine a 10 kHz tone checking in input for a level falling around -2 or -3 dB on the meter. Find the "bias adjust" pot (make sure it isn't "bias trap" or "bias erase".) Set a locate point and with the noise reduction still off, record a couple seconds of tone. Locate back and hit play paying special attention to where the meter is on playback.(this could be tricky on your edge tracks...) Record some more 10 kHz - this time turn the "bias adjust" pot counter clock-wise a quarter turn or so - play the tape - the level on playback should have increased slightly. Continue turning the pot counter clock-wise a bit at a time in record and checking the resulting change in playback. At a certain point (probably about 3 or 4 dB up at 15 i.p.s.) your adjustment should cause the level to start dropping - when you notice the change, try turning the pot clock-wise now in record - this should make the level increase again a little. Go back and forth between clock-wise and counter clock-wise on the bias pot a few times checking playback in between until you think you've found the "peak" of the meter activity. With that established, turn the pot clock-wise while recording past the peak and the level will decrease again. keep going down (clock-wise) until you've reached the suggested "overbias" amount

based on head-gap, tape type, and tape speed. Use charts here for reference but if you aren't sure about t consult the tape manufacturer or your local pro-audio d er. Now repeat this procedure for the rest of the tra When you get to the end the deck should be biased for particular type of tape. If you decide to change tape i good idea to re-bias for the new brand or formulation.

Once you've done the bias adjustment you're read shoot yourself - I mean do the record alignment. Arm all tracks and feed the machine a 1 kHz tone so the meters exactly 0 dB on input. On the same blank tape set a lo and put the machine in record for a few seconds. Play section back - ideally the tones should come off tape around zero but there will probably be some adjustment make. I usually write little notes on scratch paper like track 3 down , track 6 up etc. Then you can find the "re gain" or "record level" trim pots and make (guess?) changes based on your list. Record the new adjustm and check the playback to see how close you are. Aft while you'll start to get a feel for how much to turn the before recording to make the corresponding change playback. The "record EQ" adjustment is the next thir look for - set up a 10 kHz tone to 0 dB on the input follow the previous procedure for 1 kHz/"record gain". again, make sure you are tweaking the pots for the tape speed when it comes to EQ adjustment.

Congratulations! At this point you've probably ali your tape machine. If the deck sounds funny or the le aren't looking right, try again or call a qualified tech t you out - but don't bill us. If everything sounds great recording your rock opera based on an H.G. Wells novel —*thanks to Paul Moody and Klaus Heyne.*

Part 3

ENGINEERS AND PRODUCERS

ENGINEERS & PRODUCERS:

72	Andy Hong
74	Phil Brown
78	John Agnello
82	Jim O'Rourke
89	Oz Fritz- Visual Images
90	Jon Brion
96	Joe Chiccarelli
102	Bob Weston
108	Jack Endino
114	Adam Lasus
117	Oz Fritz- High Velocity Sound Engineering
118	David Barbe
122	Roger Moutenot
126	Tchad Blake
134	Dave Trumfio
140	Grant Showbiz
144	Dave Fridmann
150	Ken Nordine
152	Introduction to Digital Audio
153	Digital vs. Analog
154	Stuart Hallermann
156	Jim Dickinson
162	Scott Colburn
164	Some 4-track Cassette Tricks
165	Make Your Own Piezo Drum Triggers
166	John Hardy
169	Moby
170	Dave Botrill

page

8179-5

KODAK 400NC

49 KODAK 400N

photo by: Jeff Gros

ANDY HONG

BY SCOTT CRAGGS

I FIRST BECAME AWARE OF THIS ANDY HONG FELLA AFTER HEARING TH[E] KARATE RECORD THE BED IS IN THE OCEAN. BESIDES HAVING GREAT SONG[S] AND EQUALLY GREAT PERFORMANCES, THE RECORDING IS JUST BEAUTIFUL. HE['S] ALSO PUT OUT A COMPILATION CALLED IN MY LIVING ROOM (REVIEWED IN TAP[E] OP AWHILE BACK) FEATURING HI-FI RECORDINGS OF DIFFERENT ARTISTS IN TH[E] SAID LIVING ROOM. HE RECENTLY RECORDED THE WICKED FARLEYS, THE BAN[D] SOLELY RESPONSIBLE FOR RENEWING MY FAITH IN ROCK. SO I FIGURED [I] WOULD TRACK HIM DOWN AND GET THE INFO. WE MET OVER BEERS AND HUMMU[S] AT INDIE-ROCK GROUND ZERO, THE MIDDLE EAST, IN CAMBRIDGE, MA.

How'd you get started in recording?

I think I did what every kid did in the '70s, which was I went to Radio Shack and bought a cheesy mixer. Of course, Radio Shack has the 30-day return policy, so a month later, I returned it and got the next model up. I did that for three months in a row before the guys finally figured out that I wasn't gonna buy anything. That's how I got into recording. I got into music before that because I had played piano for many years as well as clarinet and saxophone. I listened to a lot of records and thought it'd be great to make my own records. So, once I realized that the Radio Shack recorder was a piece of crap, I saved up enough money and bought a 4-track, a spring reverb, a microphone, and that was that - it was all downhill from there. After that, all the money I had I spent on recording gear.

Did you go to school for recording or anything?

I actually have a degree in computer music, but when I was doing that, I had enough experience recording music that I got to go on the road as a recording engineer with some really famous people like Yo-Yo Ma...

This was when you were in school?

Yup. And then on tour I got to do sound for the London Sinfonietta, LA Philharmonic, Boston Symphony Orchestra, San Francisco New Music Players, the Ensemble Moderne - a lot of major players. It was a big change of pace from all the rock that I'd been doing up to that point, and I got to hang out with all these classical engineers and musicians. I learned a lot because the techniques they were using were nothing like the techniques I was used to using for rock.

Can you give an example of something you learned that you could apply to recording rock stuff?

Lots of omni mics.

For the room?

Not necessarily. You do pick up a lot more of the room, but you also don't get proximity effect, so you can take an omni and stick it right up into the bridge of a violin, and you won't get this boomy sound. I just did a recording with Robert Fisher and the Willard Grant Conspiracy, and I put an omni about 8 to 12 inches from the bridge of David Michael

Curry's viola, and it sounded great, it sounded like a viola. I picked up a lot of my kitchen also.

We'll get to your kitchen in a second, but the main thing I wanted to talk about is the Karate record. First of all, it sounds amazing.

Glad you like it.

In the interview you did with The Boston Phoenix, you mentioned some drum mic'ing techniques - care to elaborate, or are they top secret?

Well first of all, we did it at Salad Days, which unfortunately doesn't exist any more. The room there used to be a machine shop or something, so it had a tile floor, and the ceiling was really low in one area, and like a cathedral-style in another. We put the drums in the area with the low ceiling and got lots and lots of reverb from the area further away with the higher ceiling. It just sounded so good in the room, I thought, "What I need to do is use omnis - I don't want any proximity effect, I want everything to sound exactly like what I hear in this room." I have a bunch of Earthworks omnis and I set those up. I do this weird thing on snare drums, I don't mic the top or bottom, what I do is put an omni about a half inch from the body. I try to get it as close to the shell as possible, so I pick up more snare and less of everything else. So, depending on what kind of sound I want, I move it up and down. Further down, I get more of a crunchy, snarey sound, and if I move it up I get more of the punch.

Right, the attack.

For Gavin's snare, the mic was halfway between the hole and the bottom.

How about the kick?

For the kick, I took an Earthworks omni and stuck it way inside and just pulled it out further and further until I found the magic spot. When you find it, it's just the best sound in the world.

Where was the spot? Was it still inside the drum?

Actually no, it ended up being an inch in front of the hole.

I've never gotten anything good with the mic inside; it always sounds like "boing".

Yeah, like a basketball.

Just nothing like what the dru[m] actually sounds like.

Yeah.

His kick drum sounds pretty amazing [to] begin with...

Yeah, yeah, one thing I should say is that Gavin is t[he] most natural drummer in the world, he's fucki[ng] unbelievable. I mean that was probably the on[ly] session where I didn't tune the drums, he ju[st] started to play and it was great.

Yeah, he's awesome, we jammed wit[h] him a couple times at our house. [I] was playing guitar and I couldn['t] even hang. I just stopped. What d[id] you have for overheads?

AKG 460B, a small diaphragm cardiod.

Right over the drums?

Yep. Directly over the center of the kit. Like this.. [I] forget what it's called.

Coincident pair?

Yeah, that's it.

What did you use on Geoff's guitar?

An AKG C1000. That thing is one of the mo[st] underrated mics, it has the purest midrange [of] any small diaphragm condenser I can think [of] that's not an omni.

Yeah, his guitar is all about midrange.

Right, I wanted it to be the sweetest midrange in [the] world. We actually used a JoeMeek Meekbox as [a] mic pre for the super dry guitar solos to accentu[ate] the mids even further.

How close to the amp was the mic?

Usually what I do, is put the mic halfway between [the] center of the cone and the rim, about half an i[nch] from the grill. Then if I want more grit, I move [it] towards the rim, if I want more midrange I move [it] towards the center. And then, if it still has [too] much bite I move it back a little.

How loud were they playing? I['m] assuming they played it all live...

Yep. We kept all the basics and just overdubbed voc[als] and a little guitar and percussion. But everyth[ing] was at a pretty reasonable level, if you listen to [the] drum tracks there's almost no bleed, and we did[n't] use any gobos or anything.

And what did you use on the bass?

We weren't that happy with the bass sound actually...

Really? That's one of my models of good bass tone...

Well, his speaker was breaking up and sounded like crap...

It doesn't sound like that at all on the record...

Well, the reason why is we took a DI and ran it through, I'm not 100% sure, but I think we ran it through a Neve mic pre with the input gain cranked, and the output gain all the way down.

It didn't distort like crazy?

With the Neves, when they distort they sound good. We still weren't that psyched about the bass sound though.

Damn...

I mean, it's a good sound, it just wasn't what we wanted.

Vocals?

We tried a ton of different mics, and eventually settled on two. One was an AKG C3000, the other was the same small diaphragm AKG we used for overheads.

How close?

Mic'd his forehead. Probably four inches away, pointing at his nose. That's what I typically do for vocals. I don't like to use pop filters, to me it doesn't sound right. And also, if you take a large diaphragm condenser and put it right up on someone's mouth, you get a proximity effect that sounds good for some people, but it just didn't sound right for Geoff Farina. Also, I used a teeny bit of compression to tape, and a little more coming off the tape. What you can hear is the room reverb kicking in. He has really good mic technique, so he would back up when he sang louder. So, the level on the tape wouldn't change that much, but you'd hear more of the room, and it just sounds so real.

As far as mixing, did you do much, if anything to it?

No, we didn't have an automated board, so we assigned people to different channels to mute things on and off. We didn't want to comp anything, I hate comping. I think analog tape sounds amazing one time but after that... So we kept everything first generation.

EQ?

None.

Awesome. Mix compression?

Nope. The thing with mix compression is, if you can't hear it, then why use it? And if you can hear it, usually what happens is the kick drum punches holes in the mix. You might not even hear it until it goes through another compressor in mastering, but then you will, and I just hate that. I can't afford a bazillion dollar mix compressor; I'll let the mastering engineer put compression on it. When John Loder mastered the record, that was one of the things I asked him, please hold off on the compression because I want it to be as dynamic as possible. I just really liked the sound of it uncompressed. He did put a bunch of limiting on, just to level it out, so it's still loud.

But even still, it's not nearly as loud as a lot of other current records.

Yeah. When you hear it on the radio next to some super

duper pop record, it sounds weak, just because the level is low. But when you listen to it by itself I think it sounds really good.

It sure does. okay, enough about them. You also worked with the Wicked Farleys recently. How was that?

Well, the Wicked Farleys are the loudest band in the world...

I know. They recorded a couple songs at my house, and literally, the whole house was shaking. It was pretty great. Did they do tons of guitar overdubs?

Tons. Guitar and bass. We ended up with about 14 tracks of guitar.

This was on 24-track?

Yep.

Did you use all of those in the mix?

Yep.

Damn. Did you have to use EQ?

We had to EQ like crazy. That's one of the few records that I've done where EQ came in really, really handy.

Cutting or boosting?

Cutting. We cut lows; we cut highs. We tried to give everything its own space, so you can still distinguish the parts. I actually wanted to go back and remix that...

You guys did that really quick, right?

Two days. We mixed the second song in like, a half-hour. The first song took maybe four hours to mix, which is still not that much time.

Not at all. Did you have to compress their vocals at all?

It doesn't sound like it, but Brodeurs' vocal was slamming the compressor. I have an HHB Classic 60 compressor, it's actually made by TL Audio - it's tube, all class A, all super-high voltage. It sounds crappy for stereo compression, but for individual tracks you can hit it so hard, and it sounds amazing.

You got a really full sound on Ken's drums.

We argued a lot during mixing. Some of the guys wanted the drums a lot lower in the mix. I wanted them even louder than they ended up. Rob was saying he wanted the drums to sound trashy...

At my house the operative word was "nasty"...

I didn't really want them to sound "trashy", but I did end up bringing up a lot of the bottom snare mic just to get it a little grittier sounding.

And gritty it is. Your desert island mic choice?

Hmm, I don't know...

The Earthworks?

Probably. A lot of people complain that they have a lot of self-noise, but because there's no proximity effect, you can put them so close to the instrument and you have all the dynamic range in the world.

And those are like $1000 a pair?

Less. I think I paid about $700 for mine. But I still think the best bang for the buck is the AKG C1000s. For 160 bucks you get the sweetest midrange in the world for a cardiod mic.

Any advice for people recording at home?

That's a tough one...

Spend your money on...

Mic preamps. Because you can get decent mics, like the C1000s, for incredibly low prices.

And with a good mic pre you're golden.

Yeah, you're golden. The thing is, five years ago people used to rave about the Mackie mic pres. When you listen to the *In My Living Room* record, some songs don't sound as pristine, as sonically true as others. And it's not just me, other people can tell too. The difference is, some songs were recorded with a Mackie, some with an Allen & Heath, and some with outboard mic pres. The difference between the Mackie and the Allen & Heath was just night and day. And the outboard mic pres are significantly better than the Allen & Heath, but the leap wasn't as great as it was between the A&H and the Mackie.

Your mic pre of choice?

I have a bunch of Neve and API...

Well consider me green with envy. Did you ever try running a mix through them?

I used to have a set of Aphex mic pres, and I would send mixes through them to get that nice, even-order harmonics sound, but I haven't tried it with my Neve or API. I should give that a try.

One of the songs the Wicked Farleys recorded at my house was a cover of "96 Tears" which they wanted "extra nasty". We absolutely pounded it through an ART Dual MP. I actually thought it was a little much, but they were like "Yeah! Nasty!" If you look at it on a computer, it's not even a wave, it's like a block. Anyway, for *the Living Room* record, would you just have everyone set up in the living room?

Typically, if it was a whole band, I'd have the drummer set up in the living room and put everyone else in the kitchen or the front room.

What'd you record to?

Half inch 8-track. An Otari MX5050.

When you mixed *the Living Room* stuff, did you use any fake reverb? Like on Geoff Farina

Yeah. It's funny, because Geoff did another version of that on his solo record which was super-dry, so I asked him if I should remix mine, was there too much reverb? But he said no, he thought it sounded good. I mean, there is a lot of reverb, but I think it works with the song.

It does. But I thought maybe you were a super-purist and never used any outboard effects, in which case you would've had to have a cathedral in your house or something equally unfathomable. Anyway, our waitress is giving us the heave-ho, so I guess that's it.

Supercool. ⊕

Phill Brown has had a 30-year-long career as an engineer, something most of us are barely even capable of imagining. And not only has he been working for a long while, he's worked with some of the greatest artists in the world. **The Rolling Stones, The Small Faces, Traffic, Bob Marley, Brian Eno, John Martyn, Joan Armatrading, Throwing Muses, Talk Talk...** Talk Talk, really. If you're thinking Talk Talk was a silly electro-pop band in the early '80s, think again. They turned into real artists, and their last two records, *Spirit of Eden* and *Laughing Stock* are among some of the most amazing sounding records you will ever hear. And Phill was there. We caught up with Phill in Seattle while he was recording the next **Walkabouts** album, of which **Chris Eckman** is a member, and we got together for breakfast [thanks to **Carla Torgerson** from Walkabout] and a nice little chat on recording.

by Larry Crane and Chris Eckman

Phill: Those Talk Talk records we were making, we were doing everything in real time. So we were using five slaves for every song. Every song had five, 24-track, slaves which you could use depending on what you wanted to record. So that, some of the simplest things that became incredibly hard with that because of how much information you need. To change one of the lengths of one of our songs... .

Larry: Splice all the tape?

And redo the coding, I mean the whole thing becomes a nightmare.

They had that with Elliott Smith's record. They started splicing the master, and then all of a sudden the slaves were jumping. It can be a real nightmare... but you know, you can work it out, it just takes time.

Yeah, there are ways. On one of the Talk Talk records we had to make one of the songs longer, which is even harder. I think it did take a couple of days to put in these extra five bars. We had to start with a new master... We mixed to the Mitsubishi [digital deck] as a final master and we had all these analog slaves of what we

recorded. So we copied and made new masters to the point where we had to elongate it and then offset things in. At the time Mark [Hollis, Talk Talk leader, vocalist, etc.] went, "I need this five bars longer." Nobody thinks about the reality of it.

So you copied parts of it?

Some of it was copied and others were flown in to recreate a bass part from the bars we had, put the drums in, and build it up. Once you get those extra five bars you basically lock up everything that you have and copy the rest of the song. It is a lot of fiddling about work. This was four months into working on the album.

Those records, *Laughing Stock* and *Spirit of Eden* took a while to record didn't they?

A year to make each. In the dark.

What was Tim Friese-Greene's role in making those records?

Tim was co-writer and producer and one of the keyboard players. He's a very important part of it.

Was he an original member of Talk Talk?

The first two albums were done with other producers and other writers but I think it was their second album that they were trying to finish and Tim was brought in for a remix situation and he mixed the album and got on well with Mark. Tim's been there from *Colour of Spring* on. I came in just after that.

What was your official part in making those records?

On *Spirit of Eden* and *Laughing Stock* it's purely an engineering credit. There's been a bit of discussion on this new solo album I did with Mark because another person originally produced it and Mark got rid of him and rid of the album and we started afresh. I got what he wanted and I kind of imagined that I would be credited as co-producer. We'd talked about that and that was the agreement. Then, he thought about it a lot, and although he's given me a producer's percentage of the royalty, it's down as engineer because that's how he wants it to look.

Hopefully you still get on with him okay...

Oh yeah. We may work on a project together later this year. He's slightly tricky. I can deal with that kind of tricky because that's artistic. When it comes to doing business and all of that, the music business really pisses me off...

I wanted to ask you about that. You started as a tape operator in Olympic Studios in London and you've had to work your way up. For some sessions you get to produce stuff and for others you engineer. What do you see as the difference between those terms?

I guess I see my trade as an engineer. Even though I produce things and co-produce things I see what I do as an engineer. I tend to work the same whether you give me credit as an engineer or a producer. It's hard to say. The kind of producers I worked with originally were people like Jimmy Miller or Steve Smith (who did a lot of the early Robert Palmer stuff - we did an Elephant's Memory album together) who were producers who set up a situation and controlled thing but they were vibe merchants. Jimmy Miller was this incredible kind of energy and drive and force. He made the session feel like you wanted to be there and make music. But he wasn't a hands on producer... Growing up in the '80s the kind of Chris Hughes [Tears for Fears] or Trevor Horn sort of production. always think that they're making their albums. They're making what they want to do for themselves. I'm not saying they're not good producers, but I think that's the biggest change in production. There was more of an overall control, a bit of a vibe. They're not so much into deciding which hi-hat and which beat and all that. That was left up to the musicians and the engineer. I worked with Shel Talmy and those kind of guys. They didn't touch the desk [mixer]. It wasn't part of what they needed to do. They'd tell you what they wanted. When I worked at Island [Records] in the early '70s the vocabulary was very much into "brightness", "harsh" and "trashy". No one talked in frequencies. That all came later. I still don't talk in frequencies now.

It's all relative anyway.

Exactly. What works one day may not work another. I was working with Little Feat years ago, in the `70s, doing a Robert Palmer record, and they were the band. We were having trouble getting guitar sounds and Lowell George came in and said something like, "Three at one point eight." He left the control room and we fiddled around and he came back later and said, "So, did it work?" And I said, "No, actually it's three at two point one." He looked so puzzled. A week before he'd done a session and gotten a great guitar sound and said, "How'd you do that?" and the engineer got into the one point eight or whatever. I don't really think in those kind of frequencies. It's much easier to talk in terms of things needing to be brighter.

The term I use a lot lately is "throaty" which isn't describing a frequency...

You can run aground if you start thinking of everything in frequencies.

Chris: A lot of engineers seem to treat tracking as everything having to be pure sound and then at the end you mix. I've noticed with you that even at playback you're triggering delays and dropping the drums out where don't think they should be. It's a more playful kind of approach.

On these tracks [the Walkabouts] I'm trying to think of what... When we come to mixing it will obviously be kind of fast so to have some time to try some things out is good.

I remember when Pell Mell were working with Tchad Blake [Star City] one of the comments they had was that he set up like a mix during every tracking session

I think it makes it a little more playful. Everybody feels more comfortable because you're getting closer to it.

I do stuff in England with this guy Rollo, a producer, doing a band Faithless. We work with the SSL in mix mode and you also record. You're still overdubbing but as each thing's done it's put in to its place, reverb might be added. We've done tracks where we started in the morning with nothing but a drum loop and at 11 PM put down a pretty good rough mix. All you need to do a few days later is to recall and tweak a few things you really don't like and you've got it. At first it was a mindfuck, I tell you. It's so confusing. And even now there are days where you've got 56 channels of SSL in this configuration and you go, "I hope we don't have to track anything down" because it sounds good but what's doing what? You have to be very careful about how things are routed.

I take notes for ideas on my track sheets on effects ideas or mutes but sometimes I forget to look at the notes. I always worry that with the recall boards that we're gonna lose some of the spontaneity by working in this fashion. When you do come back to

work on a song where you've saved the mix you're gonna still be working in the same mindset. You might not have an accidental fader up that might sound good.

That's one of the main problems with digital gear. They're bringing out a new range of it now which is more analog with pots and things that you really change. I think that doing a mix on the old manual desks in the `70s - you definitely work in a different way. Things happen which you'd never recreate. We're into an era, the `80s more so than now, where perfection is something they're after. Perfect timing, perfect tuning.

Over the period of time that you've been recording have you seen people's sense of rhythm, or the concept of what a rhythmically happening track is, change?

If you look back to the kind of drumming style of the `60s, since `79 onwards the drummers I've worked with are tighter. They're learning against click tracks and computers and I think everything, like it is in all of life, is just geared up a few notches from what it was in the `60s. Back then everyone was starting to open up but now it's much more efficient really.

But not necessarily better.

Well no. When something's perfectly in time or perfectly in tune... there's something about a record where the drums speed up for the choruses and slow down for the verses that still feels quite natural.

It worries me that over the years music is losing it's feeling in many cases.

Sometimes you stumble across some guy playing in a bar and appreciate what music is all about.

It becomes a context thing. It seems there are some kinds of music where that really works. To have this very regimented beat. Like Faithless or Massive Attack. You don't want it to feel loose.

I see popular music as becoming way too sterile but maybe that's been the case in one way or another over the years. I think all of us have worked on many things that haven't become popular though.

We just won this Grammy [best album in Norway for the recent Midnight Choir album that Chris and Phill produced] but in `72 I won this award in England from NME for best engineered record of the year. In that year I'd worked on Nilsson's "Without You" and I immediately thought, "It's gotta be that." I thought that was one of the best things I'd done at that point in time. I got the award for this little pop record by Sweet which was this little glam record...

Which song was it?

"Co-Co". Not one of their best. In perspective you kind of go, "Well, what are awards? What do they mean?" "Did it sell more?"

One thing about spontaneity. I think a lot of people have this perception that if you're gonna go to 48 tracks and use a lot of reels that what you're doing is making a Def Leppard record. Like you're working everything to this fine, fine point. I've noticed with you, that you use the slave reels, like in the Talk Talk sessions, to open it up to more spontaneous creation. You're not having to distill a track down to the essence of what it is. Instead it's like, "Let's track seven takes of the harmonica" and in the end we'll go back and compile something very odd out of it.

I think once you get past 48 that should be everybody's reason for using that many tracks. It's a sketchpad to try out stuff. Also, it's that mentality of every time you put the tape machine into record you get a potential master, something that you could use. We all got screwed up in demos, things that we never could recreate, and it was after *Colour of Spring* that Mark said, "Never will I make another demo." Part of that thing is that you can always be in record. It eats up a lot of tracks that way.

How were the tape decks set up for those records?

Everything was recorded to analog, 24 track Studer, but once we had all the backing tracks down we made up Mitsubishi 32 track digital masters. Everything was slaved up and you could take it from wherever you wanted to take it Anything that we really wanted to keep was on the Mitsubishi. Then we always recorded onto analog. We would do eight tracks of whoever came in and then bounce it to the Mitsubishi. We had five slaves per song but it was really to give us that amount of freedom.

But you wouldn't have all five decks running at once.

No, but we would have the "Mitsi" and two Studers so we'd have the 32 track and 48 analog. That's around 70 or 80 tracks. It's a lot of channels. That's the other brilliant thing. If you'd walked in on any of the *Spirit of Eden* or *Laughing Stock* sessions and looked at the SSL, you'd see 50 reels of 2" and all the slaves are going and all the monitor faders would be up but you'd have just two mics up for days. We were using drum mics 20 feet away. Everything was very distant. You'd have just one mic up but at the desk you'd be changing all these different slaves.

The interesting thing is that on those records, as detailed as the sound is, the records sound very simple and open.

Yeah.

Like a band playing in a room. That's why I brought this up, because I get really tired of this knee-jerk reaction that if you're gonna use multiple machines and lots of tracks that somehow you're making this com-

pletely absurd "Celine Dion" record. "Pour Some Sugar on Me".

I just think that's bullshit. It's just how you use the tools. The other thing, about how you overdubbed those records, people wouldn't hear lots of the other stuff that was on them. You would build these disjunctive creations.

It is tricky. Part of the problem is that when you describe some of the ways we did the Talk Talk albums people just think, "Well that's bullshit." "800 tracks." Like it's crazy arrogance. But the band often didn't even meet the musician and the musician didn't even get into the control room. They'd be kind of shown into the studio. We worked in total darkness so they were really out of their element. We had oil projector lights going and strobes, there was no normal lighting. We could send them anything in their cans [headphones] like the shaker and an organ. We might say, "Play to this." Of course no one knows what the structure is since there's no melody or lyrics. We would just piece together those kind of performances. Sometimes note by note. The record ends up sounding like five guys running through the tunes in the studio. It almost sounds like it's five or six mics just capturing these five guys. On a lot of the tracks that sound like that we used 80 or 90 tracks for background atmospherics. Drums on one track, bass on one track. When people hear that it was a year in the studio with 80 or 90 tracks they immediately think it must be...

...complete overkill.

It can be.

But can you make a record like that... I've had these discussions with Al from Midnight Choir, the band that we worked with, I argued with him that you can't make a record like that in a standard kind of four week block.

No, no.

Maybe a year is too much...

I think you could probably do it, in the right environment, in three or four months. But the whole nature of working that way... you're almost saying you have no time limits on it.

You just need the time to experiment, really.

To record that amount of things and not have fixed ideas and really work out which things you want to keep. Sometimes compiling can take a while. With a lot of stuff we would record things in two or three hours; eight takes of whoever it was, on a track. It might take us two days to sort and choose and actually put together what we want to use. On "After the Flood" we had Danny Thompson come in and play bass and we gave him eight tracks, top to bottom, and we went through and sifted his bass we kept three bass notes. They weren't even together! We then brought in Joni Mitchell's ex-husband, Larry Klein, and he played. Loads of bass players came in and they were all playing different instruments. Some upright bass, some guitarron. The bass track on that, the feel is great,

and it was made up some four different basses. In theory you think it wouldn't work. I think you could do those kind of records in, maybe, three or four months if you're not quite as much of perfectionist as Mark.

It seems a lot of the creative process becomes initial conception and then sorting.

We wanted to do those along the lines of chance or accidents but not coincidence because I don't believe in coincidence. But whatever it is, that just happened. It's a fairly unique way of approaching it.

What was your initial impetus for working this way?

For *Spirit of Eden*, when I first met Mark we were talking about my background and I was talking about Olympic in the `60s and working with Traffic and Spooky Tooth. He'd left and I didn't know at that point whether I'd be working with him and as we left I dropped him off at the tube station. As he got out of the car he said, "What sums up Olympic in the `60s for you?" I said, "It's got to be one o'clock in the morning, November 1967." It was a Traffic session I did. I was 17 years old and it was a new job. That particular night we were doing "Mr. Fantasy" and there was just this fantastic atmosphere with low lights and people were a bit out, wasted. I mentioned this to Mark and he said, "Oh, cool." After a few weeks I got a phone call saying he'd like to get involved. And we met up and went into the studio Mark said, "Let's set this up as if it's one o'clock in the morning, November 1967!" So we then used only equipment that was around prior to 1967. We didn't use Dolby or anything, apart from the Mitsubishi. We actually bypassed the SSL and just used it as a monitor. We went through Neve units and some things were plugged straight into the tape machine. That, in a way, how that kind of got started. When EMI remixed some of the tracks from *Colour of Spring* it was deemed that the only way you could stop the record company from remixing your track was if all you put on there were things that were so decisive that they couldn't make any changes. That was really why the drums ended up being one track. If we just had one track of drum the record company can't remix the bloody thing. That's kind of the mentality behind it.

That's one of the best drum sounds I've ever heard and I was a bit disappointed when I heard that it was one mic.

Well, truthfully it is two mics because there is a bit of bass drum mic in there. But that caused problems as well. Once we ended up with this one mic, thirty feet away from the kit, but there's this 20 millisecond delay from when he plays to what we hear so you can't feed him that in the cans. So you've got to close mic to feed him but for all the musicians playing with Lee [Harris], we had to delay 20 ms to put them in time with the drums. So the whole thing that initially seems so simple... But with *Laughing Stock*, there was no verbal, "Let's set it up like this." It definitely metamorphed into that way of working from the drum sounds.

Initially didn't you like their sort of pop records?

Well we've just gone full circle. I loved *Colour of Spring*. I saw a gig in `86 at the Hammersmith Odeon. As it turned out it was the last Talk Talk gig, but it was one of the best gigs I'd seen. I was really bored at the time. I was working on things I didn't particularly want to do. I saw them and I said, "That's the band I want to be working with." Literally a few weeks later I bumped into Tim Friese-Greene in a studio and I congratulated him on this album and he was totally shocked that anyone would say this was a great album. Even Mark, as difficult as Mark is, he doesn't have that ego. "Well, I'm good." Two months later Tim called me up and said, "Are you serious? Come out and meet Mark." And I just mixed that gig that I saw in `86 as a live album. It's kind of full circle. A 14 year period.

You mentioned the record label remixing stuff from the *Colour of Spring*. Did they remix the album?

Quite a few things were taken off that and given to different producers. The album came out as it should have been. Then we did the *Spirit of Eden* album and that's where it all started to go wrong. We did it, the record company hated it, and they sued the band and me for "Technical Incompetence" because it wasn't commercial. It got thrown out of court. The judge was wonderful. But they changed the British production contract. It now says you must deliver masters that are "commercially satisfactory." I think that's even worse. The good thing might be that they couldn't sue you until a year after it came out! It's such a dubious clause. It's bullshit. Mark's attitude to the music business changed drastically after that.

After that you did the Mark Hollis solo album.

When we came to do Mark's album, he actually wanted it to sound like a `50s jazz album. I was sure that they basically used one mic in those eras. That's what we wanted to create. We just updated it to stereo. We set up a pair of Neumann M49's, old valve mics, cross cardiod, head high in a good sounding room. We brought the whole band in, all the people we were gonna use, which was a whole woodwinds section, percussionist and drummer. brought everybody in and played around with everybody's position. We eventually came up with a piano on the right, harmonium on the left, and marked everyone's positions and they all went home and we did everybody one at a time so we had control; well, we did the woodwinds as a section actually. But these mics were not touched; no level or EQ, they were just left there. Everything we recorded went down as a stereo pair. That ate tracks, obviously. The drawback is that, because they're valves they're not the quietest of mics. If you had everybody in there [live] and two hissy mics with nine people the hiss to volume ratio would be a lot better. We just built up a lot of valve noise.

Don't you start that album with 17 seconds of tape hiss?

The same thing with *Spirit of Eden*. It had so much background noise that we actually had to put in a hiss level.

For continuity...

Laughing Stock was pretty quiet. we used SR Dolby on that. Mark's album, we didn't use Dolby. We compiled stereo pairs. You do ten vocal tracks and then you start to compile. That's why I bought those headphones, to check that the vocal was in the middle. Things like that slowed us down. We lived in headphones a lot. That's where we lost time on that album.

Do you feel like that worked really well?

Yeah. It's interesting. It was designed, also, to play at a really quiet level. We tried loads of things. We wanted the record to always sound quiet...

You are running the opposite of the record industry!

We spent two or three days trying to find ways to make it stay quiet.

What techniques were you trying?

By making it incredibly mellow. No spikes; no leaps of dynamics. We came up with something that was actually quite good but we played it on another set of speakers and it was crap `cause it was so extreme. We came up with the conclusion, in the end, that was either put on it, "Please play quietly" or, as I tried to point out to Mark, that you've got to leave people to their own resources. If you play it at a low level and sit about ten feet back it feels like they're in the room. It feels real to me now. It's all acoustic instruments. On all these albums we didn't use any effects as such. There's an EMT plate echo if we needed any and a DDL [digital delay line]. That's all we've ever used on those three albums. All the weirdness is created in the room at the source.

Is that fairly typical?

It's typical of the way I work. I use effects for an effect but I don't like things being in there all the time just taking up space. If you're making like a real pop record you can get away with ten different types of reverb and effects. We're working with a vast amount of air and space anyway. You don't need to put it in a space. One trap we found is that reverb added on a room sound never sounds right. It sounds kind of odd. The whole room is trailing off. You set up a different type of atmosphere. I think it's kind of more a real vibe.

One thing that it requires is that you need a good room.

That is very important. It's amazing how well a drum kit will balance in a good room. When you move the mics in closer and separate the kit into nine tracks that's usually when all the problems start. Then it doesn't sound anything like a real drum kit.

The thing with room mic'ing, when you're really relying on it, is that the drummer really has to mix themselves. The burden is on the player. We can't fix it in the mix.

The other way, close mic'd, you can cheat more. You can even drop things in. If you go back to records made in the late `50's and `60's they had no effects back then. They had plates and chambers and spring reverbs but there were no other boxes around. Abbey Road built the first ADT [automatic double tracking]. They were always building little boxes then that had two knobs on it. "Try this out." They built little Leslie speakers to put things through. This way of working is moving backwards in a way. It's too easy to dial up these digital effects. I'm not a great lover of digital reverbs because it never goes off right. Digital ones always fragment to me when they get to the end of a fade. Tape loops, they're just fantastic. I'd forgotten that anyone would actually put something like that together. I remember in the `70's standing there with a pen.

When you're doing a loop for a long delay. Why'd you do that?

There was no other way. I did a lot of things with Eno, after Roxy Music, which were all done with loops and he'd bring in one's that would just go around the capstan and the playback head. Other's would be huge things...

What record was that?

It was a whole mix of things. I worked on *Here Come The Warm Jets* and side projects of Eno's in `73. He was so experimental after leaving Roxy.

What is the mic you travel with and why do you bring it?

It's not as if it's the greatest mic in the world, but I have a Sony C48 which I bought about 15 years ago. I just love the mic for acoustic instruments, room mic, overheads. It's kind of a remake of the Sony C37. I just really like the mic. It has a quality to it that really works, especially for distant micing. I'm surprised that more studios don't have them. Most studios have the same collection of boring mics.

Tell us about the John Martyn guitar sound you got on *One World*.

Chris Blackwell has this house in England that's surrounded by this big gravel pit out west of London and we did the John Martyn album out there in `76. He has these converted stables which are little flats. We set John Martyn up in one of these with his guitar pedals and amps and everything with splits all the way through there after every gadget and the guitar. We had seven or eight feeds of choice of his guitar. We then got a large PA system and we pumped the guitar out across this lake, this old gravel pit, and then mic'd up the lake basically.

And you close mic'd him too. It's this very bizarre sound. You get this very direct sound but then there's this... It's very unsettling.

I've always described it as coming from another universe. This was 4 o'clock in the morning and the lake would go almost silent. We got birds and lapping water. One of the tracks, "Small Hours," is just one guitar with a few lines of vocals but it's such a full sound. ☺

JOHN AGNELLO

by J. Robbins

When we interviewed J. Robbins in issue #12 of *Tape Op* he told us we should interview John Agnello, a producer he had worked with in Jawbox and Burning Airlines. We countered with, "Why don't you interview him?" And, to our surprise, he did. John has a long history of recording and has worked on some of my favorite records of the last ten years. That's no mean feat. -Larry Crane

So, you're my first-ever interviewee.

Really? So you're cutting your teeth on me. I'm the victim.

I wanted to ask you if you have a ballpark idea how many records you've worked on as an engineer, or as a producer ...

I think it's about 40 or 50. I don't really keep track. If you go to www.johnagnello.com you can count them on the discography. [laughs] It's got to be between 30 and 50. You mean start to finish, or just mixing, or what?

As opposed to when you started working in a recording studio, period. You started as an assistant at the Record Plant, right?

'79 at the Record Plant. I walked in the door and the first thing they told me to do was clean up the room because Kiss was starting *Dynasty* that day. It was basically just following people around cleaning up from the previous night's session. And *Damn the Torpedoes* was being done there at the same time. So my first two weeks of studio experience was, you know, seeing some heavy shit going down.

You were talking the other day about the way projects sometimes used to interact with each other there because it was a big enough facility that several records would be going on at the same time, and how that was happening at Water Music with this Error Type 11 record you're doing now and the Misfits record that they're doing in the big room there with Ed Stasium.

Oh yeah. The Record Plant was a four-room facility, and everybody knew everybody. The whole environment was a lot smaller back then, there wasn't a studio on every block, you weren't able to make a record in your house like you can now, so the people who made records generally did it for a living. It was way before the proliferation of small studios and project studios. It was a smaller, tighter community. There would be four rooms going on at the Record Plant and people would be walking in and out of each other's projects. You know how Bruce Springsteen and Patti Smith wrote "Because the Night" together? That was at the Record Plant. They were working in rooms next to each other and they were just talking and they ended up writing this song together which is fuckin' amazing. And that happened a lot back then, it was really fun, how people knew each other. An environment where you could just hang out. When we were just now working at Water Music, the Misfits were in the other studio there and the first day we were there [the Misfits] grabbed Artie and Phil from Error Type 11 to come sing on one song of theirs, and then another day we went and grabbed Ed the producer/mixer guy and got him to play tambourine on two Error Type 11 songs. I would walk back and forth, and if he was having a problem with something maybe I'd pitch in. One day they were trying to do tape flanging at one point, a three machine flange, and I spent 15 minutes with them trying to help figure it out, and then I'd walk back over and keep working on our thing. It was very loose, kind of open thing. The daily barbecues didn't hurt either.

Camp Water Music.

Exactly. Common ground: meat.

So, of any engineer that I know, you seem the most ...

Old? Mature? Unshaven?

The most comfortable with compression - I mean, I'm aware of it as a force in the sound of records you've worked on. But it breathes, it seems very musical, not destructive to dynamics. So I wanted to ask you how you approach it.

It breathes, it doesn't suck, right? At this point it would just have to be that I've been using it for so long I know how to deal with it, I can tell when it's changing the mix, pumping or whatever. [*facetiously*] You can tell when you have a song with a lot of dynamics and it breaks down to one guitar and that guitar is louder than the whole rest of the mix.

How much do you compress to tape when you track?

I never compress guitars. Very rarely. When you have a Marshall and you turn it up to ten, that's compressing anyway. I really don't compress drums at all; maybe occasionally room mics just to get them a little more consistent. And I will compress a snare or a bass drum in mix, just for corrective measures, if a guy plays really unevenly. Bass a little bit, vocals maybe a lot, but not really a lot. Sometimes I do it for effect. Although I don't really do a lot of compression, I do have the stereo compressor on the mix, and I do squash tape. More like old-school compression, not necessarily sounding "compressed."

So what I heard as a "compress-y" sound on the basics of the Error Type 11 stuff was all tape saturation?

I had the Distressor on the vocals, but that was really just tapping it. And when I mix some of these songs I'll probably use the Distressor on "Nuke" like the super-compression mode, but again that's just an effect, not the core of it. It's just the Compex or the Daking on the bus, tightening up the mix... but, a *ton* of tape saturation - that's also why I still like using 456, because unlike using 499 or the BASF tape, that really *does* compress. For example, if you listen to these old records [**Queen II**, *playing on the monitors as we spoke*], all the stuff that came out of Trident, like what Roy Thomas Baker was doing, they would slam the tape so hard that the snare would just go "Thwap!", it wouldn't go like "bink", it really had that compression edge to it, that made it thick. It was almost like distortion from the tape, and I just love that. So that's my thing about compression. It's not a lot of compression so much as it's specific kinds of compression, hopefully used tastefully.

thought the monitor mix that you had up just to do vocals already sounded like a record, like maybe all you'd do in the mix was just brighten it up a little.

ell, especially on a record like Error Type 11, where you only have like three days to mix, you can't really spend time fixing shit. You've got to get it down good when you track it and keep in mind where you want it to be in the mix. If I had a song-a-day [mix schedule] I'd probably spend more time experimenting, but I don't;

I've got to mix a song every three hours. But I think a lot of that comes from, I hate to say an "old-school" thing, but the guys I learned from as engineers were great old-school engineers and that was the philosophy, to make it sound great from the beginning, and then the players are psyched, anybody that just walks in and hears it in progress is psyched, and you can all just get off on it. It's more inspiring. I tend to like to print the crazier things I do, like the speaker - the subwoofer as bass-drum mic [*John sometimes uses a Hartke 15" bass cabinet as a kick drum mic*] - or the shotgun mic with the SansAmp on it over the snare drum, that stuff I like printing to tape that way, so it's just always there.

Using the bass speaker as a kick drum mic, or the SansAmp snare, that kind of stuff - are those things that you go back to consistently?

The speaker on the bass drum, to pick up the super low end, I got out of the Beatle recording book, where I read they had done that for bass guitar and it was super cool because you got that real pillowy sound. I've been doing the speaker thing regularly, but sometimes I move it around and it's more like a room mic that sounds kind of bizarre. On the Varnaline record [*Sweet Life*] I had Anders [Parker] sing into it for one song and it sounded really strange. I don't know how to describe it. It's on the song "Saviours". The shotgun mic over the snare, I like to get that kind of a gunshot sound... and sometimes it can be cool to go to for a breakdown in a song or something. It's compressed, and it's going through a SansAmp, to tape. To track one. I've recently developed a fear of edge tracks which I never used to have. I used to put the bass drum there and not worry about it, but now I'd put the shotgun track there because if anything happens to track one...

It was fucked-up sounding to begin with.

The only problem with [the shotgun-SansAmp combination] is you have to take some time placing the mic to make sure you're getting the most snare drum for your money there ... it's so easy for the hi-hat or cymbals to get all over everything and then it's just useless.

My friend Chad and I were recently talking about how, after all of our speculation and experimenting with recording gear, the ultimate truth of a "good production", whatever that may be, has way more to do with good songs, good playing, good instrument sounds, and arrangements. How much do you regard arrangements, helping arrange songs, as a part of your job? Obviously if it's Error Type 11 where

they're a really focused band already and you've got only a week to do the whole thing, versus a solo person like Mike Johnson, something where the songs might seem more plastic...

Although I did do a couple of rehearsals for them. But it's different for every record. There are certain things I've done where I'd go on for a week of rehearsals and re-arrange. But for example like Dinosaur Jr. stuff, there are no rehearsals and there are no demos, because everything's in J.'s head. Once he puts down the drum tracks, the song is on its way to being recorded. On your record [Jawbox] we did a little bit of rearranging, not much. It's important, it's just a question of if you have time to do it. It's different every time. As soon as I get demos I listen to 'em. It's easy for me to get demos and spend an hour on each song just charting them and getting a sense of where they go. It doesn't matter if it's a band or a solo artist. Like with [NYC band] Camber, we spent more time rehearsing and going over arrangements than we did in the studio. The songs really got stripped down and reassembled.

That sounds like my fantasy of doing a record where everyone knows the material, including overdub ideas, so well before you even get to the studio, that the actual recording part is almost a formality because you've already made the record in your heads. You could save so much money on studio time by doing that ...

They had rehearsed so much that when they came into the studio, even though it was their first record, they came in and nailed it instantly. It was second nature. It wasn't like "first day in the studio," where people weren't comfortable, "I can't hear myself in the headphones," whatever. It was like they were making their fifth record instead of their first. But everybody's different.

> **"The only room that doesn't have some kind of recording stuff in it is his bedroom."**

[Our conversation is interrupted by the beginning of Queen's "Ogre Battle."]

This is hot. When I was a kid, I was listening to this record on headphones going, "What the hell is going on?" It's just insane. But anyway, a lot of people aren't open to the idea of changing their songs, which is fine too.

I remember being resistant, on a philosophical level, to the idea of anyone "tampering" with our songs, but the ideas that you had, even if they were small, they were a fresh perspective. They ended up improving the songs, and it wasn't like you dictated them to us, it was more like asking us questions, just a little nudge in one direction or other.

I'm a nudge guy anyway. There are guys who are totally putting their stamp on a record, like, "here's MY record," but I'm more like a conduit to get where you need to go. I try to be as hands-off as possible, to let everybody do it themselves. Maybe I shouldn't say that, because I do get involved, but it's more like around the side as opposed to, "it's got to be like this." The Varnaline record was like that where at the end of the record they were listening and they were so psyched it had turned out the way it was because even though I didn't sit there and beat them up to perform, I sort of pushed them to limits they felt they hadn't reached before, just by mellow reinforcement...

That's how we felt too, that you set up a situation in which we felt like we could rise to the occasion, like we were actually outdoing ourselves.

It's also all the Ecstasy I hand out before every session.

The J. Mascis record you just worked on, is it a Dinosaur record or a J. Mascis record?

It's a J. record. He plays virtually everything. It's different. This stuff I just mixed. He started in October and did it with a bunch of different people: Phil Ek, Tim O'Heir, Dan McLaughlin, Kevin Sheilds and his engineer ... and then I came in at the end and mixed it. But he started in October and worked until I showed up in May. In his house. That's one of the beauties of working in your house, that there's no clock, just the internal clock.

Describe his home studio.

Some would say it's the perfect home recording environment. His whole house is a studio. The only room that doesn't have some kind of recording stuff in it is his bedroom. Every other room is littered with guitars, mellotrons, pianos, vocal mics, amps, drums ... the control room is in the main room of the ground floor, which looks back over the back yard. He has an Otari 24-track and a DA-88 that link up, the board is an API moni-

tor section which has no EQ; all the EQ's are outboard so you have to patch anytime you want to EQ. The board has no mic pre's either, they're all outboard too. He also has a Studiomaster 32. But he uses all API, Daking and Telefunken mic pres, and along with that, EQ. He has a fair selection of mics, a C-12, some Neumanns. It's a really comfortable environment. He was really smart because two records ago he took a fair amount of money (from his advance) and invested it in this gear and recorded in his house. He's reaping the rewards now because he can record at his convenience. Plus it's way out in the woods and it's really beautiful. If he'd only bathe his dog more often it would be perfect.

Do you ever find yourself in a position of wanting to change people's sounds - I'm thinking specifically of Zach's drums on the Jawbox record, and how he had a very specific agenda with those really small drums that he tuned up so high... that's so different from a lot of drummers in bands you've worked with.

I had a conversation with Juan [Garcia, an engineer at the Magic Shop] yesterday where he was talking about a guitar sound that he recorded through a small amp, and how that can still sound big, that a small amp doesn't have to equate to a "small" or quirky sound. It can still sound big... with Zach's drums, it was just a matter of going for a good representation of what they sound like. It's a taste issue, and I tend to not get hung up on the taste stuff.

How much opportunity or inclination do you have to alter your tried-and true approaches to recording setups?

I try different mics as often as I can, and I like putting up a mic that I wouldn't ordinarily use for certain things, but especially for shorter-term stuff, it's way more important to just get [the musicians] comfortable and get the tracks down. So there are times when I do experiment, but there are times when the moment is dictated by the need to get good performances. Also for me the days of spending all day getting a guitar sound are so overrated. You hear stories about people recording on 7 1/2 ips, 2-inch 8-track machines, and there's all this hoodoo about it, but when you hear those records next to other records, it doesn't really sound that much different. You can go overboard with that stuff. Performance is what you've really got to go for.

I just ask because sometimes that's been a lot of fun for me in recording stuff, like, "What if we move the room mics over here for this song," or "What if we turn the

guitar mic around to face the window instead of the guitar amp." But then for me that's only really fun if it's fun for the band. On the Jawbox record I remember there was a track of ambient mic'ing where you had put a condenser mic inside this giant metal cone at Water Music.**

On most things I do, I try to keep the basic tracks, for example the bass and guitar, very standard to the way I do things, very close mic'd, same mics, just to get them sounding beefy and in your face. Then when it comes to overdubs I do a lot more screwing around with pedals, different mics, mic placement, whatever. There are areas where I try to keep it really simple, and areas where I feel better experimenting. The cone thing was great because there are times when I'll walk around and see something like the big metal cone at the back of Water Music and say "Let's use that to put a mic in." But we had a cushion there, three weeks to track at Water Music so it was a lot more like we were able to screw around. But you have to balance that with getting the band going. I actually forgot about that. Those things are great.

I don't know if we ended up using any of it in the end.

Probably not.

I know I've asked you this before, but do you play any instruments?

I'm the world's worst guitar player. I don't have hell of a lot of musical background. I can sing harmonies off-key consistently, "Eeeeeeeeuuuuuuuuuuugh." I'm the third guy.

So you were drawn into this primarily as a music fan.

As a geek kid in junior high. We were listening t this *Queen II* record and it was one of the firs records that definitely blew my mind, the process blew my mind. How they did all th backwards recording, stacked vocals, the guit harmonies, sequencing and crossfading stuff The overproduction.

Did you ever find out how they did that backwards intro t "Ogre Battle"?

That stuff is demystified now. I've turned tap around for backwards reverb plenty of times it's probably just a matter of taking the time play things in time to the backwards drum which they left backwards anyway. But as a 1 year old kid, sitting in his basement, it w mind-blowing. At that point also I was workin at Eventide, and I had a lot of experience wi them, making delay lines, and there being studio above, I had contact with those en ronments anyway. But the Eventide thi evolved from me really being into music and brother being one of the chief engineers the and that's the reason I ended up getting a summer job there in the first place. I was this prog-rock music geek who at 15 was working a summer job at Eventide and all my favorite bands were using Eventide shit, Yes and all that. I was so psyched. It evolved into me getting really into audio gear, at 15 cranking tunes in my basement, shaking my house, driving my parents and neighbors nuts. And that led to the realization of records being made in a studio and that there was a process of making them and me wanting to know, and leaving college to intern at the Record Plant because I was so much more fascinated by that than by Anthropology with a Sociology minor.

And then you started assisting there.

Forever. And then it was like the pecking order, moving up the ladder, and at one point I became the main assistant. But it became a detriment, because when you were the main assistant everybody wanted you, so the studio wasn't really psyched on you becoming an engineer and leaving, because they had people who depended on your familiarity with the gear and wanted you to do that every day. We had the first moving fader automation on the East Coast, and I was the first guy to train on it. It was GML; Massenberg came and trained us on it and I got stuck in that room forever because I was the only guy that knew the automation.

What was the first record you did as a producer?

An English band called Kerosene, for Sire, not to be confused with Kerosene 454. That was right after I engineered *Where You Been*. I had been an engineer up 'til then, on Screaming Trees, Cave Dogs, what have you.

How hard was it to go from the one environment you were used to, at the Record Plant, to moving from studio to studio as a freelance engineer/producer?

I didn't and I don't really find it that bad; it keeps it interesting. I like working a lot of different places. I guess I'm thinking more from what I guess would be a *Tape Op* perspective, and from a lot of my own experiences too, where you are used to working in what may be a sonically compromised situation, like my 16-track room, and having to try to do a lot with a little, getting to a point of doing good-sounding work through your familiarity with that situation rather than because you have particularly good gear. So you get used to the quirks of a place and maybe that affects how you'd react to a different place. That perspective probably doesn't apply if what you were used to was the Record Plant.

Well, the Inferno [*Water Music's B Studio where the board is in the studio and the only separate room is an isolation booth*] isn't exactly cush; no air conditioning, we're all sweating, I'm sitting in my underwear, there's the open room thing where you're recording guitar and you're hearing it from the amp as you're recording so the only way you can tell what it sounds like is by playback. So I'd prefer places like Water Music itself, the big room, which is an amazing place; the Magic Shop, stuff like that, but I'm not really shy about going to other places. If I have a couple of pieces of gear I like, and my reference CD, which usually is *Where You Been*, so I can hear the monitors, I can tell what I'm doing. And if you have basic tracks on

"Eeeeeeeeuuuuuuuuuuuuugh."

tape and you're going to another place to do vocals and overdubs, they're your frequency barometer. If you like what you already have, you can fit in what you're adding to it. I don't really bum out about being in environments that aren't totally comfortable.

You don't bring monitors, right? You're really comfortable with the NS-10's ...

They suck, but everybody has them, and I can relate to them. Yeah, they don't sound great and you can get ear-burn from listening to them too loud too long, but at the same time they are fairly consistent and they don't sound good, which makes you make things sound better! I've bummed myself out on Genelecs and speakers like that because they just sound good. You bring up the bass drum and you get a big woody, and you haven't done anything!

What about dealing with low end on them? Because the records you've worked on generally have a really great low end.

I

guess I'm just used to them. And when I'm in New York I use my home stereo to judge what I'm doing, and from time to time in the mixing process I've popped into Greg Calbi's [mastering room] with a DAT or 1/2" to get a reference early on. But I don't do anything special to "get" low end on the Yamahas, I think I just know them. But otherwise... no clues there. A lot of bran, would be my advice.

What is some of your favorite gear?

I love Daking mic pre/equalizers on guitar, they sound really fat and they have a kind of Trident A-rangey sound, and you can dial in substantial bottom on them and they're really exceptional. You can just put stuff through them and it sounds better. Forget about EQ or anything, just the circuit really sounds good. Distressors are hot. The Eventide stuff is great. Big fan of Space Echos; I tend to like a lot of stomp boxes when I mix if I can patch in, unbalanced-wise. Memory Men, Electric Mistresses. I just got my hands on some of these Zevex guys' pedals, like the Woolly Mammoth, that's really cool. Old API consoles, Neve consoles, Trident, I love. Compexes, Neve compressors.

It's mostly pretty classic stuff.

I really care about mics and mic pres. The rest of it you can arrive at by experimentation. But good mics and mic pres, and you're on your way. Good musicians would help too. That's an aside. ☙

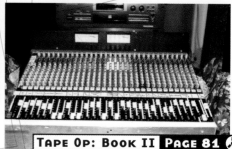

Jim O'Rourke

Story by Jenny Toomey
Art by Archer Prewitt
Photos by Nicole Radja

Jim O' Rourke is a busy fella. He's worked with so many bands it's difficult to believe he's only been producing for five years. When asked about his work ethic and prolific output, Jim always emphasizes friendship and fun, declining even to call himself a producer. Aside from recording bands Jim is a musician with dozens and dozens and dozens of releases that cover everything from Musique Concréte experimentation to elaborate pop. If you want more information on his work as a musician, you can go to his web site (http://www.cs.nwu.edu/~tisue/orourke/) which details his hundred-plus releases and archives a lot of interviews that use the word "genius." We're just talking production here. Professional titles aside... Jim O'Rourke has played a big part in helping bands like Stereolab, Sonic Youth, US Maple, Sam Prekop, Gaster Del Sol, Edith Frost, Bobby Conn, Smog, Storm & Stress, Superchunk, The Aluminum Group & others to make some great sounding records. His remarkable drive, increasing profile and (I'd suspect) reluctance to say no, has led him to work on many of these projects simultaneously. This was the case with the new Superchunk "*Come Pick Me Up*" and Aluminum Group [*Pedals*] records that arrived in my mailbox within days of one another. I popped these two CDs into my stereo with lowered expectations based on an understanding of quantity being one thing and quality another... and yet I was floored. To my ears, neither group has ever sounded better. These records positively shine on a sonic level but maybe more importantly, the song arrangements, instrument choices and performances are far more compelling and sophisticated than on each band's previous releases. For this reason, when I interviewed Jim, I focused less on the technical questions than on arrangement, environment and performance. Ironically enough, I then taped over the last five minutes of our conversation, illustrating the importance of the technical. Jim was kind enough to finish the interview a second time and I had the unique role-reversing pleasure of making a producer "do it over" because I'd forgotten to push record. The following is an interview with Jim about the recording of these records and recording in general. I've also enclosed Jim's gear-recipe for recording gold and excerpts from interviews with The Aluminum Group & Superchunk to keep Jim honest.

How many albums have you produced for other people?

Twenty. I've only done it for other people's music in the last five years. I engineered for some other stuff before that, but I've only been hired since about `94.

Producer/engineers tend to approach recording from two different camps. The predominant one is the technical; i.e. "If we can just get the right mics for the drums and the best gear then we'll make the perfect record." The other camp focuses more on the environment... techniques that create a space that's comfortable with an emphasis on collaboration and performance. I'm curious what percent of your approach is technically focused and what is environmentally focused.

I'd say it's half-and-half. I'm very conscious of environment and I'm always working to make it better. By that I mean, either purposefully making it comfortable or uncomfortable to the point of tricking musicians into doing stuff that they actually want. Sometimes it's technical tricks, like someone could be singing, and I can sense that they are right at the point where their voice will break. If I think they can get the pitch, then maybe I'll change the pitch of the tape a hair, without telling them. They won't sense it but then they will be able to sing it. So instead of constantly telling them, "Oh you're singing flat. Oh you're singing sharp," when it's only a hair off, I change the tape speed. Or like with the last Stereolab record, there was this one tune that both Sean O'Hagan (from the High Llamas who was also doing work on the record) and I knew it really needed some kind of ridiculous "hot" guitar lead. Well, Tim Gane (the guitarist) is just not into stuff like that. Over the course of the first two months of tracking I would constantly be playing hot licks while we were working. And Tim was always like, "Stop that! Oh No!" You know... it was very funny. Eventually, bit by bit, over time, his hands started fidgeting and after about six weeks he started doing it himself. By then it was time for him to go in and track it. So it's just little psychological things to get people to do stuff that... not trying to force them to do things that they wouldn't do... but getting them to do what they want to do. On the Superchunk record, with Mac (McCaughan) and his vocals, I was working with him, actually in a way he said he hadn't done before, where we actually went over the lyrics and talked about different ways they could be interpreted through the vocal performance. We talked about what combination of voices the songs might need? Does it need harmonies here? Should we lay off the harmonies here? My favorite example (of this) was Mary from

Stereolab. She had a song on the last record where she really had to sing out because the character was supposed to be this bigot. So she's singing it like she usually sings her back-up vocals. I thought that she really needed to step-up to this. She wouldn't do it. So I ran into the live room with a stick and chased her out into the street and then back into the room and immediately pushed record. When she sang the part again she was out of breath... she sang differently and it worked. So it can be anything really that works.

Did you have to do that with the Aluminum Group at all? They seem like they talk about music in that way.

We talked a lot about the implications about the way things would be done, mostly with the interpretation of the lyrics and how the performance would color the lyrics. But I tend to talk to bands about the lyrics a lot. It seems normal to some of them and for others it seems like they've never done that before... well, with engineers. But then most engineers don't seem too interested in the interpretation of the lyrics. That's up to the singer, there's a history of singers being more difficult to record than other instruments because it's more of a personal thing than playing an instrument. Most engineers shy away from that whole area.

I think that in the whole rock realm that's a bit taboo. Either because you're not supposed to care too much about lyrics, or because it's just the vessel for this angst filled, human, catharsis. Who would dare to go in and attempt to sculpt the raw emotion? Whereas, in pop music, it's just the opposite, it's all about sculpting the catharsis.

Well, I approach everything as if it was pop music.

I can hear that.

I like pop music more, although I like rock as well. In general I don't think I've ever worked with a rock band except US Maple. But even there, interpretation of the lyrics was very important because Al has a very specific set of guidelines for the way he sings. He's worked very hard at developing the way he sings. I know him pretty well, because I've known the band since the first time they played. Luckily, I was able to understand what he was trying to do. But even in that case we worked a lot on the vocals.

We're really flying through all the questions... It's good.

I'm sorry if I'm talking too much.

Yeah, I'm interviewing you and you're talking too much. Can you stick to just yes and no answers? Think like Bill Callahan. Can you talk a little bit about the difference between the Superchunk and Aluminum Group sessions?

Did you talk with Superchunk?

Yes.

Do they hate me?

No, they seemed really happy with you. I mean they teased you, definitely.

Did they?

For being over extended. For working so much and sleeping so little... for being sleepy.

I'm always sleepy, that's how I don't sleep.

From listening to the records I assumed two different processes for the sessions. I assumed that Superchunk came into the studio with skeleton pop/rock songs and they said "We want strings or horns on these parts" and you wrote those parts. I assumed that The Aluminum Group came in with arranged songs and that you collaborated with them to come up with more parts. Although both bands when interviewed seemed to say the same thing. They both said, "We came with our songs and he helped us to do some things but for the most part they were our songs and our ideas."

Yeah, sure.

I was thinking that the Aluminum Group was much more of collaboration, and Superchunk was more about selective collaboration. "We need a part for this chorus here." "Make this string part and put it in here." Etc. Because that's how the records sound.

With Superchunk they had never really tried anything like this before so in some ways they were unfamiliar with what it takes to make a record like that, and they wanted to do a two-week record in a week. I mean, you start bringing strings and horns, which aren't something that you just throw on. So in that case, of course I wasn't sleeping because I was home at night and I'd be writing the arrangements. The Aluminum Group was much more familiar with what goes into making a record like this because as a band they do it already. That said, with the Aluminum Group, pretty much all of the arrangements changed in the studio.

They said that it changed a lot in the mix.

There were also new parts. They had me replace almost all of the piano.

And the drums?

The drums were replaced. A lot of the new parts came from the original part on tape, triggering this stuff (Jim gestures at a wall of effects) and

Superchunk Interview on recording Come Pick Me Up with Jim O'Rourke.

superchunk
come pick me up

Mac (McCaughan)
John (Wurster)
Jim (Wilbur)

By Jenny Toomey

Mac: It was the same way we always do it. We set up, get the sound, which usually takes a while switching mics and stuff. Then once that's done we pretty much record the basics for everything and then start working on overdubs. In other words, for the basics we didn't do anything different. In the overdubs... that was pretty much normal. Obviously the horns and strings were not an option for our other sessions.

How was that approached?

Mac: Thinking about it beforehand. This was probably the most prepared that we'd ever been going in for a record. We had good 4-track versions of the songs from the practice space and I recorded acoustic versions of all the songs with as many vocals as I had. We sent tapes of these versions to O'Rourke in England where he was finishing Stereolab. Whether he listened to these before he started working on the record, I have no

idea. But it allowed us to have a firm grip of how the songs were going to be structured. We never really change the structure of a song once we've begun recording. We've never added an extra chorus or cut out a verse, so that all stays the same. There were two approaches to how we added the horns and the strings. With the first approach, we would have a place where the guitar was playing a part. So live, the guitar plays this part... but we would tell Jim that for the record we want horns to play this part. In those cases we just recorded it straight with the guitar playing the "horn" part and Jim would write a horn part mimicking the guitar and also one or two harmony parts.

John: "Pink Clouds"

Mac: Exactly, "Pink Clouds", when the horns come in, that was just a guitar part before. The other approach would be like in "Hello Hawk" where we weren't replacing a guitar but adding to the basic tracks. For example, each verse went three times and the second time through I knew I wanted a string part, but I didn't write a part, we just

asked for strings here, nothing overly dramatic. What's funny about Jim is that people have this idea of him as being either a "classically trained composer" or an avant-guarde weirdo who's going to sit there with a modular synthesizer and add little bleeps to everything with his PowerBook. What's funny is his references are very mainstream. He's down to earth and very specific about certain concepts, but there were other things that I thought were surprising. He's not afraid to go over the top with some things. At the end of one song I said, let's have some handclaps here and he's like, "Okay." Instead of just

that's actually what was used. On that record the arrangements changed an awful lot. The keyboard player did the strings, and I brought in some people to play the horns and I wrote stuff for that. It was always collaboration. Over the course of the record all the songs changed from the basics. The basics were actually full performances with most of the arrangements in there. Sometimes the keyboard equivalent sound would be replaced by another instrument. In general, all the arrangements were there in the beginning but by the end it was very different.

I noticed that there is a lot of play between acoustic and electronic sounds in your mixes. For example, the AG's "Two Bit Faux Construction" begins with acoustic drums and ends with electric drums. It's almost like Paul McCartney's work where he uses his voice to bridge two completely different song environments.

I think that that's one thing that we really agreed on. One song doesn't have to be this group of chord changes. It can be what someone else might split into three

or four other songs. In general, I don't want the complexity to clunk people over the head. It's there for people to find it. I don't want to foreground songs with the complexity of the arrangement but in general the stuff I do is fairly complex.

I noticed that you'd have two separate songs in one song and by the end you'd collapsed the parts together.

Some of my favorite pop music is McCartney and Sparks. That's really what The Aluminum Group are about construction wise. When we'd get to the arrangement we were usually on the same page about why this melody should move from this instrument to that instrument. I would always push it because I really like it.

I like it too. There's a lot of '70s Wings stuff happening.

Oh yeah.

So let's talk tech. Tell me some of the technical choices you made in the different sessions and tell me why...

Oh boy, I don't know where to start. In general, I'm very picky about what mic I use and I spend a lot of time with the placement. [See recipes] I set them up, hear them and if they aren't right, I change them... because you know each throwing up a mic in the little room and having us do it, he put us in the big room with three microphones and six of us spaced around the mics. And when we were finished he was like, "Okay, let's do it again." So eventually we've got six people clapping twice and it sounds great. When we did backing vocals he would have us do it three times. He would keep piling it on. I was surprised that it still sounds tasteful with all those tracks. Some producers are overly concerned with what is "tasteful." "It will only be subtle if you do it just once and we'll just kinda leave it in there." Jim's not like that at all. When I was in there doing the vocals, which is the worst part of recording for me, I knew that if I was sitting in there going, "I want to keep that but I also want to do another harmony" he wasn't going to say, " I think it's fine like it is."

Jim: He'd say that in the control room to us.

Mac: Yeah, he would sometimes say that later in the mix but while I was singing I could keep trying things.

John: In general we had to push him to do weirder stuff.

Mac: We would have to push him to do weird things, but once we got him to do it he would get really excited about it. "Yeah, come on, fuck up the drum sound." When you pushed him he would get really into it, but I get a sense that he's a bit worried about being known as the guy who makes everything weird. Maybe that's why we had to tell him to make things sound like (for example) they weren't a guitar, like on "Pulled Muscle". I think that might be why he wasn't saying, "Yeah let's put this guitar through the synthesizer."

Did he act like a producer when he was recording you?

John: He would say, "I think you can do it better."

Mac: Which is pretty much what everyone else we've ever worked with has said to us.

John: But he was never imposing.

He never said, "Imagine that you're flying in a balloon during this section?"

Mac: No, I mean it's weird because when I was doing my advance spy work before we hired him, people would say, "Yeah, he's great to work with but he's really a producer. He'll really produce your record and I'm not sure if you'll want that." So I was prepared for that, I just thought we'd deal with it if it ever came up.

John: I think he was feeling us out at the same time because we've been a self-contained band for eight years. I think he may have felt weird about...

...Over stepping it?

John: I know he did because he mentioned it several times.

How?

John: He would say, "I don't know how far "in" to go with you guys." Or "That sounded great, I don't want to overstep my boundaries so..."

Mac: One thing that is insane about him is that he is a total workaholic and I think he over extends himself, not quality-wise, but time-wise. He'll say, "I don't really sleep so I'm going to go home tonight and watch this movie. Then I'm going to mix this record for these people. Then I've got to mix another song of my own. Then I'll be back in here at 10 and we'll work till 2 am and then I'll go home and watch a video." Inevitably he'd be falling asleep in the middle of the day.

Jim: "Sleep is the bane of my existence," he would say. ☮

---

instrument... snare drums... will be different. With the Superchunk record I spent a lot of time changing mics. Especially when it came to the bass. Laura's bass has no bottom to it. It's all mid. That was a little frustrating because, of course, they wanted bottom. I had to use what was coming out of the speaker... so I spent a lot of time trying to get a bass sound that fulfilled what they wanted. I'm still not sure that I did. I think I maybe should have changed the cabinet, but it was her cabinet. I tend to spend a lot of time on all technical aspects. I generally don't use anything digital in mixing unless it's overtly digital. I like using Pro Tools; I have no problem with that, but for mixing and such, I don't use any reverbs. I don't think I used any reverbs at all on the Superchunk record. I mean if they need it, I'll only use a spring or tape delay instead of using digital reverbs or something like that.

nd your reason for that is?

hey sound like crap. I think they sound terrible and they are so horribly culturally loaded at this point that they are of no interest to me. They take away any character from the singing. It relates the singing to the reverb instead of vice versa. There isn't this equal relationship between the treatment of the vocal sound and the vocal sound. That's generally why I shy away from them. A lot of the ambience on the vocals and the drums was just from using mics in different rooms and blending them in and such. Which I

think is much more authentic and interesting sounding approach because it actually has a direct relationship with the vocal sound. It's not just a relationship with some digital algorithm. I used this stuff a lot. [gesture to wall of effects]

What's that stuff?

It's all modular voltage control filters and amps. Like on "Tiny Bombs" on the Superchunk record. The drums at the beginning, a lot of people have asked if they are played backwards, but they're not. It's actually each individual drum channel going through a voltage control amp. The bass drum triggered an LFO [Low Frequency Oscillator] and the LFO was sending out five different shapes and that shape was amplifying each of the drums. So it would trigger on the beat so the snare drum would have one envelope, and the high hat would have this other envelope, etc. Again, I think that's much more interesting because there is a direct relationship between the sound and how it's being processed. I tend to use this stuff [gesture] a lot. This was all over the keyboards on the Aluminum Group. All their keyboards are like mono, Yamaha, $200 keyboards. In order to make the sound at least a little bit more detailed they were all processed through this stuff. Especially Frank's keyboards, they were going through the Serge to "stereo-fi" it. If it's just mono, you're stuck with, basically, one option of how to mix it. You can put it off to the side, you can put it up the middle, but it sort of has a gravitational pull

to it that you can't really play with. Except for in relation to the other instruments. This way, I could put it in stereo and then create the depth that I wanted for the keyboard as opposed to the depth being in relation to the other instruments in the mix. The keyboard could actually have it's own depth which the other instruments could then work with.

I think the keyboards are really important with the Aluminum Group. They run through almost every song. While the songs on that album tend to be pretty eclectic, accessing different genres that are instantly referenced, you've got this reassuring constant of the singing and keyboards that make it all of a piece so you don't feel like you're listening to a mix tape.

Right, related to that, the other thing that I like about this is that it doesn't make this sound like processed keyboards, because it's actually making a keyboard sound with an actual direct relationship. Again, you could put it through digital reverb and make it stereo, but it's a processed keyboard then and it carries that weight. That's why I like using the analog voltage control better.

I notice you often mix an "authentic" sound into a "processed sound". Many times it's the same instrument,

you'll have real strings coming in at times with fake strings, or real drums substituting for the fake drums.

It has a narrative value. That's the only thing I like about it. By pitting these sounds together... they aren't just sounds, they have a narrative value moving from "authentic" to "non-authentic" which means that that is another thing you can use. You can work that with the song and the lyrics so that it has something to do with that.

Give me an example of what you mean by narrative value.

Well, something as simple as the song "Rrose Selavy's Valise" on the Aluminum Groups album. When the vocals change, when the singer changes, the whole mix also changes too. I mean, this is an obvious example, in that section, the drums go to electronic drums. Sometimes it's not a narrative question and it's just a question of which performance is better. I mean, almost all of the songs for the Aluminum Group record were recorded first with the electronic drums. I didn't think they were appropriate for about 60% of it so I asked them to re-record the drums on about half of the tunes. On some songs the electronic drums worked perfectly but on other songs they just drew too much attention away from the other parts. But back to "Rrose..." that first song is a real scene changer. It has real epic feel with several sort of different scenes. We tried to use the switch between "authentic" and "inauthentic" to exaggerate this idea of scene changing. I think the other song that we were

referencing the most when working on "Rrose..." was "Uncle Albert." You can use the transitions to really push this idea of changing slides. Something as simple as changing from acoustic drums to electronic drums can emphasize that scene change.

What about in a song where it happens more subtly? Like on "A Blur in Your Vision" there is an extended instrumental beginning where every two or four bars another instrument is added. Still, it happens in such a balanced way that it masks the complexity and gives the casual listener more of a sense of maybe a volume increase but not so much an increase in the number of instruments.

[We listen to the track so he can jog his memory]
Yes, you see I took out the twelve-string here so there would be room for this other slide guitar here. Also, with this cross-rhythm entering here, I thought it needed to be emptier. And there... the twelve-string comes back in there so that the effect of this rhythm moving the rhythm sort of that way [gestures from right to left], would be more effective. It just seemed more effective with the twelve-string out so that when the twelve-string came back in it had less of a sense of things just piling on.

It gets wider.

Yeah, well also it gets wider because the string keyboard was running through the Serge and here the original keyboard is on the left. So over the course of this whole section... it's

going slowly out of phase with the right channel so it is actually getting wider. I'm really heavy on mixing stereo. This sounds goofy, but every record that I've mixed, if you sit and listen to it right in the stereo spot you'll hear stuff you won't hear otherwise. I'm really heavy on exactly where to place things in the stereo and the depth. John McEntire and I had our inevitable jokey fight about the Stereolab record. You know... "You're track sounds better!" No, "Your track sounds better." We mix very differently. He mixes with that great in your face plateau.

Explain that.

He's got that great compressed mix sound where everything is up front, but everything has it's space but on a plane across your face. I think it sounds great, especially for the type of stuff that Stereolab do. Particularly the songs that he worked on - on the new album. I haven't personally had the opportunity to mix a band that does that, because the songs that I mixed for Stereolab were just entirely different. I love the way he mixes that material, it sounds great. To me, my mixes sounded like crap and his feelings were vice versa.

So what are your mixes like?

My mixes are all about depth. They are a triangle. They are all back there like this... [gestures like a diminishing point on a horizon]. I'm not saying that one approach is better than the other is. Certain material needs that, I don't know if you heard the last Smog record, but the big "Queen-like" rock song on there, that's real flat and in your face, because that's what the song needed. Even so, there is still some depth

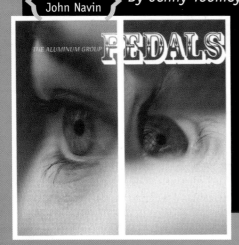

The Aluminum Group on recording their album, Pedals, with Jim O'Rourke

{ Frank Navin }
{ John Navin }   *By Jenny Toomey*

John: In collaborating with Jim... his forte' is in the mixing process. While we had most of the parts previous to entering the studio, a lot of the songs' sounds materialized in the mix. Actually, when we went in and recorded, it was a lot more electric. Then, as we began to layer it with acoustic instruments, Jim just started making a conscious decision to leave the electric out. He is sort of an editor and a sounding board for Frank and I.

I noticed that there is a lot of shifting from electric to acoustic within the mixes.

Frank: A lot of that was achieved by layering, layering, layering. We recorded sort of like we were filling up a shopping cart when you're shopping for dinner. You know... you get a shit load of things, because you don't know what you want to make. You take it home, you edit out

what you want to use, and then you make that particular dinner.

John: But you're buying a lot of stuff...

Frank: It was two weeks of laying a lot of tracks...

John: Laying a lot of stuff but not working with it immediately. So it was exactly like Frank said... laying down a lot of stuff to use it later.

Frank: 90% of the songs were completely structured, I don't know how this makes sense... but Jim did like 30% after that so we ended up with 120%.

John: Just because he would come up with these very special extra decorations that fit perfectly. It's like he doesn't sleep. He goes home and that's all he thinks about. For us, he didn't do any string arrangements because our keyboardist does that, but he did our horn arrangements. He worked really closely with our parts and the horn players. I don't know him that well, but I guess

in the drums. Almost all of my mixes are like a triangle, but I haven't really had the opportunity to do it a different way. I mean I could've with the Superchunk record , but in a way it seemed more appropriate not to do it, because that's what their other records sound like. I wanted this one to have more air in it. There is a lot of space.

What do you think about listening?

Well, how do I talk about that? Listening is the whole thing.

Though it seems to me that a lot of producers fall into a trap of mimicking.

Oh, yeah... I wouldn't want to say what other producers do because it would sound like I was insulting them. But yeah, for me it's all about listening. It's hard for me to dissect the way I do things. Not to sound like a hippie, but when it comes down to it, if the vibe isn't right, it's just not right. I mean, something can sound technically great but still not be right. The best record I've heard in years is this record by a woman called Stena Nordinstom from Sweden. Technically it's a mess but it's brilliant because the vibe is right. She's got these really badly recorded basic tracks of her singing. They are almost purposefully badly recorded [tracks of] piano and singing against fantastically recorded strings and horns, and the way the clash is what gives the record its character. I mean, generally, when I'm in the studio with a band, the only time I put my foot down is when someone wants to go over a part a million times. The more you play a part, the more you get it perfect, the more character you take out of the performance. When you think about your favorite records and you think about your favorite moments on those records... it's never the perfectly played part it's the anomaly of the performance.

It would benefit many bands to be less perfect.

Oh yes.

And for some bands it's even dangerous. Like for example if the Aluminum Group were perfect...

It wouldn't work. See that was part of my problem with some of their other recordings. They sounded too perfect... at times it sounds too programmed. That takes away from the character of Frankie and Johnny when they are being accompanied by what basically sounds like robots. There isn't an interaction between the voices and the programming. I don't mind sloppy performances, if the character is there, that's more important. I've worked with some people who will go over a performance a million fucking times to get it perfect and by that point it's completely uninteresting. And that's not just because I've heard the other performances. It's just not as interesting. Some people are interested in technical perfection.

Or when they exhaust all the spontaneity out of something...

I really couldn't give a rat's ass about technical ability because you know... it might take someone a week to learn a part perfectly, it might take them a year, but anyone can play something perfectly. It's not interesting to me. What's interesting to me is hearing the person play it. Hearing the character of the person playing, that's the overriding thing for me at all times, if I don't hear the character of them playing in there then it's not there. Sometimes it does require a few attempts to get that, other times the first take is perfect. So as far as listening, that's kind of the thing I'm always listening for... the sense that it's an actual performance as opposed to a perfect take. This is especially true with vocals. I don't care if the pitch is off a hair if the performance is there. Other times though, if it's not about being a

---

that he must work at home. It's not like the arrangements are done on the spot, or if it is it must be that he is very gifted that way. He must think about it a lot beforehand because he'll come up with the perfect part immediately, if not - within a day. He expects everybody to keep their stamina and focus. Frank was able to do that, Frankie and Jimmy worked very well together.

Frank: A lot of times I would just suggest something and then leave the room so he would have time to attempt that or find it.

John: I look back and I know how much we accomplished in two weeks, but let me tell you something; he is also soooo mellow. He's just like, "Everything will happen, don't worry," which is so reassuring. When we started we had a wish list; for example, we wanted this location harpsichord shoot. And it's like, "Hello, we're paying for studio time and we're not even recording there?" And he was like... "It will happen. We will get it

done. Whatever you want." Another thing that Jim constantly reiterated to Frankie and I was..."We're not going to do second best. Whatever you want is what we will get." At the first meeting he critiqued some of our previous work and said that he didn't want to be "present" in the final recording. He didn't want anyone to hear the record and to hear him. He wanted them only to hear us. We didn't use Pro Tools, but when we sent that quarter inch tape to be mastered, he had manually sliced and edited it to pieces. When you work on Pro Tools, tape slicing seems like such an archaic technique, but Jim said he prefers manual editing. He also always masters from quarter inch... It's analog to CD-R...no matter what band he's working with. He said that it has a warmer quality and less antiseptic. Because he's using a lot of analog mixing techniques there are moments of lag time. They aren't something that most people will notice, but

when we listened to the finished album for the first time Jim was laying on the ground and just like shaking his head saying, "Oh my god, all I can hear are the mistakes."

Frank: All organic and inorganic things are on the table for us to use and that's the point. We have more than 64 crayons now. They used to only come in a pack of eight. Now with the computer it's gotten to the point where we can even make our own crayons. My point being is that it's all available and we shouldn't shun anything.

John: We're comfortable in the studio; that's our work and we love it. This is our dream, and we are able to work with Jim O'Rourke and Dave Trumfio who are both very talented and nice too. It's like, "Yeah!" What more could you ask for?

performance, then the pitch is more important because that's the aspect you're trying to get across.

Like background vocals...

Backgrounds... or like in some of the Stereolab stuff where it's not meant to be a performance. I mean with the stuff I did with Laetitia [Sadier] we did actually go for more of a performance than she usually does. But, at other times that's not what you want...you don't want one performance blocking out or distracting from another performance, which was the case with the backing vocals on The Aluminum Group records. Often times we did go over the parts a lot because they have to remain in the background. Even with Edith Frost, the choice of having a voice double tracked has a lot of implications. She isn't singing just to you anymore.

Yeah, I don't much like double tracking. That's why I liked where you placed the harmonies and double tracks on the Superchunk. I mean it wouldn't really sound like Mac if it wasn't doubled... but...

A lot on the new record isn't double tracked.

Yes, but in those cases there is usually a harmony or something else, which strengthens the part without doubling it.

Right. I actually like double tracking but I like the implication of double tracking. Again, it has to work with the lyrics. You can remove the idea of a person singing to you. In the tiny bit of time that I've been doing that on my own records that question has been of major importance to me. Is it one voice, two voices or twenty voices?

Well that gets back to the pop versus rock dynamic again. It's strange how certain environments just traditionally allow for more ornamental approaches.

Well yeah, that contrast is of interest to me. There's sort of, well not a "rape" song, but something like that on this thing [*Half-way to a Three-way* EP] I just finished. There were so many ways that I could do it. The first time I did it super-cheerful so that you didn't notice the subject matter so it would have more of an effect. But you know, I tried different approaches to it, both with how many voices and what the tone was, because it effects the way the lyrics are interpreted so much. They aren't just words and music you know. I think a lot of people just think of it as words and music. I don't understand how you can.

I get a strong sense from your body of work that recording is fun for you. Not to imply that other engineers don't have fun recording, but that fun for you isn't just an effect, but an essential part of your recording process.

Yes, if it isn't fun, it's of no use. That's why I play a lot of pranks in the studio. If people aren't having fun then I don't think they make good records. ⊗

I approach everything as if it was pop music.

VISUAL IMAGES in the Recording Studio

By Oz Fritz

My job as a recording engineer deals with the reception and transmission of music. This involves working with musicians in a special kind of laboratory commonly known as a recording studio. The most important and yet abstract aspect of the recording process is unveiling and calling forth the creative source. In other words, where does music come from and how do we access it at will? How does it arrive on the scene? How do we invoke it into being?

There is a special class of outboard equipment that subtly, yet markedly helps to open the creative channels for everyone involved in the session. This technology is the use of fine art and other visual images in the recording studio. Light wave harmonics that may potentially instigate or aid musical trajectories in a variety of ways.

I began working with visual images in the recording studio after reading about Dr. John Lilly's repeating word tape loop experiments in his book *The Center of the Cyclone*. He would record a single word such as "cogitate"and loop it. I should mention that this was in the late '60s when the whole idea of a loop, information repeating over and over, was completely unheard of in music. People listening to the repetition of the word "cogitate," after a few minutes, would begin to hear alternate words such as "commentate" or "conscious rate" even though these words obviously weren't on the tape. Lilly had some of these alternate words printed on cue cards. In subsequent "cogitate" listening sessions he had these placed just barely in the subject's peripheral range of vision so that they could see the card but couldn't read the word on it. As soon as the cue card was peripherally shown, the person would report hearing the alternate word that was printed on the card. This led Dr. Lilly to conclude that **what you see strongly influences how you hear.**

My intention was to upscale the aesthetic in the recording studio by introducing artistic visual images of a very high quality. Many studios have a neutral, institution-like feeling about them. The exact opposite of what you want in a creative environment. I was aiming to create a space more conducive and resonant to musical expression.

I began using images from magazines and art books, usually of religious icons, mandalas and surrealistic pieces. Musician/producer Bill Laswell liked the idea and encouraged me to take it further. Every time we had a session there would be additional art on the walls but he could always see there being more. Finally, on a session with Bootsy Collins, I arrived 3 hours early and covered every inch of the control room with esoteric pictures. The studio pulsated so intensely with visual impressions that we all felt like we had taken a psychedelic. Needless to say, it led me to experiment with subtler techniques.

Shortly after that I was turned on to Objective Art as produced by a group of artists calling themselves the School of Reductionism. To quote from their manifesto: *"Reductionism treats the production of art as a science. More particularly, it is a science of perception. As a science of perception, Reductionism explores new forms of perception which force the viewer to confront new modes of perception, realities which go unnoticed, ignored, forgotten or generally avoided through whatever means commonly serve this purpose in our ordinary sense perception."*

I've worked with this artwork for over ten years now and it always seems to help bring about a subtle mood-shift that can intuitively open one up to receiving the musical current. I also find that **art adds a balancing visual counter-tension to the constant amount of listening that recording entails.**

On one occasion, in 1990, I arranged it so that the first sight Tony Williams saw when entering Laswell's Greenpoint studio was a Reductionist piece called *Star Eater* by E.J. Gold. His playing that day has been described by critics as his strongest and most wide-open in years. It can be heard on a CD called *The Word* by Jonas Helborg (Axiom). Seeing *Star Eater* was just one possible contribution to his inspired drumming that session. Art in the studio tends to open up fields of possibilities otherwise non-existent. It introduces new information and a new dynamic that can provoke and stimulate an inspired performance. In Quantum Physics, (inherently operant with all the electron manipulations going on in the studio) when you multiply one possibility with another possibility you get a probability.

More recently, I was recording Kirk Hammet of Metallica at Les Claypool's house for the last Primus release when he suddenly exclaimed "That's a great painting!" He was referring to a

E.J. Gold, *A Matter of Delicate Balance*, pastel on Sennelier, ©1977 E.J. Gold. Published as a lithograph on Arches by Heidelberg Editions International.

small canvas by Gold that just happened to be in his line of vision. It was a simple abstract piece with conte crayon and a bright yellow wash. The image could look like either a tree or the infinity sign. Later Kirk said that he was keying in to the painting and that it was helping him to focus and concentrate on the overdub.

Some of the most enlightened musicians I've recorded were Native Australians (often ignorantly called Aborigines) connected with the group Yothu Yindi. They brought in huge banners of their native art which they draped all around the control room. It made for a very intense space. Toward the end of a ten hour session the walls seemed alive, lizards and other creatures winking at me. Another natural psychedelic space induced by hard work and visionary art. The music was as equally intense but unfortunately didn't survive to see the light of day. It was deemed too noncommercial by record executive non-visionaries and was diluted and smoothed out for the pop market.

I now regard fine art as an essential piece of studio outboard gear and use it as much as possible always being sensitive to the proclivities of whomever I'm working with. It's my hope that this little essay will encourage studio owners to consider the aesthetic environment they are presenting to their clients and to themselves. ☉

Jon Brion

Producer, Session Player,
Film Scorer, etc...

by Larry Crane
photos by Jeff Cros

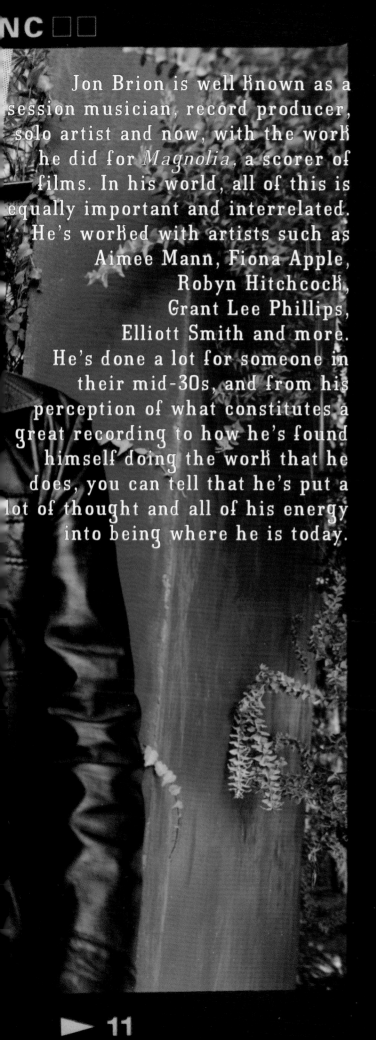

Jon Brion is well known as a session musician, record producer, solo artist and now, with the work he did for *Magnolia*, a scorer of films. In his world, all of this is equally important and interrelated. He's worked with artists such as Aimee Mann, Fiona Apple, Robyn Hitchcock, Grant Lee Phillips, Elliott Smith and more. He's done a lot for someone in their mid-30s, and from his perception of what constitutes a great recording to how he's found himself doing the work that he does, you can tell that he's put a lot of thought and all of his energy into being where he is today.

How do you get the session jobs and production work that you do?

The only reason that people get work and are working on records is because somebody has heard a record that you've done something on and they want to pull off a little of that. If you show up and you're a jerk, they'll never call you again. That's it, that's all there is. There's no other secret that is being withheld, for you or for anyone else that does it. People are going to hear some tracks that you've done and go, "I think that's cool, I want to work with that guy."

And it seems like you've got to do 20 tracks for every one track that somebody hears.

And it's not always the thing that you think. It's not the thing you're doing that you think the world is going to go, "A-ha! Mr. Crane is up to good work." It's going to be something that somebody's playing and the person they're going out with hears and happens to go out drinking that night and says, "God, I heard this amazing thing today." It's going to be the b-side of something or something that was never released – it's just a cassette. That's the reality of it.

The secret that the old engineers don't tell you is that your best work is never going to be heard. [laughter] Something that you put a lot of energy into might just be totally buried or never released.

I remember reading some things with session musicians over the years – they would grumble about how it doesn't matter what you do because it's going to be mixed too quietly or the mix of the whole record is going to not have a groove whatsoever. You work on something that was really cool when you were there and by the time it comes out it's messed up. And lo and behold, it actually turns out to be true. As a session musician, I played on so many things where I just came home out of my head so happy about it [the session] and by the time it gets released it's completely watered down. They killed it.

Did you start out as a session musician or as a musician?

As a musician, I've always loved recording. As a kid, I was fascinated with tape recorders, I love everything about them – microphones, amplifiers, all of this was magical stuff. By the time I was 13, my dad had a friend who happened to have a recording studio attached to his house. There was this local hard-rock band recording – it was a 16-track recording studio. I went nuts. I was just sitting in the control room watching them overdub. I was 13 years old and realizing the significance of an overdub.

How it's piecing the song together?

Yeah, and the whole notion of it. I totally got what it was and the potential of it and just looking at the machine and this big piece of 2" tape going by. It was the most massive piece of tape I had ever seen. It was the most monstrous, fantastic thing. I pretty much knew that I was going to spend my life being a musician by the time I was even or eight. By the time I was thirteen, I knew that I wanted to be recording. I had a stereo cassette deck and my dad had an old stereo reel-to-reel and I just used to do massive overdubbing, jumping between them. Ever since I was 13 I've had headphones on. I didn't have an amp so I used to overdrive the tape machine by plugging my guitar into the mic input. It was beautiful. A couple of years ago, somebody turned me on to the Lindsey Buckingham stuff on *Tusk* [Fleetwood Mac]. It was a very similar guitar sound.

There's that strange kind of dry, edgy guitar sound on there.

Yeah, and the other funny thing at the time was that I discovered if I detuned down to low D, I could play power chords with the fuzz with just one finger. I had this really strange proto-grunge sounding guitar stuff on these horrifically bad songs with some squeaky 13-year old singing on them.

What did your parents think of all that when you were messing around with those kinds of things?

I was very lucky. My dad was a music teacher and my mom loved singing and they had really good tastes in songs. They just sort of felt that there was no question in what I was going to be and it was useless to even fight it. So, any interest on my part, was a good thing. Most of my friends didn't have that good fortune. As a parent, it seems like a rather bleak situation. "Oh my god, my kid will starve and be a drug addict." [laughter] The fact that my dad was the breadwinner of the family at the time – they couldn't exactly say, " This is an irresponsible thing for you to be doing."

'Cause he's teaching music.

Something funny that did happen was that my mom, at some point, when I was eight or nine years old said that I might want to think about some other things or some other options just in case. It was a really serious heart-to-heart and I remember it very clearly. At the time, I was pretty much obsessed with drums. Around this time I had started playing my brother's guitar, that he got for Christmas and didn't play, so I started playing Beatles' songs on it. I took my mother's advice and basically learned to do tons of other musical things. I didn't think about becoming good at math or getting other interests. I did take her advice, I learned to play a bunch of instruments and I started writing songs. As an adult looking back, I had a good laugh about that. Funny enough, her advice probably helped keep me in good stead, because from very early on I liked doing everything.

As a kid, did you ever get a 4-track cassette unit or anything?

Those didn't exist when I was a kid. I'm 36 so...

I'm the same age as you and they weren't around were they?

No. I eventually got a used 4-track Teac reel-to-reel by the time I was 18 or 19. Around that time, the PortaStudios [Tascam] were out, but that was a new and expensive item. I got the used reel-to-reel with a Teac mixer for precious little money and I had one mic and that was it. I had the same pair of headphones that I had when I was 13. The PortaStudio seemed like an unbelievable extravagance that I looked forward to. I didn't even mess with one of those until well into my 20s.

When you first started going out into "real" studios, what were those like for you?

There was a studio that I did all of my initial work at in New Haven called Presence. It was owned by a guy named John Russell and it was in his parents' basement. He had an 8-track Tascam and a Tascam board, a pair of those atrocious JBL monitors that lots of people had at the time. They were supposed to have incredibly realistic low and high-end. I think he also had a dbx compressor and an MXR digital delay and some sort of spring reverb in a box and he had an [Neumann U-] 87. What was cool about the studio was that he was a professional keyboard player around town and that's how he bought the studio. But because of that, he had a Mellotron, which I later bought, and a lot of interesting stuff. I started going there with one of the first bands I had - we did our 8-track demo there in a couple of days. I was just going crazy, I was so happy. I was finally around a studio. I became friends with the guy who was the engineer and we ended up forming a band together and doing a lot of work at that studio. He

would produce people, locally, and he would bring me in as a session player and it's not like there's a ton of session work in Connecticut. But, these bands would come in and maybe they didn't have a keyboard player so I would play keyboards. Or if they needed guitar, I would do that. I made a conscious decision, when I was 16 or 17 that I would go to any session and do anything on it for free at any time. I wanted every opportunity to be around the stuff, I wanted to see other people doing it, I wanted any chance to have my hands on the stuff... everything. I would go in and maybe one day I would be just sitting around making tea, on another day I would be involved in something or one day I would be an assistant engineer or just wrapping cords. Any time they would let me be around, I was around. I ended up dropping out of high school right around my 17th birthday. It was really an odd, but eventful few days... John Lennon got shot, my birthday hit and I turned 17 and I literally went and signed out of school where I had hated being for 10 years – it was always cutting into my recording time. [laughter] The day that I signed out of high school, I actually went to my first paying session. My dad dropped me off and I had my guitar and I played the session. Basically, my friend's studio went up from 8 to 16 and eventually to 24 [tracks]. He also got his own building and I started working at his studio, officially, as anything. I would engineer sessions or be his assistant. I did programming, he was the only person in Connecticut to have a Fairlight [CMI, early sampler] at the time and I would program that. He was of the mind that things should be getting used, so whenever sessions were done I was allowed to do whatever I wanted. I really started getting my shit together fast. Often, I just came in and played the grand piano and I would just play it from the end of the session until nine in the morning. That's when I also started getting my own writing chops together.

Did you start recording yourself at that point?

That was never really my interest then. It was always song first and if I was just making a track to make a track, it was it's own experimental thing. After that, I ended up moving to Boston and I got involved with the people at Q Division - right when their studio opened. That's really where I sort of found myself. I did some solo recording out there before I moved to Los Angeles, which kind of cemented a lot of opinions that I have about recording and even certain styles of working.

What would you say those styles or opinions are?

The sense of intimacy with recording, which can happen even with recording tons of tracks and instruments on it. The sense of intimacy does not necessarily denote small or large. It's strictly the feeling of presence, emotionally or sonically. I'm quite obsessed with that. I also started working with Aimee Mann at that time and she was very obsessed with very loud vocals. Eventually, she totally won me over into that world and now anything I do has a vocal as loud as it can possibly be without sounding like it's a separate record.

Or without making the music incredibly puny...

Yeah, but I'm also figuring out ways of making it so that the music doesn't sound puny but the vocals are still large. These are the constant challenges that you never really get good enough at doing. I actually like to go in without a lot of structure. I like to do things... like throw paint at the wall and really not worry about them, whether it's in the basic tracking stage or the overdub stage. I'm also fearless about being able to throw things away. Rather than labor on one thing a long, long time, I'd rather do a bunch of options and look at the different combinations that come up.

When you first started working at Q Division, did you start as an intern?

When the studio had off-time there was a group of musicians - we ended up being a band for a few months. There was just always recording going on, everybody wanted to be making music and everybody wanted to be improving in their respective craft. I was writing a ton of songs, Mike Denneen, who's the chief engineer and producer there, he wanted to be engineering all the time. Everybody wanted to be recording and moving different mics around and seeing what it meant. The real moment of glory was they traded their board for a couple of Pultecs, two 67s, two 47s, two 44s, two 77s, a 49 and other things I forgot. They got this amazing deal. This was about 11 years ago and basically there was just a phone call going, "Okay, you have to come down here." I was like, "Is that stuff as good as people say?"... "Come down here!" That was it - that was the light going off. I was like, "Oh, this is why the records that I like sound the way they do."

Do you buy much gear? Do you have a home studio at this point?

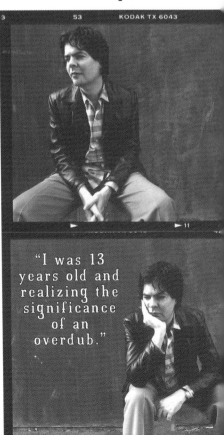

"I was 13 years old and realizing the significance of an overdub."

I do have a home studio. I have a bunch of really nice things. I've got an Ampex 1200 24-track and I also have a Stevens [deck]. I have an Oram console - John Oram is the guy who originally designed the Trident EQ. He has his own company now. They have good stuff and they have a good concept. Right now, the only things that are available to people are a Mackie or a $300,000 new console or $300,000 vintage console. There are few mid-priced good sounding things. So, they've made some good sounding consoles. I have a great deal of outboard stuff designed by David Bock, who designs gear for Soundelux [and Mercury]. I've actually got a number of prototypes of his. Things that they couldn't make on a mass production level because the parts would be too expensive.

I don't think people realize what a consideration that is.

It's horrible. This guy has wonderful ears - he makes great stuff. I'm just thrilled to know him and I like him as a person and he's up to great things. He's made a bunch of Pultec style EQs. I've got four of those and I have a stereo tube mic pre that he made for me. I don't know that he's even made another one, but its beautiful sounding. I'm obsessed about mic pres. Mark Sampson, who use to make Matchless amps, literally just dropped off to me a pair of mic pres that he just designed that are some of the finest things I've ever heard. Obviously, whatever studio I'm at I get to know the sound of their console and whatever their freestanding mic pres are. It is really possible to get onto tape, just going from the mic to the mic pre to the tape – compression if necessary. The other thing people don't do is that they don't listen to all the different compressors available. That's, yet, another EQ curve. It's not like I'm anti-EQ; I'm just anti having anything between the microphone and the tape that

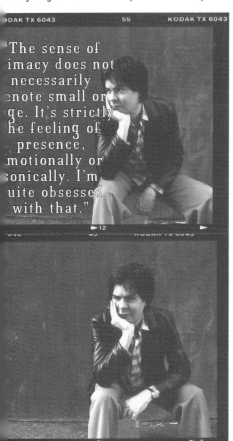

"The sense of imacy does not necessarily enote small or ge. It's strictly he feeling of presence, motionally or onically. I'm uite obsessed with that."

doesn't have to be there. If you get to know these other pieces of equipment, you're physically closer to the thing that's happening. It's coming out of the speaker and the waves have gone through fewer things, they have less coloration from other things. As close as you can get to the original airwaves is cool. I don't believe that there is any form of recording that replicates what it's like to stand in a room – or even close. I think that people, who claim that, are idiots.

I've never put a record on and felt like it's the same thing by any means.

Physically, we don't have a playback system as full dimensional as being somewhere that has even close to the resolution. The thing you can try and do is make a thing that is a nice experience to be around. When the airwaves come out of the speakers, you're happy to be near them. As close as you can get to airwaves coming from humans compiled in a nice way, the better off you are. Other than that, it's pure experimentation, since I don't feel we can have an accurate representation and we're making records, which are their own art form. The other end of the scale is to just go completely ballistic and try to fuck things up at every turn.

I thought, originally, that you were more of a musician and a session player. But, you've obviously done a lot of production work too. How did one lead to the other or the other way around?

The first thing you said is actually the reality of it. Whatever people know of me doing first, that's what they think of me as. A lot of people know me as producer first and they end up being surprised that I do sessions... People say, "Oh, you're a songwriter?" and then they think it's a producer vanity project. No, I've been writing songs since I was 8 years old. It's not particularly new. In fact, record productions, specifically the ones you know, that's much more of a recent history on my timeline. I've been doing all of these things... I've been writing since I was 8, I've been banging on things since I was 4. I'm 36 now, so that's 23 years I've been recording and coming up with songs and trying to make a version of them and experimenting with recording. To me, it's actually all one thing. All of them have their own intrinsic merits. There's something that's really relaxing, challenging and fun about being a session musician. I like going in and there's a bunch of instruments around and there's a piece of music and your job is to play it as well as possible. Hopefully, if you're doing a good job, you inspire the singer or songwriter and the producer to be more excited about the thing they have. It's really, really, fun. The other thing about being a session player that's cool or potentially uncool is that you don't know what the music is going to be like going there. Occasionally you get there and it's something traditional and they want you play something traditional. The song isn't even good, but they think it's good. It's an interesting discipline in that way. It's not your ball game, it's somebody else's thing. Usually, when you have an experience like that, you wouldn't work on those particular records again. For the most

part, it's been really good. As a session musician, I've gotten to watch amazing artists at work. I've gotten to watch amazing producers at work. I've gotten to watch terrible musicians at work and learn just as much as from them. It wasn't my session. It wasn't my nightmare where it all went wrong and everything was bad. I was just visiting and I just got to watch when they had the right basic tracks, but they did 40 more takes of it for two days. Why did they not see that they had the right thing? What are the contributing factors, psychologically? Who was fearing what? There's amazing stuff to learn if you keep your eyes open.

You pick up a lot. When you feel that a session is going really well and the music is coming out great, you see how everybody reacts and what's going on.

Also, having been a session player is really good for me as a producer. I guess the equivalent would be actors who direct. I don't know if that's an accurate one or not. I know which producers I've played best for and I know why. I know where they left me space and where they pulled in the reigns – I knew how it felt. So, it allows me to do a better job as a producer at this point... much better job. I feel like I do know how to get good things out of people.

What kind of things, do you think, help do that?

Let's give two examples. Here's an example of bad: Somebody's hired you to play. They've got demos that they've spent far too long on. Now they're in the studio making their masterpiece and you're barely getting through complete takes because they're stopping the tape and going, "Okay, the first two bars were kind of good, but we can build on that." That, for instance, is bad. Somebody will bring in their 8-track machine with their demos for you to listen to the isolated guitar track from the demos in the lounge. That's not necessarily bad, but often not the best thing. You're already trying to replicate something... it's not setting up an atmosphere of inviting a human being in to do their best for you. Let's make it simpler, I'm trying to think of the bad version, because I already have the good one in my head. A bad version is... "Don't play B flat, I don't like B flat.... Maybe you could go for a darker tone... Here, play this this way," he picks up your instrument and shows you something. "I think, maybe, it should be more downstrokes than upstrokes" Now, let me give you a good version. A good version is T-Bone Burnett on a session, producing. The band was, myself, Greg Leisz who's a marvelous pedal steel player and Jim Keltner. I was playing baritone guitar; I was essentially the bass player. I had it a little detuned on the low string so I was playing bass with my thumb and playing little chord things on the upper strings. It was a song about Texas... we played a take and it wasn't great. It was completely proficient, everybody in the room was proficient. There was no question that everybody could play and there was no question that everybody wanted to do the right thing for the song. Nobody was hot-dogging anything, but it didn't feel right. People came in to listen and it was a take that maybe a lot of people would have even kept, because it was proficient. Everything was right, not in a clinical way. It was right, it just wasn't magical. T-Bone looked around the room and said, "You guys have all been to Texas, right?" We all nodded and he said, "Do you know how when you're standing in Texas and you look around and see miles in every direction?" He starts leaning over the board and making this big sweeping motion with his arms. We all nodded. He said, "That's how it has got to be." We proceeded to march in and in one take we played the shit out of the thing. That's not an accident, that's not a bullshitty little thing. That's the real thing. To me, one of the biggest jobs of production is "taking" the people who go into the room. I think it's the most important part of production. Then there's psychological stuff, then there's the technical stuff, the tastes, and the things that people think it is – engineering, arranging. All of that is not record production, that's engineering and arranging and playing, which are some of my favorite parts of the record making process. That instruction of being in Texas was so good, it did a number of things. One: it assumed that everybody knew what they were doing. It didn't insult anybody's ability. It didn't say that anybody was bad or that they weren't good enough for this particular task at hand. It also didn't tell any individual any specifics about how to solve the problem. It just wasn't magical enough, which is completely ephemeral and a subjective thing. That instruction was not, "Hey, everybody play less." Nobody was playing a ton to begin with, but everybody went out there knowing that it wasn't a completely magical take. Everyone went out there with an image in their head and it was a solid, visual image. It was about space, and everybody played their emotional, sub-conscious version of how they represent space as a musician. I have never seen a better example of what good production is, in my opinion. What's interesting is that people have such a misconception of the job. The best producers I've seen... artists will make a record with them and afterwards go, "Oh man, I'm not going to work with them, they just didn't do anything." Artists will know that I'm working because I'm playing 20 instruments on tracks. But again, multi-instrumentalists/engineer/arranger does not mean producer. I think the job has gotten wildly skewed. Most artists want their name as co-producing on records, because they think they need to be seen as the genius and don't want people to think that somebody else has arranged their record for them. It's not what that title means. It's a horribly misconstrued thing that, I think, we need to start getting people to think differently about. There are projects that I played on where I've been a multi-instrumentalist on the record where, on songs, there will be a bass player and a drummer and 20 tracks of me playing. I'm just a session guy. I got paid for whatever time I was there and that was it. Sometimes, these things are very successful and you go. "Well, it wouldn't have been the same." That, to me, is part of a good production job. That means the producer made the right decision. He put me in the room with that bass player and that drummer. He did that, I didn't.

And, granted, while I was there I may have done whatever I did, but that's not necessarily production. Being with the artists the whole time through and making the project and understanding what their hopes and their fears are – all of that is a different thing than coming a up with a musical or sonic landscape. The job changes everyday with a different batch of people in the room.

What stuff have you been working on lately, production wise?

Grant Phillips and I are making a collaborative record. He was from the band Grant Lee Buffalo. We're writing together and we've been doing it at my studio. I'm getting together with David Byrne [Talking Heads] in about a week to do some recording. It's just, sort of, your classic trial run and if we have fun maybe we'll do more.

Is that in a production capacity?

Yeah. I'm also finishing off various records of my of my own. There were things that were just about completed and everyone in the universe turned them down and then they've laid dormant. I'm basically going through and finishing all of those off.

I know you have a solo album coming out.

Yeah, it should be out within the next few weeks. It'll be through Artist Direct, there will probably be no place, physically, where you can see it. It sort of exists in the ether on-line. I have a virtual record I guess.

Somebody sent me a promo of that and it sounded good. My friend said that it reminded him of Emitt Rhodes.

I'm a big fan of the first Emitt Rhodes solo record...

That's home recording on a 4-track for you... one of the first ones.

It's great. There are particular things that he pretty much likes on every song. Every one has a rhythm guitar and a lead guitar. He has maracas, he has the drums, and there's usually a piano and a pump organ. There are usually two part backing vocals and a lead vocal. Obviously, he had just nailed his system down of what order to do those things in. I really like the sonics of that album a lot. Once again, there's a real intimacy on any of the tracks that are on there. Neil Young records were always good on the intimacy scale, sonically. Just the feeling of... "There's a guy playing the guitar and I can really tell that's what it is." The drums are beautifully dry, those are good in the same kind of way where sonically it has nothing to do even with bandwidth. It has to do with presence.

How do you get those kinds of qualities?

The best way to get presence is to do as little as possible.

Keeping the signal chain short?

Keep it real short. With things like drums, if people play quieter you can get better mics closer. Then you've got total intimacy. If you ride the compression right, there's a place where you don't necessarily hear it, but it does allow to get you a little more intimacy. Keeping it simple. For the most part, one of things I'm really big on is mic'ing from player perspective. Everybody that learns to play an instrument, like drums, has learned the balance from where their head is. I think overheads are generally too high and I really don't go for stereo all that often.

Put a mic behind the drummer's head?

The job chang[es] different batch

Yeah, pretty much. I'm usually in a "close-to-player" perspective without being in the way of the players or putting the mic in harms way. I use to listen to records and go, "Why are all these '50s jazz records perfect?" We figured out some way to record musicians in a room in an appealing fashion. It's not truly realistic, but give us a sense of what it was like to be there. It's like looking at a good photograph. I started thinking about why records started sounding like shit in '63 or '64, and they did. All the early British rock records sound like dog shit. They have no bandwidth. Eventually I realized that when musicians started playing louder, the old mics couldn't handle the level. So, they invented dynamic mics, which you could put right up on guitar amps and drums. Then, things sounded shitty again, they could take the level, but they didn't have the bandwidth. Then people figured out ways of doing the hyper-real sound, which became popular in the '70s. You've got dynamic mics right up everything's ass and then you've got EQ and different things to get the sound together and thus began the era of hitting a snare drum for a day. You can make a snare drum sound incredible in zero time. Take a [Neumann U-] 67 and run it through any good mic pre. Let's just run into a Neve, no compression, near the drum, but a little further than you would normally put a [Shure SM] 57 or something. Don't worry too much about the bleed and have the drummer play a little quieter. You can't do this with someone who insists on having to play harder, thinking it's the only way to come off as rocking. Then the drummer becomes an important part of your chain. [laughter] At the point when somebody is playing quieter, you've got a 67, which has beautiful vocal qualities to it and great high-end presence. All of the sudden you've got all the top-end you could possibly want, all the bottom-end you want, the mid-range is appealing. Mix it dry and it'll be incredible. The thing you can't do is slam on it. If you're going to do that then you have to use a dynamic mic and you have to, in truth, have a fucked with sound. However, if you want somebody who is slamming the drums really hard

eryday with a
ple in the room.

and it has a fairly natural sound then you can back off on a good condenser and get really good mono sound or a stereo sound if necessary. I'm generally recording with 3 mics, I have one in player position which is almost all of the sound – a [AKG] D30 on the kick drum and some good tube condenser on the snare. If I want, I'll put up two room mics and track them and usually I'll do fucked up things with them. I won't try to get a normal good stereo image. I'll point one into one corner and one in an oblong fashion somewhere else and put two different compressors on them. When you put them together they do different phase things because of the different time relationship. That tends to be how I'm operating this month.

ou notice with that sort of thing, it always changes. Have you done many projects with full bands?

o, actually.

t seems like you've mostly done singers and songwriters.

have to admit I keep gravitating towards that. There are bands, in the course of rock history, I would have been very happy to just sit around and engineer and produce in the old Glyn Johns school of production – just egging people on. There aren't that many of them that I can think of right now. I can't think of too many bands that are famous for just being bands that I'd want to record. Most of the ones that I thought have been great in the past 10 years are either not doing their best work now or they've got dead members. [laughter]

ou recently did a score for [the movie] *Magnolia* too. I was wondering how you went about doing that – writing the arrangements.

was a blast, it was really hard work. In terms of my arranging, I've always worked, sort of, from an orchestral perspective in terms of how I think. Even as I play keyboards, I tend to play in open voicings. I play a C chord that has a C, E, G in it, but instead of C, E, G, you play C, skip the E, play the G and then play the

E above the next C. That's how string quartet writing has its sound. That's something that I've realized, even most people that play on sessions don't do that. Especially, with the keyboards that I play, like the Chamberlains [Mellotron-style keyboard] and the pump organs, they tended to give it this beautiful spacious sound. Over the years, I've just loved layering stuff, I love acoustic instruments – it's all of those things at once, I really couldn't resist. I just sat and watched the monitor with Paul Thomas Anderson, the director. Usually, the composer just gets tapes dumped on his doorstep and has to do something. Then he goes to the session and if they don't like it they fire him and hire someone else. Paul and I basically sat and watched the movie together and it was really challenging and fun. Once again, Paul is a great director. All you have to do is watch his movies to see the caliber of performance he elicits from people. We had long talks about a lot of that sort of stuff – we actually see our jobs as very, very similar, a catalyst for people to be at their best, hopefully. Just like the good T-Bone instructions, Paul's instructions were never musical, his were all emotional. We would watch the screen and I would learn what sort of things I could do that would represent certain things he was looking for. Once he learned he could make any emotional suggestion and I could at least try to represent it... I think it became fun for him. He had this sort of human music machine sitting there, ready to generate ideas. For me, once I started learning what represented an emotion to him, then I was freed up musically to experiment however I wanted. I'd know what would constitute tension for him. So, I would start working in that realm, but then I had all the freedom. All of the horror stories that I've heard from other composers is some director sitting there going, "Is it flute? Is that the instrument? I think it needs more flute." That would drive me crazy, that's like any of the bad session tales I could tell you. So, this is really great, I'd walk into a room with an 80-piece orchestra, that is stunning to do and it was also cripplingly sad because I heard it and realized, "My god, this is what I'm always trying to get on record. We've got 80 people acting as one organism, but you've got all these subconscious' freed up to spill into the room." It's an incredible sound and there are layers, constant color change and it also comes off as one thing, constantly. That's a hard thing, in terms of production, to get color change, to keep the listeners interest up, that doesn't feel like constant gear shifting. With an orchestra, it's very easy to get that. I thought, "This is it, that's the fucking sound." I just wanted to hear a vocal on top of it and I wanted modern records that totally rock, not post Beatle quasi-baroque string section on top of a half-ass rock track. I just hate that shit, I love it on the Beatle records and I love some isolated versions on other records, but I hate that that is the only use for this instrument that is way better than the synthesizer in creating entirely new sound combinations. Here's the problem: Any record that you get to have a string section, it means that you have to have a budget. On Fiona [Apple]'s record, I got to have 22 or 23 string players for 3 hours and I had to do 3 tracks in that 3 hours. When the first hour was almost up it was like, "This isn't quite right,

but we've got to move on to the next one." This is a small string section and it's the only thing we used. It's just heartbreaking to realize that the price and the way the whole thing works makes it prohibitive for us to make records in a humane way and use this fantastic thing which took a few hundred years of work to get these instruments perfected. It's just going to be a lost art and it's heartbreaking.

I got to watch the sessions for the *XO* [Elliott Smith] record. I think they had a pretty long day and that must have cost a bit. It all went pretty well, they had done a good arrangement job on it and they based it on Elliott's keyboard parts. Is that how you did the *Magnolia* stuff?

That's how it started. Then I would work hard on the harmony and counterpoints.

Did you have someone help you with the arrangements?

I had a guy named Thomas Positiere acting as a, sort of, orchestrator who, once I had things together, he would come and make a proper full score. He's incredibly talented; he basically works for half the major film composers in town. The more I learned about it, most of the guys can write a thumbnail sketch and they have a roomful of orchestrators that they hand stuff off to. To tell the truth, a lot of these film scores have to be written fast – you don't have time to do it yourself. Essentially what you do is you write the melody the rhythm and the harmony. They write, maybe, a 6 line score. This guy is marvelously fast and he was also great to be around. As the project went along, I had developed more of what the tonality of the movie was going to be. Thomas, as an orchestrator, had gotten to know my tastes better. Initially, I was taking time writing out every little tidbit, coming up with every little part and making sure it was right, then we would make a score off of that on the computer and make corrections. After awhile, when the tonality was together, it got to the point where we had had such a wonderful rapport where I could go, "Okay, here's the ostinato that's going to be continuing on the bottom, it'll modulate here at this bar, I want woodwinds to play this chord." But I wouldn't bother at that point anymore to say how they were going to be voiced in terms of which instrument in the 8-piece woodwind section, because we had already come up with certain tonalities and colors that worked. As the project went on I was able to trust him more and more and I actually get what I wanted. It was enthralling – that's a very unique skill on his part and it's a hugely hard job. He did a wonderful job conducting.

That must've been fun to hear stuff that you had written being played like that.

It was thrilling and depressing. It's like, "My god, the only time I'm ever going to do this again is if I do another movie."

You can't see being able to do another pop record that way...

No, it would cost so much money. You could go out and make a bunch of records for people for the cost of just making one of those. ✪

A VISITING OUTBOARD RACK

JOE'S GEAR

DAVE AND JOE

In the recording world Joe Chiccarelli is very well known. He got his big first break engineering Frank Zappa's *Sheik Yerbouti*, which turned out to be a big seller, and now he's respected for his work with Hole, Tori Amos, U2, American Music Club, Beck, Shawn Colvin, The Stranglers, Stan Ridgeway and many more. He is a classic LA producer, bringing huge racks of gear to the studio and renting more, but he is also really down-to-earth about recording, what makes a great song, and interested in crazy sounds and cool gear. Plus he's a big fan of *Tape Op*! We caught Joe while he was up in Portland working at Supernatural Sound (where Craig manages and engineers) producing an album for Five O'Clock People. He was also in the middle of recording an album for The Pulsars in Chicago at King Size Sound Labs. A busy guy. We met at Jackpot! and had a lively conversation over bagels and coffee.

JOE AND White Tape

by Larry Crane and Craig Smith

Joe Chiccarelli

One thing that I really picked up from you is that it's not about what gear you set up. I mean, it's important to pick the right mic and all that, but you go for whatever sound is emotionally compelling, not necessarily which sound is better technically.

Yeah, I really believe in that. I mean, everyone is a fan of Tchad [Blake]'s stuff. Tchad's stuff, by all standards, is tweaked and bizarre and everything else, but man it sucks you into the music and it supports the songs. I think the more I do this I find it's like this deep emotional process of stripping myself of everything I know about all this and getting to the music. Thinking, "How can all this bring out the best in the song?" Sometimes it is the super hi-fi glossy recording and other times it's the total broken, cheap microphone and tons of distortion, compression and everything else. Basically what's going to really, emotionally, make you have some kind interaction with the song.

How do you find the right approach to things like that. You get a certain amount of time to work with an artist and you're trying to get to that level. I always find that's the hardest thing for me.

It's weird. Sometimes it's a real simple intuitive thing that you instantly know, "Oh, okay, I know what will make this work." Other times it's like this process of elimination; of thinking, "Okay, this is the way I know to get to it," and you go there. Yeah, you're right, that stuff can eat up time and it can burn people out and all that. I mean, obviously, if you're producing a record you go through preproduction and all that. The thing I really try to do is to get close to the artist and try to figure them out and try to figure out what they want. The best records that I've done, in terms of that, are records where I've understood what the artist was all about. That includes understanding their weaknesses too, knowing what to avoid and where to push them and that sort of thing. I'm sure everybody goes about it different ways, but I think that the more you're in tune with the song, even if it's a really horrible song, you try to figure it out. "Okay, this is really horrible, but where's the beauty in it, where's the one great thing, how can we make more of that and less of this other stuff that makes it weak." On whatever level you are, at the time. I don't mean level of expertise, but I mean level of like: Are you connecting with the technology, are you connecting with the arrangement, are you connecting with the songwriting? What are you working on at the time? You have your catalogue of sounds in your head. If I use this old crystal mic through this piece of gear, I'm going to get this kind of result. **The more work we've done the more things we have to draw from.**

Absolutely. I know for me, personally, the more I do different types of music the better I get. It always seems like if I do an industrial record and the next record I do is a folk record that there's something you bring with you from that other project that you, unconsciously, subtly incorporate into this new thing. It somehow makes it makes it a little hipper, a little more unusual, and you don't even know what it is. It's not like you go "Hey guys let's use this distorted loop." It's just having that wealth of experience, of different variety. Any player will tell you that if he can play classical stuff, country stuff or whatever; he can bring more things to the table in terms of the nuance in his performance.

In my case I'm sort of the house engineer and studio manager. I get to watch everyone who comes in and that's a great thing. I tell you, I learned so much more from that than I ever learned from reading Mix or Modern Recording Techniques.

I think, ultimately, the best way to learn is to make the mistakes yourself, to do it. Sometimes I wish that I was assisting [assistant engineering] longer than I actually had because I loved seeing Geoff Emerick and Geoff Workman at work. All those people who are like monster guys. A lot of times when I produce stuff I won't engineer it because it's too cumbersome. It's always good getting someone like Craig or this guy in LA, Chris Fuhrman, that I work with [who's also mixing the Five O'Clock People album]. It's sort of like, "Well what if we did it like this?" "Yeah, okay sure, try it." The next thing you know it's like "Wow that's exactly what I was thinking of." Maybe a different route, but it's great. So there's a lot of ways to get to the same point.

There two things that can happen that I've found out: One is that everyone plays it way too safe. Or different ideas are introduced and people kind of feed off each other. Occasionally there's that time where somebody else is producing and I just feel like I can't do anything.

It's probably that way 50% of the time. But I love being proven wrong, 'cause then you know what the right way is. You really think you should be going down this road and then someone goes, "Well, wait a minute. What if you did this?" and bingo, you're there. Who cares how you got there or what it took in the end. It's the end result that matters. No one really cares what the process involved was.

I read in Mix, they were asking you and these other engineers about recording vocals. You kept saying "Well, try this, but really it always changes and I can't say that this always works."

There's nothing that works with vocals! The mic that works for one person, usually doesn't work for anybody else and a lot of times it's different mics for different songs. Preamps and parts of the room and acoustic spaces and motivations and headphone mixes and all that stuff. It's, once again, the performance and all this stuff is a means to that end.

The '80s were a strange time for recording.

I hated having the three digital reverbs on the snare drum and all that goofball stuff. Somewhere in the mid-'80s, after the Linn drum machine became this staple - where every record had some kind of drum machine incorporated into it - I started noticing that when people heard anything that had a drummer with real time or choruses that moved and verses dipped, that people were physical uncomfortable listening to it. They got so used to listening to these programmed beats where everything was quantized. I mean physically they couldn't dance to it on a dance floor. That's kind of sad to me. Even if you go back to all those '60s and '70s disco records that you go and dance to, they groove. They don't have perfect time, but they groove.

I find that a lot of bands think they need to add keyboards and percussion. It's always this last minute thing that ends up being the most embarrassing stuff. They realize they don't know where to fit a little thing on the keyboard, or that nobody can play the tambourine.

Percussion, though, can really make a record. It's weird, those little touches that just bring things to life. Sometimes it can totally cement a funky groove on a track. You're always looking for that glue in a record that holds it all together. The one organ pad or the electric guitar thing, whatever it is that fills all the missing holes.

You're always mixing, how you track and how you'll put something down on track and you do a lot of bouncing tracks to set levels and things.

I hate that indecisive thing. I try to approach it like, "Okay, I've got a picture of where I want this record to go" I just aim for that. So, in a sense, I'm always mixing and that means I'm putting stuff down on tape at the levels and in the balance that I want. I mean, I don't put all the faders at zero and record like that. But I definitely record things so you can leave the faders at one level and there's your record. If you know this part needs to be subtler in the verses you record it a little lower. We did that with the Leslie track - as we put the guitar/Leslie track down on one song, I sat there and rode the levels. During a couple of big sections in the song I swelled it up. You can probably do a little bit more or less of it when you mix. But at least every time you bring up the song it isn't this guess work thing of, "Where's my record, where do I want it to go." There's the song the way it's supposed to be. If there's three things on a track- there might be a background vocal in the verse a tambourine in the chorus and guitar in the bridge - I'll print them at the level they're supposed to be in the mix so that fader can sit there the whole time. You don't have to go, "Oh yeah I forgot the bridge is coming up, I've got to crank that guitar way down." All the stuff that takes you out of the picture for a second. I'll print all effects and stuff, I mean I won't print them on a lead vocal track, but any kind of guitar effects or whatever. The more I can get to the finished mix in the overdub stage during tracking. I mean I have no fear about compressing, EQing, or printing effects or whatever. I want it to be done.

When you were having me do that little mix yesterday I just pushed the faders up. It felt a little bit silly. I sat there for a few minutes going, "What do I do? I should be mixing." I put a little slap on the vocals and then it was like, "You want to look at this?"

Yeah it was like, "Put some more top on the vocal and turn up the accordion. We're done."

Part of that probably, I would imagine, would help with the overdubs stage, because when people are hearing what they're working on is starting to sound like it's gelling.

Exactly. And you go, "Okay, this sounds like the song, this sounds like the record, but you know what? The outro is missing something. That's the only part that falls short for me." I hate that thing of every time you're working on a project for awhile, if you don't commit early on it seems that every time you bring up the tracks you get a totally different balance and a totally different approach to where the song goes. Obviously, sometimes, that can be a magical thing, but for the most part it feels like every time you put up the record it's a different record.

Headphone mixes are often neglected.

That's really true. With vocals more than anything. It's great because I'll sit there and tweak a headphone mix and in the sense of like if I see somebody's really ahead of the beat or behind the beat. I give them different things to make them play differently.

And it really works, I've been really amazed at how well it works. You just find that thing that makes them lock.

I always feel bad for players, you know, having to sit there and work on headphones it's just horrible. I'll always try to bring somebody into the control room as often as possible.

I try to offer that often. A lot of times people don't want that.

Really? They feel uncomfortable?

I'd much rather drag my bass around....
YEAH! Definitely!

I don't know why people would pass on that.

I think it's kinda nice to feel more anonymous on the other side of the glass. That way you don't feel that the guy's right there watching you make mistakes.

You can blame the headphone mix!

I've worked with guys that are operating in the control room and they're like, "Okay, give me a little bit more me, and little bit more of that, more of that. Turn the overall up." Bingo! The performance is locked in.

I've had that with bass players a lot of the time. You go back and retrack their bass and you can just nail it.

Yeah, it's actually better sometimes. It's really better than what they put down. And you would always think, "Well gee, they're in there with the drummer. It's happening at the same time, they're three feet away from the drummer." It should be better, but it's not. Yeah it's weird. I have this voodoo thing about that performance thing so I'm always spooked about like that original bass track being locked in and I'm always nervous about redoing it and stuff. I'll go back fifteen times and listen to the original and the new one and well, it's better! Gee.

sor 'cause chances are from note one it's going to be great. Imagine what it was like recording Sinatra or James Brown or someone like that.

Get it right the first time?

First time? Like before the tape rolls. 'Cause they're on ya know?

It's like working with Dylan even to this day, like his best takes are his first or second takes and then forget it, he's not going to do it again. Daniel Lanois discovered that, I think, where's he's actually gotten good albums out of some of these takes. Because he gets them the first time through and builds around that.

There's something to that. I always wanted to work with Van Morrison - I always loved Van Morrison as an artist. And somebody told me this great story about where he insists that the tape machine, the two-inch tape machine, is rolling in record when he walks in the building. I'm assuming that the band is out there ready to play and Van walks in and if he feels inspired, man, he doesn't want to wait. It's great! It's obviously extreme, but there's something to be said for it. Capturing that moment. There's a Brian Eno quote somewhere about "The best engineer in the world is the guy that is ready to get the vocal before it actually happens." In other words has the sound all set up and is ready to record because chances are you might miss something if you don't.

"Put some more top on the vocal and turn up the accordion. We're done."

You put a lot, especially on yourself and on whoever's assisting, a lot of pressure on them to keep the vibe going, so when the band starts nailing a song we can get take after take in no time.

Having to rewind a reel of tape, sometimes in that minute and a half that it takes to get to the top of the reel the focus can be blown. That's the one thing that I think is different between experienced players and younger players. You have to build this momentum to this point where you will get three or four good takes right in a row. Where I think those seasoned guys are capable of delivering that level all the time, anytime. That's the one thing that I'll say about all the studio guys, they're pretty amazing like that. Usually with those guys you got to be together at capturing that first performance 'cause usually it will be the best, where with inexperienced people it's like the tenth one. It's always tricky especially with vocalists. Working with Etta [James] you'd better guess the mic pre level, you better guess the compres-

I've been really super conscious that the recording process should be really kind of hidden to the artist in the studio. I try to maintain a really low profile in a way, just try to make it seem like we are just rolling through. "Oh, let's do some vocals. Yeah. I'm all ready to go." You want to be invisible in a way.

That's a good point.

I had a band comment the other day "Everything you did was so fast, you were ahead of us, you had drum sounds. Everything was moving really good." They had never been in that experience before. They worked in small studios before.

Where everybody sort of learning as they go. So it's the whole constant process of fiddling about.

It makes me feel bad if something's not patching right. Just like, "I'm really sorry. Go have lunch."

It's true, that thing of always moving foreward, the shark.

There's Oblique Strategies that apply to most of this stuff.

I have the Oblique Strategies cards in my Palm Pilot [hand-held computer]. You dial them up. I find that stuff for me it's a little more helpful in mixing. I don't actually use it that much. It's usually more like, "Hey, let's show the band this." People would get a kick out of it. In mixing I'll just think "Okay, what's wrong with this picture." And I'll think. "What's the most outrageous thing in this record. Let's make it more outrageous" Or "What's the moodiest thing. Let's make it moodier." When you think, "Okay, this pad, or whatever they put down, is nice and vibey and stuff. It sits there and it's really doing a nice thing." Then you think, "Well why don't I even make more of that than this" Even though it's working and it's accurate. It's weird when you deliberately make moves. You know, double everything or look at the subtlety as opposed to the big picture.

Take the weakest element and make it stronger. Things like that make you go, "Let's see." It's good.

That's one thing I don't mean to transgress, but sometimes working with somebody else in terms of a mix is a good thing because you'll sort of feature one part that you got hooked on. He'll kind of look at you and go, "You really like that? This thing over here is really cool."

Just to touch on the nuts and bolts thing though. It wouldn't be a good _Tape Op_ interview without mention of equipment. You carry a lot of equipment with you, but I was surprised when all the racks showed up. Yeah, you have some nice high end stuff but you've got a lot of toys, that are just cheap, cheap stuff. What are some of the greatest things that you've found, cheap stuff, that you can find out there.

Everyone's hip to old Altec stuff now. Those Shure Level-Locks are just mondo ridiculous compressors. I use stomp boxes all the time. We'll put stuff through it all the time.

You carry a hundred of those things with you at least?

I probably have 50 or 60. That stuff to me... it's the cheap stuff to me that has more personality than the H-3000 and all that kind of stuff. It gets back to that old school thing about how those guys come up with stuff. They had to be really ingenious and they used tape loops around a mic stand and all that weird stuff. Maybe the modern day equivalent is to use cheap gear. You know, what's really good and I keep looking for: You ever see those Ibanez delays that were meant for guitar. They're this brown two rack space [AD202]?

Yeah we have one here in the studio.

Some of those early '80s things are really really good

because they bucket brigade [capacitance delay] stuff and they had a little bit of warmth to them but they had a little bit of cheese factor too. I think that stuff is great, overload the mic channel or all the obvious stuff you do.

You discovered the Audio Technica mics.

Yeah man, this has got to be the best find of the year. Those Pro 37Rs. We put them up the first day, I don't know what we started with, [Neumann] KM 84 or whatever. I used those on acoustic guitar I love the way those 37Rs sound, and it sounded okay. I was knocked out by the sound. "Hey let's try this Pro 37R." Every song we'd start tracking I would keep taking them down and trying something else. Nine out of ten cases I would come back to it.

Did you use them for acoustic?

Mostly for acoustic guitar, some fiddle, some mandolin. We didn't try it on high hats.

Larry used to use them as overheads Yeah we used to use them here.

Man these are amazing. They're punchy sounding, they're present. I talked to a friend at Audio Technica and he said the problem is as a microphone company people expect them to build this thousand dollar fancy-shmancy studio pro microphone, and when they try to pitch to people this $100 microphone, everybody's like, "You're a big pro microphone company and this is what you're trying to tell me to use?" You go to the car dealer, you don't want the bottom of the line model, even though it might be a really great car. You'd rather get the top of the line thing because you think it's got everything. That is the find of the year. I love that microphone. You never know if it's maybe that there's not much in there electronically or that maybe it's really simple. It's got this low end punch thing that's really cool.

A sort of darkness to it. That's what I always tell people.

Yeah exactly. And for these guys it works especially well cause they play Takamines, all those tinkley guitars. It's not like a Gibson, Martin, or Guild where it's got that chunky mid range thing. That's been one big challenge for this record. How can I get some kind of midrange in the record. There isn't in anything that they play. They have airy voices, bright guitar sounds, mandolins, fiddles. The record's scooped out before you start scooping it out. So it's like how do I find instruments, how do I find things in the arrangement, how do I find sounds that will fill in that gap in the record. Those mics were a total godsend.

What about old digital stuff. There's a lot of fun old digital stuff that people kind of neglect because people are rejecting digital.

We were talking about Delta Lab Effectrons. I think that thing is great. It maybe a little noisy, but for a quick little flange or chorus I think they're totally cool. I think those old Ibanez-Sony 201 reverbs are kinda cool. You can pick up one for $200 for that really slick reverb sound. They're really great.

And built like a tank. Yamaha Rev 7's.

Yeah, Rev 7s are worth $350 or something now. Yamaha SPX 90s - I live by those things. I love those. I like effects that are dark because they usually, for me, find their way in the track a little bit better than all that tinkley shit.

My effects return area over here has just a high and low EQ on it. Just roll off the high end and everything starts to fit together.

I roll the top off the reverb all the time.

It's a trick that controls noise.

Definitely makes it so much quieter. A lot of cheaper reverbs give you hiss. The [Alesis] Microverbs have fun sounds and are so cheap, but you roll off a little highs and they're cleaner and fit in.

My favorite digital delay is the PCM 41 the 42 sounds great, but it's too clean.

It has this kind of dark, distorted weird thing to it.

And even though those are a really nice Lexicon, they're only $300 too.

Actually that [Lexicon] Vortex you have sounds really good. We used that once or twice.

Did you bring any mics up with you?

I got a new [Neumann] M 147 that I think sounds really good. It sounds really interesting. It's really present in the mids, that's really cool. We have D12 on the kick, we used the Audio Technica 4060 on Drew's vocals. I thought that sounded really good for him. [Sennheiser] 441 on the bottom of the snare. That's one of my favorite things, something about that mic for bottom snare mic. 'Cause it's kinda of sizzley sounding on top and it also rejects a lot of kick drum so I really like that underneath the snare drum. What else did we do?

As far as the rest of the mics we used. We used the Sony mics for overheads.

Oh yeah the C37s as overheads sound really great. Those things sound really good. I forgot how good they sound.

Craig loaned me one of them for quite awhile. I used it on vocals. For a string band [The Dickel Brothers] we used one C37 in omni with the guys around playing. We did stuff later with a single Earthworks.

I like those mics. I only used them once or twice they're a little too pristine and sweet and clear.

They're technical.

Yeah exactly! Like that B & K thing. Like an instrumentation mic or something.

They're like a measurement mic. They're really good for overheads. Kind of center them around the cymbal you're trying to accent more. Then use a room mic looking at the drums and you get a good quick balance on drums.

We actually did that for a bunch of things. I was trying to get the record to sound as big and punchy and sort of like a balance between natural and radio friendly.

We tried my Sytek mic pres.

I thought they had a little tinselly thing on the tip top too. They had that kind almost Massenburg quality to them.

They're just so slick sounding. When I first got mine I'd been running through like these 1272 Neves or my Neotek. When I plugged those things in I literally thought that somebody had shot a lot of silicon spray into the mic cable or something cause the sound came through so much faster.

Right. They are really fast sounding. Like the Hardy's and stuff, they're super fast.

It was unbelievable - it sounded like everything improved.

As much as I'm addicted to Neve's I forget how slow they can be. Obviously for the bottom end stuff you can't get better, but even like the difference between an API and a Neve on snare drum or whatever. They're really quick. These things were even faster than any of that old gear.

They peak out really easy.

Really?

I haven't found an outboard pad that I like yet. That's the problem

I know it's like sometimes you're stuck doing that thing and there's something about it. I don't know if everyone is using cheap resistors or if it's going through... I don't know what it is but none of those things sound good.

I'm so wary using pads at all. I know people turn them on all the time.

I find it's just another sound. Like I'll bring up a fader and if I find that's it's almost like too punchy or too aggro sounding, I'll put the pad in and bring the trim up. You find that it softens it a little bit. I use mic pres like a compressor. That thing of figuring out how hard something needs to be hit. You know like the toms, like Neve's or old Tridents on toms. That was the trick that those guys did. They would bring the pres up just to the point where they were crapping out and then maybe back it off one notch. They would run those hotter, so you would get more bottom or more compression out of the mic pre.

You don't run a lot of compression on individual drums but you do a lot with room mics. You put a lot of compression on that.

I like really hearing the transients. I kind of get a little nervous mucking with it going to tape. If I compress the snare, it will be with that second mic. Very rarely would I compress the overall snare thing. Unless there was a certain thing I was really going for. But it's like, "How much excitement I can get out of the drums", ya know? That transient thing seems to be pretty important in terms of making stuff sound natural, but also localizing the beat. If you got a kick drum that's squished a little bit, you can really mess with the time. I go crazy flipping phase buttons on things. Because really you can change the whole groove of something by pushing this snare drum back a little or the kick forward. Sometimes I use it to your advantage. What should hit you first.

I can really hear that sometimes. It feels nice. The snare is outside of the mix and then bring it back in. I never make up my mind because nothing is ever 180 degrees out of phase.

Jonathan Little, who's this tech in LA that used to work at A&M for years, was actually building a box that was a two millisecond super high quality delay. That's what your doing when you're time shifting basically. So that's what he was going to do specifically for bass amp. So you could dial it in.

We talked about delaying the DI a tiny tiny bit. Line it up, but if you don't want to destroy your signals in a cheap delay.

No, but if you do it on a bass amp, it's usually a tortured signal to begin with. I always wanted something like that. I think that would be really great.

We were talking about mic pres and stuff. Have you ever come across any really inexpensive ones that are good or any kind of substitutes. You know for someone with a small set up and a cheap mixer and they trying to find some way around this whole thing.

Everyone knows the evils of the Mackie mic preamp. They're small and hard. You have to be really safe with them or you have to use them as a distortion generator. There's no inbetween.

Well you were saying you liked some of the early Allen & Heath consoles.

Yeah Stan Ridgeway, from Wall of Voodoo, and I made this record at his place and he had this old Allen & Heath console. It was this ugly brown color. He got it from Stewart Copeland. This thing sounded amazing - the mic pres sounded great on it. I was really really impressed with that console. We ran a lot of stuff through it and the record sounded really cool.

Overall I'm pretty impressed with older SoundCraft stuff.

Yeah some of the stuff was really really good. The Neotek sounds really great. Dave Trumfio's [King Size Sound Labs in Chicago] got an Elan, which is not the top of the line one. I think that thing sounds pretty good.

Yeah we were looking for one for here. We were trying find something like that.

I think that they're like 40 grand maybe.. Not cheap at all.

You can get them cheaper than that though. I've seen them down as low as $15,000. For a console that good that's cheap.

Yeah, I don't know. I haven't used PreSonus things or any that other people are building like those eight channel preamps. There's a lot of great stuff out there.

I was wondering if you had tried any of the ART mic pres.

No, I haven't tried that at all. A lot of people I know really like that. Honestly, I haven't tried that.

Bellari/Rolls?

No I haven't heard that either.

It's interesting.

Is it?

Yeah it can be really good. It can make overheads kinda come to life in a weird way. I think it adds a little break up.

A little crunch on the front end stuff. What other gear...

> **"I like effects that are dark because they usually, for me, find their way in the track a little bit better then all that tinkley shit."**

It's always fun to tell people...

The only problem doing that...

You start that cycle going.

Yeah and prices shoot up.

"Albini recommended it."

It's like ribbon mics. Trying buying a ribbon mic now? Forget it. I always think if I'm putting up a ribbon I'm putting it up for a reason. I wanted that rolled off chunky dark soft thing. King Size has this Beyer M320, which kind of looks like Beyer's version of a D12, but it's squarer around the edges. This thing rocks, it's great on guitars. It's really fat sounding but it's got a little bit of bite to the attack. IF ANYONE OUT THERE KNOWS WERE TO FIND ONE CALL ME! I've been looking for one. It really sound good. Those Altec 1591 compressors I think are really good. Those old Altecs you can get them for like $350. As a discrete compressor they're really good. Now everyone is into the broadcast stuff.

We've got some Orban things in the back.

I was mixing this record recently, and the guys wanted it to have this really tweezed '70s-'80s sort of sound, Like that New Wave sort of sound. I did the whole mix with that in mind kinda got it close, and I was like, "I don't know if this works." The studio I was working at had one of those old Orban Parametrics. I put it through that and added a tiny bit of EQ. But just going through this thing it was like phase shift city. And instantly it sounded like a Thompson Twins record or something. It was so cool. We just ran the mix through it. it just gave it this fizzely, cone filter bad IC kind of sound. It was the funnest thing. I was like, "Wow, and people used these all the time on everything."

I think that's one of the points we could even make is that, what we're saying about the ribbon mics. A lot of times being technically good, or having good specs on a piece of gear means nothing.

Exactly they just say, "This will do this and look how impressive this is.

Goes to 20 kHz.

Right, who cares! Sometimes your better off with a piano if the top is 6k. You get rid of all that weird ringing overtone, that on one particular piano might be a bad thing.

We had that $5,000 tube compressor in the studio the other day. Somebody brought it in for us to try out. And we were trying to make the thing sound good and we just couldn't. I just didn't like the sound of it. I wasn't drawn at all to the sound of it.

It's super open and super clean. If you were doing a film score or if you were doing a solo acoustic guitar, I think it would probably be great. But I tend to gravitate towards things that have a lot of character. Having this list in your brain of a hundred and ten different sounds and then going "Okay, let's pick this one for that." Maybe if you had the best bass player with brilliant tone then you wouldn't want to change it any way, then that's the best way to record. Through something like an Avalon or Massenburg. But a lot of times people bring in funky instruments or they're not great players or the particular character of their instrument doesn't work well in the setting of the song. You have to find the piece of gear that helps incorporate it. You want something that has its own character, you put it through a cheezy old direct box or the B-15 guts that you have. Have you've tried that thing he's got?

No.

Somebody took the preamp section of an Ampeg B15 and turned it into a direct box. It sounds really sweet. We used mandolin, and fiddle...

And guitar.

sounds really good.

Running a mic into it?

So we were just running the pickup into it. Just using it like a direct box, not really using the tone controls, just like going through this thing.

Where did you get that?

I got it at a garage sale, believe it or not. It was already rack mounted. It cost me $25. One of my best garage sales finds ever. I paid $25 and that same night I went and got rid of my Alembic preamp, which cost me almost $800. The Alembic just sounds like crap. I didn't want it anymore.

Yeah that's a really good sounding box. That's where the '80s went awry electronically. Everybody started eliminating transformers and all that stuff because it rings and it does this to the top end. All these new microphones, people aren't using transformers now. It's a different sound, but that's the one thing about going through those old Collins and old Gates and stuff. Even if you don't use the compressor, just going through all that iron, just rounds things out and it rings in a certain way. I was telling Craig about this time when Bob Ludwig mastered a record for me and I just hated the way the mixes sounded. I was just hating life, no matter what I did I couldn't get this record to sound right. It was off of all digital stuff, and it just sounded cold. I thought it was me - I hated the job I had done. It didn't sound right to me, no matter how I EQ'd it. I sent it to Bob, thinking, "Oh man he's going to hate me." Getting the phone call like, "What happened to you, this really sounds terrible. I had to use 40 dB EQs to make it sound like music," and all these sort of things. He sent me the disc and I listened to the disc and it sounded brilliant. I sheepishly called him back going, "Ok, read me the riot act Bob, what did I do, how bad, what did you have to fix." He was like, "No, you know I thought it sounded cold so I took this old pair of transformers that I have in the rack here, and I just ran the mix through the transformers. I didn't EQ it hardly at all." It sort of rounded the top off and rounded the bottom off and made it sound a lot more musical.

And he got paid how much for doing that?

So it takes five grand for him to figure that out. But I do think that is the brilliance of a great mastering engineer. Knowing that one final little element that will take your mix to the next point. If it's a 100 dB of compression or if it's...

You don't want that mastering engineer to go, "Sounds great." And you're like, "No, no, fix it."

Sometimes you do need that objectivity of him to say, "You know this does sound great. I'm not going to touch this. Let me even out the level of the songs, and we're done." I think that is the art of the great mastering engineer. Knowing what not to do. As a mixer, I'm sure everybody likes a large percentage of what Bob Clearmountain does. I've had Bob mix stuff for me and I think that's his brilliance, knowing what not to do. Knowing when to be subtle and when to be extreme. There's like a really great art to that. There's not a lot of old great mastering engineers left - most of them are retiring. So where are new great mastering engineers?

We've got this guy Troy we use up in Seattle at Spectre. I've been really happy because he leaves stuff alone and lets it breathe. Yet it comes out being a loud CD. I've been really happy, and he's young.

That's really cool. Nancy Hess [a Portland artist] was telling me that she loved what Tony Lash did on her CD. She thought Tony was awesome.

Tony's very good.

Tony can save things. Tony saved my band's record.

I'm amazed, having sat in on two sessions with Tony.

You know that's something for your readers, because I'm sure everybody's been burnt by bad mastering once in their life. I have no fear saying to somebody, "Look, I'm not sure who's the best mastering guy for this record. Would you do one song on trial?" Obviously Bob Ludwig won't to that for you because he's booked until November, but I think a lot of guys will do that. I think just like somebody might cast a musician for a certain part or use a certain studio for a certain sound. I think mastering applies too. I think that there are certain guys that know how to make aggressive records there are certain guys who know how to make hi-fi records. I always wait until I'm done with my mixes to go, "This record is a little wimpy. I've got to send it to Howie [Weinberg] cause I know Howie is going to make it aggressive. With a band like Five O'Clock People, I know that it's got to be really musical and hi-fi to some degree. It's got to be a little tweaky, but it has to be hi-fi, so then I send it to Bob Ludwig.

"It's how much excitement I can get out of the drums."

I do that as well, I take things to Tony, I refer things to Spectre. Different projects, given, what I know people's different strength's are.

I think that's really important. If you're a producer you would have your Roll-A-Dex of players and know that this guy is good for that. You got to do the same with mastering engineers or mixers or whatever. Sometimes you know going into it. "I don't think this guy is going to get this music." Twisted guitar whatever stuff. He does bluegrass records. He won't get it. ☮

BOB

We get a lot of requests for future interview subjects and Bob Weston has easily been one of the most mentioned. Bob is known for his spacious, natural-sounding recording style and being a member of the band Shellac (which also contains engineer Steve Albini) but it was interesting to find out that he had a degree in electrical engineer. It also doesn't hurt that he's done recordings for artists like Sebadoh, Polvo, Thinking Fellers Union Local 282, Arcwelder, Coctails, Rodan, 6 Finger Satellite, Eric's Trip, Archer's of Loaf, the Rachel's, Tony Conrad, Plush, June of 44, and Delta 72. I met up with him while he was in Portland recording an album for the Kung Fu's at Supernatural Sound.

You like to use a good room space to get sound on the whole band. That's one of the things you're kind of known for. Steve's [Albini] also kind of known for it too, using the acoustic space to get really good drum sounds and stuff like that, as opposed to just close mic'ing.

The first time I heard a record Steve had recorded I was really blown away by it. It was probably the Pixies record or the Wedding Present or Jesus Lizard. I learned a lot about that "live-room" type of recording from him and then I guess I've taken it in my own direction. But the basic recording methodology... the way I record using the room sound... I learned it from Steve. I guess that's sort of lame, but I don't know what to tell you. He's been my engineering mentor. Those records sounded really great to me and I wanted to know how to get those sounds. So I asked him how he did it and then tried to do what he described as best as I could. But of course it doesn't come out quite the same. Over the phone I would ask him how to tune drums, or which mics to use and where to put them. Obviously, these sorts of things can't be adequately described over the phone, so what I did became my version of the "Steve-method". I would try to do what he described, but would use my ears to guide me and figure out what worked best - what sounded good to me. I will still ask Steve questions and we'll discuss different things we've each been trying lately. I suppose I've moved from apprentice up to colleague. In the beginning, I would

do it all by rote. Now I understand why I'm using a certain mic and where I'm putting it and can make reasoned decisions about all this. But the basic recording method is still very similar.

More just the approach?

It's more not being afraid to use plenty of the ambiance mics in the mix and really paying attention to the live sound of the drum set. I assume you're mostly talkin about the drums?

That's where I hear it. It seems to be or other things too.

It has to do with paying a lot of attention to getting th drums tuned right, having a good sounding room and knowing where to put the kit in the room.

Do you ever feel like you're kind of ir the shadow of Steve in a way Recording wise or... You always ge lumped in with him.

When I first started doing recording it really served m well. My association with Steve really helped. Wha can I say? I've learned so much from him. He's really great engineer. He's a really great teache When I was first working in Chicago, it definitely g me more work than I would have had if I was ju sitting in Boston telling people I was a recordir engineer. That helped out, so I can't really compla about it. Yet today people will come up to me, peop I know, friends of mine, and ask, "So, are you st working with Steve?" What do you mean workir with Steve? I have never worked with Steve. I on worked for him, but that was six years ago. He and have never made a record together.

WESTON

by Larry Crane

Besides Shellac, but you're not...

Right, but we have never collaborated as engineers on a project. I was there for the Nirvana record, but I was mainly there in case something blew up. Some people assume that we are tag-team partners, or something.

Do you ever get to do pre-production with bands?

I don't think I ever have.

It'd be nice, wouldn't it?

I don't know. I've never done it so it's hard to say. It would be interesting to try that more involved pre-production thing where I work with the band before the actual recording. Right now for me, pre-production would be making sure all the gear worked right and making sure there were no hums or buzzes. Make sure the amps work and the drums work and aren't squeaking and don't have parts falling off them. I was recording this band a few weeks ago and three of the tension rods on the bass drum didn't work.

They were just all stripped?

Yeah.

No one noticed, huh?

No. It was a bummer. But with the drums, another thing I have to keep in mind is the cash situation for the band. If there's a label paying for it I'll say, "Hey, you should get top and bottom heads for the toms. You should get new heads for everything." If they're coming in to do two songs in one day and they're paying out of their pocket I'll say, "Lets just use what's already on the drums." If they want to spend a little I'll say, "Okay, we'll do the top

heads." You know, you have to balance it all out. But if the budget's available, I try to get them to get all new drumheads. Although I usually prefer the Ambassadors, certain people sound better with Emperors. If they're hitting so hard that the Ambassadors are just completely deformed within an hour, then I'll get them to use Emperors. But the Ambassador, because it's a single-ply head, resonates louder and longer - it doesn't dampen itself. If you can get the heads tuned to the resonance of the drum shell, when you whack that thing it excites the shell and everything and the whole thing is loud and full sounding.

When we were discussing preproduction you brought up a good point, that if the gear sounds good, part of your battle is already won as far as recording.

It's true. Sometimes people ask, "Oh, do you have amps at the studio?" or "We're gonna borrow a drum kit," or "We're gonna borrow an amp for the recording." That always freaks me out a little bit. I ask, "Aren't you used to your sound?" Or, "Haven't you been working on a sound that you like in the practice space for the last year getting ready for this record? Why are you all of a sudden going to change things for this record?" That always seems silly to me.

They might be uncomfortable using the new gear, too, which might throw off the performance.

Yeah, or they'll say, "When we get to the studio we can work on guitar sounds." I'm like, "Look, if you haven't

already worked on your guitar sound, I don't know what help I'm going to be. Do you want me to stand in front of the amp and turn the treble up and down for you?" I'm talking about bands that have a very limited budget. They can't afford much time in the studio, so I don't want them to waste it trying to find some mystery "perfect" guitar sound. It's about efficient use of the expensive studio time.

The idea that people should come in ready to go...

The bands that we record are BANDS. They operate as a band. They have a vision for what they want the music to sound like. They want it to sound like what it sounds like in the practice space. They've been working on the songs for a year and I assume that they want the same guitar sound they've been using. I'm surprised when they don't seem to like that sound and want to come up with a new one in the studio.

Looking at the guitar and then looking at you and saying, "Does it sound good?"

"I don't know. Does it sound good? You tell me. It's your record."

Do you think that bands that want to record the way you like to record are finding you? It doesn't seem like you're going to be hammering them into doing it a certain way.

Of course not. I'll record any way they want. And not all the bands I record want to have that live big room sound anyhow. A lot of them do, but I record a lot that don't work that way. I record albums where they want it to be more separate and dead sounding and not as real sounding - strange sounds, nonrealistic sounds. When people hire an engineer they obviously are calling someone because they have heard records he has done and they're like, "Wow, this guy sounds like the engineer for me." So, of course, if they've heard other records I've done they'd hire me like they'd hire you based on records you've done.

Yeah, I think like The Kung Fu's definitely sought you out.

They said they e-mailed me as a gag. They didn't think anything would come of it. They thought it was funny. They e-mailed me asking, "Can you record us?" And I e-mailed back, "Yeah, sure. When?"

What did they think? That because they've seen your name on records they own you were unreachable or something?

Apparently. It completely blows my mind when people tell me this. I don't have lots of work, but at the same time, for some reason, some bands just assume I won't record them. Or that I'm too busy. Or that I'm too expensive. Or that I only approach bands - bands aren't allowed to approach me about recording. I don't know where in the world this came from. I have never approached a band to record them. I get my work from word of mouth or people just calling me up out of the blue. When I hear that someone's afraid to call me or assumes they can't call me, I can't even believe it.

I think there's a lot of hero worship going on in rock n' roll. Not that you're someone's hero, but they might think that you're in a different league cause your name is on a few records they really like.

Yeah, but they don't think about the records I've done that they would probably hate. Sometimes people e-mail me saying, "I'd like to send you my tape and hear what you think about it." I'm flattered that they'd be interested in my opinion, but I'm not a music critic or an A&R guy. Why in the world do they want to know what I, personally, think of their music? They don't know what my taste is like. They assume that my taste corresponds to the records they own that I recorded. They assume that I've hand-selected those bands, and if I like their tape, they must be as good as these bands that they love. My personal taste has nothing to do with who I record. What they don't seem to realize is : 1. Those bands all picked me to record them. I didn't choose them, and 2. For every Rodan or Archer's of Loaf record I've worked on, I've done 100 other bands that they'd hate. They don't think about that part. Or the fact that I'm a Sheryl Crow fan, for instance.

You don't do every single job that anyone talks to you about?

I do. I don't recall ever turning one down.

Really? You've been lucky then, in a way.

I've been really lucky. I've enjoyed almost every single record I've worked on, even though most of the bands I had never heard of before I recorded them. I

think a lot of it has to do with being in a band and making a lot of friends over the years. When I first started recording I was friends with the guys in Sebadoh, so I got to record them a little bit. I met the guys in Polvo and later ended up doing an album with them. It was one of the first full LPs that I recorded. It was just because I'd met them a bunch of times and really liked them.

That Thinking Fellers EP [*Admonishing The Bishops*] was one of the first things you did, wasn't it.

Yeah, like the... the third thing I recorded. The Volcano Suns had played with them a few times and I had mixed them live on the radio in Boston once. I didn't totally know what I was doing in the studio yet during that EP session, but acted very confidently, like I had everything under control. I went to see them play the night after we finished and got really bummed out. They sounded so great live, I thought I had totally blown it in the studio. But I listened to that EP recently and thought, "Ahhhh, this IS ok, isn't it?" I think it was the very first time I recorded at Steve's. That was when I first moved out there to work for him as his studio tech. He hired me with the understanding that if the studio wasn't booked I could book bands in there too.

That's great. That was at his house?

It was a bungalow on the northwest side of Chicago.

That's crazy.

It worked out great. Hundreds of great sounding records came out of that house.

Apparently.

I don't know if I could do that. I don't know if I could have my house be the studio. The basement was the studio and the attic was the control room. Steve lived on the first floor. There was a kitchen, a living room, an office and a bathroom. And when a band was playing in the basement the whole first floor would be vibrating. Gratings would be going [makes loud vibrating grate noise].

Out of the bands that you've done, The Rachel's was something that I heard that was really different from the rock stuff.

Yeah I love recording The Rachel's.

Did you do a lot of that live? Or are you doing it in pieces. It seemed like it would be done in pieces.

No, most of it's live. But there's this new Rachel's album coming out where the recording is a little different. It's called *Selenography*. I know The Rachel's because I recorded the Rodan record. That's been my connection to a bunch of Louisville bands. People from Rodan are in Sonora Pine and June of 44, who I recorded. I also helped out on a Shipping News album and I've done a bunch for the Rachel's. Jason, from Rodan and the Rachel's, and I get along really well. He is really interested in recording and has picked up a lot. He's really good at it. He did all the Shipping News basic recording. So anyway, for the Rachel's we need to get a good piano and a real studio space to get the basic thing recorded. If it's a song that has piano we'll record it all live at the

studio. A new thing we did on this last session was to put rough mixes down to two tracks of a DA-88 that those guys bought. Then they went home to Louisville and filled both their DA-88s up with overdubs. We also would do overdubs onto the 24-track. So when we finally mixed this record at Steve's studio, Electrical, we used almost every fader on his 48 channel Neotek console as well as the automation. It was the only automated mix I'd ever done and it was necessary. We had the 24-track and both DA-88s running on some songs and on other songs we had only two channels going.

Oh my god.

The Rachel's are really fun to record because the instrumentation from song to song is radically different. It goes from string octet to solo harpsichord to piano, viola, cello, electric guitar, drumset. One of my best engineered records is a Rachel's record called *Music for Egon Schiele*. We recorded it at the University of Louisville in a recital hall on one of those Otari 1/2" 8-tracks. It was piano, cello, and viola. I just used six mics. I love the way that thing sounds.

Was it a good sounding space?

Yeah, it was a huge recital hall. It had a beautiful piano, as well. One of the best I've ever heard.

How long have you've been doing recording as a full time gig, just trying to get that to work?

I guess when I moved to Chicago, which was about seven years ago. It wasn't really full time at first. At first I was an employee of Steve's - his studio tech. So when I recorded bands the money went into the studio and I still got my normal weekly paycheck. I suppose you'd call that a house engineer type job. I worked there for about a year and a half until I had too much recording work and couldn't keep up with the tech work anymore. I couldn't keep everything fixed. So I thought it would be best if he got a real full time tech guy and I went freelance on the recording.

Have you worked at a lot of different studios since then?

Yeah. But I prefer working at Steve's place because I had so much to do with it and still do. It feels like home. In his new building I did all the audio system design: the wiring, layout and design, and patchbay and everything. I also designed the power system, the AC system. It's a balanced power system with some fancy grounding.

How did you learn all this?

I worked for a studio designer and I learned a lot of that from him. He designs studios, he's an acoustician, and he's a brilliant audio electronics guy. You can give him any piece of audio gear and he will make it sound a hundred times better. The other half I picked up from a radio station engineer named Grady Moates.

Who is the studio designer?

Bob Alach from Wellesley, Mass. He has a company called Alactronics. I worked for him for a couple of years. I did some architectural and electrical drafting for him. I learned a lot about studio wiring from him. He does recording studios, video editing suites, TV station audio, what else... control rooms, auditoriums, sou reinforcement, listening rooms, mastering labs and things. So I got a lot of the wiring knowledge from him. A lot of the systems knowledge from him. I still call him whenever I do this kind of work.

He knows it pretty well then?

Oh yeah, he's a brilliant man and a good friend. He designed one of the best sounding control rooms I have ever been in.

Where's that?

It's gone now, but it was at this studio in Boston called Squid Hell. It was in a house. A competing studio called the zoning board and had them shut down. The sheriff came down and made them take their gear out. All because this other studio was losing business to them. So they're moving. They're buying a building and starting over.

And it was a great sounding control room?

The control room was unbelievable. I was blown away.

I talked to Jack Endino about moving from studio to studio, keeping consistency. The problem he's found are that monitors and rooms are so different. What method do you use to get consistency?

I just read that interview and I saw that he carries around a spectrum analyzer. I've been wanting to do that for a while now. But the one that I want, this crazy Danish model, is pretty expensive. I have speakers that I carry around that I love.

What do you use?

These home hi-fi audiophile speakers. They're B&Ws - Model 805. They're the baby version of the big famous 801s, which are what all these classical music audiophile geeks use.

Are they pretty flat?

I don't know, they just sound right. I mixed on NS10s for a really long time, and Tannoys and lots of other speakers. I had these AR home bookshelf speakers that I mixed on for a while too. With every single other speaker I mixed on I always had to tell the band, "Okay, so you make it sound good on these, but you should have a little too much guitar." Or, "Don't worry that there's no low end. Trust me it's there."

Right, I say that all the time.

So when I first heard these, Shellac was at Abbey Road. We were using them and I was just blown away by how they sounded. I just tried to mix things to sound good on these speakers and the mixes translated everywhere. The mastering engineers didn't have to do as much to my work. The songs I mixed on them sounded good in a car, my home stereo, on a boombox, and to the band when they went home. It translated everywhere, so I'm like, "I'm buying a pair". I bought a pair, I bought a road case and they come with me.

Are they expensive?

They're sort of expensive. I bought mine in the UK where they're made, so I don't know what they cost over here. Probably a thousand bucks or something.

But if it's something you that can really help you.

They really help me a lot. The other thing about them that's so amazing is that you can sit there and listen to them all day and there's no ear fatigue. If I listened to NS10s for a couple of hours, I would just walk out of the control room and be like, "Don't talk. Don't make any sound, I don't want to hear anything. My head hurts." It was really draining.

I like the NS10 at low volume for mixing. Check my mixes on them kind of quiet. There's that midrange bump, it kind of helps me hear what's going on placement-wise. Then I use my Tannoys.

I've mixed with Tannoys, I don't have a problem with them. I've always wondered why there are studio monitors and home stereo speakers. Why are there two different lines made by two different groups of people? Why wouldn't you mix on speakers that the people at home will listen on? I could never figure that one out. I guess part of it is studio monitors are more robust - they can take higher levels. Maybe that's all there is to it. So that's what I use. Home hi-fi monitors work great for me. You know when you hit the wrong button and your speakers squeal, or go Ka-blam! Or you blow a tweeter on an NS10? I've had those same types of sounds come through mine and they've never even blinked. They can take more punishment for some reason. So I carry around those, and my microphones. That's all I really care about.

What mics do you like to bring?

I have a briefcase with pretty much all of my mics and I usually end up using all of them.

You have some Coles I heard.

I have one Coles mic, which I don't use that often. I love it on strings and it sounds awesome on electric guitars. But it can't really handle the chug-chug-chug guitar low end. They fart out, so I don't use them all the time. I've started using the BK-5 ribbon mic from RCA on electric guitars a lot.

Where do you find stuff at?

The first time I did any work for Steve I was still living in Boston and I flew out and wired his studio. It was long before he ever asked me to work for him full time. I wired his studio and he paid me by giving me a batch of starter mics. A little starter kit. I think the [Coles] STC 4038 was part of that starter kit. He just finds used gear, he's a real good scrounger.

I was wondering if you had any suggestion for getting a good electric bass sound for rock albums. I just want to pick your brain, see if you had any suggestion or ideas for recording that. Mics, DI, not DI, amp settings, where to put the amp...

I usually spend the least amount of time on the bass. It always seems to sound okay.

How do you do that?

I rarely use a DI. There's one mic that I use on bass almost every time. It's this Beyer mic that they don't make anymore: model 380. A large diaphragm figure-of-eight mic. Because it's figure-of-eight, it has a really super-duper proximity effect. So when you get it in really close you get really good super bottom. I

usually use two mics. If they have two cabinets, I'll put one on each cabinet. If they have one cabinet, I'll put them both on the one. The other mic I'll use is either a D112, or an AT 4033. If the bass player has a cabinet that has a bunch of different sized drivers I'll put the 380 on the biggest one and then put some small dynamic or condenser mic (maybe a 451 or a 57) on the horn, or in the ten. But even when they have that, most of the time I end up using just the 18 or the 15. There's usually enough high end out of that, you don't even need the other ones. Unless they bi-amp, which just never seems to work at all.

Do you compress to tape?

The bass? Not usually, but if it's called for.

The amp is going to be compressing it a bit anyway.

It depends on how loud they're playing. Lots of times there's speaker compression. When I play there's a lot of speaker compression.

Push it really hard.

I just like that mic, the 380. That's another one I got from Steve. They have a new version of it called the TGX 50.

Have you tried that?

Yes. It sounds a little different. I think for certain basses it will sound better. It's a little brighter and I think it's a hypercardioid.

See, I wanted some brilliant answers here, but I'm just getting, "Oh I put a mic on it." The bass usually sounds good on the things you've done. I like the sound of it. Maybe it's just bugging me. You know how everyone listening to their own recordings. You always want to be better.

I know - believe me. Maybe I just turn the bass up louder?

You're always struggling to become a better engineer and to get better sounds that you're happier with.

If I'm unhappy with the way the bass, or any instrument sound is going, I go down there with them and I adjust the amp. If it sounds right while standing in front of the amp, but wrong in the control room, I'll adjust the amp to try to get it to sound right on tape. It's always going to sound different when you're comparing the bass out of a 400 watt 15" speaker to the bass out of the near field monitors on the console.

I've done that a lot, but maybe I should just do that more.

I'm always saying, "Let's avoid EQ later, let's use the EQ on your amp." That's what I try to do.

Yeah, it's more trouble later to do.

I just said the 380 was good because you could get it in close. But I don't put it in that close. I try to keep the amps and the mics a little ways away on guitar and bass cabinets.

Like a foot or a couple of feet?

I guess around a foot for bass. Between 6 inches and a foot for bass. Between 1 and 4 feet for the guitar. I never put them in really close. I've never seen a guitar player play with his head against the amp and say, "That sounds right."

Where do you get enough room to do that? Like when you're setting up in Electrical Audio.

Oh there's always plenty of room.

What if there's a drum kit in the same room?

I've almost never had the drums in the same room with the guitar. When I record I make sure I can put all the amps in one room and all the drums in another room. Maybe a couple of times I've had them in the same room.

That gives you more room to get space.

That way you can get ambiance on the drums. I don't care as much what kind of room the guitars are in, because they're more closely mic'd. When I did this June of 44 record, the latest one that just came out, we had a lot of fun with the rooms. I'm used to having the drums in the huge room and the guitars in the dead room. So we did half the songs that way and then we swapped. We had all these room mics way far away from the guitar amps, and the drums had the super dead sound. A lot of the drums were the two-mic setup: kick and overhead. I love being able to do stuff like that.

Which sound did you like better?

It depended on the style of the song. We were talking before about the ambiance thing - about the drums in the big room. The way I usually do it is I have close mics on everything. And then I have a pair of ambiance mics away from the drums. I have some B&Ks that I always bring with me, and I put those on the floor. So they're like fancy PZMs. I just put them on the floor and that's the reverb for the drum kit. Sometimes I don't even have an overhead mic. The cymbals get picked up in the tom mics and in the floor mics. Instead of a drum overhead mic, I like to use a stereo mic looking at the kit. Kind of where your head would be if you were standing out in front, for the cymbals.

I find I like the sound of a mic looking at the kit too. Even at a lower level. About that level looking at the drums. Getting a good sound there, sort of like the natural sound. Like if you were at a club looking at the drum kit. There's a sound there. Have you ever put a mic behind a drummer?

Yeah, using their heads to block the snare sometimes.

You can get some interesting sounds there too.

There is no one way to do it every time; there are set-ups I've found that work for me. So, I'll start out with certain mics positioned the same, but then I'll experiment with a few. On this one I'll try the drum mic behind the head, this one I'll use spaced cardioids, the next one I use spaced omnis, the next I use an X/Y stereo mic overhead and the next one I'll use an M-S or a Blumlein. Just to be different every time.

Depends on the song a lot?

No, it's often just random experimentation. Or the overall type and speed of the band's songs. Or sometimes, when the drummer starts asking me to turn up or turn down certain cymbals, I'll need to use more and closer cymbal mics.

What's the latest stuff you've done?

I've been recording this band called Plush, have you heard of them? This guy from Chicago... Liam Hayes... it's his thing. Liam likes to record in an older style. He bought himself this 1/2" 4-track, an Ampex 440, that he carts around. I helped him rebuild the thing and made it sound pretty good. So we cart it around and record on location. We recorded at a film sound-stage. Very Twickenham feeling, like *Let it Be*. We recorded in his practice space - we recorded at this public radio station studio - we recorded on a rooftop in downtown Chicago. We recorded at all these different places. Steve's recorded him in a huge theater. The mic'ing is really minimal and I try to follow Liam's "old-school" aesthetic. I was using Sennheiser 441s, and would put one that's sort of the ride and floor tom mic, and one that's sort of the other drums and the crash. And then a D-12 or RE-20 on the bass drum. It sounds really good with just the three mics.

What kind of line up is it? Is it changing on all the songs?

We're doing the basic tracks: guitar, bass, and drums. Then he's going to do a reduction mix from the 4-track onto this 1" 8-track that Steve has, and do overdubs at Steve's. That's the plan.

I loved the single that he did before.

I recorded this band, Idlewild, in England. It was really fun. I think I'm going to do more work for them this Fall.

Did you get to fly to England to do that?

I got to fly to England and I got to record at AIR studios. This band has a little money. This is the first band I've ever recorded with money.

On a major?

They're on Food, which is part of EMI. So we recorded at AIR. It was one of the best studios I've ever worked at in my life - the best console that I've ever used.

That's the place where George Martin...

Yeah, it's George Martin's studio. It's amazing. It's the best drum sound I've gotten - the best drum room I've ever used. They have a custom Neve console. It has the mic preamps out at the mic panels but you control the gain at the console. It's amazing - built in the '70s - the predecessor to the Focusrite consoles. It just sounds unbelievable. Such a great studio. That session was fun. I just recorded a band from Belgium called JFMuck - they were cool.

Where did you do that?

At Steve's in the B Studio - the small studio. I don't know. I haven't done that much lately. I recorded this band in Boston called the Wicked Farleys. I liked that a lot and they were really cool. I did some records earlier this year that are just coming out now. The Rachel's, June of 44, and another Arcwelder record. I was really excited about all three bands because I'd recorded each of them a couple of times before. I'm a huge fan of all three.

I think it's a good sign if an engineer/producer gets the same bands back to work with. It builds a good relationship, you know you enjoy working together.

You build up a good rapport, a good studio rapport. So you don't have to talk as much and you know what people want to do. You can get more done in the same amount of time. You become really close friends with the people as well. That's why I like this whole thing. I like playing in a band, and I like meeting all these people. I was the A/V geek running the projector in elementary school, so it all fits together. I like plugging in cables and running tape recorders and turning knobs.

Have you ever thought of opening your own place?

I have always wanted to.

What kind of place would you want? Would you want to convert a house or...

I'm looking for a house in Chicago right now. In Chicago they have houses where in the back yard there's another house called a coach-house. I'm trying to find one of those to have a small place like Steve's basement used to be: a small inexpensive place. I love recording at Steve's, but a lot of the bands I record can't afford it and I have to find cheaper places in Chicago. And I'm usually disappointed with the gear or something at these inexpensive studios. It's hard to go from Steve's to almost any other studio - his is so great, it's hard to compare... When Steve had it in his house, it was really small, but the gear was top flight and the place was done right. It was this super fancy studio crammed into a house. I would like to be able to have a cheap place like that.

Do you have a lot of gear that you've picked up over time?

No. I have a 24-track that I bought from Mitch Easter. I've got all my mics and I have a little bit of outboard gear - I have some compressors that I like.

Would you have to get some kind of mixer?

I'd have to get a mixer. I've been really thinking a lot lately about building a console. I don't know if I'm going to do it or not, but I have a layout I've been working on. I've been thinking about building a mixer that's basically nothing but faders and pan pots. Maybe four busses, a high pass filter, and 2 sends, with a decent master section and plenty of flexibility in the patchbay. But mainly making it so I can playback the 24-track. I don't use that much EQ, so if I had a couple of outboard EQs I could just patch those in. The simpler the console, the more time and money I can spend on making the audio path sound great. I'm getting inspired lately because a bunch of the people that work for Steve have been getting into building electronics projects. This guy Bill Skibbe has built himself his own copy of an LA-2A. It sounds amazing. I think he's now building a bunch for the studio. It's really inspiring. I want to buy some from him now.

Hey, if he'll start making them, you should. If something does work good you should use it. Like the Distressor's a good piece of gear.

I love the Distressor.

But people are like, "It's all IC's and shit." But if it works..

Oh, I'm more than happy to use modern gear. I've got no problem with it if it sounds good.

Have you tried the RNC (Really Nice Compressor)?

Yep, Steve has four of them. I used it for the first time two weeks ago and I was really blown away.

I have three and I use them all the time.

I was really shocked. I even wired them into the studio, and I didn't try them for six months.

They're really fast.

They just look wrong. They look like they can't be good. But they are great, just like Audio Technica makes so many really great cheap mics now.

Pro 37R.

Tell me about it. I had never heard of it and I just tried it out at Supernatural, and I thought it sounded great. All the 40 series: 4051s, and 4033s, are great. You know it's a 451 and a 414, but for less than half the price. They sound great. I've got one of these modern UREI VCA based compressors that I really like but never see in studios. So I just carry it around with me. I don't think anyone thinks they're special. But it works really great for me.

I think one of the things people forget about gear, is that if you know what it does and how to use it well, it's more valuable then something that is supposed to be really good that you don't know how to use. The first time I had a compressor I didn't know what to do with it.

I think most of us are hip to the "vintage gear" issue, in our realm. It's not even an issue. We know we don't need that stuff. If I record a great singer on an RE20 for vocals as opposed to the million dollar U47 or C12, when it's on your stereo at home, you can't tell which one it was recorded with.

If it works right, sounds right, and the performance is there, who cares. I have a Manley tube mic. I love that mic, but I've started using RE20 for lead vocals.

Those are great male rock vocal mics.

I've been trying a lot of different things out. It's nice to get more loose when putting things up, just to see what happens.

It's totally fun to record at Steve's because he has hundreds of microphones. It's fun to go, "Oh, I wonder what this old Altec mic would sound like on the guitar?" It's fun to have that option. But when I go to a studio that doesn't have anything, I'll start with the basics in my briefcase, and mix with what they've got there and it always turns out fine. You can always use 414s for overheads... you don't need to have the Schoeps or the Neumanns.

Yeah, 414s are mics that don't even come up often enough in interviews.

You can use them for anything. I think something Steve is well known for is using a lot of ribbon mics, and I tend to do that too. I've got a lot of Beyer mics that I carry with me. I love using ribbon mics on electric guitars. But lately I've been using them for overheads, and always for strings. Whatever string instrument it is, I'll use a ribbon mic on it... any horn too.

I don't even have one.

You can get any of those Beyers new for like $500. That and the RCA BK-5 are the best guitar mics. I love the M500s - they are so great. But all those Beyer ribbon mics: the 160, 130, 260... those are all really great sounding mics. You don't need to get a Coles. Everyone's like, "Oh, I have to have a Coles. I have to have a Coles." Shut up and buy a Beyer. It's a ribbon mic, it sounds great, and they still make them.

The 201, the dynamic mic, is really good too.

Right. I have one of those.

I used them on toms. Man...They're great drum mics.

I think Steve uses them on snare. I've seen him use the 201 and a SM98 taped together. My favorite snare drum mic, lately, has been the SM98, by itself. I like it a lot. It's the talk-show drummer's mic. It's on all the drum kits on talk shows because they are really tiny. They can mount on the rim. I guess the other topic I was thinking about was just sort of general recording ideas - recording theories. I'm starting to understand that I'm more into not being in total control of everything. When you herd cattle you don't have control of every single steer: where it's going, what direction it's in. You're just kind of herding them - keeping it all together. When some guys record, they want to be in control of every single sound, like a puppeteer or something. I'm totally into the herding - the guiding. Trying to make what you've got all work together.

You don't need to think about every single detail.

People want to take every single sound and run it through a compressor and EQ the shit out of it and just beat it into submission - control and shape every single mic.

I like random things, and then you pull them together and make something out of it.

Exactly. I'll put two or three mics on a guitar amp and have the guitarist listen to them. As long as they're all useful, they don't each need to be some idealized perfect sound. If one sounds like shit, I'll change it, but I don't sit there and obsess about distance from the cone and mic angle. I throw them up at sort of random distances and see what I come up with. And then just deal with what I get, as long as nothing sounds like total crap. It makes it more interesting. I work with whatever I end up with. It's sort of a challenge to work with what you've got.

Accidental discoveries become part of the sound. It creates more variety.

Right. When people make funny sounds or mistakes, I try to get them to keep them but they almost never want to. These moments are usually really memorable things when they end up in the final mix. There aren't cool little mistakes to remember when everything is made "perfect". When I was in the Volcano Suns I learned so much from those guys at Fort Apache, Sean Slade and Paul Kolderie. Most of the basics about recording and doing sound I learned from this other engineer, Carl Plaster, who also worked at the Fort and was a great live sound guy. I would ask Carl a million questions. Carl taught me the nuts and bolts of how all the shit works. Then when the Suns recorded, I watched Sean and learned a ton about studio recording from him. So I had all this basic knowledge from these guys, and then we recorded our last album with Steve. That's where he and I became friends. That was the next step. After watching Steve and talking to him a lot I sort of said, "Ohhhh, here's a whole new batch of information about recording I've learned." All the good engineers I know are guys who've played in bands. They learn it by being recorded themselves and then saying, "Hey, I can do this". And then they start recording their friends' bands.

Yeah, I can't think of very many examples of good engineers who didn't learn that way.

I always get e-mails from people or questions at Shellac shows where people ask me about going to recording school. All I can ever tell them is: "I can't name one engineer who's any good who went to recording school. "

I never realized I was going to fall into this until I was in my thirties.

I never thought I would. I thought I would do it for fun. I was in bands and I would record people on a reel to reel 4-track for fun. And that was good enough. I'm still shocked that I now do this as my full time job, and I barely do it full time. In the summer of '98 I had almost no work for six or seven months. I was completely broke. People would be like, "What? You don't have any work? You're Bob Weston. Blah blah blah."

They don't know how hard this is.

We don't do it for the money. We do it 'cause we're music fans and we just really enjoy making records. If you really enjoy your work, it seems like you tend not to get paid as much as if you don't enjoy your job. That's the trade-off. The people who make a shit-load of money don't seem to enjoy their work as much as the people who don't make any money. Part of your pay is truly enjoying your work and getting something other than cash out of it. ⊗

This man should need no introduction. At the height of "GRUNGE-MANIA" he had recorded the records for Mudhoney and Nirvana that started it all. And he did tham fast and cheap. On the back of Nirvana's *Bleach* was the famous sentence, *"Recorded in Seattle at Reciprocal Recording by Jack Endino for $600."* Faced with 100 clone bands trying to get the same results (yeah, right) he fled to doing recording work in other countries and sticking to working with "rock" bands that he dug. He was also a member of the awesome Skin Yard, where his guitar skills were in fine form. We tracked Jack down in Seattle while he was tracking the new Zen Guerilla album for Sub Pop. at Studio Litho for an in-depth interview.

Interview & photos:
Larry Crane

Jack Endino

I'm curious about what you were doing before Nirvana and all of that. Obviously you had been recording and playing music before any of that stuff hit, and how you got going into recording in the first place.

Well, I started with an electrical engineering degree and ended up working at the Navy yard in Bremerton, Washington, for 2 1/2 years. It was a pretty stupid job after college and so I decided I was going to do something else. I had a plan. I already had some recording gear but I figured I would get some more, learn how to use it and when I'm ready I'll go back to Seattle. I lived in a mobile home for a winter with just a reel to reel 4-track machine, a six channel Tapco mixer, three mics, a little cheap drumset, a Fender Twin, a bass amp, a bass and a guitar. I just recorded myself for a few months and then I moved back to Seattle and started hooking up with musicians and found myself in a couple of bands. I ended up meeting Chris Hanzsek when he was recording my band Skin Yard for the *Deep Six* comp, which was in '85, and I said I had a bunch of recording equipment and I was looking to work in a studio and he said he had a bunch of recording equipment and was looking to open a studio so we became partners. We then moved into the defunct Triangle recording building in June of 1986.

What did you call that studio?

Reciprocal.

Oh, yeah, the famous one.

I only owned a very minor part of the equipment so I eventually stopped being a partner and just let Chris take over. In keeping with the freelance guy that I've been ever since. It never really was my studio at all, it was really his place. I was at Reciprocal for five years - that's where I worked and it was fun. The first time I did a session at another studio, with different speakers and a different room, I almost made a complete idiot of myself.

Oh, no.

This was like 12 years ago or something. I didn't realize it, but Reciprocal was a very strange room and it had a very strange, very small control room with big weird acoustics. I was totally used to compensating for it. Once I got into a normal studio, I was just floundering. Everything sounded totally alien. Now I can pretty much go anywhere and I pretty much know what to look for and how to get my sound regardless of where the hell I am. Once you work in other rooms it makes you a much better engineer and when you come back to your studio, it'll give you a new appreciation for the improvements you can make. You'll suddenly realize weaknesses that you weren't even aware of. And you'll go, "I should put a bass trap over in that corner or I should move the speakers up over there."

You did a lot of work out of Reciprocal, but it wasn't all grunge music, right?

No, most of it was rock though. There was the occasional bar band or blues band or god knows. There were some jazz people that I knew that I recorded sometimes.

A bigger variety then?

Yeah, a little bit, for a while we had to record everybody who walked in the door when we first opened up. And then as I sort of started specializing in rock, I ended up just taking those jobs. Reciprocal closed in 1991, Chris closed it down because he had pretty much outgrown the building.

I assume you'd rather being doing rock recording.

Well, pretty much. I like variety and I like doing other things when they come up, people just don't call me with other things though. There are plenty of rock bands around here, so I have no lack of work.

> **"Once you work in other rooms it makes you a much better engineer and when you come back to your studio, it'll give you a new appreciation for the improvements you can make. You'll suddenly realize weaknesses that you weren't even aware of."**

What stuff have you done recently besides the Zen Guerrilla session?

I did an album for Nebula. Zen Guerrilla just got finished. I was in Portugal doing a band for the month of March and prior to that I did a record in Mexico City in September. I did a record for The Black Halos for Sub Pop. I got to go to Moncton, New Brunswick, Canada, in November to mix a record by Elevator Through for Sub Pop. This is a band that used to be Elevator to Hell, before that they were Eric's Trip. They've got this very psychedelic record with a Syd Barrett cover on it and I mixed it and it was pretty fun. Hotrod Lunatics, RC5, Us of All were here in Seattle. Guillotina in Mexico. I got to go to Chicago in January and do a record for Thrill Jockey for a band called the Nerves. I got to work in a studio called Uber studio and made a record with no digital reverb or delay anywhere which I don't think I've had a chance to ever do before. The actual room was so good that I didn't use any reverb on anything. We just used the room for everything.

Just put extra mics up for that?

Yeah. The drums were amazing with the room mics thrown in and when we wanted room on the vocals we just put a mic back in the other end of the room and we threw a little bit of tape delay on the vocals so technically, there's no digital anything. So that album's coming out in July, I think.

How do you end up getting jobs in other countries?

All of these records I've done, a lot of them get to other countries. That's basically it. People just track me down somehow and they say, "Hey, we picked up the Accused record that you did eight years ago and we want your sound", so that's how I've ended up in nine countries other than

the U.S. Sometimes I don't make a lot of money on these things, I just go for the travel and the music is interesting and it's different from what I get around here. It has to be a decent band, obviously or I wouldn't make the trouble.

Do you listen to previous albums and demo tapes and stuff before you take on any project at this point?

At least, I've got to at least hear a demo or something. It's nice if I can actually see the band play live, it's really the best thing, I don't always get the luxury of that. It's funny, when I recorded Mudhoney, I didn't actually see the band live for like a year and a half or something after I did their first single.

No way.

I was so busy touring with Skin Yard at the time that I just never had a chance to see Mudhoney. In that time they became such a draw here that you couldn't get into their show. I still haven't seen Pearl Jam for the same reasons. I don't really care to see them in a coliseum. It's not like seeing Green River in the Ditto Tavern.

Given the stuff you're doing, you're probably not getting paid exorbitant amounts of money for production jobs.

With the kind of music I do the money's not there... it's not that the money's not there, I'd rather not emphasize money here. I do actually get major label jobs from other countries. I've got two gold records from Warner Brazil on my wall and I've done a couple of major label records in England and a couple in Denmark and I've done some major label records in Germany and actually the Mexican band I worked with was on Warner Mexico for a while. Here in the U.S. I pretty much get stuck with indie stuff, which is fine because the politics of the industry here are much more of a pain in the ass as we all know. In other countries, the major labels seem to act a little more like indies do here. They're just smaller operations and there's not all this turnover in the personnel and you don't have somebody leaning on you in the studio, checking daily mixes or whatever. I've done major label records in countries where I never ever even met or spoke with anyone from the major label. The kind of music I do in general is rock and you have to realize that rock is not that big a part of the big picture. You know? Guitar rock and roll is not that big a part of the big picture in terms of the money that's made in the record sales. Particularly in the last five or six years it's definitely not been getting a lot of the press. I'd say most of the innovation has been happening in other genres.

You want to do the kind of work that you're gonna keep enjoying over the years.

You can't work 14 hours a day, six days a week, month after month, year after year on something you hate, you know what I mean? I would commit suicide if I was doing really horrible music. It's really fun when I get a band that I really like. It's a blast, I'll kill myself; I'm a total workaholic.

You want to make something really good with it.

We ended up doing a 26 hour day on the last day of the Zen Guerrilla record. We all got sick and lost a whole bunch of time in the middle of the project and ended up in this frenzy to try and finish it because they were on tour and they had to leave town so we had to finish and we just ended up staying up all night. We were still doing vocals at six a.m. and I was mixing and it was a frenzy and we got the damn thing done. Everybody's happy and you know, I just went home and collapsed and died for about a week. It was just like, "Okay, I'm going to work all night. We are going to do what's necessary."

Do you ever have very many things that go overtime?

Nope. Damn few. Sometimes I wish I could go overtime on a few things, you know? You have to work within the time and money that's allowed.

How long did you have for Zen Guerrilla? Like two weeks?

We had a couple of weeks, yeah, it was fun. I did a record for Watt that's gonna come out on Estrus and we think we did the whole record in about five and a half days. Those guys are totally used to it; they were just like, "Okay, let's go, next thing, okay, okay, lets do the vocals. Okay, let's see.... okay, guitar, okay, solos, okay get out there, let's do the solos." It's great. I've actually done bands that did the whole thing live in like a day. And sometimes it actually sounds alright.

That's one of the things I think that friends of mine in Seattle were mentioning, when you first started getting some acclaim, was that you can get a good drum sound really quickly.

I can still do that actually. You know what? That's funny because I hate my drum sounds.

Really?

In fact I hate all the records that I've ever done. I hate music. I hate everybody. Fuck you all. Nah, just kidding. But really, I get so frustrated with drum sounds. I hate snare drums, I just can't ever get a snare drum sound that I like. Then I realize that there aren't really that many records that have a snare drum sound that I like. I don't how anyone else does it either, you know? You always end up coming back to a 57 pointing at the damn thing and you know, I tear my hair out trying all kinds of shit and I keep coming back to the stupid 57 on the snare again and it sounds the same way it always does. I

don't have the time to experiment sometimes, you know? People can't sit around there waiting for me to spend like three hours on a snare drum.

It's seems like diminishing returns sometimes too. I mean, you can frustrate the whole band and drag the project to a screeching halt trying to fine tune one little element.

Exactly, sometimes you just have to go, "Okay, we have a week to do this, let's go." You know if I have a week to do drums, that's a different story. Let's get a bunch of snare drums in here and screw around with mic'ing. What is the killer snare sound? I think most people have just given up and are just using samples these days. I'm just old fashioned, you know, I still wanna, you know, I want it to be different every record.

What records would you say have ultimate really great snare sounds?

Don't ask me, I can't even tell you.

I was just wondering if you had...

It's just some vague notion that's in my head, some ideal floating around out there that I'm trying to reach for, but...

It might not even be something that exists, you know.

You hear it on records that are like, really expensive and you go, how the hell did they get the snare drum to sound that good. I guess the best way to get a good drum sound is to have a good drummer. That seems to be the bottom line. With a really good drummer you just hang a mic over and it's amazing, no matter what he's playing. You don't get drummers like that too often. You get drummers who are just wailing on the high hat and they've got a little wimpy snare drum and cymbals all over the place and you just deal. Get rid of all high hats and see what happens. All of our lives would be so much easier. 90 percent of the time I'll record the high hat on a separate track and I'll end up erasing it later. Seriously, 95 percent of the time you'll just end up using the overheads and there's already too much high hat on it anyway.

What do you always end up going to for the kick drums?

I'm pretty much a D112 guy. It's pretty much it for me. Sometimes I'll play with a 421 or an RE20 but basically I'm a D112 guy. There just is no replacement for me.

We have both. I just keep switching them back and forth and I keep leaning towards the RE20.

They're both good mics. The D112 is a lot cheaper.

That's one thing I aways tell people if they're looking to set up a small studio.

An RE20 would be more useful overall. I like to use it on bass. I wouldn't use the D112 on anything else, except I did use it for vocals a while ago which was pretty weird. I had a female singer who, when she hit certain notes, there was this real sharp edge to

it. We tried every mic, suddenly it was like, "Wait, what about this one." And damned if we didn't end up cutting all the vocals to the D112. Who knows if I'll ever do that again, but it worked.

I've started using the RE20 a lot more for vocals, depending on the singer of course.

Ben sang through that thing on all the Gruntruck records and for that matter, Chris Eckman of the Walkabouts always sings through a 421, if I remember right. You know what I use mostly as a vocal mic? I use a [Shure] Beta58. I'm serious. I use a Beta 58 on almost all my vocals for this rock stuff. I was in a studio the other day where we had a beautiful Neumann U47 and we had the Beta 58 next to it and we put the singer up to the 47 ran it through a compressor, listened to it and hated it. Put him on the 58 and everybody immediately went, "Oh yeah, that's the sound." With certain rock voices, you get a voice that's really loud and out of control you just need a dynamic mic, I don't know why.

Do you take stuff around with you, like mics and outboard gear and things, when you go out to work in different studios?

When I'm here in Seattle I do. I don't bother taking stuff on the planes with me. The only thing I carry around with me everywhere is a spectrum analyzer. It's an Audio Control 3050A. It's made by a company up here in Seattle. It's actually to the point that have one here and a friend of mine is storing one for me in London, so when I go to Europe I can get him to send it to me over there and I don't have to deal with the customs thing. Another friend of mine in Brazil has got one down there so if I go back there there's one there I can use. When I go from room to room, let's not even get into it, I mean speakers in rooms... you might calibrate your tape deck and have the best preamps in the world, but I'm sorry, the rooms and the speakers are such tremendous variable.

As far as control rooms?

Just the control room's acoustics and speaker frequency response and how they interact with the surface of the board and how far away it is. It's all so radically, wildly different from studio to studio. It's just beyond belief. I always have my analyzer with me and I just plug it into the main output of the board right into the speaker output actually, the thing that's going to the speaker amp, so that whatever I'm hearing on the speakers including solos, in other words if solo a channel basically, whatever's in the speaker is in the analyzer.

Control room output, yeah.

I glance at it from time to time and I'm thinking, there enough bottom? I've basically watched enough records and enough of my stuff through this analyzer that I pretty much know what fairly balanced rock record looks like on the spectrum analyzer. I can sort of look at a kick drum and go, "Oh man, I need to scoop a little more here." And it really saves my ass in times when I'm not quite sure what I'm hearing in the speakers. If I think it's really bright and I look at the analyzer and it's not, I believe the analyzer.

I'll come home and I'll be scratching my head, "Going damn, why do people spend all this money recording."

Exactly, it's not gonna lie to you.

It's really saved my ass a number of times. I use it a lot for mastering as well. It's almost like another speaker in a way, it's a speaker for your eyes. It's a strange thing. I've been carrying it around with me everywhere for ten years and I've never run into any one else who does that but once I got it it was like, how did I ever live without this thing? I carry a few mics around with me because some of the budget studios around here that I work in sometimes are deficient in terms of mics. I have a couple of 421s, I've got my Beta 58, I've got a couple of D112s, I've got a couple of cheap condensers and just various oddball microphones that I've accumulated over the years and I just bring them and add them to whatever is compiled at the studio. I don't have anything fancy, I've got an Audio Technica 4033, that's like the one decent condenser mic I own and it's nothing to write home about, it's alright.

They're good little workhorses, though.

It's decent. I've used it on my own vocals sometimes and it sounds alright. I probably should have had a pair of them but, you know, whatever. I prefer a [AKG]414 and I'm not gonna buy one.

With the kind of jobs you're doing, do you get much choice of what studio you're gonna work at?

Well, I know every studio around here, so I pretty much know when someone gives me a budget and the type of music they're doing, I pretty much go, "Okay, we can go here and spend five days or go here and spend ten days. What do you wanna do?" Sometimes the time is more valuable than the equipment. You can do a rush job in a really expensive studio and it's still gonna suck because you didn't have enough time, whereas you can take your time in a really cheap low-budget studio with a Mackie and a little 16-track. If you're careful about recording the sounds properly and you've got the time to really make sure that it's played right and mixed right, it can end up sounding way better than going to a thousand dollar a day room and trying to do it in three days. Which a lot of people try and do.

I tell people that you're gonna be better off going to a small studio with someone who is into your kind of music and you'll get a really good job.

You did a little editorial in the back of your last issue and I have to say that I agree with you a hundred percent on this. The gear isn't that important if the music is good and if you spend the time and your engineering is good. The point is, it doesn't matter really what you're recording on, it's what you're recording that matters, not how you're doing it. And it's like the biggest lesson that you can possibly impart to anybody. You don't need to spend a million bucks to make a good sounding recording. But people continue to just find newer

and more inventive ways to waste money in the studio. Particularly when they get onto a major label. The producer has to bring a rack of preamps with him even if he's recording at a studio with an API board. He's gotta bring his own preamps with him from L.A. at great expense. Maybe dogs can hear the difference between these things, I can't. So let's get a rack of expensive compressors with us for tracking. You don't need a rack of compressors for tracking. Save it for the mixing. I bring compressors with me, okay, but they're just run of the mill compressors that I like using. I'm not a snob.

But how much of that is habit that needs to be broken?

I just think there's a lot of time and money wasted in the studio on things, that in the long run, make no difference. I find that the most important pieces of equipment are the room, the tape machine, the time that is spent and the guy doing it. That's all you need to record a good track. The rest of it is all bullshit. Mixing is another story, you can go crazy with mixing, but if you do that, go to a specialized mixing room where you've got a nice little place. You've got someone who specializes in mixing and has all the equipment. I've seen people waste money on recording and I've even had the opportunity to waste a bit of it myself because it seemed like that was expected of me. It sort of left a bad taste in my mouth.

Did it feel like you were just puttering around and not really getting to the job?

Yeah, because some of the records that I've spent a few months on; they're not significantly different from the ones that I've done quickly. There's a little bit of a sheen to them from just having lots of time and getting things exactly right and some of them sound pretty amazing but some of the cheaper records that I've done have a little more life to them. When I'm flying to other countries I don't bring anything. I'm dealing with customs, I'm going as a tourist, I don't want them asking a lot of questions. I deal with whatever I have and that's really made me a much better engineer. When I get there I'll whine and complain and I'll say, "Well, I really need another compressor or give me another mic" or whatever. And you try and get what you can but it's just amazing to me how I've been forced to work in every thing from Rockfield in Wales for two months doing a record (which is a legendary studio that's been there since the 60's Neve VR boards with flying faders, Studer A27's, giant rooms, a wonderful place) and then you've got like a studio I worked at called the La Cosina in Mexico

x

City which is a basement ADAT studio and the backdoor of the control room opens to the outside and all this dust comes in. The ADATs are full of this gritty dust. I made a couple of really good sounding records at this little studio in Mexico for this band called Guillotina. I'm actually pretty happy with these records and I don't even like ADATs that much but you know I just sort of forced myself to get used to them. I'll come home and I'll be scratching my head, "Going damn, why do people spend all this money recording." There's a lot of ways to do it. Frankly, I don't like recording records in two days, whether it's in two days whether it's a small room or in a big studio. Like I said, time is one of the most important factors.

What about time spent on pre-production? Do you get time to go to band's rehearsals or sit with them and work out re-arranging anything?

Yeah, I do that when I can. A lot of times it doesn't happen. They send me a tape and I listen carefully and I make comments and I say, "You know, this one's a little long. Do you realize this chorus goes eight times maybe it should go six or something like that?" A lot of times that's as far as I can go because the band is in another country. With people here in Seattle, I'll go to their shows and go to a practice if I can. I love to have a chance to go see a band practice and just sit in the corner and be a fly on the wall with my little hand metronome and see how fast they're playing the songs at practice and then go to a show with my little metronome. I have a little note pad and I'll just note how fast people are playing stuff and then when they get in the studio it's a good argument settling device. People freak out and they play everything at half speed in the studio and you can say wait a minute, here's how fast you played it the last five times I saw you. That really saves a lot of hassle.

No one's ever mentioned that before.

Really?

I've had bands that did it for themselves and it was just wonderful. Every song, we'd just print a little bit of metronome click at the beginning and then kill it as soon as the band gets going.

That's what I do because I hate click tracks. There's a Brazilian band that I use clicks with because they practice with them. They're just used to it. They used to be a pop band where they did everything with MIDI and they slowly got away from that and are now more of a guitar band but they still sort of retain their habit of recording. The drummer plays really well with a click track and when he doesn't have it he freaks out and that's fine, because it works with them really well. It certainly makes it easy to splice the different drum takes together if I need to. 98 percent of the time I strongly discourage people from even attempting to use a click track. If the drummer is good enough to play to a click track, chances are, he doesn't need it.

It's very true. Lots of times it's just like a reminder thing or something like that.

Yeah, maybe give it to them for like the first couple of measures of the song just to make sure that they start at the right speed and if they speed up a little, bit deal. It's music, it's supposed to breathe a little bit. If it slows down, that's another story. Slowing down is the kiss of death. What can you do, you know, you just have to say, look, you're slowing down. Sometimes you just have to accept. The chances are, you may hear it but nobody else will ever hear it.

That's true.

There's plenty of things on records. I was listening to a Zeppelin record and I heard John Bonham slowing down and I was thinking, my hearing is getting a little too good, you know? Maybe I worry about this stuff too much. There's a big old vocal punch in on the first Zeppelin record. I heard edits on "Whole Lotta Love".

What about tape speeds? You were saying how you would never want to record at 30 if you can avoid it.

Well, I'm just about to start a project where I'm gonna record at 30. It's a pop record for these Brazilians and the guitars are gonna be a smaller part of it. It's gonna be a lot of vocals, some keyboards, some percussion things like that. The thing with 30, it's a love/hate relationship I have with 30 ips analog. As far as recording media, I'd rather record digital than record 30 ips analog. And I'm talking like ADAT digital, 44K digital.

Anything to avoid it, because the bottom end is just too unsatisfying to me. It really frustrates the hell out me when I'm trying to get a kick drum sound and it comes back sounding like a basketball. I keep coming back to 15 ips analog for rock. There is a sound there and it's not as good... the cymbals tend to sound more grainy, the whole thing is a little bit grainier, which is kind of hard to describe to people. Machines always have an extra octave of low end at 15 ips as opposed to 30. Now the really good modern machines the Studers and Otaris, mostly the Studers, at 30 ips they're usually flat down to about 40 Hz which is the fundamental of low E on a bass, so at least you're getting all the music you're gonna get. Most of the records that we all idolize as classic rock recorded before 1973, from what I can tell from talking to the old timers that I've met, people didn't really start recording at 30 until around the early '70s sometimes around '73 or '74. There's an audible shift that you can tell in records. You can pretty much tell when people shifted from 15 to 30 because records took on a

whole different sound and I'm not sure it wa necessarily a change for the better. I was jus reading *Mix* or one of those, and there's some gu who invented some radical scheme whereby th ideal type speed is 18 ips and he's making som sort of 1 inch, 2-track or something for a ultimate mastering machine that runs at 18 ip and has this elaborate biasing scheme of its ow It's supposed to be the ultimate last word i analog recording. It just cracked me up.

That's kind of fun. It's the ultimat plus no other tape deck can rea that tape.

Yeah, I'm not sure if there was really any point to it.

So you're going down to Brazil to do th pop band?

No, they're flying up here. I've been there twice record them and this time they're coming here, I'll be entertaining some Brazilians here. I gonna be great.

What's the name of the band?

They're called The Titans. They're coming up in a coup weeks. I've got the Quadrajets next week.

It's surprising how many foreign ban you work with.

After the grunge thing I was besieged with grun wannabees. I was besieged with Soundgarden a Melvins and Nirvana clones. I blew most of the off. I was kind of bumming, this sucks. It w alright the first time around but that's part of reason I started taking all these jobs overseas.

Yeah. I remember you did a Blu Cheer album.

"It's music, it's suppose to breathe a little bit'

That was crazy. Let's not get into that. It's a terri record. You know what they did when th mastered it?

What?

They added reverb to it in the mastering! I w horrified when I got the record.

You've gotta be kidding?

Their manager decided to do it. This crazy German said it didn't sound stadium enough. The recor dreadful, I'm so pleased that it's impossible to fi

What's it called?

It's drenched in stadium reverb, the whole recor just drenched in reverb, it's just astounding. Ye well, there's been a couple of other records t they've made since then that are equally obsc But it was one of those things that I couldn't t down, you know it was just like, you kno mean, would you do it? Of course.

Yeah, sure.

"Sure. Okay, I don't care what they sound like, do the record." ☮

A Mono Proposal
by Larry Crane

Audio reproduction formats have been in flux since the first cylinder spun over at Edison's workshop. The mechanical "horn" system of playback, used on those early recorders and 78 players, gave way eventually to electro-mechanical contraptions using a stylus and a speaker. Doubtless there were listeners who decried this "move forward" as ruining the sound of music as they knew it. By the late '50s, matrixed dual channel encoding on vinyl led to the two speaker "stereo" system. Initially producers, engineers and artists ignored this "advancement", preferring to spend most of their time mixing the mono versions of albums and leaving the stereo mixes as late night fun for the assistant engineers. As stereo won over, engineers had to develop new ways of mixing to accommodate the dual speaker beast. Producers like Phil Spector, who had spent ages learning to coax depth out of a single speaker, suddenly had to figure out a new game plan for using stereo. Panning instruments in approximate positions of a stage appearance or crazily putting mics all over single instruments to make them "stereo" began in earnest. But quad was in the development stages. Soon there was utter chaos as hopped-up rock bands felt the need to pan solos and sound effects around and around in crazy patterns, with no regard for solid stereo imaging. Luckily this didn't last too long.

Now we have the beast of Surround Sound rearing its ugly head. A lazy engineer can just throw the reverb, and any other sounds they can't place, into the "rear" speakers, along with crowd noises from live recordings. Yet, there's an even bigger problem. With home stereos, people frequently have the speakers too far apart, too close, in different rooms, pointing in two different directions, and even wired out of phase. This leads to uneven reproduction of the stereo effect that engineers work so hard to achieve - in effect, all is lost. With 5:1 surround systems, where "proper" listening really only occurs in a small area, these mishaps can be multiplied into madness. This will only make the work of the engineers and producers even harder and more frustrating.

Here's the answer. Mono. If you get a perfect mix on a single speaker there's far less chance that the listener can ruin it with a mis-placed speaker and they can't screw up the phase like they can with two or more speakers. In car stereos it'll be far easier to hear complete mixes - no more vocals buried in the driver's knee. And just think, studios would only require one speaker, half as many cables, less channels of compression and EQ, and all those mono 1/4" decks would be back in fashion. How are we going to pull this off? We are the new breed of recordists. We can demand that projects be mixed and released only on mono. **We can pretend to mix in stereo but never tweak a pan knob to the left or right.** We can change the world, restoring true audio quality to listeners who will thank us for it, eventually. And just think, you'll never have to buy another "pair" of speakers again!

Deep in the industrial wasteland of Red Hook, Brooklyn, Adam Lasus has turned an old firehouse into a recording outpost called Fireproof Recording. With the pole still intact, the firehouse proves an interesting place to make records. After checking out other studios, my band North Sea Story, decided to do our record *Working for Wellness* there. Having never worked with Adam before, the time spent at his studio developed into a perfect opportunity to observe and ask him questions about many things. Adam's work can be heard on records by Yo La Tengo, Space Needle, Versus, Gigolo Aunts, Varnaline, Ditchcroaker, Mark Mulcahy, the Lilys, Sugar Plant and many others. After his start in Philadelphia with Studio Red, he relocated to New York City to discover that there is more than just a tree that grows in Brooklyn.

How did things get rolling for you?

My cousin was in Miracle Legion and I got interested watching them record. I had a 4-track and eventually an 8-track in my Dad's house and was recording my own band and Jeff's band Baby Huey.

What was your first real studio like?

My first real studio, Studio Red, was in the basement of my apartment in Philadelphia. I had an 8-track and began recording the Gigolo Aunts, Madder Rose, Versus, Chris Harford and Matt Keating at the beginning of their careers. Fortunately in 1991 a lot of the bands I was working with got signed. When they came back to do their bigger-budgeted records with me I was able to buy more gear and grow from there.

How long in Brooklyn?

Three years. When I first moved to Brooklyn, I thought I would be a freelance producer. The first project I did was a band called Muler who was on Dedicated Records. They lived in Rochester, New York so I set up all my gear in a space near them that was once a working studio. A cool thing happened when I opened a closet and found a Neumann KM86 mic that someone just left behind. I still have it. It's not the killer vocal mic they make but it's good on acoustic guitars. Anyway shortly after doing the Muler record I found this space which became Fireproof Recording.

ADAM LASUS
text and photos by Paul C. FitzGerald

Whether I do label work or something self financed by a band, I treat it the same. I'm lucky that I have a really great space and have collected some nice gear. I don't have the high fees like other studios in Manhattan and can charge a reasonable rate.

When you started Fireproof Recording, what did you have to do, physically, to get the room ready for recording?

The building is the first firehouse built in Brooklyn sometime in the 1830s. The room has 14 foot ceilings is 60 feet long and 25 feet wide, so it's pretty large. After moving in, I started immediately recording Clem Snide's first record, *You Were a Diamond*, and then Haywood's, *Men Called Him Mister*. Soon after, a neighbor knocked on my door and complained about the noise level. I was told I had to soundproof or get out.

What did you do?

Luckily my father is a general contractor and was able to design a soundproof room within the large room for me. I had to shell out a bunch of money for building materials. We framed a room and floated a floor. I did the dry wall and brought some friends in to help with the ceiling. I thought it would take a month. It took close to five. We had to be careful not to make the room too big, so as to preserve a large portion of the big main room, which has a lot of character.

Since you got to build a tracking room from scratch, what did you do to customize it?

We designed it in such a way as to make it sound natural and big. We built a bass trap in so we wouldn't have standing waves and some corner absorbers to eliminate some of the reflection. We kind of lucked out. It just ended up sounding great.

When we did drums for our record, I was amazed by the built-in sound already in the room, we didn't have to fool so much with the drum sounds.

Your drums were tuned pretty well coming in so it was pretty easy to get those sounds. Some bands come in here and we spend a lot more time on the sound and tuning. I always keep my house kit tuned well and leave the mics in place, so I can have drums ready to go in 15 minutes, for convenience's sake. I learned a lot about drums from Carl Plaster, who I had a chance to work with on Juliana Hatfield's *Hey Babe* record at Fort Apache. He has a great approach of tuning really well and not using any tape on them. I use AKG 451s as overhead mics. They sound great. I also use a Russian mic, the Oktava MK219, as a room mic and compress it as much as I can stand.

How is your room for recording non-rock instruments, like cello for instance?

Great. I produced Clem Snide's first record here, which was a breath of fresh air after doing a lot of loud indie rock records. Clem Snide has a cellist and an upright bass player and when they would bow together you got this nice orchestral sound with built in reverb. I also did a record for Leah Coloff, who is a cellist/singer-songwriter. I recorded her cello and live vocals in the big room with many room mics and was able to get a huge sound.

We knew the records you had done in the past and when we saw the space, we were definitely excited to record here. Not a lot of control rooms have giant windows in them...it makes it a little less stiffling when you're listening to a song for the 50th time, at least you can look out the window.

Part of my job, obviously, is to make the process as comfortable as possible and the bands I choose to work with, I think, benefit from that. By accident, one of the things that attracted bands is the relaxed atmosphere in which to record. When I had Studio Red in Philly, bands would often stay at my house... it was like a camp and sometimes still is.

When we came in here for our record you didn't know anything about us really and had no idea what we wanted.

That's sort of an exciting part of doing any record from the beginning. You get to experiment and learn about different working styles. That's how I've made a living for ten years. Whether I do label work or something self financed by a band, I treat it the same. I'm lucky that I have a really great space and have collected some nice gear. I don't have the high fees like other studios in Manhattan and can charge a reasonable rate.

What was your take on lo-fi especially since lo-fi is really high tech now?

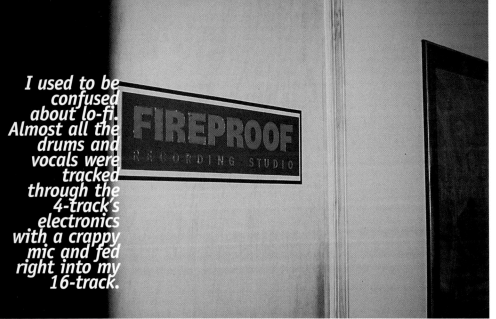

> *I used to be confused about lo-fi. Almost all the drums and vocals were tracked through the 4-track's electronics with a crappy mic and fed right into my 16-track.*

Well I used to be confused about lo-fi. I used to think that a 4-track demo was lo-fi and that when you record in a studio the point was to make it sound as good as possible. That changed when Mary Timony from Helium came to record and wanted the sound to be trashier. When we did *The Dirt of Luck* we were listening to Mary's 4-track demos and they sounded intense. The drums were distorted and the vocals had no low end. So after trying all my mics and outboard stuff to get a similar sound, I said, "Get your 4-track and mic and we'll use that." Almost all the drums and vocals were tracked through the 4-track's electronics with a crappy mic and fed right into my 16-track.

How do you feel now that you have a pretty decent amount of gear and a great space?

I have a constant jones, like anyone who reads *Tape Op* or is an engineer. I just bought a 2-track Studer A80 1/2" mastering deck. I would love to get a 24-track 2-inch and a Distressor.

What was your first real deck.

A Tascam 38 1/2" 8-track. I learned a lot on that deck, about fitting everything on eight tracks, creative bouncing, that kind of stuff. I eventually saved up enough for a 16-track.

Didn't you have a board that you had craned in here?

Yeah, an old API from 1970.

What did you do on it?

I did the first Clem Snide record, Trolleyvox, and Haywood. It was very punchy and thick. You didn't have to EQ very much because the board had such a rich sound. I had the board for a year. I was leasing it from someone, but had to give it up because the repairs were too expensive. I had it craned back out and bought a 32 channel Allen Heath Saber from the '80s with mute automation.

I heard you had Daniel Johnston in here.

He came to record three acoustic tunes. He's a really sweet guy. That was a cool thing. It wasn't really supposed to happen. He was in town and wanted to record some songs. Kramer was supposed to do it and it didn't work out. I didn't know all that much about him other than his reputation as an eccentric and talented songwriter. He came in here with his manager and pretty much played his nylon string guitar and sang. He doesn't do a lot of takes. Live vocal and live guitar. He added some trumpet and organ and that was it. You definitely feel like you're in the presence of a unique artist with Daniel. He just does really basic singing and guitar and hands the songs off to others to finish. A pretty interesting approach. He was here for four hours and then wanted to go buy some comic books.

It seems like you get to work with some pretty interesting and diverse people.

I've been lucky to work with the people that I'm interested in. I just finished a record by a songwriter named Tiffany Anders, for Up Records. Polly Jean Harvey produced and I engineered. I recently finished recording Mark Mulcahy's [formerly of Miracle Legion] new record, I also finished a nice rootsy record with a band called Violet that I really dig.

What is Tiffany Anders music like?

She has kind of an indie-country sound. Pretty mellow, good melodies and arrangements. Much different obviously than recording a rock record.

What was it like working with Polly Jean Harvey?

It was her first time producing and I have to say it was a great experience. She was really focused on getting the job done and making the right choices. I definitely respect her, not just because of her music, but for her work ethic. We would start recording around noon and pretty much have the song mixed by 10 PM. She knew exactly what she wanted. She played guitar, bass and keyboards on Tiffany's record as well.

Who else played on the record?

J Mascis played drums on a couple of tracks. He's an excellent drummer. All the stuff he played on the Dinosaur Jr. records is pretty intense and hard, while the stuff on Tiffany's records was soft. He learned the songs in a couple of passes and then laid them down a great sound to build on.

Do you ever work at other studios?

I have but it's tough because I know my studio and don't have to wonder how the stuff will come out. I've worked at the Power Station, which is now called Avatar. Massive SSL set-up with every piece of gear you could ever imagine. I mixed the Muler record there and it turned out to be a nightmare. In the end, it just sort of "expensified" everything. When I brought the mixes home, I was like, "What is this?" It sounded really flat. The record didn't need all the automation and fancy gear. We remixed everything back at Fireproof. It was a good lesson for me. I have also worked with Mitch Easter at the Drive In [now Fideletorium], which is a great studio.

When we come in here to do our second record, anything you would do different with us?

It's cool to do several projects with one band or artist because you get to experiment a little more. It's a challenge because you don't want any two records to sound the same. I think you guys have grown as a band and I probably wouldn't suggest any great departures but we will certainly experiment with different mics and sounds. On your record we did a lot with drum sounds and the guitar sounds all have a real distinct tone. Now that you're a trio, we're going to have to work hard on the vocals and harmonies a bit more. Chris Harford has done some of his records in a real straight-ahead recording style but on his new record there were drum machines and a cello, lap steel and Moog that we ran through all sorts of crazy pedals. It was great working with Chris. I could not push the sonic envelope far enough with him. We both broke some new ground in the making of his record, *Wake*.

You mentioned doing a record with Mark Mulcahy from the band Miracle Legion recently. What went on there?

Mark's not into a lot of sonic waste - delays or flange - on record, but he did some pretty interesting stuff. Lots of layered background vocals. For his record, we took the better part of a year to do it. When you work on something for that long you can really get inside it. We were able to spend the time to get all the ideas fully realized.

I see your Studer over there.

That's a great machine. It makes things sound so much better than DAT. It gives my mixes a great thick sound. The tape compression makes it sound so real and warm. I use BASF Maxima 900 tape so I can hit it hard.

Do you play any instruments?

Yeah, bass mostly. I played with Matt Keating on most of his records and toured with him as well. I was great to get out of the studio and see the country. ⊕

HIGH VELOCITY SOUND ENGINEERING

A Manifesto by Oz Fritz

"Objective music is not self-expression but a descending form of higher communication." -E.J. Gold

1. The essential aim of High Velocity Sound Engineering is clear aesthetic communication. The information communicated is music. Music is taken to be a high order language containing the possibility of evolutionary change. The structure of the communication is designed and engineered around the creative framework of the artist.

2. High velocity refers to the speed and direction of the brain and nervous system. The nervous system receives all the relevant information pertaining to the task at hand, evaluates and integrates this information, then initiates a technical/artistic approach that will successfully realize the aim. Current scientific theories hold that the nervous system functions in an electrical manner. The speed of electricity is measured at 186,000 miles per second which is also the speed of light. The direction is outlined below in paragraphs 3 and 8.

3. The method of High Velocity Sound Engineering is the exacting analysis and synergistic comprehension of all the physical and metaphysical factors that determine the architecture of the sound field. The sound field is postulated as an informational cyberspace matrix existing in various forms as an electrical/acoustic pattern.

4. The physical factors include:
A) An in-depth familiarity with all of the technology available for use.
B) All of the various combinations of interfacing and operating the technology.
C) The total acoustical behavior characteristics of the audio environment.

5. The metaphysical factors include:
A) The conceptual approach(es) to the construction of the sound field.
B) The effective interpretation of the artist's vision.
C) Consideration of the psychoacoustic effects produced upon the listeners.

6. High Velocity Sound Engineering defines the sound system as all of the factors that influence the propagation of the unique sound waves that one wishes to record or to distribute live over a particular area.
The sound system breaks down as:
A) The source, i.e. the musicians and their instruments.
B) All of the technology involved and its assembly into a working whole.
C) The acoustic reverberation/absorption effects of the environment and anything in it including the population of it at any particular time.
D) The producer(s) and engineers(s).

7. The recording studio is viewed as a subatomic particle/wave accelerator. High Velocity utilizes the latest theories and practical applications of quantum and relativistic physics to record the pattern integrity that is music. High velocity is aware of the impingement of the electromagnetic fields generated by the nervous systems of the artists, producers and engineers. Neurosomatic, neuroelectic, neurogenetic and neuroatomic techniques are practiced both to combat fatigue brought about by constant attention and electromagnetic field anomalies, as well as to metaprogram High Velocity. The most complex system of technology in the recording studio is the human nervous system.

8. The approach taken towards the construction of the audio mix is based upon the realization and the application of generalized patterns found in nature. These patterns are elucidated in the disciplines of physics, chemistry, biology, electronics, mathematics, geometry, philosophy and depth psychology. The system of geometry employed is the multidimensional "Synergetics" energy-geometry formulated by R. Buckminster Fuller.

9. The mix is viewed as a space/time event to be architecturally crafted in accordance with the above.

10. Each moment of the mix is unique and may be compared to the separate frames of a film. Each moment is given individual consideration while always maintaining an awareness of its relation to the whole.

11. High Velocity Sound Engineering is innovative and evolutionarily expanding. It may be used in any situation that requires clear aesthetic communication. ⊗

Oz Fritz's recent projects include **Tom Waits'** *Mule Variations* and a new album by **Primus.**

David Barbe is no less than a living legend in Athens, Georgia.

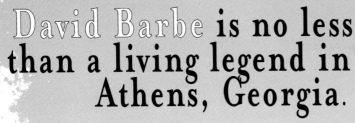

Coming from the 'old school' Athens
(and still being of sound mind to remember most of it),
he is known for any one of a number of his musical endeavors.
First starting off with the punk rock standard bearers Mercyland,
then a brief stint in the Scratch Acid influenced Bar-B-Que Killers,
then onto Buzz Hungry and then, in the midst of it, an excursion
(if you can call four years 'an excursion') with Bob Mould as bassist in Sugar.
Of course what is of greater importance to *Tape Op* readers is the fact that he's
become probably more well known for his recording prowess with bands as varied
as Son Volt, Macha, and any one of the more seedy, crusty bands
on the underbelly of the Athens music scene
(ck. Harvey Milk, Skinner Pilot, etc.).
A couple of years ago, David, along with fellow Athens recording
engineers Andy Baker and Andy Lemaster,
colluded to form Chase Park Transduction on the outskirts of Athens.
Since then, business and their clientele have been growing very well,
thank you very much. As *Tape Op* readers will no doubt notice,
what I lack for in technical knowledge, I make up for in sheer volume.
So without further ado...

CHASE PARK TRANSDUCTION
A Division of ADA Recording

160 Winston Drive #4 Athens, GA 30607   (706) 227-0(

Artist David Barbe

Engineer Henry Owings

Tempo tos by John Baccigaluppi

Song The Tape Op Interview

Reel/Location Athens, GA   Date 7-25-99

1	2	3	4	5	6	7	8
early Athens GA	learning the ropes	Sugar	Andy, Andy, and →	getting started	Son Volt + ADAT's	Mitch Easter's place	Fum is #1

9	10	11	12	13	14	15	1

So you've been in Athens since '81, did you come to school here?

Yeah I grew up in Atlanta and then moved out here to go to school. If you like rock music it was a pretty great time to move to Athens. I played in a bunch of local bands around here and started Mercyland in '85 and that's when I got serious about it. [Back then] there were only about 20 or 30 local bands and even though there are better bands now, it was exciting because it was a genuine underground. [After Mercyland,] Buzz Hungry started and six months after that, Bob [Mould] called and I started doing Sugar. So Buzz Hungry from '91-'96, Sugar was from '92-'95, sort of tucked there in the middle.

At what point did you start recording Mercyland?

Well, I had been recording stuff since I was a child, my parents were musicians and they were in the jingle business. So I've been in studios forever. I cannot remember not being in a studio. I recorded my bands as soon as we had real drums and amps. When I was about 12 or 13, I'd be recording shit in the basement. Up here, though, Mercyland went into the studio three weeks after we were a band. We had written some songs in '85 and I had been recording other people's bands on my 4-track before then. I was a really avid 4-tracker, and had a little set up in the back of my house. We would go to people's practice spaces and record. That kind of gave me the idea that I knew what I was doing, even though I really did-

"When I was about 12 or 13, I'd be recording shit in the basement."

n't. Right after Mercyland got to go into the studio, the BBQ Killers went to John Keane's. I went over there with them as "the producer", even though I didn't know what the knobs and the buttons in the studio did. I was just to be the guy to say, "Okay. That sounds good do it like that." Or, "You can play it better. The snare drum sounds weird." Once I did that, I was constantly telling people I knew more than I really did so I could go into the studio with them. So I went into the studio with a ton of bands to help without knowing shit about engineering. Most well-known being the BBQ Killers and the Jack O'Nuts and a ton of others that have since fallen by the wayside. I was also more and more, obviously, not doing the Mercyland recording. So [in '91] when Mercyland broke up, John Keane called me up and said he realized he had a need for a second person to work in his studio. I had been in that studio enough times to know just enough so that I could identify what I thought was a good drum sound from a shitty one and I could identify what I thought was in tune and out of tune. Basically, I knew what I needed to know about making some pretty rudimentary recordings, I just didn't have the knob twiddling skills. So I went over there and interned with him for a few months and then went to the Recording Workshop in Ohio, where John had been years before, which basically amounted to a six week crash course

which was the greatest thing. The first five weeks were basic recording theory and technique. It's a lot better than some of these other things where you go to school for two years and you have to take all these other classes that are somewhat related to recording music, but cover a much broader spectrum so they can charge a lot more money that way.

Was this like a recording engineer's boot camp?

Basically. Depending on your studio schedule for the day you would go from either like 9 AM to 9 PM with a couple of breaks tossed in there or from like noon to at least midnight or one. It was great, they really stressed signal flow, how the sound travels down the wires and that's what John wanted me to learn. So when I came back home, he let me do a band for one day to show him I could do it and do them for free. So I did Liquor Cabinet over at John's, did one song then John went out of town and then I was on my own. I was actually making people's records, local granted, but I was recording a week or two back from boot camp. I wasn't like making coffee or sweeping floors. He gave me the keys to the studio and alarm code. It was the greatest thing anyone has ever done for me because John just totally threw me into the fire. He also let me record really cheap, so I could drum up some business. So I did Daisy and Roosevelt who were two of the very first ones.

John Keane's is an expensive studio, comparatively speaking.

Yeah, probably now more so because he does all the major labels. At the time it was $550 a day, which now would be a steal for that studio, but at the time it was by far the most expensive place in town. The local bands couldn't go over there and record for $30 bucks an hour. So I called everybody I knew in a band, and it worked out great. I was so busy. Then from there, I got the Sugar opportunity from Bob. It was such a great time for me because I had just learned all this stuff in school, so I was totally obsessed about recording. After getting involved with John, I was really wrapped up in it and then I got to go with Bob to make Sugar records at nice studios. Those were done with Lou Giordano, who had done our first two records.

So you got to learn with them?

Oh God! Hanging out with Bob and Lou in the studio is just a different style, different part of the country, different sound studio. Just a different set of experiences all together. When we made *Copper Blue* and *Beaster*, Bob and I both stayed at the studio in sleeping bags. He stayed for about six weeks and I was up there for about a month, but it was great There has been several times like that where I've just stumbled on an opportunity to learn something else.

So when Sugar ended in '95 you just came back to Athens and started recording again?

Well, the whole time I was in Sugar we didn't tour that much because I already had kids. So a record would come out in August, and from September until right before Christmas we would be gone three weeks, home for a week, gone for three weeks. After Christmas, go to Japan for a week and that would be it for six months. So I had half the year to record. I was constantly coming back here to record and John had gotten a lot busier. I branched out, first from John's to the local studios around here. At the time there was John's, Kelly Noonan's, Mark Maxwell's Full Moon and Andy Baker's Rock Central and then from there I got a call to go to Atlanta and record Fiddlehead at Bosstown. So once I went down there and did that I was like; "Well, shit, now I'm in Atlanta. I can work down here too." It's like all these steps. I'm always thinking that I can just move into the next thing and I can just figure it out when I get there. It is what I've always done anyway. So then I started freelancing in Atlanta. Now I think that there are a lot of good choices around here for people to record with. There are a lot of things I wouldn't do a good job at because I don't know the vocabulary. I should never be asked to record a heavy metal record, I would do a terrible job. I don't know anything about it. But for a lot of these punk rock bands, I value [what they're trying to do in the studio because] I've been in these same sort of bands. I understand that somebody might want the guitars louder than the vocals or the drums to sound like you're in a room with them as opposed to some incredibly processed sound. That was good timing for me too because there wasn't a lot of competition. By the time I came back from doing Sugar, I really got steady doing it, and from the beginning of '95 until we opened this studio in '97 I really picked up the freelancing. I was working from 25 to 30 places a year just between here and Atlanta. Brooks Carter [guitarist for the now defunct Jack'o'Nuts who now lives somewhere in the Industrial Triangle, NC] and I went in together on a digital 8-track and a Mackie 16 channel board. I already had some good mics so then we started recording people in their houses.

I remember that's the way you did Skinner Pilot, right?

Yeah, Skinner Pilot was done that way. I recorded some of their sessions at Elixir and Brooks recorded some over at their house. We then took it over to Brooks' apartment to mix. The first Harvey Milk record was recorded at Paul Trudeau's [HM's drummer's] house then mixed at Brooks' apartment. I think Harvey Milk spent approximately $1,000 making that record. John let me bring my stuff into his studio and just recorded the basic tracks in that room so we could have a sound proof studio set up. We did it in one day and it was really cheap for them. Then we took all the stuff over to Paul's house and the tape machine over to Brooks' house and mixed in his apartment. He didn't have any kind of reverbs, we just ran the drums out a guitar amp out into the stairway and hooked up a couple of mics. So on that song that has the long pauses in it, if you listen closely, you can hear crickets in the background because they were coming in the window. That was an invaluable period of recording because it's little more of a challenge to make it sound good in a more rudimentary situation. Also, people are more comfortable in their houses, so that was fun. We built this place [Chase Park Transduction] in early '97 and it opened in May of '97. Since then, I've occasionally been going to other places to work. I went to Illinois to do Son Volt and a few times I've gone over to Tom Lewis' studio where he is doing sixteen track as well. So a couple of times, if we have been busy here, I've taken a reel of tape over there and mixed something or done overdubs.

Were both Andys brought in right as you opened this place?

Yes. Tom Lewis and I were going to do a studio together. Andy and Andy were going to open a studio together and we were both having an impossible time finding buildings. Tom and I decided to do our own things, it just wasn't going to work because we both have similar needs. Andy B. and I have always been really friendly so we kicked around the idea of finding a temporary space together until he and Andy could get their building together and I could build my own place. I wanted to build a studio in the woods and just do it out there. So we started looking around and we found this place. Once we started building it was obvious this partnership was a good thing and we should take this a little more seriously. It's always been three of us in partnership in the studio. Andy Le Master had a studio in Toccoa called The Furry Vault. The Vault was a small cinder block shed behind his parent's house. It was so small that the guitar over dubs would be done in a car or van. They'd back the van up to the door of the place and put the amps out there and the mics in the van. Andy learned how to record on some pretty rudimentary stuff as well. Andy and Andy decided to get together on this building in Colburn that fell through and I was going to build this encampment out in the woods. Then I finally realized that when I built the building I wouldn't have any money left to buy equipment. So we just all kind of fell together because we all had very compatible situations. That is, as a freelancer I had always bought one piece of incredible equipment at a time. If I needed some more mic pres to record something in some remote place or a studio that didn't have good sounding mic pres, well I'd go buy two API mic pres or two Neve mic pres or ribbon mics 'cause the studio doesn't have any so I would buy one Coles ribbon mic. So basically over the course of five or six years before I opened the studio, I had massed a pretty great arsenal. I had about a dozen great mics to supplement the meat and potatoes of most studios. Even the most basic studios have a few SM 57's, Sennheiser 421's, one or two condenser mics, a [AKG] 414. So what I did was bought more esoteric things that worked well with a meat and potatoes mic collection. Andy [Baker] had the studio in his house. He had a Trident console and 15 mic stands. He had the meat and potatoes mic collection and a couple of nice ones. So, when you put it together it was basic. To open the

studio all we needed to buy was a 2 inch machine cause we had everything else, but we did buy a bunch more stuff. While I was freelancing I knew I wanted to open a studio one day. I just knew that a lot of studios I'd go into there would be some regret on the part of the person that owned the studio, like, "I wish I had known what I was doing a little bit more when I opened this place up because I would have set my patch bay up differently, laid my rooms out differently. I wouldn't have bought this board, I would have bought a different one." So I sort of figured if I just bought all the really cool stuff a piece at a time, just slowly amassed it while I was sort of figuring out what I wanted out of rooms and consoles and stuff, then when it came time to open a studio all I would need was the board and the tape machine.

Andy Baker's old studio [Rock Central] was right across the street from where I lived, and that was an interesting set up.

Yeah, it sounded great. I think he completely opened up the underground recording scene in Athens. It sounded great in that house and you could work there for really cheap. I mean it wasn't slick, there weren't tens of thousands of dollars of great equipment but for what it was, it was totally great. I always liked working over there. He had Rock Central and Andy Le Master had the Furry Vault and I was just a guerrilla.

I always remember talking to Andy and he was getting very frustrated that it just seemed like he was the "demo" engineer in town. He was the one before they came to you, everyone would go to him and just do something for a 7 inch. He wanted to do records.

Right. That's what is so fuckin' great. Now that he has this place, he is doing what he was trying to do. It sort of helped everybody out that we all know twice as many people now because of all the traffic through here. Andy [Baker] could have been making great records over at his house too if anybody would have gave him a chance to do it and I always knew that. We've also started working on each others sessions a little bit. I was doing the Bloodkin record and they had gotten Moe Tucker [drummer for the Velvet Underground] to come up and sing on their record. Danny Hutchins had played in her band in Europe at one time and I was leaving to do Son Volt the day they had to do it with her. She drove up from South Georgia to come play a show and you know you don't want a mother of five to drive four hours in the car to come sing for 20 minutes. So they tried to work it out with another trip for her. It was great because there were three of us here and I could easily say Andy L. is free that day he can do it and he was totally into getting to record somebody *that* legendary. It was great for me because I knew it was in great hands but I already had a commitment to Son Volt and I didn't want to blow that off. That's just one example of how it's worked out so well.

It's like a tag team sort of thing?

Completely. Macha so far has generally wanted to work frequently like 20 hours a day. So we figured out into it that the best way for us to do it was to always keep a fresh man in the ring. There were some days that Andy B. would work from nine until six or seven at night then I came in at six or seven and worked until the sun came up. There's other days where I came in the morning and worked until five or six then Andy L. would come in at 12 and work until the next morning. They always had a fresh engineer to help them get it going on. Whereas a 20 hour day by yourself, the quality of the overdubs and hours 17 through 20 are probably not quite as good. The judgment tends to go a little bit.

How was it working with Macha?

They are so particular in such a good way because Josh [McKay, Macha 'instrumentalist'] has a vision of what it's all going to sound like when it's all done and just the instrumentation alone makes it incredibly fun to work on because it's always a challenge.

I know you worked with Son Volt a couple of years ago?

It was in '97 and '98, for about a year.

Was it all done on ADAT at their house?

They practiced in a former lingerie factory in Millstat Illinois, which is a town of maybe 3,000 and there nothing there. Jay [Farrar] lives over in St. Louis now which is about 45 minutes away from this place that they practice in out in the middle of nowhere. What they have is two 25'x40' rooms with 16' ceilings, nic size rooms to record music in. They called me in Ma of '97, [after] they heard some of those recording that I had done in the basement at Brooks', and asked me if I would be interested in coming out the and recording some demos for them. So I took dozen cool mics, a couple of Coles ribbon mics, som Lawson tube mics and few other things; a handful good mic preamps, a couple of good compressor They have a Mackie board, three ADATs and a doze or so solid standard microphones plus 5 vintage dru kits, 40 stringed instruments, a piano and 30 or 4 cool amps. They just have a ton of stuff. We record ed six songs over a course of a couple of weeks a so they asked me to come back in September and a little more. I went back out there for a couple mc weeks and we recorded a little bit more.

Was all this just demo stuff?

Well that's how it was put to me. Then I went ba in November again for a couple of weeks and that point it was like, "What are we doing? Are making a record?"

Did you ask them that point blank?

I said, if we are making a record then here is a cou more pieces of equipment that I need to get to this, their response was, "Yeah that sounds good." was great because they were doing it on ADA because the cost is really low. A two inch tape, y can budget roughly for $10 a minute for $150. minute reel of tape, there is some time in-betwe songs and what not. 24 tracks of ADAT tapes that 45 minutes will cost $18. So basically $18 for 45 m utes or $900 for 45 minutes of 2 inch tape. Two i tape sounds better, no two ways about it, but what we did is they wanted to record a record in the same manner that *Blonde on Blonde* was recorded. Where nobody really knew the songs when they were recording them, they just sort of learned it and then they would get one that would be the one where it all comes together. I recorded everything, 900 minutes that we actually kept. I would set a tape machine up and tell them it's rolling and they would play the song, finish, no recess or anything, after about 30 seconds I'd say roll again. I never turned the tape machines off, just let them roll. They would finish one whole tape and stop, listen back to what we had done and take a break and then figure out what they wanted to change. The next day we would come in and listen for a few hours and someone would say they like tracks 7, 29 and 38 and someone else would like 29 and 38, but find a mistake in 7. We narrowed it down to the ones that everyone liked. So we got it all done. I went out there a total of six times for periods of yen days to two weeks usually. We got all of the recording done and I'm 16-track here, so we had to go to a 24 track studio to mix it. We went to Mitch Easter's studio in Kernersville, North Carolina, which is a really great place. He has an Neve console and a lot of great old equipment. So we took the tapes there and bounced from the ADATs onto the 2 inch 24-track which warmed it up considerably and then mixed from that through Mitch's board and everything. It came out really great and I would gladly do another record like that. The difference in going from the digital tape to the analog rather than straight to the analog was not as great as you would think. The analog after the digital definitely sounded better than what was just on the digital tape to begin with. It totally tightened up the sound because the analog tape compresses and introduces harmonic distortion into the sound and to all of us that have grown up listening to music that was recorded on tape that sound is warmth. It's like the difference in film and video and if you perceive it as warmth well then it is warmth. I've gotten into arguments with engineers before who didn't like analog because they thought that it introduces distortion, but it's good distortion like with a tube amp. It's distortion that is fun to listen to so, therefore, it's good. We're not documenting medical records here we're making rock and roll records, it's fun. The analog tape did its thing to the digital tape and it worked out well for many reasons, it tightened up the sound overall, but, in addition, I was able to get my tape level on each sound after the performance was already done. Meaning a lot of the times you'll get set up to record a band you'll get the levels all set and then when the tape starts rolling the drummer is suddenly hitting twice as hard than he was before. After doing this for awhile you learn to set your levels low because the guy is going to hit them hard. It happens in the other direction too. You set it all up and suddenly it's a really quiet song and you have all this tape hiss because things were not recorded hot enough or everything is pounding in the red and it's beyond where you wanted to be and

your stuck with it. By setting the tape level after the performance is done I was able to really milk the analog tape for different sounds on different songs, different instruments and stuff. I knew that there was a shaker on a couple of songs and on one of them we wanted it to sound really clean and pristine so we kept it at a really nice low level where you would normally cut a quick transient attack like with a percussion or acoustic guitar or something. On another song that was kind of a rocker, we wanted it to sound like the shaker on "Mary, Mary" [which was recorded in 1966] where somebody hit the tape really hard on purpose or the meters on the console or tape machine weren't as quick and didn't know how hard they were hitting the tape. So with that we hit the tape a lot harder knowing the song is already done we have already heard all the instruments and the lead vocal we know where we want it all to sit in the mix. It was very time consuming and not something I would recommend doing for someone that wants to make a record in four days but for somebody who has got a lot of time to make a record. It was fun. They didn't have to burn any takes or 900 minutes of ADAT tape.

Which is 20 ADATs right?

It's 22 ADAT tapes is what we had so 990 minutes or something like that. So a 1,000 minutes of ADAT tape costs $600 or $700, if we would have done the whole thing on 2 inch tape it would have cost them $10,000.

Did it basically start out as a curiosity project?

I think they wanted to see how recording in the space would go. They had make records in some nice studios and I think they wanted to see what it would be like if they did it in their practice space and time wasn't an issue at all. They had all the time we could want in the practice space. I think it was one of those things that started out as an experiment to see how it would work and after the first couple of times it was working pretty well for everybody so we just kept on going.

Seems like your lifestyle is extremely mature, very grounded. You have children and a wife. How are you able to strike such a good balance between having a family and being a recording engineer?

Well, I've got a definite order of priorities. My family is first, music is second and I really don't have that many interests outside of that. There are things I like to do for fun occasionally, but I've narrowed my life down to basically those two things which fortunately are both things I love very much. You just make do. I don't really know how to explain it except that you do what you have to do. I have to support my family emotionally. I probably wouldn't be as good of a father or husband if I did something that made me miserable all day long. Even though my wife isn't a musician she is very supportive of what I do which is probably a huge factor in it. I'm sure that applies to all kinds of mar-

riages and jobs, if you don't get support from home, you're doomed from the start anyway. My priorities are clear. I don't work on weekends and a lot of bands want to record on weekends. If they have to record on the weekend, Andy and Andy do a terrific job and they're here to do it. There have been a few occasions where somebody has to choose between recording with me or recording on the weekends because I'm never going to choose somebody else over my family, but there are exceptions. If it's something I'm really dying to do and they can absolutely only do it on the weekend, especially when it's in the summer time and school's not in I can be a little bit more flexible, I generally find a way to work it out. Most people that I work with understand my situation. The exception that people have to make for me is that most of the time I don't work weekends, I've got to spend time with my family. Quite honestly, I don't have much of an interest to work with anybody that wouldn't understand why my family's a priority to me. Life is short. I take a two hour break everyday which has actually worked out to be great for the music. That is, I'll usually work with a band from around eleven to four or five then from six or seven till around eleven or twelve. There is no shortage of time spent on their recording. The thing that I've noticed is the quality of evening work is really great because everybody is fresh and rested. Everybody is on time because they've had two hours to go eat, buy a pack of smokes, if they're from out of town they can go downtown and goof off or something. A lot of people want the chance to lay around in here and not listen to any sound or if I'm recording basic tracks they can stay in here and rehearse for free for a couple of hours, get it together.

In the general day to day operation of this business who takes care of what?

The decisions are made by committee, an agreement by all three of us. I would have not gone into business with people that I didn't have a pretty similar philosophy with because it would be very frustrating. We rotate office responsibility. This week, before you came up here, I balanced the books for the week and next week I'm going to be on vacation so Andy B. will do it, the week after that Andy L. can do it. We have an outside accountant that takes care of all the real bookkeeping, we just total it up and send it to this guy. It sort of falls in different areas. I like haggling with people about equipment so a lot of the time I'll take care of that because I'm interested in seeing what is out there and what the prices are. But like I said, we rotate responsibility. I don't answer the phone when I'm doing sessions because I don't want them to wonder if they are paying me to record or talk on the phone. We have a sit-down meeting once every few months to discuss what we're doing, what we need to buy, or fix, what's not working right and scheduling wise we keep in close contact with each other every few days about what's up in the rotation, who is responsible for the books, or buying the coffee and paper towels. ☸

Roger Moutenot

New York to Nashville

Every now and then a record comes out where the production and recording techniques work together with some really unique songwriting to make a masterpiece album. The kind you listen to hundreds of times and still wonder, "How did they get that sound?" The Beatles *Revolver*, Beach Boys *Pet Sounds*, there's too many to list. While maybe not of that same scale, Yo La Tengo's *Electropura* was that sonic-awakening record for me. Roger Moutenot, the producer behind the last four Yo La Tengo records, has continually recorded landmark albums, as well as gaining success with artists such as Paula Cole and Sleater-Kinney. I had the unique opportunity to sit down with Roger and chat about his move to Nashville, setting up shop at Alex the Great, House of David and Woodland, and his adaptive recording insights.

by Kevin Robinson
photo Barbara MOutenot

How has it been working in a very music industry influenced city?

When I first moved here [Nashville], the first two years were hell cause all the clients I had in New York were like, "Well he split. I guess he doesn't want to work here anymore". And I came down here and didn't want to do country, so for two years I basically didn't work. I did a couple of little scattered things here and there. Then I got to do the Paula Cole record, and that kind of brought in other projects and a lot of traveling. I still didn't work here much, 'cause all my work was in LA. You know eight months away out of the year? But, the saving grace was Yo La Tengo always had to come down here. They love it down here. Prince's Hot Chicken and all that. [laughs]

I heard that place shut down?

more tape machines being produced. Studer ran their last production of analog tape machines. Otari does not make them anymore. There are no analog tape machines being produced right now. Then you go and you open up *Mix* and it's like one page after another... its digital, digital, digital. And I'm like, "What the hell is happening?" But with the whole Pro Tools thing, I would never use this as a stand-alone recorder. It's never going to be, "Okay, turn on the Pro Tools and let's rock!" I've got it so that I can fly something over from analog, manipulate it, process it, flip it backwards, time stretch it, and then put it right back on tape. I've found that it just opens up a whole new palette of ink. I never overdo it, but I do a session now and if the artist says, a "I want this", or "I want that", I never have to say that we can't do that. It's like, "Great, yeah let's try

How do you approach recording a band like Yo La Tengo?

We'll do it all live, sometimes with vocals that go flying in the room. And then we'll put a few things on it, put the song to bed and move on to the next one. One of the things I like about Yo La Tengo is that we never brought in people. There might have been a few guest appearances, but you know Georgia will play vibes. Georgia doesn't play vibes, but there's something beautiful about that. You don't have this guy that's just flowery on the vibes, you've got Georgia and she's just reaching for that C and is just an 8th note behind. And that's character and I love that. Spontaneous, and just flying by the seat of her pants. She's making it work somehow, but it's not pristine. In fact one time we did something really cool. I think that was the ...*Heart Beating*... record.

Really? I don't know. They found some other soul-food truck off Charlotte Avenue. They would find places that I'd never heard of. But more and more projects since have started coming down here. And this year has been great. I really like living here. I've got two kids. It's been fantastic. I've found this studio, and besides right now this time of year [July], I dig it

Well, you've had your name attached to some of the finer albums in the indie-rock scene.

Yeah, and that's what I'd rather do personally. The Paula Cole record was cool and it's fun and exciting to see it doing so well and everything. But I made her second record and, you know, they slapped so much money at her and it was such a high expectation that this record has to be [makes big explosion sound]. And that kind of pressure makes it to where you can't perform well in the studio. Yo La Tengo, Sleater-Kinney, The Pierce Sisters (my latest record) - you try to keep the budget down. You don't have a lot of money so let's just DO a record. I prefer that. Let's just dig in and get it done.

You do a lot of your own engineering work as well.

I do. Lately though, I've been hiring an engineer. I like having the producing hands on and still stepping back to let somebody else do it.

Has it been more of a cost issue or control?

A little bit of both. And I still feel that, you know? That I can't really let the whole thing go.

You've started to dabble in the digital world as well. Why the addition of the Pro Tools set-up, and what was the progression from analog?

I will never leave analog. I won't. I will never leave it and it blew my mind when I heard that there are no

it". But Pro Tools will never be my main thing. It's just that, a tool. I even went to a seminar on Pro Tools and I walked out. There's all these country guys going, "You mean I can get rid of amp noise?" you know. What the hell?

You've done a lot of work at Alex the Great and House of David, is there something there that keeps bringing you back?

I love House of David. They have this analog tape machine that they bought after the Yo La Tengo session for *I Can Hear the Heart Beating as One*. We did that whole record on ADATs. That's the only Yo La Tengo record that was ever recorded on ADATs. We wound up mixing to analog though. But I've done a lot of work at Alex the Great, and the greatest thing about that place is that anything you want, all the guitars, keyboard, organs, Acetones, vibes, piano... if you have an idea it's all there for you to use. The vibe is great and so is the rate. It's awesome. I wound up at House of David because Alex the Great was booked up. And that place has an API. I love APIs, and it's funky too. I like funky studios, where you feel like you can put your feet up or if an ash drops on the floor nobody's going to freak.

How do you usually start setting up? Say, with mic'ing the drums?

At House of David they had this drum set already set up, microphones placed, baffles set up, and I started tearing it all down and they flipped. Come to find out they haven't moved it in about four years. Like the mics even! Whenever I record Yo La Tengo it's pretty much no headphones. They can't do that. They're so used to rehearsing that way. So it's a real live situation.

We invited about 40 people to Alex the Great and set the band up, gave them monitor wedges and recorded them right in front of the people. I think we wound up using like two or three tracks from that session.

Just to get the vibe of a live show?

Yeah. Yo La Tengo is a really tense band. You know? And they work off that. If it's not tense then something's wrong. If they're having too much fun or things are going too well, then something's wrong. There always has to be a little tension. And it took me a couple of records to get into that. When I did *Painful*, I had no idea what was going on. I thought, "This record's going to fall apart any second", but we made it through and it was very appropriately named *Painful*. But since then I've realized what they go through making a record, and they realize what my thing is and it all kind of works out. But it's so cool to see that transition of recording their records.

Did you invite a crowd in on the newest YLT Record?

Uh, no. We didn't invite anybody, but we again went back into a real live situation. We'd set up things like, Ira would have his first guitar bit set up in one area of the studio, like set up some amps in the tiled room. Then he'd lay that part down and let the feedback roll a little and just walk over to the drums and start doing something with Georgia for another part of the song. Then he'd get off that and go do something else. So there's a lot of moving. James would have his delay pedals feedback on out and then leave them to go play a keyboard part. So we get a lot done in one song if we plan it out like that.

It's all happening live going down to tape like that?

Yeah, like Ira will be walking around... like when he leaves the live room and is going into this area where there's another amp set up, I'll have another set of NS10s set up playing so he can hear what Georgia and James are playing. So, it gets pretty involved.

How do you deal with the bleed?

I love bleed.

But a lot of Georgia's drumming is brush-work and soft at times and the band is often very dynamic. How do you deal with that?

It's taken me a while, because they also sing like [makes high whisper noise]. The first time I recorded them I thought the mic was broken. I walked out to the room, because I had the mic pre cranked and I was still getting no level. I was like, "What the"...and I went out there and I said, "Could you sing for a second?" And it was literally like [makes higher whisper noise], and I thought, "Okay now I get it." We really work on the vibe of the recording, and I'd really rather capture the vibe. When you let things play over and over, and you've been working on it and you've been trying to get a sound and hours are going by, you're past it. The band is lost. Especially with Yo La Tengo. In fact Ira has this saying, "This is getting tired." But as for bleed, we'll have amps set up in rooms to create more bleed. I'll put a mic over the drums, feed it into a Fender amp, put some reverb on it and have it facing back into the drums. Just put vibrato on it and stuff like that. We'll try to be creative and use the bleed to our advantage, especially tracking without headphones. I worked with T-Bone Burnett and he taught me so much about bleed. You sit down and talk with that guy and it's the best time you've ever had. He's got great ideas, like he'll get three things going on the low end. Just [makes low throaty noise]. And you're thinking the mix is going to sound awful. But then you find there is something he's going for and he gets it by taking that route. He's taught me a lot about just one mic recording. You know bleed with bleed? He loves bleed, even more than me.

What are some of your favorite toys, no matter where you go, that you have to bring with you?

SansAmp. I love it. That is an incredible little tool. I always bring my Moog. I have two Echoplexes that I always like to have along, one that is tube that I got for 25 bucks here in Nashville. I personally don't have an extensive microphone collection right now, but I have this podium mic that's just weird. It's just a long goose-necked omni-directional mic. It just sounds great. Vocals for Ira, sometimes a 57 would be stuck like this [shoves hand straight up in front of face]. Every singer's different. And everything that you're going for from song to song may be different. You might want a vocal big and just right there

inside your head, or you may want smaller and a little thrown off or something like that. So there's never one vocal mic that I always use. I try not to do that. Anything too much the same - I hate that. I used to assist this guy when I first started, and he drew me a template for his drum sounds. These are the mics you use, this is the mic pre-sets, this is the placement of the mics. So he would just walk in and it would all be ready to go. Weirdly enough, the drums almost always sounded the same no matter who was playing them or if it was a different kit.

Did you go to school for all of this?

I did. I went because I was in a band, and had a studio in my parent's house. I was recording my own band, and all of a sudden neighborhood bands and guys coming in from other towns would want to come in and record. I felt like I didn't know what the hell I was doing and I had two 4-tracks.

Would you recommend going to school for up and coming producers/engineers?

Um... I would. Although I gotta say that in the year I went to school I learned a little bit about how things worked, inside guts-wise, and hardly anything about how to listen to something. And that really only comes from experience. You know, just trying it out. My first gig was building ballasts. They asked if I did carpentry work, and I was like, "Yeah". I built these things with ten thousand nails in them and weighing at least a hundred pounds and they STILL wobbled! But they kept me on and I could easily say that in about 3 months I learned more than I had ever known before. Just by hanging out and doing alignments and all that stuff I learned so much just by watching the guys. It was an incredible education. So if you could have both, that would be the way to do it.

that, but you know, it propels me into trying to reach my goal. Where I came from, working with Arto Lindsay and all these guys that were just wacko, downtown New York, you know, just out-there... like I'm trying to mix stuff that is a half step out of the key of the song and it really taught me a lot. And I always pull from that. So I can have a pop hit and dement it somehow. Not in a way that I'm trying to destroy it, or take it away from the radio. Although personally I don't care, as long as it turns out how the band likes it. I like to produce records where I'm not just making myself happy. I've gone from Gypsy Kings, to Paula Cole, to Yo La Tengo and I love that I'm not captured into one little category.

Living in Nashville, surely you've done some work on a country record.

My first country assignment was a favor to a friend that I'd known for a while. Never worked on a country record before, and I got my first call, and I was like, "Uuuggghhh... okay." It was a favor because the engineer got sick and they were about to track this Hal Ketchum record and they needed somebody. So I said, "Okay." He says, "Great we're going to start at 8:30 tomorrow morning." What? So I go in there and there's this, "Fwap, fwap, fwap," click track going on. And the drummer's just, "Boom, tap, boom, tap." The only problem is that the song had this backbeat feel to it, and the drummer was just right on the click. And I said, "Shouldn't the snare just sort of fall? I mean everything else is just flowing". And they just didn't get it. And that's the difference right there. Fuck the feeling of the song, just get the part down. Jill Sobule played drums on her record. You know, just real simple and sometimes awkward, but the tracks just sounded gorgeous. As opposed to someone who's right there on the money.

"WE REALLY WORK ON THE VIBE OF THE RECORDING, AND I'D REALLY RATHER CAPTURE THE VIBE."

Do you have a record or project that is the closest to the sonic vision that you had for it in the beginning? A "most proud of" recording?

That's only coming about now. I'll be the first one to say it - that I'm learning with every record that I do. There's so much more to know. It has only been until the last couple of records that I feel that I'm starting to get comfortable. I don't mean comfortable as in lazy, but where if there's something I'm going for I know how to do it now. And this is the first time I'm feeling like musically and sonically that there is this whole wide range of things I can pull from. If there is something new I want to go for I feel like I know how to get there. So I guess I'll honestly say it was the last record that I did that I'm most happy with. Every record that I do is like a new stepping stone. You know, all those Yo La Tengo records I look back on and say, "Oh, if I'd only have..." and I think everybody does

That's a great mentality to have, but as a producer you must run into situations where that isn't the financially profitable standpoint to take.

Here's the deal. If you do something your way and the way the band wants it and it does hit... like Paula Cole, okay? We didn't go in and record that record to make it break. I don't really have that in me. It made it and that was the thing. Paula and I made that record in three weeks and when it was all said and done, it did well. So great. That's the beauty of it. With Yo La Tengo we go in and do what we want to do. If it clicks and people like it, then that's better. Better than you sitting there trying to make something formatted that you think people are going to like to listen to. ☮

Fear Is Not Your Friend
by Larry Crane

photo:
att Donahue @
he Clackamas River
Oregon shot
y Chris Brunkhart

The biggest enemy to art is fear. Fear causes artists to curb their vision, to play it safe, and to operate in a manner that is expected of them. In the recording studio fear manifests itself in many diferent ways. One can be afraid to try a new microphone or use a familiar one for a different purpose. An engineer can be afraid of upsetting an artist with an unusual sound. A producer may be afraid to let a group pursue a "new" direction. Record labels want you to do "what worked last time" or to "use 'so-and-so' because they had a hit with 'what's-his-name'." People are afraid of change and what lies outside the accepted norm. Fear will lead you down the safe and simple path, never pushing ahead, never bucking the norm and never breaking through to new sounds, songs and creativity.

Make sure to look for the new and unusual. Try the "wrong" mics. Talk to artists about their wildest ideas. Try to do things even if you think they might not work. Record in the "wrong" room. Play songs too fast or too slow. Change tape speeds. Put effects pedals on drums.

Nobody will admit they are afraid. Perhaps they don't even know. It's your job to make sure you never are. ☣

STUDIO
EMPLOYEE PARK
tchad
blake

PARKING
NG ONLY

The phrase "recording artist" is usually reserved for the sensitive souls who sing and play the stuff that makes its way onto those shiny little discs. But there are some on the recording end of the process who truly deserve the title. Recordists who forge a distinct creative identity of their own that manages to distinguish and enhance each project they work on without overwhelming it. Tchad Blake is among them.

In the last decade, Blake, with frequent partner Mitchell Froom, has created an aural terrain unto itself. Like a latter Beatles album or Brian Eno recording, Tchad Blake's work is usually a "down the rabbit hole" experience - the listener is transported to another realm where the sonic texture asserts itself as a part of the creative process itself.

For a recording world titan who has worked with a staggering number of heavyweight music makers from The Master Musicians of Jajouka to Tom Waits to Sheryl Crow, Tchad comes across as an unexpectedly down-to-earth guy. (I easily spot him in the dining room of his luxury hotel: he is the only one in a red flannel shirt and jeans). On a November morning in Seattle, knee-deep in the current Pearl Jam record, his hunger and enthusiasm for the work of recording is infectious. Between spoonfuls of oatmeal, we discuss, among many other things, Jaipur in the wee hours (and why you might want to pack earplugs for a visit), his predilection for high-contrast sound, and why he loves being a Latin Playboy.

But like all those who climb to creative heights, he began his trek at street level...

BY STEPHEN MURRAY
PHOTOS BY JEFF GROS

"I like to go in and... get a first impression and....just run wi[...]

So let's backtrack a little. You started with Wally Heider in LA, right?

Yeah, at what later became Filmways/Heider Recording Studios.

And that was your first gig?

Yeah, I was a guitar player for years. Not a very good one, really. But it took me years to realize I wasn't going to get much better. And I got a job at Wally Heider's, just by beating on the door, to try to stay in music. I'd just done a TV show about sharks, where I was the still photographer and boom man. It was a great experience, going out with the sharks. I got it through this young guy who was the son of the director. He was a sound guy with Nagra. I'd always carried tape recorders around with me since high school, just to record sounds. Walking through hallways, doors closing. And I just loved it. I'd go home and listen to it at night. Sad, but true. [laughs]

Were you thinking about musical applications, or were you just into sounds?

It wasn't really about music, but just noise. I put weird guitar noises to it, synth noises. And I used to love feedback. It was more avant-garde, almost like installation stuff, which I tired of pretty quickly. It got pretty stupid after a while. [laughs] But it was fun at the time. I just *loved* the sound. It wasn't the music so much. I was never a composer. I just liked sounds. So I met this guy...

The shark guy?

Yeah, great guy; Nick Webster. He used to build robots and go to the Himalayas with his dad to look for the Yeti. And he said, "You know, you could get a job. You could be a recording engineer. If you like all these sounds you could just go do it." And I thought, hmmm, really?

How old were you at the time?

About 19. I actually played a session as a guitarist at Wally Heider's and I met an engineer there who told me what I should do and it interested me. So I just went pounding on the door everyday for two or three months. One day they said, "We need someone to work the equipment room." And then two days later they said they needed someone on the phone at night down at the other studio, which was the RCA building in Hollywood. So they took me down there and showed me this set-up. It was a live set-up in this huge room, Studio B, which was a famous old room that Wally Heider had taken over. And it was the Rolling Stones and they were recording what would eventually become *Tattoo You*.

And what were you doing?

I was just on phones and running for ribs at two o'clock in the morning. I was a runner and a janitor. Cleaning up after everyone, you know. It was a great studio to work in. It totally was not about anything technical. It was just about keeping a session going, you know. In fact they didn't want you to learn too much technically. I was caught reading a manual on re-aligning a tape machine and it was taken away from me.

So you were being mentored, but they didn't think technical training wa[...] what you needed?

No. They had tech guys for that. As assistant enginee[...] you could record. But not really. Learning how th[...] tape machine worked wasn't where it was at. Bu[...] they had some really good engineers there. Reall[...] old school. But I used to just go and hang ou[...] Everyone was really friendly and the sessions weren[...] closed. I mean, you couldn't just walk in off th[...] street. But engineers would always say, "Come by [...] you want to hang out." Because they knew the[...] could get you to do stuff. "Go move tha[...] microphone, go get that other microphone, go g[...] us some food." It was really great.

So what sort of things were yo[...] picking up at that time that yo[...] could use later? When did you ge[...] your hands on the board?

The board I got my hands on right away. They use[...] to let me go in after hours. I'd take records i[...] LPs, and bring them up to the console and me[...] with EQ, fool around in the patch bay. There w[...] an old harmonizer that I'd used to tape mo[...] records and "stereo-ize" them, it made the[...] really wide. [laughs] Or we'd go into the mec[...] rooms where they did only voiceovers and fo[...] with tapes of speeches to make them say ru[...] things. Really horrible stuff. But I loved it.[...] thought I was Phil Spector.

So you had the opportunity for a great deal of experimentation?

Yeah, I'd just go in and stay up all night playing with a drum machine. I was able to bring people in to record every now and then pretty much right away. There was a guy there named Sherman Keene, who eventually wrote a book [*Practicle techniques for the Recording Engineer*] that's become a standard I think. He'd hold classes once a week and he'd talk about engineer stuff; fixing machines and things you needed to know for orchestra sessions like figuring out beats per minute. And studio etiquette. His big thing was studio etiquette. He thought that was about 60% - knowing how to make people feel at home.

What techniques did you learn?

Oh, knowing when to speak at the right times, having a studio that looked nice, make sure you have sharpened pencils. And it's all true, that's good stuff. It was a good atmosphere, and that's important.

So how long were you there?

Only three years.

So how did you make the transition from that period into a real career as an engineer?

So it sounds almost like you're leading a double life with your fascination for unusual sounds on the one hand, and working on very conventional stuff on the other. At what point did those two worlds, the aesthetically-inclined and the "normal" work, meet?

Well, not for a long time. I started putting binaural sound effects behind some things. I was always into the English progressive scene of the '60s and early '70s - like King Crimson, Van der Graaf Generator, Pink Floyd. And they were doing all that. But it didn't really come together for a long time. I loved distortion and I loved things recorded through mechanical filters; putting up papers, trash cans, boxes. But it didn't seem to fly with most music.

Probably not with Sheena Easton.

[laughs] No. I used to play stuff that I'd do and get a few laughs, "Oh yeah, that's cute." It really wasn't until I met Mitchell [Froom] that I started to use those techniques on commercial recordings. And even then we did a lot of conventional stuff for many years.

Did you work on the Del Fuegos records?

I did one record. He came in and did the first record and that's when we met. And he asked me to do the music for a play for him, to engineer it - over the

without going to a keyboard. He'll just sit there and, without even looking at what they're playing he'll say, "You're playing a D? Play this over it." And it will create a cool chord. And that's the way he thinks. He's a composer. He's an orchestrator. He can do it. He's serious. I don't want to know anything before I go into the studio. I like to go in and have people start playing and get a first impression and get the sounds and go with it. Just run with it. If I have too much time to think about stuff I'm in trouble. I like the spontaneity. I like to get a sense of the band and get that caught on record. You can't always do it. There is work and putting your nose to the grindstone, but I want to keep as much of that [spontaneity] as I can. So we really work well together that way. Because he loves to do [his thing], and then I come in and start messing things up. So it's really been a good match. Still is as far as I'm concerned. We're working less and less together these days. But I think it's just a phase. It's a good collaboration.

So at what point did you think that collaborative identity was beginning to gel and come to fruition?

[Los Lobos'] *Kiko*. We've always sort of distanced ourselves from the music business. It's not because we hate it. It's a brilliant business. And business is business. It's a bank that loans an artist money, and

" if I have too much *time* to think about stuff I'm in trouble."

Wally Heider's changed owners. He got really sick, and it was taken over by somebody who ran it into the ground. So I left and got a place called Mad Dog, which was a demo studio down in Santa Monica. Little 16-track demo studio, tiny little closet of a place. But it was another place where the owners were great, really creative. Anyway I worked for them for a while, did people's demos for about a year. And then there was an opening at Sound Factory for an assistant engineer. Phil McConnel, who had been remote manager at Wally Heider's was now the manager of this studio. And he remembered me from the Wally Heider days and asked me if I wanted to be an assistant for this engineer there who had just won a Grammy, David Leonard. He was doing really well and had just moved up from that middle area from assisting to engineering and needed an assistant. And I took the job because it was four blocks from my house. I'd just met my future wife, and it just all made sense. And I was there all through the '80s.

And what kinds of things were you recording?

Well [pause, low voice], some pretty bad stuff. I don't remember a lot of it. Sheena Easton recorded there. Greg Mathison productions, he and Trevor Beech used to be in there a lot, and David Leonard did all of their records at the time.

weekend. We were going to do all the music in one weekend. And he said I could do it any way I wanted to. So I got to do some of my "stuff", you know. And he loved it. And the play went well. It was just a small hole-in-the-wall play, but it was fun to do. So that was our first work together, then he got Crowded House and they went through 3 engineers and fired them all. During the last 2 weeks of the album he asked if I could do it with him, just finish it up. It wasn't any tracking, just overdubs: Vocals, some guitar, re-recorded some bass - which I did. And I got along with the guys really well and had a good time with Mitchell and discovered we had really similar musical tastes. And then he got the next Del Fuegos record he asked me to do it. And that was probably my first real record. That was how it all began with Mitchell and we've been working together almost exclusively ever since.

So it was then that this felt like a partnership that was going to go places?

It didn't feel like a partnership until later. But we knew we liked working together. We had the same sensibilities, with sort of opposite methods.

How so?

He's very meticulous about thinking about things beforehand. And he's really good at it. I don't think I've ever seen anyone as good at it. He's got perfect pitch. So he can always think of chords and notes, and so he can tell somebody (what he's hearing)

you make agreements with the bank. You have to do certain things if you want more money. And I don't dislike it at all. But I've always distanced myself from it because I don't want to think about it. I just want to be in the studio and hear music, you know? So it hurt us, because we didn't really have any friends in the business. A couple, but not a lot. We usually didn't allow [record company] people to come down to the studio and listen until it was done. We didn't want any input. We just wanted the artists' input and the opportunity to do what we do. And for the artist to say yes or no and let them be the final arbiter of what went on the record. *They're* the boss. That brought us to the early '90s and we were sort of tired of The records we were doing. Kinda glossy productions. I was never good at it. I hated the sound of all those records. I could never get a really good reverb sound on the snare drum. Every time I heard it I'd wince. And I'd listen to Bob Clearmountain's stuff and I'd be amazed. It sounded brilliant to me, the way he did "that sound." I couldn't do it. And I was *really* frustrated and so was Mitchell. So he came in and said, "You know, we're going to do this next record with Los Lobos and we've got to start being happy with what *we* do. So anything goes. Let's just go back to what we did for the soundtrack for the play. The first thing we worked on together. Let's just do what we do." And they [Los Lobos] were ready for it. They wanted to do something different.

That was a really bold move forward in a new direction for them. Up until then they'd been, more or less, just a really good roots/Mex roadhouse-style band.

Well, the music came from them. And oddly enough, there was just a really good coincidence. The week we started I went into Guitar Center, which I always do. Whenever I start a project I go into music stores and pawn shops, you know; tool stores. See if something catches my eye. Behind the counter was a plastic board and a box sitting on the middle of it. And I could see it had all these little DIP switches on it. I said, " What is that?" And the guy said, "I don't know, it just came in today." It was a SansAmp, the first one. I plugged in a guitar, I plugged in a drum machine, and maybe ten minutes I sat with it and I said, "Okay. I want two of these." And the guy went to look and he said, "We don't have any in stock. It's a demo." So the guy called the company and they didn't have any ready to ship for sale. I ended up contacting [the company] and they got me one and it just changed my life. [laughs] It really did.

If it's got some distortion, I can swing with it. If it's just that rock "tick"... uhhh. There's just such a wonderful quality to it, I loved it. I ended up getting another four pedals. And I started using it on bass. I haven't used a bass amp on any record since then.

Not at all?

Nope, just direct box through a SansAmp. And everyone I've used it with everyone down to Tory Levin who's... well, he's not a purist, but he's so into his equipment. They're great. I haven't found anything they don't sound good on, except I don't like it on guitar.

Ironically.

Ironically, I don't like it on electric guitar. Acoustic guitar, great on acoustic guitar.

I know you used that combination a good deal on Richard Thompson's stuff.

Richard Thompson, Ron Sexsmith. Flutes, saxes, vocals. You name it.

So I hear what you're saying about what happens with it technically, but in terms of the qualities it evokes, what do you think those sounds do for a listener?

I guess so. There is a reason, I just don't hear it.

So when *Kiko* was done, I'm sure you could see that there'd been a big leap forward in the sound of the band [Los Lobos] and, it seems, your signature approach as an engineer. How did it feel when that record was done?

Well, good. Because the thing is we made some good friendships on that record. We'd worked with David [Hidalgo] before on a song on an earlier record. And also he'd done overdubs on something else Mitchell had done. So we knew him a little bit. But this was like... we just sort of bonded. And we've stayed that way ever since.

That's evident in your work with Latin Playboys.

Yeah, David and Louie made us honorary members, because you know we didn't really play anything on the records. They're really all David Hidalgo and then Louie wrote all the lyrics and did some singing. And did some playing, but most of it is David. Mitchell was responsible for getting the tape and playing it for me and saying, "Let's take this to Lenny [Waronker] over at Warner Brothers and see what he says." He [Waronker] was, like,

For me, it's a matter of creating the atmosphere that th

And it was designed for electric guitar applications, but you were immediately using it for...?

Drums. It was drums. That's what the drum sound is. Nothing else. It's like, conventionally recorded drums with a little bit of Sans Amp sprinkled on here and there, particularly with the kick and snare on *Kiko*.

So you don't use it in tracking, but treatment afterwards?

Oh yeah, I track with it. And if I know the band, like I do Los Lobos, I just mix it in with the signal.

You track both a pure signal and a treated signal and blend them in a submix?

Yeah and sometimes I just use the SansAmp track. But with something like Pearl Jam, where I don't know how it's going to go from day to day, I keep them separate.

And what was it about the sound of the SansAmp that attracted you?

Well, there's a funny thing that happens with the sound when you bring it up on certain settings. You just play around with the settings, and there's also just playing with the high-pass filters and the way that alters phase relationships. Even just a high-pass filter with an easy slope from 75 Hz down. You just pop that in and the amount that changes things, with distortion, is incredible. So you find a setting that's out of phase. It's not 180 degrees, it's just at a weird place. It would drop the kick an octave. Hit the phase button and it would just go "Ka-BLUMPH". It would just be this "splat" but a really good splat, with a funny little crunch on top, that wasn't a "tick".

Well, if you judge by sales, it turns them off. [laughs] But if you ask me, I think it makes things more interesting. I just like high contrast. I can't stand it if something's recorded all beautifully. If everything sounds that way it's just like nails on a chalkboard to me. I want to hear contrast. That's what perks my ears up. It's like in field recording, I like noises. It's always better if there's one little thing that takes you away. Like if there's a jet engine, or a car goes by... it messes you up a little bit. So you actually hear both things better. I do anyway. Well, that happens in the music. You know, you have a really beautiful vocal and a nice guitar sound, and you put this weird bongo or drum sound to it... it sounds like it's going through a pipe - maybe it is, I like to use a mechanical filter. I'd rather have the lo-fi sound with a hi-fi sound than have it all hi-fi. Or all lo-fi, where it's all just unbearable to me.

I've heard it said that all good art either takes you to a new place or it takes you to a familiar place and makes you see it in a new way. Maybe the ambitious listener's response to conventional recording technique, as this point, is, "I've been here before," and so the experience is less dramatic.

Well, I don't know. There's a whole world out there that proves my tastes wrong because those [conventional] records are the ones that sell the biggest numbers. Like Celine Dion... Those records and that kind of recording, you know.

Well, perhaps there's comfort to be found in going to those familiar old places. Perhaps that's what *those* listeners want.

our only friend in the music business. And he said, "Let's put it out as a record." And they did. And at that point David said, "Let's have a band. You guys have to be in the band. It's just got to be us." Which was great. I still can't believe it. I'm so happy to be a Latin Playboy. [laughs] So some friendships were made there and we've made all these records since. And it's been great every time.

And so was much of the work that followed soon afterward a result of Los Lobos recommending you; was it people responding to *Kiko*?

Yes, right.

And people were saying what? This is exciting stuff, this is a sonic territory I want to explore?

Yeah, absolutely. We got work from that. And we started isolating, defining ourselves in that way. But you know, the kinds of sounds we liked crunchy sounds... somewhere between Tom Wait and the slick side, high contrast - started gettin more fashionable. I always thought it was becaus of rap and hip-hop coming up. People started usin pretty funky old records [for sampling]. And it jus broke the margin for sonics. And suddenly ther was so much more that was acceptable to recor companies. I couldn't get arrested in the '80s t mix anything. Even the Crowded House stuff wa mixed by [Bob] Clearmountain.

How are things different now tha you're working independently o Mitchell and in the "producer" role

It's different. I'm an engineer, basically. There are different kinds of producers and there's room for all of them. Different artists require different things. I think I'm best with bands who have a strong identity and a strong sense of themselves - who are good songwriters and good arrangers. I can help. I can sometimes spark a somewhat lackluster arrangement, but I'm not an arranger. If a song's not working, I can try to tinker with it, but it doesn't come naturally. Unlike Mitchell who can see the flaw in a song and a structure and say, "Here's three different options." For me, it's a matter of creating the atmosphere that the music's going to live in. With arrangement, my strength is with mute buttons. I love to capture the spontaneity on tape and then just give me mix time and I can mute for days.

And then there's the non-technical side. Sounds are important, but there's also the social aspect; how to get the most out of people. As producer you must have to take greater responsibility for that as well.

Yeah. It's really just in the last year and a half that I've started to produce people I don't know. People I sometimes meet on the day of the session, almost.

With Pearl Jam, I'd met them in New Zealand and hung out with them for a day or two and knew I liked them as people. And so I knew we could work together. But it's still different because I'm used to working with people over time. That's where it's at. I miss that, sometimes: developing *with* somebody. It's great to do three or four records with somebody. It seemed to happen a lot in the '60s - where you'd grow with an artist. Doesn't always work, but it certainly makes it fun and comfortable in the studio.

You get to be the fifth Beatle.

[laughs] Right. It's happening less and less though. Oddly enough I now get more offers to mix than anything else. Which is crazy because, like I said, in the '80s and early '90s I wasn't allowed to touch it. I've done some mixes more recently where I've really restrained myself, conscious not to get too "out." Like a single's mix where I can take it out a little and not offend anybody. And I've turned it in and they say, "It sounds a little conservative." And I go, "Man, times have changed." [laughs]

I can't help but think that you've played a pretty big part in that evolution. I think the records you've made throughout this decade have contributed to the opening of a lot of ears.

I guess it's hard for me to see that because it doesn't seem like that many people heard those records. Mitchell and I have a running joke, that we should call our production company "Kiss of Death Productions". [laughs] Because our sales figures are pretty dismal. But I've loved the records we've made. And I actually think that the records we make together are the most fun to do because the weight is distributed. And I can actually sit and listen to the music in another way. When I'm producing and engineering... I think this record [Pearl Jam] has been the hardest for me. Because it's in a new studio [Litho], which is not ideal. It's a good studio - I wish I had a studio like that. But for me it takes a long time to learn a studio and how it sounds. So producing and thinking about the sounds and engineering... I'm finding it hard to juggle. If I was at the Sound Factory [Blake's main haunt] I could be on the phone while patching something in. So it's a little more weight. So when I'm working with Mitchell it's like a vacation. And I love the tempo

and how we work. It's kind of a lazy approach. [laughs] But it's really fun. Every day you feel like coming into the studio. You wake up and you go, "Oh, I've got an idea. Let's go do it."

When you say "lazy", is that because you're just "playing?"

No, it's actually lazy. It's an eight hour day. But in that eight hours there's probably two and one half hours of breaks. [laughs] We just sit and eat and talk. Which is also a huge part of the process. With Los Lobos it's just ridiculous, but it's *so* much fun. By the time we've finished dinner everybody's kinda like, "Aw, let's play." They get up there, play through a few takes, usually the first one's the best. As we listen to some playback, Louie [Perez] is finishing with lyrics on his computer.

He's actually writing the lyrics in the studio?

[laughs] Yeah, he's got a computer in there, music playing from the other room. He gives it to Dave [Hidalgo] who sits there with two or three passes and says "Okay, let's try it." I put up the mic and, I kid you not, 50% of the time he goes out and sings it and it's *the* vocal. First time. And then we do a couple of backgrounds or a keyboard... and it's done. And we're out by nine.

When you say people are so attracted to the Latin Playboys records I suspect that the spontaneity is part of what they're responding to. When you deconstruct it, a particular cool sound is no substitute for chemistry and fun. The vibe infects every aspect of what goes to tape.

I think so. I'd agree with that. And that's been my thing - I just want to have a good time. Everybody wants hits, and everybody wants to be successful and have lots of money. But I can't think that way. And I don't work with the kind of artist who thinks that way anyhow. You just have to go with what you really love, what you really like about music, and hope it clicks. It can't be the other way around, for me. There are people out there who can do that, who are really good at it. More power to 'em. I love TLC and they're writing hits. And they're producers.... it's *amazing*. I'm stuck on that record. But my head just doesn't think that way. I can listen to it and love it, but when I'm in the studio, I just can't do *that*.

Maybe an important aspect of the whole process is learning how to be yourself, rather than emulating someone else's schtick.

Yeah, I've been through that. But you know with sounds and stuff, I'll usually think in a really, really broad fashion about what kind of sound might work on something. Maybe I think in terms of the thing at hand: the drum. It's almost like connecting the dots. And I sometimes arrive at a sound that I couldn't have imagined.

So you don't necessarily say, "I've got a sound in my head, how do I get it?"

usic's going to live in.

Sometimes, but rarely. Usually it's, "That guitar sounds too normal, put the amp in that trash can over there." And then the handle on the trash can will buzz - *but not enough.* [laughs] So then we have to put a mic on the buzz. Maybe you do the part and it doesn't work. I'll tell ya, eight times out of ten it does. You experiment and you find something you can use somehow. And sometimes it works in a way you didn't think it was going to. On a different part, maybe, than the one you were going for. It's a crap shoot.

Well, on your current project you've been working with a hugely successful band [Pearl Jam] on an enormous record label [Epic/Sony], have you felt big expectations from them?

Just from the band. I just want to make a record that's good for the band. So it's really about my own expectations. And I can be pretty hard on myself. It's a matter of working with new people in a new studio in a new town [Seattle] for a long period of time.

How long have you been at it?

I was here a month in September, it's been three weeks this month [November], and it's probably going to be two weeks in the new year. And I'm used to doing a record in four weeks, five maybe. Mixed, done. Usually in a situation when you have a concentrated time. And this is different - everybody in the band has other things going on. Important stuff, like benefits, and shows to do, or a record company to run. So it's a little bit piecemeal. People coming in, one at a time, doing specific parts. They're used to it, it's easy for them. And it's a new kind of music for me to be working on - which I really like. I'm getting to stretch a little bit here. But I'm also trying to bring some of my sensibilities to it. But hopefully not too much. So my concern is that I'm helping them make the record they want to make. I'm being careful about that. I'm talking with everybody. That's a different role for me. It's not quite as, "Let's just throw things down." It's a little more considered. It involves re-doing things that someone doesn't like a few days later. That sort of stuff.

Have you had any specific directives?

Oh no, they're open for a lot of stuff.

Lots of experimentation?

Oh yeah, they're ready to do another kind of record. And I think we're getting there.

To use a metaphor, some producers' style might be like a soup base, to which an artist adds his/her own ingredients. But some, like yours for instance, are a spicy jambalaya from the start. Is it possible that in some cases you run the risk of overwhelming the project with your recipe?

Maybe so, yeah. But I'm trying to make sure that doesn't happen here. I don't want to just come in and put my stamp on the record. I want it to be the band's project where I just add a few spices to the stew. So like I said I think we're getting there. But technically it's difficult because I think I have a hard time doing both: producing and engineering. Although Matt Bayles, who's engineering this, really is great. But I can't help [doing some of the engineering], I've been at it for too long. Sometimes I get so caught up in the sounds, say the snare drum, that I miss a verse, how the lyrics went. It's hard to split my focus. So the mix of this will be at the Sound Factory, and that's where I think I'll really be able to lighten up and fly a little bit. Because I'll be in familiar surroundings and I won't have to think about any of the technical aspects of the process.

Let's talk a little about gear. So what's your relationship with the analog and digital mediums, respectively?

I've heard both sound good, and both sound bad. And it depends on the budget. Most people I work with aren't like Pearl Jam or Sheryl Crow. They're on smaller budgets and it's cheaper to do analogue, that's changing I know. Maybe not if someone owns [their own] Pro Tools and as far as editing goes, I love cutting tape. I come from the day when that was the way you worked and I love it. So I guess analog takes precedence.

Are you tracking on tape with Pearl Jam?

Yup. But they've got the new Pro Tools system set up. There are about two songs where I've spread the drums out all over the place - a compressed track, a SansAmp track, a room track, and then all the separate [close mic] tracks. And I'm keeping that way for now. And that's taken up a lot of tracks. But some other things, like percussion and vocals, will probably go to Pro Tools directly. And then I'll find a track to dump it to on the 24-track later. We have both going. I save everything to Pro Tools.

Anything new and strange you've used in making this record?

Well, I love the new Moog pedals. I've got those. The phaser is actually very cool. It's actually like a little filter box. I've always wanted a phaser that you could actually stop. You get a filtering that you, like, in the throe of its phase modulation you can just stop and keep in that place. Very cool.

"Usually it's, "That guitar sounds too normal, put the amp in that trash can over there." And then the handle on the trash can will buzz - but not enough"

And how have you been using that?

On guitar and there's a couple of drum things I'm going to use it on. And probably a vocal or two. Oh and here's something for your readers. I've had this for years, but I've only used it once or twice in ten years where it stuck. It's a Ludwig Phase 2 synthesizer, made in the '70s. It's a big box with a pedal that switches on like a wah-wah. It's got all these settings - one that's called "vowel," one that's called 'parallel', I don't know what else. Anyway, Mike McCready has really taken to this box and he's probably gotten the best sounds I've heard out of it. Ludwig for crying out loud. It's really a lo-fi, bad, bad box and it's looming *large* on the project. [laughs]

I wanted to ask you about your use of the binaural head.

It's a Neumann KU-100. Fritz Kunstkopf developed it a long time ago. They were making these in the '60s, I think. And binaural is an old concept that I think goes back to the late 1800s, and began to be applied to recording in the 1950s. ["Binaural" refers to the concept that sound is interpreted in a unique way by the actual physical placement of the human ears, and the construction of the human head] I believe Neumann, was the first to make a stand-alone binaural head. When I started in the studio I'd heard about it and had seen some literature on it. So I built my own. I got a couple of ECM 50s and just put them in my ears and it worked really well. Not great frequency response, but you can fuss with it afterwards.

So what does it look like?

Mine looks like a broken pair of headphones with mics hanging over the ears. I actually just let the mics hang.

So it closely approximates the actual human listening experience.

It's the closest I've gotten. Except for the actual Neumann head. The Neumann head is really such a great microphone. My little set-up doesn't sound as good. The Neumann uses KU-100 mics - they're like KM 84s. A very, very fine microphone. I've used the head a lot, on lots of records. But I can't always take it and it's sometimes better to be unobtrusive walking down the street. [With my set-up] people just think I'm listening to something and it doesn't scare them. With the Neumann head people sometimes get a little freaked out. I had one guy in India who was reminded of a deity by it. Luckily the deity was a friendly spirit but he was a little startled. [laughs]

I'm still having a hard time envisioning the Neumann version.

Ah, well have you ever seen the Dada stylized representations of the guys with the slicked back hair? Almost bald and the really angular nose? Angular chin? It's a really stylized, almost "Deco" looking head. A big grey plastic thing with soft rubber ears. A nose shape, a mouth shape.

And what was the idea there?

Well, they did a lot of testing to see if hair, shoulders, etc. had much of an impact on sound.

And they found that, for the money, it didn't make enough difference, so they settled on making the head from mid-neck up. And that approximated human hearing. It does a fair job. But human hearing is so much more than what's going into two ear drums. There's bone conduction, body cavity resonance. You can't really pick that stuff up. So you're missing that and there are certain cues you don't get. But it's amazing what you do hear. It's just its own thing.

What have you used it on recently?

That's my overhead. I haven't used conventional overheads in years. I place that slightly in front of the drums, maybe a couple of inches above the top cymbal line, facing the drummer. I try to get a lot of the drums from that. Maybe use a couple bottom tom mics if I need to. Kick and snare mics, though I don't always need to. Sometimes it's just the head.

That almost takes you full circle to your early field-recording days.

That's always been my real love: field recordings. I've actually got a label for it, a sub-label actually. It's through Peter Gabriel's Nomad Select called Document. It's going to be my binaural recordings.

From all over the world?

I've done a bunch and some have already come out on Nomad Select. One from the Gambia, one from Sardinia, and those are both out. And there's one by a Ugandan guitar player, but I did that in England. Wonderful record, he just died unfortunately. But the first fully binaural record I did was made in 1994 and that's going to be the first Document release. With a little photo booklet and a CD available early next year.

Also, I wanted to ask you about your use of Shure Level Loc.

That's something I discovered on a Waits record: *Bone Machine*. We went to a swap meet and found this thing - it said "Level Loc". I heard a sound for about half a second and it blew up. I realized it was a mic-level compressor. Then I was really interested in it. So I sent it out to be repaired. Got it back and we both just flipped over this thing. It's a podium compressor - so it's made to be used for a human voice at closest 12 inches. That's a pretty low level. It's made for low-level stuff, but to keep it controlled so if the speaker varies his distance it'll stay the same. So I put a microphone into it and put the mic right between the kick and the snare drums - which is 10 times greater a level than it's designed for. And it just *flips out* in the most beautiful way. It's turned into another essential. Drums often don't sound right until I've got a little of that in there.

And you use the Empirical Labs Distressor a good deal, right?

The Distressor is great.

And what qualities do you get out of that?

The Level Loc is just a total fuck-up. It's distortion and compression at the same time. You can make it truly sound backwards. That's an effect.

The Distressor will also do that but in a more elegant way. If I don't want it so distorted I can use the Distressor. It's also a really fine compressor. You can make it sound just grungy, but it's also a really good-sounding vocal compressor. Guitars, drums. Everything. You can't have too many Distressors. [laughs] And then the ADL is great. Different compressors are good to have.

My last question is a broader, more philosophical one: Why do you make records?

I'm not sure I can tell you. I haven't really tried to define it. I don't always like being in the studio. There are certain pressures, especially in pop music, that I don't like. And they make me ask that very question every now and then - why do I do this? But there is something that happens to me on almost a chemical level. When I hear cool sounds work together, and witness someone's creativity - something I can be part of, help with, or bring to another level... maybe it takes me somewhere. There's something about the collaboration I really like. Sometimes it's difficult in the moment; it's not where I want to be. But I usually like the result. I get to sit back and listen and go, "I *like* that." Or even if I don't, I'm always learning something. These days I like it. And then I get an idea to do something else. I'm not really a musician, I'm not a composer. It's sort of like working with found objects. Show me something that's got some potential and I can take it in a particular direction. Hopefully, when I'm collaborating with someone, it's a direction they want to go in. That's what works, that's what's fun.

It's interesting that you use the phrase of "found objects" because your work sometimes puts me in mind of the artist Robert Rauschenberg - the way seemingly unrelated images are treated and assembled and juxtaposed. It has the effect of transporting you into a new dimension of perception.

And yet hopefully there's still a thread of familiarity running through it. It's funny that you say that because I'm very much into art. My wife is an artist and clothing designer and she's really taught me a lot about putting things together. I do metal work at home, I have a little metal shop. And that's helped me realize what I do in the studio. If you bring me a raw metal square I'll just stare at it dumbly for days, "What the hell do I do with that?" But bring me a bent up old spoon, or a hunk of metal that's been run over with a hole in it and just a hint of a mouth... I'm away. I think, "I could do this to that, and put this on that," and I'm off. That's why I work best with people who have a strong sense of their own identity. It's freedom. But I need that little seed. ⊗

daVe TRumFio

Mike and KEN and DAVE and White Tape

DAVE At Front Door

KING SIZE SOUND LABORATORIES and THE PULSARS by JOE CHICCARELLI

When we interviewed Joe Chiccare
for *Tape Op* #14 he was heading b
to Chicago to finish producing th
Pulsars album for Dave Trumfio ar
brother Harry. When I mentioned
we needed to interview Dave soo
Joe obliged. Dave has recorded fc
ages, starting as a home studio a
now as a pretty darn nice place w
it's own mascot to boot. He's als
done some great recordings for
Barbara Manning, Wilco, The Mek
Tsunami, Butterglory, Ashtray Boy
Number One Cup, Alternative TV,
Billy Bragg/Wilco, and more. -LC

DAVE and M320

SANDY THE DOG!

FLUBBER....

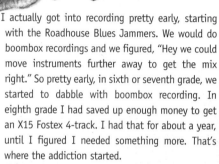

At a young age you were a guitar player. What was the first band you had?

It was called the Roadhouse Blues Jammers, and it consisted of my friend Tom on violin, my brother Harry on Tupperware (filled with different amounts of water) and myself on a Harmony triple pickup guitar.

Wow, was it a Rocket or something?

No it wasn't even that, it was "No Name", the triple pickup version from Sears with a Hohner amplifier.

So out of that was born the Pulsars?

Oh, no. The Pulsars came way later.

After the Larry Cash Project?

Larry Cash, after Ashtray Boy...

Ashtray Boy was another one of your bands?

Yeah.

Did any of these bands put out any CDs?

Ashtray Boy has actually put out five CDs on Ajax and Feels Good All Over Records. They're still together. I'm kind of a rotating.... I play when I have the time. I usually play keyboards.

And did you produce the CDs?

Usually it was a group effort, but...

So this was all done in your basement?

Liz Phair sang on our first record. As she was recording *Exile in Guyville*, she would come over after her session and sing back up. That was all started on a 1/2 inch 16-track in 1991.

This is all pre-King Size, which is your studio that you own here in beautiful downtown Wicker Park, Chicago.

Shithole.

No, no we love King Size. So before you had King Size Studios, you had the studio in your basement. What other bands did you record in your basement studio?

Mostly local hardcore bands. A band called Flesh Merchant, a band called Freedom - a couple of bands from the north shore of Chicago.

What year was this?

This was between '88 and '92. We started King Size around '92.

So around '88 was when you got into recording?

I actually got into recording pretty early, starting with the Roadhouse Blues Jammers. We would do boombox recordings and we figured, "Hey we could move instruments further away to get the mix right." So pretty early, in sixth or seventh grade, we started to dabble with boombox recording. In eighth grade I had saved up enough money to get an X15 Fostex 4-track. I had that for about a year, until I figured I needed something more. That's where the addiction started.

So the next move was to a 16 track?

The next move was to a Fostex 250, then to a 1/4 inch 8-track. Finally, out of high school and on my own, I went to a 1/2 inch 16-track. I stayed with that until about a year or so into King Size. All our early King Size recordings were done on a cheap 16-track Fostex.

Oh really?

And a Biamp Legend, 20 x 16 console.

Oh man, you really learned the hard way.

Well, I did work at a studio.

You worked for Seagrape Studios.

That's where the 24-track deck at King Size is from. There was an older Neotek prototype console... a really cool console. Most of the stuff recorded there was a lot of mid to late '80s house music. Frankie Knuckles did some stuff there, Ralphie Rassario and the Hot Mix Five, some Massive Attack remixes. I got my professional start assisting, and eventually becoming an engineer there, and learning a lot about electronic music at the same time. Up to then if we used any electronics it was a choir sample from a Mirage.

So was that where the birth of the Pulsars came from? From all your new interest in electronic stuff?

Well yeah... At the same time I was really getting into indie rock, like Sonic Youth and the Pixies. The kind of newer stuff coming out in the late '80s and early '90s. *Slanted and Enchanted* by Pavement,

Sebadoh and stuff. I had that kind of DIY, lo-fi interest. But at the same time I was making the best 909 kick drum I could make for house guys. I guess my growing up, engineer wise, was done in both genres. During the day I would do house music and at night go and record (what I like to think of as) mid-fi with soul.

How did the Pulsars get their album deal? Did you do demos or independent CD first?

Well we had a seven-inch out on Sweet Pea Records. Which is sort of the local indie-pop label here.

Who else is on there?

Number One Cup and a band called Hooker. It's run by the drummer from Number One Cup, and his girlfriend.

So that was the first Pulsars release. Did you produce that?

Yeah. Mike [Hagler] and I did.

That led to the album deal right?

Yeah, well we did a demo. We were actually making a record that we figured we would find somebody to release it. What became our official demo was going to be our record for Feel Good All Over, John Henderson's label. A tape of that fell into the hands of John Rubily from Atlantic Records, and that got the ball rolling. I guess the whole idea of the Pulsars, from the beginning, was to make over-the-top shameless pop music. Do whatever we want to do, and not care if it's not the hip thing to do. We thought the best place for this band would be a label that could support us in what we want to do. Experimenting and having a budget.

So at the time did you think it was something a major label would be interested in?

We kind of thought we would start a project that we could take as far as it could go. Not worrying about if it's going to fit into a label's aesthetic. We just freewheeled it and said we would do whatever we wanted to do. It just so happens we got interest from major labels. We said "What the hell?" We're not militant in our beliefs of independent versus major. There really isn't a difference for the Pulsars, because our music is so driven towards the commercial potential of it. The only difference between an indie pop label and a major label is the budget and the support they can give. Like getting played on the radio, which is what our goal is. If our record can get played on the radio, it would be a little a better than what's on the radio now.

So when you were making these demos did some of them make it to the first album?

Yeah.

So you recorded some new tunes, and re-recorded the demos or augmented them.

We pretty much augmented the demo ones. Just redoing some vocals. Once we had the deal we had a budget, so we went back and tried to recapture some of it at a higher fidelity. We bought a Pro

Tools system, we bought some new mics. We had a Neotek console, and we got some preamps. We cut some stuff, but some of it couldn't recapture the moment. On "Tunnel Song" and "My Pet Robot", those are all the original electronic tracks. We just redid the drums and some of the vocals.

Mainly to get better sounds?

Yeah.

You felt that it was a major label so you wanted a hi-fi sound?

Yeah and we had the time. We actually spent two or three months dabbling and tweaking. Just because we could - that was freedom. Up until then we were on a shoestring budget. Finally, we could sit back and relax. Take a lunch break and come back and tweak the kick drum for the rest of the day. It was a wank party for us.

The difference, in your mind, between indie labels and major is being able to take a lunch break?

This summer I recorded three albums which were done in three weeks.

Anniversary.

Anniversary was the last project I worked on. Apocalypse Hoboken. A couple of local bands. I mixed Sally Timms' record.

You've done other stuff with the Mekons [Sally's long-lived band]. As a producer or engineer?

Engineer. My average project is ten days. That's an album project for me. Whenever I get the chance to work on something on a major label, I jump. For instance, on the Wilco record [Summerteeth], Mike and I did most of the overdubs, backgrounds, and stuff like that. A lot of editing. They just came in at two week intervals, every couple months for about a year. It was kind of nice — we get to leave and come back. It wasn't like we have two weeks to finish this record. That record turned out great. You could tell that a lot of time was put into that record. Just sitting back and hearing where the song is coming from and being able to have that luxury. I feel the same way with the new Pulsars record we're working on. Being able to take a break and let your ears relax. It's great.

Having that two months we took off. That objectivity is great. Parts that I thought were cool feeling, turned out not so cool...

Looking at the trees instead of the forest. There's this really pretty tree, but you missed it.

Now you've done your first album. Major label, big budget. You produced yourself, so being an artist, producer; you engineered it and mixed it?

With Mike Hagler and Ken Sluiter. My partners here at King Size.

Having to wear, to some degree, all those hats. Did you really feel a lot of pressure? Did you ever want outside help or did you feel like you needed to compete because it was a major label?

Well at that point, three years ago, the state of radio wasn't where it is right now. They were taking risks. The Rentals had a song on the radio... Weezer. They were definitely taking risks with bands. Daft Punk had an instrumental hit. So we thought the sky's the limit. We could just go and make a quirky, weird audio sonic soundscape. Not make it sound like a Steve Lillywhite mix. Not to gob it up with certain name brand reverbs that sound like everything else on the radio. We just took chances, and maybe were a little heavy handed here or there. There was a pressure, though; the reality that this record would be heard by more than 5,000 indie rock fans. The main problem with producing your own record is that it's your own record. You don't have the objective ear and it's really hard to distance yourself from it. First, I couldn't listen to the record for about a year. I just recently hit that point where I could listen to it. I still get this feeling that had we an outside producer, things would have sounded different. Bob Bortnick, our A & R guy, had a lot to say on different things, which helped a lot but the day to day stuff was kind of me and my friends. Everyone thought it was cool. No one said, "No man. Stop wanking."

Give it the Frat boy speaker test.

Oh we did plenty of the Frat boy speaker tests.

The Frat boys are these humongous home speakers here at King Size. They are mounted in the back of the control room, by the couch. Kind of the living room test. If stuff passes the Frat boys you know it works.

Yeah, exactly.

So after doing the first record, was this a conscious decision on your part to say, "Hey, I want to gain some objectivity." Or, "Take some pressure off of me." To get a producer. Or was this pressure from the A & R guy, manager, or...

No. It was a combination of a lot of things. There wasn't any pressure from the label. Other than saying, "Hey, why don't you try something different this time around." Pretty much from the day I finished our first record I was thinking about an outside producer/engineer. Someone who could bring something fresh to what we are doing, and doesn't see us on a day to day basis. Someone who is totally fresh. Working with someone I respect, admire and can learn from too. Like you Joe.

Ah, thanks.

Wait! You are working on the record!

The producer interviewing the artist or how he feels to be produced.

No, it's cool. I'm learning so much from this experience. Usually I'm the guy who is engineering and producing someone else. I've never been in this position, so I'm learning a lot.

What about the awkwardness of it? What about the moments you're thinking to yourself, "Hey if I were doing it, would do something different."

I've been doing this since '87, '88 - I'm way past that. I'm at the point now where I had my chance and I did my first record. I'm totally open-minded to whatever. I like sitting on the couch or leaving and going into the lounge and then coming back to hear something totally fresh. If I didn't trust you, I would constantly be jumping at the board. Turning knobs. It would've ended after a week.

So one thing that this has brought you is bringing in a producer that has some objectivity, but it also allows you some ear breaks to gain objectivity on your own record.

It's great to be able to sit back and take the dog for a walk or just leave for an hour while you're working. I feel more like an artist. Instead of the first record which was this big ball of...

Chemical reaction.

Yeah, of Dave Trumfio doing everything and calling the shots. Bossing around his friends on the Pro Tools system.

Let's talk about your Pro Tools. This album is maybe the most Pro Tools intensive album that I've done. Usually my involvement with computers and stuff is always for edits and little fix-its here. Now it seems there's more Pro Tools. Instead of locking up a second multi track, we're going to keep it all in Pro Tools and mix in Pro Tools.

Yeah.

You started in analog. You have the 24-track. Are more of your projects, not only Pulsars, but the punk bands (and what I would think would be analog indie pop music) using Pro Tools on that?

Yeah. Actually all the records I worked on this summer it was kind of half-and-half. Apocalypse Hoboken was all analog. I left three tracks for vocals after we did all the instruments, and they are a little more stripped down. I guess the most recent records that I've worked on, like Floraline for Minty Fresh records, was done completely on Pro Tools. There were some previously recorded tracks that we put into Pro Tools, but pretty much everything we did from scratch...

All the drum tracks and everything.

Completely in Pro Tools.

Do you ever miss the sound of analog, for your drums and bass?

They were going for more of a synthetic sound. We used real high hats, but we triggered kicks and snares a lot. We used a trigger kick with a snare and maybe synth high hat. That project we did all in Pro Tools and anything we needed to get analog warmth out of we ran through a Tube Tech "Pultec" knockoff. Or ran it out through a [Roland] Space Echo. Just ran it out through an amp and mic'd it. Just to dirty it up a little. The Anniversary record is pretty much the same that we are doing for the Pulsars. We cut all the basic tracks, rhythm section, most of the guitars...

What do they sound like?

They're a mix between say Superchunk meets Human League [??!!-LC]. We cut the tracks on the analog deck and then I did submixes into Pro Tools. We did all the keyboards, vocals and auxiliary percussion.

Like a stereo sub mix to Pro Tools and overdubbed everything on top of that.

Yeah. We just worked in the Pro Tools for the overdubs. Once we were done with the overdubs, we locked it back up to the 24 so it was half and half. Then we mixed it down.

So you got the original punch and everything.

That way we didn't wear out the 24 track and it allowed me to use two or three mics on guitar amps. Their basic guitar was half stacks. So I was able to get a little crazy with that stuff. Any kind of extra overdubs we did were in Pro Tools. Even some guitars and what not.

When things are dumped into digital, the fatness and glue that you get in analog is just always missing. Having the Apogee AD8000 (analog to digital converter) really helps. It rocks; it just sounds so good.

We started with an 882 and a 16-bit version 3. That's what we did the Pulsars record on.

Oh yeah?

That was the same way. We would lock it up to the 24 track. The last record was hybrid. Synced up to Pro Tools, we actually threw a lot of stuff back to tape. We never left the 24-track analog. We never locked up two machines because we only had one machine. I totally agree that you want that warmth. There's something about drums playing off a two-inch tape.

It's just kind of real, the air between the notes. It just doesn't feel like a bunch of samples.

Some of the other stuff I've been doing is submixing the drums into the ProTools. Mixing the bass using mic or DI, kind of getting your blend and putting it in there.

Just like how you would make an analog slave tape.

Right, right. That seems to work cool too. Sometimes if you want to spice something up, lock it back up and bring in the original snare drums underneath it. Get creative with it. I think it's really cool, the new technology out there. Especially now with the 24 bit.

The 24 bit makes a big difference.

And the AD8000. I mean it sounds pretty. It does sound a little bit different when you put it back, but it does with analog as well. Apples and oranges.

What's your favorite new piece of gear that's not too expensive? What's your find; your discovery.

I guess my favorite thing is the Master Room spring reverb we have, which has an EQ right on the front of it. You can EQ the reverb and get some amazing sounds out of it. Sometimes I just run a mono signal in and a mono signal out. I'll pan the reverb off of where it is. To broaden the sound and give this really weird Link Wray kind of depth to it.

We used it, the 505, on a couple of things where we've printed mono reverb. It sounds really good; I really like that box.

It's cool. A really cool cheap reverb, if you can find them, is the very first version of the Alesis Microverb. I'm not a huge fan of Alesis in general, but the first version. Microverb I, the little kind of third space rack - there's some really great settings on there.

I like their Midiverb II, but I don't know if I've heard the early Microverbs.

If you can find them. The newer ones, like the Nanoverbs, they just don't have the same... I guess maybe it's a little darker 'cause it's 12 bit. They always have an old-fashioned reverb sound, believe it or not.

I'm all into that bucket brigade stuff and all that early digital stuff that didn't have as much fizzly top end. In a mix, that stuff always sounds competitive...

Like with Alesis, the Quadraverb always had that really fake top end. I'll tell people that the Microverb is good and they don't believe because of the Alesis name. They've usually dealt with the Quadraverb, which is a totally different animal. I guess the Effectron's...

I love those. I finally found one for myself, but I love those 1024's.

They have a built in limiter. So you can hit it & it will limit it. It's cool for room sounds. Getting a clashier sound.

Just a warm...

It compresses it.

Exactly.

So we use those a lot on our room mics. To widen the room out, depending on the tempo of the song.

I'm really curious where the future of music recording, and music recording studios is going. Do you think that it's going to be those few upper echelon rooms, with the SSL mind caves for Celine Dion and Aerosmith and all the big budget projects, while everything else is going to be done by individual producers based at home with the Pro Tools? Will King Size fit in to all this? Where do you see the future of King Size and studios?

I'm always asking that question. My roots were in the basement and I still have a nice home set-up that I record at home on. As far as the really big top rooms, I'm sad to hear that a classic studio like A&M is going out of business. If anything, I'm all for home recording and King Size is more or less a down and dirty project studio. But we still get guys who work at home. Archer Prewitt, he'll come here and he'll track drums. I'm doing a Jenny Toomey record this fall with Archer and they are going to come here and do basic tracks, then put them into Pro Tools and then they can take them home. A lot of people have project Pro Tools systems now at home. They can go over to Archer's and they can work on it. I think that's kind of the future for home versus studio recording. Accessing better microphones, maybe a room that's sound proof. For instance, in Chicago, it's mostly project studios and the studios that are the big SSL rooms, like Chicago Tracks, CRC. They're usually R. Kelly or commercials- maybe a band coming through town once in a while. I think this city is only able to support two of those studios if you really think about it. As far as the medium studios go (which King Size has graduated into that league, with our equipment) you have to have a hook, you have to have a draw for your studio. You have to have either the good people working the equipment or a room that's totally original.

Like with Albini's room [Electrical Audio]. You walk in and you know the room is going to have a great character.

That's a great example. Say I want to get a good room for strings or horns, Albini would be my first choice.

Totally. I would work in that place in a minute. I think it's awesome.

If I wanted a really smaller, kind of rock room, there's Albini's and our room. Then I would say, "Hey lets do vocals and programming at home." Even as an owner of a studio, there are certain projects I'll work on where the budget is not there. I'll say "Hey, let's spend three days at King Size. A week at my house, and another four days mixing at King Size." We've worked it so we have ADATs, DA-88s, Pro Tools and Cubase. We're able to support all the different formats, so that's really important for a medium-sized studios, especially big studios too. That they can take any format and mix or transfer it or whatever. We got to keep up on what people are using at home so you can help the people at home. It's not like it's an "us and them" mentality; it shouldn't be. You'll go out of business in two seconds if that's your attitude.

As an artist producing yourself, maybe one of the hardest things...

You drive yourself crazy?

Yeah well you usually drive yourself crazy. One of the hardest things, I would think, would be producing your own vocals. Like how do you know how far to push yourself, how do you know how to comp your own vocals?

I think the demos aren't, pitch-wise, perfect.

But the vibe is great.

The vibe is there because I usually end up going for my character rather than pitch.

So on the last album and the demos, did you comp your own vocals?

Well Mike actually helped out on that. He has a good ear for pitch. So I kind of left it up to Mike or Ken. At the same time, I was sitting on the couch for every edit and I more or less said, "Hey, I like the gravel in my voice." It goes back

to the whole producing yourself argument. If you have your own home studio, and you're putting this out yourself or you're putting it out on an independent label, you can invite friends over, play the tape for people and get feedback that way, if you're producing yourself. It's just great to have this set-up in an official form. You're going to produce the vocals, let somebody else call the shots. It's great when you can spend two years recording your record at home. But when they say, "We want this to come out in five months." I definitely prefer this way. It just goes back to trusting who you are working with to call the shots. There are a lot of bands that I work with where maybe one of the other members likes to work with the singer on pitch and stuff like that.

I find that's true; that's the case.

Maybe they 4-tracked it together.

Feedback.

That's always nice. Especially working on a budget, you have ten days to make a record. It's always good to find the strengths within the band. How they did their demos. Now I usually ask a lot of questions, "Oh, what kind of recordings have you done before? What works?" I ask a lot of questions, and you'll find that the band's usually got their stuff together. If you're a musician you should know about the basic stuff. Everybody should at least have a four track and understand the idea of punching in and comping.

I find that if you compare recording to ten years ago, it's way easier making records because there's less mystery. Everybody knows the lingo, everybody knows the process. Most people have the experience that they know the difference between the sound of a [AKG]414 and [Neumann U]87. There's so much common ground that it makes life way easier. There isn't like this voodoo thing and there isn't this element of distrust.

Well, you have a computer now so that if someone messes up you can just fix it. That's the scary thing.

Do you find that you are relying on the technology more? What would happen if the computers went down and you had to make this record totally analog?

Well, the important thing is how it sounds to you afterwards. If you go through and you cut every syllable of a word, or if you AutoTune... you have to use those things sparingly. You can tell, and I think that's really obvious when a person gives a good performance, versus when somebody is leaning on the technology. You can weed through the bullshit. You can make it sound technically right, but there is going to be a lack of soul. That's the good thing there's always going to be soul and you can tell when it's not there. Not that the Pulsars are a real soul band. Sometimes our soul is going for no soul but in a very soulful way. That's our goal.

Producing this record is hard for me, because I always find I have to walk this line between the stuff being quirky and clever, but being urgent and passionate and soulful.

Where someone who doesn't know about music too much, or just enjoys listening to music can say, "Oh this is nice to listen to." You're making music for people to listen to; not making music for engineers and producers who can dissect your album and know every trick you pulled in the recording of it.

You mixed the last Pulsars album here at King Size on the Neotek with automation?

Yeah, the Audiomate. Actually our board is the first board shipped to leave Neotek, before Neotek folded, with automation.

I like the way this console sounds. For an inexpensive console I think it sounds really, really good, especially when you do that master fader by-pass that you do. That really puts the punch back in there. What I love about Pro Tools is the effects that you would spend $200 an hour in a mixing studio...

Like the phase toms.

All that weird backwards stuff. I know that if I had to stop in the middle of mixing and work out all that, it would drive me crazy. But that was the one great thing about having Pro Tools and the plug-ins. We are premixing the whole album, which I love.

That's what we did with the Wilco record too. A lot those two-week sessions were spent premixing background vocals and shifting things around. That would normally be done at $200 an hour.

With a zillion tracks to choose from.

What I do like is that when we do get into the mix stage we are going to pull up faders and say, "Let's get this to sound really good. We got all the elements, let just blend it all and EQ." ⌘

Just Listen!
by Larry Crane

I recently spent a big chunk of my days working on a record by my friend Luther Russell. We decided it would benefit the record to mix at a different studio, Supernatural Sound. I've spent most of the last three and one half years cooped up in my own studio, Jackpot!, making records and hadn't ventured into other studios to work on stuff. I was worried - Would I figure out how to set all the compressors? Would the monitors mislead me? How does the automation work? Would I like the board's EQ? How do I program all the stupid digital reverbs?

When we got there, we had to learn the automation. This wasn't too bad but took getting used to. Then there were all of the new compressors, EQs and reverbs. What should I do? I'd developed ways of working at Jackpot! that were almost rote. I found myself in a new environment. I started pushing the sounds around with all these compressors and EQs and felt like I was battling the mix through to completion. Then it hit me - all I had to do was listen. We took more time to listen to Byrds CDs to get used to the speakers. I would put up a new song and start bringing up the faders before I inserted compression, EQ or added effects. When I had to set a compressor I would try not to look at my hands, the knob settings or the gain reduction meters. On the EQ I would turn the knobs around until sounds worked better. I tried to only listen to the differences in the sound.

We look at meters and lights - we look at where the faders and knobs are set - and from these things sometimes we assume a lot. I recently hooked up some older Quad-Eight mic pres at my studio. They don't have meters or peak lights and the controls are minimal. I set them by turning the dial until the sound is loud without distorting. That's all. Sometimes I've found distortion on a vocal track when I solo it later. The distortion created harmonics which helped push it through the mix. It is fine—stop worrying so much!

📷 Chris Wills

On the third day of mixing, we talked about how the mixes were going while on the way out to the studio. Luther and I expressed our concerns and fears. When we got there, we took out the automation and everything we'd patched in and started fresh. What was on the tape was good, and we trusted it and let it come through the board. I got more comfortable and the mixes started flying out onto the 1/2" tape. Sometimes they ended up only on DAT. We listened to both and decided both sounded fine - whatever it took to get the record done in the best way possible.

Then we spent a day back at Jackpot!, mixing some songs for the third time. Did jumping from a Trident console to an Allen and Heath Saber bum us out? No. For some songs it sounded better, which was a surprise. Maybe we had tailored the sounds to the board when we tracked through it. I don't know, but we just trusted our ears and I think it all worked out okay.

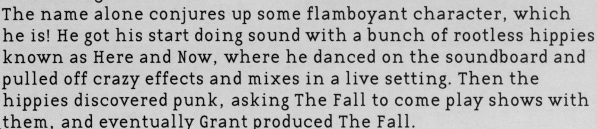

From The Fall to The Smiths to Billy Bragg with Mood Swings thrown in

Grant Showbiz. His name pops up on records by The Fall, The Smiths, Billy Bragg, Alternative TV, Mood Swings and more.
The name alone conjures up some flamboyant character, which he is! He got his start doing sound with a bunch of rootless hippies known as Here and Now, where he danced on the soundboard and pulled off crazy effects and mixes in a live setting. Then the hippies discovered punk, asking The Fall to come play shows with them, and eventually Grant produced The Fall.

by Larry Crane

It was my first professional record. I did *Dragnet* in '79 and I suppose the last thing I did was this "Chilinist" thing, which I suspect is the basic track that they still used on the single, which must have been '97. The third album with The Fall was *Slates*. Adrian Sherwood came in and did some time with it. He had the whole kind of snare mic'd up on the stairs, put through the reverb and then fed back in. I thought, "Okay, I like this. I'm not going to spend as long as Adrian does getting it, but if it happens, go with it." You've heard a sound, it's worked really well, and you spend three hours setting up in your studio and it just doesn't work. I've really learned lots of things like pointing the mic down away from the [kick drum] beater, make sure it's right in there. And then one day you don't do that, you mic it from the front. The mic is outside the drum and it sounds great, and you're like, "Oh my God! Everything I've learned is wrong." But I can look back at The Fall stuff and think, "I don't mind." It's looked upon as brilliant stuff. I think The Fall are probably the best band in the world. 20 years of sheer brilliance.

Grant's career with The Fall lasted until leader Mark E. Smith's erratic behavior and alcohol problems made things difficult.

What you see is people going over their peak. Certainly with Mark E. Smith I was thinking, "Well you're not making sense anymore." It came to head for me when we made "Chilinest". I was up there working on it, and Craig Scanlon, who was one of the great guitarists of The Fall, had gotten a clarinet and we tried really hard to get it to work, to get a good sound. Then Mark heard it and said, "What the fuck is there a clarinet on this song for?" He told us to wipe it off the track. He went back to the pub and came back three hours later. We played the mix again and Mark was like, "This is shit. Where is the clarinet? That was the best thing on the track." I've seen Mark since then and he's much more stable now and I support him dearly - the last record he made was absolutely fantastic - but I just thought it's not for me. You make a decision. You say, "I can't do this anymore!" I'm very close to Mark, I'm in contact with him eight or nine times a year. The last time I saw

him he was very, very sober after a lot of this trouble with the band and Steve Hanley finally leaving. So he cleaned up his act. He did say, "We should work together," and then I thought, "You've got to actually ask me to do this." I can't phone him up. He never did and I thought, "Okay, well, I'll leave this. I'll just carry on buying their records." As a kid, you think you're going to say to a cabbie, "I worked for The Fall. I've done about half a dozen albums. They're a seminal punk band." And the guy's like, "The Fall?"

After some of his early productions for The Fall and Alternative TV he opened his own studio. Briefly.

I formed a studio in '79 called Street Level. It was myself and a guy called Kif Kif. He was the drummer of Here and Now. We had lived on a bus together for five years. We went off and did this studio - and did a lot of great work but he really didn't do a lot after that. He's kind of out of the loop, and if he had a little bit more sense at the time he would still be making music. I hate when people do that. He was a great producer, great musician, but th tide's gone out and he's been left there. The problem I had running the studio (until '82, when it closed) was that we definitely had to have heavy metal bands in. Now I look back at those times in affection, but it was the pressure of doing too many bands like that that got to you. It was like, "I can't do this. It's too much for me." I had a 1" 8-track which is what I started working on. It got dismantled and then it was in a house that got repossessed... I never saw it again. If It was around I'd still be using it I guess.

During a lull in The Fall's schedule he stumbled across The Smiths.

I was there from the beginning. I was taken by Rough Trade to their third or fourth gig. It was me, John Peel, the writers from *NME*, the writers from *Sounds*, and the writers from *Melody Maker*. There were about twenty people in the audience. I was like, "Oh, this is really interesting." Then I went along and produced an album for them [*Rank*] and did some tracks

with Cheap Trick and Billy Bragg

or them and I had nothing written down on paper. Then the band broke up. I went back to Rough Trade and said, "I've got points on this album." They said, "What are you talking about? Of course you haven't gotten points on ." I found Johnny [Marr] and I said, "Johnny, ey're saying I haven't got any points on this cord." He said, "You've got points on this cord, Grant. I'm going to find out and tell em." If he just said, "I'm sorry, I got mething better to do. See you later." That ould have been it.

After that I managed to think, "Okay, I'm t going to leave it to Johnny Marr now." If I dn't have gotten that then, I'd be sitting re whining about all that stuff like so many my friends do. Passion and dreams will only ke you so far. Then you have start thinking out some return on it. I was so lucky that e Smiths came along. I can remember them king me how much I wanted to be paid. I

said, "Oh 13 pounds." Because 13 is my lucky number. 13 pounds a gig, and that lasted for quite awhile. People thought it was crazy. I did basically all the live sound. I must have missed only four or five gigs.

During a Smiths' concert he caught an opening set by a young man playing electric guitar and singing with no backup band. This led to work with Billy Bragg, live and in the studio.

When I did *Don't Try This At Home*, which was the "big" pop album for Bill, we did the three singles, three videos and a world tour. But at exactly the same time that this was happening, which was '91 or '92, Mood Swings took off so I just didn't do the world tour with his group. It was a very unhappy tour and at the end of that Billy got a psychosomatic illness and decided not to tour for five years. I was so pleased that I missed out on this horrible tour. That meant that I'd never done any bands [with Billy].

This new tour's been going on for about a year now. Hopefully we'll do the next album together - I really want to. I'm really excited about this band We've got Ian [Mac] McLagan from the Faces. When I was 14, I used to go see the Faces and I loved it. It was the first time I thought, "Maybe I could do something." They looked so normal and had such a good time. We've also got people like Ben Mendelson and Lu Edmunds. Lu was in the Damned and Public Image, but Ben was also in a band called 3 Mustaphas 3 who were these fake Eastern European band. They were fantastic, and now I'm working with these guys as well. So they're putting in this weird Middle Eastern thing into

the band. We've got a bouzouki, saz and a cumbus, which I had never seen in my life. We have this mix of Ian and these weird ethnic instruments. It's great. Like Bill says, we've spent so long in the studio, saying to people, "Play like Ian McLagan, play like the Faces."

Mac has got all these great stories about the fantastic tape phase on "Itchycoo Park" [by the Small Faces]. How really it was just an engineer saying, "I was just over at the Beatles session the other day and they were doing this weird thing, let's see if we can do it," and they did it. I love that shit, and I think people imagine it's all been done, all that magic and excitement is over, and now it's just a science. That just isn't true.

On *William Bloke*, the album before we did the Guthrie stuff [*Mermaid Avenue*], we had a mandolin player and we worked out the track in the front room [of the studio] with a double-bass player and a baran player and Billy. We went into the studio and after about a half hour, we went back and did it in the front room. It sounded really good in the front room. So we set up a couple of mics in a room which wasn't designed in any way for recording. Suddenly we've moved out of the expensive, spectrum analyzed studio, and we were back in the front room, with [mic] leads that were too long. Of course I have to say the engineer came back and said, "What the fuck are you doing?" And I said, "Too late, we've done it."

Along with James "Fred" Hood, Grant started an electronic-y dance band that became somewhat successful.

With Mood Swings, it was like James and I were so fed up with engineers and producers telling us what we could and couldn't do that we just built our own recording studio and did it the way we liked. If you're going to spend three months on a track, you can go and do a stoned day or a speedy day. The thing we found with dance music was if we set up all the really complicated stuff and then took drugs it was great, because you could just sit there. I think there's a period when you're smoking dope and you think, "Oh, I can smoke dope and do anything." Then you realize that mending a car engine is not very good when you smoke dope. I think that a lot of my friends who never went into the professional music business still think that actually smoking dope is the most important part of the process in making music.

When they first came out, James bought 14 8-track ADATs, and when we made the Mood Swings albums, we never had less than 60 tracks running at the same time. James is a real perfectionist so my job is to say, "It's finished. Stop." Then again, he has no gun at his head. The whole thing with ADATs is that James was just obsessed with the cleanliness of tracks. It wasn't something that interested me at all. My job in Mood Swings was to dirty things up, you know put a bit of black against the white. Now I've got three of the 14 ADATs; I bought a couple and James gave me one. I record on ADAT because it's cheap and it doesn't fuck up. I've worked with them for about eight years so I kind of know the signs of when things are going to go wrong. I know when to see an error message and think, "Fuck that, that's got to be perfectly alright."

Mood Swings is still going, but I left it when the Woody Guthrie album was gathering steam. It was really good timing. What happened was that we made three albums for Arista and we did very well, and we got paid an awfully decent amount of money. We sold about half a million records of the first album over a period of about five years. The first album is called *Mood Food*. It kept going real nicely and I must have spent ten years doing it. James is independently rich and doesn't need to make money. I'm not sure he really likes playing live, and I have this really obsessive thing of playing live and breaking even financially. So it became a bummer. We made an album and it was really dance-y. James turned around and said, "I don't want to play drums anymore." I was like, "But we're a dance band." So it was all coming to a confrontation, and then the Woody stuff came along. I think I would have stayed in Mood Swings for the rest of my life if James hadn't said anything.

He's made a new album, which is very, very good. It's got Julee Cruise, the *Twin Peaks* woman, on two tracks, and I think it's a world beater. James and I are closer now than two years ago. In fact he spoke to me last week, and said, "Maybe we should go back into the studio again."

Working with Billy led to producing *Mermaid Avenue*, a collection of Woody Guthrie lyrics fleshed out with music by Wilco and Billy Bragg.

I used to do things so you could never overdub drums later, you could never do that. Now on some of the best records I've been involved with, like "Sexuality" which was a great hit for Bill, the drums were done later. You set yourself up with rules 'cause it's such a big playing field, in a recording studio. Then, once you've got the focus you can let go of the rules, it's about getting the focus and knowing where you want to go and sometimes the rules help you. Wilco was obsessed with getting the first take of everything. One time I missed the first take of something and Jeff Tweedy was like, "You didn't record it?" From then on I realized that it was the rule: *The first take had to be recorded.* Record everything that they did and make a choice later. I never had so many reels of tape; we had 40 reels of tape, we did 40 songs and 15 songs came out. We put away about 15 to 20 songs at King Size Studios, which in a way was supposed to be a demo - knocking ideas around. Then we went to Dublin for six weeks and ended up doing one song a day.

People kept saying, "Is Woody playing with you?" You're like, "No, he's been dead for thirty-five years. He wrote "This Land is your Land", you sung it in school." "No. No. Woody did a gig last year." You're like, "Did he have long gray hair, and did he do 'Alice's Restaurant'?" We went to the Cleveland Rock and Roll Hall of Fame because Woody was being inducted. They were saying, "Is Woody going to come?" and we were like, "I hope not. It would be really scary if he does."

It was really good fun, 'cause we were all live. If we have a live band with Bill, we would put the band together so they would pretty much do what we were asking. With Wilco it was interesting to suddenly work with guys who had their own agenda. We would do a heavy metal version of a song and a jazz version of the song. Jay [Bennett] would decide that he wanted to play the drums and the drummer would come and play the guitar, everybody switching around.

He doesn't get very technical about what gear he "must have" or what works for recording what.

There are some mics that I'll ask for. Obviously mics are different, some are great and some aren't. But you know, you use a [Shure]SM58 on a vocal, bass guitar and guitar, and then you're like, "Well, it's alright." You can use it for anything. I've got a 202, which is a hi-hat mic, but I use it on the bass drum. I've got an Electro-Voice which looks a bit like an SM58, and a couple of Sennheiser 421s and that's it I think. I'm sort of going back to basics, a lot of the drum tracks are only three mics. It's more of a distraction to have 16 mics on a kit - if I've got three on the drum kit you can move the mics or something if needed. Accidents are great too, like when you suddenly realize you've been recording a vocal on the mic over there instead of the mic over here, and your like, "Wow, that was great!"

Part of what makes Grant an asset to any project is his positive attitude and youthful energy. Plus he's a rampant record collector.

The thing I think with music is that it's not good or bad, I just haven't got the key to it. Sometimes I will sit and play a record fifty times until I get it. I know it's good, and I guess I just don't have the key to it, and I want to get the key to it. I can remember doing this when I was ten. Thinking that I've got to find out what it is, because I know this is good. It's like you know that Motown is good, you know that it's great, and you're like, "It just sounds like fucking pop music to me." Then suddenly you start hearing it, and you're like, "Wow!" To me, there are two or three gods in the world. One of them is The Fall, A Green is one of the others. A lot of people say "He's just a soul singer, isn't he?" I understand that attitude because I was like that once. Soul music to me at some point in my life was like... didn't get it. "A black guy singing about love great." Then you get in to the intricacies of it all and you realize that it's just a magic world.

Despite all the time he's in the studio Grant still spends a decent amount of time on the road doing live sound.

I just love it. I love live work. It's been this way since when I started. It's great when you know the dynamics. I don't think people realize or care about the live sound engineer. But then again they don't care about the producer either, do they? They don't care. That's why you need *Tape Op* magazine. Just so people care about these things. Say to someone, "He produced this record!"

Gender...
by Larry Crane

Photos:
Engineer &
Tape Op Contributor
Hillary Johnson

As long as I have been involved in music I've had a healthy respect for women who are part of the music community.

Most of the bands I've ever been in had female musicians, I've trained women engineers, I've recorded many female and mixed-gender bands and I've worked with female writers. I don't see music as being a "thing for guys" and I've found that women often help introduce a balanced chemistry in bands and recording studios.

The recording field is obviously far too male-dominated. Just look at the interviews in a typical TAPE OP... there are a lot more men than women out there engineering, producing and mastering records. That sucks, and we're more than willing to be supportive of the women that are working in this field, so look for related articles in the future.

One thing that has been really pissing me off lately though has been some of the ads in the *other* recording magazines. I know it's not the editor's fault, and advertising sales people sometimes never even see the ads they pull in until they are run, so I can't blame the staff of these fine mags at all. But these ads offend the hell out of me. One company in particular has a recent ad campaign built around pictures of attractive young women and captions like this:

"...My guys worry about all the technical stuff. I told them I wanted something with no strings attached. Something that will put a smile on my face."

What the hell? Are they saying women are dumb? Should men make all the choices for them when it comes to audio? These ads are the worst offenders but other companies use women as sex-objects to get the reader's attention, like a certain ad with a woman getting out of a shower with the word "strip" above her. What the hell does this have to do with audio? I understand the need to sell product, but let's have the product sell it, not pictures of scantily-clad women or demeaning text. Don't these companies realize that women buy their products too?

At a recent NAMM show (a trade show for electronics) one of the companies being represented there had a booth with a hot tub full of porn stars that attendees could climb in with. What can I say? Let's just hope that some of these "guys" wake up and change their ways. I don't ever want anyone, female or male, to get a feeling that the "recording club" is closed off to them before they even get to the door. It will be a long battle.

Dave Fridmann

Eureka! or: An Account Of A Person Who's Ear Is In Constant Contact With Innovative Sounds In A Rural Setting Away From Things Like Very Tall Skyscrapers And Out Of Tune Ear Drums Wearing Suits.

by Roman Sokal
photos by
Mary Fridmann

Quaintly nestled in the western region of upstate New York, USA, between Buffalo and Erie, Pennsylvania, lies a small blink-and-you'll-miss-it town named Cassadaga; a place where maybe the most exciting thing going on might be someone filling up their vehicle with gasoline. While existence in any small community may lend itself to being very quiet and seemingly uneventful, Cassadaga in particular, just so happens to be summoning some of the world's most creative and acclaimed musical recording artists. The source responsible for this phenomenon points towards nearby Fredonia resident Dave Fridmann: producer, recording engineer, musician and an overall friendly collaborator. His perogative is different and simple - to fill up tracks.

Young Dave first hits 'Play' - the button with the arrow that points to the right.

The genesis for Fridmann's involvement in the recording arts originated from his days as a high school student in his native Buffalo, New York, suburb of Williamsville. And like many suburbanites beaming with a jaded-less sense of unlimited hope for a stable and fulfilling future, he made up his mind on what he was going to do. *"Like most recording engineers, I wanted to be a rock star,"* he muses. *"I became aware of engineering during my junior high school year through my music teacher who was an alumnus of SUNY at Fredonia. He had heard*

that they started up a new sou[ ] recording program and thought th[ ] I might be interested in it." Up[ ] graduating from the binds of hi[ ] school, Fridmann enrolled in t[ ] program to continue his pursuit [ ] rock star luminance. *"It seemed [ ] me, in a very viable and obvic[ ] way, that if I wanted to be a rc[ ] star, the best way to do that wo[ ] be to meet other rock stars, and t[ ] easiest way would be to become [ ] studio engineer because that [ ] where rock stars were. That's c[ ] way to get in."*

Fate or coincidence. Dependi[ ] on whichever belief system [ ] reader leans toward, it was cert[ ] that Fridmann would find hims[ ] in a situation that would su[ ] propel his desires into reality - [ ] the role as bass player for a ba[ ]

"In a lot of ways very much exactly what I hoped would happen did happen," he states matter-of-factly. With access to the college recording facility's Amek Angela console, Otari MTR-90 Mk II 24-track machine and a band called Mercury Rev, he would get a chance to exercise both his ears and his bass playing. "When early incarnations of Mercury Rev came into the studio to record they didn't have a bass player," he recalls. "I would record their songs and then we'd get to the point when we'd notice, hmm...

gee... we really should put some bass in there, which would be left to last and then I'd say, well, 'I could play it 'and they'd say, 'Okay, go ahead!' I ended up joining the band which worked out exactly as I'd hoped, which wasn't as it exactly turned out to be what I wanted, but that's what I thought I wanted at the time so it worked out great." The resultant product of their first collaboration was 1991's *Yerself Is Steam*, featuring the stratospheric "Frittering", which was primarily recorded at the college and mixed in Argyle, New York, at Sweetfish Studio.

Two more collections of songs were transduced onto tape by Fridmann via the college and Sweetfish Studios combo; *In A Priest Driven Ambulance* and *Hit To Death In The Future Head*, two albums by a band equally and colorfully known as The Flaming Lips. He recalls how he first became acquainted with the Oklahoma-based group. "Jonathan [Donahue] from Mercury Rev went to college in Buffalo and was a promoter there who became friends with The Flaming Lips and eventually became their tour manager. He'd be on tour with them and couldn't really do their live sound well and once they could afford a live sound person, he asked me to do it. By then I had been doing Mercury Rev stuff for a while. At the end of their first tour I knew they were going into the studio and I built up enough courage to tell them they should do it with me. They fell for it, and we ended up doing it and we have been mostly ever since."

During this formative period Fridmann began to apply a certain polishing touch and character to Mercury Rev's final product via a now nearly deleted medium - magnetically striped 35mm film. "Back in the 1950s, 35mm magnetic film sounded better than what was normally available at the time in the world of music technology," he quips. "Some of the old Miles Davis and other jazz stuff were tracked onto that simply for the fidelity. It was a more durable medium as well. That was the inspiration to use it. I thought, hey, that sounds pretty damn good." Ever since first applying that process to the mastering of *Yerself Is Steam*, 35mm magnetically striped film became a staple of every Mercury Rev album.

"Jonathan actually used to be in The Flaming Lips under the alias 'Dingus') and we've demo'ed songs for The Flaming Lips that ended up in the long run being

Mercury Rev songs," he reveals. "It's a very incestuous relationship. There's been times when both me, [Mercury Rev guitarist] Grasshopper, Jonathan and The Flaming Lips have all been in the studio at the same time working in the same music." Not only does Fridmann write with both bands, he also aids with constructing arrangements as well. "Everyone has a lot of common ideas as to what is good and what constitutes good sounds. It's no accident that there are a lot of similarities."

When time came for Mercury Rev to tour and promote themselves worldwide, Fridmann chose to bow out of touring duties. Unlike musical artists of the past such as Syd Barrett and Brian Wilson, both being brilliant yet too detrimentally preoccupied with mental 'crutches' to take on touring, Fridmann was far from being a semi-dysfunctional person. Instead, he opted to stay in the US and work with an array of groups including Syracuse's The Wallmen, Jennyanykind, St. Johnny, Grand Mal and Weezer.

The filament burns bright.

In a blessed 'right time at the right place' situation during the summer of 1997, Fridmann found himself temporarily exchanging his natural habitat for a big learning lesson in the madness that is known as Los Angeles, California. His task was monumental - to co-produce a new track entitled "So What!" for *Kettle Whistle*, a compilation disc by Jane's Addiction, a band that is infinitely distant from 'normality'. "No one wanted a normal sounding set up, so Kevin Haskins from Love and Rockets (a friend of Jane's Addiction's Stephen Perkins) brought in his home studio gear that included samplers and I also borrowed a series of guitar pedals called Love Tones from Joe Barresi." Barresi, an

engineer/producer in his own right, first met Fridmann in 1996 during the Weezer *Pinkerton* sessions, remaining great friends ever since. Fridmann considers Barresi to be the best engineer he knows, someone from whom he has learned a lot from. Fridmann continues, "I ran the drum loops through the pedals. It was the first time I ever experimented like that especially with something that was so loop-based."

Fridmann also had another concern, a large sized one. "I was very worried about how I was going to get Dave Navarro's sound [Jane's Addiction's guitar player]. I always thought he used some special big rack of gear to get his sound, but instead he shows up to the studio with only a Marshall half-stack and a few pedals. I sent the assistant to mic his amp with an SM57 and didn't even see where he put it and all of a sudden blaring over the speakers was 'DAVE NAVARRO'. And [singer] Perry Farrell became Perry Farrell screaming through an SM58." This was actually first experienced during the sessions for the second Mercury Rev album when John Ashton of The Psychedelic Furs [guitarist] was invited to play on the album. "He came straight from England to Buffalo with absolutely nothing and played only through our gear and he still sounded like The Psychedelic Furs." Fridmann excitedly expands on what he calls a major "revelation" on the Jane's Addiction incident. "What was even weirder was when Flea [from the Red Hot Chili Peppers] played bass. At one point I wasn't looking and Flea handed over his bass to Navarro who started to play it. I wondered to myself why all of a sudden the bass sounded like crap. Then I found out why. Navarro handed the bass back to Flea and all of a sudden it sounded great again. I really didn't have to do anything. The sound literally came out of his fingers!!! The sound was him."

Badminton anyone?

Once Fridmann's personal world expanded into a family unit, the idea of having one conveniently fixed studio close to home where a project can be realized from start to finish became yet another logical idea. Hence in the summer 1997, he, his wife Mary and

additional partners Greg Snow and Andrea Wasiura erected what is quickly becoming a mecca for many recording artists - Tarbox Road Studios. Inspired by Sweetfish Studios, Tarbox Road is located in Cassadaga a capillary town of Fredonia. The isolated cul-de-sac studio-in-a-house is far from its deceptively rustic shell as it boasts not only creative autonomy, but also allows a client to practice their badminton skills for recreation purposes if they see fit. It is a place to work that is situated in Dave's preferred rural setting, serving as a place to nurture focus on the work at hand, far, far away from any intrusive big concrete city music 'industry' types. *"What I shoot for most of the time is to get clients comfortable just as if they're at home working on their 4-track at 3 AM at their own pace. I may go home at midnight, but I'll leave two mics and a DI set-up and tell them what tracks they can record on. It doesn't take a genius to hit play and record. It's a great environment. People just work. They come down [from the studio's bedrooms] the next day in their pajamas and keep working, just like home."* The location also tends to make sure that a project maintains 'freshness' to avoid 'studio burn out', or worse, an age-old condition known as 'cabin fever'. *"Most bands get sick of being in the sticks, bands tend to record here only in two week segments"* he chuckles since that environment does not phase him due to residing in it for a majority of his life. For a Japanese band like Number Girl who came straight from Tokyo to Fredonia, one can imagine the culture shock.

The first project to deflower the new facility was instigated by The Flaming Lips' Wayne Coyne. It was to be a 'modest' project, one that would *only* involve the creation of four separate compact discs that were meant to play through four exclusive sound systems at once, *and* whose purpose was to shatter linear storytelling by taking the listener into a new dimension of time and space. It was called *Zaireeka* (the combination of the words *Zaire*, an idealism inspired by the country's state of disarray and chaos; and *Eureka*, the word Coyne used to describe a sudden discovery of an idea that moves forward the creation process. *"We weren't sure what would work... we set up Tarbox with* Zaireeka *in mind,"* Fridmann recalls. *"Greg [Snow], who does the tech work here, set up four sets of speakers and four DAT machines. We bought an [80 input] Otari Concept Elite console, which has flexible routing features and is massively automated. We chose it because it would work for* Zaireeka *the way it is... so it would be possible to do all four live simultaneously. He made this really cool box with four stereo faders connected together to control the playback level. It looked like an airplane thruster."* An example of what goes on with the psychotropic *Zaireeka* is perhaps best depicted in the track "Thirty-Five Thousand Feet Of Despair", which sonically *tells* the tale of a troubled airplane pilot who commits suicide in the middle of a transatlantic flight. Each disc contains a different perspective of the situation at hand. Disc one features a news reporter who awaits the landing at the airport, disc two has the pilot walking to the bathroom to meet his demise, disc three contains the downtrodden airport ambiance and disc four goes subjectively deep inside the mind of the angst-ridden pilot. As one might rapidly come to the conclusion, *Zaireeka*, now sadly out-of-print, is definitely not your everyday standard generic top 40 kitsch.

Their method of taming a behemoth of a project was approached with a need to maintain sanity somehow. *"In general we mixed each CD one at a time so as to have more randomness so things wouldn't sound too perfect. The final product [the CDs]were easy to synchronize but DATs aren't. Most of the time we were listening to it very poly-rhythmically. It was a strange event. It plays more normal for the people who listen to it now than it was for us. We thought it was weirder, which of course, we thought was cool."* In an attempt to sync the aural information so as to have things not be led too astray, Fridmann included a time cue in front of the tracks, similar to a slate used in filmmaking. *"We did the mastering at the studio just to make sure there wasn't any confusion down the line."* In the end, the experiment was deemed a success, and is now a staple for many who enjoy being taken on a ride to previously uncharted territories of perception. It also makes for great entertainment at parties and by no doubt is highly suitable accompaniment to those who enjoy ingesting substances.

On any given session, be it Mogwai, Home, Delgados, Citizen King, Creeper Lagoon or Toronto's Bodega, Fridmann assesses that the top three microphones responsible for picking up the soundwaves from instruments are the tube-based Neumann U47, the RCA 44 ribbon mic and the common day workhorse known as the Shure SM57. Before the gracing signal paths with the warm and omnipotent U47, a pair of Neumann TLM 170s were constantly employed around the clock. *"When I finally got the chance to use a U47, I was shocked and appalled over the superiority it had over the 170s,"* he excitedly reports. When he occasionally ventures to another studio to work, he is sure to pay attention and always keep on the lookout for new mics to induct into the Tarbox tour of duty. Among the ones desired are the Earthworks Omni OC1 and the Coles 4038s, of which he professes would accumulate quite a bit of sonic mileage at his studio.

Dave can see more things that should be heard.

Fridmann also believes in ghosts. Well, sort of. When a client records at Tarbox, their project is subjected to every morsel the facility has to offer. The sounds emanating from a guitar amp for instance, can interestingly transmogrify into a haunting sound in one

Wayne Coyne
of the Flaming Lips
by Larry Crane

How did you first hook up with Dave?

I think it was through Jonathan Donahue. He was going to Buffalo University with some of the members of Mercury Rev. They were all recording themselves with 4-tracks and they all had brief stints of recording in studios. I think they knew Dave Fridmann just as a friend and he was part of the recording program at Fredonia University. I think, somewhere along the way, those two connected and Dave started recording them. Jonathan, originally was sort of part of our entourage - he would go on tour with us and act like our soundman. Little by little, we progressed onward and Jonathan started playing guitar with us and at the same time it left the soundman position open. Jonathan had said that he knew a guy who was a great soundman. Dave Fridmann came out and he was our live soundman for the summer or so. As we got done with the tour, we went immediately into recording up at his studio where he was working and still doing his graduate degree or something.

What was the first recording you did with him?

It was the *In A Priest Driven Ambulance* record. The very first thing we recorded with him was song called "Unconsciously Screaming" that took us about three weeks. We recorded and did all these things to it and I think we ended up mixing it over 20 different times. After that we realized that, "This i our guy." He's so dedicated to what we do that w can't wear him down. He seemed to have thi endless energy and enthusiasm. Right then w decide it was a good way to go. We thought h would eventually come to his senses and say "These guys are too much work, I want to mak money..." but he never did. It seemed like the mo we threw at him, the stronger he got and the mo he embraced the whole concept of exploration an all of that.

I noticed that there's such a difference in sound from your earlier records.

I think we had reached a point where we were equal frustrated, but equally in awe of the ways recording. If we can't do it the way we want, we' not going to go back to the old way of trying t wear down some conservative engineer that we en up working with. That's what we would end u doing - we would get these people who knew ho to run the boards, but always laughed at all o ideas. We would eventually wear them down and 10 o' clock at night they'd be willing to try anythir we wanted just so they could go home. [laughte With Dave, we went in there with the idea of doir what we wanted. By then, we didn't feel what w wanted to do had to be silly – we could try ne ideas and not have people roll their eyes all the time. Meeting up with him at that point, with what we were doing and the kind of money that we were able to spend, it was a perfect combination. Recording is like that - you need to have artists, producers and engineers. All of that is important and people think that if you have a great song, the other parts of it don't matter, or if you have a great producer they can do anything. It really isn't that – it's a combination of everybody doing the best that they can. We see that now, with Dave, how important it is to have him being the expert at what he does. He embraces the way that we want to do the impossible. We say, "Dave, we've never done this before, but I think it would be great." You can see him sort of rise to the occasion.

What did he say when you talked about Zaireeka? Having the idea of four simultaneous CDs - what was his first reaction?

If a movie of that was ever made, I think people probably envision me in the back room looking like Jerry Lewis as the Nutty Professor where I'm concocting these ideas and then I'd walk out and go, "Here's what I'm going to do." In reality, it's just not like that, these ideas come slowly and it's because I know Dave and I could bounce these ideas off of him little by little. But we realized that we could do it, so by the time I said that we were going to do it, it wasn't like he had never heard it before. He assisted me in figuring out that we could do it. The equipment and the computers and all this stuff were coming together and I thought, "I'm not sure how we'll do it, but I think we could do it." Him, being enthusiastic and interested in it, propelled it to the next level. When you're talking about concepts like that, there needs to be this abundance of belief that we can do it and it'll actually be worth listening to once we do it. Art is like that, if everybody doesn't think it's going to work, it doesn't actually happen. You kind of have to think that it will work and it'll be good and then you have this big period where it's in the abyss of, "Well, we'll see what happens." I think, by the time I approached him about actually doing it, none of it seemed impossible. We both knew it would be a lot of work and we didn't know exactly how we would do it, but we were determined to make it work. We knew, to a certain extent, that elements of it would work. I think that's what is so great about those sort of things, you just go about them. There's no blueprint or anything to fall back on and say, "This is how these people did it." I think he really likes that, I know I like that. I think we found out a lot about each other, going into Zaireeka.

What are Dave's main strengths?

I think that his main strength is that he really knows the equipment. He knows all the ways around it. The biggest problem that most people have isn't imagining ideas. Look at something like going to the moon, it's not that hard to imagine. Cavemen probably looked up and wanted to go to the moon.

of the far corners of a room. And just in case something does go there, a mic will be present to capture the stray sound. Nothing is nothing, not "nothing is everything" as someone once preached. *"I always have both of my 24-track MTR-90 II and RADAR Otari's running at the same time. There is no reason not to use them. I have everything going all the time due to the nature of the bands I work with. Most of the projects I work on are 'studio projects'. We're not sure what it is going to be until it's done. We put things down one by one then sometimes do it all over again because minds tend to change so much. Or, you get to the point where you realize what you should have done and you start over and keep going and going. Even the simplest things I do now tend to be 48-track. Number Girl are very straightforward and play together, which is uncommon for what normally goes on with projects I work on. They're adamant about recording live at the same time and that will be the final take. If it's not good, we'll keep doing it until it is. And even with them I am into the second 24-track. I set up a million mics, arm all the tracks and fill 'em up. I may end up using two mics in the long run, but I always like to have options. You never know what might happen."* In what is beginning to sounds like his motto, he cannot help but ultra-emphasize his strict recording regiment in which *"everything is going on all the time, no matter what."*

ADD - Analog vs. Dave vs. Digital.

"When [Digidesign] Sound Designer and Pro Tools first came out I wasn't leery of them at all," Fridmann reassures, keeping in tune with his ever-accommodating persona. *"I wanted to embrace them but they sounded like crap. In general, I prefer analog, although 24-bit [digital] is pretty amazing now. We did a jazz band [the Steve Copeland 5] entirely on the studio's digital 16-bit Otari RADAR simply for financial reasons because it costs only $15.00 to back the data*

onto a tape. While we were tracking, Dave Dusman, a big mentor of mine from the college, mixed it down to a Genex 24-bit 8000 Series along with Lucid Tech 24-bit converters. He recorded the monitor mix while we were tracking and we would quietly listen back to the Genex recording... and it was absolutely AMAZING. I've been amazed by my RADAR about how quiet it is but when we did the Genex playback, the difference was night and day. The RADAR was noisy and grainy in comparison. Digital is pretty damn good nowadays." When confronted to differentiate between the digital Genex and his analog Otari MTR-90 II, Fridmann meekly assures, *"The Genex is remarkably similar, except it doesn't have any noise."* After numerous trial runs, Fridmann found what he considers are the best tape stocks to load his multi-tracks and magnetically charge their oxides with. *"These days I stick with the revamped Quantegy GP9 formulation because it's reminiscent of the old silky 3M 996 formulations. It has more of an in-your-face rock sound whereas 499 was a little rougher like 456. I still use both depending on what the project calls for. I still don't like BASF. I can't figure out why people do."*

It's always inevitable.

Fridmann and his collaborators will at one point be *left* to think what should be *right* for a mix that gets piped down the 2-track digital highway. *"Before outboard converters I used to pick flavors of DAT machines like picking flavors of tape. I still hate Panasonics because they're too soft sounding. From memory, even Tascams were better, because they at least had a crunch and attack - you could really drive them."* When it came time for Fridmann to go to the DAT machine 'toystore' for Tarbox he purchased two Sony PCM-R500 with SBM (Super Bit Mapping). *"By default, I thought they sounded best on their own, especially* with its D/A conversion. However, I haven't used built-in converters in a DAT machine in a long time." This is because Fridmann massages his projects with his older model TC Electronic Finalizer for A/D conversion with no compression or normalizing. Since 16-bit is still the all-around standard for digital, he sticks to it. His Pro Tools is 16-bit as well, but soon plans to upgrade to 24-bit for archiving. He would love to see 24-bit become the standard. *"Even a person who isn't obsessed with sound will be able to tell the difference. The sampling rate should be left at 44.1 kHz, because the 96 and 88.2 rates are kind of a hoax. Sampling rates don't matter as much and are not anywhere nearly as important as bit depth is. They should focus on that more."* He also confides his view on 1:1 digital copies or 'clones'. *"The difference is terrible. It's as plain as day."*

"Sure, there is a cinematic scope to most of the projects I work on," he admits, *"I naturally gravitate towards those types and vice-versa."* (He also admits to the hopes of taking on sound design duties for films in the future, taking his passion with 35mm film a step further). *"All people seem to care about in the big picture is 'the beat'. The guy who fixes my car knows I do something with music and asks me whether I heard a certain song because it had a good beat. Once you get beyond record sales of 20,000 copies you start getting into the 'normal people' audience very quickly. All the work and intricacies that you've put into a recording just doesn't matter anymore. People don't care. They only want to wash dishes or party to music. That's fine, I don't have a bias towards that. A lot of stuff I've been working on recently certainly has been 'weird' in nature,*

The hard part is actually doing it. I think sometim that my ideas are a lot like that. I'll tell him tha have this song that we've already recorded, bu want to insert a brand new song right into t middle of that. He knows, technically, that it's as easy as I'm telling him. I'm the caveman th wants to go to the moon. [laughter] So, I come him with these problems and he explains to what we could do. Those things require creativity it of themselves. The creativity isn't just the fr in the corner that says let's paint the room pur It's every step along the way, you've got proble that you have to solve to move on to the next th – sometimes they're technical, sometimes the musical, lyrical, philosophical or just problems objectivity. Is what you're doing any good?

"The sound literally came out of his fingers!!! The sound was hi

And while a band might be discovering new heights of musicianship thanks to Fridmann's friendly work methods and Tarbox's comfy atmosphere, he himself can be found in a perpetual state of seeking technical enlightenment. His concerns these days are cleanliness of the sound kind. *"I've been worrying a lot about noise lately. It's a private little fetish of mine. I've been testing out various sounds versus noise combinations. I'm trying to find a quiet dynamic mic so I can use my older Altec mic pres. Even with my RCA 44, it's hard to get an adequate amount of gain without noise creeping up."* Although he once temporarily discovered relief via the use of a Summit Neve Element 78, he feels there is a more universal way to go about it. The quest continues...

Dave reaches the final stage - with ease.

When possible, every stage of a Fridmann-related project is executed at his studio to be kept free of possible 'contaminants'. Keeping with the Fridmann tradition of logic, he puts his foot down. *"Let's put it this way - a lot of what I do as a producer happens in the mix stage. When it says 'Mastered By Dave Fridmann' it means we didn't change anything. When we do a mix, it's done. It doesn't need anything else. At the end of any mix session I print a CD-R and it has to be as good as a finished CD. If it's not, then keep mixing, 'cause it's not done yet!"* Eloquently put.

When queried whether he is a producer that is noted on the outside for working on projects that are more suited for 'connoisseurs', Fridmann takes a moment of silence for introspection before replying.

but we're hoping that it can appeal to a wider audience. There is a concerted effort to do that."* And with the success of The Flaming Lips' *The Soft Bulletin*, they are obviously on the right route.

Suddenly everything has changed.

When the calendar year rolled into the infamous digits that read '2000', numerous music-related publications world wide began to report that The Flaming Lips' *The Soft Bulletin* as the 1999 record of the year. Featuring such lush tracks as "Race for The Prize" and "Waitin' for a Superman", the on-again-off-again two year project was a labor of love of which everyone involved on the project will attest that it was an intense learning experience. Initially the album was planned to exist as two separate versions. One would be inspired by the positive results of *Zaireeka* format which allowed for them to potentially use all 80 tracks that were sometimes going on at once. The other mix would be what is currently available, a stripped-down stereo version. Fridmann warmly sums up his experience working on the critically acclaimed album. *"To me, the best thing about The Soft Bulletin was when there was this time period where we weren't really sure what we were doing. About a year and a half into the project we were recording the track "Feeling Yourself Disintegrate" and did a rough mix of it, sat back and listened to it. We noticed something had changed. Everyone became aware of it simultaneously. It was very strange."* And of course, being susceptible to the 'Eureka!' complex, things were always changing. *"Even at the very last session we totally changed a bunch of*

group of people that work in an intense w everybody has a strength and at the end of the if we have a technical thing, that's where Dave his thing. He's great at music and he's grea arranging and recording. But eventually, at the of the day, if there's one of these big tech questions, that's where he shines. It t everybody, pushing to the limit of what th good at. I think sometimes it shows up in music, sometimes I'm surprised when I pu something that we've done and I say, "How did do that?" and I go, "Oh, that was us." You ge immersed in it, there's so many things goin that it still is a little unknown to it's makers.

Do you like working out where he out in a rural type area?

Yeah. I think any artist, after awhile, ends up beco isolated. Even if you're in a room with tw people and you're starting to write, eventuall world disappears and you're there with your i That isolation may seem like it's easier if already physically isolated out in the midd nowhere, the way his studio is. But it's not true, you can surround yourself with your re and computers and cable TV. Even though yo be 100 miles from a real city, you can really b as immersed in all that stuff as people who li the city. Location doesn't really matter to me much anymore. It matters that Dave is whe this equipment is and if that was here, I'm su would become isolated and we would find ours alone with our problems of doing something with the ideas that we have. Even though, because it's out in the country, it looks like we are purposely isolating ourselves. I think it would happen anywhere. The main thing is, is that Dave is there and all his equipment is there that he's the master of. The situations don't really have much to do with it, it's really our problem from there on.

o you plan to work with him in the future?

yeah, sure. We look at it like it's this progression that people get to. It's like old married couples... it's Thursday and we're going to have macaroni and cheese. You don't even have to speak about it after awhile. So much of what we do is intense work, it's not like being a doctor or an airline pilot. I don't think of it as serious in that way. We do take our work serious even though we realize it's just a bunch of silly music at the end of the day. But, you do get into intense situations where it's hard to communicate what it is that you want to do, because it's new to everybody in the room. That unspoken way of working sometimes, where you don't have to be polite, you don't have to do any of that stuff. You work with each other so much that you end up being like a bunch of cavemen, just grunting. There's a lot of unspoken things that happen when people work with each other all the time. Sometimes, you're just so comfortable with who they are that you don't have to worry about the niceties of being courteous to each other, even though we try to be. Some moments, everybody's focused on the same thing and there isn't anything left to speak about. You just simply have to go in and do what you have to do. In that sense, I want to always work with him. I'm sure that if we couldn't work with Dave, we would still be able to record. [laughter] He would be the first to say that. He wouldn't want to think that if we can't record with him we're powerless. It's just in the way that anybody works together, you acquire a certain way of working that hopefully progresses to making it easier and you can do bigger things without it being, necessarily, harder to do.

keep progressing.

h. I don't know if I'm progressing anymore, but certainly he has. ✪

the songs that bore no resemblance to themselves." The end result - a meisterwerk. Hear for yourself.

Despite the similarities heard in the array of sounds present throughout any Fridmann-related project, he feels that people are usually misled thinking that there is a mystical "Trademark Dave Fridmann Sound". Fridmann himself wishes to set straight what a producer's role really is and what it *should* be. He feels that a good deal of his work is purely contextual in nature. *"I don't adhere to a formula. Under the best of circumstances, when things are going right, what you hear more than anything, is what the band wants. It happens to certainly be that many of the groups I work with like and use the same types of sounds. It makes no difference to me. I can't qualify one sound as being better than the other. My job as an engineer and producer is to find out what those people want and do just that."* He continues with a logic-laden dogma that once again recalls his 'revelation' story; *"People call me and say they want a Flaming Lips drum sound. I reply usually with a 'you mean you want to hire Steven [Drozd] to play on your record?' This is because it comes from him, not me. I just put up the mics. Sure I have an idea of how to capture a good sound but really, when a band is good, it's good. You're set. You have to stay out of the way."* He dictates that the key to having a good result in the end product begins with the artist. *"They have to have a strong idea about what they should sound like, and I've been lucky to work with people like that."* After taking one quick breath, he continues his common sense-based attack, *"Look, this Fall I've got a line-up that includes Low and Godspeed You Black Emperor! How far out of my way would I have to go to suddenly be a bad producer working with these bands? What would I do to make a Jonathan Richman record sound bad?"*

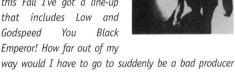

Another important professional threshold of rationale he lives by surfaces in the conversation. *"If it had to come down to it, I'd rather work with a crappy band that are friendly any day than a great band that are a bunch of assholes. This job involves working with people, so it matters. If I wanted to work with assholes, I'd have gotten a corporate job."* Given the lengthy work days that both a musician and engineer share in

close proximity, his point is very clear.

The year 2000 will definitely be a rewarding year for Tarbox Road and Fridmann, and always exciting. After the off-the-floor Japanese Number Girl sessions, his next client will be Sparklehorse. *"There are only two of them [Mark Linkous and Scott Minor],"* he explains, *"so I'll go back to having to slowly build the songs; although it'll still be organic. After that, Dot Allison (a Scottish singer) is coming in and we're going to do a lot of computer-based work. What I love, and is fun about this job, is that it changes all the time."* Fridmann is glad to be away from the cloud of the megalopolis music business and would rather just work. *"I live in the sticks. I work 12 hours a day. There is no entertainment industry here. People around here don't care if something is #1 on the charts. They probably wouldn't care unless they saw something about it on [the TV show] Entertainment Tonight."* Set aside the odd chance exposure to other's work from the outside world (he vehemently admires the production skills of Tchad Blake, Jon Brion, Nigel Godrich, Bryce Goggin, Jim O'Rourke and Brian Paulson), he is content on getting home to his family at the end of a long day and reverting to absorbing two therapeutic albums which have taken permanent residence upon his cerebral tastebuds - the eerie John McLaughlin guitar-threaded Miles Davis classic *In A Silent Way*, and The Cure's *Disintegration*.

By the way, Dave wishes to thank his mom and dad.

Sparklehorse. Low. Mogwai. Godspeed You Black Emperor! The Flaming Lips. All five are amongst the most talented and expressionate artists this planet currently has to offer. And they will all be making the trip along the New York State Thruway this year with Cassadaga as their destination. And Dave Fridmann will await their arrival at his bunker of self-sufficiency. He'll lend them his helping ear, friendship and act a conduit to their resilience. And more will follow. Oh... and add in a band called Mercury Rev to the roster. He's a member, remember? He plays bass, and sometimes keyboards. You will be let in on a secret - they have already returned and have begun to record the follow up to 1998's critically acclaimed *Deserter's Songs*. And, in the same work ethic as the late great filmmaker Stanley Kubrick, they are taking their time, as usual. *"Who knows when it'll be done,"* he says humbly, *"when it's finished, it'll be finished."* ✪

Master of Word Jazz, Ken Nordine

by Curtis Settino

Somehow, somewhere, somewhen, someone shared with me the sonic sensibilities of Ken Nordine. I was delighted with his word play (or were the words playing with him?), his deep, clear voice (an accidental hypnotist?), and the fresh and exciting music that slid, skittered, and strode in and around his sung-spoken thoughts. Nordine began his career as a radio announcer and commercial voiceover artist in the '40s. In the '50s, he started recording his own material. He released *Word Jazz*, *Son of Word Jazz*, *Next!*, and *Volume II*. The success of these recordings earned him a cult status that's still strong today. Throughout the '60s and '70s, he continued doing voice work (several hundred of them a year!) and adding to his personal catalog. In the '80s, among many other projects, he created over 300 30-minute programs for National Public Radio. Currently Nordine hosts a weekly radio program, still does commercials, creates visual and sound art, and kindly obliges interviewers who call him up asking him what he's doing.

I've been playing around with a special phone that I have so that I can make funny phone calls.

How does that work?

I have a lot of phone interviews done and I'm going to mix them with music. I'll call a friend of mine who wants to play the game, and who has the sense of humor to do it, and I'll ask him for, maybe, a brain transplant or something. He'll be Dr. Curtis, for example, and I'll say, "Hey Doc, do you have any unwashed brains?"

[laugh] Are you planning on releasing these?

I never think ahead that far. If it comes off the way I conceive it, I'll slip it into one of my radio shows. But to get back to what you're primarily interested in, what can I tell you that would be helpful?

Well, one of the things I was curious about was how you go about creating your recordings.

With the orchestrated music, I write to the music, generally. With the free form jazz, I write to the phrasing of the music. I'll say, "There's room here for something." That's one way. The other way is using live music in the studio, with the musicians listening to what I'm doing and I listening to what they're doing, and it becomes a kind of empathic situation. So if I'm doing something, as I was the other day, about the arachnid family, I'll say to the musician, "You can be the web, and you can play the attitude of the spider waiting for some food to come by." So each musician brings to the fantasy whatever they feel is appropriate. Or, in another way, I'll say, "Hey, let's get a good groove going." And then I'll do something that fits with that groove metrically. Because I work with metrics pretty much. For example, the spider thing I was working on is a 6/5 rhythm. So I knew that would work with some of the things the percussionist was doing. He did a wonderful thing that sounded like the light coming off of the web. I'd say, "It's a good year for spiders," and he'd go, "tchi-tchi-tchi" ... "Or so it seems. Incessantly weaving such gossamer schemes." ... "ur-ah-ur" "It should make one wonder what blueprint within instinctively causes the spider to spin." ... "phew-shew-phew." That sort of thing. It's really an empathic relationship between the musicians' hearing and my hearing, so there's room for them and there's room for what I do. One of the beautiful things about jazz music is that when it really works each of the players allows room for the others. So there's not a competitive "Hey, I can step on top of what you're doing" thing. Those are the groups that don't last.

It seems that there's a natural soloist quality to being a vocalist, though?

Yeah, but even at that, some soloists don't leave room. They figure they have to be singing all the time. The best, of course, is when everyone is listening and there's a relaxed togetherness. That's what I strive for.

Do you work as the main producer at these sessions?

Yeah.

Have you ever worked as just a producer and not as a musical participant or composer?

No, I've always worked on things that I'm really involved in. I've done other things where other people were involved. But the thing that's closest to my heart is doing something where there's a kind of a rapport with each other. There's nobody saying, "Hey, faster, or slower, or louder, or softer." Or, you have to change the feel of the message to fit someone's preconceived idea of what the audience is going to react to. That happens more in the commercial world. When you walk into that world you recognize that immediately.

Are you doing many commercials these days?

I do some. Not as many I used to do. I guess I just don't try as hard anymore.

Someone told me that you have a home studio where you do some of that recording in?

Yes, I do. That's where I am as we speak. I have all the things that you need and more. I did some recording here with Tom Waits, and a lot of other people, too.

I heard a recording you did with him that was a sort of Hollywood banter about trying to get a film going. I think it was on a David Grisman CD.

[chuckles] Yeah, some of that was also performed live in San Francisco at a place called Bimbos. I went out there and did a concert. I also did a concert the same way last year in London at the Royal Festival Hall with Laurie Anderson, Brian Eno, and others. I flew two musicians over with me, Howard Levy and Kristan [one of Nordine's sons], and we picked up two people in London. There was no rehearsal. I just said, "This is what we're going to do." It's pretty hard to rehearse when you have no charts!

[laugh] So, when you're in the studio, do you serve as the engineer as well?

No! My son does the engineering for me.

Is that Kristan?

Yes. We have a 24-track with Dolby, a Harrison board, Pro Tools, and all the goodies that you need to manipulate sound. The studio is on the third floor of an old, old house built in 1902.

Wow! That sounds nice!

Yes, it's a beautiful place. It's got quarter-sawed mahogany paneling, big windows. It's a little bit of yesterday in a neighborhood that doesn't know what the hell is happening—which is all right.

Are you right in Chicago?

Right in Chicago, smack dab in the middle of its heart. In fact they've even put an honorary name on the street. That made my wife very happy. "Ken Nordine Lane—Honorary," it says.

That's great! Do you find yourself getting into the Pro Tools type of manipulation more and more as the technology advances?

It still has to end up being something that's worth listening to. You can circumvent a lot of things, but you can't circumvent content. You can use technique to create all sorts of strangeness. There's nothing wrong with that if you need it. Of course, that's all subjective.

Yeah, I think it's interesting to come back to something after several years and just be surprised by it from the new perspective.

Yeah... in fact, I've been working on these things called "Maybe the Moment", which is an attempt to resurrect moments of time. The idea of "seizing the moment", you know, to see how you were. But actually, the moment is like a bird in your hand that flies off in a blur. It's that type of realization that time is probably just dimly remembered. I don't know where that part of the brain is? Do you? There's a little section there somewhere where all these things are stored in a strange way. Of course, if you've had any experience with Alzheimer's, you'd see what a sad thing it is when cognition slips away. "I'll never forget What's-His-Name." They really fall apart. Well, part of life, I guess, is falling apart. There was a great sculptor that nobody thought was great because of his subject matter. He made sculptures that would fall apart. They were strange Rube Goldberg-type things. And what would happen, right before your very eyes, over a period of, say, a month, the sculpture, because of the eccentricity of its motion, would fall apart. I guess what happened was that they [the art dealer] were trying to sell the damn things. But it was disconcerting to them, because by the time they found somebody who was interested in the thing it had fallen apart. [laughs]

I guess they needed some time-release sculpture then.

Yeah [laughs]. Do you paint or anything like that?

Yes I do. I'm also a graphic artist.

Oh, I love to play with PhotoShop! It's a wonderful way to manipulate images. Now there's a case where I have fun manipulating. You can do things to screw up an image that can make it very interesting.

Do you paint as well?

I goof around. I'm mostly in the computer now. I used to do a lot of painting. I did some rectangular Easter eggs. I put ink in my kids' wading pool and dropped canvases in there and sold them for $150 a piece! They looked rather nice come to think of it. That's a Japanese technique that they've been using for centuries. Most of the things we think of have been done, one way or another, at least unconsciously.

Yeah, but you never seem to find that out until you come up with it yourself.

That's true. I do a lot of fooling around with the [PhotoShop] filter Warp. Are you familiar with Warp?

Yeah.

I've done some things for the magazine Outré. They do a quarterly that can be a low-rent-Romeo type of a thing. Each issue they print one of my "Maybe the Moment" pieces with an illustration that I've done. I had an exhibit of this type of thing with Jerry Garcia in Chicago years ago.

It seems like you work similarly in each of your mediums.

Everything we do is a gross abbreviation of what's really happening.

I was wondering how involved you are in the sound design aspects of your work?

Quite a bit, actually. In fact, I'm working on a part for a new CD where Tick is talking to Tock inside of a clock. So we created a tick-tock fugue by slowing those sounds down. That's an old technique that started out with musique concrète.* You can do it so much better now because you don't lose quality digitally. With analog tape, you used to wind up with all kinds of surface noise.

And your editing was destructive.

Also, Ampex [now Quantegy], God love their little souls, years ago, they came out with a tape that developed traction. So we have some tapes that we did archivally that scrape off and catch on the heads when you play them now. It becomes like glue. It's a drag. To get rid of it, you have to warm them up in a convection oven. But even then, you can only play them once. So it's, "Sorry, that's all. You can't play it anymore."

Well, it's similar to the sculptures you were talking about.

[laughs] Exactly. You hate to think about that sort of thing. Of course, that's sort of what happens to language. How many people speak "Beowulf"**? Not many, Sanskrit is on the way out, too.

It's popular in the yoga community!

[laughs] I think you're right there. ☮

* Musique concrète is music created from recorded sounds rather than notation.
** An Anglian poem written Old English, circa 700 A.D.

INTRODUCTION TO DIGITAL AUDIO

A Basic Overview of Digital Audio

by Scott Colburn

Your ears are analog devices that convert sound waves into mechanical pulses the brain can understand. Your computer is a binary device, which means that it can only understand messages described in ones and zeros. In order to convert an analog signal to a digital signal, a converter executes several operations. The main objective of the converter is to sample a piece of the incoming analog signal (kind of like nibbling on a slice of cake), and then the conversion of each sample into a 16-bit binary description.

The standard sampling rate for digital audio onto musical CDs is 16-bit, 44.1 kHz, a rate that was standardized early on by a fellow named Nyquist. Mr. Nyquist determined that sample rates needed to be twice that of the highest frequency people can hear. As most people can hear up to 20 kHz, it was decided that the sample rate should be 44.1 kHz, which would give you a frequency response up to 22 kHz - a little beyond what most human beings can hear. The entire range of usual human hearing is 20 Hz - 20 kHz, with 20 Hz being the lowest frequency people can usually hear (ex: rap records try to utilize these low frequencies). 20 kHz is the highest frequency you can hear (think of a dentist's drill).

Electrically, an analog audio signal looks like wavy lines on an oscilloscope (which is a device electronic technichians use to test audio equipment). When you use a hard disc audio recorder on your computer, the program will represent audio waves in this manner:

The converter looks at the amplitude (the distance above or below the centerline of an audio signal's waveform) of the incoming signal 44,100 times per second! The amplitude is then described using 16 digits (always a combination of zeros and ones: binary code). This 16-digit number is called a word. A stream of words is then recorded onto your hard drive, and is then converted back into analog audio by the program you are using to edit your audio. In other words, every audio file on the computer is just series of ones and zeros grouped into 16-bit words. These audio files are referred to as uncompressed digital audio. The most popular file formats for uncompressed digital audio are: WAVs (Windows Audio Volume - a Windows native file format); AIFFs (Audio Interchange File Format - the Macintosh version of a WAV); and SDIIs (Sound Designer II - a proprietary file format used by Digidesign for their suite of programs, including Pro Tools, Sound Designer and AVID).

Recording audio onto your hard disc is easy with the right tools, but the file size is huge. It is estimated that one minute of stereo audio at 16-bit 44.1 kHz has a file size of about 10.5 megabytes. This may not seem like a lot of space if you have a 27 gig hard drive, but let's looks at it the way the internet sees it: With a modem speed of 28.8 kbps, each MB of information takes about 35 seconds to download. Hence, a three minute music sample will take about 18 minutes to download - not a very efficient way of transmitting data! For this reason, several companies have developed various methods of reducing audio file sizes so that reasonable quality can be maintained while file sizes are reduced dramatically.

Internet Audio Technologies

As we learned, several companies have developed methods of reducing the size of a 16-bit 44.1 kHz audio file into a more manageable size for internet distribution. Methods of reducing audio file sizes are known as a codec, which is short for compression/decompression. Remember that WAVs and AIFFs are uncompressed audio. Applying a codec to an uncompressed audio file will yield a compressed file that is smaller in size, yet (hopefully) maintains the sonic integrity of the original file. You might be familiar with WinZip or Stuff It. These programs compress computer data into smaller files that can be emailed or distributed in less time over the internet.

Codecs determine what information is unnecessary and throws it away. As a result, the file size is smaller. We learned that stereo audio is about 10.5 megs per minute. Mono audio files will be half that size of stereo audio files since stereo is actually a combination of two mono files! A codec works in this way, but it does its magic by reducing bit resolution rates (16 to 8 to 4 bits) and reducing sample rates (44.1 k to 32 k to 22 k to 11 k).

Bit resolution is an important component for the fidelity of an audio file. Each reduction in bit resolution results in a less accurate description of the amplitude of each sample. For example, if I asked you to measure a wall using only full sheets of 8.5" x 11" paper, you would be able to give me a number (say 10 sheets) that will represent the height of the wall. When you get to that last sheet of paper, you might find that the wall is actually 9.5 sheets high, but the criteria is to describe the height using whole sheets of paper, so you opt for saying 10 sheets. This is equivalent to 8-bit resolution. Now remeasure that wall with index cards. You will find that you can get much closer to describing the actual height of the wall because your measuring unit is smaller. This is equivalent to 16-bit resolution.

Sample rate reduction affects the frequency response of your audio file. Remember Nyquist? The sample rate needs to be twice the highest frequency you plan to encode, and 44.1 kHz is the standard for CD Quality audio. This means that the upper limit on the high end is 22.05 kHz, which is beyond what most people can hear. 32 k will give you a high end limit of 16 k, which is just below what the average person can hear (of course, we lose high end response abilities as we age). This sort of reduction in high end is almost undetectable to the average listener. A 22 k sampling rate will limit the high end to about 11 k. Cymbals on a drum set live in the 10 k range, so you can see that we are still at an acceptable frequency response (maybe slightly dull), but this will be perceived as good quality by the majority of listeners. Also notice that the sampling frequency is now half of it's original 44.1 - therefore, the file size is also half as large. Each reduction of these parameters yields a smaller file size but at the cost of fidelity. The race in this field is to provide a small file size with excellent audio quality, which is no small task, indeed.

There are two types of delivery modes for the internet: Download and Streaming. Every platform can be "downloaded" - you can post or send a WAV or AIFF to anyone via email. Of course, the result of downloading a WAV or AIFF is massive connect times on the internet because the files are so big, so the person you send such a file to may not be too happy about it but it can be done.

Some genius somewhere realized that they would be donned the King/Queen of internet delivery if audio files could be reduced in size yet perfect audio quality was left intact. The most common form of downloadable audio delivery is mp3. This codec analyzes audio information and translate it in a compression scheme of 5:1, with almost no detectable loss of fidelity. This means, for instance, that a 3 minute music sample that was originally 33 megs could become 6.3 megs or smaller. This is accomplished through the use of variable sample rates, variable bit rates, and perceptual coding. To explain perceptual coding, let's look at a typical song; the music begins the vocals come in and possibly the music continues by itself at the end of the piece. When the voice comes in, the music drops down in level and is at times masked by the voice itself. Codecs analyze these waveforms and give the most bits to the voice (which is up front) and less bits to the music (in the background). There is no need to encode the music in full fidelity since it is covered by the voice most of the time.

Streaming media is the ability to see or hear content on demand from a web site. This is a hot field in the internet world! The main players of streaming technology are Apple's QuickTime, Real Network's Real Media, and Microsoft's Media Player. These three companies have led the march to provide high quality media streams at the lowest bit rate possible. At one time, each company's player would only play their own files, but these days most players able to decode all the other formats. Isn't direct competition grand? ✍

DIGITAL OR ANALOG? THE DISCUSSION CONTINUES...

Pro Tools Mix Plus 24: Work of the Devil?

An Opinion by John Vanderslice

Note: If you have sold your car (and re-mortgaged your house) to buy one, stop reading and start chanting: "It's okay to record on a G4, it's okay to record..."

This is not another digital versus analog article, I promise. This is a highly opinionated, anecdotal investigation regarding the uses and misuses of Pro Tools Mix Plus 24 in the context of recording electric/acoustic instruments. While I am stridently pro-analog, I have no problem with the possibilities and promise of digital audio. I am a great champion of MP3 (the little codec that could) and hold the heretical view, at least in the analog world, that CDs are a superior storage medium to vinyl. I will focus on the *sound* (or, more accurately, my opinion of the sound) of Pro Tools, not on the supposed by-products of digital editing (i.e., decrease in the overall performance level of musicians - slick, lifeless, quantized, over-produced records), nor will I consider the larger question of hard disc recording.

I was reminded time and again by the people I interviewed for the article (many of whom, by the way, did not share my negative feelings about PT) that hearing is subjective and wholly personal. Tony Visconti, the brilliant producer/engineer who worked on over half of Bowie's earth-shattering '70s work, reminded me that hearing is a chemical process of the brain. "The bottom line is that Pro Tools is just a storage medium, just like tape, it does it in a different way." He adds, "Digital recording is still in its infancy and is getting better and better."

My studio, Tiny Telephone, has PT Mix Plus 24, and I've spent countless hours in the past two years using it for looping, sampling, recording and mixing demos. As a result, I have overwhelmingly dour feelings about this soon-to-be studio standard.

There was a time when the only projects in my studio that requested our Pro Tools rig were doing club remixes, sequenced beats, or the occasional rock band seeking Eric Valentine-like sheen [producer for Third Eye Blind, etc...]. But I've noticed a sea change in the past year: bands that have made great home recordings in the past (and who grew up listening to analog classics like the *White Album* and *The Who Sell Out*) started asking me about getting Pro Tools for their home studios. They not only wanted to do editing and sequencing on PT, they wanted to record directly into the computer. Indie bands that a few years ago would have been knee-jerk pro-analog would ask about bypassing the 2". "There's so much more we can do there, besides we don't want to buy tape..." And who can blame them? If PT sounded good it would be a dream come true, wouldn't it?

I should come clean: I have been hostile towards digital recording since buying my first ADAT (that I sold my Tascam TSR-8 to get it only made it worse). I had no idea why it sounded bad (I mean look at the specs...) but I was thoroughly uninspired to record on that loser. When I started my studio, I bought the only 2" I could afford, an Ampex MM1000. That beast sounded wonderful, but I lost much sleep (and many sessions) dealing with its idiosyncrasies (i.e., breakdowns). So let's admit it, analog is a major pain in the ass, tape cost is a consideration for any budget, and the whole thing is going the way of the wax cylinder. But while it's here, it will provide us with an important benchmark: in my opinion, nothing sounds better than a properly aligned, well-maintained 2" deck.

For low cost recording, digital can be the right choice, but Pro Tools is another matter. A functional 24 Mix Plus system with two 888s runs over 20 grand. The first thing people do when they spend that kind of cash is repress any negative feedback their ears are giving them - it took me years to admit that my ADAT was not right for me, and man I was depressed when I finally did. Let's not mince words: Mix Plus 24 is a supreme rip-off - you can start a serious analog studio for that kind of money, especially considering that MM1200 16-tracks are now selling for $3,000 and under.

I am partial to the accidents of analog recording: tape hiss, distortion and compression, bass bump and high-end suppression, to name a few. It's not the absence of these that makes Pro Tools so lame, but it certainly doesn't help. What are some of the problems, you ask?

Sonics

"Ricky Martin's "Livin' La Vida Loca" is the first single entirely recorded and mixed with a Digidesign Pro Tools digital audio workstation to reach the Number One position on Billboard magazine's Hot 100 chart."
-Digidesign Press Release

My general feeling is the more you lean on Pro Tools, whether as an editing tool, effects unit, mixer, or recording device, the further you degrade and compromise your audio. PT, for most of the engineers who work at my studio, is an invaluable and efficient editing tool. Tracks are flown from 2" tape, manipulated, and flown back. This is the least disruptive use and you'd have to be a bah-humbug Luddite to think this is going to ruin a perfectly nice, organic analog recording. "It's really best in a situation where a lot of fixes need to made," says John Croslin, my partner at Tiny Telephone. "If it's a band that's not really happening but there's some potential that makes it worth working on, that's when Pro Tools is useful." But, be cautious, "It won't necessarily have a lot of soul."

Once or twice a year, our Ampex 1200 gives out in the middle of a session. We give the band the option: you can reschedule or discover hard disc recording. This gives us a unique opportunity to A/B, with the same band, signal chain, mics and engineer. The jump to Pro Tools is a shock. Everything coming back off the G3 sounds aurally fatiguing, brittle and just plain *cheesy*. There is no center, no floor, to the drums, as if someone had patched in a mastering EQ and scooped out some low-mids - guitars and cymbals have a trashier, more volatile high end. The effect would be similar if some evil gnome sneaked into the studio and replaced the U67s and Coles 4038s with cheap mics. I can always tell when I enter the control room if an engineer is recording into PT - its sonic imprint is as recognizable as tape.

"The impact of Pro Tools is not as pleasing," Croslin adds, "if you have a drum hit or guitar chord - when it comes back it seems as if something's missing that you would have had on analog tape." Jim Eno, drummer in Spoon and studio owner, thought he was getting good drum sounds on PT until he bought a 2" deck. "It kicked me in the ass," he says, "it's like the difference between seeing a painting in a book and going to a museum." Billy Gould, ex-Faith No More member and current Kool Arrow label head, is more blunt: "After recording on Pro Tools I just don't feel very good."

One major problem with Pro Tools may be the A/D converters: many engineers I know, including quite a few who love Pro Tools, are of the opinion that the proprietary 888s are substandard and use third party ones instead. Michael Belfer, a Bay Area producer, uses his Akai S3000 sampler on the front end. Visconti feels the PT converters are "great." He reminds me that "even analog has a converter - if you play analog tape through a Neve desk, it's gonna sound different than if you played it through an API desk." I prefer the sound of the Panasonic 3800 DAT converters - not exactly a paragon of audio fidelity. Comparing a mix from our Ampex ATR 102 with the PT safety elicits nervous laughter from bands at Tiny: "Wow, we dodged a bullet..."

Things get catastrophic when Plug-Ins enter the picture. I'm not talking about hi-fi hair splitting here - program material coming off the G3 suffers deeply when TDMs get added to the signal path. There are two issues here: their actual sound and the phasing problems that develop from using many at once.

What self-respecting musician would use cheeseball amp modelers like Amp Farm instead of their own amplifier? Well, you'd be surprised. Musicians who scoff at an ART multi-effects unit will gladly load up a mix with crappy sounding TDMs. And once the mix is heavy with Plug-Ins, you will have latency and phasing problems to deal with. Latency is caused by the time it takes a signal to be routed through a TDM and back into the mix. It may be only a few milliseconds delay, but additional Plug-Ins will increase this time and possibly create serious phasing issues.

Tiny Telephone has recently bailed on Pro Tools - we're looking into Sonic Solutions for mastering. I have to admit: it was *great* for burning CDs.

Where to now?

Digital recording will be great one day - there's no doubt about that. "Obviously the more bits, the higher sampling rate, the better it's going to sound," Visconti reminds me. "It all comes down to resolution." I have heard good records done on Pro Tools, but they are not my favorites and they would have undoubtedly sounded better if recorded on a 2". I truly believe that in years to come we will be ashamed of these quantized, Amp Farmed, obsessively edited monstrosities that are coming out now. The early '80s should provide a grim reminder of what happens when the recording collective adopts new technology (early digital multi-tracks and all-in-one effects boxes) without cynically listening to the end result. Visconti counters my gloom and doom, "If you were on a desert island and you were given Pro Tools, you would find a way of making it sound great. I don't really believe that gear sounds great, technique sounds great. Always did and it always will." I agree, in theory, I definitely agree. But please, dear *Tape Op* reader, if you're considering Pro Tools as your primary format, A/B it against analog tape. You too can dodge the bullet. ✪

> **Note:** This piece originally ran in July of 2000. While most of the recording world has sided with Mr. Stenman, Mr. Vanderslice is still making records on 24 track tape.

Pro Tools Mix Plus 24: Gift From God?

An Opinion by Eric Stenman

Like most engineers, I learned my trade on various tape-based analog machines. Most of my early days were spent working on a Fostex B-16 1/2". Soon enough, I had graduated to 2" recording and spent countless hours recording bands like Will Haven, Deftones, 7 Seconds, Knapsack, and others on that format. Times have changed. I now find myself addicted to the joys of hard drive-based recording and I'm always a little disappointed whenever I have to go back. A few years ago, I decided that I wanted to get more serious about entering the world of electronic music. Instead of going the sampler/sequencer route, I opted to buy a better computer and focus on a fully hard drive-based system. After a little research and a decent amount of time staring at my computer monitor, I found myself to be quite taken with programs like Sonic Foundry's *Acid*, *Sound Forge*, and more recently *Vegas*. Very quickly, I became a fan of the newfound freedom that I had been granted. I discovered that, with a little creative thinking, any style of music could be captured and presented quite well with computer-based system. I loved the idea of being able to go from having a song idea to having a mastered CD using just one piece of gear. Added to this were the benefits of almost limitless sample time, not needing to buy expensive analog tape and being able to work on professional level projects in my bedroom. I got off to a great start on this system without spending too much money.

I now find myself working with computer based hard drive systems more than with analog machines. This process became even more prevalent last year when I recorded an album for the band, Training For Utopia. (*Throwing A Wrench Into The American Music Machine* - Solid State/Tooth and Nail Records). TFU came up out of the hardcore/metal scene and was a band that I had worked with in the past in a more traditional/analog manner. When we started to talk about their new album, both the band and I were very interested in making a much more electronically treated record. In many ways we set out to make a remix record that would, in fact, be the original version of the record. We went about this is a fairly untraditional way. The basic tracks were recorded to 2" in a conventional studio. We did this quickly not paying much attention to small mistakes. I then loaded the drum tracks, bass lines, guitar riffs, and vocal passes into my computer and went home. The remainder of the album was assembled, reassembled, filtered, effected, and mixed in my computer. Real drums were layered with programmed beats, guitars were sampled and rearranged, vocals were tampered with in any way necessary and it was all done on my Gateway PC in my bedroom using a few pieces of Sonic Foundry software.

Some time during all of this, my band Tinfed managed to get a record deal with Third Rail/Hollywood Records. Having recorded all of our past efforts myself, I welcomed the chance to work with a bigger budget and a producer. This would be the first time in seven years that I would get to be in a studio without being fully responsible for the production/engineering side of things. We ended up working with Ed Buller (Suede, Ben Lee, Pulp, Spiritualized, etc.) at The Plant in Sausalito, CA. Going into the record, Ed made it clear that he was a big fan of Pro Tools. As a band, we agreed that we were up for it as well.

In an attempt to capture some traditional analog warmth, we decided to track the drums to 2" analog tape. From there on in, however, every other aspect was handled in Pro Tools. Very quickly, I fell in love with Pro Tools-both as an engineer and musician. Due to features such as no rewind times and quick auto punches, I found that it is so much easier to concentrate capturing good performances and to stop worrying about complete perfection. With a digital editing system as powerful as Pro Tools 5.0, practices such as recording multiple takes and then comping the most unique sections are quick and easy. Musicians and vocalists can concentrate on emotive, spontaneous performances. The good flaws can be accented and the bad ones replaced quickly and effectively.

When it came to mixing we opted to stay within the system in order to save time and take advantage of the many options that it presented. Complete automation and the ability to fully and easily save multiple mixes was enough for me. I love knowing that I could pull up a recall six months later in a studio half way around the world and start up right where I left off.

And then there are the plug-ins. This entire article could be written on the joys of using all of the great plug ins that now exist. Focusrite EQs and compressors, Lexicon reverbs, Line 6's Amp Farm, Antares AutoTune, etc. There are too many to go into in this short article. In conclusion, both as an engineer and a musician, I have reached the point where I would always rather work with computer-based systems. Whenever I'm back in the fully analog world, I always wish for the freedom and options that digital editing and processing offer. ✪

Stuart Hallerman Avast! studio

by Ben London

Stuart Hallerman has run Seattle's Avast! studio since 1990. Stuart left his hometown of Chicago in 1980 to attend Evergreen College in Olympia, WA. After "the 5-year plan" at Evergreen's recording program and several years as Soundgarden's live soundman and scapegoat, Stuart realized a dream of opening his own recording stud. Avast! found a permanent home when Stuart installed an Ampex MM1200 2" 16-track purchased from Roger Fisher of Heart into an old mechanics garage in Seattle's Wallingford neighborhood. Avast! is a very comfortable room that feels more like a spacious practice space than a studio. It is filled with amazing gear yet it is still accessibly priced. Over the years Avast! has hosted a wide range of artists including the Screaming Trees, Soundgarden, Built to Spill, Hater, Bikini Kill, Supersuckers and the Evil Tambourines. I have been lucky enough to work at Avast! on a number of occasions and have always been pleased with the results.

What were some of the first releases to come out of Avast!?

The first CD release that came out of Avast! was Christ on a Crutch's *Crime Pays When Pigs Die* with Nate Mendel [Sunny Day Real Estate, Foo Fighters] and Eric Akre [Treepeople, Citizens Utilities, Goodness]. Steve Fisk produced The Treepeople's *Guilt, Regret, Embarrassment*, as well the Jesse Bernstein record which was started while Jesse was still alive and finished after he died. I was very busy doing albums, seven inches, & demos. The Screaming Trees did a round of demos here with Don Fleming for *Sweet Oblivion*. The Screaming Trees just have this sound, they're just always *themselves*. I asked Mark Lanegan jokingly as the session was concluding "Why does Epic need to hear a demo of the new stuff? Couldn't you just send them one of your old tapes?" He laughed and said, "They just want to make sure we still sound exactly the same."

What are some of your favorite sessions or bands that you have worked with?

Some highlights? One of my favorites would be the Hater record. It was sort of a moment captured on tape. It's an informal pile of mistakes and jokes that comes out so musically. There are so many unplanned moments on that record that are just gems. The Jesse Bernstein album with Fisk, Jesse reading his poetry with Fisk doing the music. That will always stand out as a classic Avast! record. A recent highlight is Maktub. I keep playing their *Subtle Ways* CD for people and they are like, "What is this, where can I get one?" The Treepeople's *Guilt, Regret, Embarrassment* has a lot of depth and

texture. A really quick record done in 5 days... tops. All the Built to Spill stuff. Doug [Martsch] has a fondness for recording here, he really goes out of his way to make sure that pieces of his records get recorded here. He consciously supports Avast! because he is a nice guy.

How did you end up in Evergreen's recording program?

If you knocked on Evergreen's door and said, "Hey, I want to study recording, and be a recording engineer," they'd say, "Go to a vocational school." What they wanted to teach you was a fully rounded interdisciplinary liberal arts education. If you mentioned that you were interested in recording they would tell you to get lost. I wanted a full education, but still had to finagle my way in there. They had very few students in the department. There might be 10-15 students studying recording at one level or another at any one time. Evergreen's communications lab building was built in 1977 and it was fully outfitted with approximately the state of the art equipment at that time. It had an Ampex 2" 16-track tape machine; it had a fairly large API 2488 console, pretty good mic collection. Neumans, AKGs, RCAs, the standard good old mics of the day. Basically what's considered vintage now is what they had then. Besides the 16-track studio they had three 4-track studios with nice recording spaces attached to them. Because there was so much time, space, and gear you could actually get hours and hours... days and days of recording experience there. It was great.

It seems that it was a real vibrant ti to be attending Evergreen?

At that time Olympia felt slightly like the center of universe. Bruce Pavitt, who started Sub Pop, there. Steve Fisk, who was just leaving, had mad real influence on the scene as performer/engineer/producer. Calvin Johnson making cassettes in his bedroom and selling th through little flyers and word of mouth as genesis of K records. During school I bought a and started doing live sound for local bands. included Nirvana, Mudhoney, Screaming Tree touring bands like Fugazi. I felt slightly mispla I really wanted to do recording but here I was d sound for punk rock shows. On the other h when I did eventually move up to Seattle I kne the early Seattle rock bands. I was acquainted them, friends with them. They knew me from d live sound and they trusted me. When it came for them to record they felt that I understood they were trying to accomplish. One of my concert events in Olympia was a punk rock s that Slim Moon from Kill Rock Stars would pu every summer out in the park. As the 1987 s approached, the bands he had originally sched to perform cancelled and he was stuck. He sa guess we'll have to call it off it unless we can some other bands." I offered, "I can call s friends in Seattle, they're called *Soundgarden*." excitedly goes, "You can get SOUNDGARDE "Whatever, It's just rock, waddaya want?" replied, "No, no, those guys are great! I really them to play!" So I got him connected. The had never played Olympia so they were in

Nirvana ended up opening followed by My Eye and Soundgarden. Nirvana was great and the show had some intensely memorable moments. After the set, Soundgarden came up to me and said, "We're going on the road in January. You have a van don't you? Would you like to come be our sound man?" We're just standing outside in the park as the sun is setting and I'm thinking about this in my head, driving my crappy van all over the US in *January*, to go to all these crummy bars, with smoke and beer and doing sound on these crap-ass PAs... "Sounds great, I'll go!" They were also promising that we would go to Europe in the Spring. I'll believe that when I see it I thought. It all kind of worked out though. That was kind of a highlight and turned into about three years of touring!

How did you end up assisting on Soundgarden's *Louder Than Love*?

I had done some 4-track recording for the band in '85 and they had loved the way it turned out. While we were recording I asked Kim [Thayil] how he wanted his guitar to sound. His answer was, "I want it to sound like Godzilla knocking over buildings." So I put the mic where I thought it might work, I turned the knobs and had him keep playing and within a few minutes I got a pretty crunchy and bold sound. Kim was pleased by how I translated his request into a taped sound that he had never actually gotten before. I brought something out of the band that other engineers had missed by trying to polish stuff up and basically wash them out. The other engineers would not respect the band's ideas. So when they were doing their first major label record with Terry Date they asked me to hang out and be a production assistant. I had no illusions that they should record with me in my living room in Olympia. I had no idea how to make a major label record and spend $80,000. They knew Terry but they didn't yet trust him. They were worried that they might get that same washed-out pop production they had gotten from other producers. They invited me along to keep an eye on him. The idea was that when I saw him do something wrong like gating the tom toms or whatever to go pull the band aside and warn 'em. I didn't have much to tell 'em though! Terry did a really great job of producing that record. In the end it was a little slicker than I think the band had wanted, but it's a pretty fun record to listen to still. There is so much texture in it.

Did you learn much from watching Terry work?

Mostly I saw that I had the right idea all along, but I did learn some great techniques from Terry. When he did the basic tracks he filled the first couple of tracks with kick, snare high hat, then he left two open tracks, and then ambience mics and stuff, and then the bass and guitars. Then up on the upper numbered tracks he recorded all the tom toms. I think it was four toms at the time, two floor toms, two rack toms, and we spent about two weeks doing all the basic tracks. When they finally had the drum tracks, Terry, Matt [Cameron], and myself sat down at the mixing

board and ran a fine toothed comb through the tapes. We listened to the tom toms and bouncing from the 4 original tracks we made a stereo mix. He added some EQ and a little compression and bounced that to the open tracks in the drum kit area of the tape. What we would do is roll through the song and note where in the song Matt hit the toms. Where he hit the rack toms we would turn off the floor toms and bounce just the racks over and vice versa. Push up the faders, pull down the faders. Matt would sit there and push up the fader every time he did a fill. It went quickly because he knew exactly what he had played. The whole record was done on one 24-track machine. It was a relatively simple kind of recording. Later I observed them in the studio with Michael Beinhorn during the recording of *Superunknown*. Matt called me up at the studio and to commiserate with me, "When we record at Avast! we get great drum sounds with like seven microphones. I've got a *forest* of microphones around me here." I used to have a picture on the wall here of that drum set up and I think there were something like 50 mics on and around his drum kit. Five snare mics, seven kick mics, three mics on each tom eight room mics, etc. Soundgarden did a demo recording with Beinhorn before *Superunknown* and Kim called up distressed and said, "We're kind of stuck here, Stuart. You have to tell Beinhorn how to get my guitar sound because we have put up seven mics, all these compressors and equalizers and every time he adds another microphone my sound gets smaller and smaller. I want it to sound huge. Let me put you on the line with him and you can tell him what you do to get my sound." Well, what I do for Kim is basically an Endino-ism. Put a SM57 on the cone of the speaker, run it through a Summit tube pre-amp straight to tape. No compression, no equalizer, just overload the mic pre a little bit. That's it. It *still* sounds like Godzilla knocking over buildings!

Is that what they ended up doing?

No, They mixed the seven mics until they were only halfway *un*satisfied.

What are some of your favorite low cost microphones?

That is a good question. One of the school standards that is still in production that you can still get is the Shure SM7, that they just re-released. It is a dynamic mic. It's like an SM57 but has a selected capsule. It is a very silky, very nice microphone. For that matter the SM57 is a very usable microphone for vocals or instruments. When Steve Fisk did the Gits' *Frenching the Bully* album here we tried out every nice microphone we had and ended up recording Mia Zapata with an SM57 because it was the perfect mic for her. It sounded right with her. Everything else was lumpy or shrill or harsh. Audio Technica makes a wide array of microphones. They make some for vocals, some for instruments, some for drums and there is something about their microphones. They are cheap, if you put them in the application they suggest they just fucking work. You don't have to hype em', EQ them, or work em'. You just put the kick mic [ATM 25]

in a kick drum and run it to tape. It is not my favorite mic - I would rather use an AKG D-12, but I always have to EQ it to get the kick drum sound I want. They have a tube vocal mic called the AT-4060. Put it up against some of the newer Neumanns, some of the better AKGs, it is a great sounding vocal mic. It is not a cheap alternative; it is just a great vocal mic. They have a new one called the AT4047 which I believe is supposed to be a copy of the U-47 Neumann. I have not heard that yet but I bet they hit the mark. They have a really cheap mic, about $140 that looks kind of like a skinny SM-58 and it is called the ATM-813 and it really sounds a lot like a U-87. The U-87 is about a $2500 dollar microphone and this is $150. You put them next to each other and you can hear the difference but it is hard to describe what the difference is. One has a golden sheen; one has a silver sheen. Is that worth the $2000 plus difference?

How do you balance being a creative person with being a businessperson?

I got into recording because I love music and I got into this business because I love recording.

Any other tales?

When I got my first 4-track rig in Olympia and four okay microphones (a couple of 421's and stuff) Calvin Johnson from K records, no, K Cassettes, was just starting his recording empire there. I knew him from around town and I saw him one day and I was like, "Hey Calvin, I just got these *good* microphones and a nice little 4-track reel-to-reel and I know you have been doing some home recording. Y'wanna record together? It'd be cheap and it would mostly be for me to get some experience, what do you think? You can make better tapes this way, not just those cassette things. He said, "You have good recording equipment?.... Nah, I'm not interested. We're doing just fine recording on cassette. Better is not something I am interested in." I was puzzled. I was talking about free recording, better equipment, how could he not want better sounding stuff? I just didn't even get it. Eventually Steve Fisk brought Beat Happening to Avast! to record and we rented a really nice microphone and were using the 2" 16-track and at that point Beat Happening had already been to the Music Source and been working their way up from cassettes to 2" tape. So over time Calvin had slowly gotten exposed to better recording techniques and he finally realized that if you sang into a really good mic, it was just satisfying. It really helps the music, and it helps the record. Calvin was becoming interested in better techniques and equipment and I was learning to appreciate the value of rawer sounds. We met in the middle and are now great friends. By that time I had been watching Jack Endino and Soundgarden work and I was really learning how to record a distorted guitar and a punk rock drum kit. I finally realized that recording has nothing to do with perfection. It is just capturing the spirit. So I went from schooled engineer, seeking 'perfection', to learning to just capture what you get... the mistakes are part of the beauty of it. ⊗

Roll, Jordan, Roll: A conversation *with* Jim Dickinson

by Philip Stevenson

Dickinson at "Old Ardent" 1966 - 1967

Somewhere on the thorny road to legend, hotel recording genius (and Eric Clapton victim) Robert Johnson wrote, "This stuff I got'll bust your brains out." While he may have been referring to the poison that took his life, he may as well have been describing the aftermath of a conversation with Jim Dickinson. An instant Memphis luminary, Jim has played with artists such as Sam and Dave, James Carr, The Rolling Stones, The Flamin' Groovies, Sleepy John Estes, Bob Dylan and countless others while simultaneously producing records for The Replacements, Screamin' Jay Hawkins, Green on Red, Calvin Russell, Toots and the Maytals, Ry Cooder and Big Star (to name a few). Some sane men go crazy after long stretches in the hit factory, becoming so firmly entrenched in the hyperbole and dissolute entanglements of the business that they can no longer hear music. Luckily, Jim is fine. One afternoon, we talked about his attempts to control nature, mendacity and Paul Westerberg in a lifelong quest for the "fuzzy little sound" that first inspired him.

Tell us something of the past. Did you always know you wanted to record music?

When I was a little kid my parents took me to Thomas Edison's museum. I didn't understand what part of it fascinated me - I thought I wanted to be an inventor maybe, but then I realized it was the recording equipment I was interested in.

There's a duality involved in making records. How did you decide to be a producer as opposed to an engineer?

I didn't separate the ideas of production and engineering at first, and it is two very different things. A lot of producers were running their own equipment, so I thought I wanted to be an engineer. John Fry told me, "Jim, I don't think you're emotionally suited to be an engineer." And he was entirely right. Engineering was a nightmare to me. It gave me nightmares - the worst dreams of my life. I was actually going to a Freudian analyst at one point because of engineering. As soon as I quit the guy declared me cured. I was going to school at Memphis State. My wife and I were living on campus, in Veterans housing. John Fry had a family home which was just a block and a half away and he had a recording studio behind it where he had made records as a teenager. The original Ardent records - four or five singles that came out when John was a teenager, with Fred Smith as a partner - the guy that is Fed Ex now. John considered himself retired at this time, which was 1965! That recording equipment was just too close - I couldn't resist it. So we did some sessions together, and I brought some people in. Again, I didn't know what production was. Fry had a partner in the radio programming business at the time named John King. King told me about Phil Spector and Motown - identified things, like the music that comes from New Orleans. I knew about the music, but I didn't know it specifically came from New Orleans. Johnny Vincent, Cosimo Matassa. King turned me on to all that.

What was your first job in the business?

My first "job" in the business was working for Chips Moman at the American studio. He had the first pop hit out of Memphis at the beginning of what they call the "Golden Era". "Keep on Dancing" by the Gentrys - a teen-age band from Memphis. Larry Raspberry and Jimmy Hart (now "The Mouth of the South", WWF manager) were in the original band. The kids that played on the record cut this very simple cover of an old R & B tune called "Keep on Dancing" at American Studios, put it out locally, then sold it to MGM and the thing was a hit. These kids were in high school, so half the band had quit with the record number 15 on the charts, and no album in the can, because they wouldn't go on the road. Well, I never have enjoyed playing live - I don't connect to the audience. In the studio I'm utterly aware of the audience, although we're separated by time and space, you know? I feel my audience in the studio - I never have on stage. So,

Left to Right: Sam Phillips, Jim Dickinson, Jerry Wexler

it was known in the Memphis music community that I wouldn't go on the road. I turned down an opportunity to go on the road with The Mar-Keys and a couple of other things. So Raspberry, the leader of the Gentrys, calls me up one night in my little cabin at about ten o'clock at night, my wife and I are sitting there, and he says, "You know, this is my situation: I'm number 15 with a bullet and my band has quit. I need to have a band and I need to have an album. Chips Moman, the producer, won't start to record until I've got a whole band. Will you go on the road with the Gentrys?" I said, "Hell no, Larry." He said, "Well, will you come down here and tell Chips that you will?" I understood what he meant, so I said, "Yeah, sure. I'll do that." My wife and I went down to the studio, and met Chips. He says, "Will you go on the road with the Gentrys?" And I said, "Yeah, sure" and then I started talking with the other musicians, bullshitting around, and before we knew it Chips had locked the doors and wouldn't let anybody out! So we started to record the album. He didn't unlock the doors until noon the next day, by which time we had recorded the entire first album, *Gentrytime*, and half of the second album. Chips says to me, "You're too good to go on the road with the Gentrys" and I thought, "That's what I think too." So, I got my first job, which was working in the original American rhythm section, which was Tommy Cogbill - the genius bass player, God rest his soul - me, and Clarence Nelson, a black guitar player who had played on some early Stax records, "Big Party" in particular -brilliantly played. He had to sweep up, and I'm not sure they paid Clarence anything. My original pay was $92.50 every other week – maybe. And "maybe" was part of the deal.

So then...

Then I quit Chips to go to work for John Fry, because I wanted to be an engineer, and I didn't think Chips would let me run the board. And the first thing he [Chips] did after I quit was to hire an engineer, so, once again, it tells how wrong I can be. But I went

to work for John Fry. We did a couple of records in his house - then his parents sold the house to the University. Then we built what they now refer to as "Old Ardent", which was the first studio outside of John's house where the first two Big Star records were cut, and where I started engineering. The first band that I worked on with John back at the old house was "Lawson and Four More". The keyboard player was Terry Manning, and Manning and I started out as second engineers to John. We did spillover R & B sessions and custom work around town. We had the first 8-track tape recorder that anybody had ever seen. It was the first "modern studio" in the City of Memphis. We ended up doing a lot of overdub work for Chips, Dan Penn, Willie Mitchell and everybody – when they realized that there were four more tracks, they were all there. So I worked for John and I quit in '67. When I next found gainful employment it was back as a session player. I started working with the band that became the Dixie Flyers - Tommy McClure, Charlie Freeman, Sammy Creeson - working for Stan Kessler who was running a studio called South of Memphis. He, and the two men who had been behind Sam the Sham and the Pharaohs - Gene Lucassi and Paul Bomarito who were liquor wholesalers were building a big state-of-the-art studio. But they built this temporary 8-track studio in this tobacco warehouse on Camilla - which is kind of in the medical district in midtown Memphis - and there was no reason why it should have worked. It wasn't even a ceiling, it was just baffles - acoustical pink insulation hanging on pikes and styrofoam crate stuffing on the wall – I mean it was very, very primitive. Misshapen concrete floor with rug scraps thrown around – it sounded great! The best sounding blues room that's ever been in the city of Memphis. And when I went to work with the band, the first thing that we recorded was the Albert Collins' album *Trash Talkin'.* This was 1968. The band kind of fell together. We did a bunch of work for Leland Rogers, who was Kenny Rogers' older brother. He was the first one who had hired two keyboard players, which kinda became our trademark.

Which did you play?

I was playing piano. Mike Utley became the organ player, although the first organ player we had was James Hooker Brown, who then became the piano player in the Amazing Rhythm Aces, but who is a remarkable organ player - played on some Willie Mitchell stuff - very characteristic strange sound he had. We played in one form or another in '68 and '69 in Memphis and as a result of that I did a little engineering, but I was starting to get some actual success as a player, so that was the road I was going.

I associate the Dixie Flyers with Atlantic...

Muscle Shoals, which was really the hottest place in terms of R & B rhythm section work, that was our real competition. Willie Mitchell was off kinda doing his own thing – he always was. There was the mythology that if you had the Atlantic account in the South, that was all you needed, and that was definitely not true, as we proved. And we got hired - to make a miserable and literally untold story shorter - we got hired by [Jerry] Wexler as a result of that Albert Collins' album (which he heard at the right place at the right time) to move to Miami and work for what he called Atlantic South. He and Tom Dowd had both moved to Miami and were trying to start a production food chain in Miami at Criteria Studios, which was kind of being refurbished. They had a rhythm section in Baton Rouge called Cold Grits who had cut a record called "Rainy Night in Georgia", and apparently they were crazy white boys, just like us, and they got fired. We took their jobs and moved down there – this is me, Freeman, McClure, Creeson and Mike Utley. And we took Albhy Galuten with us, who later produced *Saturday Night Fever* and became rich and famous. We moved to Miami and worked for Wexler in January of 1970. I stayed six months, went crazy and came home. I had never really tried to play anywhere but Memphis, and it hadn't crossed my mind that there was something geographic about what I was doing. There was something in Memphis that I desperately needed in order to play the way I play. I'm a very limited musician. What I do is kind of specific. In LA, they used to call me a "color player". I don't know what that means but whatever it is I need to do it in Memphis. After six months, I came home, converted my employment agreement to an artist's contract, made *Dixie Fried,* my so-called artist album on Atlantic, and gradually slipped back into production. I can't really tell you why, but before you know it I was back doing it. I did my first Los Angeles session with Brenda Patterson. I hired [Ry] Cooder for the session and, as a result of the session, he hired me to produce him. I produced his second and third record with Lenny Waronker, and it was Lenny, for me, who made everything make sense. By that time I had tried to produce records and had no idea what production was. In

the '60s, at Ardent, when I was producing, not only was I engineering myself, but I did all those things you hear about: I either wrote the song, or re-wrote the song - I played half the instruments - I told everybody what to do - I jumped up and down and screamed and hollered and arranged everything. And, of course, that's not production. Then I would see these other producers, great producers, and I would work with them in whatever capacity, and I'd virtually see them doing nothing – the better the producer, the less they did. I couldn't figure it out. I couldn't figure out the similarity between Jerry Wexler and Sam Phillips and Huey Meux and Johnny Vincent and these other men that I admired – what the similarity was. And I failed to see the genius of a lot of producers, like Quentin Claunch from Goldwax, who not only appeared to be doing nothing, but who appeared to be buffoons!

Left to Right: Jim Dickinson, Sean Slade, and Paul Q. Kolderie at Fort Apache Studios

The opposite of a lot of record people who appear to be doing something but actually are buffoons...

I never thought of it that way, but that's really true! Through Lenny Waronker I understood it. He made it all make sense for me. What I think is that production is invisible - you can't see it, you can just hear the result, and you can't always hear that right away. It is a nefarious activity that needs to remain so. I've probably said enough about production already!

That's the problem with a lot of modern records, you can see the production.

Well, that's because it's not production. It's over-arranging. A lot of what passes for production these days is the result of an over-active ego and a terrible personality problem. You've got somebody in there who wants to hear it his way, and I just don't think that's making a record, that's doing something else. Of course they don't even call them records anymore, so what do I know!

There's a big difference: an engineer makes a recording, a producer makes a record. The engineer's job is to record every note as well as they can possibly do it. The producer's job is to finish, and basically steal it from the artist, because there's no artist on earth who wants to give it up. Because once they give it up, it's not theirs any more. You can't even blame them. I myself as an artist – I stand at the microphone, and I don't want to give it up. Paul Westerberg looked me in the face and said, "I'm not going to give you 100% because you don't deserve it." So I had to steal everything I got from him. I got that 100%, in his case I got 110% sometimes, but I had to go ahead and steal it, and that's the producer's job. And you can't possibly let them see you doing it, or it won't work. So when Johnny Vincent - God rest his soul, I read in *Mojo* that he just passed - would turn his chair around backwards and make some inane comment about some basketball game or something, the artist didn't know that he was being produced, but he was. When Sam Philips rants and raves and quotes Bible scripture and bangs his hands on the console and makes you think he is going to completely lose control, he's just producing! It is a nefarious craft and when it's happening to you, you don't know it.

Let's talk about the record you're infamous for: Big Star's *Third/Sister Lovers*.

Third really isn't a record, more a series of recordings. We never finished it. It's not supposed to be two records and it's obviously too much for one record. Some of it doesn't fit, and I don't see who on earth could possibly be the judge as to what doesn't fit, so that's what prevents it from being an actual record. There are two reasons it endures, I think, and has become as much of a cult object as it has. One is that it's the last set of consistent performances that Alex Chilton ever delivered -

there is not a bad performance on the record, not even a questionable performance as far as Alex is concerned - and the other is a testimonial to the genius of John Fry, since it is the last project that John engineered from floor to mix and it broke his heart. He's by far the greatest engineer I ever worked with. I've worked with some of the ones that are supposed to be the big daddies, and they can't carry John Fry's slide rule. He's unquestionably the best. He recorded musical note and sheer noise as if they were aesthetically equal. There weren't even any pan-pots on the console. That's three-track switch-able. There's two echo sources, one external equalizer, two external limiters - to say "primitive" doesn't even begin to cover the way we recorded that record. What he did was microphone placement and knowledge of the room and the sheer volume of the instruments, which, at that point, a lot of people were avoiding. Even the old Ardent studio was designed for loud guitars, and at that point people wouldn't let you bring a [Vox] Super Beatle into the studio. I'll never forget watching Alex run his hands down the Ampeg amplifier and turn every knob all the way wide open, and start to play, and John just walked up and moved the microphone across the room. This was before people used a room mic on guitar amplifiers.

How many tracks was that Big Star record done on?

Sixteen.

That always struck me about it was the marriage of Beatles, folk rock, feedback, and orchestral imaging. It's a beautiful puzzle.

What I think I did for Alex was remove the yoke of oppressive production, be it Dan Penn and the Box Tops, where Alex did only what he was told and had no creative input whatsoever. Or the John Fry/Terry Manning Big Star situation wherein Alex contributed certainly, but was told, "No, you can't do that, that's crazy." See, I never told him that. If Alex wanted to do something crazy, I figured out how to do it. And, of course, as he saw me do that, he got crazier. You know, I've been accused of encouraging him, which I guess I did, but a lot of the horror stories you hear about the *Third* album are just that – they're stories. Some of it got psychodynamically ugly, but I can't think of many records that don't – especially records that go on for that long. Everybody knew Stax was going out of business. We were making this record for Stax [through Ardent Records], and nobody wanted Stax to put it out because their records were getting lost, so we figured if we kept working on the record Stax would go out of business and then we would own it, which is what happened. But then, we owned it and nobody wanted it. We took that record around to New York and Los Angeles and played it for people who would run shrieking from the room. People who now genuflect to it as if it were a religious icon said to me then, "You've ruined Alex Chilton's career." Lenny Waronker said to me, "I don't have to listen

to this again, do I?" Jerry Wexler told me, "Baby, this record makes me very uncomfortable." And I thought, "That proves it's successful."

Is this where you got your reputation for someone who works with troubled artists?

I guess that it started there, but I think the place where it at least became popularized was the Replacements. That's where it got me in trouble. After that, I did get a lot of "problem artists". I like problem artists and I like artists who are working in character. I like people who have figured an alternative reality to participate in.

That was the Replacements "high tech" record up to that point, strangely enough for you...

Well, I think that was the last record where some of The Replacements' sound, the idea of their sound is still around without rigid tempo. They had never even had their amplifiers separated before, because of course, they were punks and they wouldn't let anybody help them, and I kinda tried to help them in spite of themselves, and make a record that felt like them but sounded better. We ended up with a hybrid of technology and very primitive recording. Again, it sounds kinda funny now but I think it sounds like them. I had a cartoon concept of the Replacements in my head: I could see them performing as a trio in the middle of the Coliseum with nothing but a spotlight, just kind of falling over, and not finishing songs, and doing what they did. I still think it's better than what they turned into. And of course on my record, I didn't have Bob [Stinson]. I said to their managers, "Bring me Bob, I'm not afraid of him, I want him," and they'd just shake their heads and make the sign of the cross. I wanted to call the record *Where's Bob?* and nobody thought that was funny, but I thought that was what everybody's gonna want to know.

What about some of the technological aspects of that record?

I used a lot more Fairlight [CMI/early sampler] than anybody would ever believe, but that's because they wouldn't perform consistently. And I was using it as a device to fly vocals and rhythm guitar parts together keep it from sounding too manufactured. There are some places you can hear it. Westerberg walked in one day, caught me Fairlighting his vocal, and he said, "Is that me in there?", pointing to the machine. I said, "Yeah". He went and sat down on the couch. I took that as his acceptance of the technology. I think he realized it was making his life easier so he just accepted it.

That record was mixed on an SSL [Solid State Logic, automated mixer], and it doesn't sound like shit either.

With SSL, you gotta fight em, but the technology that's under your hands in terms of what it will do is great. You have to fool it from time to time. See, I don't buy this Neve crap. A lot of my friends are Neve fanatics, and yeah, that's okay but they're soft as far as I'm concerned.

Some are very soft. Some are not well maintained.

The center of it is just way too soft. I gotta have a little more stereo center than that. If you want a good sounding console, API's a good sounding console. That sounds good.

It "rocks".

Yeah, other than that, it's all a compromise, so I'd just as soon accept an SSL as a compromise instead of some European-sounding thing. There's a certain combination - and this gets back to the microphones and preamps - there's a certain combination of pre-World War II, and World War II German technology and post World War II British technology, that, if you intermarry it just right, you've got The Beatles. Back when EMI was making in-house consoles, back in the mid to late '60s, a lot of studios were making their own equipment. Now, if you can dig some of that stuff up, there's some damn sound! In the digital realm, if you're willing to digitize - which since you're making a CD, analog is just a process anyway. If you want it, you can get it. If you are going to face the digital reality, you gotta pick up some teeth somewhere. It's not just warmth - people talk about "warmth" - you can get warmth through any kind of tube. Teeth is different. I've got a couple of engineers, Bob Krusen and Kevin Houston, around here now who use some Helios modules, two in particular, out of the console that cut *Dark Side of the Moon*. It's instantly identifiable, as half of the early guitar that Keith Richards ever played was obviously cut to these things. They build up a harmonic accumulation: it sounds like distortion - it *is* distortion - but it's something you can accept digitally that's sounds analog. Of course any of the old EMI equipment is like magic. The Helios stuff is like magic. You know, it's pricey but you can find it. And you know it doesn't even have to be this stuff. It's anything that can make the sparks jump. With microphones, it's like they built the best ones first. I work with one engineer who's got some very interesting Soviet microphones - Russian stuff

Oktava stuff?

Yeah, especially for a room mic, it's really a remarkable sound. If you use all the same mics, guess what? It all sounds the same. Again, one of my all time favorite engineers was Joe Hardy, and if you asked him what kind of mics to put on the drums, he'd say "black mics" and mean it, and of course, black mics do sound good. [laughs] But there has to be a little more to it than that. What I do is record the motion of air in a room, and the instruments are what's creating the motion of air, but they're not what I'm recording. I'm recording the motion of air. So you use microphones to achieve depth, and you know, the more I've done this, the more I've come to lean on ribbon mics, because the recovery [time] is so much quicker. You do have a little fuzzy thing there, and you know condensers have their use, but I find that it's these ribbons that I want to hear. When I was recording purely analog, I was trying to eliminate noise. In the digital domain, you've got to encourage a little noise. As long as the noise is being modulated by the signal, it's not noise anymore. There's your Big Star comparison. We were modulating all that distortion. It wasn't sheer distortion. It was distortion that was moving as music. If you listen to old records in particular, I mean when I listen to records for enjoyment of sound, I listen to jazz records from the late '50s and early '60s, especially stuff that came out of the Columbia Studio in New York.

That's the best sounding stuff there is.

Right. Period! You can listen to classical music from the same studio - I just don't like classical music. The last Glenn Gould sessions where they've got him in the studio were done there. And if you see pictures of the session, there's no microphone closer than eight feet to the piano - I mean these people knew what they were doing. And again they were recording in mono - they were recording in stereo for his safety. When I go for sound, that's the sound I go for. If I want something extreme, if I really want space, it's *Sketches of Spain*. You see the picture in that, it's like a Daniel Lanois session - he's got the microphones in the center of the room, pointed out. And so the thing sounds huge, even though everybody's sitting in a little room.

There are "closer-in" sounding ones, like Mingus' *Ah Um*.

Sure, because the mics are straight across. It was years before I saw the pictures, but when I finally saw the pictures of *Sketches of Spain* session I said, "Oh yeah! Sure!" How else would you record a tuba, in the Miles Davis group?

How about a few specifics, I know you're a fan of the Coles mic.

Oh yeah, the Coles. Going back to The Beatles analogy, if you look at the coffee table book with all the session information [*The Beatle's Recording Sessions* by Mark Lewisohn], there's only one picture in that book where you can see the drum mics, because they're so high up, they're out of the picture. There's one shot from across the room where you see this little hockey-puck thing hanging down, and that's what it is, made for the BBC, Coles ribbon mic. They've been remanufactured [by STC, available through AEA/Wes Dooley] and the new ones sound a little different but they don't sound any worse.

Right, the Coles 4038.

I use RCAs on the room a lot.

77s?

Yeah, because that's what I've got. Of course, I'm too dyslexic to remember numbers, but there's a real interesting kind of square looking Beyer ribbon mic at Ardent that supposedly is for boxing matches, like over the ring? It distorts like crazy on loud stuff but for something like a vibraphone, it's a fabulous sound. More recently, I've gotten into ribbon mics. I used to be into old German power mics...

Nazi mics...

Nazi mics, there's definitely a place for those. But for vocals, I've had the problem of working on my own so-called project. I decided that, after 30 years I might as well make another record. I found this, I can't call the numbers, but I can describe it to you. It's EV, not the top of the line - it's like the top of the line, but with no heater or cooler or whatever that is. It's like a copy of the Sony that's got the things sticking on the side of it. Whatever the model is down from that - sounds great on my voice and my voice is not an easy thing to get a sound on. But by experimenting around for this record of mine, with that and a Joe Meek mono limiter, I've got a pretty interesting kind of period vocal sound down there.

You like the Joe Meek stuff?

I like some of it. They're almost toys. They're not serious gear so you can use it in a kind of less reverential way.

They do that pointy optical thing.

And it's very interesting on the bass and voices as well. I like the limiter a lot. I don't have a Meekqualizer. I want one though.

What about mic pres?

Well, the ones that are my own are all APIs. I use these two engineers with the Helios, and a Neve or two here or there because it does do a glassy kind of thing. [Telefunken] V72s are good as well. Early on, I used to use some Massenburgs [GML] and I got away from doing it. I don't really know why.

That seems funny for you - they're not fuzzy.

No they're not, but I had a situation where I had one real strong singer and one real weak singer doing a duet, and I used the Massenburgs to pull up the weak singer, and it was a very successful. I've done that with guitar players where there's two situations, and one is something that sounds a little "better", a little more expensive. The Massenburg sounds real expensive - it *is* very expensive.

I've always thought of you in relation to an idea of England vs. America. People now are really into what they perceive to be a "British" sound, but that sound is not as simple as using a Neve. It's not just using that EQ point. English pop music doesn't come up from blues and country the same way American pop music does. It contains other elements as well, like dance hall music. You can certainly hear that in The Beatles.

Yeah, I think it's changed over the years. There are two very different English sounds. One is the old "lab coat" sound, you know, the technical guys who record everything the same whether it's a rock and roll band or a string quartet. And then

there's the young upstart, Glyn Johns type of sound, and the tradition of that, which is basically "Fuck it and do whatever you want to - use the equipment however you want to use it - push the buttons until something sounds right," and that's closer to America. So I don't know. And now America has been so affected by the old lab coat sound, it really is interdependent. The first four Beatles albums that we heard in America had been re-mastered in America. Unless you have a European record and basically European gear, you're not hearing what was being put on the record. It all comes down to what you're hearing in your head, which is partially cultural, no matter where you are. You know the expectations of the sound are created culturally.

Are you hearing any new stuff you like?

I hear stuff that I like. The most recent stuff that I like is Johnny Dowd. I like his first record better than his second record because it's less produced.

What about producers? Are there sounds you're hearing that are influencing you?

Every once in a while I hear something where I wonder, "How do they do that?" moreso mixers than producers. I ain't saying they're not out there, I just haven't seen 'em. I haven't seen a lot of young producers who work the floor in a traditional way. There's so much ego manipulation involved now.

Do you want to talk about your analog tape-digital transfer?

Well, it's an ongoing experiment, and I do it different on every project. It depends on the budget.

Explain first, why you do it.

It dawned on me one day that the mixes I was making were deteriorating. The further that I got into measuring this deterioration, the more I realized that it wasn't in my mind, and that this explained a lot of things. Like direct-to-disk, and why the rough mix sounds better than the final mix when the final mix is done two months later, why you get your old tape out of the box and it doesn't sound the way you remember it. You assume the difference is in your head – but in reality, it doesn't sound the way you remember it. Because, if you talk to any tape manufacturer, they will admit that analog tape was never designed to be a permanent storage medium. In a digital reality, which is what we're in because we're manufacturing CDs, the analog stage becomes only a process anyway, so what I think now is that it's never too late to analog. If you record digitally, you can go through any number of analoging processes, either multi-track or to mix, but the crucial stage - if what you want is "fresh" analog, then you've got to preserve that digitally right away, because it's going to go away and the part that goes away is the little magic fuzzy stuff at the top and the big round-bottom end - the very reason everyone who uses analog uses analog. That's what goes away first and it's absolutely provable and measurable. I've made utter analog fanatics accept it because you can hear it, there's no question about it. I myself go in three hour increments, I know people who measure it in 20 minute increments once they figured out it was happening, looking for the hot spot. What happens is, if you over-modulate the tape, the bias is set to where the molecules are going to find each other, and seek each other and find each other in a certain way. If you over-modulate the tape, this can't happen. Of course, I'm explaining this like a caveman because that's the way I think, but this is basically what's happening. Those little molecules are unstable because they haven't found the right place to go because they've got too much information. As time goes by, they stabilize. They find where they're supposed to go. As that happens, of course, the sound changes. So if you're making a mix straight to an analog two-track and you want the sound that you've put on that tape, then you have to digitize it right away. The way that I discovered this in the first place was that most people who make an analog master and a DAT master do it simultaneously. Well, I noticed that there was a difference between the simultaneous DAT and the first analog playback, and the first analog playback was by far superior. So I started taking my DAT safety from my first analog playback and giving that DAT to whomever the mastering engineer was going to be, 'cause of course the mastering engineers all want to work from the analog tape. But if I have a DAT of the fresh analog tape, then they have to at least recreate – if they're not advanced enough to use my DAT - they have to recreate the frequencies on that DAT with the EQ from the deteriorating analog master. Thereby, you end up listening to more EQ and less signal, which, to me, is not a good situation. This is not like I'm doing something that other people aren't doing. A lot of other people are doing the same thing, and calling it something else.

ow, I know here, you're accepting the inherent problems with the 44.1 digital media.
yeah, certainly.
hat about 44.1 and what it does to ambiance anyway?
ll, you have to accept it because it's going to happen. I mean, what was his name, Neil Young's engineer?
vid Briggs.
vid Briggs monitored his multi-track through a 1630, the Sony thing - which sounds like shit, right? And he's an analog fanatic.

They had the idea that they didn't want to hear the music in a way no one else did.
Exactly, you've got a downstream effect no matter how purely you're recording.
But does it make you mix different because you know, for instance, that 44 is going to kill your echo?
Sure, I've been doing this 40 years. When I was engineering, I knew that when I played back my mix - my 2-track mix, or my 4-track or 8-track - I was going to hear less effects than I did when I mixed it. And when it was mastered from that to a vinyl disk I was going to hear yet again, maybe 30% less of the effects, echo, slapback, whatever, so I always mixed with too much
Right, and now in the digital world...
You have to go even further, but I think it's why natural ambiance has become so popular as opposed to digital because, in the digital domain, right away –BANG- you can hear digital echo, everybody's aware of it. Room sound and natural chambers, you don't know quite what you're hearing - there's a mystery to it, there's something that's not familiar - and digital echo is instantly familiar cause you hear it all day every day.
Is stereo a concession?
Oh yes, certainly! Somewhere in the '70s, everybody, and I was one of them, got sold the idea that everything should be stereo. I remember talking to Tom Dowd about how to make a guitar amp stereo, and watching him draw the little pyramid on the floor - and that is more valid than, say, stereo piano or stereo acoustic guitar. The way everyone mics a piano? Wrong! Two mics inside a piano, left hand, right hand, pan it out - it's stupid. It's like listening with your head inside the piano – nobody listens there. The mouth of the grand piano opens so it can project the sound about eight feet, ten feet away - that's where the sound is.
This probably explains why grand pianos sound so fucking awful on rock records most of the time.
That's because the strings are too long. When you go back to real rock records, they were made on upright. Jerry Lee Lewis played a fucking spinet in the Sun Studio! Ike Turner was playing one too. It's the sound of rock and roll.
They record better in a band...
Sure, I learned this working with Ry Cooder. The grand piano, the overtone series is so strong, and it destroys all the overtones on the acoustic guitar. Cooder was the artist, he was the star, guess what? He gets the overtones. So, I found this old upright piano that had been painted white with house paint, and had no overtones at all, and then put a blanket over it - and that's what I recorded most of my Ry Cooder on.
You once said that the way you mix is to turn up the good parts.

Yeah, that's the job of the producer, not the engineer, but the producer in charge of the engineer - turn up the good parts, turn down the bad parts. It's not always the case. Tom Dowd says if you got a mistake, turn it up real loud. Sometimes that works.
Is that true of a singer who sings off-key too?
Well, now God has provided a wonderful tuning box, which I wholeheartedly endorse, and will buy none of the detractors. [laughs]
That statement right there is going to ruin your reputation.
Uh-huh! If I'd had that box in the '70s you'd been talking to a rich man. There's certain people - and I'm not going to name names - who are now walking wreckage, who would have had successful careers with that box. Now, why should those people be less important than Shania Twain? Why should Courtney Love have an advantage those people didn't have? It's unfair! There was nothing wrong with 99% of punk rock that couldn't be cured technically, without violating anybody's, you know, attitude.
And people lie about doing it. In fact, people lie about all sorts of things they do in the studio. I've heard people say triggered drums were "just room mics."
You gotta lie yeah, that's all production is. "It's okay, baby. Don't worry."
Have you got anything else you want to say?
The reason we record, philosophically speaking, 'cause you know as you record - for me more so as a musician than as a producer - your mind wanders because you can't think and play at the same time, and you have to keep yourself distracted. So, you think about strange things, and I've thought about recording way too much. There has to be a reason why we record, and I think it's fear of death. I think it's literally a search for immortality, even if it's momentary, and I think it springs from the oldest desire of mankind which is to preserve the moment somehow, and, if possible, play it back.
Like procreation.
Oh yeah, it's definitely that - it's continuity, you know, a search for ongoing continuity. It's like the handprint on the back of the cave wall, because that's as far back as we can go as people. It's there. That's the first document, right? Also the first record. You hear the story, the trite story, about the native in the jungle who won't let you take his picture because you're capturing his soul. Well, you see, I think that's exactly what you're doing in the recording studio. And I think people understand it intuitively. That's what Edison was about, it's what Sam Phillips was about. It's what it's all about. ☯

by Curtis Settino

Scott Colburn

In just a few short years, Scott Colburn's Gravelvoice Productions has been involved with a wonderfully diverse collection of artists and recordings. His Seattle, Washington studio offers an analog 16-track, digital editing, and plenty of charm. Scott engineers, produces, and contributes musically when needed. He's also an avid record collector and for years was known as Shaggy (a la Scooby Doo) because he looked exactly like him. To start off the interview, Scott agreed to answer some silly profile questions.

What are some of your current projects?

I've been creating audio montages of each album for the Residents' web site. I'm also compiling material for a Captain Beefheart box set.

Who are some other artists you've worked with?

I've worked with Sun City Girls, Amy Denio, Bali Girls, Climax Golden Twins, John Fahey, Miss Murgatroid, Ed Pias.

How many years have you been an audio engineer, producer, musician?

I started playing piano in 1970, saxophone in 1973, then guitar in 1976. My first live show was in 1979. My first "pro" recording was in 1981 (reel to reel 4-track). I realized I should be a producer in 1990. I opened my studio in 1993.

What is your audio education?

I have a bachelor's degree in sound engineering from Columbia College, Chicago, 1989.

How many projects have you been involved with?

That's hard to really pinpoint; approximately 37 CDs, 22 cassettes, 30 books on tape, 10 singles, three 78 rpms, 19 LPs.

What has been your biggest disaster?

Moving to Los Angeles.

What has been your biggest success?

If success is measured by record sales, I project the Beefheart will beat all. If we're talking about record sales, then any Sun City Girls or Climax Golden Twins. If we are talking about personal accomplishments... *Pint Sized Spartacus*. My best sounding experimental project is Climax Golden Twins *Imperial Household Orchestra*. My best sounding rock record is the *Leatherboy* CD which isn't out yet.

Who was the nicest celebrity when you were doing books on tape?

The most professional was Adrienne Barbeau. She was also the nicest. Gary Owens was super professional.

Who was the scariest?

Michael York. He was a perfectionist to the degree that he ruined the recording. Lukas Haas couldn't read a line without a mistake. I also want to add that Kirk Douglas was the only person I worked with that star struck me. All of a sudden I was looking through the glass at him and said to myself," My god that's Kirk Douglas!"

So is Gravelvoice a full-time thing yet?

No, not yet.

Is that your intention?

Yeah, definitely. I just moved the studio into a commercial space last month. That's the first step: take it out of the basement. I'm also considering doing some advertising. So we'll see what happens. It's kind of nice to not have to rely on it to pay the bills. That way you can really choose what you work on. That's the way I've been working for the last five years. I really want to make a living at it. But I don't want to compromise. And that's hard to do. That's probably why it's taken so long to take this first step.

Well it sounds exciting.

Yeah it is! The space is big enough. It's about 23 feet by 23 feet with a control room inside of that. built it to be, firstly a control room, secondly a tracking room. I felt that if I wanted something to sound really good I could go to a different studio and track it; then bring it back to my studio to do overdubs and mix.

So how big is the control room?

It's 12' x 15'. The ceilings vary from nine feet to ten feet throughout the space. It's hard to describe how the ceiling is. It sort of dips down with these pyramids, like wedge foam, made out of reinforced concrete. It's actually really sound. There's a parking garage on top of it. I have cement walls on two sides as well. So you can make the loudest sound you want to make at any time of the night and not have to worry about it. I hired a contractor to help me build the control room walls. They're not sound proof by any means and there's no window. I chose to not put a window in because I didn't have one in the studio in my basement. And I got more comments like, "We really like it that you don't have a window," than, "Why don't you have a window?"

Just because people didn't feel like they were under a microscope as much?

Yeah. Also, when I closed the door they felt like they were practicing. They kind of forgot that they were recording. I think I got better performances that way. Ultimately, I'd like to hire someone to engineer for me. That way I could concentrate on the performance part more. But I'm so far away from that.

But you've got tons of experience doing both.

Yeah. But here's the thing: I know my studio really well, because I wired it myself. But if I go to a different studio, one that I'm not familiar with, I really need an engineer there, or at least a super competent second (engineer). One of the things that's fun about the new space though is that it's new. So I don't know where the drums sound best, or where to put the guitar so that it doesn't bleed as much. And it's kind of exciting. I was in my last studio for three years, and toward the end of the time there it became almost a science. I knew exactly where to put everything. That's good. But at the same time it gets a little boring because it's hard to break out of that mold.

How long do you think it'll take for you to figure out the new space?

Well, far less time than before. But it depends on how quickly I can get the people in there who'll allow me to experiment. I'm always working with Climax Golden Twins. I work with them twice a week. And they're super experimental. So I can try all kinds of different things with them. But as far as rock music is concerned, I need someone with a really nice kit to come in so I can try some things out. I've got a pretty good relationship with The Bali Girls now. And they want to come in and record a couple of songs. So that will be good because their drummer, Randy, is one of the most pounding players I know, and he's always very concerned about the way his kit sounds. He wants them to sound really big. So he'll scrutinize every drum sound and make comments, and I like that. He's great to work with. So they'll be good for the rock sound. Then I just got to throw a jazz combo in there and try that out.

What other surfaces do you have in the tracking area?

Well, like I said, it's concrete on two walls and wood for the control room wall. The other wall is a Japanese-type screen that slides open. It opens into another space which is where the Young Composers Collective rehearse. It's a huge space for an orchestra to play in. Technically, it's their space, but it can used for isolating instruments, for a bass trap, or things like that. It can also be used to change the acoustics of my room just by opening up the screen.

how is scheduling work with the Young Composers Collective?

It goes really well, actually. They have permanent rehearsals Wednesday night and Sunday night. So I have all the other evenings, plus some day time slots. So that's pretty good for right now. And realistically, most of the people that want to record have day jobs and aren't going to want to record during the day.

Are you still doing your own stuff as well?

Not really. I did do a live show a couple months ago though. That was the first live show I'd done in about ten years. I've done about ten albums worth of material. But they've always been released on cassette, and in very few numbers. I like doing it. And I'm excited about doing it. But what I really want to do is work with other people and record other people's music that I like. Because I feel that they can do it better than I can. But the live show was a lot of fun. And it kind of whet my appetite for doing music again. One thing is that Climax Golden Twins consider me a part of the group. So I get to play and create with them. And that's what I've always wanted to do. It's really fun!

That's great.

Yeah. There's two kind of people that I work with: One is somebody who approaches me and I check out what they're doing, and if I like it, I'll decide to record the album; the other, I guess I would call

career investments. For the Climax Golden Twins, especially, I see a progression in what they're doing, and I'm willing to put the time into it, and be a major participant in helping them achieve what they're trying to do artistically. Because I see that as a way to go onto bigger and better things with them. I don't see them becoming stagnant. They're always progressing. There's always a lot of different projects coming up. We've done CDs that are straight music. We've done installations in art galleries. We've done live shows. And that's really interesting to me. I like that better than doing one-off records for people.

The thing that's nice about that is that you both get to grow in your own areas.

Absolutely. I have a similar relationship with The Bali Girls. I did a demo for them and then we did a CD. And they're already talking about the next record they want to record and I'm developing that too. But most rock groups don't experiment that much. Climax Golden Twins are working on a CD for a Japanese label right now. And the concept is to make it all electronic. And we're doing it all on the computer, which we haven't done before. The other stuff we've done has been analog recordings heavily edited in the computer. But this one is being created totally in the computer. It's exciting, but it takes a lot of time, even more, I think, than recording analog. Well it's easy to get sucked into the micro-tweezing, just because you can. Yeah. That's my big job; saying, "Let's get the basics down first, we can go back and nit-pick at things later." We've got about twenty minutes of the CD done. We did that in about eight sessions, which is pretty good. But we got another twenty to go!

So what's the process?

All three of us have supplied different sounds. They may be sounds that were recorded separate from the group, or stuff Jeff and Rob have done together, or samples from other records, sometimes 78s. We're big on 78s right now.

Do you have a 78 player?

Yeah, Jeff got a Victrola Low Boy. They've actually released a series of cassettes called Victrola Favorites. We record them right off of the Low Boy straight to DAT. There's five volumes so far. One is all Japanese. One is things we like. And I just finished my set, which is a companion to The New Session People CD (*Famous Songs From Days Gone By* - Amarillo). That CD was inspired by the 78s in my collection. So my set is the actual songs we covered on that CD. Sometimes people come over for the recording of the 78s. It's kind of an event. The mic's live so everyone just keeps quiet. Every once in a while a chair creaks, or something like that. But that stays in there, because that was the moment. My mind's just reeling thinking about all the 78s I've passed by, especially at estate sales. Oh yeah. You know it's amazing to hear a 78 played on the Victrola. It just sounds so much different than on a modern phonograph. It sounds so good.

We change the needle every other disc to keep it fresh sounding. Setting up to record the 78s I discovered that, oddly enough, the low-end comes out of the veins at the bottom (of the Victrola's horn) and the high-end comes out of the veins at the top, even though it's just one little horn. But there is a difference in sonic quality as you go up and down the veins. I took two mics over there one time and put one up high and one down low. The other times I've taken a stereo mic and positioned it mid-way. For me it's great to hear my collection this way. It's always, "Wow! I didn't think that sounded like that," or, "I never heard that before!" Actually, there's some later 78s, not the vinyl ones but the shellac ones, that are amazingly hi-fi. You can really hear depth in these full band recordings that you don't hear on a regular turntable. It's amazing what they were doing with just a single mic. They were spending a lot of time sliding chairs around, adjusting players positions. Which I like and wish more people would get back into.

I'm into that in a way too. I'm not a big isolation fanatic. It's like, there's really no reason to eat your peas separate from your mashed potatoes. They just get mixed up in your stomach anyway. So you might as well eat them together and enjoy the complex flavor. [Laughter]

Oh, I had a recording technique I wanted to tell you about. It's not actually one that I developed, but one I read about and tried. The name of the book is *Practical Techniques for the Recording Engineer*, I think. And the guy's name is Sherman Keene. He's got a flying microphone technique too*. This technique requires sending a signal through an amplifier. You then swing two microphones in front of the amp: one in a clockwise direction, and the other counter-clockwise but in a bigger diameter, and record what's coming out of the speaker onto two tracks.

So this is concentric circles parallel to the floor in front of the amp?

Yes. So the microphone comes close to the amp then further away repeatedly. I used this technique on a Sun City Girls track. We played a harmonium part through the amp. Then I laid on the floor with my head up by the speaker and my arm straight up and swung the microphone around my arm. And then Alan (of Sun City Girls) took a microphone on a pole and swung it around my circle in the opposite direction, and it really worked! You take the two channels and pan them hard left and right and what you get is a sound that flys around in your head and in the stereo spectrum haphazardly. It's so much better than trying to create the effect by panning.

I can see some cool choreographed swinging being used too. Maybe it's haphazard in the verses but then the two microphones synch-up in some way during the choruses.

Oh yeah! But it was really hard to do it. It was a five minute song and my arm got really tired. [Laughter] I guess you could probably rig up something that was automated. But I think that the human interaction was the key thing. Because my arm would get tired and I couldn't keep the same speed going all the time. This other thing I wanted to tell you about was this Indian music I recorded. I got to record this guy named Vishal Nagar. He and his mother come to the University of Washington every year or so. She teaches dance there. When I met him he was 16 or 17 years old; and he was already considered a master on the tabla. He'd already made guest appearances on a couple of releases in India. But he'd never had his own solo recording. So my friend, Ed Pias, brought him and his mother into the studio. While I was setting up I found out that a tabla sounds better when you place the mic in between the two drums, pointing down at the floor, rather than trying to mic the two heads. So I'm using that technique and he's listening to it and says, "No. I don't like that." So we moved it around, tried a few different things, then all of a sudden he liked it. But then he says, "There's no echo on it." I sat down and explained to him, "We're not in New Delhi. We're in Seattle, Washington, and this is an American technique. I'll put plenty of echo on here if you want. But what is our goal on this?" And the goal was to make it sound good on cassette! And that's why they put so much echo on

their recordings. So I put some on. Actually, I used a reverb with a slight echo on it. Then he said, "You got to put more on." So I put a little more on. And he said, "I want more still." So I said, "Hey Vishal, why don't you go in there and play a little bit? I'll record it and we'll throw it on a cassette and see if you like it." He did and he really liked it! So we were ready to go. They had an electronic tambura going, and his mother played harmonium. She was playing this one melody line over and over and over again. The run was about 45 to 60 seconds long. He performed his premiere tabla solo over that; and it was an hour long! It was simply amazing! And when I walked out from the control room after it was over you could feel the humidity in the air because he was sweating so much! [Laughter]

Did you use much compression?

Yeah. I actually compressed it quite a bit. Plus I had some ambient mics around as well. When you listen to the DAT of it you think, "That's pretty good." But when you hear it off of a cassette you go, "Wow!" I was really glad I got to do that recording.

So that was it, one take straight to DAT?

Yeah. There's a couple imperfections in it though. He would play these incredibly fast runs and at the end of them he'd raise his hands up really fast. And a couple of times he hit the mic. I was talking to Ed about it. Ed has a doctorate degree in ethnomusicology. And I said, "I'd really like to take those

mic hits out of there. But I'm afraid I'm going to mess up the music." And he said, "Oh, you don't want to take those out! You don't know how many tapes and CDs I have from India where people start hacking up lung in the middle of the performance and they leave it in because that's just what happened. That's what they're into." [laughter] So I didn't bother with it. But it bugs me to this day. [laughter]

Here's another technique I wanted to tell you about. It's called the "Schizophrenic Microphone Technique". We used this in two places. One was *Dante's Disneyland Inferno*, which is a Sun City Girls record, and the other was on Charlie's (of Sun City Girls) solo record, *Pint Sized Spartacus*. The technique involves two microphones. I have this old AKG mic. I don't even know what the model number is. It's not a great mic by any means. It's all crackly and trebly and the top of the windscreen is missing. I put that on a mic stand and then taped a Shure SM 57 on top of it. The 57 was set back a bit behind the remaining half of the AKG's windscreen. I ran the 57 straight to one track. The AKG I ran into this small tube amplifier and miked it with a PZM hung from a stand. So Charlie would sing into the AKG for this crackly personality, and then move to the side a bit to get a cleaner sound from the 57. He just played with it as he did his vocals. It produced the effect he was looking for and was really fun for him to do. ✪

Some 4-Track Cassette Tips

by Leigh Marble

Here's two routing tricks for cassette 4-tracks:

1) When recording, bypass the channel mic inputs and instead use line or aux inputs whenever possible. This can audibly increase the clarity of the recorded signal. For mics, obviously, this will only be possible if you have an external preamp. But even without an external preamp, you can still use this method to help your line-level signals (e.g. from a keyboard or sampler), as the benefits stem from more than just using a higher-quality preamp. There's quite a bit of extra signal path in a channel input (EQ knobs, pan control, fader). On a cassette 4-track, these won't be made from the highest quality components. Signal degradation adds up quickly, especially when passing through cheap capacitors. So even on a line-level signal, where you would have the channel's "trim" or "gain" knob all the way down, you are running that signal through more stuff than it needs to experience. If you have simple, non-preamped and non-EQ'd inputs (like line inputs 5-8 on a Tascam 424) use them whenever possible, because it will save your signal a fair amount of dampening and muddiness.

2) Cassette 4-tracks usually have, at best, one aux/effect send per channel and no insert points. Flexibility in routing is not the strong point of these machines. If you're doing a mix you can have a reverb or a delay hooked up to the effect send. But what about adding compression to a track during playback? Without an insert point it's pretty hard to do. There is, however, a routing trick which will work with many machines to allow you to add an "in-line" effect like compression. You need a "sync out" jack on the machine - a special, direct output (from track 4, in every case I've seen) that was put there to route FSK or SMPTE sync codes out of the machine. If your machine has a noise-reduction (dbx or Dolby) switch, DON'T switch it to "sync", because this will remove the noise-reduction from the signal that we want. Plug an RCA cord into the sync out and voila, now you can put that signal through a compressor and feed it back into the mix via channel 4, switched to take its input from your (now compressed) mic/line signal instead of direct from tape. Note that this will of course only work for whatever you've recorded onto track 4, so it takes a bit of forethought. For a small home studio with only one compressor, this technique can help enormously. Here is one sample application: recording a vocal and guitar performance with two mics (or a mic and a pickup). Put the vocal mic through the compressor while recording it to track 3; put the guitar signal direct to track 4. Then, during playback route the guitar signal out the sync out, into the compressor, and back into channel 4. That way you get two passes of compression with only one compressor. ✪

Make Your Own Piezo Drum Triggers

by Leigh Marble

Ingredients:

- piezo discs (at least one for each drum you want a trigger on, preferably more in case you screw up)
- small gauge, double-stranded wire (about 6" of wire per trigger)
- speaker wire or patch cord cable (however long you need your trigger cables to run)
- 1/4" male jacks (one per trigger)
- soldering iron, solder, electrical tape, etc.

To make any of this worthwhile, you'll also want some kind of drum module or keyboard with "trigger ins" on it. You also may be able to rig up something if you have a MIDI device with an "external clock" or "sync" input on it. More on this later.

Where to find them:

Piezo discs can be found inside small black buzzers sold by Radio Shack, but there are far cheaper ways to get them. I got a handful for about 5¢ each at an electronics warehouse in Portland. Many cities will have a place like this. Your other option would be mail order from a place like Mouser or All Electronics. If you can't find any try buying one of those Radio Shack buzzers and tearing it apart to get the piezo element though it's expensive and more trouble than you need to go through.

Tech background:

The purely pragmatic amongst you can skip this part and just chalk the workings of piezo triggers up to some form of magic. In short, piezos work by creating electricity when physical stress is applied. When placed on a drum, a piezo disc translates the energy of the stick or pedal hitting the drum into an electrical pulse. Piezos are also used in under-the-saddle pickups for acoustic guitars. Again, the same principle of translating physical energy into electricity is at work here, although with guitar pickups what is sent out electrically is a continuous signal, analogous to the vibrations of the guitar strings. With drum triggers, we're not interested in using the piezo as a musical pickup, just as an indicator of an event. Let's get to the activities section...

How to make it:

Making a drum trigger from a piezo is theoretically straightforward. It's as simple as soldering a wire to the disc. That's it. The physical reality requires a little more work — soldering wire to a piezo disc is a bit delicate, and needs to be done with small gauge wire. However, you probably don't want to have long runs of such small gauge wire, because of its weakness. Your trigger runs will probably wind up getting stepped on at some point, so it is better to use tougher cable for the length of the runs.

1. Cut a 6" length of the small gauge wire and strip both ends. You only need two wires, so if your cable has more ignore them. You can use shielded cable, but it's not really necessary.
2. Repeat the above with the speaker wire, but make the piece as long as you want your trigger run to be. Again, using shielded cable is optional. In considering length, at some point (maybe in the hundreds of feet), the resistance of the wire will be too great for the trigger pulse to overcome, but you don't really need more than twenty feet of wire, do you?
3. Solder the small gauge wire to the piezo disc. Solder one strand to each of these two points: *[see fig. I]*

Use a light touch with the soldering iron. We're using small gauge wire so that it won't take too much heat to get the solder to melt onto it. Piezo discs aren't fragile, but too much heat will mess them up. When the wires are solidly attached to the disc, wrap electrical tape around the disc once, covering the wires. Stress relief for these wires is very important.

4. Now solder the small gauge wire to the speaker wire. Make sure to insulate the two strands of wire from each other, and then wrap the whole thing with more electrical tape. Again, stress relief is the name of game here.
5. On the other end of the large cable, solder the 1/4" male jack. Pretty or not, you've now made your first drum trigger.

What to do with it:

You're now ready to try out your drum trigger. Tape the disc securely to a drum head, somewhere where you won't be hitting it directly with a stick or pedal. Plug the 1/4" jack into the "trigger in" on whatever drum module you have. Depending on what kind of electronic gear you have, you may have to fiddle with a trigger sensitivity setting, or do other stuff to get the module to make a sound when it detects a trigger pulse. Read your instruction manual. If you're SURE you've got your electronic gear working right, and you're not hearing anything, go back and check your soldering connections. Remember that for a solid connection, both surfaces being soldered must be heated up enough for the solder to run onto them — you can't just melt the solder over them and hope they'll stick together. It's also possible that you got a dud piezo disc, or that the disc was heated up too much during soldering. If so, try, try again.

What else to do with it:

I've figured out one more way to get MIDI gear to listen to drum triggers — using an input called "external clock" or "sync". This is more common on older gear. These inputs were the only syncing options for keyboards and drum machines before MIDI came along. They are designed to detect various analog clock signals — pulses sent 24, 48, or 96 times per quarter note. Gear that has both MIDI jacks and a sync jack can usually be coaxed into sending a MIDI clock message out whenever an (analog) clock pulse is received by the sync jack. (This MIDI clock message consists of a single byte, 248 in decimal, F8 in hexadecimal.) So if you have a sync input, you can possibly use it to generate a MIDI message every time you hit your drum. You'll need to figure out what to do with that MIDI message next. Depending on your setup, you may be able to record it into a sequencer or route it to some piece of hardware/software to trigger a sound. I've written a small program in Cycling 74's MAX environment to listen for those clock messages and trigger sounds from them.

(See netspace.org/~leigh/max.

Sorry, Macintosh-only for now.)

In conclusion:

So that's all there is to it — a couple bucks of hardware, a few soldered connections, and your drumset has entered the MIDI age. Feel free to write in with any stories of success, failure, or other things to do with these drum triggers. ☕

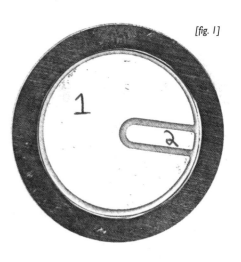

[fig. I]

990
DISCRETE OPERATIONAL AMPLI

John Hardy
Builder of Mic Preamps
Interview and Photos
By Steve Silverstein

John Hardy runs The John Hardy Company out of the basement of an old and pretty house in Evanston, a few blocks north of the Chicago limits. His M-1 preamp uses a transformer-based, discrete solid-state signal path to produce its famous clean sound. I stopped by his house to tour the facilities where he builds pre-amps and runs his small company. I got to see his vintage Hammond organs (while not a very active musician, he'd rather be known as a bass player) and discuss the merits of soda in glass bottles. In the midst of all that, Hardy found the time to share some stories about himself, the M-1, and the company that bears his name.

"I can remember doing just some crude recording of bands that I was in, mostly just a couple of microphones or something like that. I might have had a Shure mixer at some point, something like that. Of course wondering why this didn't sound at all like it's supposed to sound - the usual chaos and confusion and gross stupidity as you start off not knowing a thing. Little by little you learn, for example, that gee, there is such a thing as a low-impedance microphone. Not all microphones have a quarter inch phone plug at the other end of the cable. So we all learn little by little. I was playing in bands; I was doing a little bit of crude recording with the bands. I was, in my own stupid way, building speaker cabinets and learning how to make them better and better as time went on. And working on different electronic projects, and I built a four channel tape recorder back in 1969. It worked occasionally. Little by little, you know. You blow things up, you learn from that. Electrocute yourself, you learn from that. Little by little you learn, hopefully you learn. Hopefully you don't keep electrocuting yourself every day for the rest of your life."

"It's just more of a hobby really. I was lucky to get out of high school at the rate I was going. I was well on my way to crashing and burning. Fortunately graduation occurred before the plane hit ground. I think I had one semester of high school electronics and that was the limit of my formal education. But there are other ways, and little by little, you learn this, you learn that, trial and error, talking here, talking there, talking to whatever, magazine subscriptions" all provide useful information. "Some of the semiconductor manufacturers are just, they're willing to give you a world of knowledge just in their data books. I have to show you my library where there's just book after book, free books from National Semiconductor or Analog Devices or whatever." I later saw the library, where bookshelves full of manuals and other electronic information occupy most of one room in the basement. "So there is much to be learned, various textbooks that have come out, so that's how little by little..."

"The first major project of any kind that I had done, I think, would have to be a couple of consoles that I built for DB Sound, based here in Chicago, back in 1977. Those consoles were specifically done for the group Kansas. For some period of time, DB had been working with the group Kansas, before Kansas was a real big band. The way I understand it, when it came time for that fall of 1977 tour, Kansas said to DB Sound, we're a bigger group now, we're getting bigger exposure. You've got to upgrade your equipment. I had done some smaller projects for DB at different times, and they came to me and said, 'We'd like to do a console, and we'd like you to do it.' In the fall of 1977, miraculously, two consoles got built, a front-of-house and then a stage mix console. The main modules for those, I built as modular as I could. There was a particular module common to both consoles that had the line input section, the mic preamp section, and an equalizer, all in one module. I called it the IM-200 module, just the Input Module, IM-200. Rationality at work there — simple to remember what they are. Some of those modules have been made available as sort of vintage Hardy equipment or something. Oh, jeez, the nightmares I could tell you about that whole project, but at any rate they're still around. In fact, I've got a box of about eight or ten of them under that table over there that one of the guys who is still involved with DB sound, Harry Witz, wants me to fix. So I still will fix them; I'll offer repair service for people that have those. Even though they're 22 years old at this point, I'm happy to keep them running as much as I can. That was my first real, substantial product or project, but that was fall of '77." At that point, Hardy still used monolithic op-amps.

The January/February, 1980 issue of the Journal of the Audio Engineering Society included Deane Jensen's article about the JE-990 Discrete Operational Amplifier. The article contained specifications for the op-amp and directions on how to build it. Jensen stated, "The circuit is 'public domain' and can be used for any purpose without license or permission." Hardy felt that "Deane had this great circuit design for the 990," so he began building 990 op-amps. In 1981, Hardy began making the MPC-500 mic preamp card, a replacement card for MCI 500 series consoles. It included the 990 op-amp. "I became aware of the Jensen JE-16-A input transformer. And it was originally only available in a round can, which made it larger in diameter than a square can would be in length and width. So I bugged Deane long enough and I suppose some other people did too, to make a square can version, so it would be more space efficient. That made the card possible, because otherwise there wouldn't have been enough height for a round can to be sitting in that opening. This is a direct plug-in for the MCI 500-C and some of the D series consoles. Just plug it in and you're done." Hardy followed it with the MPC-600 for MCI 600 series consoles and then the MPC-3000 for Sony MXP-3000's.

While the good feedback that he received pleased Hardy, he was surprised by just how much his preamp cards pleased some people. At the time, there were a lot fewer mic preamps available than there are today. "I don't know when the Massenburg came out, but the Massenburg and maybe the Sontech by Burgess MacNeil, but there were maybe a couple of others. Maybe the API preamps might have been available in some kind of somewhat usable form back then." With fewer options to choose from, some people who "were either crazy enough or dedicated enough" added boxes and power transformers to convert them to stand-alone preamps.

Hardy applied the basic design principles of his replacement cards to build the preamp for which he's best known, the M-1, which he began selling in 1987. "There are three main things that show up in my various ads for the product. The first thing the signal sees when it comes in is the JT-16-B input transformer, which is the top of the line Jensen input transformer. I just think Jensen makes the absolute best audio transformers, and this is their best mic-input model. So the signal first sees the transformer, then it goes into the 990 discrete op-amp. The third feature is that there are no capacitors, coupling capacitors, anywhere in the signal path. Capacitors can cause problems; they can cause degradation to the signal. There's a problem with capacitors known as dielectric absorption. A capacitor is just two conductors separated by an insulator. Literally, speaker cables are capacitors; they are also resistors, and if there's any kind of curve to them they're inductors I suppose. There's always an insulator between the plates. Now you can get capacitors that have Mylar as the insulator, or polypropylene, or polycarbonate or polystyrene, or Teflon or this or that or on and on. And then there are the larger electrolytic capacitors, which still have an insulator, but it gets into a whole different territory. The dielectric can actually absorb some of the signal as the signal moves from one plate to the other. You want to block the DC voltages; that's the main reason for using them in a signal path — DC voltages will creep in and you want to stop that. So the capacitor blocks the DC but lets the AC through. But that dielectric in the middle there can absorb a little bit of the signal and then release it a short time later, and that can cause a little bit of smearing of the audio signal. It's better or worse depending on the type of capacitor. I know there are all kinds of transformer-less mic preamp companies out there, and they would probably say 'Oh, transformers, you know, they're terrible, all sorts of phase shift and ringing and core saturation.' Sometimes it comes down to, well, who's got the biggest problem, is my transformer a bigger problem than your capacitors? So I'll just leave it at that. Your mileage may vary." He feels that the Jensen JT-16-B which he uses in the M-1 "belongs in a category all its own. Part of the deal is it's not whether it's transformer-less or transformer-coupled, part of the deal is, 'How well is the design executed.' That's true in so many things in life."

"When I first started making the M-1 mic pre-amps in 1987, I just crossed my fingers and hoped that anybody would even kind of like them. And it just seems that most people like them a lot. I've heard some people tell me that they have many preamps to choose from, but they find themselves going back to the M-1 much more often than any other preamp. So many people, they're beating their heads against the wall, trying to get things just to sound right. I remember bringing an M-1 to a local studio in the earlier days of the M-1, and the engineer, Danny Leake, he's a local engineer here in Chicago and he's got an excellent reputation. He's traveled around the world doing all kinds of things. He was expecting me to bring an M-1 up, and I brought it up. He was in the middle of doing some vocal overdubs. This was at Universal Recording, while they were still in existence. He was using one of these legendary old Neve consoles that everybody seeks, and thinks it's the greatest thing to come down the road. So as soon as I walked in, he stopped the vocal overdubs, he patched the microphone into the M-1. Instead of being in the old Neve and a Pultech equalizer—he had been using this combination of the

Neve and a Pultech equalizer to get the high frequencies back where they belonged after the old Neve had screwed them up. So he listened to the M-1, he said, 'All right, take '71 or whatever. The vocalist was singing, and after about eight seconds, I heard Danny say 'Whoa.' And that was his way of saying whoa; this is just great, just by itself. This is so much better than the old Neve and the Pultech equalizer. People are just looking for; I think 97% of the time they just want things to sound the way they sound. And the M-1 seems to do a much better job of doing that than most pre-amps. Everybody is entitled to their opinion, everybody can get the kind of sound they want to get."

"Another quote was 'Even the producer could tell the difference.' I like to poke fun at producers, you know. A true story, a long story but a true one, where even the producer noticed when they switched from the M-1 back to an old Neve in fact. A whole other story where it was an M-1 and an old Neve. So, to make a long story short, an M-1 failed. The engineer called me in a panic. I sent him a new 990 because I figured that was the problem. Gets off the phone realizing that he's not going to be able to use the M-1 for the rest of the day. So he plugs the stuff back into the old Neve, which was one of the reasons they went to this particular studio in New York, A&R Studios. And called everybody back in, they started recording. And everybody, including the producer, noticed the difference, and they refused to continue the session until the M-1 was fixed. So you know, there's an example of an old Neve."

"I keep thinking of Blind Melon Chitlin, the Cheech & Chong fictitious character. It's this fictitious old blues harmonica player who's just this burned-out, practically just a pile of dust for a human being. But somebody like that I imagine, they probably have some just beat-to-crap microphone they plug into some guitar amp; that's the mic preamp is this guitar amp that's probably 50 years old and the tubes are about to fall out, and everything about it is screwed up completely. And it gives him exactly the sound he's looking for. Well, for something like that, fine. You do the Silvertone amplifier, you know, the Sears Silvertone amp, with a horrible microphone and it's great. But the guy that wants to then record that, if they manage to hire a recording engineer to do this Blind Melon Chitlin album. He might put some fine microphone in front of that amplifier, plug it into an M-1 mic preamp to capture it exactly the way it's supposed to sound. Anything anybody wants to do is fine. If it works, salute it. If it doesn't, you know, try something else. There are only like two or three hundred mic pre-amps to choose from these days."

"When you get into the details of a discrete design versus a monolithic design, you realize that there is at least a potential for much better performance. Now again, there are better and better monolithic op-amps as time goes on. And there are certainly ways that you could make a discrete op-amp so badly that you'd be better off with a monolithic op-amp. Just being monolithic doesn't mean anything, other than the fact that it's monolithic. It could be bad monolithic, it could be great monolithic. I mean discrete, well, whatever - either way. Evaluate and make up your own mind. But there are lots of reasons why this circuit could be better and in fact ends up being better. I write at somewhat great length in my 990 data package that I include, I explain to people that if you were to look inside of a monolithic op-amp, you would find a little chip of silicon that's typically about a sixteenth of an inch square; that's the whole circuit. And somehow on that sixteenth of an inch square of silicon, they have to put dozens of transistors and resistors and diodes and capacitors and whatever else. And it's amazing that they can get all those radically different kinds of components fabricated on one tiny chip of silicon. Now it starts off with a 6-inch or 8-inch wafer and they cut 'em up into thousands of little op-amps. But how in the world are you gonna get the world's best input transistors, where the signal first comes in, with the very unique requirements that those transistors have," into a tiny silicon chip? "That's a very unique set of parameters to make the input transistors. Meanwhile here are the two output transistors, meant to handle lots of power and whatever, radically different requirements. They're made in a substantially different way. Well how do you get the world's best input transistors and the world's best output transistors on the same 16th of an inch square chip of silicon? It's just... you can't do it. There are going to be compromises. It's like trying to have one vehicle that's both a Porsche 944 or whatever, and an 18-wheeler, over-the-road. So there are going to be limitations in monolithic op-amps, and oh, by the way, you need some real resistors on there as well, and some capacitors. So you certainly have the potential with a discrete op-amp of having much better performance. You can have much higher output current, which then allows you to use much lower-value resistors in the surrounding circuit, which then can give you even lower noise. And just one thing leads to another, and you can get much better performance. The trade-off being it takes up a lot more room, and it's 50 dollars versus maybe 50 cents. But we're not talking about building clock radios for the side of your bed, where who cares what it sounds like. This, in theory, is part of a business where people are pouring their heart and soul into the music that they're recording. And so the difference between a 50-cent op-amp and a 50-dollar amp is not nearly as important to them as it might be to someone shopping for a clock radio for their kitchen or something. They don't want to spend more than 9.95 for the whole radio, much less... You can do good preamps with monolithic op-amps, [but] I think judging by the reaction from my customers, this discrete design offers something superior. But again, your mileage may vary and your personal preferences are yours."

"And then vacuum tubes, that's a whole other area, of course. You can get 12AX7 tubes, or ECC83s, whatever, from ten different sources out there. There's lots of companies that make them now, and each one has its own sound qualities, so how do you deal with that? There are usually coupling capacitors in tube mic preamps. I suppose there's a way to do without them, but usually you need them, so there's that potential compromise. And one thing about [the JT-16-B] input transformer, which is a real important point, I think, is that it has a very low impedance ratio. 150-ohm primary, but just a 600 ohm secondary, which is an ideal match for the 990 op-amp. The 990 likes to look back and see low impedance coming from whatever is before it. So that transformer matches perfectly. Well vacuum tubes get their best noise performance when they look back and have a high source impedance." At this point Hardy pointed to a Jensen JE-115K-E high-ratio transformer. "That's the kind of transformer that you would typically find in a tube circuit as well, with a high impedance ratio to match better with the requirements of the tube. The trade-off being you get more voltage gain out of that transformer, you get about 20 dB of voltage gain, compared to 5.6 dB out of this, but [the JT-16-B] will perform in a much more linear fashion. If you compare the specs of this transformer to that transformer, you'll find that this has wider bandwidth, the distortion is

lower, the phase response is more linear, group delay, however you want to look at it, better specs—simply because the lower the impedance ratio. Laws of physics at work here - the lower the ratio, the better it will perform. So most tube circuits, I don't want to speak for all of them, but typically tube circuits require a high-ratio transformer. So you've got the compromise of a high-ratio transformer. You've got the variability of all kinds of different tubes out there. You've got coupling capacitors in the signal path, so there are some of the potential problems. Again it becomes a matter of execution and how well somebody does a particular design. But all things being equal, that transformer will perform better. And no capacitors should sound better than capacitors. Again, I don't wanna step on anybody's toes too badly."

"When I was designing all of these things, and really particularly with the M-1 I guess, because that's a ready-to-go product, you don't have to invent your own boxes and power supplies and stuff. So it's the first really mainstream kind of product. I knew that it was a great op-amp and a great transformer, and with no capacitors in the signal path it ought to be beneficial somehow. There are so many great designs that people come up with that just fall flat on their face for whatever reason. It may even be a great design but there's something about the packaging or the look or there's a vibe there. You know, we're dealing with human beings here; you just never know. I've had a lot of people compliment me on the metering of the M-1 for example. That seemed so important to me that, when you've got a signal of some unknown quantity coming into the preamp, this is sort of a great unknown. You really need to know, well how am I doing here? What kind of levels are we dealing with?"

Since when Hardy designed the M-1 he was unsure in what genre it would find its niche, the broad range of styles for which the people use the preamp has pleased him. "One of my earliest customers is a guy who was in Southern California, now he's in Nashville, last I knew - Michael Wagener from Double Trouble Productions. He's doing what I would call, and forgive me if it's the wrong terminology, but heavy metal kind of stuff. You wouldn't want to be anywhere near the guitar amps without serious hearing protection, that just real high level kind of stuff. There's that kind of stuff going on, there are people doing spoken-word, voiceover kind of stuff, talking books. But there are all kinds of M-1s down in the Nashville area. There are people doing classical work, people doing jazz work. You name it. Whatever there is to do, it seems like the M-1 does an excellent job. It doesn't have a certain sweet spot and then everywhere else it kind of falls apart. It just seems to do well whether it's at the lowest gain settings or the highest gain settings or whatever. Again, I had my fingers crossed hoping people would kind of like it, and it just seems like it fits in everywhere, for which I'm grateful."

After Hardy designed the M-1 preamp, "Deane Jensen asked me if I'd be willing to build his concept of a preamp, but using my packaging as the basis for it." The joint collaboration resulted in the Jensen Twin Servo mic preamp. "On the Jensen there are two 990 op-amps per channel, whereas the M-1 uses just one. For two or three years, I sold that directly to Deane Jensen and then he would market that as his own preamp. But sadly Deane died after a couple of years of marketing [it]. And after a

few years the folks at Jensen finally said to me, the people who took over after Deane passed away, they finally decided, well hey, you're the mic preamp guy, why don't you sell the Jensen twin-servo mic preamp? We're up to our necks in transformer orders. We do transformers; you do mic preamps. So we'll sell transformers. I certainly tip my cap to Deane Jensen. He was extremely helpful over the years. I certainly miss him, and I think the industry as a whole misses Deane Jensen and his contributions."

Hardy designs his preamps on old Hewlett Packard 300 series computers. "A guy I used to be in a band with back in the early '70s, at some point in his life decided to write a CAD program." Hardy wouldn't name the ex-bandmate, because he abandoned the program over ten years ago. The anonymous programmer started the CAD software in the late '70s, before personal computers, so he wrote it in the native Hewlett Packard Pascal environment. Today, Hardy runs it, and maintains it himself too, on several Hewlett Packard machines, which he can buy used for affordable prices. He showed me some of his current designs in the CAD program, ranging from re-worked versions of his old replacement cards with better grounding patterns to a redesign for one of the bedrooms in his house.

Hardy finds running a small audio company challenging but worth the effort. "It's frustrating and there are so many things that divert me from designing stuff. I'm behind on things I'd like to get designed. But I certainly like it a lot - I mean, I don't think I would trade it. I was in enough bands where there were insane people in the bands generally screwing things up and causing chaos, and working for other people at various points, that I just decided I've had enough. I'm gonna just do my own thing here and call it the John Hardy Company. And that way I don't have to answer to anybody, I don't have to drive to work because I work here, and I like it a lot." In addition to selling Hardy's preamps, the company also distributes a German direct box, the AMB Tube-Buffered Direct-Injection Box.

He has a small staff helping him. "Just a few people, part time people that do assembly work. And I let them do as much as I can, but when it comes to the final testing and quality control and everything, that's what I do." His employees install the cards and the chassis, attach the knobs, and cover the unused areas with blank panels. "But then I come in and start neatening things up and give it a good inspection and some last little bits of soldering I have to do. And then power it up and make sure that everything is working right, calibrate and test it. Stick it in a box and ship it out, hopefully to a customer that will live happily ever after and love it for years."

"As I'm designing more and more preamps, at least until I see some reason to change, I will be using those same basic ingredients. I'll have different versions of it, for example [a preamp with] a variable high-pass filter. I've had various people say, 'Well the M-1 is great, I wish I had a mixer, it's like an M-1 with pan-pots, maybe and a high-pass filter' - So a high-pass filter. I'll probably add a switchable resistive pad on some models, whatever I come up with in the future. Offer more choice, but still based on the same basic principles, the same transformer, same op-amp. Variations on a theme, yeah - if it ain't broke, don't fix it."

"I'm much more comfortable recording at home. I know my equipment so well. Outside studios make me uncomfortable. They're so expensive. If I have a week where I get nothing good at home it's not that big a deal. If I've been spending two thousand dollars a day and I get nothing good after a week, that's the end of the world."

   -**Moby** *on recording at home*

Moby's album 'Play' on V2, was recorded and mixed almost entirely at his home on two ADATs.

photo by
Joseph Cultice

The db of *David Bottrill:*

Transatlantic Aural Architect

![Capital A]At any given instance in time, David Bottrill partakes in one of three activities. He is either submerged in the realm of slumber, routing signals on a recording console or is seated in an airplane high above the ground. In fact, he travels so often that the next time you gaze up at the sky and see a plane scrawl across it, he just might very well be inside it. And where would his destination be? A place with a recording studio no doubt. And on an aeroplane, one can sleep.

Story and photos by Roman Sokal

From an early age the native Canadian found himself in the intimate work habitat of musical vanguards Brian Eno and Daniel Lanois. He was not only responsible for skillfully operating world-class equipment, but was also forced to push his own creative envelope. A few short years after his indoctrination into the studio he relocated to Real World studios in the UK, where he worked on such notable albums as Peter Gabriel's *So*, *Passion* and *Us*. Bottrill is renowned for being diverse with a forte of applying his techniques to a wide range of artists: liner notes in albums by King Crimson, Clannad, Tool, Nusrat Fateh Ali Khan and even Kid Rock immortalize his boniker.

His exceptional talents as engineer, producer, programmer and ace of spacious mixing keeps him from staying put musically and geographically, as he constantly shuttles back and forth from his decade-plus home base in the UK to locations across North America and Europe. This is perhaps the reason why his verbiage remains free of infiltration from British colloquialisms. Well, almost. At times he is heard referring to a console as a *'desk'*...

The blueprint that depicts Bottrill's entry into the domain of wires and microphones traces back to the dawn of the '80s in Hamilton, Ontario - a modest-sized blue collar Canadian city known for its skyline plumage of industrial smokestacks. *"It's a curious story,"* begins an energetic Bottrill. *"I grew up in Dundas [a bedroom community outside of Hamilton] and, like most people, I was unsure what I wanted to do with my life for the most part and tried a lot of different avenues, including going to Mohawk [Community] College for a Business Administration diploma. I never actually finished [the program] because two personal and significant events occured that kind of woke me up to the fact that I wasn't really heading down the right path."*

The year was 1983. Bewildered in a premature version of a mid-life crisis, Bottrill decided to seek medicinal refuge in the ever-secure world of music. *"I was always a guitar player and in a bedroom-basement band and I was always interested in trying to do something with making music. My girlfriend at the time said her uncle had a recording studio in Hamilton and said to go look if there was something there for me as an opportunity. So I went to Grant Avenue studio and her uncle was Bob Lanois [co-owner and brother of producer/engineer Daniel]. The first time I walked into that studio, having made an appointment, and looked at the control room and spent a little time there I thought, 'Well this is a pretty fantastic thing to do!' They didn't have a job for me at the time but said I could hang out to learn. So I spent the day doing odd jobs - washing windows and so on to make money so I could go in at night and assist at making coffee, sweeping and eventually I got to plug in microphones."*

In a true existential moment that combined both his intrusive enthusiasm and curiosity with the chance element of being in the right place at the right time, Bottrill stepped into a vehicle that would take him on a life long journey. *"The first session I was involved in at an assisting capacity was Brian Eno and Dan [Lanois] doing the 'Apollo' soundtrack. That was a major influence in how I was to work ever since."* It was no question that at that precise moment Bottrill knew he was on and in the right avenue. Next he participated in many a session *"in eclectic-land"* by Teenage Head (an infamous local punk band), The Parachute Club, Luba (*Secrets and Sins*) and yet another Brian Eno soundscape opus, *Ambient #4/On Land*.

By 1985, Grant Avenue studio had earned the status of fame due to its comfortable atmosphere and the aura left by reputable artists that had channeled their souls onto tape there. That year the brothers Lanois decided to sell the studio, and explored many options including the possibility of dismantling it and selling off the equipment. *"We felt it had a heritage and didn't want to see the studio die,"* he recollects. *"We began to rip out and dismantle the board and at the 11th hour Bob Doidge [current owner] came up with the money to buy the entire studio and we spent the whole night plugging it back in. Without any prior experience, what I ended up doing was finding the way the wires had been bent into each connector and tried to line it up again - it was very funny."* Having been once again blessed with a continuous electrical current running through its wiring, Grant Avenue ended up as Bottrill's official place of work for the next few years. Eventually, he became promoted to official conductor of the studio's MCI console and JH-24 tape machine beginning with the recording of Roger Eno's *Voices*, which was followed by avant garde producer/guitarist Michael Brooks' debut, *Hybrid*.

West Meets East Meets West...

The second step in the evolution of David Bottrill, the engineer, involves British Airways and Peter Gabriel. In 1986, Daniel Lanois asked Bottrill to fly to England to aid in the recording of Peter Gabriel's ground-breaking album *So*. The session was taking place in a cow shed near the town of Bath. This session was the first where equipment and time were unlimited, thus allowing everyone's creativity to run rampant. *"At the end of* 'So' *[Dan*

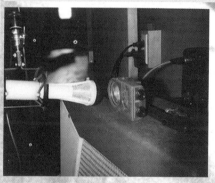

Lanois and I] were supposed to do something with the Psychedelic Furs, but at that time they didn't have the songs written yet. Dan had just spent a better part of one and a half years getting songs out of Peter [Gabriel] for 'So' and he didn't want to go through that process again," bares Bottrill. *"Dan is a man of the moment and likes to capture the performance and excitement and doesn't like to dwell for long periods of time, I don't think. He wanted to work on the development of the music and not on the songwriting, which he would have to drag out of people."* Gabriel, like any tour-de-force, had his own eccentric approach to creation. Whether it is always compatible with an outside party is a different story. Bottrill explains the friendly clash between the two giants. *"Peter likes to take much time to get it as right as he can because he has a lot of things on the go that distract him from writing lyrics. There*

was a time when Dan got so upset with Peter he ended up nailing the door shut from the inside of the studio where Peter was writing lyrics so he wouldn't be able to leave to make another phone call!"

The faltering Psychedelic Furs project posed a question mark that lurked over the immediate future of Bottrill's career. "Dan didn't have any more work for me and he suggested I either stay here in England and look for more work or that he would help me find some back in Canada. I decided to stay." By making that bold and fearless leap, Bottrill quickly ended up working for Peter Gabriel. He accompanied on the subsequent So tour not as a live sound engineer, but as his keyboard tech. The choice led Bottrill down a passageway which soon led him to help develop a concept called Real World, an edifice in which he deeply immersed himself for nearly a decade.

Situated in the village of Box near Bath, the idyllic Real World recording facility was the brainchild of Peter Gabriel. He converted an old mill into a hi-tech shangri-la for musical luminaries from around the world to record at. The Real World concept also grew into to the Real World recording label. Gabriel is a pioneer in incorporating obscure unconventional and unique instruments into his own music. Influenced in part by 'world-music' artists, he felt that the rest of the world should be enriched and exposed to this wide spectrum of music too. Sadly, without such a label, most of these artists would not be heard outside of their own domain. Initially the studio was armed with the equipment dismantled from the cow shed. "Peter had an SSL desk and two Studer A-80 [24-track] machines. One [of the Studers] was customized with electronics built by Colin Broad. It could have been a revolutionary machine except for the fact that it didn't work very well. Like an SSL, you could set up a gate on the output of every channel, because each channel had one built in it."

It was there that Gabriel's eastern-influenced, instrumental breakthrough album Passion [1989] was executed as the label's flagship release. The album was conceived specifically as the soundtrack for director Martin Scorsese's The Last Temptation of Christ - an acclaimed and stunning feature film depicting an alternative portrayal of the life of Christ. A plethora of musicians from all walks of life and styles of music were invited to play on the album, including percussionist Bill Cobham, vocalist Youssou N'Dour, double violinist Shankar and guitarist David Rhodes.

Many of the artists involved hailed from exotic locales where their music is ensemble-based, non-electric and where the English language is non-existent. Bottrill had to innovate in a way to make sure things would work. Unexpectedly, he wound up validating the virtue that extols music as language unto itself. "The most important thing at the time was to make sure the musician playing in the studio was feeling their most comfortable in how they were able to do their performance," Bottrill explains. "We'd get them into our good-sized control rooms and turn it into a performance space. They couldn't speak English very

well a lot of the time so communication was really important. We had to get Peter's musical point across. We would have to use every communication technique available. Sometimes it was using handsigns, or we were pointing. Anything like that is easier when you're in the same room. We record almost everything in the control room. We were trying to make sure we could communicate and you could look at someone and that would make as much sense as it would trying to talk to someone on a talk-back mic. Giving a look does a lot more than a mic with headphones."

In order to make this feat technically possible, Bottrill conferred with the studio builders and made suggestions as to how the control room should be constructed for such occasions. "We would also modify things, like being able to change the absolute phase of the speakers so when you're recording with a mic you could put them out of phase, and it helps to cancel out more of the sound when the rest of the track is in." The 48+ individual tracks used to build Passion involved more than just an organic process. He quickly and methodically learned how to maneuver the incorporation of MIDI sequencing and sampling technologies, which at the time were still in infancy. Fortunately, the technically-inclined Bottrill had a working familiarity with programming Linn Drums and Emulator IIs and IIIs back during his tenure at Grant Avenue. Vastly employed for Passion was the MPC-60 Fairlight as well as software-based systems such as Performer and Cubase. Complexities were inherent due to the larvae-like stage that the technologies at during that time period. "Usually there was up to 64 tracks going on at any time that mainly involved peripheral programming. It was a lot

more of a process to do it back then than it would be now. These days everything is done through Logic Audio and Pro Tools. Now all you do is plug in a hard disk and there you go. It's a lot easier."

When listening to the end product, one is enveloped by a sense of spaciousness that is a result of Bottrill's keen sense of microphone placement and atmospheric mixing. "It was definitely an education on learning how to record different types of instruments. All of a sudden I'd be presented with an oud, kementché, or a mazhar and I'd have to figure out where the sound came out of it and how to mic it. It opened up my ears to the new styles of music that I would never have an opportunity to hear otherwise. It was a real education." Passion is a prime specimen

of Bottrill's deftness at blending and mastering the art, science and politics of music recording - a skill that he lends to every project. The disc also functions as a quality reference vehicle for many of today's top producers and engineers. It is no surprise that his name is credited directly on the disc itself, which is highly uncommon for record companies to do. By doing that, it made Bottrill's name synonymous with craftsmanship.

Immediately following the completion of Passion, work would begin on another seminal and highly personal Gabriel album, Us. The Lanois-helmed production spanned over two years as Lanois cyclically went back and forth between Us and U2. The venture was perfectionist and gargantuan in scope - it requires a dedicated article unto itself - occupying two 24-track machines and a 32-track digital machine that often ran with various other computer-based programs. "It was possibly the most intense three years of my life to date, and encompassed some of the most involved recording sessions I have ever experienced. It was the culmination of my career with Peter."

As chief engineer at the studio, Bottrill's expanding duties began to earn him the status as a 'producer' whilst engineering, mixing and editing a handful of titles for the label. These included Qawwali master Nusrat Fateh Ali Khan's Shahen-Shah, Exile by Geoffrey Oryema, and the Drummers of Burundi's ensemble Live at Real World. He expresses a clear opinion on what the title of 'producer' stands for - "a 'producer' is anything from the person who puts musicians together in a room to the person who books the studio and assesses the performances to the person who is the DJ or the programmer. A lot of producers today will find a single but the music will be the producer's. That's not my thing. There are so many ways someone can be called producer that it's almost irrelevant to be called one because it's so wide it doesn't mean one thing. Ultimately, I use 'producer' as like being a director on film. They help the artist to achieve the music they are trying to make. And by having worked in other studios and made albums before, the producer understands where the artist wants to go. I work with people who are good artists and musicians that write songs that I like. I help them realize that. I don't do the writing, although I will write with them if they need it, like a bridge melody or chorus. My strength is making arrangements into a more concise format so that the song is crafted a more cohesive way. People, as musicians, aren't good self-editors. They'll go over and over and do section after section and I'll say, 'You know what? You've said what you needed to say here and here.' I spend a lot of time in pre-production with artists doing that. You can edit down or lengthen songs when necessary. It depends on the intention of the song."

When convenient, Bottrill will invite an artist to his home set-up before the main production commences, for efficiency. His home is modestly equipped with Pro Tools, Logic Audio, a small collection of mics fired by API pre-amps, valve compressors and "a small desk." For the sparkling clear, ember-warm vocals that exist on his recordings, his preferred choice of microphones is quite narrow. The Neumann M7S which he describes as having a "Nuremberg Rally lollipop-style look" tops the list. With a manufacturing period that predates W.W.II, the mic's characteristics includes a "full body" adding "presence without being too sharp." The classic Neumann U47 mic serves as an alternate.

Having been exposed to the best technological accoutrements for the recording process, Bottrill has had to rationalize in order to avoid overcome by an infinity complex that could lead a session astray. "I find myself more and more wanting to make decisions so you can spend the following days not making decisions and having to cover your ass. I'll only use up more tracks than I need if I feel I might be missing something. I have been guilty of piling it on and cutting it down later." His deduction is simple. "If you make things work in rough mixes then they should just work! If they don't, then there's more of a problem than just piling on the shit!"

The way in which Bottrill claims to have legitimized himself as genuine 'producer' beyond the job's regular clinical functions of the job happened ironically. He had been hired originally as engineer only on *The First Day*, a stellar 1993 showcase collaboration between ex-Japan founder David Sylvian and legendary guitar guru Robert Fripp. His duty as engineer expanded to the point where he became co-producer by contributing to the rhythmic framework. "I had to fill in as the rhythm section when their drummer was sacked halfway through," Bottrill reveals. "I'd try a bunch of different patterns and loops until they liked what they heard!"

The *First Day* undertaking also became a talisman and would sound a beacon that summoned two more vital projects which together would form a triumvirate of recordings that anchors the Bottrill legacy: King Crimson's *THRAK* and Tool's *Ænima*.

Thrak: the reawakening of the King.

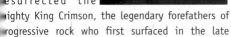

In 1994, nearly after a decade-long truancy, Robert Fripp resurrected the mighty King Crimson, the legendary forefathers of progressive rock who first surfaced in the late

1960s. Leader and guitarist Robert Fripp assembled a new court of established musical entities for the resurgence. Their goal: perfection. The collective included the resilient Adrian

Belew on vocals and guitar, bass magician Tony Levin, drum syncopation master Bill Bruford (an original Yes man), the alchemic Pat Mastelotto on an additional drum kit, and Trey Gunn, a revolutionary instrumentalist of a *"different kind"* who strikes the Warr guitar. This musical apparatus functions as a tapping instrument, similar to the Chapman Stick, with a harmonic range that is just as wide.

The first new King Crimson to re-emerge was the Bottrill co-produced litmus-test EP entitled *VROOOM*, which was quietly unleashed onto the public by Fripp's own label, Discipline Global Mobile. *VROOOM* was done at Applehead Studios, a very small studio in Woodstock, New York, and we had to push it beyond its limits by bringing in another multi-track" reports Bottrill. Based on the triumphant praise and demand warranted by the EP, the full-length *THRAK* became its successor, only this time they converged at the Real World studio.

For both sessions, the task of containing the radiating collective of talent was Bottrill's prerogative. *"The way Robert works is very immediate and performance based so I was required to set them up so they can play live. It was difficult because they had two drummers, a bassist, and Trey on the Warr guitar. Adrian sang and played guitar, and Robert played the other guitar, and his sound is huge. So having to fit all that together was an interesting scenario and trying to actually record it and have everyone be able to hear what was going on was another challenge. Everyone was in the same room except for Pat so as to isolate the drum kits from each other. Otherwise, cabinets were isolated in separate booths. We had a monitor engineer specifically for the headphone mix. He was able to make eye contact with the players since I couldn't see them because the desk at Real World faces the other way. I'd set up and each time they did a take it would be vastly different - sometimes halfway through we'd edit together different versions. Their discipline is to the point where they are methodical yet non-flippant with their improvisations. They spent so many years playing that they are beyond technique - the pure performance was able to come out because they were in tune and in touch with their instruments."*

Bottrill amicably departed from the Real World homestead in 1996. Backed by his enormous credibility, Bottrill ventured into another kind of *real world* his association with *The First Day* and *THRAK* projects would escalate him to the next echelon.

The cleanliness of Ænima.

It began with a phone call from Los Angeles. Bottrill recalls with humor and irony how his involvement with the band Tool came about. *"Funnily enough, they called and asked if I would work on [their new album] and they sent me their 'Opiate' [EP] and 'Undertow' record. I listened to them and thought 'I've never done anything like this before... why would this kind of American metal band be sending me things when all I've done was English art-rock music?' At first I thought they had me confused with someone else, so I spoke to them and asked if they were sure they had the right guy. As it turned out, Danny [Carey], the drummer, was a HUGE King Crimson fan and Adam [Jones] the guitar player's favorite album had been 'The First Day.' The singer, Maynard [James Keenan] was a huge Real World music fan. A lot of the stuff I worked on happened to be their favorites even though they were musically doing different things. They thought I wasn't an 'American rock producer' but they figured they already knew what area they wanted and that I would bring something else to their music. So I met them in Los Angeles, sat in on one of their rehearsals and right away, we hit it off. It was an exciting rehearsal despite the fact that I sat beside Danny's ride cymbal, which kind of made me deaf by the end of the day. They knew what I could do, they knew what they and their fans wanted, so I went along with their confidence."*

For the most part, Tool creates a genre of music that is their very own. Its fabric contains threads of epic, progressive dark compositions, yet weaves in ethereal and mathematical structures. At times the thematic content deals with 'disgustipation', oppression, struggle, rebirth and self-realization. Even though their strange biomechanic arachnid tapestry of sound makes them perfect for post-production tinkering such as sequencing and editing, Bottrill dispenses an ironical fact. *"They're extremely well thought out. Nothing was done to a click track or through a computer. It was all live with overdubs."*

For almost four months Bottrill and the band incubated themselves in Ocean Way and The Hook studios in regional Los Angeles before eventually sealing themselves at Larrabee for the mixing stage. From the first track "Stinkfist", with its crescendo, one is immediately brought into a spacious yet well defined environment, especially with the lively drum sounds. Bottrill reveals his modus operandi, *"One of the things on that record, as well as with other rock bands I work with, is that I'll get a small PA in the same room as the drummer and place it behind him facing forwards. The close mic'd signals that are on the kit's snare, tom and kick are run through the well-EQ'd PA so you get this added volume and weight. When you use your ambient mics they pick up the PA so it* becomes overall a much bigger sound with an exaggerated volume. Danny also had extra programmed electronic sounds that would play along with his drumming so we put those through the PA as well so the sounds gelled more together with the kit." The capturing of the chromatic guitars was done in a logical manner as well, allowing organics to be the backbone for the calculating song structures. "[The] guitars generally took multiple takes, doubling and tripling with different guitars so as to allow for tonal changes by featuring different guitars as opposed to EQing differently for different sections."

When scrutinizing the credits of many Bottrill-related projects, one might also discover that he has provided a touch of his own musicianship. Take for instance Passion. He is credited for providing 'drone'. Perhaps the most peculiar example of his involvement as a musician lies within the morbidly dark and humoristic track from Ænima entitled "Message To Harry Manback". The track features delicate, sparse and melodic piano playing with atmospheric beach sounds, which ironically is accompanied by... a death threat. Bottrill reminisces, "It was me playing the piano. The threatening Italian person was leaving a real answer phone message on Maynard's roommate's machine. Basically it was from a guy who had recently been kicked out of the house for being the guest from hell."

The manner in which Bottrill deals with natural sounds via his world music experience combined with dexterity in the high-tech realm suggests that he should be dubbed as a 'World Engineer', one that merges the 'best of both worlds' for which the Tool project acts as a bonafide example of. And Bottrill agrees. He considers Ænima as a monument that rests on his curriculum vitæ as a producer, engineer and mixer.

Select discography featuring the audible feats of David Bottrill:

(year/title/artist/function)

2000 - *Waters Of Eden* - **Tony Levin** - Mix
1999 - *Blue Green Orange* - **I Mother Earth** - Mix
1999 - **Europa String Choir** - Mix
1998 - *Devil Without a Cause* - **Kid Rock** - Mixed track: "Bawitdaba"
1996 - *Sound Magic, Vol. 1* - **Afro-Celt Sound System** - Mix
1994 - *Damage* - **David Sylvian/Robert Fripp** - Mix
1994 - *Exotica* (motion picture soundtrack) - Mychael Danna - Mix
1993 - "Kiss That Frog" (CD single) - **Peter Gabriel** - Remix collaboration with Massive Attack
1990 - *Mustt Mustt* - **Nusrat Fateh Ali Khan** - Synthesizer, Djembe, Surdo, Record, Editing, Mixing
1986 - *Kafka* - **Nigel Kennedy** – Engineer

When the name Remy Zero is brought up, Bottrill's voice melts with adoration and respect. If you have not heard their 1998 album *Villa Elaine*, or if you perhaps have not heard of them at all, well... now you will. "Remy Zero are from Mobile, Alabama," Bottrill vehemently states for the record, "They're great songwriters who make really great interesting and credible pop music in the same area as Radiohead and are a little like the Verve. They have an amazing singer that could bring tears to your eyes. When I heard their demos it captivated me so much that I stayed in LA for nine months just to work with them, and LA isn't my favorite place. When my friend offered me the gig I had already been itching to go back to England! I did some production and recording and Alan Moulder did some remixing on the album. Sadly, hardly anyone got to hear it as they got lost in the shuffle and weren't really promoted when [their record company] Geffen was swallowed by Interscope."

As of the past few years, Bottrill is increasingly being summoned to mix pre-recorded projects. Therefore he keeps his cochlea well-groomed for the occasion and for accuracy. He notes the advantages to only being brought in only to mix. "You're able to come at it from an objective viewpoint. You have no agenda attached to any of the parts because you haven't sat in the studio for three days working on it. Its another chance and angle to alter what you're doing as you finish things off. Of course, sometimes its a distinct process when you're working with a lot of programmed music and reprogramming and changing structures is part of the process. These days there is less of a line drawn between the record and mix process."

The fundamental components of a Bottrill mix is a grand sense of unification, transparency, a virtual three-dimensional presence, and when context dictates, force. In fact, the mixes appropriately sound so sterile that one wonders whether he wears a white lab coat when executing a mix just as his British predecessors did in the early 1960s. "What is really important is to make sure there is clarity of hearing all the parts in a song. Each thing has a meaning and music is the sum of all those parts. If you are unable to hear some of the parts then it makes half of them irrelevant, so, you're not getting half of the music. Dimension is very important. It has to spread across the speakers but the depth has to be there. It's all about being able to catch and feel where things are recessed and when they should be up front. Both are difficult to achieve. What I usually do for depth is to use short and long reverbs, wide panning, dry on the left or right and making it reverberant in the middle or back. Somebody once said to me that they felt that when they listened to my mixes they could reach around behind the speakers and reach into the mix. When I start off a mix I'll try and listen to the style of music that the people are doing. I find out what else the band listens to and listen to that as well." The prerequisite for an

Danny Carey of Tool © *Syd Kato*

Testimonials

"I have had the pleasure to work a few times with David Bottrill. I love David's drum sounds - very big, open and dark. David also has a keen sense of symmetry and helped me with the "Walking On Air" (*Thrak*) drum arrangement. And, he is one of the few [engineers] I have ever seen dance to King Crimson (I mean *really* dance, even in 15 or 11!). His bouncing and bopping provided great adrenaline to our mixing. Best of all is 'Dave's Whiskey Emporium' (so named by Trey Gunn & myself) - David is a member of a cask club and let us enjoy his collection on several nights. David will put hair on your chest but not on your head."

-**Pat Mastelloto** (drummer – King Crimson, Mastica)

"I only did one album with him, but he was great. David was obviously a scholar and a gentleman. Besides, he lived, and probably still does, in Bath, so he's definitely okay."

-**Bill Bruford** (drummer – King Crimson, Earthworks)

"It was his ability to capture all the ethnic instruments in the past doing a lot of engineering on the *Passion* album and all that. That was what attracted us to him. We had all these producers climbing down our backs at the time and everyone we talked to said, 'I'll do this and I'll do that.' When we came to David he was like, 'Why do you want me?' And that was such a cool attitude to have you know - he wanted to know what was going on with the band and what we were about rather than just, 'Oh Tool's a big name, I'll record them!'. That's what really won us over."

-**Danny Carey** (drummer - Tool)

Bottrill mix session involves particular gadgetry along with what the studio has. "I'll try to get gear I'm comfortable with using, like an Eventide H-3000 harmonizer and a DSP 4000 - for reverbs I like the Lexicon 480-L and AMS gear. I bring my own Anthony DeMaria stereo compressor, some nice mic pres and Pro Tools plug-ins like the Waves [series], especially the limiters, as they allow for extreme volume. Also, I have recently tried the Wave Mechanics soundblenders. Very creative plug-ins. AutoTune is always useful, as is Soundreplacer and AmpFarm." Technical specifications aside, Bottrill deems that an environment and the make do with what you have' ethic takes pecedence. "I try to work in a studio for its sound and with what it already has so my sonic interests are kept up."

When committing a song's schematic of sounds to 2-track, Bottrill applies a strict definitive 'dogma' to the procedure. "I always mix to 2-track analog 1/2" tape. You have to. I'll mix to DAT at the same time, but its negligent to only have your mix on DAT. When DATs go wrong, they go horribly wrong." He prefers Sony's 1030, R500 or R700 models, and at times Prism A/D converters or the newer Apogees, which he really likes. The 1/2" machines of choice are an ATR, Studer or Otari machine loaded with Quantegy GP9. He embraces 24-bit technology for its increased clarity. "You don't need to go much further than 24-bit. After that it becomes a question of storage. You get conned into buying more storage space!"

Even during the finalizing period that is the mastering process which involves tweakage and assembly of the final running order of a project, Bottrill's rabid obsession with achieving THE mix will continue when dealing with the mastering engineer. "We talk about sonic problem areas from wherever it is that I've mixed. I have the fortune or misfortune, I'm

not sure which, that every project I do I usually end up mixing in a different studio. So I try to learn a new studio every time. When I go into mastering I say, 'Well okay, what do I need to know about this studio that I just mixed in - what the sonic problem areas are'... and so on. I like to rely on a mastering engineer who has good ears and knows his room and he tells me what to work on in my mixing technique in terms of strong and weak points. I like [the mastering] stage because I can listen to the music as a whole album and learn from them each time. I hope that stage never goes away!"

His voyages have taken him to world landmark studios such as Olympic, NRG, Bearsville and Abbey Road. His recent accomplishments include mixing for London-based the Infidels and Belgium's dEUS, which he describes as "a curious blend of angst rock and Abba-style pop." He recently returned from a stint at The Warehouse Studio (owned by Bryan Adams) in Vancouver to mix the aptly named Unified Theory, featuring members from the defunct Blind Melon. "They have a lot to offer," concedes Bottrill. He travels next to Paris to work with Spor, a loud beat-driven Belgian band that incorporates some rap/rock elements with "interesting sounds." Although constantly busy, he still manages to find time to listen to other's work. He respects a multitude of fellow producers and engineers, and cites Kevin Killen as somewhat of a mentor, from whom he admits learning a great deal during the recording of So. Alan Moulder, Flood and Tchad Blake have also left an imprint on him. "Tchad's stuff doesn't sound like anyone else's. You put it on and you have to listen to it. Everything has a character to it and his sonic characteristics have a sensibility of how sound ought to be. They have a real sound. It's ear candy."

Bottrill's amassed a wealth of expertise and working familiarity with top-notch consoles such as SSLs - the Neve Flying Fader and the Euphonics systems. He is smittenly inclined towards the new 24-bit Sony Oxford digital console for its ergonomics and proficiency. At the time of printing, only four are known to exist worldwide. Peter Gabriel acquired two of them, which logically means that the two have reunited for yet another collaboration, this time for the Millennium Dome in London. "It is a structure on the bank of the Thames river as a celebration and exhibition for tourists and family outings. Peter wrote the music for a performance that goes on three times a day and is kind of a bit Cirque du Soleil and a bit musical show with floor dancing and aerial flying and the like." Given the console's capability for spacious 5.1 or 7.1 (an addition of left center and right center channels) mixing, Bottrill was the ideal choice for creating a surround sound mix of the music during the dome's construction, thereby adding an eccentric irritant edge to the job. "It was mixed inside the Dome while two huge cherry pickers, angle grinders and cranes worked away - it was an adversarial process. The project was mixed down to Pro Tools, and plays back from that for the show. The subsequent mixes for the album of the show's music was mixed to the new Sony [professional PCM9000 Master Disk Recorder] Magneto Optical drive." Usage of the device is standard practice at Real World and Bottrill observes that it seems to sound better than DAT especially with its depth and bottom-end characteristics.

Dawning upon nearly two decades of experience in the recording studio domain, David Bottrill appears to be constantly moving forward, having bypassed any signs of succumbing to a tiring or detrimental formula that some artists might fall victim to with time. His demeanor seems to be devoid of a crippling ego, (one wonders why he doesn't speak in the third person) which no doubt serves as a passport to merge with other craftsmen worldwide. By osmosis his exposure to the planet's finest talents pushes his creative envelope, and the end result manifests in a highly enveloping experience for the rest of the world that listens. In spite of the fact that he ventures to a potpourri of locales, his Canadian identity remains relatively intact as the avid skier tries to keep up on the progress of the Toronto Maple Leafs hockey team. "Shit! The Leafs lost to the Senators!" he griped, interrupting our conversation at one point (upon learning the final outcome of the game).

In any occupation diversity is the key to survival. Authoritatively, Bottrill stresses a straightforward reasoning - "If a band hears what I do and they want to work with me then that is where I get my inspiration from. I'd rather feed off the band and their sound and put a little character into it. I want good quality but it always has to sound different. I mean it's good to have a 'sound' , but if it goes out of fashion, you're out of work, aren't you?!" ☒

Sparkleh

Sparklehorse interview
with **Mark Linkous**
by Adam Selzer

On a farm somewhere in Richmond, Virginia, next to the house in an adjacent annex, Mark Linkous (aka Sparklehorse) is wiring up his 16-track studio. He has released two records on Capitol, *vivadixiesubmarinetransmissionplot* in 1995, and the long anticipated *Good Morning Spider* in February of 1999. Most tracks on the first record were recorded at Sound of Music (David Lowery's studio) and others were done by Mark at Static King, his home studio. The recordings are very inspired, utilizing unconventional vocal sounds, manipulated drums, and sound samples while maintaining a cohesive feel that contains a mix of creative pop and more sparse, beautiful slower songs. On *Good Morning Spider*, Mark decided to record it all himself and invested a couple of Tascam D88's, among other gear. I called him while he was still setting up his studio at a recently inhabited farm. We talked for about an hour and when I was transcribing the interview, I realized that his demeanor was very important to what he had to say and how it should be interpreted. So please, if you will, insert a soft spoken, very humble voice with a sweet southern drawl to get a bit closer to what actually transpired.

Are You playing all the instruments on your new record?
On most of the songs I do. I had a couple of days off in London on one of our last tours so I went into Church Studios and recorded the drums for "Pig" and "100 Sparrows."

Did you play the drums on those recordings?
No. My drummer Scott Miner did those. He operates the sampler a lot live and plays keyboards and all sorts of stuff really.

So you recorded your new record at home, is that right?
Yeah, I have two Tascam D88s.

photos by: Danny Clinch

Was Capitol hesitant to you doing it on your own?

With producing it myself? Well yeah, we had to trick them into it.

It seems like your recording aesthetic is so important to the outcome that they would have to agree to it, it wouldn't be Sparklehorse any other way.

Well, the first one was produced by me and David Lowery [Cracker, Camper Van Beethoven]. He's producing Counting Crows and all this stuff now, but I wanted to produce this myself anyway.

Did you learn a lot from working with him?

Yeah, the way I started was David would come out to my house with this Tascam 688 cassette 8-track and we would record stuff. Actually, that's when the original version of "Sick of Goodbyes" and "Happy Man" were recorded, without all the radio noise. So they were recorded even before the first record but I've done a lot to them since then. Then David would go away on tour with Cracker and I'd just have his machine out there with nothing but a compressor. By not having any access to any outboard gear I got really used to just using a compressor and eventually started not liking reverb on anything.

Yeah, I don't hear a lot of reverb in your recordings. It sounds like you got quite a few different keyboard sounds on the new record.

I wanted this record to be more keyboard based than the last one, just soundwise. Theres a lot of Optigan on there. I have a couple of Wurlitzer organs that are kind of messed up and that's why they sound good. I have a Magnus Cathedral organ, its a fancy Magnus in a wood cabinet with a tube amp in it. I also have just little Casios... the only pro keyboard I have is one of those Roland JV heads but you've got to get so inside of those things to make them sound not so shiny and pro.

What are the string sounds you have on the new record? Are any of them real?

Yeah, a lot of them are real. Usually things that I can't fake, like violin or cello I'll have someone come in and play. The cello is someone we toured with, her name is Sophie. And the violin was played by Melissa from my brother's band.

What band is that?

Spike. They're a Richmond band.

So, when did you realize that your recording aesthetic would have so much to do with the way the song is perceived?

I guess I got really tired of pop music when I was living out in Los Angeles, just being in bands for so long that were trying to get signed. I was ready to totally give up on it, but I was totally re-inspired, and it saved me by some Tom Waits records that someone turned me on to. The Island records. Also, Daniel Johnston's homemade tapes. I just spoke to him last night for the first time which I'm very excited about. I was so intrigued by that stuff. The field recording, just document stuff, Daniel's aesthetic, and the junk yard vibe of Tom Waits. I wanted to make pop records that sounded as cool as Tom Waits records. He was actually supposed to be on *Good Morning Spider* but he called me the day after it was mastered.

That would've been great. Maybe for the next record.

Definitely for the next one. I was just going to have him sing over the telephone.

Do you usually track things over and over or do you try to capture things more spontaneously?

Well, sometimes I'll program the drum machine or get some kind of rhythm thing going like on "Hey Joe"- that's just a little Casio SK-1 with a sampler in it. It distorts pretty much any sound you put into it. I'm just making a sound into the mic there. So I like the foundation to start with something interesting, not just a drum set with reverb and a compressed snare. Everybody's records sound like that.

Do you envision how the song is going to sound recorded when you're writing it?

Not specifically. The aesthetic I imagine in my head, but not specific sounds in an aural way. I think I picture them more in a film way, and how someone will be affected by them. What kind of film is it going to inspire in their heads.

Your records are very visual in that way.

And in the context of a whole album, imagining the album is a galaxy and the songs are planets. Some of them don't orbit correctly and some of them are a little bit off axis.

How did you decide what kind of gear to buy for your studio?

Joe Henry, do you know him? My manager managed him and I talked to him over the phone. He had a couple of these (Tascam) D88s. It seems like everyone had ADATs. I didn't really want to have those. I'm not to crazy about Alesis stuff anyway so I ended up getting the Tascams. I didn't get the total low end equipment, I got the mid range stuff. I mean, the nicest piece of outboard gear I have is one of those Distressers.

Who makes that?

Emperical Labs. I think because I use compression as an effect more that anything else it works really well. You can hit it harder than any other compressor I've ever heard.

What other pieces of outboard gear do you have at your studio?

One of those Joe Meek things, the Meek box.

Do you like it?

Not really. I think I'm going to send it back and get some kind of remote for my Tascams. I have an Ampulator, its a tube amp rack thing. An [Alesis] Quadraverb, a Midiverb, a TL Audio valve interface thing. It's pretty basic. Every year I want to try and add on to the studio. I'm trying to work it so I can get my advance so I can get more gear and start working. I really need to get some decent mic preamps.

It seems like a lot of your sounds are direct into the board.

I guess the only time I use a mic is for singing and acoustic guitar. With the electrics, I started to go direct out of necessity for fear of not waking up my wife, so I kind of got used to that. If I want it dirty I just run a stomp box in between the guitar and board. The sound - I love it.

How are you getting that trademark vocal sound that appears so often on your records?

That kind of distorted, or aloof sound? I started by using toilet paper tubes over SM57s and just cutting them to different lengths and experimenting with how far you put them on.

Are you distorting them at the board?

Sometimes. That's one reason I want another mic preamp is because I can't distort the pre amps on this Mackie board that I have. But the old (Mackie) 1604 was really nice because you could slam it twice. A lot of times I'll sing through a mic and run the mic through a little micro amp with a speaker built in. I think its a Boss or something, its old. I've never seen another one. I'll sing through that and then mic that. Or sing through one of those battery powered Marshalls.

Those tiny little amps you can hook on to your belt?

Yeah. And then I have a whole box of just shitty microphones I just experiment with.

Those seem to work well if you really put your mouth right into them.

Yeah. Sometimes I'll get in there and slice apart the diaphragm with a razor blade.

How do you record your vocals when you're going for a clean sound? What kind of mics do you use?

The best mic I have is an [AKG] 414. I think its fairly unforgiving. I want to get a really good mic for the next record. As much as I like the cheap Radio Shack mic, I'd love to get a Neumann or a Rode. And a good tube preamp. I'd really like to hear those Manley things, they look so cool.

Oh, the Vox Box. Yeah. I called Manley about those the other day. They list for $4000.

I figured they were.

That's way out of my range right now. What kind of Mackie board are you using now?

The 24 channel, 8 bus. I got it because I could try to keep everything modular. I could get another (Tascam) D38 and get an expansion thing for the board.

Are you running out of tracks?

I'm trying to be disciplined enough to keep it at 16 tracks.

Do you end up experimenting a lot, layering, and then taking things out, or do you keep most of what you track?

No, I do a lot of punching in and out. I don't really ride the faders much when I mix. Sometimes there will be a couple of different instruments on one track but I kind of arrange it when I'm recording.

Are your doubled vocal sounds actually doubled or a lot of times do you use a delay in the opposite channel?

The majority of the time its two vocals.

They seem so exact I was convinced it was a slight delay.

I want to try that live. I was just listening to *Good Morning Spider* the other day on headphones and there is quite a bit of that on there so I'd like to figure out how to do that live. Have the sound man do it, I'm sure he could. Just split the signal or something so it's hard panned.

It seems like there are more pop songs on this record compared to the last one. Was that a conscious decision or did it just happen that way?

I intentionally saved "Happy Man" and "Sick of Goodbyes" for this album because I wanted to establish my style as being something other than pop. More like "Spirit Ditch." I wanted the first record to really establish that style, then I thought it would be more safe to do some more pop songs on the second record.

It seems like it would be the other way around.

Well, there are still a lot of quieter, more deconstructed songs on the new record.

Sure. Songs like "Saint Mary" and "Sunshine". Is that a Mellotron sample on that song?

No, its the flute sound on this Roland. I'm always trying to emulate the flute sound of a Mellotron.

Yeah, I love the Mellotron but there is no way I'll ever have one so I'm trying to find a way to get a sound as close as possible. I borrowed this mid size Casio and the flute sound was the closest thing I've come across. Just put a little tremolo or vibrato on it, or other effects just to tweek it out a bit.

Well, I just went to Memphis and recorded a song with Eric Drew Feldman from PJ Harvey's band - he produced Frank Black's first two records. I wanted to go down to Easley because I like the sound of those records done there by Pavement, Guided By Voices, Cat Power... and also I knew he had a Mellotron. So I took my little 4-track

down there and recorded this waltz with just Mellotron and Wurlitzer electric piano. I'm trying to get PJ Harvey or Nina from the Cardigans to sing on. Its kind of this country waltz thing. I've never played a Mellotron that wasn't sort of shaky and fucked up, and his is pretty fucked up so it came out really nice.

How do you like recording at a regular studio that that as opposed to your house?

It was alright. One thing is that I wanted to learn more, especially about mic'ing acoustic drums so I paid a lot of attention. The drummer is the guy from the Frank Black records. He's actually the drummer on the Hansen record and his day job is drumming for the Donnie and Marie show so he was dying to rock. I liked it alright. Easley is cool, Sound of Music is cool. I'm sure in every city there is a decent recording studio that isn't too sterile.

Does David Lowery still run Sound of Music?

Yeah. Its grown quite a bit and gotten a lot better. It certainly hasn't evolved into any kind of sterile studio.

Do you still do a lot of stuff down there?

No. I did one song there. I'm not too crazy about the board down there.

So tell me some recording tricks you've been using lately.

Well, I have this Hohner tape echo that's really nice if you use it as a return on another channel and just peg the preamp on the return. Its kind of fucked up anyway because its an old tape echo. A lot of that is on "End of Sunshine." Its kind of a weird sound, like on that PJ Harvey record *To Bring You My Love*, it kind of sounds like a distorted bass guitar going through a little Marshall with a low battery, and then being played through a disc man with low batteries. The signal is just struggling to even get through. I've always been blown away by that and I kind of found a way to fake it here. I don't know how that guy Flood does that.

Did you just stumble across that or did you conceive the idea in your head?

It's usually accidental. I just built my studio on the farm we just bought - it has a little building that's just big enough for my studio.

So its separate from the house?

Yeah. I can actually play through amplifiers and sing. The first time you called the other day I was actually wiring it up. Two or three things I actually wired up wrong and it just sounded amazing so I wrote it down.

Were you wiring a patch bay?

Just wiring the entire studio. I would fuck something up, have something too loud or wire something wrong and it would just amaze me.

Do you think you'll keep recording this way, on your own, or do you have any desire to do a full studio record?

Not an entire record. I'd like to keep adding on to this studio every year. Not have a whole lot of

stuff but just get some nicer gear. Maybe get rid of some of the Alesis stuff. But I would love to go into a studio with that guy Flood or someone like that. There are some producers that I just love what they do. I'd like to do a song or two with people like that.

Have you had a chance to hear the new Tom Waits record yet?

No, I didn't even know there was one?

Its not out yet, I haven't heard it either.

That guy is even more low tech than I am. I was asking him about Kurzweil things and he didn't know shit! But he told me how the Optigan worked - I didn't know about that.

Those run on discs, right?

Well, they run on big LP sized floppy discs. I thought they had a stylus on each chord button but they're optical sensors.

Is Capitol pretty much letting you do your own thing now?

Well, I had some pressure to give them a song that they could "take to radio". They thought that "Happy Man" would be a great single but I was really opposed to changing it. We reached an agreement to keep it the way it is now on the album and then I would go down to Easley to record a more radio friendly version of it. I don't even know if it will be available commercially.

I remember a few years ago there was a collaboration 7" released under the guise 'A Loose Confederation of Saturday City States'. How did that all come about?

David [Lowery] introduced me to Vic [Chesnutt] and I wanted to go down there, he was down at Keane Studios. We just went in there, hung out, drank whiskey and recorded. That's about all there was to it. Vic is on my new record, on that song "Sunshine." That's him on the telephone.

Do you think you'll ever work with him again?

Oh yeah.

It seems like you two are a good pair to work together.

Yeah, he's great. Did you see him on Conan O'Brien the other night?

No, but I heard he played with Lambchop.

Yeah, there was about twenty people on stage. It sounded amazing.

Vic is starting to get his studio set up. He just bought the house next to his- I can't wait to see it.

He's going to put a studio in the new house?

I'm not sure. He got a really good deal on this old Victorian house. They've been doing work on it for quite a while.

So who is playing in you band for your upcoming tour?

Scott Minor has always played the drums for me. Jonathan Segal, who used to be in Camper Van Beethoven, is playing violin and guitar and some keyboards, and singing a bit. ⊛

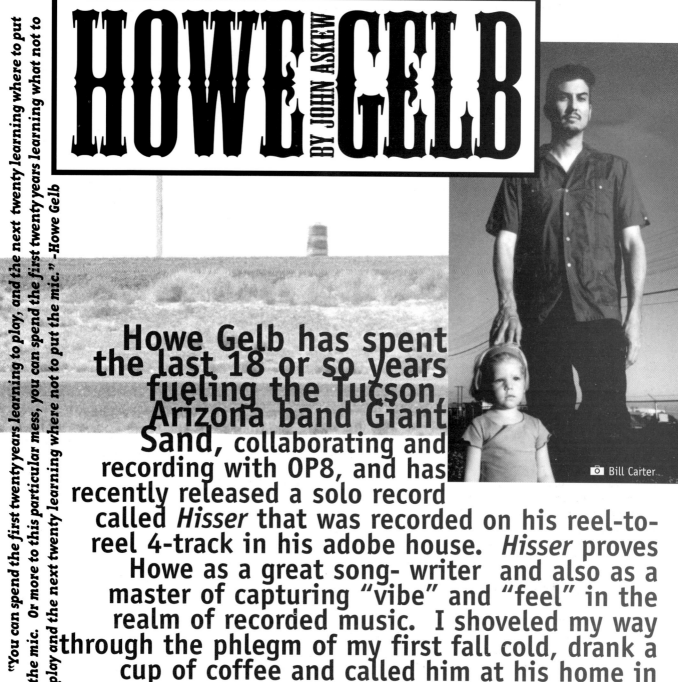

HOWE GELB

BY JOHN ASKEW

Photo: Bill Carter

"You can spend the first twenty years learning to play, and the next twenty years learning where to put the mic. Or more to this particular mess, you can spend the first twenty years learning what not to play and the next twenty learning where not to put the mic." -Howe Gelb

Howe Gelb has spent the last 18 or so years fueling the Tucson, Arizona band Giant Sand, collaborating and recording with OP8, and has recently released a solo record called *Hisser* that was recorded on his reel-to-reel 4-track in his adobe house. *Hisser* proves Howe as a great song- writer and also as a master of capturing "vibe" and "feel" in the realm of recorded music. I shoveled my way through the phlegm of my first fall cold, drank a cup of coffee and called him at his home in Tucson. We ended up talking for almost two hours about his new record, some history and recording philosophy of Giant Sand and OP8, and yes, of course, the desert.

How's the desert?

Deserted.

You talk about the adobe house that *Hisser* was recorded in. How relevant is this place?

The sounds that I get... um... adobes... well, they're pretty ingenious, structure-wise. The old ones are the thickest and with the tallest ceilings. The old one I used to live in had a lot to do with me even buying a house, with the lack of right angles, because I realize the virtue of the sound in a place like that. You know, I'm akin to it. It just makes good sense for every day conversation or living; breaking glass sounds better. They feel better. When I was in Chicago a few months ago I heard that Steve Albini lined his new studio with adobe.

Really? So in terms of your record, am I hearing the adobe?

You are probably hearing the sound of the room, the tone. Fortunately the less sophistication you have with recording, the more natural and room-like sounds you're gonna get. You use fewer mics, cheaper mics and put mics in technically wrong spots.

Are you spontaneous when you are recording? Or do you think a lot about it?

No. I like to forget about it as much as possible. I have mics set up so when the notion hits you in the middle of the night you can just walk into the room, push down the button and just start playing... and capture something. I think this is very inherent in many songwriters. You get a song idea on the way out the door, late for something, going to work, picking the kid up, somebody is waiting for you somewhere, and then advertently you get a notion for a song. If you have a Walkman around normally you'll throw it down. The result of that over the years is that I've lost the cassettes. I just filled up cassettes without ever learning the songs... just with these notions. So one way around it is you have it set up on 4-track to capture it on tape... you can go back to it later. That's what I tried to do with Hisser. Like "Shy of Bumfuck", they were ideas that I literally threw down really quick when I was walking out the door, the kid was outside, the door was open, and I just turned on the tape deck as if it were a giant walkman and quickly put the song down and left. You don't ever get moments like that on big studio recordings. Because you are always there for intended purposes. I like that off-handedness. I think that off-handedness even lends itself more to the room. The more you don't think about things, and DON'T think about recording, the more you can actually get what I think are the most honest recordings.

A lot of Hisser seems to be almost like it was a super-8 camera going. You can't erase Super-8 film, so you just turned it on, caught a feeling, printed it and watched. Did that come easily on Hisser?

Hisser is a licensing deal. If you get a real big recording deal you get a large amount of money to deal with. Which includes a large amount of people to deal with. That way of doing things is okay, there are certain advantages, but it's just not so instantaneous. So with licensing deals there is less money involved. The money for them (V2), that they spend, drops down to next to nothing. I just have the freedom of recording for next to nothing and doing whatever I want. So a lot of Hisser is just the allowance of me not having to deal with the "loop" [of big label bureaucracy] and to keep pushing some frontier in instantaneous recording.

That seems like the ideal of recording...

I know it is... and it only took me about 18 years. [laughs] Yeah, it seems like the nightmare of recording deals is dealing with people who don't care about music. Business people... Everyone has an adoration of sound or melody. Whether or not you fit in that camp, or whether or not you make a mess that they can relate to, you just want them to be moved by it. Then there is a connection and you feel good about everything. The lines of communication are now opened.

Was Hisser recorded first and then presented to V2?

No. I started doing what became Hisser mostly in light of John [Convertino] and Joey's [Burns] Calexico adventure. A few years ago things got weird... like 1996 and parts of 1997 were really fucked up years for a lot of people. A lot of that was happening around me and with me in the middle of it. And there were like five insane situations going on at the same time and it just took me away from everything. So in the interim John and Joey started having their own troubles with Friends of Dean Martinez so they were recording in their house. We all live in adobes. Joey lives across the street where we all had lived at one point singularly and now it was Joey's turn to have it and he started recording in that place and that's where most of the Spoke record was done. More evidence to the wonderfulness of adobe. So anyway, they had something going on and I was able to completely be removed from everything... and say, "Well, maybe it's time to set up a little 4-track in the living room." So I did, and I started coming up with these little bits and pieces. They were all way too slow and mopey. I did that for about a year and then it started changing, there was a little more spark in life and in the material. So when I realized I was coming up with this record I approached V2 with this notion.

A lot of really great records have come out of Tucson lately: both Calexico records, OP8, Hisser, Richard Buckner's Devotion and Doubt. There is something about the vibe and warmth of all those records that feels really good. My friend and I call it "desert core." Do you think the desert is really influential?

I think that whatever choices you make along the way, how ever you decide to live, whatever you end up going through while you live there, will influence what will happen next. Like in the next year. So in a sense... if I had never lived through a flood in Pennsylvania I might never have wanted to come out to the desert where there was no water. Whatever... I wasn't aware of it at that time. Turning John and Joey on to this place, did a lot for them being able to find sounds they liked or tapped them into some form of imagination. I see Joey taking a lot of different parts of things that already exist and mixing them up. If we didn't move down here, would he have made sounds like on the Calexico record? I doubt it.

Sometimes in order to fuel creativity you have to ditch the notions of being a "band" and just make a record out of it. Is this what it was like for the OP8 record?

Yeah. It was a better blend. The whole idea was really a chance for us to come to the table on equal terms instead of having to deal with

seniority like in Giant Sand. It was burdensome. When someone new comes into the band I don't know if they are going to be there for a year or ten years. So if I assume that they are an equal member of the band, what I have learned is that I am setting myself up for disaster. Because I want it to be more of a unit. If you don't know their staying power and they end up becoming a big part of the sound and they leave, then you're kind of fucked. When Giant Sand formed in 1980 it was an equal membership. One by one we split and by 1983 that didn't exist anymore. That notion always seemed the most appealing. Like R.E.M. or U2 that had all got together at the same time and stayed together.

Does this seem like an impossibility these days?

No, it did with Giant Sand though. Slowly I was able to figure what or what not to do to find the next idea that would feed some form of record or inspiration or sounds. Or whatever. Then when John came in 1987 it was like the band kept changing now and again and then I verbally offered up a partnership saying, "You know this could be great, to start all over again." To only having a drummer as a full partner. So with me and John doing a two piece thing. It was great. So free. And then from that point Joey came into the mess a couple of years later. Didn't know if he was staying or going. And then right when, [?] years down the road, "We're ready to initiate ya." That's when he started, more than ever, picking up side projects. I mean they were all related. They were all things we had become involved in. That was part of the wonderfulness of the cred[it] of Giant Sand, was the coming and going. Whether it was Victoria Williams coming and sitting in, or Lucinda Williams sitting in, o[r] Julianna or anybody...

It still seems that way, like it's a "cooperative."

Yeah. The other thing with Giant Sand was the fear o[f] incorporating too many sounds by too many othe[r] people, and then if they weren't around wha[t] would you do? OP8 allows us to come to the tabl[e] as equal, 25% partners. It makes it easier on y[ou] and also more effective. Because it just isn't s[o] heavy-handed. I think the result is really cool.

So does this mean that the new Gian[t] Sand record is a "project?"

No. You have four working bands within this on[e] band. Finally. Depending on the moniker we'[re] playing under you have to be psyched about th[e] band. Otherwise, it'll be unfocused. So if it's on[e] of us, it's just me, if its two of us it's Calexico, [if] it's three of us it's Giant Sand, and if its four of [us] it's OP8. But the tricky part is letting the oth[er] shit go enough, to then come in and trick yoursel[f] into thinking, "Oh yeah, all we have going [on] right now is Giant Sand." So it sounds like it whe[n] you record. Right now we're having op[en] discussions in the band about this because if th[is] can't happen then there is no point in doing it

Hisser CD cover

Do you still have touring to do as "Howe?"

That's sort of set up as an open door where I can jump in and out of that when I know I have free time. Or when I know for certain that Calexico will be gone. Normally when Calexico plays it's just the two of them. The irony is that Joey is playing the exact same guitar that I used to play when John and I were a two piece and he's playing the exact same amp.

What? Did you lose a bet with him?

When I saw him using it and it sounded fine, you think, "Cool." But then in the next instant through your head you think, "Am I dead?" And it's totally his own spin on it. You know his assembly of what he's heard through the years and what he's discerned that he likes. Which is what everybody does and they put together their own thing. But it was part of the surreality that it happened during those trouble years. One particularly bad night, I went to this little gallery downtown, I knew that they were having something in there and I walked in and John and Joey were playing in the corner, and the first feeling was like, "...Ah... warmth, comfort, home, friends, family." And then I go through and the brain starting deciphering things a little bit differently... "Wait a minute. That's John playing the exact same drumset we played as a two piece, Joey playing the guitar and the same amp. What is twisted here? It sounds like the same tones that we got!" The certain vintage of those things sounds good, just like the adobe walls do. But it was Joey's slant on things. It was weird.

Yeah, John has a way. His kit. Whatever. There is just something about the way he plays.

Yeah, John has a poetic delivery. He has a real knack for tone that he acquires.

Those drum sounds on the OP8 record are incredible. Your record has great sounds too. Especially the tune Grandaddy backs you on...

Yeah. The Grandaddy thing was a good evidence of us... me then getting something back from John. The advent of trajectory. You know, we get stuff from each other. That's why we hang together. Being with John allowed me one stoney day to trip over this drum set that was for sale outside this second-hand clothes store. I realized there was something about it that felt like tone... like something. I ended up buying it for $200 and it turned out being this really old '50's Ludwig drumset that when John saw it he couldn't believe it. I was like, "Yeah, man... it just felt like you were there." He helped me set it up and it was in the corner of the room. So when Granddaddy came in they just used those drums.

Did you use that kit on all the other drum tracks?

Yeah. I had that kit over at Wavelab when [Winston] played on those piano songs.

What is that sound on the beginning of "Explore You" and on the OP8 record? Sounds like the tape starting up or a laser or something?

Yeah. It's the tape starting. I did it intentionally three times. I had the pedal steel player Neil Harry, who I've used since the '80's but you've also heard on the Calexico records... that's another thing...

Ah... there the incest continues.

Yeah... but I had Neil just sustain a chord on the steel (because I was just recording that at the time... it was just me and him in the studio). So I started up the machine and I said, "Okay try it one more time" and I rewound it and said, "Okay just try it once more" and rewound it just a little less and did it so you got that "Boing, Boing, Boing."

In an interview with Craig Schumacher [@Wavelab] a friend did a few months back he talks about the train that goes by. Its the same train that's on your record, right? I mean are you guys all neighbors or something?

Yeah we all live pretty close. We all live in the old section of Tucson which is downtown. Well, his studio is down here... an old warehouse. Yeah, you hear that train. When you're blessed with the train coming in just right its like a cross between a free horn section and trajectory being on your side. Lining in and mixing so well. There are so many times when the train goes by and you're like, "Oh... if we could've just been recording that right then..." So I kind of forced the issue and went out there and recorded it going by and came in and with the Walkman and put it on tape intentionally. Hoped it would sound like you wanted the train to happen right there. Like a horn section.

Hmmm. The desert.

You know I remember you bringing up the whole "desert" thing before. I remember for years always talking down the effects of the desert on the sound.

How so?

I always figured it would be so fucked to um, to say you play "desert rock". It always sounded so stupid. To just blame your sound on where you live. I don't know why I feel that way...

You still do now? I mean it's too late... ha.

I definitely used to make it a point of saying, "Don't blame the desert on our crap... If we lived in New York it'd be the same." I mean I was born in Pennsylvania. I just feel more comfortable living in the desert. The flood was in 1972 and that's when I started coming out here... moved everything out a few years later. But now I think, I told Joey this the other day, that you come here from California, from the coast, and you're totally sounding like some Italian representation of a Western. And that's cool. Because it's sort of screaming at this

point. Instead of saying, "Yeah... [mopey voice] we play desert rock", it's just like "YEAH. Here's some Desert Rock for ya'!... BBRRRLLLLAAMMM!"

Yeah, funny, Portland is like the opposite of a desert. It rains nine months out of the year! Not to be cliche' but your stuff just feels like a desert. Even from the photo on the cover of _Dreaded Brown Recluse_; the car on a lonely, abandoned desert highway.

Yeah, but something that kind of woke me up to the point that it doesn't matter or feel bad anymore if it's Desert Core or Desert Rock or Desert anything. Life is too short to think it's cool or not cool. Somewhere along the way I realized... you know as you get older you kind of figure a few things out... ha... whatever it is, somebody has to refer to something in a category. It always seemed like the first instinct to a category is to rebel against it. It's in the very core of whatever rock is. But somehow it makes sense to them... and it doesn't mean that you know more about what's going on with your stuff than they do. So it's become a favorite pastime of mine lately to basically drop the issue. To be "Yeah, you're probably right, it probably IS desert core." Another thing that sort of backed me up on this somewhat is whenever you run into someone that is older and talk to them (because the older you get the less you run into people that are older and are still around). Like we just got done recording the Giant Sand record: we did half of it here in Tucson with John Parish and that was really cool and we did half of it down in Memphis with Jim Dickinson.

Who's that?

He used to be a session player for some of the early Stax recordings and he produced the third Big Star record. But for me... he played piano on "Wild Horses" on [the Stones'] _Sticky Fingers_. He's got a legacy. So we were talking when he came out here, when we're going to possibly use him as a producer, and he started talking about the sounds of the region. And he was talking about Memphis like a snake oil salesman. Almost like a swindler. Talking about how the sound sticks to tape in Memphis, because of its moisture. He said, "It's too dry out here. You won't get those sounds out here." [He sings...] "You gotta come to Memphis!" And I couldn't call him on it. I mean, if you're going all the way out there and spending some coin to record with him it's because you're believing what he's telling you. You don't doubt it. And I've listened to the Memphis stuff and the Tucson stuff and there are some weird differences... and what it is exactly?... you can tell me and you'll be just as right as me. ☸

MAYO
THOMPSON

by Steve Silverstein

The singles "Totally Wired" by The Fall, "Nag Nag Nag" by Cabaret Voltaire, and "Fairytale in the Supermarket" by the Raincoats share more than their importance in the history of British punk. They share the same producer, Mayo Thompson, who a decade earlier had created such psychedelic-era classics as the Red Krayola's *Parable of Arable Land* and his solo record *Corky's Debt to His Father*. One of the few people involved in underground rock through virtually its entire history, he continues to make relevant music with the Red Krayola today. I talked to Mayo during his Chicago visit last fall, between an afternoon in-store at Reckless Records and a concert that night at the Empty Bottle.

The Red Krayola first recorded a single for a label run by *"Keith Stefek, a local man in Houston who had made some money, and he was investing making records. He backed us up to make a single, but it didn't work out,"* and the single never came out. When Lelan Rogers of International Artists agreed to release their debut album, **The Parable of Arable Land**, they returned to Walt Andrus's studio where they'd recorded the single.

Andrus was *"Houston's most famous recording engineer. He had recorded everything. He had worked at a studio on Broadway, which was modeled on Gold Star Hollywood. He had a first class engineers ticket. He had worked in the first TV stations. He really knew his onions. He had a wonderful studio."*

"He did everything. He did the [13th Floor] Elevators' albums. He did us. Lost and Found album was done there. He worked with Euphoria - a guy named Wesley [Watt] had a power trio, one of the first power

trios in the mid '60s, before anybody else started doing this kind of stuff. First class sessions were being done in that studio all the time."

The Parable of Arable Land alternates conventionally structured songs with noise segments that share the title *"Free Form Freak-out"*. *"We had started off as a group and there were five of us. And then one night we got another person that was playing and it seemed like we'd be the six. So Steve [Cunningham] and Rick [Barthelme] and I decided we didn't want to be a band in that sense, we wanted to do something else. So we took it back to the three of us. But the Familiar Ugly were these people who still came along to all the gigs, and they got to be quite a sizable bunch, of variable size. So when we were playing at the battle of the bands where Lelan [Rogers] discovered us, playing in this mall, he heard this music and he came to us and he said, 'You know those crazy guys, you know, you could mix that all up.' And we*

said, 'Yes, that's what we're thinking.' So we went i the studio and it was just, was very straightforward because he had an idea, he understood, w understood. Everybody knew, we agreed that we we gonna try to do it this way. It was coherent. It was th right way of dealing with the stuff. Wanting to make point there that the difference between a song and th other stuff - song sounds like this, this sounds like th but it's the same stuff, the same material."

"We did all the freak-outs in one session, in or evening, in two halves. We exhausted one master tap and took a break, and put another one on and we back and did another session for 30 minutes like tho So we had an hour's worth of freak-out material, th free form material, with the Familiar Ugly. A guy w riding down the street on his motorbike and there we 50, 60 people standing outside the recording stud and he's going, 'What're you all doing?' 'Well we going to go in here and make a record in a minu

'Really, no kidding. That's interesting. Y'all are in a band, that's a lot of people.' 'No, these are our friends and... you wanna come in and bring your motorbike in?' 'Oh really? That's cool.' So this guy brought his chopper in. We said, 'Okay here's how it's gonna start. Ricky's gonna start the chopper, and when he starts it, everybody hits it. When you hear that thing kick in, everybody jump on it.' And there it went. Then you just filled up the tape and then somebody walked out and said, 'Okay, tape stopped,' and it's over. Everybody went out and had a cigarette and then came back in and tried it again 30 minutes later."

"The Familiar Ugly stuff was done 50 people down to eight tracks. There were eight microphones set up and all that down onto one channel. So it mixed itself, its organic self. That was all happened. We went back and pieced it together so that it would have a flow to it and all the while we were naïve. We went in the studio, if we'd had our druthers, we would have multitracked the free form stuff, because we could have done more of our own thing. As it was, it was just frozen. It was a documentary relation, documenting the recording."

"And then over the next couple of days we went in and did the backing tracks - we played them live," with few overdubs. Vocal tracks on some songs, such as "War Sucks," were also recorded live. "When we had the backing tracks, Roky [Erickson, of the 13th Floor Elevators,] was invited in to play the organ part on 'Hurricane Fighter Plane' and played the mouth organ part on 'Transparent Radiation.'"

Andrus's studio "had a beautiful room, you could get a really lovely sound in it. He had Ampex gear, and [used] good old-fashioned Neumann microphones for the vocals. Had a real echo chamber, a concrete floor, and a microphone and a speaker in it. Change the echo length by going in there and moving the microphone."

"Our first album was recorded mono. [The simulated stereo mix] is Walt Andrus's studio wizardry. We made the mono version and then like two days later I was around the studio, and they said, 'Come here, what about this for a stereo album?' And I sat there and listened to it and I said, 'Sounds okay to me. Crazy, but sounds okay.' It's not ricky to me. That was when people were finding out about things like phasing vocal sounds and all these kinds of strange devices, gimmickry. We were not making electronic music, we were using rock n roll instruments, but sometimes the music was related to electronic stuff."

"Walt's studio had these baffled walls. And also buckets of sand distributed here and there. Strange. Is that for fire, or for cigarettes? Or is that for acoustic reasons, or what is that? That's where the line, 'On the shelf I have six buckets and they are for you,' that's where this comes from. I can remember I'm standing there playing that song, I'm thinking to myself, I just thought, "On the shelf I have six buckets and they are..." You don't know what they're for, I don't know what they're for, but they're for you." He never found out the purpose of the buckets. "I like mysteries sometimes."

For **Coconut Hotel**, they returned to Andrus's studio. It "was done in a slightly more leisurely way, but we recorded all live in stereo, a pair of matched condenser microphones. They were set up in stereo in this room. It had a lot of space, it had a lot of natural acoustic depth and space, so you don't need a lot of reverb. The first piece, the idea is that we want to play these keyboards. There's no plan, we're gonna play 'em, we're gonna play 'em for awhile until we get tired and see what this piece does and see how long it goes on. The development of it is not in the usual musical way - there's not a melodic development, there's not a rhythmic development, there's not an intensifying of the dynamic strategy or anything. It's just always more or less the same. And then the next piece was built around the idea of an improvisation which had some kind of "kitschy" poetic elements. Like clarinets and playing into the water. It had a lot of atmospheric, koto going 'wunnh', strange, exotic instruments. And also the agreement on being abstract. The decision was taken to make an album that was obviously 180 degrees out from **Parable of Arable Land.** No drums, no songs, no rock, no rhythm. A hard-ass record, an experimental record in the sense of is there anything possible? Is there anything left to play? Is there anything to do with pop music at the time? Yeah. 'Hey man, peace and love feeling' - is there anything more than this going on in this music? Does it have more of a role in life than, 'Yeah, you're a good guy, you like good music. Doesn't that make you feel good? Yeah, that makes me feel good.' It makes me want to puke. Hippie positivism is really repulsive. Not because they were repulsive, it was a pleasant sentiment. It was a kind of sentiment. At the time it was a really highly charged atmosphere, because of the politics of the '60s, people claiming that they knew what to do. How could you know, I don't know. I don't believe you know. **Coconut** was a real effort to push the topic."

"**Live 1967** is what we were doing around that time. When we'd go to play live, it was not with the purpose of making terror - it was with the purpose of the artist as the agenda. This is on the menu tonight, what do you think of that. When we were in California, we borrowed a machine, a 3M stereo portable machine that was really cheap. [We used] that kind of bronzy colored, real thin tape, and recorded on both sides. And just did it very primitively - had a couple of microphones and just put 'em there, and let the frequencies sort themselves. We learned that that would happen by doing **Parable.** We knew that we would be alright. We were satisfied also with the sound, it just worked out. We dragged this tape recorder with us for the three or four or five days that we were there and recorded everything."

"The only thing that happened bad on that trip was we recorded with [John] Fahey in Sierra Sound, we went and did like two hours worth of 16-track recording of the same kind of stuff, of him doing our thing. He knew what we were doing, it was his thing - he was doing the same thing. We came to California and we were asked, 'Who do you want to meet?' and we said John Fahey, he's the only one. And

they said 'John Fahey, that's interesting.' So happened that the guy we were staying with knew him, so we were able to meet him, and have John sit in with us, but those tapes were lost, alas. They were done 16-track [at] Sierra Sound. I don't know what kind of stuff he had at the time, very early 16-track. All that West Coast bunch were friends of John's, we didn't know anybody."

For **God Bless the Red Krayola,** "we had some tunes. When I came back from California to make that, we'd fallen out with IA over the stuff with John Fahey, and then they got in touch with me because **Parable** had done business and they really wanted to go on. They said, 'Would you like to make another album? Please come back.' So I went back to Texas, but they wanted to know what the songs were, and I didn't want to tell them everything. So I had some tunes, I played some tunes for them. Went in and made a demo at Walt Andrus's with Frank Davis, but luckily Frank Davis is out there. On the day that I went in there making the demo, he had an idea that we were going to make an experiment using slapback. So the demo is just, I wish I had this demo - it's insane. I was trying to play with the gaps and the delays and so on like that, to demo these songs which are on **God Bless.** It was insane. When [IA] heard it, they just went kind of like, 'Oh oh oh oh okay. Just go to the studio and do it.' So a lot of it was written on the fly, on the feet. Pieces were improvised and made up. Go home at night, and 'I got an idea.' A lot of that stuff is sorted out in the studio, raised in the studio. It took us about a month to make that - we had a little time to make that. Engineer was Jim Duff. One time, when we were recording "Victory Garden", he suddenly lit up. He like woke up. Suddenly he started doing some things and then all of a sudden we had this classic sound. Hey, that's it, what is that? It sounds like real country and western music, you know? He started talking about his own songwriting. He had written some like 250 songs for his wife"

"That was back in that studio that had been modeled on Gold Star, where Doug Sahm had cut 'She's About a Mover'. That was a real recording studio in the grand style. It was modeled on Gold Star. It had like the little Gold Star room and then it had the big Gold Star room. So it was okay, the gear was a bit primitive. IA had bought [the studio]. They got tired of, they thought, 'We're not gonna pay Walt anymore, we're gonna have our own studio. **God Bless** was recorded like 7-track. Mostly we recorded 4-track, but when we needed extra tracks we could fly in 3 outboard tracks from submixing stuff. The other thing that was going on there was we were in this, for us, kind of technical wonderland. We eschewed all technical embellishment. EQ was all set flat. We recorded flat. No reverb on that record until the very last tune. 'Night Song', it drifts, the reverb is jacked up, very obviously, but before that there is no reverb. All you hear is just the acoustics of the room."

"Then I fell out with IA again after that was over. I went back and started working with Walt and made my solo album, **[Corky's Debt to His Father]**, at Walt's place. By that time it had gone up to Ampex 8-track. He had just beautiful gear. He had some really high-class speakers. They looked, funny cabinets, they had this kind of decorative stuff on them. They didn't look like this technological aesthetic - they looked more domestic and had beautiful sound. The board was good, rooms had good sound, mixing room had a good sound to it. That took 3 1/2 months to make. Frank [Davis] said, 'I don't think we should crash this record, I think we should take our time on it.' So it took us 3 1/2 months, some hours a day for 4 days a week, and then we would take 2 or 3 days off to think about it. The other difference was that I had written all the tunes before we got there. Like 90% of 'em I had the tunes there. I talked to an arranger about what I wanted to do. Lined up the musicians, and we recorded it with different ensembles - the idea being to have variety of ensembles but unity of sound."

For the Saddlesore single, he returned to the "same studio, but then the studio was starting to fall apart. We were working around, piecing it together. [Walt Andrus] had started Gulf Pacific Records, he was like a week away from being a very rich and powerful fellow, and then it kind of like all collapsed. He had a soul singer, a white soul singer, who was signed to CBS contract so he was doing things that were making a lot of money. He had fun doing other kinds of things like doing stuff with us. He had a plan, a really wonderful plan, to record music really fast, topical music, and he liked working with me probably because I could work fast. [He wanted to make] music based on the news. Make it one week, press it and bring it on the street. In the next week you're selling out of the back of the truck. That was his idea, way ahead of the times. But we had to kind of put the studio back together in order to make the Saddlesore single. That was another one of those things that sat on the WEA A&R table for a couple of weeks. They were tempted, almost bit, almost liked it, didn't like it. Frank sang because people didn't like my voice on my solo album. Some people either loved the solo album or hated it. The reason most people hated it was because they didn't like my singing. The way we'll get around that, we'll have Frank sing. Frank had been a hero to me - I learned a lot from him. There's a lot in common we had in terms of the vocal sound and the pitching and all that sort of stuff, just attack. And so he [sang], and then that didn't go. So I just quit for a while. I stopped. I just thought I must be misunderstanding something because I had been under the impression that the idea was to get into the game and push the envelope, try to do interesting things with it. Turned out that people want you to get in there and deliver known goods, that seemed to be the point - still is. I understand that, but I still play the game. Feed a few familiarities but put 'em in a funny shape, because I'm still looking to see, is there anything else? How many ideas are there?"

Corrected Slogans "took three years because we didn't have any money. It took awhile to finish it off. The political infighting in the organization, inside Art & Language, also meant that it had a certain kind of shape. Plus I was living in America and I was

working mostly with people in England. Some of the basic tracks I recorded at home on a Nagra - set it up, limiter is off, really crash it, load the tape up with sound. Some music was recorded in a basement studio which later became, which is now Philip Glass's studio in New York on Greene Street. As I recall they did have a Neve board in there, some first class gear. So we recorded some of that stuff there, and then we finished off a lot of the stuff in England with the Art & Language. [We did] the vocals in Stonesfield in [a] studio where they were working on the prototype of the SSL desk. The first SSL desk."

"Every time we could think of how to use a gimmick, we used it. Some funny reverb or some funny delay or some funny this or that or the other stuff. It's hard to tell because it's pretty well integrated, synthesized in there as a gimmick, but it is also an index of gimmicks, studio gimmickry, made present as gimmicks, for novelty's sake. 'Hey, listen, here's a funny noise.'"

"And I guess then after that I started the band again. I started playing Red Krayola again. Jesse Chamberlain got a deal with Warner Brothers, with Radar Records which was financed by Warner Brothers."

About the same time, Thompson began to produce records, starting with the Monochrome Set. "What happened was Rough Trade was getting started and they said, 'Do you want to produce a record for us?' Sounds interesting. I never had really produced any records before myself, in the usual sense." He cites mixing as a central part of his role as a producer. "I didn't set up the microphones and run all the lines, but I mixed Stiff Little Fingers' first album. I mixed Raincoats' first album. It was hands on running the board, before boards got so sophisticated I couldn't run them anymore, or they wouldn't let me. I mixed some singles for The Fall, 'Fiery Jack', 'How I Wrote 'Elastic Man'', 'City Hobgoblins', 'Totally Wired', those singles.'"

"Different bands have different requirements. Stiff Little Fingers was a matter of setting it up, because they knew what they were doing. They were a bar band basically. They were a BAND that could just play that stuff in its sleep. So it was a question of just making sure to get everything straight up. Other times, like with Monochrome Set, it would be arguing a little bit about this or that part. Same thing with the Raincoats. I gave a suggestion to Vicky about the violin playing when I first heard them. So I was involved in all the stages of the development of the album there. Sitting in at rehearsals, talking to them about songs, talking about arrangements. Saying, 'The violin, have you ever heard of the Velvet Underground?' No, Vicky hadn't heard of them, did not know about John Cale and didn't know about Tony Conrad or LaMonte Young or any of that stuff. She was a trained classical fiddler, so she tried to familiarize herself with the aggression and evil that had been done with this instrument which was also interesting. The other thing that I think I brought to production was performances. If a musician trusts you, wants to work with you, they'll put out. You can help with it. Nobody held my hand in a studio when I first started, but people were very friendly. Always

watching, so you learn bit by bit. It was that kind of a process. Try to do as little as possible - try not to interfere. I never had a Mayo Thompson sound. There is not a Mayo Thompson touch to all kinds of recordings that I've ever made. My criteria has always been to be true to the music that I record that the band has played, and to say something if I had an idea where I thought it was something off or wrong. At least to say 'Do you want it this way because here's what I could think. This could sound like a mistake to somebody.' Or 'What if we did this next?' those kind of things. But mostly hands off."

"I worked in Kingsway Studios, which was owned by Deep Purple. Did a lot of work in that studio, which had a very nice Trident board and a good Studer 24-track, fantastic machine. That's where we recorded the first [Raincoats] single and mixed some of their album, even though it had been recorded at another studio up in Cambridge. We also did Stiff Little Fingers. It was done in a really primitive basement recording studio setup. Primitive in the sense that it was clean, it was coherent, it was a good recording, it was a good tape to signal ratio, and all that other kind of stuff. It wasn't like fighting a battle to record with improper gear. It belonged to the days of punk. We got there, we went up to look at the studio, and arrived in the session before us, the Mekons were making that first single of theirs ['Where Were You']. It was a good place. [The Red Krayola single] 'Wives in Orbit' was recorded in Olympic Studios. It was an old church in St. John's Wood. It was just part of the Commonwealth, people knew of places to go."

"The Fall, I met them in England. We worked with them up in Rochester, in a studio just outside of, a bit north of Manchester, toward where Mark lived, Mark Smith. They had been with IRS before - they'd made **Dragnet** and some other stuff. I had seen them, and they were riveting, really good. Mark was really good, and really knew what he was all about. I saw them play the Palladium one night and somebody doused him with a bucketful of water and he didn't say anything. He triumphed in this war. He was a fister, and a very smart guy and a hard guy. And then one day Geoff [Travis, head of Rough Trade] said, 'Oh, you're gonna do some stuff for The Fall.' Geoff and I had kind of like a little distribution of functions. Geoff also inspired confidence in bands when he was there because he was really committed to the stuff. He was behind you. So his presence was always conducive to a good atmosphere when I was recording things. He trusted me. I think the only thing, [it] kind of came to where he and I kind of had a parting of minds, it was on drum sounds. Because there came a moment where he was hearing music and thinking, well the drums are they never did 'em very well. Which I don't think is true at all. I think we always were true to our drummers. think our drummers were not always fantastic. But that was when it was getting into, that was venturing off into a domain where we were saying, 'We're going t have an ideal'. We're going to have an idea of what kind of sound we want. Rather than here's the sound th band has got, or here's the sound and let's see what w can do with it. Which takes you into the domain [where] this sound needs to have a syntactic quality to it. People recognize that this is modern because the drums are way up and really loud and big. And also it was making allowances for the fact that a lot of people who were recording music, they're going into Abbey Road but they can't sing technically. 20 years before the idea of going into Abbey Road and recording something would have been just like, 'You wanna go to the moon?' just as unlikely as that. But after [punk] then anybody could do it. It was proven. You had a really high quality sound of recording and some very poor performances in some cases, but rich in feeling frequently. Poor musical attributes maybe it's understood, but powerful nonetheless, really powerful."

"I did [James] Blood Ullmer's album [Are You Glad to Be in America?] I'd met him in the same studio where Philip Glass later recorded in New York. I had met him because Ornette was recording Body-Meta in there. I was in New York, and belonged to RCA and supervised all the tracking sessions. I had been going to rehearsals every day, listening to the band, listening to the arrangements, learning the tunes, and knowing what was going on. Go to the RCA and we were going to cut 12 Blood Ullmer tunes in one day. Some of them were eight [or] nine players and some of them just three or four. They're working with the tracking engineer, just making sure. Lost one bass drum track where the mic slipped and I missed it, I didn't catch it. I had to patch it."

"There was a Space Station [Ursa Major] reverb, [which] played a big role on that. We did lots and lots of layers of reverb with tiny delays behind them, makes them sound huge. The standards we were working to were, when they're talking about Blood, they were calling him Hendrix, was he gonna be the next Hendrix. There was a criteria on getting the guitar to be really powerful and big, so it was so big that all the other instruments fit beside it. Because he had a wonderful guitar sound, just a killer guitar sound, and we built it all around that whole thing, and then this voice occasionally."

"'Nag Nag Nag' [by Cabaret Voltaire], that was in, I can't remember the name of the studio. I did a lot of stuff in there. The Blue Orchids did their single ['The Flood'/'Disney Boys'] in there. The thing that's funny is when we recorded 'Wives in Orbit', Geoff was there, Edwin Pouncey was there, and [Steven Mallinder], and [Richard H. Kirk], and Chris [Watson] also. The one I got along with was [Mallinder] mostly, and wound up having a progressively kind of like a real difference of opinion with [Kirk]. He had a difference of opinion with me. I didn't even know we had fallen out - I found out eventually. But got to work on "Nag Nag Nag". It's the only time I ever worked with them, and I always say it was their best song. They made some great stuff. I have some cassette recordings and stuff from the '70s that nobody's ever heard. But "Nag Nag Nag" is a great tune. That was one of the first times working also with Adam Kidron engineering. Very good engineer, he was great to work with. In fact, it was through working with him that I stopped working so much with Geoff. I

started kind of like moving in this direction. By the time we started making Kangaroo? I was absolutely trying to get away from this other position. Not get away from, but just change it."

"I wish I could remember the name of that studio where we mixed Kangaroo? - same place where we mixed Blood's album. They were doing a lot of funk music in there so it was very up-to-date. Good tech, expensive. Right by the British Museum. I forgot the name."

"Mastering records for me was like the final step, and the key to the thing. I always worked with Porky, Porky Primecut. And Porky had this little pair of brass

> "EVERY TIME WE COULD THINK OF HOW TO USE A GIMMICK, WE USED IT. SOME FUNNY REVERB OR SOME FUNNY DELAY OR SOME FUNNY THIS OR THAT"

scissors and a pair of really plain vanilla bland little speakers. You would get in there and you knew that's what it really sounds like right there. No matter what anybody's system worldwide, this is objectively the problem, right here. So, what's the last thing we can do? Always aspiring in the studios to get everything to be able to take it into a master room and cut it flat, because you couldn't be there every time. But Porky was great to work with. And for me, that's the only room I'm kind of interested in, someplace where if it sounds good in there, it's gonna sound fine anywhere. That's the thing that always struck me also about high-class recording, really good technical recordings. You listen to a record like Thriller, Thriller sounds great on every system. The important stuff comes through on every system. It's been recorded correctly. Every picobel is just perfect. By contrast you take a lot of these independent records and you put 'em on one stereo and they sound like something and you put 'em on another stereo and they sound like it's busted, something's wrong with it. The big meat and potatoes is in between the busted sound and the high end sound."

"I don't have any problems with noise. Some people don't like noise, I don't care - doesn't bother me. Tape noise, hiss. It can be distracting if it's the first thing you notice, that there's a lot of crackling. On the whole, my game has been to try to make the most out of what little there is."

"In England, in the industry, a lot of places you would go into, they would have an Allison board, or something like that - that would be the range you could rise to. Or they would have some kind of Craftsman board. Or a Soundcraft board - Soundcraft were very popular in UK studios. I recorded in a 16-track state-of-the-art Auratone studio, that's where we did [Red Krayola single "Days of Future Pilots"]

for example. Which was completely strange sound. We're now going to the small box to record this record. They had some big Auratones. It was a completely strange setup. They had big Auratones and little. It was a unified Auratone system. I'd never heard anything like it. Auratone speakers, you'd find them in every studio, it's like here every studio you find [Yamaha] NS-10s. And then in England, you would find NS-10s, and sitting next to them was a couple of Auratone boxes. And this was sort of like a worst-case scenario, here's what it could sound like."

"I suppose my experience of recording has been largely, like everybody else's, shaped by the technological developments. What does this mean to me, what does that represent a way that I've got all of this potential? Trying to learn how to use it, trying to find out if there's something that it can do that could teach me something I don't already know but that I might also be able to learn how to integrate."

"I'm one of those guys who, if they said to me, 'Can you record de, de, de in here?', I'm more than likely, even if the place is fucked, gonna say yeah, because I don't care. I mean if I had my way, I have some equipment of my own that I've bought, I have ways of working. But one is always operating within material constraints as well, no question about it."

"Blackwing was a great studio. Vince Clark was a partner with Eric [Radcliffe], and by that time they were even starting a label and Vince liked it. Daniel Miller, I've known him since the days of the Normal and Rough Trade and stuff. It was through him that I got asked to work there. I did two records there."

"[One] thing I learned from Eric which was very good, working at Blackwing, was to go to mono. Which was something I had kind of lost track of. When we first started recording, we recorded mono, because of sound from the Phil Spector recordings. He reminded me of that mono. It was after working with him I got to the point where I would take all the records and at a certain moment I would take a mix and just put it in mono and listen to it for awhile, just to see what was going on and make sure the frequencies were organized right. That was the other thing I learned progressively more and more about was mixing by frequencies, and the master of that for me was Conny [Plank]. His whole technique was built around frequency mixing, which was perfect for me, because my criteria in mixing alternative music and punk music was to make sure that you could hear everything. My imagination was digital was going to be the perfect mode to make punk records in, because you would have the technical presence of all frequencies but they would not be competing with each other. They would just be there and you could really jack it up and you get a lot of color out of it. Even though it would be cold sound, it wouldn't matter. I have tried it; I was wrong. There are no rules about that. There are no easy algorithms that run along the lines of, 'Oh, this is a perfect format for this.' Maybe it depends on the tune."

"Conny was really fun to work with, although he had this strange way of talking about things in terms of pictures all the time. 'I'm trying to get the picture of this mix, let me see.' 'I've almost got the picture together.' This figurative use, is he talking Lichtenstein to me, is he talking about some picture theory representation? What is going on here? I didn't know quite what he meant. It was coherent in the way that he did it. He had a real ear for experimentation, will to experiment. And a love of music in general, that didn't mean that he felt like he was wasting his time if it was something that was not going to make a million dollars - he was still interested. Met a lot of strange characters there - met [Holger] Czukay, met Jaki Leibzeit, met Rene Tinner."

"Worked in Can's studio, that's another studio that's quite an interesting studio. I did some advertising music in that place, and I tried to make a couple of singles in that place, one with Robert Gorl from DAF mixing, producing. Failure. But wonderful sound, wonderful room, an old cinema with canvas stuck on the walls, and it's kind of set off by baffles here and there. You can draw the curtains around, but it's just like a big, open quiet room. Of course, because they're German hippies, there are stars painted all over everything. They're strange. Rene Tinner is a Swiss. He's the tech man behind all the Can records. I wouldn't exactly describe him as a hippie. He likes to drive his Porsche 928 at 160 miles an hour."

Part of **Three Songs on a Trip to the United States** was recorded live by Plank. "He brought his mobile out, and set it up outside this place, and recorded the gig. On great big reels, not 2" reels, but the next size, the ones, 'There's a machine that takes these things?' They're like wheels of trains. The three songs themselves were done in his studio but not with him, they were done with the engineer of Einsturzende Neubaten, their producer [Jon Caffery]." Thompson attributes the drum sound of those songs to the room at Conny's studio. "It was a funny setup. There was a room that was about the same size as the control room and [also] kind of a half-room, but there was no wall [between them]. And there was a big rest of the room and there was a grand piano and an organ. It was like a synthesizer museum, he saved everything he ever had. The drums, just set 'em on a rug in this thing, and there was a wall with these baffles behind it, and you could open these things or close them. You'd get a hard reflection off the back or you could open the baffles and get absorbed."

With Pere Ubu, "I was like the guitar player on those records. The unhappy guitar player on **Song of the Bailing Man**. By that time the really miserable guitar player. I kept thinking to myself, when Anton Fier was saying to me, here's this little thing [sings baroque line]. As I understand it, all I need to do is get one of them right and you could fly it on to the whole session. Why don't you play it? It was that kind of a session. And we need some more tunes. Why doesn't someone just write some more tunes? I was ready to go home; I was pissed off. They hated me and I hated them by that time - it was just a miserable mess. Ravenstine doesn't talk to me still. But wonderful guys, great band. Fun to work with in a strange sort of [way]. They were

operating at a higher niveau than I'd ever worked at before. Going on tours with bands, big-time managers making lots of money as well - we did Ubu well. I learned a lot working with them. Painesville studio [Suma Recording Studio], for me, it was, it already had a lot of problems. When I lived in England, I worked in shoestring operations, improvising. Let's win the war, that kind of insane mentality attached to it. And then coming back to a comfortable studio in an old barn, with carefully chosen old pieces of wood here and there, and a fireplace, and a perfect piano. And over there the kitchen. It just reeked to me of this American riches and fat-ass luxury for no fucking good reason. I hated it at some level. At the same time, Ken and Paul [Hamann] were salt of the earth greatest guys, no pretense. They're just doing it because this is the best way to do it. Nothing against that studio."

"Recording with Ubu was a different kind of thing. My job in there was to write tunes, to write guitar parts. Typically all I had to do was write a guitar part for David to take it over and use that as the vocal melody, and then I had to go and find another guitar part. That got to be a problem sometimes. I would get a guitar part and then that would be the structure of the tune. In the Red Krayola, that's the way Red Krayola tunes are built. With him, the voice goes down here and suddenly we're duplicating things. And my harmonies on my guitar are eating up harmonies that the voice needs to be heard properly. So I've got to go somewhere else in the mix."

> # "THIS WAS LIKE THE ESSENCE OF POP MUSIC, THAT'S THE ELEMENT WE LIKE, THE CHEESY BIT."

"The Art of Walking [was] a really interesting session. It was done in the wintertime. It was kind of cobbled together. David has a very dramatic relation to production in general. He's an intense and very serious fellow, and so he's moody as well. He'd go up and down and you didn't know if you were getting it, was it good, what did it sound like. It came together, but I had no oversight. I was already in a difficult situation because in England, where I was playing, you had people like Paul Rambali saying that I was the guy who was killing Pere Ubu, because I had ruined their sound. I was making them arty. It was an ugly situation the whole thing, but it was kind of fun."

"The recording of [Song of] the Bailing Man was slightly different because it was really done in pieces. Adam [Kidron] would have somebody over from the office and they would sit there for a couple of hours and do something. It was not a band tracking in the usual sort of way. Sometimes we would be

doing band tracking, and tracking is, like on **Corky's Debt,** the song "To You", which is the first song on side two, it took us all day. We spent one day trying to record that. We made 30, 40, 50 takes of this tune, and still didn't get it. We walked out at the end of the night thinking we didn't have it. But with Ubu, there was not this kind of possibility. People would go nuts if you had to play it 50 times. So it was more, sort of a pretentious atmosphere I would say. And there's a tune on there I wrote the structure of, I can't remember what it was called [sings "Petrified"]. We played a version of it, and we were in the mixing room, and Adam had it all up. And then we came to this [sings heavy part], Anton was playing the toms, and he jacked up the volume. It sounded... to me it sounded fantastic. This was like the essence of pop music, that's the element we like, the cheesy bit. 'Yeah, push it up right there, that's the groovy bit, right?' That never happened. That mix didn't exist. It didn't go down on the record like that. It didn't go down with any color, life, or excitement. So I call that record the 'Song of the Boring Man'. It's a good record, it's just not something I listen to."

"The Chills record **[Brave Words]**. The record I'm dissed for my production on. Yes. I plead partially guilty on the grounds that I was working on an extremely strict budget. I was told we want to do 16 songs and we've got three days. I said, 'We're gonna track 16 songs, three days, no problem.' 'No, no, no, track and mix.' The last recording session was 20 hours long. My ears were bleeding at the end of the session for one thing. The other thing that happened was I didn't master that record. I handed over a tape that was balanced. In my opinion, it was ruined in the mastering room. In the sense that it became muffled, something technically happened there. Now the guy who was their manager, who organized it, apologized to me for that, and said it was not your fault. Martin [Phillips] seems to associate this, he makes it out to be my responsibility. I hope not, because I enjoyed working with him, very much. If I had been in a position to make a red hot commercial record, which is what they were talking about, I would have had to do a number of things. Number one I would have had to hire a drummer, because she couldn't play the tunes and hold the rhythms. She'd get playing and then she'd get tired and then they'd want to make another take. I'm saying, 'What we've got to do is we've got to make some takes and when we get a good drum take, then we've got to go back and build on this, because she ain't gonna make it. If she has to play long enough until you get a perfect guitar part, you're never gonna get there.' It was definitely a really interesting, strange studio in Victoriaville. It used to be a morgue. It was haunted and they had to perform an exorcism in this studio in order to be able to even get in there and record. We didn't get the good ghosts on our side, apparently, when we made that record. Although that record has got some chills in it, which is that it does have that effect - that physiological, epiphenomenal. I don't mind it at all. It maybe doesn't sound as good as it could. The thing would be nice to have the tapes and go re-master. I'm sure one could make a very acceptable piece out of it. Sold maybe 6000 copies, I made a little bit of change from that one, that was good."

The Shop Assistants' *Will Anything Happen* "was done in Scotland. That was when I was working with Geoff [Travis], and Geoff just said, 'Why don't you go to Scotland tomorrow and produce this album?' So I got on the train and went into Scotland and worked with that band. That was another one of those difficult bands because the guitar player wants to play his Les Paul, and he's playing one clean track, two fuzzy tracks, one dirty track, and one harmony track. He hears all this guitar stuff that's going on there. He's massing the guitar. I know how that works because that's how I built Primal Scream [*Sonic Flower Grove*]. There's no way to get Jim McGuinn 12 string guitar sound in 1987, anymore, it's just not there. For one thing the Rickenbacker 12 string doesn't have three pickups anymore, it's only got two. Technology has changed. Those sounds are gone. They just don't exist anymore. You can simulate 'em, that's what we had to do. Same thing with the Shop Assistants. It was a question of electronically, trying to keep the power of the guitar but without blowing out the delicacy of that woman's voice. Deal with various, diachronic relations of ability to play. Some can play and some can play less well. Shop Assistants were very nice people to work with. I enjoyed making that record, it was easy, and Scots have a real grasp of the pop syntax. I had a really strong feeling that I wanted to make a really interesting two record set with them, one which had a lot of power and punk and then some other tunes were unplugged acoustic, where the quality and delicacy of her voice would be allowed to shine. I tried [to get both on the album]. Tried to showcase a little bit, had a few fights."

"Some interesting mixing problems with Felt's *Poem of the River*. First mix I made of it, I had a true American pop record. I had Lawrence's voice out there like Frank Sinatra's. It was just right there. Freaked him out, he wouldn't have it. So we had to go back and try to remix the goddamn thing, to pull the voice down and still keep all the power relations. Upsetting to me to have to go back and remix that record. But I played it for [Alan] McGee [from Creation] and McGee said 'Yeah. I don't know if we'll convince Lawrence, we'll try to.' Lawrence wouldn't have it."

"The self-titled [Red Krayola album from '94] was done here [Chicago]. That one was done in Albini's [old house]. We tracked everything over here and mixed everything over there. The record where we started doing things ourselves was *Amor. Amor and Language* was the first record where I really started producing ourselves in a home - recording at home, taking it in the studio and finishing it off if necessary, doing the mix there. That and most of *Hazel* was recorded that way. *Fingerpainting* is more various because *Fingerpainting* represents some recordings from archival material from like '66. From gigs where we recorded, we had a stereo machine, and didn't have enough money and didn't have enough tape, so we'd record one night on one channel and then record the next night on another channel."

"When we record these days, I've got a digital 8-track, a D-88, Tom's got one, and Albert's got one. So we have 24-track capacity. We rent ourselves a Mackie, a bigger Mackie. I've got a Mackie at home, a little Mackie 8-channel which is good enough to do the basic track layouts and stuff. No reverbs, no graphic equalizers, no nothing. Just counting, straight empirical tests, that's what it sounds like. Is that Okay? Yes? No? And then mixing it up, also using analog bits here and there. Some people don't like digital sound - I don't care. I know that analog is richer, and if you put on a vinyl record and you've got yourself some gold cable and [a] platinum stylus, and piece of little cedar there, you're bound to hear some real stuff. That's the ideal listening circumstances, where fidelity is a trivial issue, because then it's possible to strike the relationship between a high-fidelity and some other kind of fidelity. If I had lo-fidelity it doesn't mean that I can't afford it or I'm lousy, it just means I know I got that, I wanted it. I want that sound."

"If I had a lot of money I would buy myself a matched pair of AKG condenser mics; I might buy a good Neumann. I used to have a Sennheiser shotgun mic which is really a very nice mic, I had an AKG barrel mic, it's got a tube in it." Right now, he just has a Shure SM 57.

"When I go into the studio with Albert, for example, I get concerned about vocals. It's always been a bugbear for me, because some people like the voice and some people don't like the voice. If you've heard the band live, you know that I'm expressive. On stage, I push it. But in a studio it's all cooled down, more abstracted, notated versions of a lot of the tunes. Albert, he doesn't like when I want to do too many vocal versions. This kind of perfectionism to get absorbed in, [he considers it] the wrong approach. At the same time, you don't want things to sound wrong. So you do just enough to get beyond that threshold, and then trust also the fact that even the best run in the world and 100% clarity of judgment still could make a mistake. 20 years from now I could hear something I don't like. I listen to *Parable of Arable Land*, 'and it's mine', I sing some kind of tone to the side at the end of 'Hurricane Fighter Plane'. 'And it's mine', a sort of strange kind of jazz interval, and I always thought, wow, people are not going to like that, it just doesn't sound right, because most people are not familiar with something that suspends like that, generally not in pop music anyway. I'm so glad I that I didn't cave to the cliché."

"The other thing is that instinct and intuition play a big role, and you trust yourself. If you hate it later, that's the way it goes. But not having any is bad. There's no record we've made that I'm ashamed of at all, nothing I'm embarrassed about. *Black Snakes* is a hard album for some people because it's a mean record. Did that in Blackwing, in London."

"Sometimes I go in the studio and mix, but I like to mix at home. The 'Chemistry' single of ours, that's mixed on a Trident board, in a 24-track studio. I can drive the Trident board so that it distorts. It's got a sweet distortion too. It's got a nice little funny little note in there. People tell me I mix funny. People tell me I have a funny ear. *Fingerpainting*, we did all the sessions and then handed the tapes over to Jim [O'Rourke] and he couldn't mix 'em, not to my satisfaction, so we had to take it back and mix it ourselves. Albert mixed the freak-outs. I mixed the tunes. I mixed parts of the freak-outs and then sent it over to Albert."

"I have two little Sony speakers that are [small]. It's got a little cardboard speaker, and that's what I mix it on. Foolproof, I check it with headphones just to make sure the balance is sometimes like that, and then I'll make a mix. And then I'll find out if I can trust it by taking it away and trying it in some other place."

"Marina Rosenfeld. She works in Austria but she's an American. She graduated Cal Arts. What she's doing for me is she's assisting me in an opera. The Art & Language/Red Krayola opera, which has been 20 years in the works now, it'll come out in 2001, next year. I'll have it ready more or less. She's trained, [can] sight-read. I write music but I can't sight-read worth a damn. I also wrote some of that stuff so long ago, I can sit there and laboriously work out what it is. The other thing is I can dictate to her more or less, I can sing, I can say I want it to go like [sings] and she can write it down. So it's gonna facilitate things a lot. She makes interesting music on her own. She does something similar to what we; do she comes from completely other side of the thing. She starts with fields and colors and harmonies and blocks of sound like that and builds up everything out of [them]. She rarefies or synthesizes some bits. I start at the other end, I start with the bits that I want and everything else follows from there. Because Miles Davis is my hero I suppose. I've learned a lot from Miles, the way he organizes sounds. I've learned a lot from just the idea of jazz also, of organizing from the top line down. She's more field oriented, a little more chromatic field, harmonic field. Plus the other thing with her music is she's using samples and presets."

"Helped mix [her record **Theforest-thegardenandthesea**], did some mixing with it. I did produce, I recorded one of the sessions where some of the music was put down. I made a mix of it, she made another mix of it, and then she took that mix and did some trickery and put them together. There are some bits that I worked on that are in there but I didn't have overview of the whole time, it was her thing. She's doing really interesting things with turntables, and doing interesting things where she presses acetates, discrete numbers of records. Keeping alive the various stages of the history of the whole process, understanding that it's a very physical process. It's happening in real-time."

Thompson's plans for the near future include "making a boogie record. Got the follow-up to *Fingerpainting* sorted out more or less, got the structures in mind, in shape. We're beginning to process that. The record after that make a boogie record. I wanna make a solo album. I've got some soundtrack stuff I've been doing. I don't know. I'll keep you posted." ⊕

FUGAZI

Brendan Canty & Guy Picciotto on the recording process

Fugazi is probably one of the best rock bands on the planet at this point in time. Really. Their new album, *End Hits* is one of their best, proving that a band can grow over ten years without becoming a bloated parody of itself. Part of what makes this a great record is the band becoming more familiar with the studio and the recording process, as they talk about below. Brendan (drums) and Guy (vocals/guitar) also have been involved in a lot of extracurricular recording activities, many revolving around the Pirate House, which is now being manned by Juan Carrera. Anyway, Dewey and I met up with Brendan and Guy at Portland's Crystal Ballroom before the Need, the Ex and Fugazi blew the roof off the place. Dewey asked the real specific questions regarding records they'd worked on, I talked about gear, and we had a great time.

Larry: So what's the Pirate House?

Well, it's kinda just gone through a transition period right now, but I'll tell you how it started. For ten years, up until last year, it was the group house that I lived in and about four or five years ago, Fugazi had invested in a SoundCraft board, a reel-to-reel and some mics. Our soundman helped us buy some stuff because we really didn't know what we were getting...

Dewey: It was an 8-track?

Yeah, it was an 8-track. That was original set-up, an 8-track and we had it set up in our practice space. We then kept moving into an impasse so it just kept sitting there not getting a lot of use. I just started offering it up to bands in the neighborhood if they wanted to record, because in D.C., things have kind of changed where there really wasn't a cheap recording facility like Inner Ear was in the early days. Things have gotten more expensive, so for a lot of the young bands that didn't really have any money and were just starting out, we were like, "Well, we've got this equipment and we'll let you use it." So for about five years

we've ran it as an 8-track at a house and it's called Pirate Studios and a bunch of records actually came out of tapes that were made there. It's surprising because it was really just a row house and we were running a snake upstairs and recording in the living room. Something set up in the basement, but when I moved out last year, Juan Carrera who runs Slowdime...

Yeah, I know Juan. I met Juan when he was out with the Spinanes and we talked about what you guys had been doing.

He bumped it up to a 16-track and he got a new board. It was kind of half and half, it was 16-track but we still used our old board. And most of all outboard gear but now at the Pirate House everything from this point on is all Juan's basic setup. And Guy is actually recording a new Make Up record there with Juan's gear but it is a new era. He's done some building, my old bedroom has become the control room. He's really expanded.

So Juan's taken it on now?

Yeah, it's his set up now. And our 8-track stuff is at Joe's house and we're all recording bands there.

It kind of seemed like from just like the earlier Make Up record... you guys are getting more equipment and it's progressing and you can really hear that in the recording.

We're still learning. When we started recording bands we had no idea what the fuck we were doing. The Make Up stuff, I was scrambling to record like 14 songs with seven people living in the house, trying to move all of their furniture around and record really quickly then try not get into anyone's hair - it was pretty hectic. With neighbors on either side. The neighbors were actually pretty cool. Amazingly, you can still pull it off after this many years.

What kind of equipment were you guys using? Those earlier singles have a really overdriven garagey sound.

It's a lot of a mishmash. Most of the Fugazi mics we bought all at one time - we decided to get a bunch of stuff to record. Fugazi went out - at our house we've got a Tascam 58, an 8-track reel-to-reel, a SoundCraft Spirit board with 16 channels and then our mics were just standard [SM] 57s; some SM 81s that we've used pretty liberally for the

overhead drums. I love those mics. They work really well for making the kick and other drums sound great. We also have a [AKG] D112 and a bunch of those little bullet mics and those little Yamaha mics that look like little claws - they work alright.

When we first started, like in the early Make Up recordings, we just set up mics on each record in a different configuration. "Yeah, we'll put mics on the ground or up high on the ceiling," and it was all really different. As far as outboard stuff we had one Alesis Quadraverb reverb and a compressor

A [DBX]166... a lot of that had to do with how the actual house sounded. For the drums, they were sitting right in the middle all by themselves in the dining room and the band would be buzzing in the living room and all the vocals were recorded in this stone room where a woman had her preserves collection. It was a really cold stone room so the vocals had this really good sound. That room is my favorite room in the house, it's actually a solid concrete bunker and you put drums in there with on SM 81 and it sounds incredible. In fact on the new Fugazi soundtrack record, there' three songs on there that are recorded that way. The room is so loud in there. You can just barely stand up in there and you could probably just lie down in it and the concrete makes shit crash around. The upstair rooms are made of really thin plank wood. It more looks like a basketball court and just sounds great.

The wood kind of has an absorption.

I guess so. I think that house is th greatest.

So Juan is still working the studio out of there?

He's trying to set up a monitoring situation which is better than when we use to... before, it was like complete chaos because the band would be so loud you couldn't really monitor what you were mic'ing, you just had to tape and then listen back to the tape... it's so annoying. So I would just close the room and try to make a decent setup before.

And everybody in the band is looking you as an authority figure, as if you knew what's going on and they can't hear any thing!

I literally did not know what I was doing when we started recording the Make Up

by Dewey Mahood and Larry Crane. Drawings by Jeff Kriege

mean we used to overdub and it was the most heinous crimes that you can do. I really started to sympathize with engineers who used to piss me off now that I've done everything awful that you can possibly do, like recording over vocals.

Been there. So you were able to record yourselves then, I assume at that location at the old Pirate House.

Yeah, some little pieces are on *Red Medicine*.

With that gear. But, that gear moved to Ian's grandparent's house in Connecticut and it is just an old kind of farmhouse built in 1814. So, that gear has traveled around.

So you were able to stretch out. Have some space and spend some time recording with it out there.

guy   brendan

We spent a week moving it around to see how that works. Recording demos.

And so there is an album that came out with the video too?

Yeah, it'll be out in April.

And it's got a lot of unreleased songs?

It's all instrumentals, demos, practice tapes. It's more of the 8-track kind of stuff.

It's songs you've heard, but in that vein. With or without vocals or like the original demos of it which are...

Yeah.

It has Ian playing a piano song.

Wow! Really different!

Like whole songs that we never got to.

Yeah. That's great. That should be really good.

Did the All Scars project kind of develop out of just recording, experimenting...

All Scars developed out of a concept... me and Jerry and Doug were playing together and Chuck started playing with us, started singing, but really the idea was to write a set of music, 20 odd minutes of music, play

it, record it and move on. We tried to do that as quickly as possible.

Was it pretty improvised?

Well, now it is. Now I think they're improvising a lot more, but when we first started, we would improvise. I would bring a little Tascam 234, 4-track that I'd bring to practice and I'd just tape and tape and tape and we did it for Fugazi. I was carrying it from my house to Fugazi practice; I have like buckets of tapes at my house of all that stuff, but you know we did get a lot of tape, find pieces we liked. The difference with the All Scars was we wouldn't try to make them into songs, you know, like verse chorus, etc., we just keep it like linear. Keep it moving in just one direction until we have an end result. We turned into one big song. You've heard the record?

Yeah.

Those were two different sets.

It's real different sounding, kind of..

Well both of those sets we recorded live at the Pirate House.

We were running live off of Chuck's mic.

He was singing in the room with us, so whatever he had on the delay, everything had some delay on it.

Did he have some pedals on the floor and stuff?

Yes.

Like run a mic into that and then out...

Right.

Oh cool.

And he'd just leave the shit on because it works and I only doctored a little bit of one of the tapes a little bit, one part that was kind of boring. I took a live tape of the same part and flew it in and doubled it up on that. Because that was the only thing. Then I messed with the speed of it. It's the second piece of music on the first set on that CD. You can hear it toward the end of it. The guitar stuff splitting and flowing downward. That's the part right there. Yeah, so those were all pretty much done live but not much effect or overdubs at all and Guy recorded the second one. And there's another one still that hasn't come out yet because we were in that process and we were writing a lot of music, and it's like,

"Okay! We have another show next week, let's get another CD together!" We sort of started booking the shows before we had the songs ready. I think that even made it more manic. It was like now we have to get 25 minutes of music in a week.

I was wondering, Guy, about your recording of Blonde Redhead for "Slogan" [Serge Gainsbourg tribute compilation and 7"] and there's a lot of echo and things on the drums...

The way we did that was he set up two snares and one snare had a mic on it that was just running into a digital delay and then while they were playing I was just fucking around with it. I just did it all on the fly and it came out. It's one of those delays that has a bunch of program numbers and everything's preset and you just get it around so you get some feedback on it and then you wanna roll. I tell you, they're an amazing band to record because I think they were the first band where I started feeling more confident about what I knew in the studio and then they were just... their sound, they just know their instruments so well. When they set up it's not a lot of like tearing your hair out trying to get them to sound like something. They just have a really good sound and they're really like trained musician type people so they kind of communicate in a very intense way and they kind of cut to the chase real quickly. So they were fun as hell to record doing that album...

Especially on that last album... because it's so different from the previous one...

Right. Well it was an interesting experience because John Goodmanson and I had never met before I was involved with that record so I just kind of showed up there and I deferred to him. I think he is an established producer, he has a stronger sense of engineering, so I was really not gonna try to... I had made a decision that I was, you know, gonna be kind of laid back about it, but he was so cool about letting me get on the board and I think in the end we ended up really well as a team together. A lot of that session, the songs really hadn't been shaped, so John and I gave them a lot of helping them arrange the songs, building a lot of stuff.

Was that more of the band's idea?

I think it was just a mixture between the songs that they were writing and... the studio that we were in had such amazing amounts of gear - they had Mellotron, crank pianos and organs. We didn't have a bass amp so we were using a lot of pedals on the organ to get the low end... it was just a really good experience. The gear was so different from anything I had worked on before, so there was a lot of stuff I wanted to fuck around with and John had tons of ideas. Just a lot of ideas.

Just experimenting in general?

Oh yeah. Totally. Totally. They were writing and rearranging songs as we were recording.

Taking advantage of the studio.

Right. And all of the gear that was there. It was the first time I had seen a Mellotron. I was very excited. The first time I had ever worked on a Neve board.

Oh, yeah. What studio was that?

It was called Jolly Roger in Hoboken. It's run by this guy Gene [Holder]from dB's. And it's really, really great sounding and has a really, really incredible mic collection. Gene would come in, open the studio and just leave and we'd be just sitting there, trying to run all of this gear and stuff was catching on fire all the time. He was totally cool about it! I think it's an amazing studio, it's got a great sound, it has tons of different rooms and it's really cool.

Oh, Brendan, for you, The Make Up, the, what do you call it. The one with K...um...

"Detroit"?

Yeah, "Detroit" and I forget the other songs...

I don't know, they didn't give me a copy of it.

But that one had a different sound than the other one. It just has the overdriven live sound, it's warmer, with the backwards guitar and everything. I think it was also recorded at Pirate Studio, so I was wondering how...

That was a switch over to 16-track. I tell you the 16-track makes all the difference. Being able to not, you know, to monitor it's not that great, just making sure the levels are right and then fixing it later it helps a lot. Also all those extra tracks to throw on three separate backing vocals, I mean backwards guitar and then you can...

Can comp them...

Yeah! It just makes everything sound so huge and it's like you would...

It's such a warm sound.

They would do a dub and then they would say, "Let's super size it" and then we would just double it. So it would come out... so I was always, "Well, while you're at it, just double it, just in case." I was always confident that we could have it in stereo and redub stereo but I think it makes a huge difference.

What kind of 16-track did you guys end up with?

It's uh, what's the numbers? I don't know. It's like a Tascam. It's like the...

An MS-16?

I can't, I really can't remember what it's called. But yeah, I thought that session went really well because we did it, literally, in two days. With five songs in two days. I was really cracking the whip.

You're more productive that way?

Yeah. And then I am actually working on an album for them right now and it is going well although it is a full 13 songs so it's hard to concentrate. It's taking a long time to do each song justice that way. I felt like that tape... the basics went down really fast.

They're prolific in a way that completely blows my mind. They just crank out the records.

When they did *In Mass Mind* **they went in with nothing, like a few riffs and a few ideas but nothing really finished at all.**

I mean, I think there's a concept where you just go into the studio and make something and then don't be too precious about releasing it. A really interesting.... very different tactic, say like Fugazi, we always are very selfconcious and take a long time. We really labor over some things. It's kind of inspiring to work with them because there is a real freedom and they're really into trying ideas really quickly and they're not really hung up.

They were putting out a lot of stuff for a while.

Did you buy most of them?

Most of them... yeah. You know how it is.

Weird. Some day there will be like a CD set of all the...

Well, they're putting out the singles on a double CD.

Oh, that'd be great.

Guy sequenced it. So he would know, I would imagine it'd be great because it's so diverse.

It's really a wild listen, I really loved it.

I always say that those make great records sometimes because compilations of a good band and a bunch of different singles from different sessions all thrown together...

All kinds of things going on. And we're moving into the Pleistocene era or whatever.

Exactly!

...I love those kind of records. The Bikini Kill singles collection sounded so great.

That's really good. The Versus *Dead Leaves* **I really like.**

Yeah.

Yeah, so that's gonna be a double album too. Chock full.

They have really good ones... some of my favorite songs on them.

And it sounds great. So I think you're right, I think it'll be, it'll make a great album. It is tough, you know, that's the difference, you know. You do a single or you do a couple songs and you can really concentrate on the setting or the room. Then you sit down with 13 songs and it's just so much harder to to focus on each one. Plus you also lose... you record all the basics at the same time. You don't have those variables in the basic tracks, you don't have that weird drum sound that you got from that one day.

Yeah, I find that really hard that's what I do for a living, I record bands and I wish you could just come in and do a song a day, strike everything, come back the next day, set up. I mean, it's a lot of energy and it a lot of extra work but it's just amazing to me how that can actually work out. When you do an album from several different sessions, even in the same studio with everything the same, it gonna feel different.

We did that with the Blonde Redhead, last record. There were certain songs that we knew we wanted the drums in a larger room so we recorded that and we knew there were songs that once you try drums in a smaller, dry room like, so actually we tri three or four types of songs and it ended up being really good.

Yeah, even if it's not completely obvious sounding, it's just like it helps with the whole definition of different things and working them. I wish there was more room for that sometimes.

It's just a time problem.

Yeah, time or money. It just depends.

Yeah.

Definitely. With Fugazi, you guys were talking about dragging the 4-track cassette around, and stuff, do you guys do a lot of the writing by taping bits of practice and then listening back and then keeping good ideas from your own tapes?

All the time.

That helps us trying to relearn songs that are on tape. When we have no fucking idea what the hell we are playing.

Especially when you have it on of 4-tracks. If it just has it on 2-track, I'm like "What the fuck am I playing?" If you have it on 4-track you can isolate the bass and the drums and now, but these days, now that we have moved the gear over to our apartment space, we just set up. We leave the mic set up, we have it set up behind plexiglass, you know, have a good monitor set up, so at anytime we have a remote access. We just turn it on, you know what I mean, and keep it.

Do you have a bunch of blank tapes stacked up?

Yeah, a whole box. So I find that completely invaluable.

I'd rather listen to our new soundtrack record, which is primarily 8 and 4-tracks, than I would like listening to our records which are recorded on 24-track. The stuff we recorded in practice is has a certain energy or vibe, a non-self conscious type thing happening with it that for me kind of makes it more enjoyable to listen to. So now that we have this thing set up, we've recorded a lot more. It makes a lot more sense.

It could be a high enough quality to record your next album too which is like... the difference between a 4-track cassette and your new studio.

It sounds pretty good.

How often are you working with other people in the practice studio environment?

I just did a tape of a band called Deep Lust which is Alison from Bratmobile, her new band, and that hopefully will be coming out soon. It's an amazing tape. I mean, that was like, they hadn't practiced or played together in six months and they just showed up. I set them up and within an hour the thing was done.

Wow!

It was fuckin' classic. It was way cool. It was the rawest, most... it's not the best recorded thing because I just threw this shit up but it's just, the vibe is outrageous, it rips your face off. The only overdub on it is a wheelbarrow that he's like hitting with drumsticks.

How were you tracking the vocals?

She was in the middle of the room with a bullet mic live with the band. She was screaming her ass off. For that kind of thing, if it works, it's the best. They just kick ass.

So just an occasional project?

Not all that much in the new studio because we just moved all the stuff over a few months ago. We're just getting it together. Our idea is that if the shit is just set up, people can just come in if they wanna use my drums and stuff and just do it. In a few hours or whatever.

That's what Sonic Youth have been doing too.

Yeah, that stuff sounds great.

Are you planning to do your next record on the 16-track?

We may do it on the 8-track. There are advantages to more tracks because of the freedom it gives you but I don't think it is necessarily an audio or aural preference to it but there is a certain amount of scope or size but if you have something that works well and it sounds cool...

How much of the sounds on your last album were done in the mix? There seems like is a lot more reverb and all kinds of effects on it.

Different mics were used at certain times. We would drop out everything but the bottom snare mic... at the end of "Floating Boy" it's all just bottom snare mic. If you have all those mics set up and they sound weird, then use them.

We also got into overdubbing the entire drum set with one mic and then changing the pitch of the tape.

When "Closed Captioned" was recorded, the basic tracks to it are all to a drum machine and then I overdubbed two different drum sets on top of it, which I love doing. It gives distance to a song.

"Version" on *Red Medicine* is a - stand-out track. A real departure musically and also the way it was recorded, the whole sound of it. It's so much more atmospheric and not really following the whole verse, chorus structure or anything.

We had the music for a long time, but in terms of the vocal and the idea of putting in the clarinet and the feedback, there's a lot of weird vocal stuff. Like the clarinet track, we listened to it and then we laid in two different clarinet tracks and then we listened to it and we realized that if you pull this part it kind of segues into that part and it turns into, sounds like a solo! Accidentally. In the studio, for me, that is what makes recording fun. If you know what you're shooting for, then you're trying to nail a specific thing. It's so much less interesting than showing up at the studio, everybody kind of being game to listen to what's happening, coming over the speakers to see that and to go with it. Inevitably, when we start recording we come in with a bunch of songs and stuff that we're demoing or whatever. It changes so much, the way we play together, the way I play. All the different sounds and the beat.

It's taken us six records to stop hating the studio. Because we've always been an intense live band, we always came to the studio as if it was an unfortunate laboratory we have to enter and we had to get out of there with something that we hoped would be like the the live show. But we really had a backwards concept. Now we are really much more comfortable about trying to get loose and spontaneous, attacking the mixes a lot more energetically and letting it be a different experience than the show. We always were thinking that the records were the menu and the shows were the meal. ✖

J. Robbins -Jawbox

Burning Airlines, Inner Ear and more.

By Larry Crane with Jane Cowan, Photos by Jeff Gros

Tape Op gets quite a few letters and emails suggesting people that we should interview, and recently, J. Robbins had to be one of the most requested names by far. J. was in Jawbox for years, a band with integrity and a strong work ethic, and is currently leading a band with the Eno-ish moniker of Burning Airlines as well as producing records for Promise Ring, Jets to Brazil and others. He came into recording and producing through being in bands, much like myself, and I had a great time chatting with him in the back of Fellini's before Burning Airlines took the Satyricon stage and rocked our worlds. And did I mention how nice he is?

How did you make the transition? I assume you were playing music before you were recording. You worked with a lot of cool people on the Jawbox records. There's quite a few different people all recording in different ways. Was that something you were doing, working in that respect, and then started thinking you'd be more interested in doing recording on your own?

Yeah, I think from the first recordings that Jawbox did I was always compelled by the recording process, but also really intimidated by it too. I have always been an incredibly insecure singer, especially. When we did our first full-length record with Eli Janney, I was going, "Oh-my-god, Eli's a total genius", just really inspired by the way that he would do things, but then I was so busy freaking out about singing that I never really got a decent grip on it. Also, because we had to work really fast, I never felt like I got a grip on the nuts and bolts of recording. Some of the 8-track stuff we did with Barrett Jones was a little bit more relaxed because it was at Barrett's studio, it was really cheap and Barrett's really mellow. So I definitely started being interested from a musician's standpoint. I was always interested in the abstraction of how to translate a song into a recorded version where it becomes a little world instead of it being so much of a performance. For a while I lived in a group house with Geoff Turner, who runs WGNS in D.C., and this house was the second incarnation of WGNS Studios, the 1/2" 16-track version. I got to look over Geoff's shoulder a lot. I didn't actually start engineering-recording until Jawbox signed to Atlantic and we got to spend seven weeks in the studio [Oz] with Ted

Nicely, and I got to really pick Ted's brain. Drew Mazurek, who was the engineer, is an awesome engineer. Then we bought an 8-track and started doing demos in our basement and that's when I sort of started to really pay attention to what mics to use and where to put them.

The actual nuts and bolts.

I'd gone into the studio with other bands and anytime anybody would ask me to do it I'd be really psyched, but then I'd also be cursing myself, sort of self-flagellating because I'm just this guy who's sitting there with opinions. Meanwhile there's an actual engineer who really knows how things work, and I would be just like, "Oh, that's the same microphone that you used when you recorded us, isn't it?" I felt like such an asshole that I was so glad to have an opportunity, finally, to learn to actually engineer.

Like know what to do and just kind of hear what does what right? On the other hand, too, it can be productive to have someone producing, or in charge of the session who isn't so technical, that's just kind of helping the band to get the feel of something.

Yeah, I think when we worked with Ted, when Jawbox did *For Your Own Special Sweetheart*, at first I kept giving him these side-long glances because he wasn't interested in engineering. Whenever there was a dispute I would always side with Drew, who was the engineer; but now that I've actually worked on a bunch of records, I have volumes of respect for Ted because he knows exactly what role he wants to take. It's good for him that's he's not bound up in the technical matters and he's interested in translating things in a more ephemeral way. I don't know if that's necessary for everybody, for every band, I don't think it is.

The production team kind of thing?

Yeah. But I have a lot of respect for it now.

In a lot of cases, especially on an indie level, you don't get a chance to have an engineer and a producer.

Yeah, 'cause there's no time, too.

Yeah, there's no time and there's no money.

I always think that's kind of a crime, in a way, I know a lot of people who feel that way too. I think Juan [Carrera] feels that way; that it's kind of a drag that bands with no money don't get to spend a lot of time and mull over their songs, how to interpret them and craft them in a recording. I definitely feel that way. It's weird that people don't spend more time in pre-production when you've got no money. There are so many bands that go to the studio and they are like, "We have two days to do everything, so let's just bust it out", but they could be making their record in their heads for a month before they ever get into the studio. But not too many people think of that.

Practicing, taping your rehearsals, listening to your stuff, editing your songs.

Really thinking about it.

Fixing your gear.

Yeah! Intonating your guitars or charting out what overdubs you want to do or whatever.

Definitely. In Vomit Launch I was the guy in the band who would say, "Okay, guys, we're gonna do this and this and this and I'd run the band through rehearsals, we'd work on the arrangements from the beginning to the end so they would record well. I became the intermediary in that band and got really into the recording process and was able to help our band focus on the recording. Were you kind of getting that role in Jawbox a bit back then?

No, in Jawbox, the stuff that we did with Ted on *For Your Own Special Sweetheart* was the first time that anybody came to us and really encouraged us to pay attention to the really nitty-gritty details of performance. That was the big learning experience for us. Before Bill [Barbot, guitarist in Jawbox] and I, it was really me doing that stuff, if anybody did it. When Bill joined the band he and I ganged up, but everybody was trying to pay attention. Jawbox was super concerned about having our shit together, almost to a fault. On a daily level, it was really frustrating because we would do takes and Ted would say, "You realize the drums are behind the beat, but the guitars are rushing." And we were like, "What does that mean?" And we were already doing the record then, but we had a long time to work on it so it was an education because it was then that we were able to listen to the takes and be like, "Augh! That's what he means. I can hear that I'm pushing on the guitar". You learn so much. It was difficult, but we learned a lot. So after that experience, we all collectively were able to pay attention to stuff like that.

Everybody was more tuned into it.

Yeah. It's actually really remarkable. I'm really psyched when I think about it. The difference between rehearsals and writing songs for that record and then the incredible difficulty of understanding what it means to be ahead of, or behind the beat or what a good ensemble performance is... and then getting out of it and doing demos at home and applying all that stuff.

When did you start the full-on engineering?

I produced stuff like Antimony, which was the band after Circus Lupus broke up. It was Circus Lupus without Chris Thompson. The first couple of Kerosene 454 records and the last one I got to do a fair amount of engineering and I mixed that record. The first proper engineering I did was the 8-track demos of Jawbox stuff and then I started working at Inner Ear a couple years ago just because the guy that was running the B studio there quit. I know, when you guys talked to Don, he told you a little bit, but it's like the Fostex B16 that he modified. It's got this awesome monitor board that he built from scratch that sounds so great. It's just pots and toggle switches. There's no faders, there's no EQs or anything. There's an old Tascam board that's kind of terrible. Don didn't know what he was gonna do, whether he should just sell all the stuff or get somebody else to run it and Ian MacKaye knew that I had been doing a bunch of 8-track stuff, because I was basically doing anybody that I knew that was in bands, I was just like, "Come over to my house, I'll record ya'!"

We're you charging them?

No. Occasionally, barely. Like five dollars an hour just because occasionally my housemates would get pissed off that there was so much noise and so I could say, here's 50 bucks for the house funds. Buy some cleaning products or whatever. So, like Kerosene 454 would come over and do demos or what have you. So Ian suggested that I start the 16-track and I dove in and did it. It went well. It's weird to me because I've always had a great deal more respect for engineers or the idea of engineering than I have for producers, but I've been in a position of producing records. I've done that more than engineering up until the last couple of years. So I have Ian and Don to thank for giving me a chance to get in and record people.

Is the room in one building?

The B room and the A room are wired into the same live room and the live room is awesome. Everything in that studio is designed according to Don's desires and it's a cool space because the live room is a big figure 8 shaped room and one side of it is paneled in open plywood. It's got a drum riser so it's real live. The other side of the room is carpeted. The feeling is like you're in a living room - it doesn't feel huge but it's got 18 foot high ceilings. There's ways to set up in there that everybody can aim towards each other and nobody has to wear headphones but there's still decent isolation.

Yeah, less rattle.

A little bit, but he's got a 24-track room that has automation, so you can deal with it. There's things that I run into occasionally, now that I've been to a bunch of studios, that frustrate me, but when I think about how good it feels to play in that space, I probably wouldn't trade it for anything. It's just such a comfortable place to play. You can do anything you want in there. It's a really fun place to work.

It's important for people to feel comfortable when they're playing too.

It's crucially important. There's a little isolation booth off to the side and I've been putting guitars in there and redoing guitars or whatever. The live room feeds into the 24-track control room and into the 16-track. The 16-track goes way down to the end of the hallway. Like way towards the front door. So when I engineer in the 16-track I have to run back and forth all the way down the hall and I don't get to see the band play. You can only talk back and forth via a speaker and a microphone.

So you could be mixing in there and tracking in the live room?

Yeah, sometimes Don is mixing in the 24-track room and I'm tracking in the 16-track and we're running back and forth and overlapping. I recorded Mike, our bass player plays in another band called Jack Potential, and we were doing that record while Don was mixing the Down By Law record. It was cool because the Down By Law guys got the Jack Potential guys to come do some backing vocals while we were mixing the Jack Potential record. It's a little bit too small of a place to have everything overlap but for some reason it seems to work out.

Do you have a lot of rumble if you've got a whole band playing if you're trying to mix in the control room.

Yeah, but it hasn't been a problem so far. You can envision it being a real nightmare but it hasn't been.

Have you done work at any other studios recently?

I did. Any time I've gone to other studios I've felt like I didn't want to bluster my way in and be like, "I can engineer your records!" because people don't have time. I would rather respect people and their desire to make the best record they can make rather than waiting for me to get used to another studio. The Promise Ring records and the Jets to Brazil record I worked on were done at Easley and Stuart Sikes engineered both of those records. He's a fuckin' awesome guy and really great engineer. That studio's amazing. For both of those records I was much more of a producer. On the Jets record it was especially cool because I got to know the songs way ahead of time and they invited me to participate creatively and to suggest things. It was so fun. Easley, that place blows my mind. The Promise Ring EP we did at Smart, which was amazing, and that was cool because I got to mix at Smart. I did a Roadside Monument up at Robert Lang Studio in Seattle.

Is that the one with a stone room? Quasi did a couple tracks up there.

Yeah, and he's got these API consoles that he modified so there's LED's that show you for certain whether you're using it. That place is beautiful. Once I again, I felt hesitant to engineer. At Inner Ear, I've worked there so much I feel like I know it very well and I feel extremely confident to engineer there. I want to engineer at other places now because I feel like I can now. But for the last two years it's been getting so it's like at Inner Ear. It's so nice to be able to walk in and to just know that place and to be so comfortable.

It sounds like you did the Burning Airlines record on the 24-track.

Yeah.

Did you use a half-inch 16 on the other?

Yeah, it's a Fostex B-16 and a really old Tascam 20 X 8 with the Playskool knobs. It's weird because it's proof to me that anyone can do good work if they get to know the equipment really well.

That's the *Tape Op* motto!

It's really true!

When we get home from this tour I'm gonna record a new Promise Ring record and it's my dream come true because I'm gonna engineer it at Inner Ear and then mix at Smart. It's the most neutral sounding control room I've ever been in. You know what I have to do? You know what I feel like really, really, conscientiously bound to do?

What?

If anything I say is going to appear in print regarding recording I have to say that John Agnello is like a god to me. You know we were talking about the comfort level of recording? John Agnello was the first person that Jawbox ever worked with who really was able to make us feel really comfortable in the recording studio. It was never a question that we were going to achieve the best possible things that we could achieve. It was just a matter of how long it would

> ## "It's proof to me that anyone can do good work if they get to know the equipment really well"

Just take time at learning to get good sounds with what you have. You go from there.

But I think this summer I'm gonna go ahead and take the plunge and really revamp the whole 16-track room. I may put a Soundcraft board in or something. Don and Chad Clark are both really pro-Mackie. The Soundcraft - I know enough people that use them and they sound really nice.

Those are pretty nice. My friend has one at a studio here and I've played with it a little bit.

It's weird, I haven't known how much of an investment to make in the 16-track because I keep getting to do 24-track projects and I really love going to other studios. The minute I went to Smart studios I was so bowled over by that place.

I bet. It's amazing.

take. He's an awesome engineer and he's been a great friend ever since we worked with him. I think the record that we made with him is the record that we felt represented our band the best. He came down and he and I mixed two thirds of the Burning Airlines record together and he brought a bunch of outboard gear. He can take a great deal of responsibility for that record sounding good. I endlessly give props to John because he's an awesome, awesome guy.

I interviewed Trent Bell from the Chainsaw Kittens and he had done a record with him. He is the same way he's like, "You've got to interview John, he's the best."

You should.

I think he did the last Varnaline record

Yeah, he did.

They were raving about him too.

Especially for that wonderful, ephemeral thing about feeling comfortable in a recording studio.

In what ways did he do that?

I don't know. It's like the process of recording when we work with John; the process became really transparent and he was a friend who was on the side of us and our songs. He really made me believe that I was a good singer, which was not an experience that I had had up until then. I would get in front of a microphone and just freeze and be looking through the glass in the control room and

"I've always had a great deal more respect for engineers or the idea of engineering than I have for producers"

thinking, "Let me count all the people whose time I'm wasting." This record was so awesome for me because I did the vocals all by myself, just in the control room late at night. I was so happy to do that. Agnello has endless patience but he doesn't make you feel like he's being patient. People should be beating down his door to work with him.

You should interview him for us.

I would love to do that. He has great stories. He has amazing stories about the bad old days because he worked at the Record Plant or the Power Station or something like that in the '70's when people were snorting lines off the mixing board. He recorded the Outfield.

I saw that in a Goodwill bin the other day! Oh, they were horrible.

Indeed. But their record sounded great! Well, for the times. I don't know, I never heard the record but, I guess...

Do you have a favorite brand of microphone?

You know what is a great microphone that people don't appreciate enough is the CAD E300. That is a fuckin' awesome microphone!

They're cheap too!

They're cheap and when we did the Dismemberment Plan record, we went to Water Music, which is a gorgeous, amazingly great studio, and the band was used to recording at Inner Ear where the E300 was really the hit vocal microphone. So we borrowed Don's E300, we took it to Water music and we AB'd it against stacks and stacks of microphones. It sounded identical to a FET U47. Which is kind of like, that's right, it's good. It was just a lesson in not fetishising the good equipment. I think that's a wonderful microphone. It's weird, my Inner Ear experiences made me familiar with a lot of microphones that are maybe not standard, because Don has bazillions of mics. He's got these Philips omnis that are like twenty-five bucks a piece and sound fantastic. He has the CAD100 which is an incredibly great kick drum mic. Not a lot of people's first choice. I bought one because I loved it so much and that was the kick drum mic on the Jets to Brazil record.

Do you put it in real close?

About half way in and aimed at the shell, actually. But not by itself.

Yeah, like something else in close to pick up the tap.

No something further away actually. It's all trial and error.

I'm always amazed in interviews where people describe how they do their drums or vocals.

Like, "There's a right way. I have a way, it always works." You know, like that.

Yeah, I mean, it's just things you try or what you can probably start with. I'll be like, "I'm just using this one mic" or other times I'm using all these overheads. I had ten mics up one day and then the next day I'll have three.

Yeah. I remember when I started doing stuff at Inner Ear and I was so hot to use a lot of drum mics. Don used to kind of poke his head in and be like, "Hmmmm...", sort of look quizzically, and I was pretty happy with the results. Now I realize that with two thirds of the amounts of mics I was using I can get a better drum sound. I love that it's trial and error. It's one of the most fun things about it.

The randomness of recording is something I really enjoy. I'll be on the talkback and accidentally hear something over the wrong mic and go, "Hey!" I'll put that to tape.

Yeah, it becomes like a beautiful feature.

What are your plans recording-wise, are you planning to fix up that room at Inner Ear or...

Operating the 16-track room, which mainly involves getting a new board and just sort of redoing the patch thing. Because I've been doing it, I've been working in there in a way that is not entirely healthy. Just sort of getting to know the foibles of the room and working around them. I've been really pleased with how things have turned out at this point, I want it to be easy to make things turn out well. The main thing that it would take is just to get a really good board in there. I also have a bunch of projects coming up in July and August. I just got demos for the Promise Ring record and we've been trading notes back and forth. The whole band is very sort of production inclined at this point, but Dan their drummer especially is. I'm thinking about the Promise Ring songs, drum tunings and instrumentation and stuff. I'm really looking forward to it. I'm gonna let them take over my apartment and I'm gonna stay with friends. Keith, who plays drums in Burning Airlines, works at this equipment rental place so we'll be able to rent stuff if we want to. Xylophone overdubs or whatever. I'm kind of on the edge of my seat about it. There's other things

too, actually, because we're doing SuperESP which is Casey Rice and Damon Mocks, who used to sing in Trenchmouth. They're doing some remixes of Burning Airlines stuff, for a record that we want to do, hopefully by the end of the summer, where we'll record some new songs. Hopefully they'll be a little more studio intensive, like some of the stuff on *Mission Control* but maybe more so. We'll put that together with the SuperESP. I have no idea what they're doing, I mean, I just sent them some mixes, like individual tracks and then certain things together, and based on the SuperESP record, I imagine it'll be a little far afield from the songs. All I know is Damon said that he put some of the *Planet of the Apes* soundtrack in it.

That's fun to see what comes back.

Yeah. It's extremely exciting to see what comes back.

Yeah, it could be completely different.

Yeah, I hope it will be, I mean, I'm sure it will be. ☻

DJ

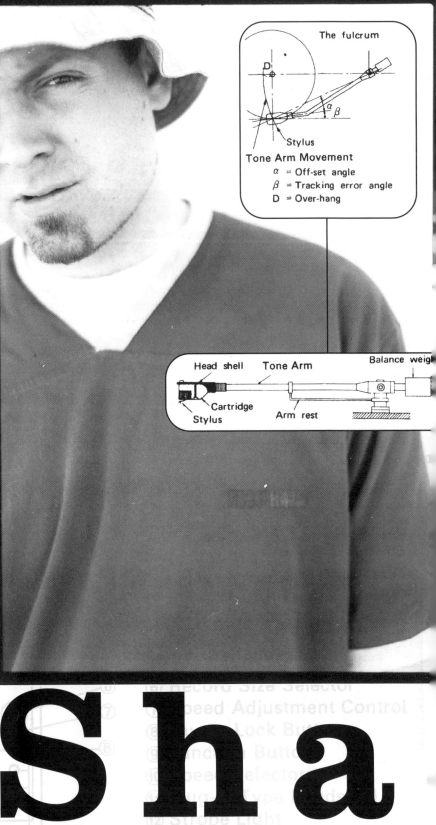

The fulcrum

Stylus
Tone Arm Movement
α = Off-set angle
β = Tracking error angle
D = Over-hang

Head shell   Tone Arm   Balance weigh
Cartridge
Stylus   Arm rest

Home recording has taken some serious leaps during the nineties. A 4-track and a couple of cheap microphones used to be the standard setup; nowadays it's just as common to find a sampler, turntable, and an ADAT, Pro Tools or hard drive recorder. This "Do-It-Yourself" ethic is very prevalent in the sample based DJ/Electronica world. Is it more chic to go out and buy a sampler rather than an electric guitar? Electronica is the new punk rock, and there are no rules for this subculture's art form.

DJ Shadow (AKA **Josh Davis**) is a perfect example. Here you have a middle class, white kid from suburban **Northern California** that grew up listening to hip-hop. Most of his work is done at home using only a few pieces of equipment. Shadow's debut album, *Endtroducing* (Mo Wax Records, 1996) came out of nowhere. It sold quite impressively, and launched him and the rest of the DJ world into the plain view of record buyers worldwide. Shadow's flavorful, sample driven combination of huge breakbeats and spacey organ and bass loops landed his album on top ten lists everywhere. Shadow has now released a new album under the name Unkle. Unkle is Shadow's collaboration with Mo Wax Records founder, **James Lavelle**. Shadow has been quoted as saying, "He's the director and I'm the DJ." What this translates to with Unkle is this: Shadow creates the music while Lavelle brings together other artists such as **Radiohead**'s **Thom Yorke**, **The Verve**'s **Richard Ashcroft**, Beastie Boy **Mike D.**, and many others to add vocal and instrumental collaborations. I was able to sit down with DJ Shadow and talk about some of his gear, his approaches to music, and the making of Unkle's new album, *Psyence Fiction*.

Sha dow

What is your set up like, equipment wise? I'm sure you've been asked many times.

Well, I don't mind talking about it anymore. Mainly, I just use an Akai MPC-3000.

Will you continue to stick with that sampler?

No. I think it's time to move on. When I first started using my MPC-60 Mach II back in early '92 it was so new. No one was using them. Everyone was still so SP-1200, SP-1200, SP-1200. Now, it's time for something new. I think that when you change your instrument, you change your sound. But, I still want to keep it simple. I don't want to fall into the trap that a lot of producer friends of mine fall into. A lot of people that I look up to make the same mistake. When they are having a hard time making music, they spend a lot of time and energy on getting new gear. They feel that because they are reading manuals, they are working. However, they aren't making anything. It's easy to get caught in a tech trap where you never put anything out, but feel like your new piece of gear is going to put you on the top. My home studio would still fit on a dinner table. Turntables and my 3000.

Did you use the same equipment for Endtroducing and Psyence Fiction?

No. For Unkle I upgraded to the 3000. I made my own album on the MPC-60.

I've heard that you never use computers. Is that true?

"To be inspired, you need to live a little bit."

The only time I use Pro Tools is for the editing and sequencing of the album. For Unkle, it was just used to de-click some of the really noisy samples. At the very beginning of making the Unkle record, I was feeling very self-conscious. I was hearing all these chops on drum and bass records that I couldn't do on the 3000. I played around with Cubase a little but then I decided that I already had my sound and that I'd stick with it for a while.

How much multi-tracking do you do?

Endtroducing was recorded to ADAT because that was all that we could afford back then. The Unkle album was multi-tracked to 2" analog. Jim Abbis did the actual mixing but James and I were there for every minute of it.

What about outboard gear? Any certain pieces that you like a lot?

The MXR Pitch Transposer. It was something that Mario Caldato Jr. from the Beastie Boys introduced me to. That's one of the few pieces of outboard gear that I've ever sought out and bought. I used it a lot during my DJ set when I was touring Europe with Radiohead.

Are all the sounds you sample already pre-recorded? Would you ever commission musicians to come in and play parts that you have written?

Jason Newstead from Metallica played live bass on one of the Unkle songs. That was because I couldn't find a bass line that I liked. That was the only reason. I used his bass line because after working on the beat and guitar sample for six months, I still couldn't find a bass line to sample. It was too strange of a melody. I grew up on sample-based music. Breakbeats are the foundation of what I do. I like the fact that, even though it doesn't always sound the greatest, someone could go out and find the beats. They are out there. Everything I use can be found somewhere else if you look hard enough. I think that makes it very interesting. I love finding other people's samples. It's great to not only find the sample but then to also see how it was used. It's great when people aren't lazy and take the sample as a whole. I like it when people chop up stuff and flip it around.

On the Unkle song Nursery Rhyme you made a piece of music that is entirely made out of samples sound like a rock band. Someone who didn't know better would assume that it is just a rock band playing that song. Was that your goal?

Yeah. As rock bands try to sound more sampled, I've wanted to make songs that are 100% sampled and feel live.

It does. It even has the stick click four count.

Exactly. I had to go through about 30 records to find the stick clicks. It could have been worse if I hadn't known to look for them in punk records. That was a fun song. It was a milestone for me on the record. It came together faster than anything else.

Interviewed by Eric Stenman
Photo by Jeff Gros

Will there be a new DJ Shadow album in the works anytime soon?

The thing is this. I finished *Endtroducing* in June of '96 and started Unkle right away. I did *High Noon*, toured, and then worked on Unkle all the way up until now. I haven't had any time to relax or reflect since '95. I think that for the sake of me making good music, I need to take the rest of the year off. I need to just DJ and not make music. If I started another record right now it would sound like Unkle. To be inspired, you need to live a little bit. There's a lot of bait for me to work, work, work. Strike while the iron's hot. I can't buy into that.

I'm sure that you could do a ton of re-mix work if you wanted to.

I don't really do re-mix work. I have done a few. They have to have really influenced me in a major way and be friends of mine. Some people make their whole living doing re-mixes and do a really good job. Someone like Fatboy Slim. I think that's cool. For me, I don't look at music that way. I have a hard time with it. I still consider myself a consumer of music more than anything else. As a consumer, I think that a lot of re-mixes are rip offs. Rarely will something hit me the way the original song does. Usually it's spare beats and two days in the studio. It's the same reason why I didn't have many re-mixes done off of *Endtroducing*. The Cut Chemist re-mixes were the only ones. It just doesn't seem like a good idea for me.

What other current producers do you really like?

I like Timbaland. There's a producer from Miami named Gray Strider that I really like.

Are there any new pieces of gear coming out that you are excited about?

That's a good question. I'm really not a techie. When it comes to me building my new set up, I'm going to have to do some investigating and call around. It's hard because the MPC turned out to be a very classic, standard machine. There's not much around that's been an improvement. I'd have to find something that is better. I don't want a new piece of gear just for the sake of having it. It's got to be able to do at least what the MPC can do. I've always liked the fact that it's all in one box. *(pause)* I can't believe that I have no Akai sponsorship. I've talked about Akai for so long. I don't know what's wrong with them. I don't know what's wrong with me. I should be calling them. ☺

Neutral Milk Hotel began in the early '90s as a 4-track cassette project by **Jeff Mangum**. Since then, he's released a couple of albums on **Merge** records (*On Avery Island*, *In The Aeroplane Over The Sea*) and assembled a "band" to take the show on the road. We interviewed Jeff after a Neutral Milk Hotel show at the **Portland** rock dive, **Satyricon**. Despite having been booted from the stage after a scant forty minutes due to club scheduling problems, Jeff was still up for talking *Tape Op* trash. After assuring us we weren't bugging him, we got underway with a few questions.

Neutral Milk Hotel

By Larry Crane and Leigh Marble

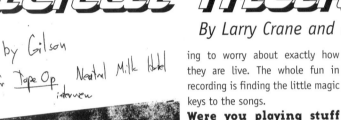

Have you had a long day, Jeff?

Long day... Don't sweat it, you're not pestering me. I really like your zine a lot.

Thank you. Well, these are the questions I was thinking of. Your first single was the Cher Doll Records one, is that right?

Yeah.

I really like that. I heard That whenever it came out, someone sent it to me to review. And I was thinking that you're, even still, oriented towards recording being really separate from live. So I wanted to head in that direction with questions, as far as your band being a band. Like on the new record, how many of the people who played with you tonight appeared on that record?

All of them. Jeremy plays drums on the album, Scott plays all the horns, Julian plays accordion and saw, and Lauren plays the silver saxophone and the xitherphone.

So you headed up to Robert's [Schneider of the Apples In Stereo] house in Denver to do the recording?

Yeah. The whole band approaches recording in a very... recording is such a magical thing, it's fun to see the songs grow and take shape as you're working on them and not get too caught up in try-

ing to worry about exactly how they are live. The whole fun in recording is finding the little magic keys to the songs.

Were you playing stuff off the new album live before you went to the studio?

We played 'Ghost' a couple times, and that was it. Cuz we got the band together up in New York City after ...*Avery Island* [NMH's first full length] came out, and then we toured for a while. Then Jeremy went to Chicago, Scott went to Austin, Julian stayed in Long Island to start his album on his own, in his grandmother's basement. I went to Athens and started working on some of the songs for the next record. And then Jeremy flew down to Athens for five days and that's where we worked up 'Ghost,' in the garage, and then he went home. The other songs we did after he got back from Chicago, we worked on them right before we went to make the record and then we worked on some of the stuff in the studio.

Just worked it up a little bit and then recorded it?

Uh-huh.

What did you record on this time, did you use the 8-track?

Yeah, 8-track.

You did the first one on a 4-track, right?

Fostex 4-track, reel-to-reel.

Damn. Didn't he have the 8-track at that point, when you were out there for *Avery Island*?

Yeah, we couldn't afford the tape.

That's a wild reason. An extra eighty bucks or something.

Well, Robert's been eating rice and beans for both

records. We basically ended up living off a credit card for half the album. And plus I was only used to cassette 4-track at that time, so it was a step for me into something still comfortable.

And they can sound great. Has it been nice working with eight?

Yeah it's great.

How'd you hook up with Robert in the first place?

I met Robert in third grade, in Louisiana. Will from Olivia Tremor Control I met in seventh grade, and he moved away when he was eighteen. See, we were always trying to get out of Louisiana, we always knew it was a place to leave. We were always surprised at how many people who lived there didn't have the same idea that we did. So he ended up moving to the Virgin Islands, thinking he was going to sit on the beach and drink martinis and write Hawaiian music. And he ended up homeless on the beach, broke. His plane ticket was round-trip, so he went back to Miami and called our friend Lisa in Athens, who went and picked him up. So one of our friends had actually broken free of Ruston so we all flooded to Athens immediately. I ended up moving, though I've moved back to Athens three times, this is my third time to move back.

Where did you move between?

Denver, Seattle, and New York City.

I thought you had lived in Seattle like when the single was done or something?

I did the single in Athens, then went to Seattle, found out about Cher Doll records and sent her a tape.

So at that time you were 4-tracking at home?

Yeah, working at some crappy theater job. Giving away free popcorn. Constantly.

To friends, or anybody?

Anybody who looked interesting. Some guy would buy ten bucks worth of food, give me a ten-dollar bill, and I'd give him ten bucks back in change and say thank you. *[everyone laughs]* They'd look at me completely confused. And then everybody quit and there were three fifteen year-old kids there that were asking me how to pop the popcorn and looking to me for guidance and I couldn't take it so I left. Yeah, I lived in Seattle for a while.

Before that you'd been 4-tracking, when you lived in Athens, right?

Well, I started 4-tracking when I was around sixteen. And before that I had a little York stereo with the left and the right input and a little K-Mart mic. It had a double tape deck so I'd record one track on the left speaker, and then put the tape in there and hit play and record the right speaker and you had two tracks.

Yeah, we all start with something like that and it just goes to hell from there. On that first single, that has the most distinctive guitar sound I'd heard in a long time and that was the first thing that blew me away. It sounds like you just plugged into a distortion pedal and plugged straight in. Is that how you were getting that sound?

That was the Fostex X-18 that has a remix button on it which feeds, if you're remixing on track one, it'll feed it into track two and back into track one. So I plugged the guitar into the four track and it's supposed to be on "line," but if you pop it *[the input level switch]* into "mic," the signal is really hot. And then you put it through the remix and the whole thing just starts looping on itself. Plus I had a guitar with a pickup that was really hot.

So you just did it straight in, no effects or nothing? That was my favorite guitar sound in a long time, it kinda blew me out of the water. I was starting to 4-track, living up here in a basement, and that single made me feel good about doing stuff on my own. It was great. You had really simple drums, sounded like just a snare and a ride cymbal.

And a floor tom, I think.

Yeah. Just really simple, probably one mic?

One really crappy mic. I think it was a K-Mart mic, one of the seven dollar microphones you can buy, plastic with a plastic mic stand you can pop on there.

I just found one of those at R5D3, this really strange store that has a lot of radio surplus and weird shit. It's the best place to find weird things.

So they have any Space Echoes?

Yeah, I wish.

I really want a Space Echo really bad. *[into tape recorder]:* If anyone reading this has a Space Echo, please let me know.

Contact Jeff now. I'll take one too. *[laughs]* **So after that, were you still four-tracking up to pre-*Avery Island*, doing stuff on your own? When you're writing songs, you're putting them together on tape?**

No, all the songs are just in my head. Now I just record shit for the fun of it. Unlistenable noise. But now I have a 1/4" 8-track.

Oh, cool. What kind?

Fostex, mid-eighties model.

Do you have a mixing board?

I borrowed one, I haven't bought one yet.

What are your plans for recording stuff in the future? Recording with Robert?

Hell, yeah.

You said he's listed as producer. How do you guys interact? You have the songs in your head, all the musicians, you're there, Robert's there, you've got a tape deck...

Start with the drums. We get there, sit around in his living room playing records. And I'll pick up a guitar and say, *"Hey man, these are some of the songs that are going to be on the record, will you tell me what you think?"* Sometimes I'll play him songs I'm not so sure about. Robert is a really beautiful person and I don't understand where he gets all his stamina from. I'm so amazed he can engulf himself in the record as we're making it, from basically two in the afternoon until three in the morning. He wakes me up and says, *"I'm going to the studio to play the piano for a couple hours,"* and I'd show up around two.

Is it fun?

It's a blast. He wakes you up all freaked out, *"I heard these sounds in my head, I know how we can get this done, I had this dream and I heard all these sounds, and I figured out how we can make it sound like that."* He'd say, *"I love you, I love you, I love you,"* kiss me on the head, go, *"Wake up, coffee is downstairs, see you in the studio in two hours." "Okay Robert!"* So it's just really great. They gave me a room to live in, and he's got all his books on Eastern religion and philosophy to look at, so it's a pretty cool experience.

What is songwriting like for you? Do you have a bunch of ideas and then say, "Okay, it's time to sit down and flesh them out", or are you writing constantly, like you finish a song and then move on?

It's hard to say. They all sort of morph themselves into different shapes. Sometimes I can't remember where they got started. Different pieces will cram into each other. But I'm constantly writing, there's constantly words that come into my head that sit there a while.

Do you travel with a typewriter?

No, I pretty much keep it all in my head. Usually when I write with a typewriter it's so Dada, you can't look at it. I've written pages and pages of typewriter stuff that is such nonsense that no one could possibly make any sense of it.

Is there anything else you'd like to say about the recording process?

All the little stockpile of sounds that I came up with on the four track were accidental things that happened, and then I brought those ideas and those sounds to a bigger recording situation with Robert. For me, recording is like I can sense these waves of the up and down of the music, the dynamics in the music, and I get this feeling of how things are happening musically and try to guide the songs and the albums themselves, to make the waves even and work well.

How do you communicate that with other people?

I'm surprised at how well they understand already.

They seem to be really responsive to what makes your songs work.

Yeah, we're really fortunate that we're good friends and we get along so well.

And that you're all able to be out on the road at the same time, not tied down to jobs.

Yeah, well it's rice and beans on the road. Looks like it's going to be rice and beans for life. ☺

Mercury Rev

is one of the best bands in America

Fact.

by Kevin Coral
Photos by Steve Gullick

Another *fact* is that last year they released one of the best American records in a long time, *Deserter Songs*. Recorded by the hot producer of the day, Dave Fridmann, it was an instant classic. We were lucky enough to talk to Jonathan and Grasshopper on their swank tour bus when they rolled through Cleveland. They were very forthright and honest with their answers and really seemed to enjoy themselves. It was a great show, as expected. Thanks to the boys, Roberta at V2 (for all her help and patience) and Jason for holding the recorder!

First things first: Your record is great. I know everybody has told you that but it's really true. Anyway, you recorded this record at three different places, right?

Mostly at our studio in the Catskills, and Dave's - a lot of the mixing was done at Dave's. A lot of it was just done at our house - the bass and overdubbing.

Dave's place is Tarbox, right?

Yeah.

Is Tarbox sort of a big place - dimension wise? Is it his house or...?

It's a converted house. A really large place – sort of like a barn. Not an old house, a new one. A big vaulted ceiling where the living room used to be. Dave's partner, Greg, sort of re-vamped the house and moved some walls and stuff.

The record has a really big sound to it, like on the drums, and I figured you were laying those down in a pretty decent sized space.

Well, the space is large and there's a slate floor. Most of the drums on our record, and I know Wayne's [Coyne, of the Flaming Lips, who also did their record at Tarbox with Dave Fridmann] too, we only used two mics.

There are a lot less guitars on this record than on the previous ones and that seems to be happening, lately with you, the [Flaming] Lips, and to a lesser extent, us [the Witch Hazel sound]...

Well, I think most people tend to change a little bit. I don't think anybody would want to be stuck with just orchestral sounds...

Yeah, it just seems to me to be a real zeitgeist. Obviously we aren't calling each other up to find out what the next thing is. It just seems to be happening naturally...

I think it's just laziness, [laughter] you know? I think it's pure laziness on the part of not really wanting to spend 20 hours fiddling with guitar pedals - finding an amp that works...

Yeah, plus it's just plain fun to recor[d] strings...

Yeah...

Lets talk about gear.

You know, Dave's studio is relatively basic. He doesn[t] have a lot of bells and whistles - he just has a grea[t] ear. I think that he has gear which he fee[ls] comfortable with and not a lot of sirens an[d] foghorns and things like that. Anything of tha[t] nature, the band probably brings themselves.

It's more of the environment...

I think so. He has a wonderful big, black mixing des[k] - Otari I think it is - a big old thing. A lot of it, [I] think, is from him doing so many records he sort o[f] pares down to what it is he feels comfortabl[e] using...

He knows what works.

Yeah, and a lot of the other stuff, he just doesn't fe[el] any charm towards.

Is there anything significantl[y] different about the recording of thi[s] record than from the previous ones[?]

I think on the past records it was actually more helter-skelter. We would just sort of go in at night, when we could get cheap studio time. I think the first two records were probably mixed on an old Peavey board. [laughter] A lot of that, (with ourselves, Dave, Wayne and Michael) we were all cutting our teeth and actually learning how to work within the studio because we never really had the money to have a great studio - where it just came through a great preamp and it sounded good. It was always sort of fudging around. It half worked and half didn't - there were things you didn't know anything about. We've all sort of grown up as our bands have all gotten bigger, but the mindset is still there - that you never really trust equipment. It helps that Dave owns his own studio now, in that he can

"It's not what you play, it's what you don't."

do whatever he wants. It's all his equipment. He knows what he has and that makes it all the more easier, and quicker, than going to a bigger studio.

You've pretty much worked with Dave exclusively. He's good at what he does, but I assume the comfort level you have with him is appealing too, right?

It just began as him playing bass with us in the band and he was the only one who knew what the different knobs meant. [laughter] He was a student at Fredonia University [near Buffalo] doing engineering classes and he would have some of that free midnight to 8 a.m. studio time - our first record was his senior project. *Yourself Is Steam* was handed in as his senior project.

That's a pretty good senior project. [laughter]

o, the same with the stuff we were doing with the Lips and things at that point. It was basically, "I have some cheap time at a university studio. Not much gear but you can mess around with it. Come

on, let's go." That also helps that at Fredonia there are kids who go to music school. If you want horns or strings, they're eager to come and play - that's kind of a plus.

Were there any records or anything that you had been listening to that made you come to Dave and say, "Oh, I really dig this sound." Do you ever come in like that?

We're all pretty close. He [Dave], and I and Sean [Grasshopper] are all pretty much on the same wavelength. We really don't know what it is we want. We generally know what it is we don't want. Those are the things that when they rear their ugly head all three of us will reach for the panic button [laughter] and press "erase" quite quickly. Sometimes there is a battle there, but for the most part you just sort of listen to the music and try and not repeat yourself too often. If some of our earlier records were a bit more aggressive and even abrasive in terms of their tone, then this one was probably a subconscious effort to make it sound like a really worn-out cassette. Something that had a comfort level immediately by putting it in.

Probably my favorite part of the record is the little instrumental things, like segues between songs. Did you ever feel like you're sitting there surrounded by glockenspiels [laughter] and wondering, "Does this belong on a rock/pop record?" Does that ever come up?

It does, but only in the way of how you present it. We don't really think of them so much as instrumentals, sometimes they just act as nice segues to give the listener sort of a breather from

something that is either 2/4 or 4/4 or heavy orchestral, something so that you can step out of it. We really haven't done many instrumentals in the past and I think that probably some of these would have had words but it was laziness. [laughter] You're forced to really express yourself without words. It sort of ups the challenge to say, "Well, is this instrumental really kicking our ass or is this just muzak for the sake of it?" Generally, people can tell the difference quite quickly on the first listen, "Does this sound like filler or does this have a purpose? Is it setting up another song quite well?" I think, for those reasons, it's something we're all quite conscious of. We could do instrumentals out the ass for the next 30 years but is it really doing something? Is it saying something? I think the same thing that runs through anyone's mind certainly runs through ours if not more, because we're in a sort of high public eye. Every little thing tends to be over-analyzed when all you can say is, "Hey, we were just having fun." It was not meant to change music, it's really to just have a little fun for two minutes.

I see that *Deserter Songs* was mastered by Greg Calbi [of Masterdisc]. The reason I bring that up is that when we did the interview with Don Dixon he mentioned how Calbi is the only guy he uses for mastering. Is that the same with you guys? Or did Dave or the label point him out?

No, Grasshopper had just seen his name around. There's another guy there who is equally as good as Calbi, but for whatever reason, we worked with Greg and it seemed to work out. He had a few ideas that certainly helped the record out - in that process.

So many musicians don't seem to understand mastering. Could you talk about what you think the mastering did for this record or what you think of mastering in general and why you think people should do it?

Well, there are a couple of different schools and we talk about it quite often. There are a lot of groups that record a bunch of crap and believe if you send it to Bob Ludwig, he's going to turn it around and make it sound like *Sgt. Pepper...* or *Pet Sounds*. That's really not the case. There's other bands that sort of do their record and send it to someone else and say, "Well, put your stamp of approval on it or give us your sound."

Give us your sonic imprint!

Yeah, so that nineteen different Howie Weinberg records all sound somewhat the same. I'm just using names for whatever reason, but for us, we go in there and we're very meticulous. We spent a year recording, why would you go in for the last two crucial days just get fucked up and do nothing or send it in the mail and hope it comes back? We're there and we always tend to look at the masterer as somebody who can articulate your ideas in that final step. Maybe someone who will give an alternative or something you hadn't thought of. Greg would do that, we'd say, "Well, it's not warm enough." He'd say "Well, I can do this or I can do this," instead of just saying, "I'm gonna do this the way I do it and fuck you." You have to listen to other records, basically. You'll find a continuity there amongst maybe even one guy's records, either Neil Young's or John Lennon's records. You can say, "Well, that's really good, and probably Greg Calbi had a lot to do with those Lennon records." So, why not? If you want a "modern rock" sound, there are guys who just do that sort of sound.

I remember when we were mixing our last record that we were using *Hawaii* by the High Llamas as a reference disc and we were commenting on how great it sounded and that the guy who mastered that at Abbey Road did a great job. Everything was there. It was warm, all the frequencies were there, but nothing was overbearing. We were just stunned. That's the kind of record you play for people to let them hear what mastering and recording is about.

I know Sean O'Hagen [head High Llama] is very intelligent in the way of knowing records, especially Beach Boys' records. You can hear a lot of that spatial influence within the High Llamas, things are spatially appropriate. People think that, "Well, just because it's stereo, you put one here and one here and that makes it a wide sounding record." It's not true, it's the depth perception that gives you that and that's just through experience. Good records are generally associated with people who made a lot of poor records, including us. Meaning records that didn't stand up to what you thought or hoped they might've been at the time. You learn and sometimes people think you throw a pan program on and that makes it spooky or psychedelic. It's just not the case. It's always "less is more". It's not what you play, it's what you don't. Once you develop that confidence in the band or even working with producers that can give you that confidence to say, "You know, you guys have got some really great parts, let's work with them. You don't have to write 32 more." That's where you begin to move forward.

Is there a favorite mic you like to use for your vocals?

Umm, Dave uses big, tall silver ones. [laughter] Probably Neumann U47s or something...

C12s maybe, too?

Yeah, I think there might've been. It's gotta be something Dave would know. But, yeah, they are usually big old things. They have a warmer sound. I have a lot of sibilance in my voice so he has to sort of shield that...

When you lay down vocals, do you sing with effects in your headphones?

Maybe some slight reverb here and there depending on the song, but for the most part, we really don't effect them much.

When you lay down vocals, do you sing in a small space or do you set up in the big room?

It's just out of laziness, wherever the mic is...

Have you even recorded in the control room, just sitting there listening to playback?

Yeah, literally. At some point I think you can understand where certain rooms are better, but for the most part it's really just the voice and you've got to try and work your best wherever it is. If the mic is out in the big room, than that's where I go. If it's in the kitchen, thats where I go. [laughter]

A very scientific process...

It's just the way we grew up making records. There never used to be 14 isolation booths and 32 padded rooms. There was only just a kitchen and a garage or this and that and you just went up there and gave

it hell. It's just like playing a bigger club now or a smaller club years ago, it's like, "Okay, there's no monitors, fuck it." You do your best and go up there and kick it out - letting everything else get to you sort of defeats the purpose, at least for our band and some of the groups we've been associated with. The mics are just sitting there on the drums or on an amp anyway, so we just pull it over... [laughter] Dave has an ear for things, but even he's not too particular in certain instances. You know, it's, "Are you gonna go do your voice?" "Yeah, what mic should I use?" He'll say, "Just grab one off the drum kit."

That's funny because our studio is a lot like that and sometimes we get an inferiority complex when you look at these massive, mega-studios, but in your case for example, you don't really need that...

Well, it just breeds imagination and creativity. If everything is done for you and there are three

guys to walk a mic out there for you and two to hand you a Reese's peanut butter cup, you tend to lose focus. We've worked in many big studios and BBC studios and all that and it just boils down to the song. I think certain gear helps certain engineers get there faster - rather than dicking around for three hours with poor EQs or crackily wires - that makes a difference, but for the actual performance of the song...

I think another strength of our situation is like Eno's philosophy. He was quoted as saying, "There are too many options in a modern studio." You can almost use your limitations as a strength.

Yeah, like Pro Tools. There are a million things you can do, but how much...? You can be there for hours dicking around, but if you don't have that, play the part right the first time...

When you're faced with near infinite options, what's a sane person to do?

Infinite options also get people to think, "Well the snare is not exactly on the click 40 bars in there." This was one of the first records we began using a click and it's valuable to sort of have some consistency, but at the same time you don't want to be a slave to it - where everything sounds so perfect. Then you're getting into Peter Gabriel-land. And that's just somewhere...

Well, don't the songs that sort of speed up at the chorus sound better?

It just depends on the music and the band. A lot band may have a hit record their first time out and they really don't realize what it is that they did on the record or how they can grow. They just hear the song on the radio and turn to the producer and say "Let's just do it again." The same thing over and over. A lot of groups, like ourselves, and the Lip and other groups - you know, commercial succes hasn't been banging our doors down. So, you're forced to create your own sort of world, your own paradise where all your songs are hits in your mind. [laughter] That drives you - you say, "Yes, I know the Supremes had hits, but they're great songs. Let's look at the good shit. Let's not listen to the bad shit. Let's look at some of the good things." I think in all our minds, we are deluded but you sort of have to have self-confidence to say, "Well, our songs could be hits, maybe in the '40s or in the '30s, but they could've been, they should be." When you have that approach, you really try hard. You just don't think, "Oh, we've got three hit songs and nine fillers. Let's concentrate on three songs and we'll leave the rest for some other guy to mix." For all of us, we work so hard at every little detail and most of it's just erasing constantly in the studio. [laughter] For every part that's on the record, 400 have been erased - blatant, miserable failures. Things that were... "That's a great idea, that's really gonna rock this world." Then you hear it the next morning and you're like, "What the fuck were we thinking?" It's the things that you're most afraid of on your record that strike people the hardest. The things that you're really unsure of... "Did we push it too far? Did we do something that even we don't know what's been done?" Those are things that stand out. The things that we found that we're most confident in.. "Yeah, we nailed it. That's

a rockin' one." Everybody just goes, "Hmmm, okay." And it's the things that you thought were kinda scary. Those are the things that stand out. The more balls you have, the more you find your record is filled with frightful things to yourself. Things that you didn't imagine you could do or you don't even know how you did.

hat was it like working with Levon Helm and Garth Hudson [of The Band]? The drums sound exactly the same way as they do on *Music from Big Pink*. I was just stunned by that...

e just sits down and it's instant Levon, add water... Yeah, I was stunned by it. It really must be the player, you know? Because here we are 30 years later and the drums sound the same. But Levon has a funny way of playing. He's not a heavy hitter. He doesn't wail on them, so that was one song that Dave had to fudge with a bit in terms of the EQ because

Levon hits very lightly, very dynamically. So some kick drum [hits] will be very quiet and others will be like, "thud, thud, thud". So Dave's riding the fader like mad...

I read somewhere that Tom Dowd [famous house engineer for Atlantic Records] would ride the fader all the time so he didn't have to use so much compression.

That's what faders are for. You move 'em and shit happens. You sort of have to get over the fact that the board doesn't run itself. [laughter] Then it frees you up to this other world of like, "Yeah, that guitar is quiet here and now it needs to be loud even though it's still quiet." For us, anything they tell us not to do, we do. Like, you can't run DATs into the red on the machine. The first time we got it in at Fredonia with Dave he said, "You guys can't run it in there [in the red], you'll get distortion." We were like, "Fuck that." [laughter] Then you realize it takes a lot to overload a DAT or tape or something. So, then you learn by experience.

I've learned not to be so afraid of distortion, at least in the analog recording stage. We use a lot of old gear. A lot of old tube crap and stuff. There's these two preamps I got out of an old Ampex tape machine that I just love and you can distort 'em.

It can add character - sibilance and stuff. Aretha Franklin, you listen to anything she sang and her sibilance is beautiful the way it adds the character to it. The Motown records have so much bass, you think it's going to knock the jukebox over. But those were people who realized, "Well, the bass is the booty. People shake to the booty." That's what you accentuate. That's something where the guitars might lose to the bass on this track or on this part. Not everything needs to win. Music is not a democracy when done at it's best.

Don [Dixon] said something like that. To the effect of, "You don't have to hear everything." It's more about how it's felt there. If it were taken away you would know, but it's not readily apparent on the first or second listen.

The rhythm guitars and things... you don't even realize they are there. But if they weren't there totally, you'd notice it. But if they're slightly in there it changes the mood and stuff...

Anything else you'd like to say?

Just to anyone recording, there are no rules, break the rules - do whatever. You are the producer, you know? As much as the title can mean something in a larger way, to be in awe of something, even as great as Motown or Stax or something. Those were people not unlike anyone here in this room. People who are learning, people who are trying something out. Especially for your readers or for anyone - you are in control. This is the one point

in your life when you will have some control. [laughter] Exert it, because everything that goes with the record after it's in the stores, you have no control over. Where you play, whom you play with, and how much money you don't make. All of that you have no control over. Exhibit something so you can sleep well at night. Say, "Yes, I put my soul into it. If people hate it, fuck it. Because it really lived up to what I had hoped it would." That's why people sleep well.

Speaking of that, do you have anybody else you'd like to work with someday?

Well, Dave has always been a part of our group. He plays on the records. So, as Mercury Rev goes, Dave goes with it. But at the same point, I think Dave is always up for collaborating with people. It's not so much to have some imaginary British producer come in and sort of throw lightning bolts - it's really just to work with somebody. For us it's important to work with the older people. The Jack Nitzche's [god-like arranger of all the Spector stuff. Also produced Neil Young, among others] of the world. And people like that where you can collaborate with them and say, "This is one way we were doing it, if it's in your hands, what would you do?" And to be there physically and watch him and ask him these questions. Not just send him the mix and say, "Do something." You want to learn from the horse's mouth, which is one of the reasons we got Levon and Garth in. Why get a drummer to parody Levon, why not get Levon himself? [laughter]

That must be one of the nice benefits of having success...

Well, it's not even so much success, it was the fact that we just asked. Because a lot of older people really aren't working much. The label didn't even want us to use Levon and Garth. They just thought, "Well, these are just old guys. We can get you some 21 year old kid who knows computers." You say, "Well, these guys are Levon and Garth and these are people who, yeah, haven't had a hit since '67 but they're valuable." Those are people that we hear. The Bob Johnston's, the Jack Nitzche's. It's more of a collaboration to say, "Well, we've got some ideas and this time we're not going to go in there and turn every knob ourselves. What would you do? These are some sounds we've heard on your earlier records, was it magic? Was it accidents?" Usually they'd be honest with us and say, "Look, I was fuckin' wasted at the time in '64 and I can't even remember doin' that record." You say, "Okay, let's pretend you are and work from there." Those are the people who are self-taught. It's in the mind. It's people who might say, "Half the shit you recorded on the song is utter bullshit. Take it off and you'll have a good song." That's more valuable than anyone turning up the high-end on a hi-hat. The best producers will try and simply tell you what not to do. Through their own experience they'll say, "I know what you're trying for, maybe stay away from that and try this road." That's just what we do with each other. Bring out the best performance in each other. ✸

CALEXICO

by: John Askew
photos by: Val Cañez

The first time I tried to reach Giant Sand, OP8 and Calexico drummer/multi-instrumentalist Joh Convertino at his Tucson, Arizona home he didn't answer the phone. It seemed only natural tha when he called back he told me he hadn't heard the ring because he was playing the drums. H and the other musical head behind Calexico, Joey Burns, have been busy. With the follow-up t their first record *Spoke*, the latest Calexico release *The Black Light* has kept them on the roa in Europe and around the States, seemingly around the clock. But in addition to their rigorous roa diet, they have managed to play and record with artists such as Richard Buckner, Barbara Mannin Doug McCombs and their musical alter egos (with long time friend and Tucson music-ma Howe Gelb) Giant Sand and OP8. I talked to both of them during some of their time off and aske them about the recordings, the bands, the music business, and Tucson.

First I talked to John

ll these great records have come out of Tucson that you've been a part of. Is Giant Sand sort of the hub of the wheel of projects so to speak [OP8, Calexico, Giant Sand]?

/e heard other people use this word a lot, like Howe especially: *reinvention*. I think as a way of being able to survive as a musician you have to be able to reinvent what you do. If I scale it down to what I do as a drummer... if I set my drums up different or use a different drum set or even if I just turn a cymbal upside down it will just automatically make me think and play a different way. With that same concept if it reverberates out and you do something as drastic as change the name of the band even, it's going to totally change what you

do. I think Giant Sand kind of centered around what Howe would bring to the table and Joey and I would add our ingredients to the dinner. OP8 was originally Howe, Joey and I experimenting with different ways of putting songs together. You know I'm playing vibes now and accordion, and Joey's playing guitar more now. So it was branching out on different instruments. Then Lisa Germano jumped in there and it became a whole record.

How did Lisa get involved?

Her record company at the time was wanting their artists to work with different musicians. Since we met her in New Orleans, when we [Giant Sand] were doing the *Glum* record, we all got along really well. So when the label challenged her to work with other people she said, "I wanna work with the Giant Sand guys." Her label didn't really like what she was doing with us so that freed us up to finish it, do a whole record and then shop it around. That, consequently, got the V2 [records] thing going for Giant Sand.

So I heard the new OP8 is not going to be with Lisa Germano?

The idea was to try and bring in different people. To leave it more open.

You and Joey seem like the dream session players for so much stuff. You did the Barbara Manning and the Richard Buckner records. Do you promote yourself as session players?

No, it just pretty much happens. If a person hears something they like and they think we can work with us they contact us. Although there are people I'd love to work with like Chan from Cat Power. I really like that record [*Moon Pix*]. I think she would be a great OP8 candidate. I'd love to work with Lisa again but it's hard with schedules. It's hard to force these things. You kind of have to allow them to happen. That's like the first OP8 record. It's weird when things get forced and expectations get put on it. It ruins it.

The new album that you just did... did you write stuff like you always have in Giant Sand or more like "reinvention" of an old band?

I think Howe really had to dig deep and go into different more territories than he has before because he was working with a major label. I think they were wanting something more specific than Giant Sand has ever had to come up with. More radio friendly. For me personally it was a more difficult thing for me.

In the recording process?

Yeah. There were ideas that I had that weren't really able to happen because we were working with a producer and on a major label. It just wasn't as free. The label [V2] put up a budget. It's all in the contracts. The studio and the producers all have to be approved by both sides: the band and the label.

Your Calexico records came out on Quarterstick, an indie label.

Yeah totally independent, practically no budget.

You're able to have total freedom when you record something. How do you feel about having more money to record?

With *Glum* [Giant Sand] it was neat because we got to go to New Orleans [Kingsway Studio] and live in the studio and work with really good mics and a really good engineer and get good sounds. That was a great experience. That was when big budget worked for Giant Sand. Then it was kind of interesting. The day our record was done our A & R person got fired and the label kind of went bankrupt. Even though the record didn't get promoted very well, at least we didn't have to pay back that huge budget.

What did you spend on *Glum*?

I don't know, $75,000. For us that was big. Mostly, just being able to be in that big house there in that French Quarter, living there. When you woke up in the morning and you stumbled down the stairs and there was your drum set all mic'ed up and the engineer was already buzzed on three cups of coffee and ready to go. It was great. I think with this new Giant Sand record it was fractured because we never really had that place. We recorded some of it in Memphis, some in Tucson, some at home. it was more mixed up. Ultimately it is going to present a very interesting and diverse sounding record.

You and Joey did the first Calexico record, *Spoke*, and the new one, *The Black Light*, yourselves right?

Yeah. Craig [Schumacher, of Wavelab] helps a lot. Even with the *Spoke* record, although we recorded at our houses, we took it to Wavelab and threw a lot of stuff into Pro Tools and did editing.

How do you feel about Pro Tools? You know digital editing and using computers?

I think it's great. It's exactly what it is, a tool, you know. Another way of helping things along. You just have to not let it be a master of you. For me I just want things to sound real. You gotta have that feel to it. Psychologically, it took me awhile to come to grips with the digital world. It's so weird that the music is going into these boxes. Like with the *Glum* record, the engineer [Trina Shoemaker], she did most of the editing on the 2-inch tape right there. With a razor blade. She would be tapping her foot and slice the tape. It's hairy but I dug it. I loved the reality and the instantaneous of it all. There is a margin of error there. The digital world is super clean.

Yeah I just bought a computer a couple of months ago. It'd be cool to be able to store mixes.

Yeah, and I like being able to loop things too. There's those accidents that actually wind up being the coolest part of a song and you can build a song out of that. Even if it is just looping it to remember it.

In terms of the records you've played drums on, there is a definite link between all the recordings and the sounds of the drums. The drums are totally unique but they have a "feel". I like to A/B the OP8 and Calexico records a lot when I'm mixing. I associate the recordings of those records mostly with your drumming and the drum sounds.

Well, it could be the sound, the actual sound of the drum set. That has something to do with it. But I think more than anything it's capturing performances. And this is something we've all learned from Howe more than anybody. The way he plays and the way he comes up with his music is very in the moment. And if you don't capture that moment it's pretty much gone. A lot of the stuff that was recorded at Wavelab, whether it was by Nick Luca [the engineer] or Craig, they were astute enough to tell when something was happening, really happening, when the band was playing and to press that fricken' record button. You know? It would be like I'd go out to the drums, Howe's startin' to play guitar and Craig would go, "Oh this is happening" and he'll press record. Instead of saying, "Let's tape this - let's make this a take." Stopping the band. A lot of engineers make the mistake of going, "Wow that was great, let's take one." Then it's gone. You can try a go again the same way and it just does not work. It's bizarre, the whole sound, the physical sound of the drums and everything starts changing.

Would Craig be rolling tape all the time?

Yeah. Sometimes he would have a DAT going. Something un-tangible happens. I think John Coltrane may have said it once: "You will always play different when the tape is rolling." When we were recording the *Glum* record Malcom Burn would say, " Yeah that was great do it again." And we just couldn't. I would think I'm a lame-ass drummer. I can't come up that groove we were just playing. A lot of times a producer won't take no for an answer and you'll spend the whole night working on the song and it's really just a waste of time.

Are you good at knowing when that's happening?

No. I'm not. There were times when I thought a take was really good and it sucked. In that Memphis session [for the new Giant Sand record], we did a take, then did a second take, then a third. And we all agreed that the second take was the best. Then the engineer rewound the tape and went past the second take and we were listening to the first take. We were all going this doesn't sound like the second take but we were all diggin' it. It was a happy accident. We listened to the second take and it really sucked.

So do you and Joey both have studios in your house?

No. I'd like to. The *Spoke* record was done on 8-track that the Friends of Dean Martinez had bought. It was in Joey's apartment for a while and then in mine. Just two microphones. This house I'm living in now has an amazing sound. It's got 14 foot ceilings, all stucco inside. It s just a regular brick house. It has this weird hallway, you know? Rooms with lots of doorways leading into this hallway with this high ceiling. Lots of room for notes, sounds, to go off into a little corner and circulate. You put mics around in different corners.

The drum sounds, specifically the kick, are all so similar. You can tell it's the same drummer. But there seems to be a specific mic approach too. Is it something you picked up from Craig or is it the way you like to hear your kit?

> "If I set my drums up different or use a different drum set or even if I just turn a cymbal upside down it will just automatically make me think and play a different way."

I got into this thing where I didn't want to have anything in my drum. I got this Ludwig kit about twelve years ago that has this sound. I think it has something to do with the fact the the shells are thin. When you hear the Ludwig, the bass drum opens up. It's an open sound. You're hearing like this subsonic reverberation. You're feeling it more than you're hearing. It's just a double headed bass drum with no hole cut in it. I think a lot of it has to do with heads too, made in the '60s.

Does a lot of that sound come from the warehouse at Wavelab?

Yeah, it's a great sounding room. And in the house here too, it sounds really good. There are some things about that *Spoke* record that I like better. More open. You hear the air.

The drums sound incredible on the first song on the Buckner *Devotion and Doubt* record. Especially the kick.

Yeah, I think that was a first or second take. You have to give Craig credit too. He would just go with that. He's got a lot of enthusiasm and energy. If it's not happening he'll just move mics around and put them in different parts of the room. He's not like, "Take the front head off, blah, blah, blah."

Experimenting is good.

The bottom line is just getting things to reverberate. I gotta feel like the wood is vibrating. When Joey's playing the acoustic bass you can walk right up to it and put your hand on it and feel it vibrating. When we were on tour on with the Dirty Three I just had to walk up to Warren's violin and put my hand on it.

Then I called Joey...

How important do you feel the recordings are, as aesthetic, to your records?

I try to think of the recording process as another band member. The silent band member. Doesn't watch, just listens. Depending on what machine you record on it can give your album a totally different vibe.

The *Black Light*... unlike *Spoke*, you did at Wavelab. What was the main difference in terms of your involvement?

We've worked with Craig and Nick Luca (Wavelab engineer) so much. Those guys are so used to us that a lot of times they set us up with a few mics and say, "Alright, we'll see you guys later." During the Friends of Dean Martinez records and the

Calexico records we'd be engineering ourselves. Craig and Nick would help get the basics and we'd jump in and do overdubs.

Would they help you mix?

Yeah we would all mix together. It was hard because the budget was minimal. We were kind of pushing our limit as far as time in the studio. Not only that... there is a certain natural time that feels good to be in a studio and if you go over that it can pretty devastating. If you're going over and over on a take it can completely ruin the song. You might as well call it a day and go and get some Mexican food. Go watch the sunset and come back later that night or the next day. The tape doesn't lie, it's going to play back whatever you do. On the *The Black Light* we wanted to have a little better sounding recording. *Spoke* is a different vibe, more like a home vibe.

So you don't necessarily have a preference?

No, it depends on the song. What you want to paint.

If you had had more of a budget for those records would you have wanted to spend more money and go into a big time studio?

No. Wavelab moved recently.

Oh really? So now what does that mean?

That means no more trains on the recordings. Right next door there was a dance studio. So a lot times we had to wait for the train to go by, and then wait for the dance class, or go over and say, "Hey we're going to record this song could you just hold off for five minutes." Sometimes they would, sometimes they wouldn't.

So did Craig get a nice new space?

It's still a nice size room. He's built a small dry room. He doesn't have a wall for the control room. It might be nice to have some separation from mixing. Right now it's pretty open and we like it.

Have you tracked a lot in there already?

We did a project with this guy named Jean Louis Mirat from France. And then I did some stuff with Doug McCombs of Tortoise. We got a great vibe, great sound. Just set up some mics, sat around in a semi-circle, threw up a couple baffles, and it all went to tape.

Do you and John always start recording with the two of you playing live?

Yeah, well we just try and get a good take. With *The Black Light* I decided I wanted to try and do some stuff at home so I borrowed a 4-track and did some rhythmic stuff. I wanted to break up the songs and the huge amounts of orchestrations with really simple, monotonous things. To put you in the trance state. John came over one day and picked up the bass and I hopped on a pot or a pan or a shaker and recorded a couple of songs like "Fake Fur" and "Chach".

Is there a lot of improvisation on *The Black Light*?

Yeah, but I wanted to go more away from improvisation and into orchestration and arrangement.

Like the "Where Water Flows"? It is so beautiful.

Just vibes, guitar and cello on a 4-track at home. Sometimes on these records there's a lot of stuff. There'll be like an accordion, old world, Italian waltz. John has been doing that for a while because that's his roots. There's a tradition that comes through on each record. It's got that flavor. For me it's like the Spaghetti in the Spaghetti Western. We have all these different styles. Sometimes I think we could do a whole record of stuff like "Where Water Flows". I wanted to utilize all these different instruments we've been collecting, like marimbas, vibes, mandolin, the accordion. Here where we live it's called Barrio Viejo. Some of the oldest buildings in Tucson are right here. So you have a lot of old Mexican families here, the music blaring on Sundays. The family coming by, the low-riders crammed with kids. The life down here breathes a completely different kind of breath. At times you can lose yourself. Am I in Mexico or in America?

So how did the whole Richard Buckner connection work out for his record *Devotion and Doubt*?

We were all down at SXSW a few years ago and Buckner came to our show and John checked out his show. We had met JD Foster [producer and ex- True Believer, etc.]. I had heard about him through Craig so I was really interested in meeting him. They liked what we were doing. We enjoy playing with other people because you really get to focus in and listen to that person and back them up.

What was JD's role in terms of your playing?

He was great. I really liked the way he was inside of Richard Buckner's songs. He knew everything about the songs. He did his homework. Also, he really made us feel that he liked us as people and that he liked our playing. There was no such thing as a mistake. JD was like a conductor when we were doing takes.

Again, it was all done live?

Yeah.

Did JD encourage all that sparsness and space or was that Richard?

I think a lot of that record has to do with Richard and JD getting in the car. Driving to Texas, driving to Tucson. Being in New York. Those guys have a great rapport. We're only on a few of those tracks. Which is so beautiful. When you hear the band come in it sounds so great. Then, just like leaving a town out here in the desert, you drive away and you're in the middle of nothing. Like an instrumental that's like maybe 30 seconds long just fits in so perfectly between two songs. Bridging songs together by way of transitional snippets or sketches.

Yeah you guys do that on the *Spoke* record.

Yeah, an ice cream truck in the barrio.

I asked John this too, what is your perspective on indie vs. major, no budget vs. budget?

I think indie is more realistic. At the same time it's nice when records get out there. But in the major label process of putting records out there it seems like the people that end up working on your album have no clue as far as who you are and what you do. That to me is a big sign. It's like, "Okay, there's someone selling my record that doesn't know jack shit about where we come from or what we like musically or what we like aesthetically." Whereas Quarterstick/Touch and Go is the best label I've ever worked with. They've got their shit down. They're the most friendly people and most honest and sincere people. And they're putting out great music.

Are you happy with what happened with the new Giant Sand record?

I still haven't heard the final mixes. V2 has a certain criteria that they want to see met with the Giant Sand record. They want to get it out there as much as possible. So they need something they feel they can work with. That was where I had to step back from that whole process because it just feels very strange.

And the new OP8?

I just talked with Lisa Germano yesterday to say hello. Talk about studio save. That girl, she knows what's going on. I learned so much from her approach. I mean she kind of took the bull by the horns. Like getting in there at 11:00 every day. We were all like, "Let's get there at noon... alright lets go get some lunch." She really helped us with the discipline. You know, "Move on, next thing... great take John let's go. Howe, I want you to do this... okay that sounds great." There was this woman in the studio that has got everyone wrapped around her finger. She's learned a lot from the recording process. When we worked with her it showed. This was when the machine ran at both 30 and 15 ips. She would do things like on *"It's a Rainbow."* She got this old accordion down from the wall and played the bass notes... sitting down on the ground... recorded it at 30 ips and then put it back down to 15 ips. It was like a bellowing organ. She's a master of getting vocal sounds. Craig would get things set up and she would come in and do her own vocals. Seems like that works better.

What's next?

Well there's some touring to do as Calexico, the new OP8, the new Giant Sand is coming out so we'll see if there are any tour dates with that. There's Bundy K. Brown of Isotope 217, Pullman and that whole Thrill Jockey circle of friends. He did a mix of some of our stuff. He got Doug McCombs of Tortoise and Rob of Isotope to play on it. It's really ambient. It goes off on that tangent. So we're working on a B side to that. ☉

DEATH CAB FOR CUTIE

Death Cab For Cutie attacked me when I heard their first album, *Something About Airplanes*. I was floored by the melodies, and the overall sound of the entire album. Their first album was constantly in my CD player for five months; I was afraid of wearing it out. The best part about the album was that it was recorded by band member, and all around nice guy, Chris Walla. When their latest album, *We Have The Facts and We're Voting Yes*, came out I sacrificed food for a couple of days to be able to get it ASAP. Through an almost constant bugging through email I was able to get to meet the band and from there I arranged for Chris and I to sit down in a Seattle coffeehouse and talk shop. Afterwards I gave him an old Revox I had and he gave me a TEAC M-2A mixing board. I picked Chris' brain and realized that the mysterious sounds I heard on the new album weren't so mysterious.

by Bryan Bingold // photos by Chris Wills & Kelly Huckaby

hen did your interest in recording start?

remember being six years old and listening to *Sgt. Pepper's* with a pair of headphones going, "Oh there's something over here and something on this side. Why is that?" It used to drive my mom crazy 'cause I would balance everything to the left and listen to just the horns like in "Good Morning Good Morning" or something. I didn't know it at that time, but that's when I got interested in recording. Then in high school I got a little further into it. I've always have been putting together Radio Shack adapters with crappy microphones. When Nathan and I met we just wrote songs and recorded them together. I did a lot of crazy shit. Like those three dollar Radio Shack microphones, we used to stick them inside the hi-hat and then close the hi-hat and hit it and get this awful noise - it was great.

'as there a distinct point where you bought a piece of equipment and said, "Now I'm committed. Now I know this is something that I want to go into."

ot really. I got a 4-track either my senior year of high school or first year of college. I don't remember. It wasn't really a conscious thing. I guess I've always been interested in recording, but I never knew that I was interested until I started doing 4-track stuff. So I guess maybe the 4-track, yeah. And I was also making mix tapes for people.

Once you got the 4-track did you start accumulating different outboard gear, mics and stuff like that? Was it a snowball effect?

Kind of. For a long time all I had was a 4-track and a [Shure SM] 58, and I guess my parents bought an Alesis MicroVerb for Christmas one year. I didn't even have a guitar amp for a long time. I had a guitar and a Rat pedal and that was it. So I went direct on all my guitars, like maybe a little bit of delay from the MicroVerb. But I didn't even put a mic in front of a guitar amp until like three years ago. I didn't really start amassing stuff until I was out of school, out of Shoreline [University].

Did you take any classes in recording? Read a lot of manuals? Or was it just a matter of getting the equipment and fiddling around until you got something good?

I went to Shoreline for two years and did the recording thing there. Failed both of my recording classes there. Most of the reason for that was that there was fifty people in the class and one studio, so getting any time in the room was a total miracle. The instructor was great and it's a good class and I learned a lot on the book side of it, but I figured out really quick that the only way I was going to get any time in the studio was to not go to recording class. So I would not go to class and

screw around in the studio instead. Record direct guitar and drum machines and crazy stuff. Like write songs just to be able to record them.

So when did your Hall of Justice recording studio start up?

Funny, it's not actually a studio. It's just a bunch of half broken stuff that roves around from place to place under my direction. It's wherever you want it to be.

It's portable? It's mobile?

It's not really mobile - that's the thing. It's all this big cranky, clunky, old, old state of the art mid-'70s analog stuff. It's all temperamental - like knocking on wood all the time to make sure it works. After I got out of Shoreline and when I first met Ben [Gibbard] he had some songs he wanted to record, and I had some songs I wanted to record. For a long time it was just a matter of renting stuff and driving up to Bellingham, because I was still living down here. I would just rent stuff and go up there during the weekends. Like American Music used to have this reel to reel 8-track analog package. So I could get a TSR-8 and a Mackie 1604 and a couple of mics for like $250 bucks for a week. It was super cheap, because it was right around the time when the ADAT thing was happening and no one was interested in the 8-track anymore. So I would just do that and screw around on the 8-track. We recorded on two or three different occasions, and then I decided that if I was renting this stuff all the time, that I could drop $2500 or $3000 and get a couple of mics and machine and a crappy board and cables. Eventually that's what I did, I just maxed out a credit card, bought my 8-track, board and a couple of mics, which was what we recorded the first record on.

The name "Hall of Justice" is there a story behind that?

I'm a "Superfriends" fanatic. A big fan.

Were you recording other bands as well at this time?

No, not really. The great bulk of the recording I've ever done has been stuff that I have been involved in on a first hand level. Like stuff I'm playing on or contributed to. The first Death Cab tape was really the first thing I recorded that I didn't play anything on. That was really easy, because Ben is just real chill about recording. It was understood that he was writing and playing the songs, and I got to do what I wanted on the recording end. We were both guinea pigs for each other and that worked out really well. And somehow or other that's still how it works. He's the songwriter and I'm the recordist, more or less. I don't ask him any questions and neither does he. So it works out. I mean we definitely both contribute with one another. It's still really hard to record other bands because I still don't have a good solid dedicated space to do it. Recording spaces have always ended up in really compromised places. Like in Bellingham, it was our house, and there was always a roommate there who wasn't a musician, who was a senior and studying for finals. All the roommates were super supportive, but even so it's hard to charge other bands to come into your house when it's very much a house-house and not a rock and roll house to do some recording. So I mean, even getting someone to come in on weekends for free was an ordeal. The place we're in now doesn't have heat and there's no bathroom. It's unlivable.

Is that your practice space?

It's the practice space we have now. It's this little cinder block box, but it's working out okay. It's a totally recordable room, which is nice.

Analog versus digital? What's your choice?

Man, the *Tape Op* question. Given the choice I would always pick analog. The thing is that I'm discovering quickly, for where I'm at, it's the idealism versus practicality argument. It's very much about finances. If you have the financial ability to keep an analog machine in order, then you're doing really well. But if you're in a situation like I'm in... I never know what my 8-track is going to do. I haven't any idea. I mean it's not like a Studer or an Ampex MM 1200 where they're still, to some degree, pro-machines and there's parts for them everywhere, and there's always someone who knows how to work on them,

particularly the Ampexs, Studers and Otaris. But then you get into the sketchy semi-pro basement stuff from the '80s like I am used to. I have a 1/2" 8-track and it's like pulling teeth to get parts for or even someone to work on it. I've had some really bad experiences with some people in town. Even when I have a service manual to give to people. It's seems like five or six years ago people still knew what to do with that stuff, but the whole 1/2" 8-track stuff is so far out of phase that if you take one to someone for a transport [problem] you're just fucked. It's going to sit there for months, they won't be able to find the parts and you're going to wait and wait and wait. It's just a drag. But given the choice I would choose analog. And I'm rediscovering that again as I'm finally learning the space between compression and distortion on a piece of tape and different pieces of tape. How 456 is different from the GP9 and stuff. Which is something I've never gotten to before and now I'm understanding. It makes sense. And I love to hack up tape, I love to drag a razor blade through a piece of tape, and you can't do that on any practical digital level.

Have you've ever thought of picking up some old electronics manuals and learn to repair some of your equipment yourself?

Yeah, I've thought about it. But I also thought about getting burned and breathing in lead fumes. I'm a terrible, dismal, pathetic electrician. I don't know anything - I can barely solder together a guitar cable. It's really a bad situation for what I do. I have all this old equipment and whenever it breaks I have to take it to get repaired. I mean one of these days I'll take an electronics class and figure out what's going on, but I'm hopeless until then.

What piece of outboard gear can't you live without?

This has changed just recently. It used to be this little preamp I have called the Newcomb Pathfinder, but I don't think it's the Pathfinder anymore. I'm starting to think it's my board. It's an Allen and Heath, The Mix Wizard. It's just this 16-channel board. It's actually the Allen and Heath equivalent of the Mackie 1604, but it does some really weird stuff that I'm really, really digging a lot. It does stuff that I haven't been able to hear on anything else. I mean its just this little portable board that's built to do anything you ask it to do. It's really awesome. The EQ section is so fun. One of my favorite things to do I got into on the last record: The EQ overlaps so much - there's two midsweeps and they overlap between 500Hz and 1K so you can zero in on things in that range and boost them like 30dB and overload the channel. It's just this ridiculously gritty, awful, brittle sound. It's really fun. And I like to take the pad off the channel, just totally drive it so it's red, then white. Then you can put an effect on that and place it way down in the mix so that's it's just barely there. The Allen and

Heath has all these cheesy effects built into it and you can't control any of the parameters. It's like having a guitar with built-in effects. It's like "Cathedral" and you don't get to adjust the amount, or the time of decay, or the brightness or darkness. It's just "Cathedral". That's all you get.

There's only one "Cathedral" sound and that's what you're getting?

Exactly! That's kind of cool though. Sometimes the less stuff you have to fuck with is better.

In "Title Track", in the beginning of the song, there is a huge level change. Is that just a level change?

Not at all. The first half of the song we recorded bass, drums, and guitar all together live in a room into one microphone and then we doubled that same performance. Ben went back and added his guitar and vocal, and then we just stopped at that point in the song. Then I had Ben go and play the drums. We did that to click track, basically the entire album was done to click track. So you have those two tracks and then it opens up, and it's all on the tape like that. We ended up mixing that song a lot. I mixed a version of the full song and then I went back and mixed the first half of the song and then mixed the second half of the song, individually. Then when Tony [Lash] mastered it we slapped the two together and then Tony dumped down the beginning a little and narrowed the stereo image a bit to make it more drastic.

On "The Employment Pages" it sounds like you used reverb on Ben's vocals. Was it one basic reverb or a bunch of them?

There's really no...

I mean did the "Cathedral" make an appearance on this album?

Anytime there's a reverb sound on this record that is ridiculously bombastic it's the "Cathedral". I mean BOOM! But there's really no artificial reverb on this record, it's all just room sounds. The vocal on "Employment Pages" and all the delay on Ben's vocal is from my little analog delay pedal, that and a little digital delay pedal I have. Ben got really into the slap delay on his voice for this record, and there would be times where I wouldn't want to use it. But Ben would get a little defensive and say, "No! I want it there." So with that song, I ran his delayed vocal to my guitar amp and put a mic at the other end of the house and sent that back to another channel in the board and compressed it to shit.

On "405" there's a pulsating tone that travels throughout the song. Is that a phone tone, a keyboard sample?

That's Dr. Sample. Man, Dr. Sample is the key.

Is that one with like 24 second sampling time without a memory card?

It's this little black box with orange buttons. Boss makes it and it costs 300 bucks. It runs on batteries, on AC, it's got RCA ins and outs. It's got 1/4" in and 1/8" out.

Do you play with the waveform buttons?

Oh yeah. That machine is destined to be a piece of equipment like the Roland Space Echo is today. It's kind of weird and twitchy, but it's so easy to use and it does a specific thing and it does that thing so well. It's great.

How do you usually pull samples? Do you mic things? Do you take them from CDs?

On "405" that pulse is actually a sample off a little Yamaha keyboard that I have. I distorted it into Dr. Sample, and then it does that repeat thing. So that was a quarter note and then I have a quarter note delay and then I had to manually line it up to the click track. We've been pulling samples from stuff we've recorded. Like the drum loop in "For What Reason" was from a different part of that song and just tweaked like crazy.

On "Company Calls", right before the chorus, there's a backwards swoop. Is that keyboards? A sample?

No, it's a backwards tom. I took a SM 57 on the tom hit and then turned it backwards then sent that through the "Cathedral" and brought it back on to another channel. Then I turned the tom hit back around so it's normal, but you get this pre-verb sound. A big suck up sound. And I know there are easier ways to do that, but... Then there's an EQ sweep on that as well.

At the end of "Company Calls Epilogue" it sounds like a very distant mic'd recording of Ben and his guitar.

That song got recorded the day before mastering. We recorded another version of that song and it's going to come out on an EP later this summer. But that ending was the old scratch acoustic guitar track from the other version of that song. We ended up keeping that and with the click track Nate [Good] could play drums with it. It just turned out really well and it's almost a seamless transition at the end. That scratch track was recorded with a cheap four dollar mic, through my Rat pedal and then back into the board.

The thing that impressed me the most was the drum sounds. Do you have a set mic'ing pattern for the drums? Or do you just throw up anything?

No, drums are like anything goes. This record we had a lot of problems with drums. Ben can play the drums really well, but he is not a drummer. I mean he is, but he doesn't have all the things that comes with being a drummer, like being able to tune the drums, and being an endurance drummer. Some of the songs were cake, but two days into recording the snare drum went flat, and it became apparent, really quickly, that none of us knew how to tune a snare.

Not even Nathan?

Well Nathan wasn't even supposed to play on the record because he was out of the band at this point. But we called him in the day before mastering because we decided to record two more songs. Both of those songs got tracked and mixed the day before mastering - it was insane. I think

that this is the record where I found what works and what doesn't work for me as far as drums go. Up until now I had been trying to do the Steve Albini/photographic realism sort of thing. I've finally figured out, I think, when it can work for me and when it can't. I think that most of the time it doesn't. There's this record that I'm doing now for the Revolutionary Hydra where I'm just doing something completely different. Most of the drums on the Death Cab record are either three or four mics. One in the kick drum and then two mics somewhere in the room, always a big, wide, and noncoincidental pairs. The Hydra stuff on the 8-track is done to a click track so 7 tracks open then I mix that to my CD-R and then bounce it back to the 8-track as 2 stereo tracks. I've just been close mic'ing things in lots of different combinations and learning that it can work for a lot of different things. Photographic realism, if you're a genie at it, that's all you do and it's awesome, but I don't have a consistent enough situation to figure out how to make it work, not room wise, equipment wise, not player wise. So I'm starting to get into the "anything goes" style.

So you aren't the type of recordist that will spend three to four hours placing a certain mic to get that certain sound?

No, no. I am so impatient. Terribly impatient. I've gotten used to recording Ben and Ben is always ready before I am. When I first met Ben there was a big imbalance because he knew exactly what he was doing as a songwriter and a singer and I just bought all that equipment. I didn't even know where the plugs went and I just had to totally catch up with him. I think just doing that has just made me feel that I have to move fast. I think I'm at a point where I can move fast and for the most part get some good sounds. I like to over-compensate as well, I mean if you have more mics than you need then just erase it as you go.

What's the most important thing about recording for you?

I would have to say it's doing right for the song. As a sound geek, it is easy to get tied up in something because it sounds good. But if it sounds good it doesn't necessarily mean that it compliments the song. It could very well be doing the song a great disservice. My whole goal is to keep the songs focused on what is best for the songs. If the recordings are interesting to listen to then that's cool, but the recording, at least in rock and roll, shouldn't be more important than the song. It's my job to get whatever on tape that best showcases the song.

Any last advice for those frantic home recorders that read TAPE OP?

I guess there are no rules to speak of. That's something that is easy to say, easy to hear, but very tough to practice. It's hard to let go and say, at least for me, "Oooh, can I do this?" and the answer is yes - of course you can. You might blow something up, but it's worth trying.

It's the consequence you'll pay, as long as you got the sound of it blowing up on tape.

Hopefully you did, to use later on.

Why does Chris produce all the albums? Have you ever thought of getting an outside producer?

Chris: It's definitely been talked about. I mean I like to record and this band has been a guinea pig for me for a long time and they're very nice to have been the guinea pig.

Ben: Well we were going to get that one guy who recorded "Heart of Glass" by Blondie [Mike Chapman]. We need that kind of guy. I mean Chris is all right, he is doing his "recording" and his "stuff" but...

Chris: We were in touch with Steely Dan for awhile.

Ben: We need a producer that will turn the song around and make it a hit.

Chris: We're almost there.

Ben: We need the type of producer that will just swing us a hit.

Chris: I think for the new record, it definitely turned into "my project". I got kind of defensive about it and maybe at the expense of the record. In hindsight, it might have been a good idea to have someone else mix it or have an ear on it. By the time we got done with it it had been on the plate for five months.

Was Tony Lash [the mastering engineer] telling you what you should have fixed?

Chris: No. Tony is really cool that way. I had a talk with Tony about that very same thing and Tony said, "I hate when people say, 'You should have done this that way and you should have done that this way.'" That's not how you do it. The only way you learn how to change things is just by doing it. People make suggestions and you take what you need from that.

Ben: At this point there is no reason to find another producer if Chris is happy doing it. There's been maybe one or two points in the entire history of the band where Chris has done something on the recording and the rest of us were like, "No". All of us have been in bands before where you go into the studio and someone starts twiddling with stuff and you're just, "Ehh". But we are all on the same plane as far as the way we want things to sound. When Chris says, "I'm going to do something really messed up here and make this sound really sketchy." We say, "All right man, go at it." Usually 99.9% of the final product is tight.

Chris: Being a producer while being in the band... We all are learning about being in a band together as we go. We are learning what works and I'm learning on the recording level as well. I don't know how I would feel about going into a studio with somebody who knew exactly what was going on. I don't know if I'm ready for it. ☿

DJ Spooky

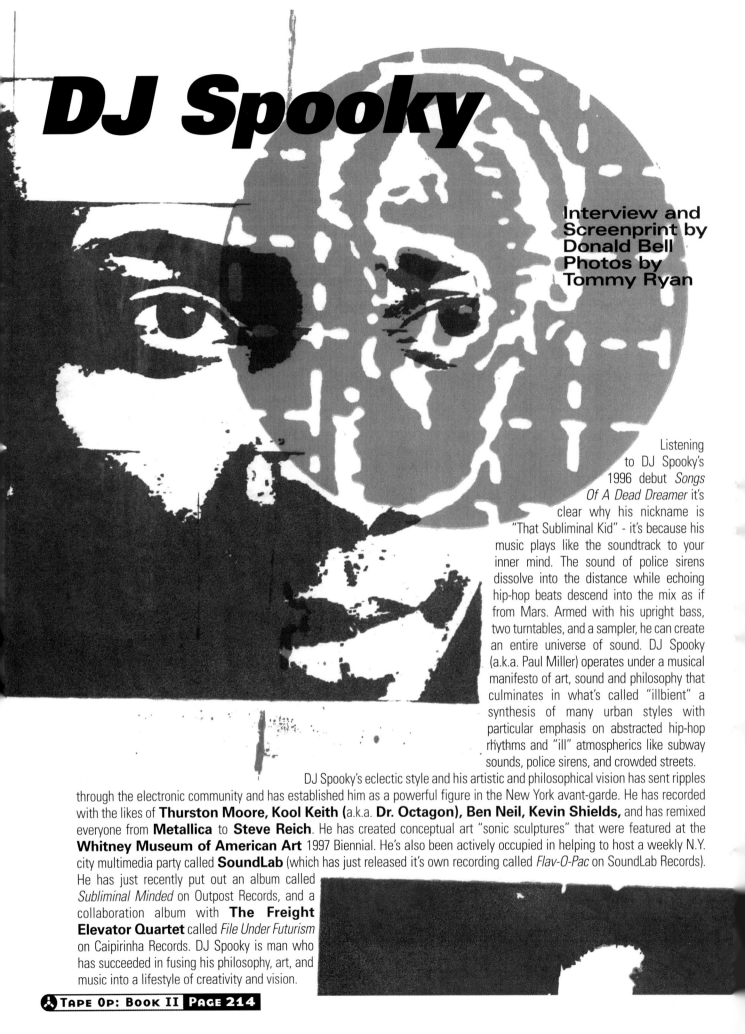

Interview and
Screenprint by
Donald Bell
Photos by
Tommy Ryan

Listening to DJ Spooky's 1996 debut *Songs Of A Dead Dreamer* it's clear why his nickname is "That Subliminal Kid" - it's because his music plays like the soundtrack to your inner mind. The sound of police sirens dissolve into the distance while echoing hip-hop beats descend into the mix as if from Mars. Armed with his upright bass, two turntables, and a sampler, he can create an entire universe of sound. DJ Spooky (a.k.a. Paul Miller) operates under a musical manifesto of art, sound and philosophy that culminates in what's called "illbient" a synthesis of many urban styles with particular emphasis on abstracted hip-hop rhythms and "ill" atmospherics like subway sounds, police sirens, and crowded streets.

DJ Spooky's eclectic style and his artistic and philosophical vision has sent ripples through the electronic community and has established him as a powerful figure in the New York avant-garde. He has recorded with the likes of **Thurston Moore, Kool Keith (**a.k.a. **Dr. Octagon), Ben Neil, Kevin Shields,** and has remixed everyone from **Metallica** to **Steve Reich**. He has created conceptual art "sonic sculptures" that were featured at the **Whitney Museum of American Art** 1997 Biennial. He's also been actively occupied in helping to host a weekly N.Y. city multimedia party called **SoundLab** (which has just released it's own recording called *Flav-O-Pac* on SoundLab Records).

He has just recently put out an album called *Subliminal Minded* on Outpost Records, and a collaboration album with **The Freight Elevator Quartet** called *File Under Futurism* on Caipirinha Records. DJ Spooky is man who has succeeded in fusing his philosophy, art, and music into a lifestyle of creativity and vision.

Can you give me some idea of what your home studio looks like?

Well it's mainly an Akai S-3000, a Macintosh Quadra 800, I use a Pioneer DJ M500 mixing board because it has built-in sound effects, of course turntables, and some Yamaha monitor speakers. There's also software like MetaSynth, there's a program called Digital Cathedral which is a really cool piece of software that lets you do bugged out reverb effects and stuff like that. Hyperprism is another effects program, it lets you do real-time manipulation. There's a whole bunch of other stuff, but that's just what comes to mind off the top of my head.

How often do you find yourself recording?

All the time. Just about every other day.

Is there anything that particularly inspires you to record, or has it become like a ritual?

No, I'm mostly an ideas person y'know. I try to come up with a concept or an idea and try to figure out sonically how to engage it and just push the envelope in that direction. It's about trying to conceptualize a framework around art and music, because that's my whole kick. I mean I'm mainly a writer and artist, and DJ-ing was meant to be an extension of that kind of stuff that would allow me to build and develop and create a forum for conceptual art as DJ-ing.

And now look at everything it's become?

Right, it worked, but now a lot of people think I just do music, which is a real drag.

Do you have any kind of ritualized process when you're building up a composition? Do you start from the drums up, or like, a loop that catches your ear?

Nah, I mean it depends on what project or focus I'm working on. I don't really have a set routine.

You play upright bass too, what are you using to record it?

Just a piezo-electric pickup. It lets me go direct into my mixing board. That way I don't have to bother with a bunch of amps and mics and stuff, because I like to travel really lightweight.

You use a lot of field recorded sounds in your recordings, like police sirens, and subway rattling. Are you recording these yourself, and if so what kind of gear are you using to record outdoors?

Just a pretty high-end mini-disc recorder and a microphone.

I've read about a recording experiment you did using a group of friends who would run around the city recording sounds and then bring them back for you to incorporate in a live DJ mix. Can you elaborate on what you were doing?

Yeah, it's like a game y'know, hide and seek. The idea was just to try and disperse the creative process both

amongst people and across geographies. Almost like the internet when you send files back and forth. I like the idea of always having a continuous, changing configuration of people involved with things y'know. Which keeps it kinda' fun and keeps things fresh, gives it a sense of humor.

Are there any similar kinds of recording experiments you've been involved with?

Yeah, my installation for the Whitney [Museum] biennial was like that. I made a musical map of Mexico City's Zona Rosa where again, the whole geography of the place was turned into digital code, which was turned into music.

That's so cool. I know you've got a new CD out that is a compilation of recordings from your SoundLab parties. Will you explain a little about what SoundLab is?

Basically, it's a conceptual art party amongst a group of people who are really annoyed with the conventional music scene in New York, which is mainly based on balkanization. People limit themselves into one little niche or scene, and to me the idea was to try as much as possible to build bridges between different scenes and styles and show people that it can work. I used to do a party called Molecular, and SoundLab was kind of just an extension of that. But it's also its own thing, if you're curious about it go to <soundlabrecords.com>.

With so many people involved how are you going about recording SoundLab? Is everyone just plugged into a giant mixing board or what?

Yeah, sorta' like that - a big mixing board where different signals from different people are routed through it and dumped out. It's kind of a pun on the whole Soundsystem thing. Again, I always look at that as a metaphor about the internet and how people can be geographically in different locations but everyone's checking the vibe, y'know?

If there's a bedroom DJ out there right now who wants to get started making and recording his own music on a tight budget, what essential piece of equipment would you recommend they buy? Sampler? Computer? What's going to give the most versatility value?

It's a difficult thing to say because there's so much different equipment and everybody has their own style and way of looking at things. The basic thing you need is a mixing board of some sort. Whether it's a DJ mixing board or a line mixer, everything is about multi-channels. That's the basic component, and everything else, whether you get turntables, CD players, a laptop, etc. etc., it's up to the individual. You just need stuff that allows you to fluidly and easily play with what you're into. Because at the end of the day it's all a game, and if you are bored with the game you gotta figure out the pieces you want to play with, y'know?

Exactly.

And so these are all just variables, pieces of a puzzle. You can make an interesting puzzle, or you can make a simple one, but whatever helps you...

Not get bored with it.

Yeah.

Is there anything that you do in particular to keep yourself from getting bored, except for just mixing things up and keeping things from getting too routine?

Well, like I said there really is no routine. So like, if I have an idea or some sort way of thinking about things I'll use music or writing to explore that, and it just helps me get driven.

Is there a particular piece of recording hardware you're lusting after right now?

Nah. Whatever comes across my path, if I think it's interesting, I'll check it out.

Would you recommend Mac or Windows as a more powerful sound tool?

I used to be an IBM guy, but a lot of software I wanted to use was only available on Mac a couple years ago. But now that's changing, I could switch platforms but at this point I'm so involved with Mac it would be a drag to switch back.

Have you ever thought that calling yourself a "DJ" has limited how people perceive your music?

Yeah, the whole DJ thing is playing on expectations. People see the word DJ and they think it automatically has to be about just clean dance music. I like playing with people's expectations, and so I can use the word "DJ" and then all the sudden have no beats or anything. Everyone's conditioned to think along certain lines about music, and to me it's just a real drag to see how most people so conservative about their own expectations and the way they project them on other people. So I'm considered sort of a trickster in a way and I like doing that. ⓐ

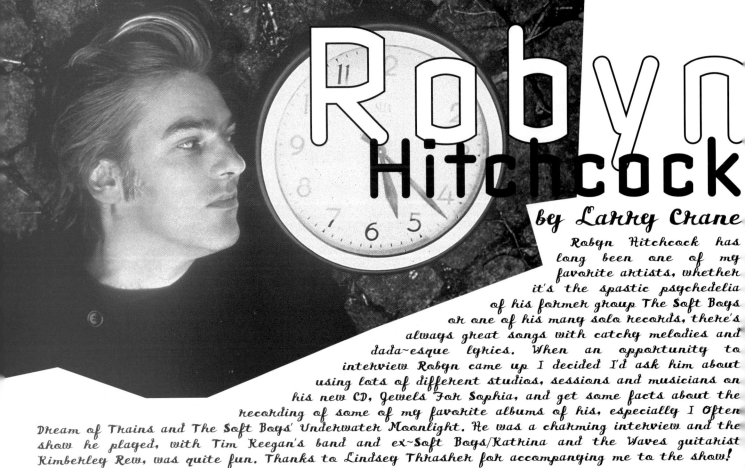

Robyn Hitchcock
by Larry Crane

Robyn Hitchcock has long been one of my favorite artists, whether it's the spastic psychedelia of his former group The Soft Boys or one of his many solo records, there's always great songs with catchy melodies and dada-esque lyrics. When an opportunity to interview Robyn came up I decided I'd ask him about using lots of different studios, sessions and musicians on his new CD, Jewels For Sophia, and get some facts about the recording of some of my favorite albums of his, especially I Often Dream of Trains and The Soft Boys' Underwater Moonlight. He was a charming interview and the show he played, with Tim Keegan's band and ex-Soft Boys/Katrina and the Waves guitarist Kimberley Rew, was quite fun. Thanks to Lindsey Thrasher for accompanying me to the show!

I wanted to start by asking you about the new record. It was recorded in different places.

Three songs were done in Seattle, two were done in London [at Milo Studios] and the rest were done in Los Angeles.

I noticed in *Moss Elixir* too, that you also had a kind of pattern of going different places to record.

I've always liked moving from one place to another. It has nothing to do with the technical quality of the studio – it's simply a psychological thing. I think if you get locked into doing a record for three months, you completely lose perspective of what you're doing. You drag your friends in and they say, "That's very nice, do you want to go out and have a pizza?" Or you take the tapes back home and you listen to them while your blind drunk and think it's great. You're too close to the project. For the last two A&M albums, there wasn't enough time between starting the thing and the final mixes to assess them. At the time I thought they were great, but that's just because I became a part of the collective hypnosis of making a record. Prior to that (except for an album I did called *Groovy Decay*, which was similarly done in one sort of spate and I also thought was disastrous) I've always done things in bits and pieces - right from the Soft Boys up to *Queen Elvis*. We tended to only work in one studio in one town, we had certain haunts. But it was all in little bits so you can listen to what you're doing, take it away and live with it for a couple of months and then go in and overdub and mix it. You really appreciate it.

Make sure it's the right basic take of the song.

Yeah. It's also like having hundreds of children, you can't focus when you have twelve songs running around your heels. You're just trying to get them in order. If you've got just three songs, you can cherish them more. It's just more exciting - I appreciate the recording process so much more if it's broken up like that. With the most recent records, I know people in studios all over the place. I can't afford to fly the Young Fresh Fellows over to London, but I can afford to fly over and record with the Young Fresh Fellows, or go record with Grant Lee [Phillips] and Jon Brion in LA for a week. It's just fun to have different people. I wouldn't have wanted to make this record with any one set of people. The whole thing, especially at this stage, should just be fun to make. I'm not looking for any other element - if there's fun on tape, then it should come through to the ears. I think this record is one of my enjoyable, confident records. It's not as somber, it may be the songs, but it's also just the fun of it.

I was surprised to hear a song like "Viva! Sea-Tac". It feels like an exuberant, off-the-cuff rock song. It something that you can obviously do, but it doesn't always come out on your records.

I actually wrote that song in London, but it was obviously a good candidate for recording with them [Young Fresh Fellows] in Seattle [at Hanszek Studios].

I wanted to throw a few different names at you, from different people you've worked with in the past. One of the most obvious would be Pat Collier.

Pat Collier sidled up to me in 1977 after a gig somewhere I remember he came up to me in a club and said, " saw your set and I kind of like it." I thought, "Thi guy's very suspicious." It turns out that his father wa a policeman. About two years later we started workin in his studio - it was very cheap. He also understoo how to make really great 4-track recordings b bouncing things down. He was a real student of th '60s, he wasn't part of this "Steve Lillywhite" 24-trac thing. We were just scuttling away in this dank sort c archway beneath the railway line at Waterloo. Ther this special kind of fungus that grows there and if yo take your guitar away - you can take it 6,000 mil away – unpack your guitar and that fungus come wafting past your nostrils.

Was that Alaska?

Yeah. He then sold Alaska to someone else, I st occasionally rehearse there but... I had a guitar the which had been there for a year and it stunk so bad left it somewhere. I actually gave it to Pat to keep his house until the fumes went. He had a big phase the late '80s, he got quite trendy... doing people li the Darling Buds. I don't know what he's doing no but he was always a really reliable guy to work with

I put on [The Soft Boys'] *Underwat Moonlight* and I was thinking which songs were done on 4-track an 8-track... the fact is that you can really tell and some of the 4-track stu sounds better than the 16-track. think Pat did an amazing job and I w curious about how you guys we about doing those kinds of sessior What would you track first?

Photo by Ferriou Sanjar

I think the bass and... Well the guitars wind up being in stereo and then the bass and drums... he probably just recorded the whole thing in stereo and then... it's a good question. I know that by the end of it there was very little flexibility. The more important thing was that he did get a terrific guitar sound.

It was an example to me, when I first started recording, that you don't need 24 tracks to do really good recordings. You just need some ears.

That's good to know that it seems that way. I think at the time people were just getting out of punk & they were starting to get high-tech again. People wanted expensive drum sounds and all that. We couldn't afford it and frankly I didn't care anyway. I was more interested in the song than the sound, which I know is a failing in making pop music, but something about sound has always eluded me. Maybe I think it sounds okay and I imagine the rest and really I should put something else on that I'm imagining is there and it's not.

What do you find the difference is between working in a session producing yourself or having an outside producer like John Leckie?

It depends who they are. I'm very much at the mercy of other people's ideas. I don't go around telling everybody what to do. I sort of take the consensus of whoever is in the room. If there's nobody else I have to make those decisions myself and sometimes it's very important to do that. On the whole, I can work with whoever is there and get a good result. There are times when I feel like I've been steered by other people and maybe I'm not happy with the result in the end. At the time it seems like a good idea, it's not like anyone has ever hi-jacked me and put a gun to my head. It's always been the kind of thing I've wanted, but maybe the approach is the consensus between the other musicians and the producer and it gets swayed. It always winds up being by committee and I like to, every so often, pull away from everyone else and call all the shots myself. I think it's just partly my nature – I'll leave decision making to other people and that's a flaw. You've got to be able to make snap decisions or the whole team will be machine-gunned.

Do you feel like there are people you've worked with who have made decisions that you have been very pleased with?

I enjoyed working with Jon Brion a lot, because we're both quite impatient. He throws an idea at the take and if it doesn't stick he lets it fall off, he doesn't sit there with an agenda... "Now, let me try my idea, this is really... what I want to do." Sometimes you talk to people and you know they're not listening, because they've made up their mind that they're going to do it a certain way. They smoke pot or something and they don't listen to anybody anyway. I would say that I really don't like having drugs or alcohol around in a studio. I think that's one of the counter-productive things, especially if you're living with the music. I use to drink at recording sessions... the vocals on the first few Soft Boys sessions - I was drunk for all of those. I just thought that's what you do, you go to the pub and then carry on. My heart sinks if I walk in and there's a

bag of weed on the desk for the engineer. Some people can all get stoned and do lovely ambient... I guess my stuff isn't stoner music. It's not drug music.

Not for the creating part it, maybe. [laughter]

No, maybe not for listening either. I'm not an ambient person in that respect. I'm more concerned that the performance is lodged well between your ears. The purpose, in a way, is to make people feel less lonely, not to give them a soundtrack. You've got to listen to what I do or it'll annoy you, like a baby crying in the background. I don't make good-time music where you put it on and say, "Yeah, that's nice, let's get some friends and have a couple of beers." The idea of being partied over is sort of insulting to me. People often put on their favorite records for the background and I don't like doing it with mine.

One of the records that came up quite a bit with other engineers was *I Often Dream Of Trains*. It's not a party record by any means, but everyone voices it as being a real favorite of theirs. That record has some very heavy mood to it, even the songs that are lighter, like "I Wish I Was a Pretty Girl" - it still has this somber late-night feel. When you were creating that record, was it anything like that?

No, I wanted to make a record that cost less than a thousand pounds and I wanted to do it within four days. I recruited Pat [Collier], because I hadn't worked with him in three years and I had a rather... the *Groovy Decay* sessions had been really difficult, because they were done late at night, by committee and often not in a very sober state, but not in a happy state either. It was a party atmosphere. It wasn't a healthy atmosphere and I don't blame Steve [Hillage, the producer], but it was just a combination of people. I wanted to make *I Often Dream Of Trains* really simple – get away from anyone who had been influencing me. I trusted Pat wouldn't try to peddle anything... "You could be great if you did this!" I wanted to make something very un-state-of-the-art, not whatever was going on like the Thompson Twins, Frankie Goes To Hollywood. I was listening to it, I don't listen to the radio now, but back then, I still did. I knew what was happening, but I wanted to stay completely away from it. I think that's the secret of its success, there wasn't any attempt to please anybody but myself. Songwriting... you know James Taylor, Lou Reed, Gene Clark, Leonard Cohen - its all dark, dark stuff. In a way, I'm not sure that I want to produce that kind of thing anymore. I think being some reasonably successful white middle-class person, what the fuck have I got to complain about? [laughter] I can find things, but I'm trying to get out of adolescent self-pity. When I made ...*Trains*, I was 31 and I was still very adolescent. It's my ultimate teenage record, which is probably why people like it.

It's easy to connect to.

Yeah. It was this feeling isolated... earth, humanity and then there's me.

How were the sessions?

They were great. They were sober, daylight sessions with Pat Collier.

You demoed those songs too.

I did some on 3-track in a barn and some on a 4-track in my house. My only technical information I can give you: The Fostex X15, I bought it for 300 quid and it was a revelation. It was very simple to operate and that was as technical as I've ever gotten. I had a microphone and I borrowed a friend's spring reverb. I just sat there writing, making up songs with the headphones on, singing through the reverb. By then, Pat Collier had gone 24-track, Alaska would still do it cheap and 24-tracks were dirt cheap. *I Often Dream Of Trains* had much more technology than *Underwater Moonlight* [by The Soft Boys] did. Again, I think it was the simplicity of it that worked.

I wanted to ask you about the Dub Narcotic session that you did... the single with Calvin [Johnson]?

How is he?

He's doing good, he's got a new space and he bought a 16-track 2". But compared to a lot of your recording exploits in the same time frame, that sounded like a pretty different trip, going to Calvin's basement.

It was lovely, we started upstairs and then they wanted to make supper so we moved down into the basement. I think he had an 8-track. As we mixed the tracks we went out to the car and listened to them on cassette to see if they were alright. It was only a day, but by the end of it we had been very close to the songs because it was impossible for us to lose focus. I really enjoyed it, because it was quick. There was none of this, "Well, I think we might need to send out for a few XK16s", or something like that or "Another pair of JBLs to check it." I suppose I'm impatient, I just don't want to be held up by machinery. I really enjoyed those sessions with Calvin Johnson and I'm so glad it came out on 7".

And on the album.

Yeah. I should have left that off - I should of put "Trilobite" on that album. I should have left the Dub Narcotic thing as an intact unit. I was a little swayed by an A&R person to put that on. I knew it was mistake.

Don't ever listen to A&R. [laughter]

Geoffrey [Weiss] had some very good ideas, he's right about lots of things, but he's not there anymore.

Another one of my favorite recordings was *The Kershaw Sessions* CD, which is kind of knocked out too...

That's it you see, that's great. The Egyptians were always much better live, I think. There was a tension there and there was an intensity. We played very well off each other without needing to overdub. In *The Kershaw Sessions* there was no time to overdub. Whereas, I think the studio efforts were all attempts to recapture ideas that had been worked out before. I never felt the studio records were more than blueprints. I thought the live three-piece was excellent. I agree, I thought *The Kershaw Sessions* was definitely the best. Some of it was actually done in Andy Kershaw's kitchen. Our soundman had an 8-track mixer and it just went straight to it... Andy Kershaw was having a party in the next room and we just did it. ⒶⒷ

Interview by
John Baccigaluppi

Elliott Peter Earls

In theory, the proliferation of low cost multi-track recording devices has democratized the recording process and put these tools into the hands of many people who previously didn't have access to them. All of these people would then go on to create works of musical art that would amaze and gratify, as these musical geniuses were heard for the first time. In practice, if you had to listen to all the recordings made on 4-track cassette recorders and low cost digital recording systems, you'd surely want to die. Like the hapless protagonist of *A Clockwork Orange*, who's forced to view the terrible acts of humanity for hours on end, you'd beg for it to be over. Admit it.

Occasionally heroes emerge from the mist like Beck, with his Top 40 single recorded on an 8-track and cheap sampler. But reason says there must be more, just like reason says that we just can't be the only intelligent life in the universe, right? Well where are they then? Maybe they're hard to find until they're overexposed like Beck and the dead aliens of Roswell.

Elliott Earls is one example of an artist doing great work that very few people have heard. His music and art would probably exist without the proliferation of the digital tools he uses, but it would be quite different and it's even more likely that you'd never hear it. No major label in their right mind would ever open their checkbooks for Elliott like they do for N'sync and the Spice Girls. Most music these days is pretty cookie cutter and predictable, but Elliott produces unique and experimental but ultimately enjoyable pop music that is very original. A bit of a novelty in 1999. While original, his influences are still present, just mixed in and regurgitated and disparate enough in the first place to keep things fresh. Immediate references would include hip-hop, music concreté, funk, spoken word, slice and dice, and contemporary practitioners of the above like the Beasties and Beck. Standing on top of this all is a passion for the English language and wordplay, and a deep respect for Henry Miller.

Elliott has two more or less self released multi-media CDs available, *Throwing Apples At The Sun* and *Eye Sling Shot Lions*. Each CD is not only a full music CD, but also has a rich multi-media layer. If you think that a lot of multi-media is boring and soul-less, these CDs will probably change your mind. Instead of trying to create bad TV-like imagery you can control, Elliott strips it down to the basics and fucks with the constraints, turning weaknesses into assets. One nice thing about working with, as opposed to fighting the current technology, is that these CDs run fast and never crash your computer.

The only slightly surprising thing about all this if you enter into it from the music, is that Elliott has no training or background as a musician, but is an internationally renowned type designer and graphic designer, albeit an eccentric one who will probably never reach the mainstream status of someone like David Carson. Once you know this, the visual brilliance of the CDs and the eclectic variety of the music begin to make more sense. At this point a more familiar reference point might be someone like Brian Eno, a brilliant musician, and a practitioner of many forms of art.

You studied at Cranbrook, probably one of the most controversial and influential graphic design and art programs of this century since the Bauhaus in Germany. What was that like, and how did it help to form your current aesthetic.

After four years of art school, I found that I was 25 years old, wearing a tie and driving a Saab 900 to work each day. I looked at my life and was utterly revolted. Here I was designing corporate communications for a living, paying my car payment, and looking forward to my two weeks of vacation. I felt the only way to get my life back on track would be to have a few years to really examine my values, and develop some real work. I started to look for the most fucked up anti-establishment art school I could find. It turns out I went to a graduate school for two years that has no teachers, class, grades or any of the other complete horse shit that fucks up the educational process. The mythology of the place stated that you could study anything you wanted as long as you worked with passion. That's what I did.

"I found that I was 25 years old, wearing a tie and driving a Saab 900 to work each day."

How did you move from graphic design and the visual arts into music? Was their any kind of music program at Cranbrook that you were involved in?

For two years I worked on "many-media." I'm not talking about the complete crap that you see on the CD-rom that came with your Acer-XT. I'm talking about nonlinear digital video, spoken word poetry mixed with typographic experiments, still photography and cell phone conversations. So from the very beginning of this process I began to investigate music composition, pop song form and sound. I read a million books on music theory and composition. I made sure that the books I read were one of two distinct types, either extremely simple, or so esoteric that they were nearly impossible for me to understand. This was intentional. Books like *David Harp's Instant Rhythm Kit*, or *Music Theory Made Easy* by David Harp, were over simplistic and would map the territory; in other words these books would clearly spell out the rules. For instance they would explain the blues in an almost formulaic way. It would talk about 12 bar blues form and maybe what key the blues would typically be played in among other things. The point behind this exercise would be to do what artists have done since the beginning of time; fuck with form. Now that I had an elemental grasp of the stereotypical form, I'd start composing around that form and try to twist it and bend it. Simultaneously, I would be

reading *The Computer Music Journal* [MIT press] or maybe *The Elements of Computer Music*. I'd take an extremely sophisticated program like Tom Erbe's SoundHack[1], and I'd convolve two of my simple tracks to get that groove bouncin'. It's very important to me to clarify at this point: I believe in reading absolutely everything you can about theory, music and technology. I believe in rigorous exploration in a systematic way. But, and I can't stress this more strongly, at the point I'm directly working with the music, all that shit is gone!! The song, the tone, the vibe, the groove is the thing! All the preliminary work is gone, if the shit don't bounce, if you can't move your ass to it, you're fucked! And all the books in the world won't help!

On a higher or meta-level, what are the differences and similarities between music and art; design and sound? How is the act of creativity universal to all art, be it visual, literary, musical or otherwise? Or, how isn't it?

It's all the same, man. I find no difference at all on the deepest level, between writing a song, building an instrument, designing a typeface or editing video. They all come from the same place. It's the manifestation that's different, and that's so minor. To me it's all about mastery. I'm aware of how ridiculous and traditional that might sound, but at the point the artist has come to a profound and deep understanding of his craft, he no longer is constrained or controlled by it. He's able to transcend it. He's able to control it. So back to the David Harp books. It's all about the fundamentals, whether it's in music, painting or computer programming. I'm a student, man! I'm working hard on my skills everyday! Be they logic structures or understanding the Dorian mode. Everyday towards mastery, towards a deeper and more meaningful form of expression.

Describe your song writing and recording process. Do you go through several drafts of songs? Do you sit down with a guitar or something? How much of a role do your recording tools play in the actual writing and creating process of songwriting?

I've really been thinking a lot about this recently because I'm currently writing the music for my next disc/performance piece. I would have to say that the recording process was a prime element in the construction of both discs. And this is precisely where I've decided the new disc will break from the past! A little side note: I'm not saying this to score points. *Tape Op* is honestly one of my favorite magazines. I just became aware of it about a month ago. The focus on small studios and how they are working makes it invaluable. I used to really love *Recording* magazine. I would buy every issue and look for their articles on "Making a Broad Band Diffuser" or some other equally interesting topic that would help me be a better recordist. Anyway, about a year ago, I realized that I was picking up the magazine on the newsstand and looking for that one article that would really make me need the magazine. It seems that almost overnight they became this 4 color rag dedicated almost exclusively to reviewing VST plug-ins or the latest Windows sequencing package. The magazine is terrible. My point is that I feel this is a reflection of a broader problem in music today. Take a look at *Keyboard* magazine as an example. They would have you

"Make sure that shit is bumpin with no effects, no technology, none."

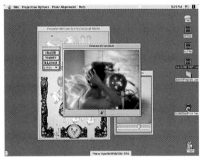

believe that the composition process should be something like this: First select a premade sample off the "Extreme Ethnic Explosion CD-ROM," get Cubase VST with the "Brazilian House Party" plug-in and you patch it in line with the "Hyper-engine-Mondo-Mod-Reticulator" plug-in, then run it through "Recycle," then you're done. Give me a fucking break! So for this, my third disc, I've been writing songs with my strat. No groove up Teddy Riley shit yet. My plan is to finish writing the joints. Make sure that shit is bumpin with no effects, no technology, none. Then take a week and find a beautiful room. Use one of those laser measuring tools from the Home Depot, calculate room fundamental modes and shit. And cut the tracks. At that point, I'm sure I'll get retarded with the mixes, maybe warm up the old D-110 editor and SoundHack. But as I mentioned before, I'm consciously playing with the algebra. I feel good about the new songs I've written. They rely on guitar, harmonica and bombastic beats when I play them live.

What kind of gear did you use on your first album? Describe your set up and the processes involved in recording that first album.

My first CD was recorded entirely on a Macintosh 660av with 16MB of RAM. A Mackie 12x2 board. I had a Roland D-110 as a sound module. I should add that as much as that module sucks, if you get an editor for it and really get deep into it and twist it, it has this dark, metallic vibe that's beautiful. I was using Opcode Studio Vision Pro, a really crappy 30 year old Japanese 3/4 scale guitar, a SansAmp and an $80 dollar Shure microphone. I think it's important to state that virtually every track on that disc was processed in some way through SoundHack. I realized that with my limited equipment, I ran the distinct risk of coming off like a bozo. Coming off all Yanni or worse, like John Tesh. So I deeply fucked with the every track on that disc. I would convolve a horn track onto my bass track. Or phase vocode the vocals, pitch shift the drums, whatever it took to create a sonic palette that was dark 'n lovely.

What kind of gear did you use on your second album? Describe your set up and the processes involved in recording that album. How did it evolve from the first and what prompted that evolution?

On the second disc, I got a DigiDesign AudioMedia III card. A Macintosh 72/75. Some Paradigm Mini Mk2's. A Strat. An Alesis D4 drum module. Sony PCM 2600 DAT. Sony TCD-D7 DAT Walkman with a wide field stereo mic. An old Harmony tenor guitar. An Alesis compressor and MidiVerb. One reason my equipment is so mundane is because we're only talking about my audio based equipment. My work consists of video, programming, video projection, photography etc... So for every Sony PCM 2600 I buy, I've also purchased an 8mm Sony video camera, and a LCD projector etc... Have you priced a good LCD projector lately? My God! My studio has got to be a be able to handle broadcast quality after effects spots, 4x5 photography etc. The recording processes on the two albums were very different. It's quite odd. The musicians and artists who I respect are those who are very versatile. I'm very interested in attempting to work through interpersonal "movements" in the work. In other words, I wanted my second disc; the vibe, the beats, the tone to be completely different from the first. I wanted the accompanying nonlinear digital video spots, the typography, the visual programming all to be different. So I did everything in my power to work in ways that were counterintuitive. In any artistic discipline, if you modify the method or process you modify the result. It's like algebra. The first disc had this dark slow atmospheric vibe, that I was really in

love with. Therefore on *Eye Sling Shot Lions*, the second disc, I wanted to attempt to create something that was a bit softer and cleaner. I was well aware of the danger in this, "soft" can obviously be quite a bad thing. Anyway, I wanted to work within those constraints. I wanted to try to convey the same intensity and passion but through the contradiction of a lighter sonic palate.

What kind of music if any would you do if you didn't have the access to the tools and recording processes you have?

Currently, I'm investigating a sort of fluid guitar and harmonica playing thing. I love the contrast between my extremely technologically sophisticated performance stuff, and this simple harmonica guitar thing. I've been working hard for the past two years on the athletic aspects of being a musician.

You use a lot of spoken word type things in your music and in general, your lyrics are more than just something to hang the melody on. Describe your background, influences and approach to lyrics, poetry, language, literature, etc...

At Cranbrook a classmate of mine, Brian Schorn, was this poet from Brown, who used to organize these poetry readings in the north studio at night. I only actually participated once, but because my crib was in this small room called the north studio, I got to observe. Over the course of that year we became tight. Brian would say, "Hey dude, check this shit out." Then he would play some extremely obscure video from "Sacred Fire" featuring the work of a poet I'd never heard of. Brian and I would discuss our work and focus on the linguistic aspects. At some point in our relationship I realized just how good a poet Brian was. I also realized that he kind of enjoyed some of the shit that I was hitting him with. After I left Cranbrook I worked on *Throwing Apples at the Sun* for a year never really letting Brian hear anything off of it. That whole year, I worked my ass off on the linguistic aspect of the disc, all the while keeping Brian in mind. I was hoping that when he first heard the CD he would be proud. That he would be shocked. I guess it simply boils down to the fact that I love words! I love language and I love word games. I take it extremely seriously even when I'm having fun.

Your CDs have a lot of really unique vocal effects. What are some of the tools and techniques you use to achieve this?

Well, It's odd because I read your interview with that cat from Sparklehorse. I just love that guy. And on a very superficial level I'd say that some of the sonic character of his vocals is very similar to the way I handle my vocals. I point this out because I was surprised when he discussed how he treated his vocals. He seems to do a lot

of very lowtech hardware manipulation to achieve that sonic signature. I always attempt to record my vocals straight through the Sony PCM2600 DACs with no processing at all utilizing the shortest possible signal chain, then digital to the hard disk. It's at this point that I fuck with the timbre. I mentioned my love of SoundHack. Well the beauty of the program is that it is very difficult to use. Unlike a polished commercial release, this program will allow you to enter parameters into the program that will so severely mangle the audio that it becomes useless. The key, I found is to keep entering "wrong" parameters but do like 35 tests on very short files, until the audio sample is right at that critical point of intelligibility. Then I would either convolve that track back onto its original unaltered file for a bit of clarity or I'd mix the original and the mangled versions together to taste. The other thing I do a lot is to build up a lot of pressure in my throat when singing. It sounds stupid, but for some reason, if I really stress my vocal cords through what I can only describe as pressure, it comes out sounding very distressed. I know I put the smack down on the whole plug-in thing, but there is one set of plug-ins I don't think I could live without; the Waves Pro Bundle or whatever they call it. With the LT-1 Ultramaximizer and that EQ you can really fool with the sonic character of your voice.

You are now building your own instruments. Describe some of these instruments and how and why this came about.

Well, I've been doing these performances for about a year and a half now. And what they are is not like a rock concert or a hip-hop show, or a rave. They 're a kind of mixture of theater, movies and poor musicianship utilizing CD-ROM and LCD projection. It's quite hard to explain, but essentially *Excerpts from Eye Sling Shot Lions* is an interactive digital composition conceived and constructed around the Quicktime Media Layer, Max and Supercard technologies. During live performance, a melange of typography, sound, video fragments, interactive digital video, simulated live performance, short films and pop music are controlled via MIDI and interwoven with live poetry, sub-urban hip-hop and spoken word texts. I've custom built interface elements like gold boots that trigger samples that link me to computer controlled video and typography. It's all based upon piezoelectric elements. You know, those three dollar buzzers at Radio Shack. Well if you cut them apart, they have these little discs inside that when struck give off a faint electrical impulse. This signal can be used to control video, audio, smoke machines, cell-phones, scanners etc... All you've got to do is get a soldering iron and spend about three years of your life learning to program some fairly sophisticated shit in a scripting language. Anyway the instruments you refer to are more like interface elements. They are boots, and drums and electro-magnets, and horns and lights, that feed signals back to the Macintosh. The Mac is listening for these signals and alters the film that's playing, the base audio, turns on some lights, switches off the smoke machine, etc. While all this is happening, I'm playing the guitar/harmonica, telling stories, hiting ya' with some spoken word etc...

What was the impetus that led to you recording your first CD?

Well, after I got out of grad school I went to work for Elektra records at 75 Rock in Manhattan as a designer. I met a few people that I really liked. Some unbelievably good cats working on what amounts to a slave ship. Generally, I felt like this was one of the most amoral outfits I'd ever seen. I couldn't believe the way the corporate culture treated people. I found out they would fire like 25% of the staff every 3 months. It took them over 120 days to pay my initial invoices! I couldn't believe it. Anyway, I got fired 6 months after I started. I was told later that there was a small uprising among the women that worked in the art department with me. Apparently, they went to my boss, and said, "Either he goes or we go." At least that's what my boss told me. Get this, the last project I worked on and the potential last straw was a European release of the *Eagles Greatest Hits*. I simply couldn't bring myself to give them that dorky *Hotel California* vibe they so desperately wanted. They showed the band my comps and I was told that Don Henley hated them so much he pulled the package from the art

department, and had an outside designer do it. Needless to say the chief was none too pleased. Anyway, I mention this not simply because I now find it humorous, but because upon being fired, I immediately started my own studio, The Apollo Program, and began to record music that I liked rather than the crap the A+R department was having a hard time shoving down the throats of the American consumer. I decided to become a "prosumer" of music. I decided to base my studio upon my music, performance, typography, video, posters and do business the way I thought it should be practiced. Fuck the multinational-musico-hamburger-pushing establishment until they treat me with a little fucking respect.

What's next for you and what are your current projects??

I was really fortunate that last month The Wooster Group in SOHO gave me an Emerging Artist Grant and I was one of the featured performers in their Emerging Artist Series. This was an amazing experience, The Wooster Group has been around for something like 30 years and has played a critical role in avant-garde theater and performance art in New York City. The people helped me tremendously. I mention this because during that week, we had two top of the line Sony 3 CCD Digital Video Cameras, a Hi-8 mm and one straight 8 running. And over the course of the past year, I've been collecting interesting documentary footage including my first poetry reading based performances in New York City and a private performance I gave at Bennetton's research center in Treviso among others. So I've been working on a documentary. I don't quite know what form it will take yet; I'm hoping to put it out on DVD. I've also been getting calls from all over planet earth to perform, so that should keep me busy for a while. And, of course, I'm hard at work on my next CD. ☮

(1) SoundHack is a super cool shareware program for the Macintosh. Just search for SoundHack on your WWW browser and you'll find it. -Ed.

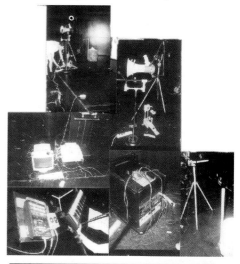

Throughout her career, Ani Difranco has put out albums at an amazing rate, averaging about one release every nine months. Her fourteen albums have all been self-produced, and released on her own Righteous Babe Records. Despite working at such a clip, her production style has been anything but predictable. Since her first release in 1990, her sonic palette has expanded from a solo guitar and vocal sound to one incorporating drum kit, bass, accordion, and banjo, having also stopped off at various points with horn sections and sampled drum loops. All this studio work is squeezed into an aggressive touring schedule.

I met up with Ani and Andrew Gilchrist, her partner in life and production, at the Congress House Studio in Austin, TX. There, they were mixing Ani's second collaboration with storyteller and union troubadour Utah Phillips. For many hours they waxed poetic about ADATs, instant studio gratification, and the eternal struggle to get a decent acoustic guitar tone on tape.

AG: We recorded this album down at Kingsway Studio in New Orleans. It was done as nights of live performances, we had an audience of about thirty people in there. The last four tracks are just live room mics. The first two are near where the band and Utah are, and the last two are in the back of the room on the other side of the audience. They picked up all kinds of crazy shit, whispering and rustling. Unbelievably, there was a dog at the studio and during the performances he wandered into the audience and his tags were rattling.

AD: And at one point he just sat down in front of Utah and started chomping on this bone.

AG: The dog is definitely on the record. We actually set up a small PA in the room, that was being mixed at the back of the room, it was a very strange setup.

Was that for monitors for the players? Or did you use headphones?

AG: The PA was for the audience. Nobody was on headphones, except the drummer, cause he was way in the back. Most stuff was happening pretty quietly and everyone could pretty much hear each other. Utah sat and told stories, Julie [Wolf] on keyboards, Jason [Mercer] on bass. The trumpet that you hear is Dave Pirner from Soul Asylum, who happened to be there, and he's taken up playing the trumpet. We said, "Come play on this track!" and it's this really warpy crazy trumpet. So off to one side of the house you've got the control room, which is very open. The whole concept is that there is no control room, there's no glass, you don't have that kind of separation. Off the control room there's another big room with a piano, and there's another room off that, and that makes up one half of the house. The house is symmetrical, and on the other half of the house is the big live room.

Has Kingsway been a studio for a long time?

AG: No, Daniel Lanois set it up, around '89. He came to New Orleans to do this Bob Dylan record, rented a house, set up a bunch of gear, really liked New Orleans, and then found this house, which was vacant at the time. So he bought it and basically installed a studio. But it's still very open. Until very recently, there was just a hundred foot snake that came off the back of the board and wherever you wanted to record you just ran the snake. Now they have, in a few different places,

some remote boxes. That compressor there, the TubeTech, is a key piece of gear. Utah's voice is going through that. And pretty much any of the vocals that have been on the last three Ani records have gone through it. It's real transparent, it just adds a presence to it. We've been using the FMR Really Nice Compressor [RNC] too, they're actually made in Austin. Mark [Hallman, the head engineer and owner of Congress House] got one as a demo and I bought it off him. They're amazing, I use it a lot on drums, run it on the overheads. I pretty much don't use it in the "Super Nice" mode, because it's so transparent, it freaks me out. I was suspicious of it at first. I used to use that Valley People compressor (the Dynamite) that's sitting next to the RNC, it does the same kind of radical pumping, but it's really noisy. Now I've changed over. [The track Ani is mixing ends.] We're actually mixing this new Utah record in order, it's a very strange way to mix.

AD: Why is it strange? Just cause we've never done it before! Of all the records I've done with lots of crossfading and stuff, to figure out first how it's all supposed to flow... you know, Living In Clip, it was like, oh well, I guess this should be the order. And then it was, well, this song stops dead, and this one starts like this.

AG: No, mixing in order totally makes sense. Your instincts, which I really like for mixing, you do all the starts and the fadeouts. Most people don't do that, they leave it for mastering. All that junk, applause at the end, or count-ins and stuff.

You're using automation with this board?

AG: Yeah, it's not flying faders though, it's VCA controlled. Automation saved our lives. We do four copies of each mix, two at 48 and two at 44.

AD: We have to do 48 and 44, because you never know what's going to happen in mastering, and you can't do them at the same time.

AG: And since there's two machines here, we might as well do two of each. We just had our first major DAT fuckup in a long time. I think it was for "Providence," we had an unplayable DAT.

AD: Oh, yes. The DAT machines at Kingsway were doing a little dropping out, bink, bink.

AG: They're new as well, they're two [Panasonic] 3800s and the drum hours are really low. I don't know what is wrong with those machines.

Bad day at the factory.

AD: Yeah. And Kingsway has some crazy monitors. I feel like I have a blanket over my head at the board there. They have huge, what are they called? Like custom Tannoys.

AG: It's a fifteen [inch speaker] with a concentric tweeter mounted on the cone, two of them, so there are four in all.

AD: But basically there's no high end and there's no low end. These huge, muddy, low-middy speakers are in this room with a ceiling fifteen feet high, and a tile floor.

by Leigh Marble

ranco

AG: There are curtains behind the board, but if you close them off it's very small in there. There's also these huge foam blocks that you can make walls out of. I did that, I closed it off while we were tracking.

AD: It's amazing to me, that Dan's whole thing is very low-mid oriented, very warm, except that that's all you can hear there!

AG: I know, what do his records sound like on those speakers? It must be insane. And when we're getting sounds in that control room, my instinct is I want to dip 200 [Hz] on everything.

AD: You're trying to clear up the bass and you do things you shouldn't be doing just 'cause you're listening through water.

AG: You just learn, it's going to sound big and muddy, and you get used to it. But if you put up the foam wall, close the curtains, and monitor real loud, it gets better. That's what I've been doing. It's so funny, it's like the Ani way: whatever is available to be used, she has this way of maximizing it. For this record, we were going to record to sixteen tracks, but we decided because ADAT's are so weird and because it's a live performance thing, we got a spare. And then suddenly, it's all on twenty-four. It's like, where did that spare ADAT go?

AD: But the last record, *Up Up Up Up Up Up*, was on sixteen tracks, and that seemed fine for that record.

AG: The *Little Plastic Castle* record, we did sixteen tracks of ADAT as beds, did all the transfers to two inch, overdubbed on two inch, mixed on two inch. And that was the idea, we went into *Up Up*... doing that.

AD: But then we started saying, why are we bouncing to analog?

AG: Well also we never got beyond sixteen tracks. So we ended up keeping it on sixteen, mixing on sixteen. I don't know, you could go on about that for a long time too, about working on eight tracks, working on sixteen, working on forty-eight. There's something about working on sixteen tracks.

AD: Well, I think for the Utah project, if I could speak for the engineers, because they were live performances, to

have different instruments on their own tracks [made it easier]. 'Cause when you're comping stuff...and it's all happening one song after the other without any like, wait, Okay, is this line working.

AG: No, and I can't imagine that there's any mix on there that's more than sixteen or eighteen tracks.

Who were the players on this album?

AD: Me on guitar, Jason Mercer on bass, Julie Wolf on keyboards, Wurlitzer, and Darren, who's my new drummer. This was his first gig! We went deep right away. But he did so wonderfully. 'Cause it's a crazy gig for the players, it's like, Okay, we have to play with this guy who is very arrhythmic, and you can't freak him out but you've gotta groove hard. The whole collaboration was heavy, and we were just making it up as we went along. And Utah likes the doghouse bass, as he calls it, he doesn't like electric, so Jason played his upright the whole album.

Did Utah play any guitar?

AD: Yeah, there are some things where he was leading and we set music to his playing. Let's play you some mixes...

That moment where the drums drop out [on "Shoot Or Stab Them"], was that done live or was that a dub thing?

AD: That was in the mix. Yeah, we were supposed to do three nights of performances, but we had to cancel the third night which is unfortunate because it wasn't until the second night that things really started to come together. So let's see, what else is there....

AG: There's that crazy "Bread and Roses" thing that you did with Mark the other night.

AD: You know I don't really like that [mix], it doesn't have the vibe of the rough mix.

AG: Is it 'cause you don't like the bass?

AD: Hmm, yeah, I don't know. And also his voice.... it's too loud. It was really teeny and squanky before. Yeah, so this is a story that Julie was playing piano to and then it went into this song, where the performances we did of were just not happening. It was a bunch of people trying to follow Utah, kind of careening along. So then I sent Darren in as an overdub to just groove on the drums and try and smooth over the rhythmic pushing and pulling of the song. And he laid down this great groove. So when the song starts we sucked Utah into this teeny little box of an EQ. And now in this mix I overdubbed a bass which now I'm not sure I like.

Did you take anything on this project and pull it into samplers and do a total remix?

AG: No, "Shoot Them and Stab Them" is pretty much the only non-literal one, he had just spoken that stuff and we laid that over the music. But really it's pretty far away from the other approach. Okay, this track is "I Will Not Obey."

That's a really deep, warm guitar on there.

AD: That's my baritone guitar.

AG: And also going through the dbx 120 subharmonic box. That thing's amazing.

Do you run the 120 live?

AG: We used to a lot. Before there was a bass player.

AD: Yeah, now I gotta move over. I kind of miss those days when I just toured with Andy, and people thought there were taped bass tracks or something.

Ani and Andrew continue mixing, later working on an grooved out version of the labor movement classic "The Internationale".

AG: We're running a 40ms digital delay here on the guitar amp for some stereo imaging. Pan the original to one side and the delayed signal to the other. It stops becoming a pinpoint signal and spreads out. You just have to watch it when you collapse to mono, with the phase cancellation. You can do that with an amp, take a 57 in front of an amp, and if it's an open-backed amp, put a mic in back of it, so that when the speaker throws forward on the one mic, it's throwing back on the other mic. It sounds big if you pan one hard left and the other hard right, but collapse it down and it's gone. This Roland Reverb box (the SRV330) is totally amazing, it's one of the best sounding and usable reverbs. Real simple, it's got around four hundred

"It's so funny, it's like the Ani way: whatever is available to be used, she has this way of maximizing it"

presets in it, not a lot of weird stuff, just reverbs. Lots of really short verbs. We use it a lot.

AD: It has that 250 plate thing. Our friend's studio in Hamilton has an actual EMT plate reverb, with the big levers. It's so excellent, you can make it so transparent, it takes away the sound of a microphone and it sounds like you're there. And this Roland box has a 250 plate emulator.

When you did [the live album] Living In Clip, that was all to one ADAT?

AG: Is that true?

AD: Yeah. Three people in the band, one ADAT.

AG: Oh yeah, it was one. We're now carrying two.

AD: But it's worse than it used to be, 'cause nobody i monitoring the recording process. Back in the days o one ADAT and no compression, it was less things t fuck up I guess. It was kick, drum overheads, guita vocal, vocal, bass. Everything generally went to tap at really low levels, so everything was low and nois until that one big hit where it would go crack!

AG: Then too, you had three guitars but they were a plugged into one [input], so the guitar could just g straight to tape. Now, you've got all these differe guitars and they all have to get grouped.

AD: And Julie [Wolf], who plays organ and Wurlitzer an clav and accordion...

AG: And those all have to get grouped to tw tracks, maybe...

AD: And now, we have two ADATs, we were just mixi some stuff from them, half the instruments it's lik oh well, that didn't go to tape. 'Cause nobod watching them. He just patches them all in and mix the show and meanwhile.

AG: And Julie's melodica has a little mic in it, which we leave up and on, and suddenly it's all over everything. I just had a big conversation with Klondike, which is our sound company, talking about revamping the ADAT setup. Every night, for Steve, there's all these cables where it's like, Okay, this plugs into aux one, and this goes to group out three, and this one goes straight to tape, and apparently it takes him half an hour to set the thing up, and sometimes he gets it right and obviously sometimes he mispatches things. So we're talking about creating a little interface box. Building an Elco, so all that stuff just lives in the back on the board, and we can just plug a snake in. And that'll also provide an opportunity to revamp how the whole thing's working.

So are you continually taping shows?

AD: Yeah, you know what happened? So, we carried an ADAT around for a year, pieced together a live album, and then I was like, OK, no need to keep taping shows, we made a record. That was the whole reason to get the ADAT, baby's first ADAT. And then what happened is that Chuck Plotkin, who is like Springsteen's pseudo-manager / producer / buddy...

He did Dan Bern's first album, right?

AD: Yeah, hence, because Dan was on the road with me and so Chuck was with us for a little while. And Chuck was talking to Scot [Fisher] my manager one night, like, "Son, this is what you need to know."

AG: He was blown away by you and started saying, "Oh my god, I've never seen a performer this vital since Bruce."

AD: And so he says to Scot, "Document! There's very little footage of Bruce from his heyday," and there's very little this or that and Scot's like, "Oh, okay." So then after the live album came out, Scot's like, "What, it just gets loaded on the truck, it's just one more box, you just turn it on. Tapes are cheap." He insists. But it's

just gotten so fucked up, it's two useless ADAT's per night of line hum.

Did you record *Up Up Up Up Up Up* [Ani's previous solo album] here at Congress House?

AD: No, we recorded it all at Kingsway too, and mixed it here.

What was the recording process for *Up Up...*?

AD: It was pretty much live. We went down to Kingsway. I had been down there for Jazz Fest and fell in love with the place. So then I decided the thing to do would be to go down there, not bring our mics or amps or anything, just our instruments, and use what was at the house, really try to utilize the house. Which was a bad idea when it came to amps. You realize that the room full of amps there were left behind by Dan for a reason! But it's incredible, because the house has fourteen bathrooms, for starters. So you're talking fourteen tiled room 'verbs. We just started walking around the house listening to rooms. Each song was different.

AG: We just kept moving around. It was like, okay, drums sound really good underneath the stairs and we'll use a certain tiled area for this...

AD: Apparently, according to Ethan [Allen], a lot of bands just go in and they set up in the main room and they just stay there.

AG: That's why they put those snake boxes there, because it was like all the time they were recording there, and it was a drag to have to pull that snake out to the same place all the time. The control room as well. The weird thing is that it's always been where it's been, but in theory, everything can move.

AD: 'Cause that was Dan's thing. "It's not a studio, it's just a house," and there's some gear in there but nothing is hardwired. Everything has to be floatable.

AG: So you could just literally take a rack and unplug it and move it, if you wanted to.

AD: But the thing is, you don't want to move the whole fucking board and the tape machines - nobody's ever moved it! But it can't be installed. Which makes for some...

AG: It makes for some fucked up wiring! I mean, I know everything that's a problem on this record is my fault, but there was really funky [wiring]... the patchbay leads to really strange places. Instead of just putting in a patch and having it go to a preamp, it actually goes to a weird little snake box where the preamp is temporarily plugged in. There's so many connections in that studio it's scary. Around the back of those racks, there's all these weird snakes, so that anything could go in and out, nothing is hardwired to anything.

Did you get a lot of noise problems?

AD: There's a lot of radio hum....

AG: RF on things. And crackly things. The board is a 1970 API console and it's in good shape, but it's from 1970.

AD: So every now and then channel one disappears. And you don't notice that the kick drum hasn't been there for a couple takes, or something. And you just have to get into the bleed. Make it bleed! The album was very much about performances, playing together.

AG: The other aspect of that record was that it actually took place over a long [time]. Most of those songs were also recorded in June, and a lot of those were recorded in February, by you solo.

AD: Yeah, so this is my big theory: Because I'm instant gratification slut, I just play it once, Okay, fucked up the lyrics a little bit, whatever. I just can't perfect things, I just can't deal with doing things over and over. So, you know, you make quick recordings and live to regret most of them. So I thought, Okay, make quick recordings, since I can't stand to take too much time on things, and do that in different places, different times of the year. I had this bunch of songs, and we recorded most of them here first. I thought, compare and save the recordings. It was cool, because you learn a little from the first times, but then we ended up just taking most of the Kingsway recordings. It just had a whole vibe.

AG: It definitely flavored the record in a big way.

AD: Yeah, mad Kingsway flavor.

AG: It's a great place to work. There are certain kinds of music and certain kinds of records that you just would not be able to make there. To try and work against that studio would be a real drag, to try and have lots of isolation. The whole place just lends itself to working in a certain way, so that's how you end up working when you go there.

How much time did you spend down there?

AD: A week and a half. The band was there for five days, and we were there for another three. So I guess that's just a week. But fuck.

AG: There's all these stories of people spending a month in the studio or two months. I don't know.

The new Rufus Wainwright album... two years in the studio!

AD: Wow. So that's what you can do in two years! It's so complex, there's so much going on. Alright then, if anyone's going to take two years, you might as well have a million strings and stuff. I just don't have the attention span.

I think with any project, you get to a point where you just start to lose momentum.

AG: Yeah, like after the first eight months. [laughs] The way we did this one was very cool, because we were breaking it up, you did demo versions in February, out on tour, back in June, out on tour again, back to Kingsway. So it was kind of like spending a year or six months to make a record but not in the studio [the whole time].

Was that the first time you had done a demo-like process?

AD: Yeah, totally. Usually it's like, write the songs, play them live, drive around, do gigs, drink beer, and go in the studio for a week and make a record. I think it was making the live record that made me realize that the songs sound much more like themselves onstage. The songs that turned up on the live record probably sound totally different from the way they were recorded in the studio. But the studio was just a fluke! It was what that song sounded like at that moment in that studio, depending on... But the songs onstage are more indigenous, that's where they live, you know? And then getting the ADAT's into the studio then got it more like live. With two inch tape it's like, ok, rolling, go go go, and then it's do we keep it, do we do another, ah! Now because the tape is so cheap we can just keep rolling, keep all the takes. It's less pressured. But I have a very love/hate relationship with ADATs. We get error messages all the time. They're fucking VCRs. One of the great things about the Kingsway setup is that Ethan, the engineer there got these little sixteen channel Mackie mixers for headphone mixes so everybody's got a little rolling cart. We're all like invalids with our IV, rolling it around.

AG: And then [in the control room] there's a patch section with sixteen little inputs to send them to all the mixers, split from the tape outs basically.

AD: All the musicians can change everything in their headphones whenever. So the engineers at the board spend no time, like you were saying, after every take, "Can I get less organ?"

AG: "But you're sharing a headphone mix with Julie and she needs that organ." So this setup was just ridiculously easy.

AD: It is much more like a live recording in that you're not dealing with the needs of the musicians all the time.

AG: And with everyone in the same room, it's just making sure the preamps are connected properly and it's all going to tape.

AD: But Kingsway is up for sale now. It's been having a really precarious life the whole last year. Since we started going there, you never know, any moment a truck could show up and take all the gear away 'cause Dan has been wanting to get rid of it. This Utah record was supposed to be officially the last session.

When you did the previous Utah album [The Past Didn't Go Anywhere], what kind of sampling setup did you use? Or did his voice just get flown to tape?

AD: H3000! Eventide H3000 SE. It's all about that box, that whole record. You can get it with a stereo sampler upgrade, so you can do sixteen seconds or something like that. Everything went through that box. All the drum loops.

Sixteen seconds? That's like old school hip-hop production.

AG: And it wasn't MIDI'd up to anything, it was just triggered.

AD: That album's sound is very much the capabilities of that machine. If you set up a loop, then press record [on the tape deck], and record five minutes of a drum loop, and then you want to set up some other kind of loop, eventually, in five minutes, they'll be out of sync with each other. But there's a triggering function, so I would set up a trigger for each track.

So you used a click as a trigger?

AD: Yeah, basically, or I'd record one instrument and that would trigger all the other loops.

AG: Or the kick from the beginning of a loop, you can use that as a trigger.

AD: But mostly it was just sampled drums and then I played everything else. It's a little Luddite.

The results don't sound too Luddite, I was thinking it was done with a whole digital audio system.

AD: I would go from a DAT of Utah's voice, which had transfers of all this stuff he had sent me on cassette, but cleaned up some at a mastering place. And then into the sampler. For the drums, I could only do about a four bar drum loop, but with a trigger I would have alternate drum loops so I could go back and forth. But listening back to it, the sound of that record, it's pretty simple stuff. I was learning my way around the H3000. It's a digital machine but it has an analog front end. If you overload it you can make some really crazy, cool distortion happen. And that was my big thing for a while, when I first discovered how it would distort, and then fucking Mr. Burst - My - Bubble - Guy here comes along with the Brian Eno diary, the *Year of Swollen Appendices*.

AG: There's one little entry where he's like, [in stuffy British voice] "I've recently discovered that distorting the inputs of the H3000 produces this..."

AD: Blah blah blah! And I've had this inherent anti-Eno sentiment, only because I've toured for too many years with these enlightened Church of Eno Canadian boys. "There's not enough Africa in my computer." It's like, fucking bite me right now. And then he shows me this chapter, oh look, you and Brian...

Do you feel more in harmony with Brian now?

AD: No, it's just my animosity towards him [points to Andrew] has grown! [laughs] Yeah, so that first Utah record, there's not a lot of complex sampling going down, it's like set up a loop and pound it.

AG: It's funny, I've recently been buying old LL Cool J and Run DMC records and fuck, talk about simple. It's like a drum machine plugged directly into a board, a guy yelling into a microphone, and some eight bit orchestra shot samples. And it's got such a vibe to it. There's no big production happening, except that in itself it becomes this big thing. But it's deadly simple.

AD: When I last checked out that Utah records, I was struck by the basic loops, they don't really evaporate or dissipate or tonally filter.

AG: Yeah, when we do remixes of stuff, I'm always trying to plan, Okay it's going to drop out for these bars, and we'll put an alternate pattern here.

AD: The other thing is that, on our board at home, the mutes actually...

AG: It's some kind of damping, it's not a hard cut. You don't get a pop.

AD: It's like a quick fade. But on this board to mute something, it's pppt!, it pops every time.

AG: And then you're using the automation and you get it at a certain place, but because it's an analog board, it's slightly different every time.

AD: You'll be trying to mix down and things will be popping randomly. So all the remixes of my songs that we've done here, it's a very loose idea of remixing. Basically it's like set up a drum loop then replay all the instruments and re-sing a vocal, and if you want to drop something out stop playing.

AG: I think people are doing that more and more, with the remix as a redo. That whole Björk remix album, all those vocals are redone. They pretty much used elements of the songs to create the new tracks, and then she redid the vocals. I think what we do as remixing is closer to the classic remixing than what a lot of people do.

AD: Remixing is supposed to be taking the original tapes...

AG: Yeah, but the remix of "Jukebox" is like that.

AD: Right, we took the actual drums from the song. But we have no sampling gear so to take tracks and edit them, shift them around, it's kind of tough.

AG: I remember a while back when we were doing remixes, having that hellish time trying to sync everything up, and you were like, what are we doing wrong? And I was like, people don't remix like this, I mean, we're remixing to two inch tape, flying elements over to the tape (from ADAT) and adding stuff. People don't remix like that, it's done with a pair of headphones and a hard disk system.

AD: And we're discovering the hard way why all that fucking gear was invented!

AG: Yeah. If we're working with the two inch tape, we'll print SMPTE onto the last track, and then the ADAT can sync up to that. That's another reason we're using the BRC, because it will either sync up to SMPTE or generate SMPTE, which is something the ADAT's won't do by themselves.

Do you ever use the track delay function on the ADATs? Like to get drum overheads in phase?

AG: Yeah, but usually just for getting stuff to time. Usually for the bass track, if I use it. If the bass is a little late, you can delay everything else and [thereby] push it forward. You know what I feel like I'm just learning about? Documentation. For me it's like a lost world, my focus has never really been there. But the things we do have been getting more and more complicated. All these ADAT tapes, and doing the *Up Up* record over a series of months, just keeping track of stuff. Everything I'm used to doing is like, here's your multitrack tape and here's your DAT and that's it.

What is your current approach to recording acoustic guitars? That's something that obviously you've been dealing with forever.

AD: You know, I really wish I could tell you. I feel like I get worse and worse at it.

AG: I was going to say, it's almost like we've been avoiding it. You know, like let's just send it to an amp.

AD: The past however many records I've done, I always mic it, maybe stereo or maybe just a single mic. And then take the DI to a channel, which you can really get a good bass out of the higher registers sound a little magnetic on the DI. And then send it to an amp. That's been my whole thing, I think that's the only thing I know how to do, get different acoustic guitar sounds through amps. But in terms of mic'ing it, I feel so disappointed, over and over again.

AG: It terrifies me, every time we go in. If you want to get the bottom out of it, it sounds all boxy. And then you get rid of that boxyness and it gets all shrill. We tried that thing of hanging a blanket between the two mics...

AD: Yeah, everything, baffling between the two mics. I have gotten some good acoustic guitar micing sounds in the past.

AG: We use (AKG) 414's a lot, for whatever reason. It's funny, people talk a lot about micing acoustic guitars, reading your basic *EQ* magazine, and all they ever talk about is how to get that crisp...

AD: ....sparkle, all that fucking shit that I hate on an acoustic guitar! That brittle...

AG: Basically you could just retitle the article "How Not To Record An Acoustic Guitar."

AD: My whole quest is how do you get a full, warm, percussive, but still present sound.

AG: Without being tubby or boxy

AD: I don't know. I'm still wrestling with it. There's some EQ'ing involved definitely.

AG: It varies a lot, even the same kind of guitar, or the same guitar played at a different volume. I used to think we had kind a kind of technique, down at the bottom, on the wood, off the soundhole, and then sometimes that totally sucks, sometimes the soundhole is terrible.

So you're still at the mercy of nature and the wood.

AD: And ignorance and experimentation. And I've been playing the same guitars for years and I still don't know how to mic them. That's the other thing about being my own producer — that's the last thing I worry

about so often. I'm worrying about drum sounds and the buzz on the bass, and the arrangement, and getting the whole vibe. I feel like I've been neglecting the acoustic sound the past few years. Listening back to some of my old records, before I had any ideas about sounds at all, and the sounds are all very suspect and haphazard, whatever engineer was working on them. But there are some acoustic sounds that are like...

AG: The other night we were making a tape for Darren to learn a song and I was like, that guitar sounds good!

***Out of Range* had some great guitar sounds. Big, sweeping, natural...**

AG: That's what it was! That's what we were listening to and I was thinking the same thing.

AD: I don't remember. I don't know. I've no idea.

AG: I suck, that's basically what it is.

AD: Yeah, it's all his fault.

AG: Maybe it's once we discovered all these cool amps and other ways of getting really interesting sounds.

AD: And also the past three years of having a bass player onstage, the level of the guitar has come down on stage and in the house, and it's one of many instruments, it's no longer playing the drums and the bass. I used to be so focused on the sound of it and now I think on stage my mission is how can I play less and make more space.

AG: There's a good side and a bad side to that. Live, your ability to play less, to sit back, it's great.

AD: There's a definite liberty to that, I can lay out or do something much more sparse and the song is still there. But you know, I was listening to some older songs, and I thinking, wow, I used to be able to play guitar better.

AG: You had that super percussive, breakneck speed crazy guitar.

AD: But now that would just be too busy cause there's a bass player and a drummer, so I find myself playing less and less. Generally it's stereo micing, in the vicinity of the soundhole. Some people put a mic on the neck to get that shimmering stuff that I hate. Generally I find mic'ing the body gets woofy or boxy, so I try to get a stereo image on the soundhole. I've spent many an album baffling between the two mics, but then if you're singing live, also a baffle here (under the chin), so it's a T-form of baffle, to get as much separation as possible. And then also always taking a DI separately and sometimes, on some past records, even EQ'ing the DI to tape so that it's just low-end punch.

AG: If you're going to send something to the subharmonic synthesizer, it's always the DI. You get the definition.

AD: And the acoustic mic'ing gives it its texture and its shape and the DI gives the punch. Often times the amp will give it a meat or a tone.

AG: Sometimes that'll be to tape, but I love sending things from tape to amp. I was talking about that before, finally having that spring reverb, so we don't have to send the signal to an amp to get the spring reverb.

AD: The good thing about having four or five channels of one acoustic guitar is that you can have more amp in the choruses, and more of the mics in the verses.

Do you have a studio in Buffalo currently?

AD: Yeah, at the house in Buffalo, we just have a big room that's a control room and [live] room. And we're just amassing stuff. We've got the famous ADATs, those poor things, they do duty out on the road, and then they sit in the house, and we haul them out here. We take them in for service a lot cause they get real bashed around.

So it's a one room setup?

AG: Yeah, we recently hung curtains and carpets because it's a very live, big room.

Is there anything from there that's going to be released?

AD: Yeah, actually, on *Up Up* there's some Dust Bowl Studio tracks, that's what we call the place in Buffalo. The fucking house is covered in an inch of plaster dust, everything. There's a lot of construction at our house, when I bought it there was no kitchen and no bathrooms, the whole place was gutted.

AG: And we've been trying to do the studio thing. For the first six months all the stuff that we had stayed in its cardboard boxes, because it's so dusty and finally it was just, fuck, let's set it up and then we would cover it in tarps.

I'm sure that keeps the ADAT's going in to service.

AD: Yeah, I hate to think of our spanking new board.

AG: Soundcraft, their kind of version of the Mackie board, which is called the Ghost. It's nice, it's fairly clean, well set up, little analog console, a real functional eight buss board. I think it sounds a lot nicer than the Mackie boards. The EQ is real subtle and really musical. And I'm a terminal gearhead so I collect stuff.

AD: Yeah, every day off in Des Moines is a trip to the pawn shop.

AG: I don't even play guitar and I have more guitar pedals than anyone. So many.

AD: He has to bring me around with him to all these crazy shops just to check out every pedal.

Last year you produced the Dan Bern album [*Fifty Eggs*, Sony/Work], which was the first big project you produced of someone else's music. What was that like?

AD: I have great aspirations of putting out other people's music, now that we've got a mechanism to do that with. I fell in love with Dan's songs and I think that he's got something special, and I was trying to convince him to make music on Righteous Babe Records. But he's doing the Sony thing. He had made his first record with Chuck Plotkin and then it was it expected that he would do the second record with Chuck. And then we met and Dan wanted it to it with me, and Chuck very graciously said, "Hey, whatever you're into." So we made the record, and we both learned a lot.

Did you go into with specific ideas on how you were going to produce the songs?

AD: Well, we share a booking agent, and Dan opened a few shows, and then a few more, and pretty soon Dan was a fixture on the old bus there. So I knew all the songs pretty intimately from touring. I just got together musicians that I know, Andy and Jason and Sara Lee, who used to be my bass player, and then Denny Fongheiser, a total session cat out in LA, a drummer who's played on more albums than any of us could begin to fathom. So it was a collection of people and it was all about the Congress House and the vibe there.

Did you use the ADATs with Dan?

AD: Yeah, and then we bounced to two inch. That was back in the bouncing days, when I was still determined to end up on some kind of tape that had some weight. It was really cool for me to be able to step back from the music, stay in the control room and listen and figure out what was working and what wasn't and how to make it work. Producing your own stuff, it's hard to put down all the baggage. Like that track we were listening to earlier ("Bread and Roses") that I overdubbed that bass on, I don't really like that bass part so it's mixed kind of low. And typically with my mixes you cannot hear the acoustic guitar half the time because I'm playing it so I don't like it. It's really hard to listen to a mix and say, "it needs more acoustic guitar," even though you played it, and it sucks, turn it up because that's what the mix needs. It's so hard not to be emotional and immediate like that. I'm always turning down whatever I'm playing, just cause it's a closeness thing. So it was really cool to have a somewhat more objective view of what was going on. I feel with the first Utah record, it was so nice working with somebody else's voice and somebody else's ideas, I felt so much more at liberty to love it and really get off on it. I didn't have the tortured, self-loathing obstacle. But in all of my idealistic aspirations of working with other people and their music, I always come to the brutal realization that working with other people's music involves other people. [laughs] Which always seems to be a challenging proposition!

AG: Whatever baggage you may have working with your own stuff is only...

AD: Oh, fuck, baggage! We need to build a new wing on the Congress House to fit all the baggage that comes in. I only ever had to accommodate my own psychosis before.

What is the new speaker system you're using live?

AG: Live now we're using this new V-DOSC system. Traditionally with speaker systems, you don't want the speakers to overlap coverage areas because then certain frequencies will be emphasized, and whenever you hit a note in that range it'll be much louder than everything else. That's called coupling. It's something the Grateful Dead were experimenting with. They had sound systems with huge numbers of speakers, very tall, but not necessarily very powerful. And the whole idea was to get them all coupling, to throw the sound out. Bass specifically does not travel well forwards, high frequencies travel better.

But if you can get bass frequencies coupled they'll actually move in a line. So V-DOSC, they're from France, they spent a lot of time and money figuring this out, and they've come up with a sound system that uses this coupling and they've got it down to a fine art, positioning speakers in relationship to each other so that they couple well. And then also, this is the part that freaks me out and where my understanding of it drops off, being able to tightly control the dispersion. You know, PA speakers are always rated in dispersion, whether it's ninety degrees or sixty degrees. The stuff we used to use, the AW 850's or the EV stuff, they were different cabinets, some of them were sixty degrees and some were nineties. What you don't want to do is start throwing a lot of sound into the side walls of the theater, or the roof, or the floor, or across the other side. You try to control the dispersion. And this system, the dispersion is controlled to the foot. You can focus it, it's like lighting. You position the box, aim it a certain way, couple it with the box underneath it, and you can keep the sound... it's so hard to even understand.

AD: My understanding of it is very experiential. From the vibey front man's perspective, what I'm used to hearing at the front of the stage, especially in these huge sheds (outdoor arenas), these cavernous barns, is just low end wash coming back from the balcony or the far back wall. It's just this sort of chaos, low mid to sub frequencies. Somehow with the V-DOSC you can tune it to throw but not reflect back. And the result is that you can be walking down the outside aisle of a shed and be able to hear the vocal totally as clearly as if you were mid-audience.

AG: A lot of it has to do with side-to-side too. If you were in a big basketball arena, and there's all that space to the side you're not using, you can walk out of range and it just drops off. You can keep it off the ceiling, you can keep it off

the side walls. In a standard theater you have the orchestra section, and then the balcony rail, and then the balcony.

AD: It's balcony that always fucking kills me.

AG: You can actually stop it from bouncing off the front of that balcony, so that it's going down into the seats in front, and then the other boxes are aimed up at the balcony, and you don't get that throw off the balcony back to the stage. It's amazing.

AD: What I think is really admirable about the way the V-DOSC people are working is that it's all still very new and they don't just sell you the gear, 'cause if you don't use it right.... so a V-DOSC technician has to come out and teach you how to use it and how to calibrate it to every room that you're in. But it has made such a difference. It's so funny, little folk girl touring around with this really high tech sound system.

AG: You have very specific problems that have to do with the fact that you're trying to get all these low frequencies out of the acoustic guitar. The only other person I've ever seen trying to do that is Luka Bloom.

AD: Yeah, he's got that smiley EQ: tons of low end, tons of high end. But Bruce Springsteen was like that too.

AG: But Luka Bloom has a closed body guitar, with no soundhole.

So he's cheating.

AD: Yeah. So the trick is how to crank between 60 and 125 Hz.

AG: It's basically a recipe for disaster what we're trying to do live.

AD: Every night, yeah. The acoustic guitar, you're talking about a really thin, resonant piece of wood, so what I have to contend with at the front of the stage is the kick drum and the bass guitar washing back off the very back of the house, the low end just keeps existing and existing forever. By the time it gets back to me it's pulling my guitar into feedback. So the V-DOS system has meant my level before feedback onstage has really gone up and the clarity of what I hear, I can start to hear the sidefills and the wedges without being consumed in wash. And we got to learn it on the Dylan tour, 'cause he's been traveling with that system for a while. Steve, who does my front of house, he had to start using the system. So contending with the sheds now it's a world of difference.

How much extra time is it to set up?

AG: Believe it or not, there's software that comes with it. That's what Larry, our PA tech, does now, his first job of the day is to come into the room and he literally, with a three hundred foot tape measure, does the whole room. And he enters all that info into the computer and it creates an image of the room, and then figures out where to hang the system. And there are these pieces of wood that go between the speakers, and the thickness of the wood corresponds to a certain number of degrees. You still tune it by ear after it's done. But the software will tell you, Okay, hang this many speakers for this room, tilt this one two degrees and this one five degrees, and put a spacer in.

AD: And now friends who come to the show, they come backstage after and say, this is the best sounding show we've ever heard here, this is a terrible place. And we've been carrying our own speakers for a while anyway, there's only so many years you can, like in the days of just me and Andy, they'd see the rider and say, Okay acoustic guitar and drums, it's a folk show, and so we'd get speakers on sticks. And underpowered teeny little wedges. Despite that fact that the rider says fifteen inch speakers and a certain amount of power.

I read a while back about you wiring monitors out of phase to help knock out some bass on stage. Does V-DOSC take care of it so you don't have to do that?

AD: Yeah, that was before V-DOSC. And we used to take the front house subs, and juxtapose the EQs?

AG: That was sort of the second generation of doing that. The crude way of doing it is you just take the left sub and the right sub and put them out of phase with each other. So the people on the left and right are getting good bass but straight down the middle where those two meet they literally cancel out. And that's where you stand on stage, at the center.

AD: That made a big difference in the bass wash that I got back off the balcony in those theaters. Theaters with aisles down the middle, hopefully it was narrow enough, but standing houses with people right down the middle...

AG: You always knew that there were a bunch of people down the center who were getting this weird phased bass thing going on. Right now Meyer has just come out with this thing that's a directional subwoofer [the PSW-6], which nobody has ever done before. It's the same kind of concept, it's massive, the thing is the size of a Volkswagon. There's a certain number of twenty-one inch speakers facing forwards, and then there's half as

many facing the other direction, and very simply the ones facing the other direction are out of phase. So you've got the throw forward and then the other way you've got these other speakers pushing real hard to try and cancel them out. But they use massive amounts of power, they're extremely heavy, and they're exceedingly expensive. Klondike, the sound company we work with, demoed a pair, but the problem they had with them is that they were too big to tour with.

AD: Yeah, we would have to get another truck.

AG: And also the power requirements too, because you're using a lot of power just to cancel.

AD: But for that matter, V-DOSC is pretty insanely expensive.

[For more info on the theories behind the V-DOSC system, check out www.coxaudio.com]

Andrew, what was your production experience before you got hooked up with Ani?

AG: I lived in Toronto for years and years and worked at a place that was really cool, it was a venue and a recording studio called the Music Gallery, specifically devoted to experimental music. In Canada there's all kinds of government money that goes into music and arts. So this place, I used to tell people, if you take everything that you know of as music and draw a circle around it, all the stuff that fell outside that circle, that's what we did. John Cage, Philip Glass, Steve Reich, that whole world, that's where that venue came out of, and then it expanded into free jazz, world music — basically anyone who was not mainstream enough to be playing in clubs.

Were the performances in the same space as the recording studio?

AG: Yeah. As a recording studio it was pretty limited, basically a one inch 8-track machine that never got used. There were a couple grand pianos, a really nice live space. I spent a lot of time doing demo tapes for classical musicians, which you need if you're a student at a college and you're trying to get a job in an orchestra. It's basically you on your instrument and a piano accompaniment. And it's got to sound really good. So that was my bread and butter for recording, doing that just live to DAT. And the combinations were crazy, you know, soprano voice and piano, tuba and piano, chamber orchestra and tape. People would come in with their instrument and I'd be like, how the fuck do you mic this? So I was there for a long time. And Andy, who used to play drums with Ani, he was kind of plugged into that scene because he played hand drums and did all these things. He would get these weird gigs at this place, he would get hired to do recordings and do gigs. So I met him when I started working there and we kind of became friends and hung out and he got me doing all these other projects, I started recording some acoustic pop music, which I knew nothing about. He figured it was a cheap studio, and I'd let him in for free. We'd finish shows, I'd coil cables 'til

midnight, then he'd come in with some Cajun trio and record until four in the morning for free. I did a lot of that. So then Ani was looking for somebody to help drive the van, sell CD's, and do sound, sort of tour manage. And it came at a really good place, when I was making really bad money, the hours were really long, it was five shows a week and then recording on days off. And the guy who was the head engineer there was stuck in his ways and I was not going any further than that in that world. So I was actively looking for other things when that came up. Ani brought me out for a week-long tour in the northeast and the rest is a long and involved and varied history...

AD: Sordid.

AG: Yes, sordid. It was not a direct or smooth path from that time to here but here we are. But I feel fortunate and pretty proud of that background. I know a bunch of people who did the recording studio thing where you're like the whipping boy in some commercial studio and you coil cables, watching the same setups every day, "This is how you mic drums, this is how you mic a guitar amp," and then eventually you get to push "record". What I got to do was working with minimal equipment in a weird space but being asked to do anything and being expected to do anything, being thrown all these challenges and being presented with music that was way out there. It was cool and I certainly learned things that you wouldn't normally learn and it gave me a mindset to be able to experiment.

AD: See, and this explains the highbrow/lowbrow war of art that has gone on in our musical marriage.

AG: I definitely have this weird highbrow art background, conceptual...

AD: Meanwhile, I'm busting ass in bars for ten years, strumming along, smiling with my acoustic guitar. It's a whole different world, the whole Music Gallery, government funded thing. If only, man, welcome to America... It's good, we balance each other out. You have all these insecurities: does this have a right to exist, masturbatory, high art shit. And I come from the other end of the spectrum: am I the most simple, inane, lame-ass, lowest common denominator, prop her up in the corner of the bar and play cover songs bitch? Somewhere in the middle there's got to be real specific, challenging art that exists in the world, which is not born of some elusive aesthetic, real art moving things, air molecules and people, but also on a grassroots level.

I see the dichotomy now, between you.

AD: It's Art Boy and Folk Girl! ✿

Three Looks into The Ex

❶ an interview with guitarist Andy Moor **❷** the studio "Het Koeienverhuurbedrijf" [Cow-Rent Company] **❸** Steve Albini on recording *Starters Alternators*

It made sense that in the summer of 1999, the 10th anniversary show of the current line-up of The Ex took place in Amsterdam and included Shellac as well as a host of great experimental Dutch bands and performers. Shellac's Steve Albini has been a loyal fan of The Ex for years. Why? Because The Ex have developed their sound so meticulously over the years, through rigorous touring and recording and maintaining their steadfast politic, that it is hard to liken The Ex to any other band ever.

The Ex solder political poetry to searing guitars, driving bass and mesmerizing, tribal drums. Since 1979, they have changed members and adapted their sound over and over again, but somehow the band has steered a rock-solid-punk political course supporting freethinking and social critique. They have always toured with and supported dissident underground, punk, and avant-garde musicians, as well as with politically outspoken bands and artists over the years, to name a few: Dog Faced Hermans, God is my Co Pilot, Tom Cora, Thurston Moore, Lee Ranaldo, Ab Baars, most recently with Chicago post-rockers Tortoise. The Ex have toured in Europe and in the US regularly, and have released countless numbers of recordings. The Ex's popularity in the USA led to an offer from independent label Touch & Go in Chicago, to record with Steve Albini for 1998 release *Starters Alternators*. The Ex's live shows — visceral sonic attacks of part-improv-part-scored music, to the ecstatic energy proportions of Zorn's Painkillers — lead one to wonder, how on earth does such a band approach recording?

I had the chance recently to sit down for an interview with Andy Moor, one of The Ex's two guitarists. Originally from the UK, Andy was the guitarist in Dog Faced Hermans and joined The Ex in the early '90s. He became a full-time member in '95 (when Dog Faced Hermans unfortunately split up). Andy's highly-creative style of playing guitar uniquely combines avant-garde techniques with punk rock. By adding pieces of metal to contort his old Fender guitar (a la Fred Frith), and by using unusual tunings and volume control, Andy avoids using affects pedals or other devices to achieve wide ranges of incredible guitar sounds (a la Steve Albini). On a typical sunny/rainy February day in Amsterdam, I biked over to meet with Andy. We spoke for two hours, surrounded by tea pots, a wilily rigged archaic 4-track, an old stereo, piles of cassettes and CDs and Andy's two guitars.

How do you guys create The Ex's sound and music and how is your music is recorded?

The energy thing of how we make the songs, what happens live and what happens in the practice room are really two quite different things. I mean, we don't jump up and down a lot in the practice room at all. We talk quite a lot, we play things over, we try to create a frame or a structure that later on will allow us to jump up and down. We don't try to make it too imprisoning so that when we play you can't breathe. We leave the possibility that once we start playing it's going to get looser and people are going to be able to breathe and play. The first gigs are a bit weird or stiff and slowly you find the right way to play it. Very

quickly after one gig you know, "Oh this bit works or this bit doesn't work." You can't really tell this in the practice room, because you're sitting down and you can hear everything so everything sounds allright. When you get to a gig, you hardly ever hear... we can't hear each other, there are sounds from the audience, I can't hear Terrie, or... it's a completely different state you are in. You adjust the music that's been created in the practice room to the gig conditions, which are completely different. The sound is different. So the music changes. That's nice that we really react to the sound. When I go to the States, I have to use a different amp, and it's completely different, I mean there's bits that sound the same, but then there are whole sections that I have to adjust to, because the whole reason I had decided to play those parts was because of a sound that was coming out of the amp, and suddenly that sound is not there - it's not there from Terrie, it's not there from Luc, and you get a bit disorientated and it takes a few gigs to get adjusted and you never ever feel it's as good. I think we're going to try to bring our own stuff over, because every time we tour in the States we suffer from that.

How does that translate into recording your music? Is recording more like playing live or playing in the practice space?

It's another third space that I am usually unsatisfied with, because it is neither live nor like the practice room. What happens is we play the songs for quite a while live before we go into the studio - the only time that The Ex ever recorded straight after being in the studio

was *Dead Fish* and they recorded that live directl[y] onto DAT. John Langford just set the mics up, the[y] spent a whole day and then he recorded it directly But I didn't think that was the best sounding E[x] record, partly because the songs hadn't been playe[d] in a bit and you could hear that, they got much bette[r] later, those songs. The sound was a bit over-reverbe[d] - the live room they did it in in this great studio i[n] England [KGM Studios, in Wakefield]. It has a grea[t] live room but it's a bit reverby and when you recor[d] the whole band live in it, you can hear... I don't kno[w] if you've heard that record, but I think that's th[e] result of a band going straight from the practice roo[m] to the studio rather than taking their music out o[n] tour first. Because then all these really fine playin[g] things, you don't even realize you are doing it, th[e] more you play together the more the sound move[s] and you do it by talking about it by thinking abou[t] and you don't even realize you are doing it it ju[st] happens, and it's to do with wanting it to work. I[t's] nice because usually when you try out something li[ke] most times everyone agrees on what works and wh[at] doesn't, most times everyone feels it immediately. [We] also get a reaction from the audience, which we ta[ke] quite seriously. Even if we like something, if we'[ve] played it three or four times and we notice th[at] people are a bit confused by it, they don't react, w[e] I don't think there is something wrong with t[he] audience there is something wrong with how we a[re] putting the idea across. Which is very different I thi[nk] from a lot of the stuff in the improv jazz scene. I thi[nk] they don't take so much from the relation with t[he] audience. It's a bit of this thing, "it doesn't matter what the audience thinks, it's all about the music if the audience likes it well good but if they don't..." I don't think that's true. I think that when you play before an audience they are intelligent and they can feel when something works and when it doesn't work, and that's a really important aspect. That's why playing live is so good, it's like having ten practices in terms of how the song will suddenly improve and sometimes it's brutal it doesn't make it and you've worked on a song for weeks and weeks and you take it on tour and somehow you've lost it, you've done all that work... If it doesn't work it doesn't work and it's better not to play it. But it's difficult because you have old songs that are in really good shape and you have new songs that you are trying out which are always going to be a bit more fragile and you have to be careful that you don't throw them away too quickly because the old songs sound good and the people in the audience know them... That's what we are busy

and that's what he managed to do. I can't really give you much information about gear though, I didn't even know what the name of his mixing desk is, you should ask him. He really likes it, he said it was analog - I didn't even know you had digital mixing boards nowadays.

Yeah, they've got all kinds of crazy stuff, big stuffy computer screens where you just sit there and basically can just go "whaa!" at it and it makes a song!

Yeah? Well, there you go! He's not really into that though.

I bet not!

But he has all these mics, I don't even know what kinds he used with us, but he's got Russian mics and old '50s mics and Chinese mics - really an incredible collection.

How many would you say he has, roughly?

a video or have a chat rather than struggling. I think it went well, it was really fast and painless.

What would you say that you learned most, that you took away from the experience of working with Albini - it seems that The Ex working with Albini was a really really good match of circumstances.

Certainly. We knew he really, really liked The Ex, When we asked him, he said he'd known The Ex since nearly their first single, and he knew that at some point he'd work with them. So when we asked him he was immediately into it. He had all the old records as well, which was really quite nice, because he's a big fan. When you are playing and when you are recording that feels good, you feel like you're in really good hands working with someone who really likes your music and isn't just doing it... Sometimes I've recorded with people who I think just don't like the roughness of our sound and they try to clean it up.

with the whole time, balancing these two things and trying to keep the set alive so it doesn't feel like we're playing the same songs...

Working with Steve Albini, were there specific things you wanted to achieve by working together, and what kind of gear did you use to achieve these things?

Well, actually microphones are everything - they are his specialty He seems to have hundreds of different kinds of microphones. He doesn't use much gear at all - he has a simple analog mixing desk with a little bit of EQ on it, and he hardly EQ'd anything. Whenever he thought something didn't sound good, he'd change the microphone rather than trying to put it through a compressor. He spent a lot of time in the beginning positioning microphones really with incredible detail. A couple of times I bumped a microphone and it moved like five cm and he could hear it upstairs and he came down and looked like that (furrows brows) and moved it and that sound coming out was like "thhhrhrrrrr" (a really noisy part of the song!). It sounded like in the whole room it wouldn't have mattered where you put the mic, but he really could hear that something was changed. When I saw that, I was like, "Wow."

This is a guy who knows his mics.

Yeah! And his ears must be really really finely tuned to that. I guess if you have that level working in that way then you don't need to use all the other stuff. All of the other stuff is a bit compensating for if you can't get it on tape sounding good in the beginning,

Four or five hundred. He basically spent the whole first day working with the mics and then we went ahead and played our songs the way we play them. When we went to listen they really sounded more like The Ex than most times I've been recorded. It sounded like The Ex in the practice room, a beautifully recorded version of what we sound like in the practice room. Really clear - you could hear everybody, and the way the sounds kind of mix is the way he managed to get it, there was no instrument that sounded unfamiliar to us... He's like a kind of field recorder, he tries to capture our sound he doesn't try to produce it the way he wants it. He does the levels afterwards, that's a different thing. But to do the actual sound of the instruments, he tries to really get the sound that we are, that we have, and he's not trying to push us into some "style" or something. I think that's great and for us that was quite a pleasure. It meant that when we recorded it already sounded good, so that when we mixed it was already there, we just had to do a bit of levels, and it went really quickly, we didn't get sick of listening to the music. It wasn't spending hours gating reverbs and all this stuff

How many days did the recording take?

We did it in seven days I think, so we recorded three or something. Mixing was only two days, and it was very kind of relaxed, we'd stop and play a game of snooker, or was it billiards? and have a little bit to eat and come back. It was very relaxed. I think also from experience, knowing that your ears get tired quickly and it's better to stop for twenty minutes and watch

That's frustrating, isn't it?

And you try to explain to them that that's not what you want, but we're not great at explaining those things, we're not a super-articulate bunch of people in that field at all. We know with our ears when it isn't good, but it's very difficult to explain that because you are in the process. and usually engineers make out that they know much, much more, that it would sound better if you did this this or that, and after a while you... you kind of give up a bit and you let them deal with it. I think he [Albini] liked that roughness and tried to open it out and make space in this kind of noise and encourage it, and that is great. It wasn't like he was thinking "the guitars are too noisy or scratchy." He made them noisy and the thing that's strong about The Ex live, he managed to capture that... there are dynamics, and sometimes they are loud, I thought it was good for that, and it wasn't to do with equipment, I mean of course he has great mics but that wasn't the thing that impressed me the most when we went into the studio, it was the way he worked with these things...

And the next recording plans?

We'll be recording again with Steve in February. It's going to be quite an operation - we've got to get all the way out to Chicago and the flights alone cost as much as the recording. But the last one went so well and it's so good to get out of Amsterdam when you're recording, there's no distractions, you're in an environment where you can totally focus on the music. ⊗

"Maybe some people think that The Ex play a lot of 'noise', but The Ex have a touch that is not like other bands. There is a lot of sound but somehow there is something pleasant there. You could listen to them for three hours and never get that buzzing in your ears!" - Zlaya

Where do ya go in Holland if you're a great punk, rock, or noise-rock band and you're looking to record? Well, surely there are many studios in Amsterdam, Rotterdam, and even maybe in Utrecht where you could find yourself a densely-equipped new studio for your high-tech needs. Or, if you really seek to become part of the real fabric of Dutch punk/rock history, you'd seek the firm farm walls of the most recent standing version of Het Koeienverhuurbedrijf... that is, if you can find it! Best translated as "Cow-Rent Company" studio, this one-level farmhouse out in the flat-flowing-farmland of Purmerend is not so far from Amsterdam in miles, but certainly exists in its very own place in time and space. Over the years, there have been several incarnations of Het Koeienverhuurbedrijf's in different locations. Thus, the studio is geared up with equipment compiled over the years, from squat studios, donations, and purchases by fans and friends. Far from high-tech, far from digitally hotwired, far from the slickster modern age of computer processing and burn-by-joystick accessorization, Het Koeienverhuurbedrijf is a no-nonsense center where like-minded musicians make a gang of great noise!

The segue here is of course the band The Ex. At the various Koeienverhuurbedrijf's, The Ex made many a recording themselves and with friends, most recently with Chicago's Tortoise. In the earliest of the studios, The Ex recorded *Disturbing Domestic Peace* '80, *History of What's Happening* '82, *Dignity of Labor* '83, *Tumult* '83, *Blueprints for a Blackout* '84, and in the next two Koeienverhuurbedrijf's they recorded *Pokkeherrie* '85, *Too Many Cowboys* '87, *Joggers & Smoggers* and *Scrabbling at the Lock* in '91. The Ex's other albums were recorded elsewhere, such as *Aural Guerilla* in the UK and *And The Weathermen Shrug Their Shoulders* which was recorded in Amsterdam. Those who have recorded and produced The Ex include Dolf Planteyt [most albums], Jon Langford, Steve Albini, and Zlaya and Colin, who recorded the Fishtank project with Tortoise.

Het Koeienverhuurbedrijf is basically run by three individuals, one of whom is full-time producer/engineer Zlaya. I went out with Zlaya on a hazy cold and windy day in March 2000. Zlaya himself is originally from Sarajevo, and is one of many talented music-ex-pats from the region who have formed their own whole sub-scene within the rock, avant-garde, and punk music circles in Holland in the last years:

How long have you been recording here and how long has this studio been here?

The studio has been here now about 6 years, that's when I started working here. It took 7-8 months of lots of work to build, back in 1994.

Where did the gear come from?

Mostly from the studio's previous locations, and the

squats. This is the first location that intends to be semi-professional/semi-commercial. All the previous locations had a lot more to do with the squat scenes - more about having a place to record and not really bothering to make them 'perfect'. Whereas this one is sort of in half-way. I personally still do things on the basis of, "Okay, I like the stuff, I want to record it", but I still have to make my living from it. It really matters, of course, what kind of music you want to be involved with. That is basically the kind of attitude that people remember this studio by. We record the stuff if we like the stuff - that's basically the attitude we have. The gear is pretty sufficient.

What are some of the main recording equipment here?

The main piece is a Soundcraft mixing console, and just a few small bits and pieces. 2" 24-track we got 2 years ago. And the Rane desk we also got two years ago.

What is that one used for now?

Right now it's an old Telefunken mastering machine, a 2-track analog mastering machine. It hasn't been used in the last 2-3 years. I always tell myself that I'm going to give it a try again, clean it up and get it working again, but... well... It looks great, doesn't it?

It sure does!

This studio is not really vintage because as you know vintage costs. It's very much analog orientated, I mean there's a computer in the corner but it's hardly ever used. The best part of the studio is the live room, because it's stone walls and a good heavy sound. It's a good recording studio, not a great mixing studio if you're after automation and a fancy clean-sounding place. But for recording the likes of The Ex it's a very good place.

What are some of the projects that have been recorded here?

The Ex recently did their Fishtank recording for De Konkurrent here with Tortoise, and there were other Fishtank recordings here like with Guv'ner, June of 44, Zion Train, No Means No, Ne Zhdali - I don't know if you know them, they're an Estonian band?

Actually, yes, I'm a huge fan of Leonid Soybelman...

Mostly bands from Europe and Eastern Europe, Russia, from Belgium like Perverted or Tryptik, Croatia called Gone Bald who live here now - the most known names would be those on the Konkurrent series, Tortoise, The Ex. That recording sold 20,000 copies in two weeks!

What was your involvement with that recording? Did you handle all of the production, or how did that work?

Well, the Fishtank series recordings are meant to be really 'free' orientated, the band is given kind of all the freedom to do whatever they like, which they wouldn't do under a regular release. It's basically a lot of fun, those sessions I enjoy the most because every band walks in having absolutely no idea whatsoever they are going to do! Their limit in time is 2-3 days, mind you those are long days like 3 hours of sleep max, and the bands just start making music. My job really starts with just

engineering, helping the band set up and doing the technical side of the work. With some, like with June of 44, I even played a little bit of tone generator on it, I am part of the creative process of making the recordings. Usually, bands come here right after a tour, so they are a bit knackered and tired and all, so it's kind of a very peculiar environment for making music. So far we've had really good results because the idea is good. Basically, I do engineering, mixing, and then mastering, but that doesn't happen here.

The Fishtank project is really cool.

Yes, it's a really strong connection between The Ex and the Konkurrent bands. The idea of the place here really is like you should feel at home here. I always feel much better recording in a place that is not so clinical, where you are not afraid to touch something. So that was the idea here, to have a place that is comfortable where you can feel at home. I like having a kitchen here, for example.

What kinds of mics do you usually use in general?

A whole collection of different things, depending on what you want to do. We've got about 40 to 50 mics, we use a different one for each instrument depending on what you want to get. It's probably the most important part of the session is where you place the mic. Condenser mics, dynamic, just a few ribbon mics unfortunately.

What are your favorite mics?

It really depends, I mean my favorite mic is the Shure 57. It only costs about 100 guilders, but if I had to pick one that I could take anywhere and you've got these mics you could spend 4000 guilders on, but they won't necessarily do the best job on each sound source. 57s are my favorite. I always go for it when I am micing the snare drum, a combination of an expensive and a cheap mic combination to try to make something nice out of it. The placement of the mic is more important than anything else here.

Were there any special uses of mics or equipment that really added an extra something to, say, the Fishtank recording with The Ex and Tortoise? I mean, it would be hard to remember exactly but...

No, I do I do actually. Those sessions I always remember. For this one, there were 12 men in the room! I mean, we had three drum kits, 3 bass amps, 3 or 4 guitar amps, xylophone, tons of stuff and you've seen the room, it's not a very big room. Basically you want to get a live feeling of the room so it's not just about micing every instrument separately. It's also about the total complete sound of the room. So that was the key thing.

Difficult with three kits and...

It was really tough, the room was always full saturated with sound. Luckily those guys are good and they knew what they were doing and they're not just banging things at the same time, they made good arrangements. It went really funny -

the first half of the day nobody did anything, everyone was waiting for the other to start! They didn't have anything prepared of course, and they only met here. It wasn't like a bunch of people who knew each other well from before. They all started in the afternoon, like, "Okay, we'll just lay down a few tracks and then we can pop in and do some stuff on top of it." And that's how it went. So, Colin and I together didn't really have the time to bother too much with anything technical - our job was to keep an eye on who was doing what at what moment, to get everything mic'd. You just don't have the time and conditions to do neat precise work, that comes with such improvising, you hope it all comes out good!

And how about mixing?

Mixing took, well again, not very long, 2 days, Tortoise had to leave for home. Mixing was tougher cuz we had piles of stuff on tape. You don't have time to select things and play them again, you just take everything that was there. Mixing became more of a selective listening to bits and pieces. There were tons of instruments on tape, it was really very interesting. Those recordings could have come out hundreds of different ways, you could have picked different bits and pieces and put them together. It was about mixing. That was an interesting session. June of 44 was very peculiar as well - we slept a total of 4 hours in 3 days I think. They came straight from being on tour, and they were tired. One of the guitar players was really sick as well, and they had to leave straight to Chicago after the session. Everything was made up right here, all the songs - just sort of jamming in the room and putting them together. Very interesting, but very intense.

On your feet work.

Yeah, that's for sure.

Anything else about the studio?

Well, it's pretty boring to talk about technical things but if you're asking I love the Rane desk. It's brilliant, the EQ, mic preamps, everything on it - it's a thing that you can't abuse basically. You can crank up the gain and still sounds musical, you can create distortion on it that still sounds musical, EQ is musical even though it's really kind of set at 15 dB +. It's very open sounding, I mean it's an old thing comparable to a Neve. The 2 " machine is great as well - I usually drive it really hot, I use lots of tape saturation and tape compression and that's what people know me for. I don't bother with rules so much, as long as it sounds right, I don't care. That could be sort of the common thing about this studio - that you are allowed to do anything. I mean I've been to places where they are like, "Hey man, the meters are hitting pretty hard" and I'm like, "Yeah, I wanted it that way!" Not everything of course, but things I want to sound that way just put them onto tape and then it works... it's really a matter of attitude. The room is really important here - the most important thing is if the recording sounds good in the room, if it sounds good there it sounds good here. ⊛

Steve Albini talks about recording The Ex

It's one thing to be an incredible, time-testable, almost-beyond-critique band and it's quite more to have fans that include the likes of famed producer / guitarist / socio-cultural-critic Steve Albini. When The Ex were offered to record with Chicago label Touch & Go, their choice for a producer could not have been better. *Starters Alternators* **was recorded at Albini's Electrical Audio studios in Chicago, and here's what he had to say to my probing questions about working with The Ex... and a lesson for us in the kick-ass use of kick-ass mics! Thanks Steve!**

Andy Moor has raved to me about working with you. How would you describe your impressions of recording with The Ex?

I am nearly a 20-year fan of the band, so it was a fantastic experience for me. I love their playful approach to music and life, and they are all exceptional musicians. It was an absolute joy.

Was it challenging to work with The Ex, as their live sound incorporates (sonic?) (kinetic?) improv? or, was this not the case at all?

The nature of the expression doesn't have to change the technical aspect of recording, so the spontaneity didn't require any special consideration. If I had developed a "standard" method, I may have been on unfamiliar ground, but I have generally tried to be prepared for anything, so it was no obstacle.

What were the specific mics and gear that you chose for working with The Ex to best record their sound?

The only really tricky thing about recording the Ex was capturing all the action on Kat's drum kit, since she uses so many pieces in a non-standard style, and anything could be hit at any time. It required using quite a few microphones. When there are two mics per drum, I normally combine them to a single track per drum. The exception is a bass drum, where the balance of the two is better determined during mixdown. Kat was using Gretsch drums (one of the kits we have here at the studio) with additional percussion pieces and a tiny little toy tom tom she uses for accents. Over the drum kit I used a pair of Schoeps 221b mics (small diaphragm tube mics with an extended low-end) as a spaced omni pair, and a Beyer 160 (used to fill-in the stereo image between the 221s.) I think (though I'm cloudy on this) that I used an Earthworks TC40k in the vicinity of her percussion blocks and

bells. It may have been an Audio Technica 4051. Normally, I use two mics on each tom, top and bottom. I used Josephson C609 mics with side firing capsules on most of Kat's drums. I used AKG 451s on the tiny little tom tom, and on her floor tom I used two 414s. On the bass drum I used a Crown GLM 100 dangling near the beater and an AKG D112 on the front head. On the snare drum I used an Altec 175 (a small tube mic with an excellent sound in this application). The room ambience was recorded with a pair of Altec 150 ("coke bottle") mics, with 21d capsules. With this setup, I could be assured that whatever Kat did, it would be recorded. Luc's bass guitar was recorded through a Traynor TS50B bass amp and 15" EV speakers. The mics were a Beyer M380 and an Audio Technica 4033. I don't remember which mics were used on Terry and Andy's guitars. I seem to remember using an STC 4038 and an AKG C28 (with CK4 capsule), but there must have been others as well. Jos's vocals were recorded with several mics, according to whether the vocal was meant to be dry and direct or booming and ambient. His stentorian delivery has an almost percussive quality at times, and the choice of mic and room (dry or ambient) has a great effect. Unfortunately, I don't remember the precise choices we made. I know there were an EV RE20, a Neumann U67 and CMV563 in play, as well as an interesting mic made by Capps: The mic has no official name. It is a prototype commissioned by Capitol records to be a low-noise omnidirectional mic for general-purpose recording. Electronically it is very much like a C12, but it is an end-firing, metallic diaphragm with an interesting, peaky sound. I don't know if it would make a suitable "general purpose" mic, but it occasionally sounds great. ⊛

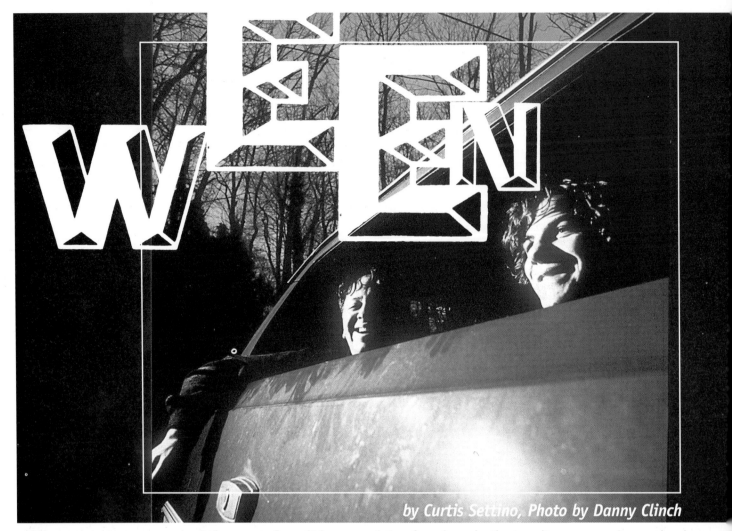

by Curtis Settino, Photo by Danny Clinch

Ween gets away with murder. It is one of the few bands that writes, records, and releases exactly what it wants. The group's songs can be daring, funny, offensive, and tender. Composed of *Mickey Melchiondo (aka Dean Ween) and Aaron Freeman (aka Gene Ween)*, Ween has released nine full-length records so far. Mr. Melchiondo was kind enough to share his thoughts on recording when he should have been shoveling snow.

Okay, the first thing I have to know is what the hell is the end solo in "Voodoo Lady"?

If I remember correctly, [producer] Andrew Weiss did a lot of that. I think it's a [Yamaha] SPX90 or an old rack mount Effectron-type delay that has knobs you can turn and hold buttons. So you can go, "WAHH UNH EEH AHH!" and scroll through the programs while turning the knobs. A lot of the stuff we do, especially when we do things with Andrew, has tons and tons of tracks. And then when it comes time to mix, you just sort through it. It's sort of the P-Funk way, except white. [laughs] It's actually a huge part of our listening. Up against The Beatles, Parliament Funkadelic has been my favorite band since I was a teenager. I started buying the Funkadelic records when they were still a quarter. Andrew turned me onto them.

So you've known him for a long time?

Yeah. We've known Andrew and been working with him since around '85.

I was curious about what his role is exactly. Calling someone a producer can mean a myriad of things. How early does he get involved in the production?

We didn't work with Andrew on this last record actually.

White Pepper?

Yeah. But in the past, except the country record, he's had a huge, huge, huge role in all the records. And it's been different every time. For the first album, we went to his house, sat in his living room and made *GodWeenSatan* for about a year. We did tons and tons of songs starting with the first track. While we were doing that, we were also working at home. Aaron and I lived together then, and we were doing things on the 4-track. But the stuff at home was more who we were, because we did it every single day. So when it came time to do the second record, we decided to

use the 4-track stuff rather than re-record everything at Andrew's. So we did the next two albums that way, except Andrew mixed all that stuff and made it sound a hell of a lot better. In my opinion, *Pure Guava* is one of the best sounding records done on a 4-track–because of Andrew mostly.

So that's a cassette 4-track record?

That album and *The Pod* were done on a Tascam Porta-3, or Porta-4. It had these dial faders on it instead of knobs.

What were you using for mics?

Just a Realistic Highball. We used this one sucky mic that we got at Radio Shack on all that stuff. And it wasn't because we were trying to have a lo-fi aesthetic about it. Later on, everybody was "Oooh lo-fi." But, to us, we always thought it was dog shit. It was just the mic that we had. We didn't even have a [Shure] Beta 57 or any other standard mic.

It's interesting–over the years Radio Shack has had some gems.

All my shit is Radio Shack at home, not my receivers. But my speakers have always been Radio Shack. I used to have this little mixing console that we used to do every thing on. It was for DJs. I would DJ school dances and parties with that. But in the early days, before we even had the 4-track, we would use that with two tape decks and bounce back and forth. We also have one of those cheese-dick reverbs that they made back then. It's a Realistic reverb unit with only one setting. And we got a Realistic "Moog". Have you ever seen one of those?

No! When did they come out?

I guess in the '70s. *The Mollusk* CD is done with that thing – a lot of the synths on it anyway. It was licensed by Moog to Realistic. It's really small.

They've increased the recording resolution from 16-bit to 20-bit.

We bought the first batch of them and recorded *Chocolate and Cheese* on them. We spent more money trying to undo that record than we did making it.

What do you mean by "undo"?

Well, we bought three ADATs and rented a studio. And we – me, Aaron, and Andrew, started going out there every day to work on the record. And all along it was like, "Why does this sound so bad?" It sounded like glass or something. Nobody knew about ADATs at the time, and they were real buggy and they would break. So we took the whole record when we were done and threw it to

We bought a Tascam 16-track tape deck for that. We took some of the advance and invested in that because we knew we didn't want to use ADATs anymore. I guess it's an ATR60.

Is that a 1" machine?

Yeah. And we had bought a board to do *Chocolate and Cheese* – something we could afford. It's a CAD [Conneaut Audio Devices]. That record we did differently than the other ones. We went back to just Aaron and I during the recording. We holed up at the beach house. There wasn't a lot of gear. We just threw it down and gave it to Andrew to mix. But once he started mixing, he was, "Look, you gotta redo this. You gotta redo that…"

"On the song 'Candy' we put Aaron with a wireless mic in the trunk of my '76 Cadillac, and I drove him around the parking lot going about 60 miles per hour while Andrew was recording him inside! There's a lot of really stupid stuff that we've done."

Cool. I was wondering what you guys used for a synth. So going back to *GodWeenSatan*, you said you were working simultaneously at home and at Andrew's.

Yeah.

Were you re-recording things at Andrew's that you had come up with at home?

We brought in all of our 4-track tapes and re-recorded everything for *GodWeenSatan* in Andrew's living room. Except for a few songs at the end, like "Birthday Boy", [that] were from our home tapes. But then for the second record, *The Pod*, and the third record, *Pure Guava*, we decided, "Fuck that." And to this day, the concept of demos sucks to us. So, we decided to have Andrew just mix our 4-track stuff and we'd put that out. So, he was just mixing the stuff then. But he was doing so much to it as he was mixing that he got producer credits on those records. So the second and third records were done at home.

It's amazing how clean they are.

Yeah. *Pure Guava* especially for some reason. The thing was though, for us a 4-track was just 4 tracks. We very, very rarely would do bounces. Because then it would sound like shit. It's impossible to make it sound good when you start doing that.

Are you still using a cassette 4-track?

Yeah. We're not making our records that way. But I still have my 4-track. I have an ADAT, too. There's something about the 4-track. When you record something on it, it does something to the sound of it. It has an instant vibe. It's really, really weird. And then when the ADATs first came out, we were really excited about the cheap 8-track format, but they sounded like shit. I've heard that since then, they've made some improvements.

tape. We ran it through tube mic preamps and stuff. There's the expression, "You can't polish a turd." Well, that's what we were dealing with at the time. So we got Howie Weinberg involved. He's a mastering engineer at Masterdisc. And he said people were coming in every day with the same complaint. When it was all done, we were so frustrated with it. We hated it. But now I like it a lot, now that I'm away from it. But we were really upset because we had worked really hard on the music for that for a long time. After we did that record, Howie, who's a Ween fan, said, "If you can get me involved in the process a little earlier on I'd like to help."

The country record was analog right?

Yeah. That was totally analog. They were amazed at the studio that we wanted to use the tape machine. I think because Nashville is such a music factory that everyone wants to do everything digitally. But we didn't, and the engineer was like, "Great! I'm glad." The funny thing about that record is that they have such a system for doing things down there. They had all the gear in the studio already. Everyone uses the same shit. They have one of those little Ampeg – I forget what they're called – B-15? It's one of those fold-out cabinet amps and a [Fender] Twin and a piano and a drum kit. And these guys [the musicians] just walked in. The engineer spent about half an hour getting sounds and that was it! We just worked with what the engineer was comfortable with, and what the producer, Ben Vaughn, was happy with. We wanted to let them kind of dictate where it was going to go, so it wouldn't sound like a contemporary record but like a Nashville record.

For *The Mollusk*, I read that you guys rented a house on the East coast to record. What machines did you bring out there?

Just because some of your engineering wasn't up to snuff?

Our engineering fuckin' sucks! [laughs] I can engineer on a 4-track but… I don't know. It's terrible – especially if it's just the two of us. Because if Aaron's doing a track, I have to engineer, and if I'm doing a track, he has to engineer. You have to do everything yourself. I think this is why we enjoyed making the country record so much. For the first time, we didn't do anything. We wrote the songs, and we sang. And I played guitar on a few songs. But that was about it. But on *The Mollusk*, Andrew threw a million synthesizers on it. It's our synthesizer record.

So he added a lot of analog synth after you guys?

Yeah. We added a lot during the recording. But when he got it, he just went to town. He loves to collect [effect processing] boxes, toys, any old broken down synths he can get his hands on. He's got the shit all over his house. And when we were done, it was almost like a gurgling diary or something. [laughs]

I have to ask, which of you is the Jethro Tull fan?

That's all of us, actually. We call it the "regal factor", you know, Fairport Convention, Steeleye Span, Tull, even the more foul shit like Gentle Giant, ELP. We've listened to tons and tons of prog rock.

And you came out of it okay!

Not really. [laughs] We haven't even released the most heinous of that shit that we've done. We've made some very unlistenable prog rock. But we do want to make a record that's basically one tune in fifteen parts at some point.

You mean something "epic"?

Yeah, totally.

What's the new record, *White Pepper* like?

This record we did at Bearsville Studios in New York. We rented a cottage on the ocean up in Maine last summer and wrote there. After that, we took some time off. Then we rented the same house that we used for *The Mollusk* and wrote the rest of it there. This record is all songs. There's not a lot of jams on it. We were trying to go for a more Beatle-y thing. It's very melodic. We played all the songs on tour last year. And we did it more as a full-band format instead of just the two of us. It's very... I don't know what to say about it. It sounds like Wings, basically. It's like the Beatles but not quite as good and with more distorted guitars. [laughs]

So the people you've been playing with live went into the studio with you?

Sort of. Mostly it was Aaron and I with our drummer. Our keyboard player plays on some tunes. And our bass player plays on a couple of tunes.

Is there any drum machine on this record?

No.

Do you see yourselves evolving into a more traditional band?

On this record, definitely. But now I want to head back in the other direction. This record is fine. But it's not ugly enough. And I realized, that in order to do that, we need to revert back. We try to keep it interesting. That's what Ween has kind of been about. Even for touring, we change our configuration every year.

Just to keep it fresh?

It's what you have to do if you want to keep going at it for a long time. So for our next record, we want to get a warehouse and set up permanently. I don't like going to a place for a month to make the album and being on the clock. Everyday there you're spending your money. I prefer to do it like we've done with the majority of our records; to always be working on our record. So every song that we record is in contention for our album. Then when it comes time for our next record, we have 500 songs, or whatever, to choose from. The notebooks come out and everybody writes down what they like. Then you just mix it and fix it.

I'm not sure if Andrew will be involved in your warehouse space or not, but it seems like with all of your experience 4-trackin' and, now, in bigger studios that you and Aaron should be getting more comfortable as engineers and with the results.

How good something sounds is relative, too. You should be able to make do with whatever you have. In theory, you should be able to make anything sound good if you can play at all. We do everything direct. I don't know anything about microphones at all!

I was wondering if you have any interesting techniques that you've come up with? What's it like when you're doing your 4-track stuff?

Fast, very, very fast. That's our motto: "Quantity, not quality." [laughs] If you record five songs, chances are you'll have one or two good ones versus slaving over one that probably sucks. If you have to slave over it, it's probably no good anyway. Aaron doesn't like to do vocals after one or two shots. My guitar playing definitely gets worse after the first or second pass. If you've recorded yourself as much as we have, you learn what you're capable of and what your limits are and when it's counter productive. We sent Aaron out in the snow in his underwear on the first record to sing. On *Chocolate and Cheese*, on the song "Candy" we put Aaron with a wireless mic in the trunk of my '76 Cadillac, and I drove him around the parking lot going about 60 miles per hour while Andrew was recording him inside! He couldn't even hear the track. So all the stuff you hear on that song was from him being slammed around in the trunk! There's a lot of really stupid stuff that we've done.

That's the stuff I love, though. So why did he have to sing in the snow?

For the song "Bumble Bee" on *GodWeenSatan*. Aaron had been mowing the lawn and he ran over a bees' nest, and he got stung, and we wrote the song. We were 15 or 16 when we wrote that song. So when it came time to redo it at Andrew's, it was the dead of winter and the memory of the bees had been gone for almost a year. So it was like, "Hmmm, what would Sinatra do? How do we get Aaron in the original spirit?" So he agreed to take off his clothes and go outside in the snow. And we were just staring at him through the living room window while he's trying to sing "Bumble Bee". [laughs] It's just stupid. It's more funny to us I think than it actually is. For the ballads and stuff, like on *The Mollusk*, we sent Aaron out to the ocean. And he would do his vocals with the waves crashing around him. We always carry a couple hundred feet of cords with us for a microphone and headphones.

I was wondering about "Cold Blows the Wind" (a traditional ballad on *The Mollusk*). Where did that song come from?

That was from the first night at the beach house we rented. We went there in the winter. The beach is really magical and intense in the winter. It's a totally different thing. It's freezing cold, no one's around, all the houses are empty. And we were right on the ocean at the end of this island. So we came down and set up all our gear that afternoon and were waiting to start recording that night. But we didn't have anything to record. So Aaron had this book with him that was like 15th century folk ballads or something. And that was a tune we found in there. So he started singing it and playing it. And it was like, "Fuck it. Let's just do this." And it came out pretty well. But as we continued on writing songs for the next few months and recording, that song ended up being more in the spirit of the record than some others that we had done. So we just used it.

So did you guys really use up 3,600 hours of tape for *The Pod*

Probably. If you add it up, I think we would have had to record eleven hours a day for the two years we lived there. Something like that. That was all that we pretty much did at that point.

Are you intimate with what's on these tapes or do you forget after a while?

I have really no idea what's on them. It's stupid. We made the mistake of saying that on the record. So everybody wants to know why we don't put it out. But we're kind of wary of any retrospective thing while we're still making new records. So I never, ever listen to them. For all I know, the tapes are decayed. I have two big computer boxes filled with these tapes. There's no labels, or cases or anything. Someday someone is going to have to sit down and check 'em out. There are reasons why you don't release things. Most of the time, it's because they're abominably horrible. But I'm sure there's some great stuff in there somewhere.

Also, you guys are probably still too close to it. Sometimes what the fans want is totally different.

That's what I've found. Every time we make a record, I'm sure everyone's going to hate us. With the leap from *Pure Guava* to *Chocolate and Cheese*, where we weren't making the records on 4-track anymore, I was sure that everyone was going to think we sold out because we made a multi-track record. But then life went on. Then after that, we made the country record, which I knew everyone was going to hate. There was no question in my mind. But as it turns out, it was a great experience and it's a cool record. I have the same feelings about this new record. Now we've made a hi-fidelity record at Bearsville Studios. It's thundering. It's really melodic.

Your stuff has always had lots of melody though.

I think at the core of everything is songwriting. Regardless of how you make your record. If you record over some band's demo on a normal bias tape and it's a good song, it doesn't really matter. People don't really listen for that stuff so much. So I think we've gotten by on our songwriting.

Well, also, the way you produce each song is a big part of your appeal too. You always seem to be able to define a mood or a moment or an idea very concisely. It's always about what the song wants or needs. I guess that's why you have to genre hop so much.

We're not even conscious of that. We don't set out that way. We don't say, "We have to have a little bit of this and a little bit of that." We just pick the best tunes. I think that's why most of our records – the ones recorded over time instead of in one month in a studio – play more like compilation records. With *The Mollusk*, fo example, those songs were written during a very defined time frame. When you start writing like that, you get onto a certain vibe and feel and tendencies for a while, six months to a year. A lot of it has to do with what you're listening to at the time. And when you're all done, sometimes it can be very cohesive. *The Mollusk* is my favorite Ween record because it's the most complete thought. From the art work to the sound of it to the songs and the lyrics, it was done with one vibe.

It sounds like the new record is similarly focused.

I don't know what to say about the new record. Because, right now, it's the last record in the whole world I want to hear. It's like our wives and babies record, because we have both now since the last record.

Did you have to adjust your approach at all to work at Bearsville?

Not really. That's why we got the guy that we did. The Dust Brothers were going to do our record at one point. And Todd Rundgren was going to do it at one point. But these people have such a "thing". So, do you take a chance, spending all your money to have someone else's "thing" over your "thing"? In the end, we decided on Chris Shaw, who's just a great engineer, instead of someone who's going to put their stamp on it – like Daniel Lanois. These are all great producers, but we decided to go with an engineer and to produce it with him. So, no, it wasn't hard to adapt to that environment. Recording in a studio is really no different than doing it at home. I mean, when it comes down to it, I don't play any different because I'm in a studio. ☸

Ween discography:

1. *The Live Brain Wedgie* (Bird O'Pray Records, 1988)
2. *GodWeenSatan: The Oneness* (Twin/Tone, 1990)
3. *The Pod* (Shimmy Disc, 1991)
4. *Pure Guava* (Elektra, 1993)
5. *Chocolate and Cheese* (Elektra, 1994)
6. *Twelve Golden Country Greats* (Elektra, 1996)
7. *The Mollusk* (Elektra, 1997)
8. *Paintin' the Town Brown – live* (Elektra, 1999)
9. *White Pepper* (Elektra, 2000)

Ween info: www.ween.com

Modifying your Yamaha NS-10 Speakers

By Jef Brown

Recently, I've been asked a lot of questions about getting the most out of your sound recordings for low dollars so I figured writing some articles on sound improvement could benefit the masses. Today the subject will be about the monitoring system and the only speaker

I trust, the Yamaha NS10. I once asked a fellow audiophile what his opinion on improving the NS10 was and his response was, **"Well, you take a stick of dynamite and..."** You get the idea. A lot of fellow engineers complain about the speakers' harsh high end and "ear fatigue". I have to agree with them, but I haven't found any monitors as flat and accurate as these. Here's a simple solution. The high pass capacitor in these is a cheap and crappy 8 mfd electrolytic. Most speakers use these or equally crappy Mylar capacitors. They sound like ass so replace that cap with an oil cap of about 6-10 mfd or a high quality polypropylene cap of a similar value. Either way, it'll zap that harshness right out of there. My preference is simply a motor starting oil cap easily obtained at most electronic surplus joints. If that's too smooth sounding for you, try the tin/poly Angela caps available through Angela Instruments. Look up their website at <www.angela.com>. Experiment with both types. Remember that any type of harshness is distortion and the less distortion you have to deal with, the more honest your mixes will sound. Improvement #2 is the actual monitor amp itself. We're fortunate enough to have a Marantz model 8-tube amp to mix on here. I figure that a lot of engineers used these marvels of Jet Age technology back in the day so why not use some today. Perhaps the best tube amp for the dollar is the famous Dynaco Stereo 70. They made about a million of these and you can still find them at yard sales for a buck or two, or find ones at used high-end audio stores for $200 to $400. A properly serviced and re-tubed example can easily outperform a modern solid state amp sonically costing much more. Well that's it for today, peace and happy recording. ☸

I saw XTC live on November 23, 1980, at the Masonic Temple Auditorium, Detroit, MI, USA opening for The Police. The only problem with the show was that I had no idea who XTC was. I remember a visually jarring slide show (or was it a film?), Dave Gregory walking over to play keyboards once or twice, and two rabid fans begging us for our front row seats just to see the opener (the seats weren't ours to give but we let them have them anyway). This was my first concert. My folks had dropped us off and had dinner downtown while we endured and basked in the raw rock experience that was the Police in those days. My dad asked how the opener was and I said, "They were alright." Twelve months later, thanks to a late night, Sunday only, new music program called "Radios In Motion" airing on the legendary WWWW radio station out of Detroit, I had become a huge fan of XTC. A couple years after that, I was lamenting that XTC had stopped touring when I realized that I had seen my heroes live and didn't even know it! This is where I'd cash in my time travel tokens in a second.

All that aside, I've remained a fan all these years, bought everything I could, scrounged a few bootlegs, and evangelized their greatness to all who would listen (why do we force our likes on other people?). Like many fans, I was very excited when *Apple Venus* was released in February 1999. Despite several years of record company battles and personal crisis they had delivered another outstanding album. But I surely can't be trusted to be objective. Now, in May 2000, they've released their follow up (really volume two) to *Apple Venus*, *Wasp Star*. Where *Apple Venus* was orchestral and sweet, *Wasp Star* is guitar driven and compelling.

With parts of both albums being partially recorded at their home studio, I thought it'd be interesting to hear about their process.

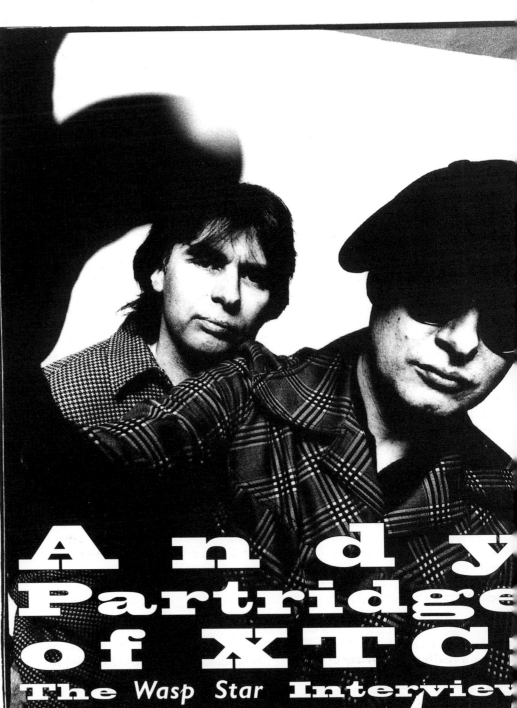

Andy Partridge of XTC!
The Wasp Star Interview

by Curtis Settino // photo: Steve Gullick

So the new record was done at home?

It was actually done in our own studio. *Volume 1* was done in a mixture of all sorts of places. It was done in kind of a converted stable that Haydn Bendall had, then we did some in Abbey Road and finished it off in Colin's living room. And this one... I think that we realized that recording in Colin's living room had great results. You know, as long as you have nice quality gear you can just about work anywhere. So having decided that, it was just a case of, "Well, look at that big double garage out there that you don't use. It's just full of junk. And look at the room next to it that you

just store coal in. Why don't we get converting." So this is the first album that we've recorded in our own studio, which was Colin's double garage.

That's great. What kind of gear do you have in there?

We have a Radar.

A Radar? [laughs]

Do you know Radar?

No, I don't.

Oh, you don't know Radar. Well, it's hard disk recording. 24-track.

Oh, okay. I thought you were making a joke.

[laughs] So we can detect people coming up t drive there.

Well, you were saying earlier abou recording at Colin's house an being afraid someone would con in the front door.

I think we've got over a lot of problems like that n because it's kind of a dedicated studio space. I not actually his house. Before he had to give ov the front half of his house and we had a mixi desk and some bits and pieces in one room an mic stand in another room or in his hallway. I this time we had a dedicated space to do it

It's a great luxury. It's better than throwing a thousand pounds a day at somebody else's studio.

And you can work in your jammies.

Exactly. You can sit there in your slippers picking your nose. It's a luxury not to have a clock on the wall that's going, "100 pounds, 200 pounds, 300 pounds, 400 pounds."

It seems like the record is a simpler record. I knew you were recording at home so I was thinking we might have another *The Big Express* on our hands, as far as a lot of stuff in the production.

No, we wanted to make a more stripped sort of record.

So there's a lot of single guitar rather than two-part guitar stuff.

What happens is people say, "Oh, that's nice stereo guitar." But, actually, a lot of the tracks where you think there is one guitar, it's an electric guitar with a microphone on the solid body, so you have just the sound of the strings coming out. Then you take a DI and treat that and that becomes the other channel, so you have a wide, schizophrenic sound. In one channel you have this very thin, ultra-present sound which you can't get down pick-ups, and that becomes, say, the left channel, for example. And over on the right channel you have a kind of fuzzy, deep, electrified sound which is the DI part of it treated. Then you blend them together and you can sort of put your head inside a four-dimensional guitar sound.

Did you have any trouble with time alignment on that thing?

No, because it's all happening as is. The DI is pretty instantaneous. By the time it comes down the mic it's the same time it takes to come down the DI. So I don't think we were changing phase or anything like that.

You guys recorded guitars like that first with the song "Beating of Hearts."

Yeah, that's right. That was also weird tuning on that one. That was every string tuned to the note of E. But yeah, we mess around with guitars a little bit.

There's a really great variety of guitar tones on this record and I was wondering if you have a bevy of amps at your disposal or...

No, I'm afraid it's a bevy of Pod, it's a brace of Pod we have at our disposal. Uh, it's probably the [Line 6] Pod then going out through my little Sessionette 70, which is a pretty crappy solid state amp. Or through Colin's bass equipment. Sometimes, if we want it with a little extra deep poke, we put it through his Gallien-Krueger bass setup. But it's usually Pod and, as I say, a lot of the guitar tones have this mic'd up-close, dead sound in there as well for ultra-presence. But yeah, I think we have to thank Pod for a lot of those tones. It's highly recommended. I think everyone whose tried one out has bought one. We also put a lot of stuff in the mix through it as well. A lot of drums went through it. Any keyboard things we probably put

through it. Vocals went through it, guitars all went through it, bass went through it - you name it, it was going in there. "Stupidly Happy," the devil voice is singing through the Pod. Plus, we used a little bit of Pod on some of the mixes to give it just a very little bit of very smooth tube-y distortion on some of the vocals. "I'm the Man Who Murdered Love" I think had a little bit of that. So Pod, I think is one of those beautiful things that you can just about flatter anything when you use it.

So the whole CD was tracked to disc?

Yeah, we recorded everything to Radar and we planned to use two Radars in the mix. So we started recording on Nick's, filled up what we needed to fill up, sometimes we only used one. But as we got near the maximum of the 24-track Radar, we said, "We'll, we're going to get one of our own in any case," so we bought one of our own second-hand. Just ran the two of these together, giving us 48 tracks.

Is this a stand-alone or do you need a computer?

It's all self-dedicated. It's excellent quality and in practice it works like a tape machine, so you really don't have to read the manual. You can sit at it and away you go.

Do you know what the recording resolution on that is?

Sheesh. No. You're going to have to look that up. That's out of my depth there.

It sounds great. I was wondering if it was tape or not, because this morning I was doing a shuffle with *Nonsuch*, *Apple Venus* and *Wasp Star*, and trying to see how well they went together, and the sound quality is different but it's all very contemporary feeling.

Yeah, it is different. A lot of that has to do with the engineering as well. I mean, *Nonsuch* is possibly... it's a bit of a toss up between that and *Oranges and Lemons*, possibly the best engineered record we ever had. That was Barry Hammond at Chipping Norton Studios. Unfortunately, he doesn't engineer anymore. He gave it all up for computer. And this one is Nick Davis who - god, this sounds terribly insulting, but it's not meant to be - but I don't think he's as good an engineer as Barry, but he's certainly a fantastic mixer, so... it's got a different sound. It's a harder, more wasp-y sound, damn it.

So did you do any of the engineering? How involved are you in the whole recording process?

Pretty total. For example, mostly it will be Nick, but occasionally we brought in Alan Douglas, who's a well-known engineer in England, to do things like the drum tracks. He also did the string quartet and oboe on "The Wheel and The Maypole".

So that's a real horn on that?

Oh yeah, that's Kate St. John playing oboe. And it's a string quartet tracked up twice so it's eight piece thing - two violins, viola and cello. But most of the

engineering was Nick. A little bit was by Alan Douglas, a few bits and pieces were left over from the original sketching out sessions with Haydn Bendall, and a couple of bits were recorded by Barry Hammond. I think Barry was responsible for recording most of "My Brown Guitar", cause we initially started a whole lot of these songs in one session cause it was supposed to be a double album. But we just ran out of time and money and had to divide it up into two discs. So imagine it as a double album with a year between finding the other disc at the back of the package.

That was part of the reason that I threw those three records in at the same time, 'cause I think some of the variety that you've broken up between the two new discs is kind of on one disc on *Nonsuch*.

Yeah, see *Nonsuch* was a bit schizophrenic and I think that if it has a fault it's schizophrenia.

Oh, I don't think so.

Really?

Not at all.

Oh, good man. Well, it also contains some of our better material, so I'm pleased with *Nonsuch* as far as songwriting goes. But I don't know whether it suffers from its schizophrenia. I don't know whether stuff like "Rook" and "Wrapped In Gray" and "Bungalow" sit well with things like "Ugly Underneath" and "Peter Pumpkin Head".

Yeah, well I think "Bungalow", that one definitely sticks out a little bit, but I think if you go back through all your records there's always the song or two like that, where people are going to be distracted by it. Like on *Mummer*...

Probably the odd one on *Mummer* was "Funk Pop a Roll," which was sort of the first song that was written for *The Big Express*, if you see what I mean. You could see where I wanted to go with that one.

Yeah. I was thinking that I've listened to this music so much that I don't question it anymore. If there is something that sticks out, after a while it's just part of the record. You absorb it and take it as a whole.

Right. I can't think of an album, anybody's album, that doesn't have a stick out track on it, whether you're Captain Beefheart or Joni Mitchell or The Beatles. I mean there's always at least one track that doesn't feel like it belongs with the bunch.

And it's usually the last tune. Hidden. [laughter]

It's usually the George Harrison one. But no, there's usually something that even on the kind of most joyfully banal records like The Stooges *Funhouse*, I mean "LA Blues" is just four minutes of feedback and screaming, it doesn't even have a structure.

On the new one then, what do you feel is the odd duck?

Uh, hmm…

You can change your opinion later.

Probably - it's either "Standing In For Joe," because I know - that's cheating really - I know that it wasn't written with this album in mind.

That's an older tune, right?

It was actually written for the bubblegum project. Colin didn't want to throw it away, and I can't blame him 'cause I think it's a good song. We just kind of did it in the way that it demanded to be done, without doing a bubblegum pastiche or anything. We just kind of did it. It's either that or "The Wheel and The Maypole", but that's cheating really cause it's two songs that are glued together.

Are you playing harmonica on "In Another Life"?

It's not me. It's actually Colin. There's a little story behind that. Colin did a demo of that, and I think he was playing two harmonicas, either two harmonicas at once or he dubbed one into the other one. He did it on a 4-track cassette machine. He either lost or broke one of the harmonicas. It was like a cheap Chinese one. It was probably 99 pence. It had this great rasping, wheezy, punctured sound and he either busted or lost the thing and we could not get that sound again when we went to do it for real. And we said, "Look, I don't suppose there's anyway we could take this cassette demo, take the harmonica off of it." And Nick did it, by putting it into Radar and chopping it up. I think we changed the tempo a little bit, but he just edited it so that it fit the track. And everything else was brand new, apart from the harmonica which was, I think, a combination of a blues vamper and this cheap Chinese harmonica which was on a cassette demo.

So since you've got the home studio you're probably not going to be demoing as much anymore.

No, I will, 'cause that's how I get to know a song. I have to.

Really?

I have to demo it because that's how I get inside the song and can put it on and can wear it. I know my demos have been getting very polished over the years, but that's the process of finding out what works. And I don't think I can do it in front of a room full of people. I think I have to be on my own, making a lot of mistakes and making decisions that - it's part of the writing process. I can't leave demoing alone. It's built into writing a song I think. You discover what works or what doesn't work in that stage of the song.

So are their earlier versions of demos then…

No, they probably get worked out on a mono cassette, you know, structurally, so it works with one guitar and me stamping my foot and yelling into a cassette machine. Then when it feels good like that, it then goes on to, "Does this work on electric guitar? Should it be on piano? Should it be on acoustic guitar? If it's on acoustic guitar, should it be on electric guitar? Or a keyboard or an organ sound? What should it be?" And then you can start that process of finding out how to wear the song properly. But it's got to work in idiot-form on a cassette machine for me first.

That makes sense. But all the demos of yours that I've heard don't sound much different to me from what's on the record.

No, well that's the process. Finding out what works. Then when you've found out what works, you don't have to go so much further when you get into a proper studio. But now we have a proper studio. I don't know. It might change. It might make me lazier, I don't know. I don't want it to. I want to stay vigilant. But the demo process I think is very precious for almost psychiatrically understanding how the song should be.

I see. So you're not concerned with losing the demo charm?

No. That's its own world, it's kind of trapped in that world. I don't think too much when I'm doing the demos, it's just lazy engineering and lots of sloppy playing. You get to know that, whatever, a fuzzy sound will work there, a keyboard will work there, whatever it takes - you get to know a trumpet is needed there. That's the sort of thing you can suss out on your own time without other people sitting around playing with their thumbs. I think it's a habit from being in expensive studios in the past. You know, I want to find out what works before I bring it along to everyone else.

It's economics. It will be interesting to see if the luxury changes the process.

Mm-hmm.

What's in the works now? Do you have any ideas for the next project?

I think the next project from us is going to be a lot of demos that were never released. You know, fans have got bootlegs of this stuff and it sounds pretty awful by the time they get it. So, I thought it would be quite nice to let them have better quality things, or slightly better quality things. But as far as the next official recording, I honestly don't know, which is frightening and exciting. It really is a blank sheet now, because *Apple Venus* and *Wasp Star* were a long time in writing, a long time in putting together. And, initially, it should have been a double album. But finance, and the speed of certain people and personality problems, contributed to not making it a double disc in the first place, I think this kind of rectifies it now. We've recorded the other disc that is part of the package.

What are you going to be doing to support it, as they say?

Well, for my part, it's just going to be talking. But to be truthful I'm finding it tricky to talk about this record because it's just a bunch of songs. They have no deep inner significance. And it's not like a comeback record or a record made on unusual instruments. It's just a real solid, honest-to-goodness Sunday dinner.

Well the last two records, since they were such a long time coming, seem like very solid XTC-type records, in the regard that they don't have the pastoral setting of *English Settlement* or the hyped up machinery of *Oranges* and *Lemons*. They're more just kind of like you guys, to me.

Yeah, I know what you mean, but then again, I could certainly explain the atmosphere of any of the albums, and why the circumstances made any album have that certain atmosphere. For example, *English Settlement*, to me, part of the charm of it was the fact that it felt sort of sprawling and unfinished. And that was the first time we'd worked without a producer as such. We just had Hugh Padgham - "No, record this Hugh." So hardly any editing went on. It was also, that we wanted to broaden the palette. And you can hear that. Acoustic instruments start creeping in, keyboards start creeping in…

And the fretless bass…

Yeah, and then the fact that I didn't want to take the thing on the road kind of literally released me from having to make an album that could then be shoved in the faces of an audience and that it would sound similar to the record.

You guys ended up performing some of that, though.

Yeah, but I wasn't happy with it and it never sounded right. So, I can take any album and say why it sounded like it did. It's not a mystery to me. The circumstances and the personalities involved at the time and the instrumental choice and whatever's the flavor-of-the-minute instrument-wise. I mean stuff like *The Big Express*, I wanted to make a noisy record. Most of the songs were written on open-E tuning so they have sort of a blues-y edge. We just bought ourselves a Linn Drum, so you can see this already starting to form a picture. It's going to have a harder, blues-y edge, with a blues kind of tuning. There are mechanical drums for the first time. They're tougher, simpler songs, but they're done with a producer who had a thing for orchestral arranging. So, you throw all these ingredients in and that's the sound of *The Big Express*.

I know that you're legendary as a controller…

I'm not too bad, actually. I usually get this rep from people who have disagreed with how to give birth to a record, and therefore they think I'm just a control freak. Actually, I'm not a control freak. I just want my music to come out how I hear it. And if anybody has an idea that's better than my idea, I'll hear it, and if it's better for the song we'll go with that. But if it's not better for the song, I won't allow them to use it because I feel it's degrading the song. So, I suppose maybe you hear that from people who had crappier ideas than I do.

Well, I think it is a result of it seeming like you have a full vision of the song ahead of time, probably because of the extensive demoing you do.

It's the demo process and the fact that you hear it kind of semi-formed in your head. So by the time you've squeezed it through the stage set, how the stage is going to be set during the demoing process, you have a pretty good idea of the play that you've finished up with. As I say, if people have better ideas then they do get used, but that's not always the case.

Would you ever be willing to write a batch of songs and kind of hand them off and see what someone does with them?

Um... I don't think so, because I don't trust anyone enough, because it's life and death for me. It's just a job for anyone else.

I see.

You know, Mr. Producer, "Oh, it's just a job. They're my next project." But for me, I have to stand by that record for the rest of my life. I have to believe in it a 1000 percent. I have to know that all the sounds and all the words and all the things were how I really wanted it to be, or else I couldn't live with myself when I shut the bedroom door at the end of the day.

Well, how did you feel about the Testimonial Dinner recordings in regards to having other people cover your music and re-interpret it.

I was very flattered by sort of the idea of it. But I think only some of the tracks were any good. I especially liked "Dear God", by Sarah McLachlan, and Ruben Blades' "The Man Who Sailed Around His Soul". I thought that was a great version. It makes me want to drive a car. And I don't drive. I want to be cruising around the hills of Monaco in my open-top sports car. But I wouldn't be my passenger if I were you. I'd have us over the cliff in seconds. I actually think that the Verve Pipe's "Wake Up" had an idiocy that I liked. But you know, some of the tracks worked, and some of them I thought, "Oh, why bother."

Yeah, there have been so many of these tribute albums in the last ten years.

We get asked about once a month to do a tribute album. The latest one we've been asked to do is a McCartney one. And as nice as it would be, as nice as it would have been to do the Kinks one, or The Bonzos one, or The Beach Boys one or whatever - as nice as it would be to do these things, you could do them and do nothing else. That's all you'd be doing.

If you were to do the McCartney one, what tune would you have gone after?

That's a tough one.

For most people the first choice would probably be between solo or Beatles.

I think probably Beatles, because he had something to prove when he was a Beatle and he had someone saying, "No, I've got a better song than that and it goes like this." So only the cream of the cream I think got through. But on the solo stuff you also got the clots as well as the cream. I mean some of those latter solo discs I can't listen to. I have a fantasy that he'll ring me up and say, "Look, I can't write anymore. Please help me."

He called Elvis Costello, didn't he? [laughter]

"The demo process I think is very precious for almost psychiatrically understanding how the song should be."

So, tribute albums - they're a nice idea, but it has to be said that if you're paying tribute to somebody, you either have to do it exactly the same or so different that it can never be compared. And if you do it exactly the same, you do a carbon copy, what's the point?

Well, your [Captain Beefheart's] "Ella Guru" was kind of a carbon copy.

Exactly, and that's kind of how I learned the lesson, because I couldn't envisage it any more wonderful being any other way. I just thought, "Well, I'm going to have to try and un-pick this and make the same thing." And that became a personal piece of fun, to make it as close to the original as we could, given the drum machine and a reluctant bass player and another guitarist who didn't want to be involved in the session. Then you find out that the only way is to do a carbon copy of it and then, ultimately, what's the point? You might as well have the real thing and not denigrate it by having a second-generation copy. So tribute records are a no-win situation.

One thing I was curious about, with the Apple Venus record, since it is sort of orchestral, do you have any classical composer in particular you enjoy? Do you have any influences in that realm? Or is it just your homespun orchestral music?

Probably not so much classics as show tunes. If you were my age and you listened to radio as a kid,

there wasn't any such thing as rock 'n' roll radio in England or even pop radio until the mid-sixties. It was all light entertainment, and it was usually something orchestral, like songs from musicals or orchestral treatments of what you'd call "light music". Because I wasn't really exposed to the classics until I was much older, I think what shaped me was hearing these things from shows, "light" entertainment... I suppose you'd call it easy listening.

I think the era and the location you're talking about, has a real particular sound.

I mean there wasn't any pop radio in England until '67. When Radio One came along. Until then you might get the odd pop tune that'd creep through. But as a kid the thing that I thought was the best thing on the radio was novelty songs.

Yeah.

Songs that would make me laugh or just have weird sounds on them.

Any of those you remember?

Stuff like "I Am A Mole" by The Overlanders, which had kind of a beatnik rock 'n' roll thing. [sings] "I'm not a rat or a cat or a bat/I'm not a gnu or a wee kangaroo/I'm not a fox or a lox" or a whatever and then he goes really reverb-y and he goes "I am a mole and I live in a hole." It's kind of this bizarre sounding beatnik rock 'n' roll thing and I thought that was particularly spookily interesting. That and "Martian Hop" by The Randells. Stupid space-noise rock 'n' roll, and those records by people like Vout Stainhouse, which is like this multi-tracked sped-up guitar it sounded like Venusian pop music. I loved all that. If you ever find the Danny Kaye album, *Mommy Give Me A Drink Of Water*, it's all orchestral arrangements with Danny Kaye singing these kids songs and the orchestral arrangements are achingly beautiful. They really are good. I would have liked some of the stuff on *Apple Venus* to have been like that.

Do you think you're ever going to make the bubblegum record?

No. That went onto the backburner for so long it's just turned into goo.

I think everyone needs a real fine version of "Bumper Cars," though.

[laughs] Well, I think when we do the demos, the *Fuzzy Warbles* set, that's going to make an appearance on there.

Well, it was listed as a track that was supposed to be on *Wasp Star* on the internet for a while.

Yeah, I got out-voted. Because when we were originally recording all this it was supposed to be a double album and we voted on everything. That one just didn't get in.

I think the first stuff you let go demo-wise was "Find The Fox", "The Troubles" and "Terrorism". What inspired you to let go of that stuff without "proper" recording?

I think the record company was pressuring us for more material and we couldn't afford to go in the studio. So we said, "Let's use the demos." People seemed to like it. They didn't mind that it was lo-fi.

Oh no, I adored those. It's a great testament to your songwriting that they work on that level.

Did you ever hear those things on *Jules Verne's Sketchbook*?

I've heard bits and pieces. Some of the stuff I got a hold of was totally different - weird collections of a lot of that same material. Some of your MIDI/solo instrumental music, stuff like "Do the Dwarf".

Those are just jam sessions from the *Mummer* recording. Yeah, I don't feel too bad about people hearing that stuff these days. 'Cause nobody says, "Hey, it's bad quality."

Are you still using the 4-track cassette very much?

No, only to clean up these old recordings for the *Fuzzy Warbles* project. *Fuzzy Warbles* is a line in *A Clockwork Orange* that I thought was so good when I heard it. He's trying to pick up the girls in the record shop and he's talking about the pop music that they like, and he refers to their pop music as "fuzzy warbles". I thought that was a fantastic phrase and I thought, "That is going to be an album title." So that's going to be our demo project. Hopefully it'll be four albums worth or more.

Released as one monster?

No, four little monsters, 'cause you can really lose a whole lot of money paying to make box sets. It cost us a fortune making the box sets for *Transistor Blast*.

Well, you guys want the nice packaging.

Yeah, it costs.

Now, you art direct a lot of that stuff, don't you?

Oh yeah, I insist.

Do you do any visual art aside from that?

I paint occasionally. I doodle more than anything else. But I do insist on packaging us for the rest of the world. It's like choosing what the records going to wear to be seen forevermore. I think that's important.

All your covers have been really nice. I think especially some of the singles. I really like the "Push once button" picture for "This World Over."

People think it's an atomic bomb button.

I did.

It's not. If you live in England, a very subtle, very well known object is the bus stopping request button on every bus, and if you really need to stop it says "push once". And everyone in England knows this button. But because it's red and it says "push once" it seems final. There's a great atomic paranoia about it.

On the Chalkhills web site there's a dictionary for all us yanks, cause we don't get half of your references, but it spoils it a little bit.

It undoes the magic for you.

Back to the music, it seems like you've done a fair bit of this MIDI/sequencing music.

Not too much, but it has been very influential in latter years.

Is there any idea about doing an instrumental record? Something akin to the *Through The Hill* [collaboration with Harold Budd]?

I think I got that out of my system for a little bit with that, but I'd like to work with Harold again, I think he's very inspirational.

It's a great record. It's one of my favorites.

Well, thank you. You know, I can't listen to it, and I'll tell you why. I was making it at a time where I was going through a divorce and it plunges me back into it a very dark state of mind when I listen to it. Although some of the music on there is kind of up, it does sort of a Pavlovian trick where I hear it and I feel kind of depressed again. And that shouldn't be the case, because the music is blameless - just for me personally.

Yeah, I understand. Maybe with time.

Yeah. I actually put it on the other day wondering if it would still have the same effect, and it did. Although, I prefer some things more than others. I think "Natural Track Through The Hill" is nice.

It's a great record. I was thinking about how you'd approached Brian Eno early on and you did the "Andy Pants Brian" thing on "Battery Brides". So, have you any desire to still try and work with him.

No, because I think from what I know of how he works, he tends to work with people who don't have much idea of what the hell they want to do.

Like U2?

U2, and The Talking Heads and people that make stuff up from jams. He sits there and says, "Oh, that bit was good, what was that? Okay, we'll make that the verse." Then they jam for another 20 minutes and he says "Oh, that bit was good. Okay, tone up and that can become the chorus." And for me that's the antithesis of the very structured way I like to work.

Well, some of the "Through The Hill" stuff...

Yeah, they were largely improvised on little springboards, parts to jump off from, that we had worked out about three days before.

I see.

And we probably threw away half as much material again, thinking it didn't work.

Hmm. I really like it. It was a pleasure when it came out.

Well, good man.

Lastly, I hate to ask, but what about the rock opera.

Tummy, The Arm-less, Leg-less Boy. He's just a stomach. He's a stomach that plays Cluedo. I see it now. "Tummy can you hear me," and then really loud rumbling noise. No, no rock operas. What a daft expression that is.

But what about something with a big story behind it?

I'd like to do a musical in the Hollywood tradition of the '40s and '50s. Some of the best music ever has been stuff written for musicals. So, I'd like to do that. But there are 101 things I'd like to do. The world's for playing with, so let's have some fun. ⊛

Discography:

Wasp Star - 2000 May
Apple Venus - 1999 Feb
Nonsuch - 1992 Apr
Oranges and Lemons - 1989 Feb
Skylarking - 1986 Oct
The Big Express - 1984 Oct
Mummer - 1983 Aug
English Settlement - 1982 Feb
Black Sea - 1980 Sep
Drums and Wires - 1979 Aug
Go 2 - 1978 Oct
White Music - 1978 Jan

Books:

Chalkhills and Children by Chris Twomey - 1996
XTC: Song Stories by Neville Farmer - 1998

Web:

http://www.tvtrecords.com/xtc/

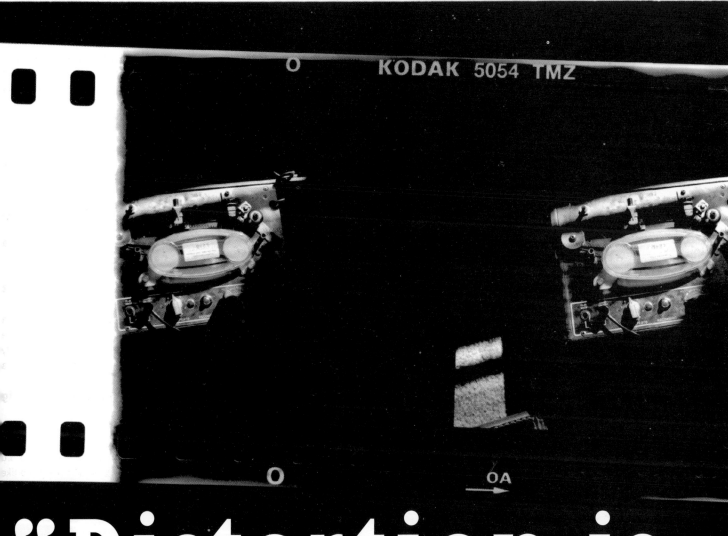

KODAK 5054 TMZ

"Distortion is usually your friend."

-Rob Schnapf in Tape Op No. 9

Photo by Sonny Mayugba

SPOT

When I was in high school, I knew a lot less about music than I do now, but even then Hüsker Dü's *Zen Arcade* seemed to jump out of my speakers. It certainly sounded a lot different from anything else that had crossed paths with my teenage ears. I remember reading in *Rolling Stone* about how quickly and cheaply it was recorded. The album's engineering credit included the terse identity 'Spot', In the years since, I'd encountered like-minded punk groups of the era whose albums included Spot's name. It's hard for me to imagine anyone whose taste resembles mine not owning something he's recorded. When I moved to Chicago, I saw listings of Spot playing solo at clubs in town. I finally made it to one of these shows and interviewed the man known as

by Steve Silverste

SPOT.

Spot first started recording at a young age when he was living in Hollywood. "It all started way back when, I bought an old Sony reel-to-reel recorder. I had borrowed recorders from people before, just sat down and taped myself. Just sounds, noises. I bought a Sony tape deck, I think it was an old model 350 reel-to-reel deck, 2-track, 1/4 track, stereo in both directions. I bought that and some microphones and tape." After that, "I had gotten my hands on one of the original Teac 3340s. Those machines, they caused a revolution. Those machines might be what created the whole independent record scene. I realized early on that really all you needed was a tape deck and some commitment. You could record pretty interesting stuff if you knew what you were doing."

In 1975, he moved to Hermosa Beach and got involved with the nascent Media Art Studio. "When I moved there, I found out about a studio that was being built and that was exactly what I wanted to do, was to get myself in a studio situation so I could record myself. These guys were building a studio and I immediately saw that the potential was there, and I just started helping them." He came to be involved as staff engineer, which initially led to him recording a lot of projects in which he had little interest. "Can you say disco? There was a Mexican record label in town that did a whole lot of stuff. At that time, most of what was coming into the studio was either lame disco or lame light-rock songwriter stuff. Stuff that was really not that much fun to record."

"Everything was either light and easy or progressive and just overblown. Back then people were coming in wanting to sound just like something they heard on an Elton John or Linda Ronstadt record. I learned a lot from that, but I just couldn't understand the concept of trying to make something sound that much like something else."

"I had gotten so sick of these Top 40 musicians who would come in and record these demos, where it would start off with a click track and everyone would play to the click track. There were a lot of songwriters who would come in, lay down a click track with a guide vocal and guitar track. There was this group of local musicians. They played in Top 40 bands and had a lot of experience. They were good musicians. They would come in and start doing these song demos for various people. Basically it would start with the click track and what you'd call a single voice. Lots of times only one guy could come at a time, like the drummer would lay down his parts, and then everything else would get played on top of that, usually one track at a time. It was interesting, but damn it was tedious. And I got so sick of the single-finger synthesizer or String Machine pad that people would put in. I hated the sound. This was back when they were making, aside from Mini-Moogs and that, synthesizers that were starting to get really cheap sounding, and I hated the String Machine. I think Roland made it. I'd love to maybe get my hands on one nowadays just so I can totally subvert it. I hated that stuff."

His favorite sessions of this era were jazz projects. Spot's explanation for liking jazz projects, oddly, was that he always liked rock 'n roll. For him, the jazz sessions involved live playing, which more closely matched his ideas than the carefully constructed productions which the singer-songwriters with whom he worked generally demanded. "They just didn't nit-pick over something." He fondly remembers working with a Dutch pianist named Rene van Helsdingen. "He would come over to the States where he had some players that he liked. They would always come in at midnight or so, whenever there was open time, and just record these compositions. He was a piano player, and he had these really good bass player and drummer working with him. I loved those sessions because you just set 'em up, get sounds and levels, hit 'record', and just let 'em play. They would take up one whole roll of tape with maybe one take of one piece."

"I recorded some classical players once where the session started at seven in the morning. That was when I lived down at the beach and was skating. I had been out skating the whole night before or something. So I was all sweaty and sticky and stinky. I was living in the studio; I woke up at about six in the morning, it was during the winter, and it was cold. I walked down to the beach, where there was one of those showers you wash the sand off you. I walked down there to the shower and just took off my clothes and took some soap and took a shower in this cold water. I walked back to the studio and I was wide awake at that point. These guys come walking into the studio at 6:30 with their coffee, and I'm like [animated] 'Hello, how are you?' Sometimes getting up that early in the morning can really be productive."

He remembers Media Art as a "really great space. The place was like a block from the beach in good old surf city. It was upstairs and they had it on like a five year lease. The rent was something like $325 a month. We had the entire upstairs space. The studio itself, between the recording room and the control room was about 1200 square feet, which is a pretty good size. The rest of the place was at least 2000 square feet. There was another room that actually became a little overdub room. There was a bathroom that had been converted into a darkroom. I spent a lot of time in there. One room in the back was kind of like maintenance. There was a waiting room area, office space, and another back room."

The studio started with a 1 inch Sculley 8-track. "We had gotten a machine that had suffered a lot of abuse. I think it had been dropped out of a truck once and had been in a fire, so somebody completely cut away all the cabinetry of it and built a whole new custom cabinet for the transport and the electronics. We got it from Paramount Studios up in Hollywood, which then was on Santa Monica right off of Vine. It was pretty amazing." About 1977, the studio upgraded to a 3M model 56, a 16-track 2 inch. "Those are cool machines. I don't really remember the order that we got these in. Eventually we went 24-track and had a 3M model 79,

but then when we built the studio B, which is where I spent a lot of my time, we had this old Ampex MM1000, which was like the very first 16-track that was ever made. The size of a pizza oven, it was huge. When they're working right, you just can't beat 'em."

"I think the original board we had was a Speck. A guy named Vince Poulos was building boards. He was up in the Valley. The first board, this was with 8-track, was a 16 channel board. Then we upgraded to the next board that he put out, which was also a 16 channel. I don't remember the model numbers on any of those boards. I know that the first one was black, the second one was blue. They worked. When we went to 16-track, we got a Tangent 32-16 console. To this day that's actually one of my favorite boards. They were not really fine boards, but there was something about the electronics where you could record really beefy basic tracks. For mixing it somehow didn't seem to do the job, although just bringing signals back through the monitor section of the board, avoiding the faders and all the EQ, was really clean and really punchy. Then after that, that studio lost the lease and was shut down."

"We were really lucky—we had some really good microphones. We had at least one pair of Neumann U67 tube condensers. Those things sound great. They look just like a Neumann U-87; basically the 87 is the later version of it, the solid-state version. We may have had about four of the 67s. And then we got some 87s, and then for a long time we were using the 87s just because they were more convenient. I remember on one session I needed another condenser mic, and I pulled out the 67 and until that moment I had never realized how good the 67 was. I had a chance to compare it. I was so used to the 87s that suddenly this thing sounded like, 'Man, my ears must have been clogged up all this time.' We also had, naturally, Shure SM 57s, EV RE20s. We had some AKG 414s, some of the original 414s, and the 451s. I guess they're now the 460 or something. They're just little pencil mics. Some Neumann KM84s. An assortment of dynamics, none of which I can remember. One of my favorite mics we had was a Shure SM53. They're silver, they don't look like a 57 or a 58. They're kind of slim, most of the body is slim, and then it kind of angles out into a kind of cylindrical head with a triple windscreen all around. They were real popular at one time. There was something about those mics, I always liked them. I liked 'em for vocals—they were real smooth. 57s and 58s were not that smooth, but a 53, and sometimes it's a 54 depending on which windscreen you screw on to it, those are real smooth. I've always liked those, recorded all kinds of stuff with them. We had a pair of Sony ECM 377s, condensers. They look like little Neumanns. Those were neat for overheads. Then there was a set of mics I really would love to get my hands on again, some Sony 56s. Also a condenser, they look kind of like a U-87 where you cut off part of the body of it. Those things had a sound to 'em that I can't describe."

"The downfall of the studio was that we had a terrible monitor system. We had these JBL 4320s. They were a 2-way system, 15 inch woofer and a horn tweeter. When you cranked them up, they sounded great, but because that 15 emphasized the bottom end so much, most of the mixes went out bass-shy. People got it sounding really great in the room and they'd take it away and there was no bottom end on it at all. We had some 4315s. I don't know if that was a 3- or 4-way system; they were really elaborate. They sounded too good. And of course Auratones. I learned to hate JBL monitors. At least 4311s, at least I knew what they sounded like. If a studio had 4311s, I wasn't happy, but at least I knew what I'd end up with. But, the monitors were just not up to snuff."

"Back then, there were a lot of people that insisted on mixing on headphones. A lot of producers, 'Oh, you gotta hear it on headphones.' I think that was more because they were smoking pot or whatever, and the headphones were real intimate. Before I ever got in the studio, I had a really good pair of headphones and would listen to stuff off the home stereo. There were occasionally some mixes that would amaze me; this was just listening to the radio. I remember one night I was laying in bed and I had the headphones on and the cord stretched across the room. Some song by BB King was on. Where the guitars were in the mix was just really cool. I remember, there was some old David Bowie stuff, that just really had really animated mixes. Not to impress you with the fact, just really good stuff." Despite these early experiences, Spot hates mixing with headphones. "I've tried mixing on headphones before, I can't do it. Mixes that I've made on headphones that I thought were just incredible, when you play them into the air, they sound like shit." He also complains about the physical inadequacy of the headphones he's used. "Most headphones that you find in the studio, they're inadequate. They break all the time."

As punk bands became more prevalent in Los Angeles, some of these bands started recording at Media Art. Spot remembers some of the early Dangerhouse bands recording at the studio. Sometimes he was the engineer on the records, but in a lot of cases he was not. In those cases, he "was just kind of like the engineer in there on call. Lots of times they'd bring their own engineer in. Some of those things Geza X was doing." He has trouble remembering which specific bands he engineered. "That's a tough one, because back then I was doing so many different sessions. I would do sometimes four and five sessions a day, back to back. So by the time these guys would come in at maybe midnight or one in the morning, I didn't really pay a whole lot of attention to who they were. At that point, I was tired, and lots of times because they had their own engineer, I wouldn't have anything to do. I would be out in the lobby asleep in the chair until someone needed me. I think I remember seeing names like the Bags and the Eyes. I know that the Plugz were in there at some point."

"At that time I wasn't just working up in the studio, I was doing a lot of photography back then, and a lot of writing and skating. I would spend just about all day skating and taking pictures. I would skate sometimes 20 miles a day. Between the studio and the skate shop down on the Strand, I was living between these two places. I remember all these experiences, so I don't remember all the people who were there." The increased chances to record bands that he cared about coincided with Spot's increasing enthusiasm for his work at the studio. "About '79 I started getting really serious about it, because the skating thing, it wasn't satisfying me as much. That's when I started making myself available to work with a few more bands." He says that the SST bands were his neighbors, and that "it was just kind of a natural progression of work that happened. Maybe I could just say we were all in the right place at the right time."

The punk bands' philosophies coincided well with his ideas about music. "Most of those bands and musicians were not interested in sounding like anything that was on the radio, which was fine, because I wasn't interested in trying to make things sound like stuff on the radio." Their approach to performing and recording also fit with the recording approaches which Spot preferred. "With the punk bands, I tried to put these people into the studio even without headphones. Just say, 'You put your amp there, you put your amp there' and just turn it up and just play. Let's not even worry about a headphone mix. They were playing so loud in the room it was like being in a practice room. Meanwhile I had everything close-mic'd and was able to deal with things." This approach was quite different from the ideas of many of his contemporaries in LA. "Everyone was worried about separation, they didn't want any leakage. Fortunately, we had recorded some things where we had to deal with leakage. There were some larger bands that had to play live. If you know how to set up the microphones, you can really minimize leakage with baffles and what-not. I wish I could remember what sessions they were, but there were some sessions that taught me that leakage is not a bad thing. Sometimes people who didn't have a lot of money, they had five hours to record three songs. So you had to set 'em up, wham bam, get the stuff down, so by the end of those five hours, they had a rough mix with vocals and the whole thing. I had to cut a lot of corners, so I just started going for the real basic stuff, and it was learning that, well, you can do this. This is the way all these old hit songs were recorded."

"I was always trying to do something new. Every session I tried to do something new." Sometimes these new ideas went horribly wrong, but he considers those his best learning experiences. "When you're first getting into recording, you have to try everything out. One thing is that you have to make mistakes. You have to record things that sound bad, only so that you can figure out what not to do. Most of recording is knowing what not to do, rather than knowing what to do. That's the thing I've learned."

Despite this open-minded philosophy, his approach to "real basic stuff" led Spot to developing somewhat consistent techniques which he employed. "I've ended up kind of reversing that procedure and going back to a more standard approach. There's a reason there's a standard approach. It's not because you have to do it, it's because it works. At some point you have to find some kind of a formula that you can rely on. From doing all those other sessions, I learned a lot of the real standard approaches, and by god they work."

Spot's combination of standard approaches with trying new things left room for variations as his opinions changed and depending on the nature of his projects. One obvious example is his recording of bass guitars. "I know that there were periods of time when my ear would tell me that the amp sounded better, and then there are times when the direct sounded better." While his early session musician work usually involved running bass direct, a lot of punk and metal bands wanted to mic their amps. In a lot of cases, including many of the famous records he worked on, Spot "would usually both mic and go direct on the bass." For mic'ing bass amps, "I always liked RE20s and I may have used some Shure SM 87s and AKG 414s. A lot of people liked the Sennheiser 421 on bass, I've never been that crazy about it. It's used a lot. If I have my choice, whatever mic I use on the kick drum, I wanna use on a bass amp too. That seems to be a good combination. They're both picking up the same frequencies."

"When it comes to snare, I'm always going to start with a 57 and usually I'll end with a 57. One microphone I've always liked is the Sennheiser 441. I love it for snare. I've seen times when I was having problems getting a good snare sound, it just wasn't sounding thick enough, a 441 usually just fattens it up. Nice thing about a 441 is it's kind of hypercardioid. I like it for vocals too. Has a good kind of raspy sound to it. And they're great on guitar amps. I wish I had some of those again." Spot has a fairly spartan approach to miking a drum kit. "A lot of people like to mic snares from the top and bottom. I find that in most situations, the bottom mic is just, you don't need it. A separate hi-hat mic, you don't need. Just in the overheads and leakage into the other mics is plenty for the hi-hat, I find. I usually tried to not close mic cymbals. I usually tried to pull the mics back."

"Overheads, usually any good condenser does the job. Sometimes it's fun to put the overhead mics in an omnidirectional pattern. If you're in a live room, they can pick up the whole room, it can be really neat." He would use two mics for stereo, sometimes in an X/Y pattern, but "mostly I spread 'em out and put 'em in omni and make sure the phase is right on them."

Spot's general philosophy of compression fits into the bigger picture of the recording. "It's one of those things you just have to use your ear and have some kind of vision. I think that's really the key of it, just having some kind of vision on what you're doing. That way when you do something that's a re surprise, at least you've got a context you can relate to it in." He explains places where compression can fit into his general vision: *"There've been times when I've compressed some drums. Sometimes you can get a really good, tight sound on toms by doing that, but I try not to. Compressing cymbals, overhead tracks can sometimes be a lot of fun, but it usually sounds, you usually notice the compression at that point. Maybe that's what you want to do. I've compressed just about everything at some point or another. But I think that really, the best thing is just to try to record the tracks right in the first place, use the right mics and get good signals and then you don't have to use as much compression. Some things compression can really help. I've compressed guitar tracks before. Every once in awhile, a guitar track sounds better compressed."*

"I've used so many compressors. The old Urei 1176s—I think that's the standard which every other compressor wants to live up to. The dbx 165 was a good one. It didn't seem to color the sound as much as squash it. Actually some of the less expensive compressors like dbx 160s and even the Alesis compressors, they actually do a pretty good job, but you just have to really be careful not to compress them too much. With the old Urei, you could really compress the hell out of them and it would still sound like a bass. But the cheaper ones, as long as you don't use too much compression, you're fine."

Any story about Spot would be incomplete without a discussion of some of his best-known work. He tends to remember big issues about the famous albums that he worked on, but not some of the minor details from the sessions. *"There's a lot of stuff that happened and it just all went by so fast, I can't really say what it was anymore."* Nonetheless, naming records did bring some great stories to mind.

The first band I asked about was Hüsker Dü, since they were my first exposure to his work. On at least one of their early records, *"the bass itself had a cracked neck. There might be some songs where it kind of seems like everything is going out of tune, and that's why."* Zen Arcade had problems with the very tape it was being recorded on. *"Back in those days, everything was recorded on used tape. Studios in Hollywood would have these supplies of tape that they would just have to, all the old projects they'd have to just throw them out. So they sold all their used tapes, anywhere from 20 to 50 bucks a reel for the 2". And I had found some pretty good sources for used tape. Good tape, never had any problems with it—but that one! They were like these safety masters from a Bee Gees special. And for some reason they recorded some tracks on a 16-track machine and some tracks on a 24-track machine. When we got everything set up and then did the first playback, suddenly, at the end, as everything is fading out, you hear the Bee Gees singing. It was leaking between tracks. See, we didn't have a chance to bulk-erase those tapes before. What I would do is I would just run the tapes, erase the tapes while I'm setting up all the stuff. What*

I had to do, I had to take every track and erase it again. That slide that I was using tonight [for more conventional purposes with his guitar playing] was part of that recording. I had to put the tape on the machine, put every track in record, with the machine in the repro mode. I took that slide and just sat there by the machine and just held my finger on it and pushed the tape up, so that it physically slid up. I got it to this point where I didn't hear anything, and I just had to go on faith, and I had to do that with every single tape. I was sitting there by the machine, just holding my finger there for about two hours while the band went in the studio and took a nap."*

"This was at Total Access. Media Art was gone at that point. It was just a studio that I worked at. They had, it must have been an MM-1200, and then later an ATR-124, Ampex machines, 2" 24." He explains the raw sound of the acoustic instruments quite simply. *"The record was all recorded so fast, we didn't have time to make everything sound good."*

New Day Rising had even bigger frustrations. *"That was a pain in the ass session. When I walked in there for the first day, the studio wasn't put together. They were building a new room in the studio, is how we got the deal that we got. So, half the studio was filled up with boxes of equipment and shit from elsewhere, where they were doing the construction. And the board wasn't put together. They had gotten a new board or they had done maintenance. I walked in, half of the modules were out of the board and none of the outboard gear was hooked up. And where they put the board in the room, you could only hear one speaker. That was the first time I had to tell a studio, you have to move your board. I don't know what they were thinking, but of course we did get an incredible deal. It was probably an MCI tape deck."*

He remembers a big difficulty from an early Minutemen session. *"d. Boon's speakers in his amp were out-of-phase. two 12" speakers, there were two different types of speakers. I remember once I recorded, I put a mic on each speaker, I was gonna record stereo. When I recorded stereo, I put it down to mono, the guitar just completely disappeared. 'd., we've got a problem here.' It didn't keep us from recording."* His clarinet playing from the Minutemen radio broadcast, reissued on Politics of Time, did not present technical difficulties, but was memorable nonetheless. *"I just walked in there and played. I think half-way through when I was doing that, I pulled the bell off of the clarinet. A friend of mine who was there watching it, he said that at one point, I didn't realize, huge gobs of spit were just dropping out of it. He said it was really gross."*

"I like that record." was Spot's initial memory of Slovenly's Thinking of Empire. *"I think that's one of, insofar as how albums ended up sounding, that's one of my favorites. I'll tell you one thing about it, I didn't get any sleep before doing it. I had just driven down from San Francisco and I couldn't hear a goddamn thing when I walked into the studio."*

"That was at Music Lab in Hollywood. It's a studio that, I don't think it exists anymore. It was a pretty nice place. I had a pretty good rapport with them; I got fairly good deals. They had a lot of gear; they had a really incredible mic selection. The guy who owned the studio actually owned one of the old original Telefunken's. The one with the Iron Cross pilot light on it, I think he actually owned one that Hitler himself spoke on. At least that's what he said. They had a lot of old Neumann's and AKG mics."

He remembers a Neumann M 49, which he used there (though not with Slovenly) as *"one of the best sounding vocal mics I've ever used in my life. I used that on some techno thing that some guy had hired me for. And I had never used one and it was just there. I said 'Well, let me try this one.' Man, it sounded great."*

The Descendents' Milo Goes to College stands out to him because he had enough time to record vocals properly. His biggest memory of that record, though, is his difficulty in reaching the studio. *"I think most of the sessions I was riding the bus to it. I think that was when I had the car that all the water poured down the carburetor."*

The first Meat Puppets record was a challenging experience, but he's happy with the results. *"That recording is the epitome of what studio recording is not about. They had this manager at that time, and I had set the guys up in a reasonable studio fashion, with some separation and what-not. And they were not gettin' it, they just weren't playing well. They just couldn't get into a groove. So the manager just goes into the room and pushes all the instruments together and says, "Well, let's make it like your practice room", and so that thing is leakage-city. And that record sounds great. I wasn't gonna argue with him. Anyone with any sense would have just walked out."* Their second album was recorded more conventionally.

One of the last punk albums which Spot recorded was the Texas band Not for Sale, whose album was on Rabid Cat. When the opportunity came up to record them, it motivated him to move to Texas, where he still lives. *"I couldn't live in LA anymore, and ended up getting evicted out of a good house, because the owner decided to tear it down and build condos, and at that point I had had it with LA. I just threw everything in my van and said I'm just going to go to Austin, do this job, and worry about it later, and I stayed there."* Spot remembers Cedar Creek, where he recorded the album, as a *"great studio."*

"I blew out the high-end driver in one of the speakers. They had these baby Westlakes, really great speakers, but sensitive. They had a midrange driver that was really bright, so, well, I just didn't notice it. I know that's gonna sound terrible. We mixed the whole album, and then when we took the stuff home, and we'd gotten some great mixes, so we thought. We listened to it at home, and there was something really lopsided about it. So, I had to bite the bullet on that one. I

mean, it was my fault. I had to remix the whole damn thing. I really tried to save it. I was hoping that maybe it could have been saved in the mastering. It was too far gone. I had a long conversation with John Golden, who was mastering my stuff then. I sent him a copy of it, and he said he could make it better, but it's not gonna be what you mixed. It'll never be that." The album's mixes continued to cause problems. When the band received the new test pressings from John Golden, they were slower than the cassette dubs that they'd been listening to. The tape deck in the studio had been broken, and the band's dubs thus played faster in their own decks. They preferred the sped-up version to their own performances, and asked for the record to be re-mastered at a faster speed. Spot disagreed with their opinions, but the finished album plays faster than the original recordings.

"I just couldn't understand the concept of trying to make something sound that much like something else."

When he moved to Austin, Spot's enthusiasm for working with punk bands had faded, and he, ironically, sought recording work in the singer-songwriter community. A record which stands out to him from this period was for a songwriter named Terry Clark. "He's a English/Irish songwriter who about 10 or 12 years ago came here to the states to play and was basically 'adopted' by the Lubbock songwriter contingent—guys like Butch Hancock, Joe Ely, Jimmy Dale Gilmore, Terry Allen. He hooked up with JD Foster, an ex-bassist for Dwight Yoakam, whom I had gotten to know as a then-current member of the True Believers. At that time I was looking for new, non-punk, types of projects to work on. I mean, you can't keep doing the same thing and expect to be happy. Anyway, JD wanted to get into producing, and Terry Clark was gonna be his first project. I was pretty flattered and excited when he asked me to engineer the sessions. It was a very Nashville-style session where the musicians learned the tunes right there in the studio, and I had a great time hanging out with them. Some of the sidemen were Flaco Jimenez, Erik Hokkanen, David Grissom, Rich Brotherton—all very well known players in the 'Texas music' realm."

"We did the whole album over one weekend at the Firestation in San Marcos. The studio had actually been a fire station in an old brick building. It was a very big, live room. Their claim to fame at the time was that they had one of the first Sony tape-based digital multitrack machines—I'm pretty sure we recorded analog, however-er. And they had a fancy-shmancy board. Neve? Trident? Damn, I don't remember, that, well, had a lot of problems. Every module seemed to have something on it that didn't work unless you chanted mantra 558 while driving a midsize Chevy backward on a Tuesday morning

that followed the new moon, but only if the last eclipse could be seen from dryer number four at Pearl's Beauty Salon on Main Street if it's a day when Flo wasn't complaining about her husband Harry stayin' out all nite. And the patchbay had more shorts and intermittency than any patchbay I've ever worked on. Oh well, at least we got the record done."

"The studio was real proud of some MIDI drum voice rack module. They tried to get us to use it, but we really didn't need it. On one song, though, the drummer found the box that it came in and started playing it with brushes, and we all said in unison, 'That's the sound we want! Let's mic it up!' Yeah, it was a very fun, memorable recording session. I wish I had a copy of the album ['Call Up a Hurricane'] but it was one of those European deals that went outta print a long time ago."

"One of the best things I think that happened when I got sick of doing studio stuff, I really, after about years and years of studio stuff, I went back to playing around with 4-tracks. Got an X15 Fostex, and I was still working in studios at this time. This was around the time I did the Slovenly record. And I started playing around with the X15, recording my own ideas and that. I just like the way a lot of those tracks sound so much better than studio stuff. I really got into that real personal thing again. And it was one of the best things that ever happened to me. It made me re-align my ears with my whole philosophy on things again. I've got one of those Tascam 238s, 8-track cassette. I'm putting out an album; everything on this album is recorded either on this 8 track or on the old Fostex 4-track."

"I've got a real minimal setup. I've got some good outboard gear—nothing fancy but good stuff. Microphones, I've got a bunch of 57s, some 58s, some direct boxes. I've got some old Sony condensers. There was a Sony condenser that they were making back in the days when the Teac 4-track was like the big thing. I don't remember the number of those but I've got a pair of them. Somehow I ended up with some omni capsules from some old Altec condensers which screw right on. Either the Altecs were made by Sony or the Sonys were made by Altec. All of that stuff serves me well. I've got this amplifier, it's a solid-state Fender with a preamp out. I've recorded so many tracks through that thing. Using it as a preamp and just going right to tape. It's a Studio Lead. I have a whole slew of old tube amps, but I probably use that Studio Lead more than any amp I've ever owned. I've used it as a mic preamp. It's just a matter of, just tweaking it in. I've actually gotten some pretty, nothing outstanding, but I've gotten some good tracks that go down to tape really well."

Aside from recording himself, Spot doesn't do much engineering any more. "I'll put it this way, I tried not to record anybody for a long time, but lately there have been some situations that have proved worthwhile. I just did this

band called the Shindigs in Austin. What happened was that they came to me with some stuff that they had recorded on 16-track ADAT. It was recorded kind of quick and haphazardly and was basically a practice that they recorded. And they wanted to take the good stuff and finish it and record a few new ones. And I liked the band and I liked the people and I said, "Sure, let's do it". It was the worst situation I've ever had with an ADAT. One of the machines would not sync up. I've always hated the way you have to wait for one machine to catch up with the other. From analog, you go back and you just hit play, so that you're sitting there waiting for it to go. They have some older ADATs and one of 'em needed a lot of servicing. We lost an entire night. That's the one project that I've done recently." He elaborated even more on ADATs. "VHS is a shitty format; I don't think it's good for video, I don't think it's good for audio. I wish that Alesis had never used the VHS format for ADAT. If someone gave me an ADAT machine I'd be happy, but they suck."

Spot's amazing memory for his years of recording reflects the diverse experiences of a veteran engineer. It's amazing with everything we did discuss, we didn't even get to the Big Boys, the Dicks, St. Vitus, Overkill, Saccharine Trust, and so many more notable bands that he's worked with. It was also a surprising but fun experience to match the name I've seen on so many records with the musician I saw on stage. His fingerpicked guitar style and Loudon Wainright-like narrative songs are light years away from the records with which I associate his name. The most interesting part for me, though, was learning that someone who made such unusual sounding records during the punk era had once worked regularly with songwriters who wanted to sound like Elton John. ✆

Top 10 Recording Tips

By Barry Rudolph

#10 ALWAYS DOCUMENT THE RECORDING SESSION IN SOME WAY.

Take numbers, mic placement, effect settings, date of recordings, song titles, artist and writers names, reel numbers, BPM and SMPTE Song Start Times, track assignments, tape setup info, lyric/music sheets, phone numbers and good Thai take-out places. They are all important. Maybe even keep a studio log.

#9   DEVELOP A STYLE.

That is to say, a routine or method to your studio madness. A lot of studio work is repetitive... doing it over and over until it is right, and it's important to establish good working habits that work for you and the people who work with you. Style is also about organization.

#8 RELATIVE STRENGTHS AND WEAKNESS' OF PEOPLE AND EQUIPMENT.

Everyone's ideas and opinions are valid in some context. The trick is to evaluate their worth in your particular situation. Likewise, all recording equipment has better and worse qualities in certain applications. Check out what works for other people who are on the same creative track as you.

#7   LEARN YOUR EQUIPMENT.

There is nothing worse than working with someone who is inept. Even if you are like me, a klutz, you need to really focus on what you are doing right now at this moment. Mental concentration is a valuable asset in the recording studio. Restrict outside interruptions (phone calls and domestic intrusions) if you have to. If you are hopelessly at odds with yourself as a recording engineer or MIDI programmer then hire some help. This would free your mind up and allow for more vicariously creative thoughts.

#6 NO PRECONCEIVED EXPECTATIONS.

Expecting something to happen just because you have conceived it in your mind might lead you to be disappointed, especially if you are working with someone new to you. A realistic expectation of what is going to occur in a given session can be surpassed if the session vibe is good. If it's up to you, then you have to make it happen. If you rely on outside help, then just allow things to happen by establishing an atmosphere that brings out the best in people.

#5 GET THE BUSINESS STRAIGHT FIRST.

Unless you are just "doing a hang thing with your buds", then have some sort of understanding when you go down that "co-write" or "co-produce" trail. Without a doubt this "understanding" will evolve as your relationship grows. It can be verbal if all parties are okay with that. Just remember all the countless stories about getting screwed over misunderstandings and forgotten details.

#4   MAKE DECISIONS.

If there is anything for sure then it's that the technologies (MIDI, Multi-track, digital) allow you to put off making production decisions if you want to. Recording and production are analogous to building a house. You can't decide to move the foundation around after you have fully decorated all the rooms. Frequent decisions and living with them is the sane approach to good sounding and good feeling recordings.

#3   THE TIME THING.

Allow more than enough time to do things. You must respect everyone's time constraints and their sense of time. Some people are always late so you may have to adjust if you are always on time. People are going to work at different speeds then you. In an amicable recording situation, your time is not more important than anybody's else's. The session moves at the pace of the slowest person or the slowest process.

#2   DEMOCRACY DOESN'T WORK WELL IN THE STUDIO.

Even in an equity band situation, where everyone has a say in writing and production direction, there has to be a person with "the plan" or "the concept". Generally, the person with "the vision" will keep the direction of the session/project on course, on time and on budget.

#1 PATIENCE, PATIENCE, PATIENCE.

Rarely does the "magic" happen immediately. It may never happen. It may have happened and you didn't know it. It could happen in the next moment but you gave up on it. Just be patient. ⊗

MACHA

By Larry Cran

Macha are a different band. Their use of Indonesian and other "ethnic" instrumentation within the format of what you would call a "rock" band is rather unique. The instruments add a texture not available from guitars and they utilize them in a way that doesn't call up the soppy tripe of "world-beat" or the pretense of Dead Can Dance. Their recent album, *See it Another Way*, was recorded at Chase Park Transduction by David Barbe and the boys in Macha's hometown of Athens, Georgia. I caught up with Joshua Mckay and Kai Riedl in New York and saw an amazing Knitting Factory show a few nights later.

David Barbe has a thing about having to take a two hour break and not working weekends; did you guys encounter that when you were working with him?

Joshua: Yeah, definitely. He was the daytime shifter. The way we had to do our recordings was on a small budget, too little time to do it at home and too small of a budget to do everything that we would like. When we get our six days allotted for making the record, it needs to be literally six 24-hour days. We developed a system where I would come in at nine in the morning and work with Dave until 6:00. At 6:00, Andy Baker, who has a little nighttime stamina about him, would come in from six to two. Andy LeMaster, who's the wild man, night animal would come in later.

You don't hear about that too often.

I don't think it's so common, it's tricky for all parties involved, and there's a certain element of uncertainty...coming in cold. Fortunately, all three of them seem to have their individual perception and they work great as a team. Usually it was very systematic. I had to chart out all the instruments that were going to be tracked so we could have an idea of how we were going to get it done in time. We didn't get to experiment a lot; most of the experimentation was with getting the sounds.

Like how to mic something? You've got some unusual instruments.

Yeah, and they really change in the sound environment. We learned a lot from the first record. The first one had a more elaborate

recording situation. On the second on[e] learned from the mistakes on the first one [-] the shape of the room and the mics we c[ould] The big thing with the first record was ge[tting] really nice sounds, because I was doing a l[ot of] overdubbing one instrument at a time. [When] you're getting a nice sound in the room, o[ne at] one by one, when you pull them all toget[her it] sounds a little too diffused. After the first r[ecord] they built these really great, huge baffles [that] can make a little room inside the big room[.]

That's a good idea, I do that with of[ten] **panels, you can get them used.**

These are just towering things that you hope[...] don't fall on you.

Do they lower them down from [the] ceiling?

No, they just have them on wheels. They've g[ot the] physics right - what seems like a very sh[ort] base for such a huge baffle somehow sits [...] Those guys work hard. They're so into findi[ng a] way to the greatest sounding recording s[...] They really, really think about preamp[s and] compressors, not effects racks.

What kinds of things were [they] pulling in when you w[ere] working there?

Kai: They had this plate reverb that we tried to [...]

Was it working?

We used it a little bit but it was on the blink. I[...] it was on the blink on the second record.

It was in mono, wasn't it?

No, it was in stereo the first record.

Yeah, but on the second record it was mono.

One channel wasn't coming back?

Right.

In the sessions did you start out with a basic scratch track or rhythm track to build the songs on?

Generally it's two people laying down basic tracks.

Do you have charts to figure out what's going to be added when?

The arrangements are definitely worked out. We record demos at home on cassette 8-track. A big part of the stuff I talked about with the engineers was how I could get it to be a "not-so-professional" rock recording. I was really trying to get the sounds of our wooden room at home, and the good tape compression of a cassette multi-track. I'm really a fan of getting what you want with the sound that's going to tape. There tends to be so much that isn't decided until mix time and not a lot of mix time to do it. I'm really just trying to create the sonic panorama, I don't really want to be thinking of the sounds, themselves, too much. We're really kind of into the "true" sound, the way the instruments sound in the room with a wooden floor at home. We're in love with what we got. We use distortion or mild stereo delay. We really don't go too wacky with changing the sound; it's more like combinations of them to cause some kind of interference.

What are the non-rock band instruments you are using?

The vibes are in there a lot, the hammer dulcimer, the Fun Machine is in there a lot.

The what?

A Fun Machine is this organ, a Baldwin '70s home entertainment organ. You're at the skating rink if you listen to it straight up. Plug it into an amplifier and it goes wild.

What other instruments do you use?

The Javanese zither, the songs "Salty" and "Submarine Lover" both have it. It's that kind of twangy, zingy sound. It's a beautiful instrument from Central Java; you play it perpendicular to yourself. There are long sets of double strings with two legs at the end of it with a big resonator box that gets wider towards the end. We've got nipple gongs, which are tuned smaller gongs with a big strong nipple in the middle. Steel drums get a lot of use. We have a bunch of double reed horns.

Do you take a lot of stuff on the road?

Yeah, we take enough, more and more. Recording instruments is the live translation of everything.

Do you have little pick-ups on things?

Little pick-ups, we haven't been able to invest in proper amplification. We just slide a couple of Dean Markley acoustic guitar pick-ups in under the strings of the zither. We use a clip-on mic for the hammer dulcimer.

I thought there was some stuff you did with micro-cassette recordings on the first record.[self-titled]

Our first 2,000 copies of the first record came with a free second disc that was 70 minutes of Indonesian recordings. The pieces on there from Bali were from my first trip to Indonesia. I got nine hours of Indonesian music and sounds on micro-cassette. Some of it sounds really interesting because of the way it was recorded. I have so many micro-cassettes and I'm trying to find the hi-fi micro-cassette player. The only recordings that have been done in Western Java were done by the government for the Library of Congress. This is a cultural group that's kind of refusing to modernize, they haven't learned the national language, and they don't have any electrical systems of any kind. Certainly the sound of the music is quite different than anything else. It's much more like Aboriginal music all over the world. The rhythms are much more simple pulse rhythms. You could almost mistake it for Native American in some ways.

With a cultural group like that you're obviously an outsider. How do you go about...?

That's a special situation. Basically, we had to get a government escort to go into the place. It was an unusual circumstance; these people have kind of defied their government and modernization. It's like going back 200 years, they're still animist - they haven't accepted a modern religion. Indonesia is really weird; you have to declare one of five religions to be a citizen. So, you go and get a government official to escort you. We had this really great guy named Arif, he had been there many times, and he knew the language.

Where did you put your recorders and mics in situations like that? You probably wanted to be kind of unobtrusive about it.

Exactly, but it was just one mic.

Did you carry it on you when you were recording or did you set it up?

I carried it on me, circumstances would change in a lot of situations - there would be random people coming in. This one couple that we met had been married for 25 years; they played music on the street and he made zithers and she had a really beautiful voice. We went to their house to record them in their living room. On their front porch some neighbors were skinning this huge snake; they were completely wasted with this snake in their hands. We had to kind of move around them to get into the house and this guy followed us into the house. He sits down and starts singing along when everyone starts performing. He was so completely out of it, it was really wild. How do you work a set up for that situation?

With a situation like that, do you offer them some kind of compensation?

No, they welcomed us, I think he knew that we were going to buy some instruments at the time. We're talking of a place very different with interactive time than what we're used to here. Everywhere you go everybody says hello to you.

It's not like New York, huh? [laughter]

We went to Taipei for our somewhat contrasted Asian experience. We played a couple of shows in Taipei, going through Taipei, you look at people and they were always just looking away, they seemed scared of us.

How did you end up getting a gig in Taipei?

This band called Ladybug came from Taipei to Athens [Georgia] and I was curious to see them and I ended up hanging out with all of them. I invited them back to stay at my house. There manager who works for this label called Crystal Records in Taipei, Randy Lynn is his name, he was trying to bring in American indie bands over to Taipei. He wanted to bring us over, it was really cool, and we were the fourth band to go over.

This whole band... The sound of it and everything is completely different, yet your working with world instruments but your not playing the safe ethno, world beat band thing. Is it just a combination of your guys' interests in music? I assume you like rock stuff too.

Oh yeah, basically it's the satisfaction of bi-polar personalities. It's just listening to world music all the time for years. It's kind of affected my orientation, like Thai food - you try it the first time and you want it again until it's part of your diet.

How did you mic your instruments in the studio?

We tried everything, I think the mic that got the hardest work was the Earthworks "anal probe."

The TC30?

The OM1 actually... The OM1 got a workout with the snare drum, all my vocals, most of the string instruments although the Sony Handycam video camera actually was the most preferred acoustic instrument mic, it really allows the overtones to take off.

So how do you do it? Do you just set on "record" and take a tap out?

Yes, it has left, right on it.

What numbered camera is that?

They discontinued that one because of the controversy in Japan. In Japan some intelligent fellow discovered that there was a red filter that you could put on it so you could see through women's clothes, so they stopped making that particular Handycam. Another mic that was really nice was were the Coles ribbon mics.

The 4038s?

Yeah.

Those were great for the guitars and for any loud sounds that had an edge that we were having a hard time getting rid of, like the steel drum. The steel drum was the hardest struggle to get the sound. We set up six different mic's and we went and listened through and found the one. It turned out to be a combination of two and we didn't know which ones they were. For some reason something got moved or something didn't get written down and we spent the next five hours trying to get even close to what we had again. We never got the sound but we got to the closest proximity to it with the Coles. We use [Shure SM] 58s and the video camera at home. On the new record, "Mirror" is obviously the lo-fi sounding one, it's a very old recording that went from an 8-track demo to a 2" 16-track. The mix is two years old I put it together in a half-hour to get over to the radio station and have something to play. It ended up getting laid onto our sophomore struggle; it's just what it is.

Was there other stuff you did on the first album that was different, recording wise, from what's on the new one?

It had a little more flip-flopping between the DA88's for stacking up tracks and bouncing them down to two on the 16-track. The horns especially, I'll lay down ten horns, like temples, they've got all these horns going.

Did they sync them up... the DA88 slave off the sixteen?

No, that time we didn't have it synced so we had to get the touch right. They're now synced up at the studio and now they're 32 track. We definitely want to explore more with flipping and bouncing back and forth and changing the sounds, especially editing. We've got a couple of samplers that we've needed for getting some of our instruments into the live shows that we can't bring with us. I guess another thing that was really different between the two records is that we mixed the first record at a different studio in Nashville.

Were you doing it at David [Barbe]'s place originally?

The first record, we mixed one song at David's and the rest was in Nashville with Mark [Nevers, at Wedgetone], who's worked with Vic Chestnutt and Lambchop. The second record, we mixed it all at David's.

What were the advantages and disadvantages of both of these kinds of situations?

I just wanted to go to different room because I didn't feel like mixing on KRKs. The place in Nashville was a mixing studio; it sounded really ideal. The guy had worked all kind of different sessions and was in a band that was experimental. It sounded like a good ideal circumstance, it was going to be a little more money so there was a lot of pressure to do it all over the weekend. We weren't sure what we were getting into. It turned out that the studio had automation, which put us in the position of having to sacrifice one of the sixteen tracks for timecode. If we hadn't had automation, that record would have not gotten mixed. The way we recorded, I had to stack up four different instrumental events on one track.

They had to come in and do different things at different levels.

Yeah, with automation it separates it out to six channels of all the different versions. It saved our fucking asses; it was such a godsend!

Have you guys ever done really different remixes of your own stuff?

Some guys in Athens have remixed some things on their own; somebody said they heard it in a club. I'm anxious to hear it. The beauty of remixing is that you can take out something and show it in a different light. I have asked this one DJ, a guy named Hahn Rowe who's an all around amazing musician. He used to play in a band called Hugo Largo. He's also a really gifted sonic manipulator and he goes by the name Somatic doing a pretty straight up drum'n'bass kind of thing. He's just gifted - he does remixes and he DJ's.

Do you know if people do remixes off anything other than ADATs?

I did some stuff with Anthony [Saffery] from Cornershop, the sitar player. We worked together on a record and I sent him a song dumping tracks off onto DAT, the whole song two tracks at a time. He took that and threw it into Pro Tools and made something new out of it, which I don't know if he ever finished.

For us, I really want to just go from the tape to Pro Tools.

If it was a 24 bit Pro Tools, you could get a little more clarity out of it. What people are throwing into their sampler are these little bits of songs. With these remixes, they get a drum loop out of some section that you did and some other sounds from different parts of the song and build something new out of just these little things, it's all sampled down to 16 bit anyway.

They're getting the ADAT tapes to have all the pieces that he prefers and manipulating the samplers. It depends on the DJ, whether they have something like Pro Tools, or just one sampler, or whether they have multi-track tape.

Have you thought about setting up your own studio for the band?

We want to get it to where we can record basics at a studio and bring it home and spend the time that's right, then go mix it somewhere.

Recording drums is definitely a lot of work, getting that kind of stuff down, but it seems like with a lot of your instruments you could use the Handycam or pick up an Earthworks and a couple of mics and some good mic pres...

We get the sound that we want at home, we get things at 2 AM in the bathroom that can't be replaced by any time constraint. Back at home, the stuff that we have on tapes are the source materials for what we really sound like. There's a way we sound in the studio, but the way we sound at home is what we really sound like.

Do think it would be a little less shimmer-y in the end?

Definitely, the cassette recordings and the micro-cassette recordings have all the distortions that come in those formats and that's what we tried to recreate in the studio. We couldn't get it. We kept driving compressors and driving the preamps and the tape, we still couldn't get that cassette power. That's definitely going to be made available to us. We won't do the record unless it's afforded that.

Then go mix at Chase Park or somewhere?

Somewhere that's got a good, true room so we can know what we are doing with all of this.

I like the kind of hybrid things that are happening now, when people record some at a studio, take it out and add things and come back, using the studio when you have to and bringing the creative parts back in on their own time.

One thing I've wanted to do is a complete multi-track, micro-cassette session with all these different song pieces with the instruments down on micro-cassette. The micro-cassette is as "field recording" as you can get. Our stuff will start out as this field recording and then it'll evolve into this studio sound.

What about mastering?

We knew something wasn't right with the first album but we couldn't pin it down. On the second record we got in touch with a man named Glen Schick, Glen Schick Mastering. He loved our stuff and he wanted to do our next record. We went to do the second record and we realized how much we were missing aesthetically and professionally. He (Glenn) had already heard a lot of Indonesian music so he kind of understood that we didn't want anything clogged or...

Where does he work out of?

He's out of Atlanta; he's our golden gem.

He is! His room is a fantastic place to do what you're doing.

He's also like David Barbe, trying to continually upgrade his situation. He's crafting his sound space.

I like the record, I think it sounds great it jumps off the CD sounding really clear like the high end is kind of shimmering, and it's got a really good sound.

Thank you.

You're welcome. That's why I'm sitting here talking to you guys, if it sucked I wouldn't be here. ☮

A few tips on drum setup, new heads and mic'ing

RECORDING DRUMS.
By Darron Burke

Setup/Getting sounds

When I first started recording I used wonder how long I was supposed to take when setting up and getting drum sounds. Sometimes it took one or two hours, and other times it took... well, a long time (with the rest of the band standing around getting impatient). I wondered if I was being "professional" enough. I just didn't know how long the "big studios" took. Now that I've made a few records where we positively had to get a good drum sound, I have a few ideas I can share on the subject.

In my early sessions, if drum sounds weren't coming along after an hour or two I used to just go with whatever sound I had and then sort it out later when mixing. Sometimes it worked, sometimes it didn't. Now I know if I concentrate on getting a good drum sound before I start recording I will have a better idea of what my finished product will sound like and not be so surprised when it comes time to mix.

Setting aside a full day or two just to get drum sounds is not uncommon for a high-expectation recording. I like to take the first day to set-up drums and mics, record a sample and then go home. I use the second day to make final adjustments and listen to the tape from the day before. Having that time away makes problems really obvious, and the clarity of mind makes it easy to get to work tackling the things we need to fix. (I can also grab a new head or any hardware we might need on my way to or from the recording site). When everything's cool with the drums I move on to other instruments and start tracking.

Before I start a new session, I always check with the band to see what condition their drums are in. It's pretty hard to get beautiful sounds out of a drumset that's trashed and has 200 year-old heads on it. Worn heads lack life and tone; new heads can give drums the sonic clarity to fit-in nicely or jump right out of the mix. Replacing heads on the bottom of drums is as important as the top, After about eight months even a head that isn't struck can start to lose its life just from being under tension. Tuning is another important consideration, but that is beyond the scope of this article. There are a few books and videos available at music stores or by mail order to help you master the art. I have a video, called *Drum Tuning*, by Bob Gatzen - it's a little corny but I definitely learned a few valuable tricks from it.

Replacing Drumheads

If the drums and hardware are in good condition then the heads are next to be checked. Probably the most common head combination for toms is Remo clear or coated Ambassador on the top, and clear Ambassador or Diplomat (a little thinner) on the bottom. Remo Pinstripe heads (a clear 2 layer head) are pretty cool for the top and can give you a little more of a smacky-thuddy attack sound. Try to stay away from thick or specialty heads until you get used to the aforementioned types. Snare heads wear-out pretty quickly and get a weak spot in the middle that forces you to keep tweaking the head tighter and tighter. Eventually it looses its zing or ability to respond to lighter playing. A worn snare head just can't compete with the brightness of the hi-hats - to really cut through, you need a fresh head. For head replacement a coated Ambassador is a good place to start, but experimenting with different types and thicknesses may lead you to your own favorite. For the bottom use a snare-side head (a thin type made specifically for the that purpose). The bottom head of a snare doesn't need to be replaced as often as the top, sometimes the more stretched and dull the better because it's less ringy. If I had to make up a guideline I'd say change one bottom for every three top heads. Kick drum heads can last a pretty long time, but if they've been on there more than a year and a half it's probably time for an overhaul. Almost every major head manufacturer makes a pre-damped or "EQ'd" head to control ring and get a good "thud". With these heads you don't have to over-stuff your drum with tons of pillows and furry creatures and such. I really dig these type of heads. Check out the Evans (Genera Dry) or Aquarian brands.

Getting a more defined sound

When recording drums, the amount of bleed can be quite severe. The snare mic picks up so much hi-hat that you don't dare turn the snare up in your mix - If you do, the hi-hat is overpowering, and no amount of EQ can be used to fix it. The same is true for tom mics, the loud crash and ride cymbals can force you to bury the the toms, in effect, ruining the bombastic drum sound you had planned. One economical and creative way to gain a little more control of your drums is to use pieces of cardboard or other material to isolate the mics from the cymbals. For close-mic'ed snare, cut a piece of cardboard large enough to fit between the mic and the offending hi-hat then use tape to hold it in place. Tape the cardboard directly to the snare drum and/or the hi-hat stand. The idea is to block the cymbal's bright sound from entering the mic. Variations on this method of isolation include using cloth or cloth/cardboard combinations. I've even heard of someone using a plastic trashcan cut to fit around the snare. Other ways of cutting down on cymbal bleed are to adjust cymbal heights out and away from drum mics, or asking the drummer not to strike the cymbals quite so hard or just a little less often. Different playing styles can dramatically alter the way a recording sounds. To affect change, the performer can listen carefully to the tape playback and make adjustments in their playing to "give the tape what it wants to hear". For instance, hitting the snare more evenly in the center or harder might give you the sound that best fits the music you are recording. and the way the recorder is picking-up the instrument.

These are just some of the ways you can prepare drums for recording. Taking your time and shooting for a sound that is nearly "finished" will make the rest of the recording that much easier. Good luck!

Jeremy Enigk

The first time I heard Jeremy Enigk's Return of the Frog Queen I was absolutely floored. I think it was "Explain" that keyed me into his very idiosyncratic and original vision; the acoustic guitar that opens the song picks an optimistic pattern, a sort of major key Wall-era Pink Floyd riff. But the recording of the guitar is brutal: it's so saturated with tape distortion it sounds like it's eating up the tape. And then the voice, distressed beyond belief (I could almost see the PZM taped to the basement wall), floating along like some spawn of Syd Barret. Enigk's voice follows it's own haramonic logic. He's one of the few singers whose melody lines surprise and puzzle me. And this is before the 41-piece orchestra comes in...

I was so obsessed with this record that I tracked down the engineer, Greg Williamson, and plied him with questions about the recording and production of this art-rock masterpiece. His advice was key in the early gear decisions of my studio, Tiny Telephone. He agreed to record my band (the recently dissolved MK Ultra) and eventually this led to us doing two Sunny Day Real Estate Tours. This record affected my life in so many ways and has influenced many other musicians I know.

Jeremy's approach to recording is refreshing: he places the song over the technical considerations, letting his intuition rule the entire process.
—John Vanderslice (I took the photos too, except the one on this page by Ben Werth.)

Describe your current home set up for recording. Whether it's sketching or for recording ideas or demos or beginnings of songs like a few of the songs that you recorded yourself on *Frog Queen*.

Frankly, what I have is pretty simple because I don't really like compressors and stuff. I get really confused. I like to get it down as fast as possible and then for the real thing, I'm letting the producer take care of the compression. I have a Fostex DMT8, one of those new hard drive things. It's an 8-track and it's basically what I use and I have my dual cassette and then I have a drum set and a couple of amps laying around. I just try to use that as best that I can. A little bit of the EQ on the actual Fostex.

So that's a console and recorder all in one?

Yeah.

When you were doing sketches for *Return of the Frog Queen*, what were you using then for your recorder?

I actually have a Tascam 4-track that's totally wasted. It's fallen off the top of an upright piano and it still works. It's a Tascam Porta-5 that I got ten years ago. One song off *Frog Queen*, "Fallen Heart" is actually recorded directly from that 4-track.

And that sounds really good.

Yeah, it sounds alright and that's the cool thing with an actual tape and analog machine - it records on both sides and you just flip it over and it's backwards.

And what were those sounds that were backwards? We're some of those piano sounds or what?

They were just guitar and vocals. That's all I used. I recorded that song years ago when I first got my 4-track, forwards, obviously. I always would have fun with that song by playing it backwards because it sounds so neat backwards and so that's always how I listened to it. I thought I should try to put forward stuff over this because I knew The Beatles had done that and I should mess around, but that I should be careful because it's an old recording. I didn't really want to destroy it. So I flipped the tape over backwards and figured out what track went to what track. Then I put forward vocals and a new bass line over the backwards guitar and vocals that were there and it ended being pretty cool.

One thing that struck me the first time that I heard *Return of the Frog Queen*, was "Explain", and it was the saturated, distorted sound of the acoustic guitar that opens it and your vocals when they come in and I had never heard anything that sounded like that. I thought, and I still do, that it was the most original recordings out there. Where did you record "Explain"? Was that one from Bobcat?

No, "Explain" was done at Greg Williamson's [Enigk manager who recorded and engineered *Return of the Frog Queen* and *How it Feels to be Something On* by Sunny Day Real Estate] basement.

So that was done and you guys were just hitting levels really hard, and that's just part of that sound.

I think that's Greg's whole thing. He loves to push it right before it distorts or right when it starts distorting. And that was done on a 4-track because it was originally going to be for a single so we thought, we'd do it on a 4-track and save money. But we really liked it and wanted to make it a serious song.

At that time you were doing a lot of your vocals on the Realistic PZM mic.

Mainly, except for a few songs on *Frog Queen* that we didn't use that mic on.

But generally that was your mic and even on the new album you have one song on there. Which song on that did you use the PZM or which songs did you use?

On *How it Feels to be Something On*, we used the PZM.

Jeremy and Dan Carr from MK Ultra

I remember singing up against the wall because Greg would mount the PZM there . I'm not fully sure if we used a PZM on that album, because what, I think, we used mainly, was a Neumann U 47.

What do you like about the PZM?

It's totally smooth.

I think it's a phenomenal microphone. I just modified one myself and it's justifiably a famous mic and it's amazing that they discontinued making it.

The new one is not even comparable to the first one. It's got a really nice smooth high-end to it too, but yet you can get the lows. It's really versatile, you can have a lower end if you mount it on a piece of wood. But if you just hold it, it's more of a high-end type of thing. So you can physically change the sound of it without ever touching the EQ in the first place.

Because if you mount it, isn't it picking up the resonation of whatever is touching the wood.

It also picks up everything in a circle, like a dome. What I like to do whenever I do my rough demos at home (I only use a PZM, unless I'm doing drums and multiple things), but first if I'm playing acoustic guitar I always put it on my right knee and then I'm doing vocal and acoustic and just kind of bend my head down and I sing into the mic and it mixes it nicely. There's nothing that's too loud or too quiet. For the drums it's unbelievable. I put it either over and a little bit in front of the tom or the cymbals, like hang it over it or put it right in front of the kick drum and it picks up the whole set. Just one mic on the drums. It sounds fine for demos and in fact I've had really good drum sounds.

Speaking of drums, you played drums on the songs "Return of the Frog Queen" and "Lizard". Did you put down a click? When did you record the drums in the scheme of things?

I always record the drums after the music and rarely did we use a click. I play drums on every song that has drums on it except for "Abigail" which William plays on. I don't know why I asked him to do them on that song. I think it would have been good if he would have come in on some of the other songs but, basically, that kind of made it have that raw sloppiness about it. Because there's no click for the most part, and it's more of take after take because I'm not a drummer and I can't nail it. In one case, on the song "Carnival", we recorded a drum track and it was a great drum track soulfully, but there were a few gnarly misses on the kick drum and various offbeats and stuff. So we recorded another drum track over it so there's two existing drum tracks on that song and it kind of covers up some of the mistakes. They kind of cancel each other out, or help each other out, rather.

The vocal sound that you seem to like in a lot of your recordings is a very close, direct vocal sound and there's very few effects. Is that how you like them? Just to hear the vocals, straight ahead?

Not really. That's just the way that it has happened. The people that have produced the albums, they probably like it that way. But I really want to go more into effects, not too much, but I want to be able to do really big stuff. Like big room sounds, but I think for some reason people like to mic me up close. when I demo stuff, it's a lot different. The music is generally a little bit more up front and the vocals are more spacy when I record it.

The intervals of the harmonies are so surprising and original like on "Lizard" and "Return of the Frog Queen". How did you write these? Did you sketch them out on a 4-track or did you do it in the studio?

It all kind of comes whenever. I usually write a guitar line first, not a whole song, but just something that makes me wanna sing and the melody pretty much comes right away after I have something to sing to. It's always gibberish, I'm never singing lyrics, but the melody is pretty solid and then I move the lyrics into it after I have an established melody line. On *Frog Queen*, there wasn't a song on there that I made up the melody in the studio. Everything had been written years before, some recently. For *How it Feels to be Something On*, I think that there were three or four songs that I came up with the melody to in the studio. Because Sunny Day works a little bit faster and I don't really have time that I would have normally with my solo work to come up with the melodies. But as far as harmonies, I'm really poor at harmonizing, and I think that kind of basic, obvious harmony, I don't really have a deep understanding of that. So I don't have that core kind of feeling, so a lot of the harmonies are kind of weird sometimes. Some are appropriate and some are weird.

As far as the layering with the orchestral instruments and the strings, you worked with Mark Nichols. How did you write them? After the fact? At some points I know that you had something like 48 tracks going on and you were slaving ADATs and it was just a wealth of melodic ideas.

Ultimately, I would go to Mark with my basic concept and he didn't understand where I was coming from until I mentioned the Gary Numan sound that I was after. Mark is brilliant and unbelievable. He really made that thing work, but there were many different songs, for example, "Call Me Steam". Where I would actually sing the string idea and the flute idea to him and he would just write it out because I didn't know how to read and write music at the time. He

would always write an underlying support to it that way that it would work. He made the magic, I just had a few ideas here and there.

How did you feel about going from project studios in basements into Bob Lang Studio where you recorded your last record. It's 48 track, API console, they've got great mics, a nice live room and I was blown away when I saw his studio.

It's a great sounding main room. For me it's almost like home. It's totally natural because the first time I was in a studio I would say I was uncomfortable, I wasn't singing on key because I wasn't used to the vocals coming out of my ears. But after that first recording with Sunny Day, *Diary*, which was really the first time, truly being in a studio, I think that going to the studio has always been like going home. It's just a bigger, more option type of place. Lang's had this weird vibe. When I first went there I was creeped out a little bit because I felt there was a kind of ghost type of presence in there and some weird stuff has gone on in there from the past. It creeped me out and it's a dark place, but in a really positive way. Only good things have come out of there.

It seems to be built out of the side of a mountain. It's like a cave just walking in there.

It was like the bat cave or something. But it's a great place as far as the vibe and the creative energy that's floating around. There's a piano in there and anytime there's a piano for me to just be able to jam on that makes me feel better about any other thing I'm doing whether it be singing, guitar or whatever.

I remember the first time you came to Tiny Telephone you sat down on the piano and played "Imagine". That was great.

That was fun. You were showing us your studio and Joe and I didn't get past the keyboard room. It was just like, "Oh, cool studio."

Getting back to your own situation at your house. Do you miss hitting tape or do you prefer the convenience and the quickness of using hard disk recording?

I prefer tape. I like the hard disk, but there's one thing I don't like about it and that's the fact that you have to erase everything that you've recorded on the hard disk and you have to download it to a DAT machine or to Jaz drives, but that takes a little time. I have an hour of time on mine and I have to go through each song's mix and whatever to get it down on there or whatever. I'm not too familiar with it. I'm used to tape and having that tape forever and being able to go back and mix it any time you want just by popping it in.

And it's physical. It exists, it's there.

And it's analog. You have the option of the backwards thing. I don't think it works like that, I don't think you can play it backwards.

No you can't unless you have a Pro Tools set up.

But I think for an actual technical, if you're gonna be really into punching and then doing that kind of stuff it's amazing. It's better in that way because I think you can do the editing stuff you can chop your song apart and rewrite it kind of like Pro Tools, but not as good, but you can look at it. You can hear it, and look at it. You can't look at it like on Pro Tools. But you can hear the frequencies and just slowly move it to the point where you want to punch in and you can set the time on when you want it just to punch in; so you can do it by yourself. It's really good for the technical stuff, but that's nothing I really use. I just like to do it over if I screw up.

What are your plans for the next recording and what direction do you want to go sonically?

We don't really know when we're going to record because we're not on a label. I think the band really wants to do something a lot more polished and produced. We come from punk rock, kind of raw type of thing. Our last album is excellent, but very linear. Every song has the same thing going on with it. The same recording. I definitely want to get out of that and I want to go more into a brilliant, bright recording that's very versatile.

You want to integrate strings again and keyboards and piano?

Definitely! We want to go more into that. Instead of how we've done it in the past, bringing my songs to the band and then everybody doing their instrument and jamming and it's all heavy and whatever, I want to bring the songs to the band the way that I originally recorded them and perform them that way and get the band to mold themselves into that, but obviously do what they need to do and what makes them happy, but try that direction a little bit more. I'm tired of us just doing our parts and we record it and it's done. I don't want to do it that way anymore.

That's true. It does make it linear because you're guaranteed two guitars, bass and drums. That's what everyone does.

This is our first album back so we weren't ready to take a major dive into that, but talking to Dan, he's agreed with me and he's into starting to open it up a little bit and William has actually expressed concern to me how he doesn't know what he's gonna do because the way I write some of my songs the drums aren't really about power and sometimes there's no drums and yet of course, he's gonna be there. I think it's really gonna open his eyes to a whole new way of doing it. ✲

By Darron Burke

How to get cool audio gear really cheap and add a unique angle to your studio collection

Gear

People have been telling me for years now that bargains in the audio world just can't be found. They say stuff like, "You're not going to find a Neumann mic for under five grand" and "You may as well give up looking for anything, all the good stuff is gone." These people can be quite discouraging. But I haven't stopped looking, and I've found enough stuff to keep my friends' and my studios brimming with some very interesting and useful gear.

Call me paranoid, but I view music chain stores as the enemy of the recording studio. If I had purchased all of my equipment from these stores I would never have been able to open my studio. The prices are outrageous! I rarely step into these establishments except to buy a reel of tape or to find out how much everybody else is paying for something I just found in a trash dumpster. I don't talk to the store personnel because they often take the attitude "if I haven't heard of it, it can't be good" or "why do you insist on wasting my time with this outdated technology?" Then they want to tell me that what I really need is the newest blah-blah self-powered computer-controlled remote access flapadapa chug ploop. No thanks.

Over the years I've developed a few tried-n-true tactics for hunting-down used gear. By buying equipment from friends, schools and businesses and snooping around back rooms and storage areas, I've been able to learn a lot about mic pres, compressors, EQs, tape machines and much more. I trade or sell equipment I don't need to get the things I really want. If I take a look at the stuff filling my studio and home, I can't believe I own it all! Especially when I thought I'd never be able to afford even a single compressor or mic when I saw the prices of equipment in mail order catalogs and stores.

I once found a metal box containing seven rare Shure Brothers ribbon microphones for $15 at a yard sale. From a radio station I got an awesome Canadian stereo compressor called an Orange County for well below its market value. Simply keeping your eyes wide open is a great way to get extra mic cables, mic stands, headphones and other peripherals that can cost big bucks elsewhere.

Whatever you might need for your studio, be it a mic or a reverb, it may be sitting on a shelf waiting for you in a radio station or college music library. Here's one method of finding older equipment that you could give a try. It has worked for me on more than one occasion.

Go through the phone book and call local commercial or college radio stations and ask for the chief engineer. Ask them if they have any old equipment you can buy, and mention that you will even consider purchasing broken equipment. That will start up a conversation and get things rolling. Tell them what you want, and be specific, if you are too vague they get antsy and end the conversation before you can get your foot in the door. Tell them that you are a recording enthusiast and are into the "old-style" of recording. Lots of radio station engineers

appreciate that kind of thing. If they are receptive to the idea of you buying their old stuff, make an appointment or lunch date to go over and see it. (You can bribe 'em with a meal, a trick that works well with most audio-types!) Once you're in the equipment room, you can peek into the corners and find the really cool shit! The unexpected discovery of something everyone else has overlooked is my favorite part.

Making an offer can be a little tricky. You want to get the stuff cheaply, but you don't want to piss off the seller or ruin the possibility of future deals. If you don't know how much to offer for something you see, you can find prices for a lot of odd pieces online. You don't have to buy anything that day; you can call back later. But beware; if you wait too long it might be gone. I have a couple of regrets because I missed-out on something good when I didn't jump on the deal.

Hopefully you can get a compressor or other piece of gear that's worth much more than the $10, $50, or $100 you paid for it. You may be lucky and find a well-known collectable item or just a box that you can drive a signal through for a cool distortion sound.

P.S. I probably shouldn't be telling you all of this because nothing will be left for me, but I've been lucky so I shouldn't be greedy. ⊛

the Go-Betweens

by Larry Crane

The eighties were a strange time of change for recording practices and for bands. Studios went from the extreme isolation of instruments and drums that were favored in the seventies to the use of analog and digital drum machines, click tracks, and heavy-handed synth overdubs. Many artists were lured into this world, making records that sound as dated today as they sounded "modern" back then. The Go-Betweens were a band from Australia, in the late seventies who were originally looking back at the sixties for inspiration and soon found themselves moving to England and spending ten years or so courting success in the music industry that always seemed a short step away. In the early 1990 they disbanded, after moving back to Australia. Recently, a compilation of their more popular songs and a collection of early recordings became available, prompting a short tour. I was lucky to catch Grant McLennan and Robert Forster, the core of the band and both fine songwriters, who performed an amazing acoustic set, and chat with Robert extensively about the Go-Between's experiences in the studio.

When was the first time the Go-Betweens went into the studio?

We went to a studio in Brisbane that's now called Sunshine Studios. It was a 24-track studio we just found in the directory. We didn't know anyone that had done any recordings. Now, it's easier to put out a CD. Records were harder to put out, it was a more difficult process and people didn't record as much. There weren't as many studios and we didn't know anyone that had actually ever been in a studio to recommend us one.

Did you have friends that were in bands?

When we started, no one. We didn't know anyone in bands. We soon met people at gigs and met other bands, but when Grant and I started, we didn't know anyone in bands. We only met other bands and musicians through playing.

What was the studio like? What was the experience?

It was a good experience. It was sort of doing a lit-

tle bit of country and jingles. The Saints had recorded their first album there... I don't know if you've ever heard of a band called the Saints.

Oh, yeah, I like that band.

They recorded their single there.

"I'm Stranded?"

"I'm Stranded" was recorded there, but we didn't know that!

That's great!

We just had an engineer [Colin Bloxsom] and we were in and out in like four hours. Recording and mixing.

Was that just the first single?

We were overwhelmingly happy, you know it's the first time we had ever played with headphones on, it's the first time we ever played and went back and heard our music over big speakers. It's a very overwhelming experience. It's a wonderful experience. It's an experience that you never forget. It was not a big room, but it was big enough, it was a one-room studio where you're paneled off from the control room so it's

just two rooms, but the desk was quite good and they had a decent mic collection. The guy that recorded us was a hippie guy, and hippie guys in the '70s, most times, knew what they were doing, know what I mean? It could have been a lot worse. We could have had some hideous rock guy or some guy that wanted to turn us into a top 40 band. We walked in off the streets, had money to pay for the session, and he was good. He actually engineered our first three sessions because we went back to the same studio. We went back in October, '78 and we recorded a song called "The Sound of Rain" which is on *The Lost Album* and then we went back and recorded "People Say", which was our second single. We did all of those at the same studio using the same engineer and then, many years later in 1992, I went back to Brisbane after recording my first solo album in Hansa Studios in Germany.

The one you did with Mick Harvey?

Yeah. It was a huge big studio in Berlin. You know, Bowie did *Low* and *Heroes* there and Iggy Pop did *Lust for*

Life. After I was in there, U2 went in there and did *Achtung Baby*. Very famous studio. After that I went back to my hometown in 1992. I went back to the same studio and it hadn't moved and it was the same desk that I recorded my second solo album, *Calling From a Country Phone*. It was a little bit like Sun. I always imagined it was a little bit like those studios that Buddy Holly did his first recording... you know, sort of a small studio, come in and do a bit of country, we do jingles and it's not the best gear but it's got a certain sort of little funkiness about it.

Those things sound good too. For a very young band that you were at that stage they don't sound like you were being dragged along in the wrong direction; it just sounds like you sounded.

Exactly. Not a particularly polished sound but almost a funky sound.

The other songs that are on the lost album are 2-track recordings in your bedroom or something. Did you have a friend that brought a deck over or something like that?

Yeah, exactly. It was a little mixer on cassette and he had microphones. He was a friend who had been in a studio and it was really, "Wham-bam" you were on the mat. This was done in my bedroom where we used to practice and write all of the songs. It was like having a friend come over and just go, "Hey, I'm gonna tape. Just set up, I'm gonna tape your whole set." Which was really good, for a songwriter like myself, to hear back all of the songs I'd written. I just got to that one step removed that was really nice and I've always liked that way of recording. Just sort of playing live.

I've heard there were some other bootlegs or something of even more early stuff that was unreleased.

There's a bootleg record as well, that our record label put out and that was put out extensively in the states and it was quite embarrassing because it was like our first album, which is not particularly strong anyway and we were so hungry, this is fast-forwarding to 1980 or 1981 but we were doing demos for our album and we recorded the album in July and we threw a number of songs we didn't put on the album and so he sort of had this other recording in a way. It was all just done in one day. It was done in a different studio in Brisbane. More of a demo studio.

Not very professional? After that, you worked with Tony Cohen in Australia.

He did *Send Me a Lullaby*, our first album. When I went back to Brisbane to do the album back in Sunshine Studios in '92, Tony did that too. So I went back to my first day at the studio and I went back to my first ever producer.

How did you hook up with Tony?

He did those early '80s Missing Link records. Tony was doing everybody. Tony did the Birthday Party, and Birthday Party were on this label too, and so Tony was the only guy seemingly under the age of 30 in Australia who was adventurous in the recording studio and was sympathetic. He was very good also. So Tony made a lot of records and recorded the Birthday Party and we had heard what Tony had done with them so we were happy to work with Tony.

You were songwriters and the focus of the band. Through the '80s, one of the most horrible recording eras that I can think of, you managed to maintain a pretty good natural sound. You kept things down-to-earth sounding, like a real record, not using big huge gated drums or terrible things that were popular at the moment. And to that end, it's only a handful of producers, like John Brand and Richard Preston that you used quite a bit. How did you hook up with them in the first place?

Very good point you've made which not many people realize, and I appreciate you making that observation.

The records hold up now.

Yeah, because it's true! And everything you've said about the '80s... don't forget we were in London which was where some of the most hideous crimes that were ever committed to recording. We could have easily turned into the Thompson Twins. But John Brand... we were in London in 1982, signed to Rough Trade records, who were a great label at the time, and they picked us up after the first album, after working with Tony Cohen engineering. And we came up to London. This was gonna be our big album and we were not happy with our first album, we didn't particularly like it. But somehow we got a deal out of it. So we were very much, "We've got to make a great second album". And we really wanted to. John had worked with a lot of Virgin records, in the late '80s, had done a lot of engineering on, I can't remember the groups, but it was a time of the Simple Minds, XTC, that whole sort of Virgin records in the late '70s, when they were a big label. And John had got tired of that and wanted to produce and he made a quite astounding jump. He just went to the biggest indie and the most well-known indie in town, Rough Trade and said, "Hey, I'm a commercial engineer..." He used to work at the Manor, where all the stuff was done up in Oxford in a huge, big studio. And he was just working with all the budgets that were fifty thousand pounds, a hundred thousand pounds and he said to Rough Trade, "You know, I'm commercial, I've worked with Virgin, I've worked in big studios, I wanna produce, I'd like to work with some bands and with you." and they played him some stuff and the first album that he did was an Aztec Camera album. And we were friends with Roddy [Frame of Aztec Camera] and everything and then they said, "Well, the Go-Betweens are gonna make a record, do you want to do them too?" And he came to one of our practice sessions, liked what he heard and so John did us too [*Before Hollywood*]. He had this deal where we went down to this place called ICC, down in Eastbourne, which is a Christian studio and in a way it was a little bit like Sunshine... a funky one-room, not too big control room, I can't remember what desk, good mic collection and really cheap, like two thousand quid a week, like four thousand dollars a week. We did the album there and he was great. He was the first person, ever, who worked, when we were rehearsing, walked into our rehearsal room and taped us, and then came back the next day and had the whole songs written out.

Charted out?

Yeah. Completely. Like this one song, there's an eight bar introduction on it, okay, which was really great, like we went, "Uh huh, so this is what he just does." You know, like Tony never did that. We had never done that on our singles, obviously. And John was very pro. It was the underground weird band with the slightly commercial producer, and somehow we made him sound interesting and he made us sound better than we were in a way. It was a nice marriage.

You enjoyed working with him?

On that album, yeah.

You worked with him after that too.

On the next album.

Was that *Spring Hill Fair*?

Yeah. It was not so... we couldn't decide, and had a larger budget and John went back to his old ways, we were suddenly in SSL, huge big studio-land. He was like, "Now we're going to make a proper record." and I was like, "Our last record was very proper and was very great." It had worked out the first time and then we went down and then we spent a week of him trying to gate the drums and set click tracks. The first and second albums, there's no clicks. It was just really natural, this is why this record stands up, you know, it's all Hammond organs, acoustic guitars, real drums and it's really super, it's really tight but it's a hundred percent natural and it just comes out of it.

It's a standard, real sound.

He must have started to smell the Top 40 and he sort of gets back to his Virgin background more.

Was that a struggle?

Yeah, huge.

How was Lindy [Morrison, the band's long-time drummer] with that sort of thing? Was she hating having to play with the clicks?

Yes, she was. It was just John and us at the studio and we spent the first week just messing around with drums. Now that I look back on it, we almost just told him to go away, but we were down in the south of France where John had booked this studio. The studio was owned by a guy named Jacque Lucier, who is very famous in Europe. He made these contemporary versions of Bach that sold by the truckload and he built the studio down in Provence, down in southern France. He'd built a studio in his chateau and he had his own vineyard. So we're down there drinking his wine but it kind of went into a storm. There was a breakdown, there would be John on the phone to London with the manuals out, and we're sitting there going, "We should be recording..." There was a French guy who was co-engineering and we should have just told John to go away and just work with the French guy.

It feels like such a drastic move, at that stage of the game. I'm sure that's hard.

Between those records we recorded some demos. We went into a small studio in London in 1983 and we did some demos because we thought we were going to do the next record on Rough Trade. We went to a studio called Pathway, which is where Elvis Costello did his first album, and it's a very, very funky 8-track in London. Great little 8-track and we met Richard Preston who was the house engineer and these demos sounded really good. After the fiasco with John, on *Spring Hill Fair*, we just went, "Let's go back to Richard" who we really enjoyed working with and so for our next album we wanted to go back to basics and none of this bullshit.

Like click tracks?

Yeah. All of that, we just decided to just skip.

I just thought that was funny because when I first started buying all of your records I always thought that maybe *Spring Hill Fair* was a later record than it was, because of the sound of it. When I figured out the chronology of it I thought that was curious and now it totally makes sense.

We sort of went back to a more smaller, funkier studio in London. We went back to acoustic guitars, vibraphones, piano, accordions. This was in late 1985.

Do you feel that, in any way, instrumentation-wise and in the way that you were looking at it that it was a reaction to any other stuff that was going on at the time... or was it more your instinct that made records like what you had listened to?

It was more instinct. It wasn't "Everyone is making synthetic, bing boingy records" that we had to do, we were just following our instincts and we were following the things that we loved.

You think of records that you always liked.

Yeah. And I can't begin to tell you what we would have been listening to.

I always thought of things like, you were saying, that it was possibly Television.

Ah, shit yeah.

Or your voice was the first I had ever heard that reminded me of that.

Yeah.

Or even in some ways things like, you know, Dylan or The Band and stuff like that kind of stuff.

That's exactly what we we're listening to.

Just some things that had a natural feel. You listened to The Band and those guys wouldn't blast it and they sound great.

Yeah, definitely.

So you did *Liberty Belle and the Black Diamond Express* and what was after that?

Tallulah.

Were those both with Richard?

Didn't Craig Leon do a little bit for it.

Yeah. They were not happy sessions for me at all and not for, in general, the band. The problem was *Liberty Belle...* went so well, everyone went, "Hit single time", okay? And we worked with Craig and at Tony Visconti's studio called Good Earth in Soho in London. Craig and Cassell [Webb] had just done Zodiac Mindwarp with a remake of "Spirit in the Sky".

I remember that.

And it went to number one and so they were hot. We met them and Cassell had played tambourine in the Seeds, Craig had done the first Ramones album and the first Blondie album and they're really nice people and they had great pedigrees and they're in London, but Craig was just so... he played keyboards and they were just so fixated on a hit record and that goal. I mean, we paid them the money to do what they wanted to do, but it was soulless. And also, they didn't get us the hit and we sort of looked into that void and it was not something that we wanted to do.

To pursue it?

No.

Those songs they did were shimmery.

It was sort of like, you know, one person doing their bit for eight hours while the rest of the band sat around in the back room and the next day. It took something like nine days to do two tracks. It was just ridiculous.

After that was the "final" album *16 Lover's Lane*. You did that with Mark Wallis and it's a pretty slick album in retrospect. It's probably the slickest of the lot but it does work for you well.

It works great. He was English. We met him when he was a remix specialist. He remixed some of *Tallulah* and we were just astounded with what he had done and so when we were going to make the last one, we thought we should get him and we wanted to do it in Australia. He came down to a studio called 3.0.1. which is a very famous Australian studio. They had an SSL desk but a monster live room, good gear but SSL, and he had just done the Talking Heads on their *Naked* album. You'll find his name on whatever U2 album that they made around then.

The name sounds familiar but I wasn't sure.

He was great. Very English, very meticulous. We spent eight weeks on the record which is an eternity for us. But somehow his English meticulousness and his thoroughness, normally that can kill songs if the songs are not great and sometimes, the English groups are not great songwriters [remember, we're not talking about the 60s]. The records sound good but we gave him ten great songs and so he could fuel and craft it and weave around and it worked. It's a record whose estimation has gone up in my mind over time and in a lot of places it's regarded as our best album, which I don't think is true.

I talked to somebody else who is a big fan of the Go-Betweens and I said, "You know, I'm gonna ask them how they

were able to hold it together" and they were like, "Yeah, even the last album [which didn't sound right to them] still had amazing songs on it. It's still a great record." So the songs are always the things that survive.**

You see, the thing was, everyone wanted him to go down. Our management especially. He had worked with U2, he had worked with these other groups and it was like, "Go make them a rock record." And so he came back with a lot of acoustic guitar, it's really soft and it was like, "What happened?" And Mark just said, they were the songs and that was the sound that the songs needed and so it worked out. It's very slick, it's very smooth and the next one that we were going to make before we broke up, well, the one I wanted to make was a reaction against that. We were going to go down and make an album with Tony Cohen.

So with the band breaking up you started your solo career. The first record, *Danger in the Past*, sounds great. That's a Mick Harvey production for sure. There's so much reverb on that record which is usually something like an '80s thing, a real dated factor. But that record still sounds really great. Was that natural reverb from that studio?

Yeah. A lot of it is and that record was very much the direction that I wanted to go in, especially with the Go-Betweens. That was where I wanted to move to, where we're playing together in a big room with a good desk, a good engineer and people standing around playing. I always did like it. We did that record in 12 days. The recording room is an old ballroom and so you're talking aircraft hangar size. This place is so big that they also hold gigs there very occasionally on this stage where you could fit an enormous band with ceilings that are 100 to 200 feet high. I went, "This is the room!" and we were just a three piece, myself on guitar, Mick Harvey on bass and Thomas Wydler, of the Bad Seeds, playing drums and we would just sit up in this room just playing, with Victor Van Vugt engineering, a New disk with microphones and that was the whole deal. My philosophy is you don't need time, if everything you're recording sounds great then you spend so much less time fixing it up. If it goes good down to tape, every chord and every sound is good, then that's recording your way. And I loved the sound of that record and don't think there was much reverb coming from the desk. I think a lot of it was in the room.

I always listened to that, thinking that it couldn't be digital reverb it wouldn't have sounded that good.

No. It's the room.

It's a beautiful sound, it's really spacious yet it doesn't sound like giant, huge stadium rock or something. It's very spacious and draws you in.

Spacious. It's loud, it comes to you but because it's analog there's that softness that you can lean into. It not like that hard-edged, slapping around the face type of sound. I really love the sound of that. We recorded it in 1990. When the Go-Betweens had been on tour in Berlin in '87 I found out about the studio because Bowie and Iggy had recorded there and I just thought I would come down and have a look. I got in a cab and I went down and I just went, "I'll come back here one day." It amazed me and then two and a half years later the band had broken up, I'm suddenly living in Germany and it was like, "Let's go to Hansa." A strange prophesy came true.

Did you enjoy working with Mick Harvey?

Yeah. Mick's great. I love Mick's philosophy of recording and I just agree with him and I think he's fantastic. I love the way he plays instruments. He's a very good piano player... I love the way he plays drums. He's just someone you could give a trumpet and somehow he'd play it and maybe do one little thing on the record and it'd be great. He's just great.

And you agree with the way he records?

Towards the end of the Go-Betweens I was getting into the Nick Cave and the Bad Seeds records, the way they were sounding, and they were getting all of these old keyboards and everything sounded natural. I was just going, "This is the way I want us to sound". I don't want to make a Nick Cave and the Bad Seeds record obviously, with Nick's lyrical thrust and everything like that, but the sound of his records... I wanted the Go-Betweens to approach recording like the way the Bad Seeds do it. And I thought that we were also a band that could do it. And the Bad Seeds record, the sound of it and the way they were recorded lies a lot in the hands of Mick Harvey, definitely, especially at that stage in the '80s.

That came out really great. The record I don't have, your second solo album [Calling from a Country Phone], where did you record that?

It was at Sunshine. That was going back to Brisbane, the one I did with Tony Cohen. I just wanted to go back to my hometown and record after the big Berlin thing. The material that I was writing just lead me in this direction, I just wanted to go back to a studio that did jingles. That might do the odd country act. I wanted to get back to that. In my personal life, my wife and I wanted to move back to my hometown and I started to go out to venues and look at musicians in my hometown and I made that type of record.

Are you happy with that one?

I am. The songs probably aren't as good. The songs probably aren't as strong as on Danger in the Past. I like the sound of it. It's a smaller, homey sound. It's like a Neve desk and a small recording room. It's a little more boxy which is the sound I wanted to go for. I didn't want to make another big record. The sound of the record is more important to me. I wanted to go for lo-fi later on. It's the way I wanted to go. I wanted to make more Brisbane, let's-put-a-couple-of-mics-up-around-a-lounge room record. More casual, a little bit more time. I should have followed my convictions a little bit more. There's a record of mine that

I produced, I did that. I should have maybe of gone a little bit more funkier. I like it. There's sort of a dark star of everything that I'd gotten.

Then there was Warm Nights, that last record, with Edwyn Collins producing, right?

He is a complete and utter studio sound obsessive. He buys gear on the road, like when he's on the road he goes to vintage sound shops. And buys things that he takes back to his studio. You know, like, the record company people are trying to get him to do interviews and he goes off and buys gear. He's got a 16-track Neve that he bought years ago for a ridiculous price that people would now pay in the millions. He's got a great microphone collection.

You did the whole record on his personal studio?

It was the first record that he had done in the studio. I just wanted to go for more rhythmic sound, a lot more muddy sort of "Creedencey". I was listening to a lot more Atlantic records like the late '60s, early '70s. Just two mics on the drums and a really warm bass.

The title sounds like the sound of the record. I always think of that one as being a fuzzy warm record.

Edwyn's always been a big Al Green fan and he's listened to and appreciates a lot more 70s black music than I have. It's a lot more swampy and a lot of it we just did as a three-piece like the drums, bass and guitar. We kept everything like most of those tracks were just the three of us playing and then we'd come in and we'd overdub really lightly. I really like that record. It's my favorite... I have to say Danger in the Past is my second favorite.

One of the reasons I thought about doing the interview is that the Go-Betweens records and your records had a real different feel to them.

Yeah, my three albums of original material have been Berlin, Brisbane and London and it's been Mick Harvey, myself, Edwyn Collins producing. With records it's really like casting to me, the songs start to get a feel. I want to talk about form. I can imagine going down to Tucson, there's a feel in that Calexico album and it's just amazing. You just get into it. You know the Band albums that you were talking about. You just get into a feeling and you've just got to follow it. Sometimes you might want to make an '80s digital gated drum-type record.

It's ironic.

Now it's ironic. Edwyn and I will be recording those drums and Edwyn will just go "bum, bum, bum" and he'll get the gated drum sound just for a joke. He is really lucky because when his studio opened, people would come in, like the big producers around town would go in and go, "What the fuck is going on here? We're never gonna bring anything in here." But the good thing about is he had earned enough money off "A Girl Like You." He built the studio he wanted to build and so he doesn't have to buy all the latest toys.

To sell the studio.

Yeah, to sell the studio. Because he doesn't need anyone else to come in. His studio reminds me a lot of Lee "Scratch" Perry with his studio in the 70s. It's exactly the sort of thing it is and it's personal. It's like, "This is the sound of the studio and not fishing for top 40 acts. Not fishing for some sort of generic indie rock thing. This is the way I want my records to sound" and it's a very personalized thing and that's what I love about what he does.

I like that. It had a great feel. How long did you spend on that?

It was actually quite long. It took about six weeks but he was still involved with the promotional period of "A Girl like You". This was still going on. And so, there'd be things like him taking two days off to go to Sweden and then he'd come back and then "This TV show wants you..."

A lot of interruptions while you were trying to work on it.

And it was the first album he did so when I walked into the studio on the first day, he had a soldering iron and was on the ground. I was like, "Okay, alright, we're not gonna be getting sounds in the first two hours." But that's what's great about Edwyn, he's very much a producer/engineer and he's very much out there on his hands and knees putting the mics beside the Fender speakers. He's very hands-on.

The only other solo record is the covers record which you produced. Was that done with Tony Cohen?

No. That was done at a studio, a good studio down in Melbourne. The record I'm not that keen about.

It's not your songs, first off, you know. I think some of them were great, I think the Grant Hart cover is one of my favorites.

Yeah, that's good. There's a few good things on it, but I hadn't written any songs for a long time and there were a lot of songs from around 1989-90 and I recorded the album in 1994 so it was already past the period that I was covering.

You were infatuated with these songs?

Yeah. It was about five years old, I don't know what I was doing. It was one of those things to start things off that I shouldn't have done.

The title is from Jonathan Richman. But you didn't do that song on there.

No, no. I tried to do one of Jonathan songs but I wracked my brain for months trying to think of songs and I wanted to do a song of his called "Important in Your Life" because it was like a great song. ⊛

Eric "Roscoe" Ambel

Eric Ambel started his professional career writing and playing guitar as a **Blackheart** and a **Del-Lord.** Now a producer and musician, he has worked with many great artists including **Nils Lofgren**, **Mojo Nixon**, **Steve Wynn**, **Blood Oranges**, **Blue Mountain**, **Syd Straw**, **Simon and the Bar Sinisters**, and **Go To Blazes.** He keeps busy producing records out of 33 1/3 Recording Studios in Brooklyn, which is housed in a turn-of-the-century bank building with 2000 sq. ft. and 20' ceilings. The studio is based around a vintage Neve console, modern tube and discrete Class A analog recording gear, and an extensive collection of vintage guitar amplifiers and keyboards. In his spare time, he runs two clubs in NYC and Raleigh, NC, called 'The Lakeside Lounge.' Whew, what a busy guy! I met up with "Roscoe" in his amazingly-quiet East Village apartment where he lives with his wife, Mary Lee Kortes (whom he also produces) and his soon-to-be-setup mini studio...

interview and photo
by **Hilary Johnson**

What
is your role as far as the technical aspects of recording go?

Most of the records that I produce I don't engineer. I'm pretty involved in the mix. I've worked with several people over the years... I really believe in producer and engineer being two separate jobs and if one guy is doing both of those things that one of those jobs is suffering. And I work with bands... I really love bands... and when you work with bands, it's not so much... sitting in there with one person overdubbing all the time. That kind of thing a guy could be engineering and producing but what my specialty is... I like to

work with bands, I really respect bands. I think the way most record companies... ya know, they go to see a band play and they love the band, then they sign the band and they put the band in a recording studio with a guy who starts overdubbing them one at a time. It really reminds me of the police interrogation. Where the three kids get arrested for writing graffitti on a wall and they take 'em into an individual room, one at a time and hopefully their stories will match up. That's what the overdub process reminds me of. "Didn't you fall in love with this band because you saw them play and sing at the same time?!" It's really hard for me to understand. That answer's

probably pretty wide and all over the place... I learned about engineering, I think the way a lot of people do from having a 4-track and breaking it down to the basic elements of recording which are, to me, EQ, compression, delay and reverb and putting the signal on tape. If a person can learn those things then you've pretty much demystified the whole process. And everything comes from there.

Did you learn about the technical aspects of recording when you were in the studio as a musician with the Del-Lords in the '80s?

A little bit... I was in Joan Jett and the Blackhearts and then the Del-Lords, and being in bands in the '80s it was kinda the dark years of recording guitars. There's, uh...

...a lot of buried guitar...

...yeah... like here we were with the major label record deal and we're in there, in an expensive studio in LA and our money is being used by some engineer who's trying to figure out how to run the big Lexicon 240 whatever and I really vowed that I would someday be in charge of this thing so that wouldn't happen to me or the people I was working with.

So, it was you, the band, and an engineer, no producer?

No, there was a producer. He was excited about that big Lexicon box too.

How did you get hooked up with the producers that you worked with in the '80s?

With the Del-Lords, our first record was made with this guy, Lou Whitney, from the band called The Morells which became The Skeletons, and I still work with him to this day. This guy has a studio in Springfield, Missouri [The Studio]. His band backs a lot of people, like they back Syd Straw and Dave Alvin and Jonathan Richman, myself...a lot of different people on their solo records. That guy did the first [Del-Lords] record then the next couple we did with Neil Geraldo, who's Pat Benatar's husband and producer/guitar player. Great guy... something that I'll say fairly often is,"The rule is there is no rule". One of the subheadings under that is, "What worked for the last guy may not work for the next guy". He was applying what he was doing with [Pat] to us. In hindsight I don't think it was the best way to deal with a rock band.

So how did you start producing?

In the '80s I started seeing some bands around here. There was an afterhours bar called No Se No down on Rivington St... an unlicensed place... and the Del-Lords were already kinda happening, we had a coupla records out, and I started seeing these young bands and following some advice from Lou Whitney... if you got a band and you wanna record, one of the most basic things that you could do is find somebody who's already done it to help you. I'd already been 4-trackin' at home and I just knew that I could help. I have a background in music in that I took piano lessons as a kid and I played trumpet from 5th grade all the way through college at the University of Wyoming. At the same time I taught myself guitar. There's a lot of skills that, even coming out of the punk rock era when training was not so groovy, the training that I received helped me a lot in being able to help bands with their arrangements and hooking up harmonies and stuff. So I started producing some of these bands from No Se No like the World Famous Bluejays and The Clintons. My own personal goal was to try to make the bands sound better than they were and make the recordings sound like it cost a lot more than it did. Make the bands sound better with them doing everything, not with... me or somebody else playing everything.

What did you grow up listening to?

Well, I will be 42, I'm of that era where... you have to have graduated from high school somewhere in between '74 and '76... Those are the only people that will tell you that they really like Grand Funk. When I grew up it was AM radio in Chicago so you had WLS and WCFL and... it would be like The Stones and The Kinks and The Who and The Beatles, and if one song sucked you'd just punch the button and go to the next station. So it was a lot of those really great records, that sort of AM radio and the beginning of FM... I think Creedence was one of the first bands that you could actually, without a lot of trickery... make yourself sound like... The Grand Funk thing is kinda funny, because Grand Funk were... I mean, it's a joke to say they were an American band but they were an American band

when this English thing was really dominating. And they were kinda like a hard rock Creedence. They were like a hard rock band, but you could... successfully play their songs and sound like them. It was exciting.

So from listening to that how did you get into the whole roots rock revival of the '80s?

That was real simple. The stuff that I like and the stuff that I still like... I don't know about roots or country or blues or anything, but most of the songs that I like and most of the bands that I work with - their songwriting takes place on the guitar. And there's natural stuff that comes from writing songs on the guitar. Like when I was a kid and you're listening to The Beatles, when The Beatles went from their guitar songs to the piano songs... with the descending bass note... that to me is when it got not-so rock and roll. So if there's any generalization, that would be it. I really love the guitar. Also in the '80s when you had people playing synthesizers and stuff... it's so same-y sounding. But you can... plug a Les Paul in a Marshall and have ten people play it and it'll sound different...and that's not the case with the electric keyboard really. That's why I really love the guitar and what it can do.

Who are some people that you're listening to now?

Well, I work on music a lot. I work with bands and the producer job, it's a very difficult job. Sometimes I don't get to listen to enough music.

What were the last five CDs you bought?

Well, I got the new Tom Petty record and I... went out looking for the new Tom Waits record but they didn't have it so I bought myself a copy of T-Rex *Electric Warrior* which I didn't have on CD - I bought it when it was new when I was in junior high but I really like that. I was really surprised, I liked the new Richard Buckner *Since* -I think it's called... Oh! And I love this Houndog record! Have you heard that? David Hidalgo and the guy from Canned Heat... Mike I think his name is... [Mike Halby] It's really creepy... it sounds like Don & Dewey and Jimmy Reed only slowed down. I think David Hidalgo is probably the most musical guy of my generation... It's really good, it's really wacked out. He's got like an 8-track cassette rig... the Fostex version of my old rig which is a Tascam 688. I think that they did this thing on a cassette machine.

...lot of tape hiss?

Yeah, and slowed down stuff. They have their picture in what looks to be a real control room, but I think they're fakin' us out! And I've just recently been working on this apartment, my wife and I moved in here and I just recently set up my spot and I've listened to more music in the last week than I have in the last year.

What speakers are you using to listen to new stuff?

It's funny. People complain about Yamaha NS-10's. I think that they're among the best home stereo speakers. They really do sound great. And then I bought myself these little cheap Radio Shack Optimus deals for my desk. The Optimus 3 or Pro 33 or something. I got 'em on my desk and I've just been enjoying it like crazy!

Not a lot of low end?

Well, the low end is coming from the floor. I don't have subs. I recently had a positive experience with subs. I mixed the Bottle Rockets record with this guy Paul Ebersold in Memphis at Ardent. Ardent is a big facility, been there for a long time. They got some really nice rooms. Every one of their rooms has Yamaha NS-10's and a Yamaha powered consumer subwoofer. And I'm telling you the Yamahas, if they aren't trying to do what they can't do, which is reproduce below 60 or 80, if they're not trying to go down there, they sounded fantastic! I couldn't believe it. I mean I came in there and this guy started playing me this stuff and I thought the bigs were on, and it was the Yamahas with the powered sub.

Did the sub have a crossover in it?

Yeah, it has a crossover and basically the only controls on this thing. It was very bonehead-friendly, which is why we're talking to *Tape Op*. It had just volume and the crossover frequencies so you could pick. And at Ardent they had it crossed over at 80 and you just dial in enough volume.

What do you think one of those things runs for?

Not very much. I think it's probably under 500 bucks. I got the Yamahas at home 10 or 15 years ago because I wanted to get my ears acclamated to the way that I would be listening all the time anyway.

...other than room acoustics...

Yeah, they don't really sound great until they're turned way up and that can wear you down.

Do you listen to yours loud or low?

At home? Not that loud. In the studio, whatever it takes for the inspiration to happen.

How do you approach recording conceptually? Sonically? Do artists approach you? Do you approach them? Or both?

Sometimes it's both. Say you're in studio and there's a band playing. In there, you've got the band in which there's a songwriter guy, there's a hot musician guy, there's the rhythm section. Then in the studio there's the engineer, and the producer and then there also might be some hot side guy that's brought in. I have sat in everyone's chair and hopefully I can help, because of my understanding of everyone's different role, hopefully I can help everyone to be doing their best. My favorite producers don't necessarily have a sound. They help the band get THEIR sound. Every band is different. Pre-production is of paramount importance. Which really means going through the songs and picking the songs. That's an A&R guy's job sort of by definition, but there's not too many of them that actually do it anymore.

Do you go to rehearsals?

Oh yeah, absolutely. I'm not making huge budget records and if there was a huge budget, you don't want to waste time in the studio. There's something about getting everyone together and now is the time. I think that those bands that go way overboard and spend days and days and days...

In terms of sonically approaching a record... We know the answer to this question, but do you prefer recording to analog or digital?

I don't think digital is ready yet. But sonically the thing is that a lot of times when I'm working with bands, their rigs are touring rigs and a lot of my sound or what I try to help a band with is I have a lot of equipment myself, like I have a lot of good guitar amps and I have most of the basic food groups of guitars - I have a great tele and I have a great Les Paul with P-90s because I've been a guitar player for most of my life so a lot of it in the pre-production is maybe looking at the guy's gear and making sure that there's a little money in the budget to get his guitar fixed or get some new tubes. There's a saying that goes "shit in, shit out" and that's pretty realistic. "How do you get a good guitar sound?" You get a good guitar, that's how.

And a good player...

Yeah. But the analog/digital thing. I've had positive experiences with digital. Sometimes when I'm out at Lou Whitney's place in Springfield, Missouri. He's got one of those big format dig machines, like the early Sony 3324-S which is a 24-track digital machine. And I'll cut the band on 2" 16-track analog and we don't listen to that tape more than twice. Cut the band, if that's the take then we dump it into the dig. On those big format dig machines, I've heard some pretty thrilling stuff. Say you record background vocals on a big format dig machine, when you're mixing, it's great to have tracks that there's nothing there and then the singing comes out. I mean that is positive. I produced a Nils Lofgren record in '92 and for part of that record we went out to Neil Young's place and did some work with him and I learned a lot about dig out there. Even though he will come out and talk against consumer digital, at the time when I was out there in '92, he didn't have an analog tape recorder in the place. He had the big dig machines and I think the best way to do dig is you have to put that sound down finished the first time you ever do it. You can't count on going back to EQ or compress the thing, you really have to run it through all really good gadgets and put it down finished the first time. You gotta get it how you like it. Sometimes I'll talk about the "kneerub" - analog gives you "kneerub." Like they have these bars in New Orleans, they're not really strip clubs, but you go in there and some girl sits next to you and [says], "Would you buy me a drink?" and these girls are in there drinking

these $9 champagne cocktails which is just champagne and 7-Up. I went and did that one time - I went in there and bought the girl a drink, my friend was there, and we bought 'em another drink. We did get something out of it. After the second drink we got a little "kneerub." It was like, "Oh! that's cool, one more drink and I'm out of my 20 bucks that I had with me but that was fun." I believe that [with] analog you can get more than you give, which is beautiful. And there's some tape that I really like. I used to like that 3M tape then they stopped making it. I had the opportunity one time to listen to the difference of a couple different kinds of tape, just printing their noise and I really liked the BASF tape - the 900. I'm not gonna buy any tape that changes their name like this [rattles my 'Ampex vs. Quantegy' DAT case]. That was the first name in tape! And now that Quantegy... I mean, "Where did you come up with that name? Did your wife come home and tell you you were supposed to change the name of the company or something?" I don't get it. I really don't get it. But, just like that magic combination of the Les Paul and the Marshall, I met these BASF guys and they have this thing - and it might be of interest to your readers, a lot of people that have an old 8-track Tascam - BASF sells their own formulation of the 468 which was the first hot tape in the '70s and what it is it's a reissue formulation from the AGFA 468. Just like the Les Paul works with the Marshall, that 468 works with that ATR 102 - the 1/2 track tape machine - so good that when I'm using that tape machine with that tape and I'm mixing, the whole reason I'm mixing is so I can get done and listen how great it's gonna sound when it comes back off of that 468. That is really something else.

My experience with AGFA is that it sheds.

It's funny how people will talk about some of these things that were corrected. Like Neotek. They built a console around 1985 for one year that had a shitload of bad switches in it. And it's taken them all this time for people to kind of forgive them. It was only one year, and it was only twenty consoles, but it was bad. And that AGFA thing, people talk about that but I think that BASF 468 is really, really cool.

Have you used the new Quantegy Red, whatever that number is?

GP9. Yeah, somebody tried to get me into that. I just don't like the idea that they changed their name. But, if you could get one reel of that stuff, which they seem to be giving away to try to get people hooked on it, the reel is red and it looks really cool and you could use it as a take-up reel!

Tape Op readers probably won't have exposure to the nice 48 dig machines. If you had to cut costs, where would it be? Would it be digital vs. analog? Would it be in the studio? Would it be on time spent?

Well, it's funny. I've never used one of those big 48 machines. My friend who has the 24-track had to do that in a market where people were calling up saying that they WANTED to record digital. "Oh, you're not digital?" Because they just thought that it was better and actually for Lou on that 3324-S, he does a whole album project on one reel of tape, they're 60 minutes and it costs $50. For cutting costs, I think the best, biggest cost cutter is to do some pre-production. And even if you're recording your own band, you have to kind of have a plan before you go into the studio. Even if it's your own studio, you have to have your time mapped out. "Okay, we're gonna spend this much time" and I think for a band most times, if somebody is the producer because you're talking about a group of people working together. Somebody needs to be in charge. Somebody. And if you have that meeting before you start, that can save you a lot of money. To really have a plan before you start. It's unbelievable. When I hear horror stories from people about going over budget or this or that it's like, "Well, you didn't even have a plan when you started."

As a musician do you think pre-production, in terms of doing demos, getting them on tape in any format; 4-track, or an 8-track digital DA88 kind of setup or something like that, do you think that is valuable or do you think it's more important to spend time talking and rehearsing?

When I work with bands, by the time I've decided to do the project, I already know that they're a great band. I've seen them play. My experience with demos is when I'm producing a record. I never ask the band to do band demos. By the time that we've decided that we're gonna work together, then, like say, with The Bottle Rockets, Brian Henneman is the main singer guy but everybody writes so he'll make a boombox tape for me. He'll get the songs from everybody and he'll make a solo acoustic tape of every single song. The solo thing is the most difficult thing to do but it really lets you know when a song is finished. If you got a song, if you can't play it solo then I might argue that you don't have a song. And also for me, I'm gonna do both, I'm gonna do rehearsals also, bu for me, if I sit around and listen to that solo tap a bunch of times, I might come up with an ide that no one would have thought of if we were jus tweaking their existing arrangement. The othe thing is that it's dangerous to record. You record demo on your 8-track or something, you might d the greatest version of that song ever and then could be very difficult to get it back. Now that kind of the beauty of the ADAT thing is that eve once in a while somebody does do somethin usable, it's in a usable format. For the songwriti demos, what I usually do is I don't play everythir myself on a record, but I like to at home, on my home writing rig, I like to completely overindulge myself and put five guitar parts on there so I can take it to the band and break it down and just play the best part through the song.

What do you have as your home setup?

Well, I had the Tascam 688 and I had various bits of outboard gear that is now in my pro studio. I had sort of a writing rig and right now I'm really close to finish the spot but really what I want to get is the smallest portable thing that I can get. So I think I'm gonna get myself one of those VS-1680 things.

The Roland?

Yep. And a pair of little powered speakers, and one keyboard that has all the rest of the sounds in it and that's a pretty powerful rig right there. With my little computer and I haven't really used one so much but I might, in keeping with the way I feel about digital, if I brought home a pair of Telefunkens and the Manley LA-2A, I'd be putting it down just fine. I hope to be sitting there doing that in three weeks.

What software do you have in the computer? Is it sequencer software?

I don't have any sequencer software. I'm gonna need to get some. I used to have Performer.

You just had a Mac Classic or something in your old studio to run it?

Yeah, Mac Plus.

And I see that you had a patchbay. Was that definitely helpful?

Absolutely. If you don't have a patchbay, you don't have a studio. I'm older I can't like, get on my knees all the time. [A] patchbay is cool. It's not that expensive, takes a little time. When you have somebody over and you're feeling like you've gotta impress 'em when you can go [insert patchbay sounds here] "boop boop boop" it's very good. Albert Caiati helped me wire up my old studio. It was really great to have that patchbay in there.

Other than your own material, what else are you going to be working on by the end of the millenium?

I'm looking at some projects. I usually do a few bigger records a year and then I might do some of my own stuff and I try to keep the local thing going too.

Are the local bands what inspired you to open The Lakeside Lounge(s), here in New York and also in Raleigh?

Yeah, My partner, Jim Marshall "The Hound", had a radio show on WFMU for over ten years and he manages this band The Pristeens now. We had helped a few bars, promoted events at different places and helped a few rock clubs in this area that are really big and well-known get going. Like my band was the first band ever to play at Brownies when it was just a little bar. I lived around the corner and I went in there after they opened and we started playing in the corner [of the club]. I

also helped the Mercury Lounge with the design of their stage. Also, I turned them on to the booking girl that STILL does the booking for both the Mercury and the Bowery [Ballroom]. And after helping these other people, we felt like we should just have our own joint. And then I really kind of approached the bar a lot like producing a record. One way to look at producing is if you can get rid of everything that sucks, you can have a great record. And I think the bar is a lot the same way. It's not a boast for me to say that I've been to a lot of bars in my life. From being on tour forever. So I wanted to have a place like that where the jukebox is kinda the star, where only one band plays one set a night. After playing CBGB and stuff, and having to organize a whole five band thing and then you get there and they've added another band and my manager who's trying to get me signed has taken four A&R people out to dinner and they're all there and it's all going on my tab and I got this band where I'm paying the guys and I'm paying the guy to drop the equipment off in the van and then by the time I go on an hour and a half late, all of these A&R guys, none of them saw me. That was kind of the last straw, I figured I'm gonna have my own bar and the one-band thing has really worked out well for us. We could have more business by having more than one band. I like it. One band. That way you go to see your friends play, when they're done you can hang out, you're not getting run out by the next band. Over at Arlene [Grocery] a lot of people get equipment stolen cuz there's so much stuff going. I like [Lakeside], it's a nice little place. I have the house equipment, because it's the right size. A guy who's playing gigs maybe doesn't have a small bass amp. Maybe they don't have a drumkit with a 20" bass drum but the Lakeside is quite hi-fi and it's because everything's matched. Vocals-only PA. That puts me right back in high school. That's why my lighting system is one red lightbulb. That was me in 1973 in the basement.

Do the bands that play there fit into the "alternative country" category?

Not always. If you had to categorize, which I don't like to cuz it is like putting someone in a box but this stuff is for sale and you have to put it in a box to sell it; I'd say that if you're gonna generalize about what we have at the Lakeside is that we have some of...the alternat[iv]e country action and we have some of the garage rock. That would be the circle I'd say.

Your publicist wrote on your discography that you were the "center of the East Coast and Southern 'scene' of musicians." How do you feel about that?

Oh, I don't know about that. I've been playing for a long time and I know a lot of people and I've played with people or done gigs with them and it's fun to help people even if I'm not producing your record if you are looking for a place that has

a 16-track machine with a 2" headstack. I think I do perform a resource kind of function for a lot of people and the bar has been helpful for us and for other people, like say if there was some band that I wanted to see and they couldn't get a gig, well, "I'll get ya a gig, c'mon up here and play." Or if we need a place to have a meeting, or also say there's friends of ours that are trying to get into CMJ [Music Seminar] and maybe they don't get accepted, "Well, you can play at the Lakeside." [I] try to help out.

And how do you think that those things are different from the whole mainstream-popular culture-record business-getting gigs kinda thing?

I don't know. I really don't know. But what it is is you like to have stuff that you can. Control is a word that kinda gets misused - stuff that you have yourself, you can optimize. Like I've got the Lakeside optimized for a certain thing. It's a nice small place. I've seen a lot of people in New York City - they have an idea and then they don't stick with it. All of a sudden they get sucked into doing something bigger than they really could do. The Lakeside is a really nice little formula, really nice. With the super-cool jukebox and the bandstand with the house equipment, photobooth, Steve Keene art on the walls. That's why when we did it with my friend in Raleigh it was pretty easy to boil it down to the essential ingredients and moving down there too.

Is there anything you'd like to add for *Tape Op* readers or anyone starting their own studio?

Starting your own studio. After you figure out how much you think it's gonna cost, double it. That's pretty standard. Sometimes when you read articles about studios, I know myself, that at some of these really big facilities, the quality of the people that are working there is really fantastic. Like at Ardent. Ardent is almost like when I first got to New York and there was Media Sound and Sigma and stuff. In those places, the assistants were totally overqualified. People did a lot of work to learn how to be an assistant and then nowadays with the engineering schools and people having their own home studio, they show up at the studio and they're ready to start punching in and telling the drummer to change his kick drum part and it's like, "You gotta slow down and try to learn and listen." And that was impressive when I was out at Ardent. Their assistants are full-blown engineers and it takes some time. Those recording schools, I think they're really good for a personn- not to learn about recording but to learn whether or not you want to pursue recording. Cuz you're not gonna learn how to do it from that school, but you could learn to if you wanted to... ☮

Photo by Larry Hirshowitz

Story by Larry Crane

Live Radio Engineering and More

How did you end up with [a] job at KCRW? What's th[e] university it associated with?

Many years ago our general mana[ger] walked in saying, "Hey, I have a visi[on] I want to take this tiny station and t[urn] it into a community service." KC[RW] started out as a training facility [for] returning veterans in 1948. We [get] special breaks because of that. So [we] stay here, but we are not part of [the] tutorial aspect of the college. We [do] have interns, but there is a sepa[rate] broadcasting department in anot[her] part of the campus.

So you're separated financia[lly] from the college.

Yes we have our own budget, we ra[ise] our own money. We just got d[one] with our fund driving; we raised c[lose to] a million. We have two fund-raise[rs a] year. Because we are in LA and [the] industry is here, the musicians [are] here, and people who get it live h[ere.] We are very unique, very fortunate [and] very thankful to the people who g[ive] us money. We are able to afford thi[ngs] like the Amek board. The gear that [we] have is professional quality. Many ba[nds] walk in here thinking it's going to b[e a] couple of mics and playing in a clo[set.] They are just blown away by [the] equipment that we have.

How did you end up worki[ng] there?

I started out in broadcasting. I was at K[CRW] for a little bit, and then I went t[o a] company called Digital Planet, doing a[udio] production. The company was funded [by] venture capitalists and they pulled [the] money out from underneath us. I wen[t on] vacation and came back, I was told "By [the] way, you don't have a job." Which [is] lovely. Then it was a whole timing thi[ng. I] lucked out that the director was lea[ving] from KCRW. That opened up a slot, and me being a mus[ician] since I was five. Being around microphones and m[ixing] boards, it all came together. Everything that I had lea[rned] so far came together when I walked into KCRW.

The station was doing live broadc[ast] before you showed up.

Yes, and there is some amazing stuff. They've got old [Sonic] Tractor live. The things they have just blow your mind. [Back] then they were recording it to reel to reel still. They sto[pped] that. When I got here they were recording them to [DAT] simply because of lack of space. If we had everything [that] we've done on reels, it would take up a lot of room.

That's true, it would be kind of big. Is [the] show once a week?

No, it's every day, five days a week.

Well, no wonder your tapes are piling up [if] you're there every morning?

Years ago a friend of mine sent me a cassette with a live broadcast of the Go-Betweens, Downey Mildew and Glass Eye that he recorded off the radio from KCRW (public radio 89.9FM) in Santa Monica, California. These weren't crummy recordings by any means, and when I saw that compilations of tracks from KCRW sessions were being released (via Mammoth records) I wasn't surprised. The show is called *Morning Becomes Eclectic* and Scott Fritz has been one of the main engineers for the show for the last eight years.

e usually, on average, have four bands a week. Sometimes more during touring season. There are two other people that are also engineers here. Bob Carlson and J.C. Swiatek. Then there's the DJ, Nic Harcourt. I do other things than just the bands. There's regular audio production, and what's also great about this place, I'll be working with Yo La Tengo one day. The next day I'll be recording a radio drama down at the other end of the studio for the BBC.

good variety of work.

xactly. Mic'ing a radio drama is a completely different thing... getting it to work in a stereo spectrum.

ave you studied up for some of these things that you had to do?

or the radio drama stuff, most of it comes naturally. You know what you want. X/Y [stereo mic pair] for the radio drama stuff. You've basically got to tell the director, "Look we are working with audio, you're doing visual." Stuff like that, trying to get them to switch gears. Trying to get them to not look. So if you don't look and you're listening you catch weird things.

ind of like the first time you hear your voice recorded. You are used to hearing your voice in a certain way. But when confronted with how it really sounds, it sounds strange.

eah. It's a bit of a Foley [sound effects] thing that you need to know to get that sound. It's not really tricky microphone activity really. It's just getting the actors to get up, intimately close to the mic and then away from the mic. A lot of proximity stuff that you have to be aware of that the director doesn't even get. You have to go through the script, before, and find where and when you need the proximity.

o do you still have to spend a lot of time researching scripts, and deciding how it's going to be laid out?

ou just have to go through it the weekend before you start on it. You just go through the script and mark those for yourself. If you go through a scene and a director changes something, you need to remember where mics and actors were.

o you keep continuity charts?

eah, little notes to yourself.

hen you're doing something like that, do you record in Pro Tools, so you can fly in sound effects and things?

e have Sonic Solutions here. We still record to DAT with it and then dump it into Sonic. Either that or sometimes they will take it with them and the BBC will edit it over there. Add stuff to it.

re these things you broadcast?

h yeah, they are broadcast here and on the BBC as well. LA Theater Works is another company that we work with and that is just strictly LA. What's great about it is that you think, "Radio drama. Nobody does radio drama anymore." But we get these great actors and actresses who give these amazing performances.

My friend does post production all the time, and he's always raving about the really good voice talent.

It's the same thing with instruments. You got a shitty sounding guitar, you put a really good microphone up to it, you're going to show how bad guitars can sound. It's the same way with actors. If the emotion is not coming out of their voice and they're not feeling it, it's very apparent.

And harder to fix than a bad band.

You really can't EQ that out can you?

Compress it.

EQ in some emotion.

Describe a typical scenario of a live band session. Beginning to end.

Every band that I do, I research the record, I listen to it and figure out what they are about, if I don't already know. We get an input list from them. Sometimes you send the input list back, because there are too many things. It's a 20 by 20 room, but nine times out of ten we are okay with it. The night before I set everything up. Position things in the room. The drums in a certain spot, mics and everything. So when the band walks in everything's ready to go and we just need to get their gear up and mic'd. We have bands come in at 9:00, the show is always live at 11:15.

Don't bands complain about being there at nine in the morning?

Yeah. three out of ten bands drive from San Francisco. This is how hard the record companies make them work. The will play live in a club in San Francisco that night. Drive down to LA that night and play in the morning, and then go to sleep. I know it's a great thing to play here, but god you're going to kill these people with this schedule. They're really tired and grumpy and they don't want to play. You do get some of them, where it really is early for them. With that in mind, a lot of bands are late. Which makes my job ten times harder. There's this band Air, who is actually on our CD. There was no soundcheck. This happens, and I've gotten to be pretty good at it. They had a huge set-up, and because they use all vintage equipment they were having problems. We go on at 11:15, and about 11:30 the producer is climbing the walls. I keep telling her, "Five more minutes. We're not ready yet." At 11:45 we went on the air. They were almost an hour late, add that to the amount of equipment and the problems they were having. This just wasn't your straight up four piece rock band. You can actually hear in the beginning of the track, the drums are really low in the mix. Just due to that was the first soundcheck. So late bands are stressful challenge. But we're going to make it happen. That's my whole thought process - give me an obstacle, I'll find a solution. We may go on late, but we aren't going to go on until the band is ready.

I got a tape of Downy Mildew, years ago, off of KCRW. There's this piano and vocal song and it's half through and then finally the vocals come in. A mic must have been out or off or something.

That's back when we had the Neotek board. In the days of the Neotek it was like, "Don't use fader nine, or thirteen. Fader one will work, but you need to turn the trim on it a couple of times." It was really a kind of dodgy board.

You got a new Amek board.

It's actually now a couple of years old. It's a 32 channel Amek with virtual dynamics on every channel. Which is a godsend. It's compression, limiter and a gate. The EQ is on the board.

So this is some sort of computer.

It's virtual, so the dynamics are done by the computer. For vocals I use the 1176s. We also have a couple of LA-4s. So, I'll bypass the board compression on vocals. But when you have mega-inputs, synths, samples that are sampled at different volumes, the virtual dynamics help.

I'm not sure people realize how hard that is to mix a band live. I find that mixing from tape you get a little bit of compression. But you don't have that happening with your set-up. The virtual dynamics take place of that.

Yeah. Exactly. We don't have the tape compression 'cause we are going to an Apogee convertor to a Panasonic 3700 [DAT]. We are going live on the air and recording two track onto DAT. People say; "Why don't you multi-track every session?"

Who's going back to mix all that?

Exactly. It's just too much, and it kind of takes away from the fact that this is a live session. This is how the listener heard it on that day, not from post production stuff where everything is perfect and slick.

What do you do from 9:00 to 11:15, from the time the band gets there, until the show begins?

The band comes in and they usually have their people setting up amps and stuff like that. Sometimes the band, sometimes a crew that comes in. I just basically get them AC, get the mics in position, and start soundchecking stuff. I usually start out checking the drums first. You get line checks and kind of go from there.

Do you have them run through a few songs?

Once we get everything up, we have to get monitors, but we don't have monitors we have headphone mixes.

So it's just like being in the studio for the band.

Right. Some of them don't like that. Playing with headphones is an art. Some of them love it cause they can hear themselves. Then I get other people who throw the headphones down. "I can't play with these fucking things. Where's the monitors?" They whine and moan, but once you play around for awhile with them, it starts to feel better.

How many headphone sends can you get up?

Well here's the thing. We have six separate headphones. Mono. I also begged and pleaded and finally got in a Furman headphone monitor system. On this the band can dial in their own mix. We can't use it for the nine member bands, but for small groups, it's great.

I always wondered if that would cause more trouble or would it work out?

It actually works. It works out well, it saves time. While they are getting their headphone mixes going, you are getting your mix going. I used it today with Billy Bragg.

I've seen those, but I always wondered if it would work. Sometimes people can't even comprehend the five knobs I have on my headphone amp.

This was one of our concerns. It had to have knobs and not faders. We forget that a lot of musicians haven't been around recording equipment. A four track maybe. But it needed to be really user friendly, and knobs are easier than faders. We tape it off as well. "This is this and this is this, etc." So it works in some applications really, really well. The band is supposed to be there at nine, so you don't start sound checking until ten. From ten to eleven you are checking individual instruments and then pretty much, from right around 11 to 11:15 is a full song, and then you're on and you got to be right there with it. Sometimes you're late, and you just have to allow that.

Do you ever get really nervous yourself? As the clock's ticking away...

I used to get more tense, not nervous, but more tense. Now that I'm seasoned I don't become that intense and the energy is more focused.

With the drums, do you go for a simpler live approach for mic'ing or do you go in and close mic it all?

With the drums, what I do depends on the sound of the band. But my main thing for drums is an RE20 on the kick, the rest using [AKG] 414s (this freaks a lot of people out), a Schoeps on the hi-hat, and a couple of AKG D224s on the overheads. I'm a drummer myself and I really like to hear that I'm behind the drums. I guess I'm saying that I pay attention to the drum kit when I'm mixing just as much as any other instrument. It's amazing, even if you took a 414 off of the snare and put a SM 57 on, like most people use. It closes the kit up, a little bit more. With the 414 the kit is more open and raised, like you're sitting behind the kit. I've been doing that for a while, the 414 on the snare and toms.

How close do you get them in there?

Right in there, like you would with a 57.

Do you have to pad it?

Yeah 10 dB pad on everything. The one right on the mic.

Wow that's crazy.

I know that it's crazy, but it sounds amazing. Then what I do, is I take that and send it to a two mix [buss] and then a two mix into a Valley compressor and back into the mixing board and

then mix that with the rest. So you still get the spikes, the percussion spikes. But it thickens the drum kit up all together.

I've done that before. Just fill out the entire sound of the drums.

The other thing I do, the alternative Scott drum mic'ing technique, is a 57 on the kick and an American D22. Do you know that mic?

No.

Oh, it's funky looking. It's an amazing microphone and you compress the hell out of it and put it as an overhead. So you have one overhead and one kick. It's gives you this really great lo-fi, Beatlesque kind of sound. The American is kind of an old microphone. It's really good and has a narrow bandwidth.

What do you use for vocals?

Everything from a U87 to a Beta 58. Depending on style. We get so many different bands. So whatever fits the bill.

And you have to make all these decisions before the session starts.

That's the thing, you can't A/B three different vocal mics on the person. You stick with one and make it happen. We have RE20s, Coles ribbon mics, and 57s. We got a really nice AKG C-422 stereo mic. TL 170s. Neumanns. A bunch of 414s.

What's been a really good session, what makes it smooth.

You know it's usually the sessions where people are really professional. The sessions I have problems with are the "rock star" attitudes. It's amazing to me, in the style of music that I work with, that it even exists. Because it goes against the whole vibe of the music. I think it would be okay to be a rock star if you're into the Top Forty environment. But when that's not what you're supposedly about, and you come in (um, Dandy Warhols) with the rock star attitude. It's just really.... They come in going, "You're the enemy, it's you against us." From that stems a lot of stuff. "I'm not going to play. This isn't right." "No, I'm moving my stuff over here, I'm over here." Yeah but if you're over here, it's going to bleed into this acoustic guitar. They don't work with you at all and don't listen to what you're saying about the sound. They don't care. They have no respect. Those are rare though, I've had three bad sessions out of all the sessions I've done here over eight years. The rest of them are great, and when they are really, really great for me is when it's a band that I've been in love with forever.

I think Yo La Tengo would be a case like that.

Yes, Yo La Tengo was amazing and Mazzy Star, because I've been a Dave Roback fan ever since Rain Parade. That session, they didn't speak a whole lot. They weren't very chatty, but they were very professional, and I just melted behind the desk. Stereolab were another great great band; Luna another one. So really these bands were good and we won't mention the names of the bad ones.

You can say Dandy Warhols though. They'll love it. I think I've heard tapes of the show on people's record. "Here we are on *Morning Becomes Eclectic.*"

Several bands have put stuff out, that I've recorded here. I just got an email saying that Cake is going to put out some stuff. My favorite is that the Pale Blue Saints put something out that I mixed here, and I am a huge fan of Pale Blue Saints. It was when I first started working here and they broke up right afterwards. It was good to capture that. Possum Dixon, Poster Children, King for a Day, Soul Coughing, Stereolab, Tendersticks, Grant Lee Buffalo, Geraldine Fibbers...

That's a lot of cool stuff. I thought that this article wouldn't suit *Tape Op*, but the irony is that this has everything to do with recording. I mean the music is out there, on albums, and you seem to be bridging the gap between recording and live music.

That's exactly what it is, it's the blending of those two types.

Are there plans to keep doing archive releases.

We have about five or six CDs out that are al compilations.

Who is on the new album?

Air, Freestylers, Ednaswap, Mercury Rev, Brad Mehldau, PJ Harvey, Morcheeba, Joe Henry, Buffalo Daughter Cake, John Martyn, Angelique Kidjo, Pink Martini...

That's a really wild mix. Have you done any work outside of the station?

I've done remixes for Kristen Hersh, Fiona Apple an Luscious Jackson. I try to keep my fingers i anything to do with audio production. I'm alway open to opportunity, and I never take it for granted I've never taken this job for granted. It's easy to d when you do it every day. I know it's a very rar thing in my life, it's been great so far.

Have any full radio performances from the show ever been released?

Rufus Wainwright released the full session, th interview and the music. It was a limited releas See we never know if it's going to be just tracks the entire session. But bands are always welcome t release anything they want.

Do they have to purchase it?

Oh god, no!

With the BBC or John Peel you have t buy them.

Oh really? That's just wrong. You've got to buy th session? What is wrong with that picture?

Have you've ever seen bootlegs of stuf you've done?

Get on eBay.

Really?

Get on Ebay and look up KCRW.

Oh my God. Is it tape trading, or CD-R?

Both. You know "so and so" sessions live on KCRW. Some guy's making them in his room. ☺

"Notes from Under the Ground"
By Eric D. Morrison

I am standing on the precipice of realizing a magical dream that I have carried with me since my youth. You see, I have recently purchased a basement. There is, of course, a house attached to the top of this basement for my wife and I to live in, but that is really just icing on the cake. I own a basement. And if you fall into the correct demographic for this publication, you know where I'm going with this... basement studio!

I've been living for three years in a tiny little 1-bedroom apartment with an MS-16 deck, a Mackie 32-4 board, a rack of outboard stuff, about 150 gallons of assorted cables, a wife, and a cat with a huge ass. You can understand my joy at the prospect of a more spacious workspace. The aforementioned inventory (with the exception of my wife and cat) was purchased by my band "Home" with two record advances. And while we still have a wish list longer than my arm, we've got the basics covered and have been biding our time since 1996 to find the space to build a proper temple for what we call "The Devil's Isle Wet Lab".

Step 1: Waterproofing

The first thing you need to know about waterproofing a basement is that there's no such thing. Hurricane Floyd taught me this lesson four days after we moved in. At first sight of the three inches of water that covered my basement floor, I called out for a pox on the lying SOBs who sold us the house with the assertion that it was a "dry" basement. Upon visiting with the neighbors the next day, however, it became clear that our street had indeed been flood-free for nearly ten years, and I had to recall my pox \request. Luckily I hadn't loaded any equipment downstairs yet, and only lost several rolls of extremely ugly carpeting (it has become my opinion that God sent Floyd specifically to force me to dispose of this atrocious floorcovering).

That being said, there *are* steps that one can take to keep moisture out of the basement in between hurricanes and monsoons, and to keep damage to a minimum during these acts.

. Location, Location, Location

Try to find a house on a hill; water only travels in one direction, so no matter how much rain you experience, the water saturating elevated property will have no choice but to slink away. Explain your intentions to your house inspector, ask him/her to check for foundation cracks and efflorescence (mineral deposits that indicate water seepage). Also, if you are legally able to buy flood insurance on the house, it means you're located on a flood plain and should probably keep looking.

. Gutters

Don't overlook these simplistic marvels; they do a world of good in keeping water away from your house in the first place. In addition to keeping them unclogged, make sure they lead out at least five feet from the house, farther on the upstream side of the property.

3. Sump Pumps

Being originally from Florida this was a new one for me, but a sump is a hole cut in the basement floor and lined with semiporous tile. When the ground gets saturated the tile allows water to fill the hole, but holds out the mud. Now, add to this the deliciously fun to say Sump-Pump - a float triggered water pump. When the water level rises to a certain level the motor starts pumping out the water. Simple enough, but here's the trick... Find out where it's pumping to! Following my run-in with Hurricane Floyd, I spent several days sweeping standing water down into the sump and making no significant progress. Finally I crawled under the deck (face down in soft mud) to investigate the problem, only to find that the sump-pump was piped out to less than six inches from the foundation, creating a pointless water-cycle that I was foolishly perpetuating. Your sump-pump, like your gutters, needs to lead away far away from your foundation and to a lower elevation when possible. The other solution, which is illegal in most towns (meaning I would never officially suggest it), is to pipe it into your outgoing sewer line. One final note on sump-pumps: get a back-up generator in the mix, because heavy-duty rains are often accompanied by electrical outages.

4. The French Drain

This solution fell outside my budget restrictions, but from what I've been told, the French Drain offers the closest thing to a "dry" guarantee as you can get. The basic premise includes digging out your entire foundation and installing underground drains that lead away from the property. If you need this kind of security, have it done first as it will completely fuck up your landscaping.

5. Up and Away

Returning to my opening statement; there is no such thing as waterproofing, and it behooves you to keep everything off the ground. If you follow the basic precautions above, you will not be facing a swimming pool in your basement, but rather a few inches at worst, which is easy enough to guard against. Unless you are following some wacky feng-shui design, most of your dearest equipment will be up on a desk or in a rack anyway. Cables, stompboxes, tape reels, and the like should be stored at least six inches above the floor, and risers should be used for drums and amps (risers are also very helpful sonically).

Step 2: Soundproofing

Phew! The first thing you'll learn about soundproofing when you hit the bookstore or the web (outside of the fact that it is even harder to achieve 100% success than waterproofing) is that there is far FAR too much information on the subject. You'll need to be very specific in your searches or risk being lost in a sea of industrial hooha. In an attempt to not add further to this saturation of advice I am simply going to recommend any book by Frederick Alton Everest and give a brief run-down on what we decided would work best for the Devil's Isle Wet Lab.

1. Floors:

Because of the low ceilings, we had little choice but to simply install some wet/dry carpeting to kill off a little bit of hi-end standing waves, but mostly for comfort. If you are lucky enough to find a basement with enough headroom, a false or floating floor (a floor built a few inches above the foundation) is preferable.

2. Ceiling:

We filled the ceiling cavity with R-11 acoustical fiberglass insulation (incidentally, if you have not worked with fiberglass before, tuck your sleeves into your gloves, and DO NOT RUB YOUR EYES!) and installed a hanging ceiling of 5/8" drywall. The ceiling offers the most challenging drywall job thanks to all the ductwork, cabling, and assorted utilitarian aparati that gets relegated to the basement. You will need to build framing around these unsightlies with 1X2s.

3. Exterior Walls:

In the basement setting, exterior walls are a snap. For the most part, the typical foot of cinderblock wall leading out to the earth offers plenty of sound blockage even for those pesky long bass waves. In order to bulk up the upper two feet of wall (which is above ground) we installed Georgia Pacific Soundboard, a specialized type of particleboard. Over this we used construction adhesive to apply 5/8" drywall. Purportedly, by not nailing or screwing the drywall to the foundation wall, one allows for more vibration absorption.

4. Interior Walls:

In addition to troublesome ducts and cabling, most of a house's vital organs are kept in the basement too. For us this meant building freestanding walls to isolate the performance and control rooms from the heater, A/C, washer, dryer, and (whee! I get to say it again...) sump-pump. The design of sound-resistant walls varied very little from book to book, filling me with the confidence to pass the plans on to you.

The key to this wall is its staggered 2X4 joists. By keeping contact between the two faces of the wall to a minimum, you can avoid simply transferring those unwanted soundwaves to what would be an oversized membrane. A strip of felt above and below the 2X6s adds some cushioning and helps keep the floor and ceiling from working in concert with the wall.

5. Finishing:

If you're anything like us, on the happy day that you finish construction and take a triumphant tour of the facility, you'll notice that somehow all of your angles aren't quite square and certain parts of the wall don't quite reach the ceiling. For the most part, don't sweat it, it's amazing what can be done cosmetically with joint compound and tape. However, before you take on this final step, strap on a caulk gun and your best set of eyes and fill every hole you can find. It's astounding how much sound can go through a small hole or crack, and the old adage *A Chain is Only as Strong as its Weakest Link*, is certainly a mantra to utilize while caulking.

Now then I will be extracting Liquid Nails from various parts of my body and wishing you all the best. ⊛

Open Letter To A Friend
by Larry Crane

25 REASONS NOT TO OPEN YOUR OWN STUDIO:

1. Freelance engineers. They always complain about your choice of gear, especially speakers. They also point out what's broken on a regular basis. damn.

2. Toilets. You have to clean them unless you get an intern and then you feel bad asking them to do that.

3. Interns. They're not so bad, when you get one and they work out well, but you'll get calls from people wanting to be one every frickin' day.

4. Taxes. I pay more in taxes than I pay in rent. I don't understand that at all.

5. Repairs. My tech costs $75 per hour. Everything falls apart eventually.

6. Potential customers. People will call and grill you, book lots of time, and then cancel mysteriously a week before. You'll never know why.

7. Actual customers. Your love of music may be put to the test on occasion.

8. Headphones. They always blow out, proper mixes for tracking bands are impossible, the extension cables fray, plus they get sweaty and gross from the drummer's head. And decent ones are $100.

9. Shopping. Buying stupid stuff you would have never thought about - like toilet paper, hand towels, pencils, tea, sugar, condiments for the fridge, the fridge itself, bottled water, Q-tips, etc.

10. Stocking. Having to keep numerous CD-Rs, cassettes, reels, DATs and such in stock because no band ever remembers to pick any up.

11. "But what does it do?" Buying a $500 power conditioner and spending $1200 to hook it up,

12. Ads. Feeling like you better run them even though you're pretty sure no one notices.

13. Responsibility. Do you really want to get paged/called at 1 AM on your birthday with news that the deck is down?

14. 9 volt batteries. People "borrow" batteries like they grow on trees.

15. Theft. They also steal your E-Bow, guitar straps, SM 57s and break your glass slides.

16. Really crappy bands. There are more than you ever guessed and they'll call you. If you work with them they'll call again.

17. Really great bands. They end up having sessions with you right after you recorded the crappy bands and you're exhausted.

18. Exhaustion. It *is* possible to work 35 days in a row - I did it once. You get kinda crabby.

19. Relationships. You might not have one soon with all the time you'll spend at the studio.

20. Patchbays. Did you know you could easily spend $1500 on a cheap setup? They're really fun to wire up too.

21. Scheduling. Every band always wants to record at the same time of year/month as everyone else.

22. Down time. There's always one dead month in the year but you never know when it will be.

23. Trends in recording gear. "What do you mean you don't have _____?"

24. Debt. You will learn to embrace it as a close yet feared friend.

25. Food and sleep. You will never again conform to any semblance of a normal routine. Meals are of random quality and at odd hours. Sleep is rare.

ONE REASON TO OPEN YOUR OWN STUDIO:

1. I like this job. This has been the most exciting and engaging career I've ever had in my life. I never know exactly what I will be doing day-to-day, which I adore (no rut). There's a wall of CDs I've worked on that I can stare at when I feel beat down. I can schedule time off without a boss getting mad - and hopefully fill the schedule with freelance engineers. And once I even got paid to record The Go-Betweens. That's enough for me!

TAILS OUT...

Congratulations, you've made it to the end of *Tape Op: The Book About Creative Music Recording, Volume II*. I hope you enjoyed the various interviews and articles that make up this book.

The other day an interviewer asked me if there was an underlying manifesto for my recording studio. I didn't have a solid answer for this. I think as any venture or business moves forward in time it changes, but there are usually root principles that keep the venture on course. *Tape Op Magazine*, to me, is always changing - finding new people making new records, interviewing people we once thought "inaccessible" and covering subjects I might have once scoffed at (like digital recording). But I also see a continuity in the approach - placing an emphasis on songs, technique and feelings over recording equipment, searching out people who make interesting albums and overall a desire to learn more from others and walk into the recording process with open ears and an open mind.

I started this magazine because I wanted to learn more about the recording process. I'm still learning every day. I get letters (and CDs) from people constantly telling me how much *Tape Op* inspired them while recording and how much they learned through the magazine.

That's all the reward I need.

-Larry Crane

P.S. If you liked this book and you haven't already subscribed to *Tape Op*, the magazine, your should do it now! It's free! There's more info on the next page.

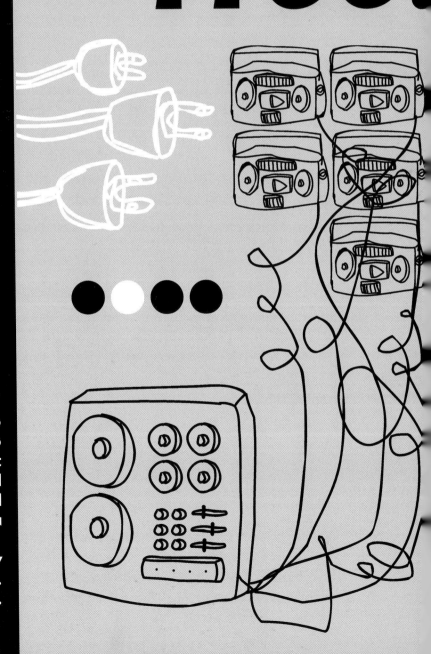